Theodore J. Lowi

American Government

Incomplete Conquest

Theodore J. Lowi is
John L. Senior Professor of
American Institutions at
Cornell University

The Dryden Press
Hinsdale, Illinois

Anna and Jason—my children
Janice and Alvin—my parents

Things must change
If they are to remain the same

Design by Stephen Rapley
Photo research by Jo-Anne Naples
Copyediting by Judith Lynn Bleicher

This book is set in Linotron
10 point Century Schoolbook by
Black Dot, Inc., Crystal Lake, Illinois

Preface

WHALES, GOVERNMENTS, AND PEOPLE

One of the annual college rituals is the apology American government professors offer their students for the text they are about to receive. These texts are frustrating because of the unwieldy nature of government as a subject of study. Government is as extensive as the economy, but it is a more particularistic subject than economics. It is acceptable in introductory economics to treat multiples of facts in a few universal generalizations. Introductory government or political science tries this sort of thing at its peril. Many abstractions about actual governments are an affront to the facts; a purely factual treatment of governments or politics can be a front for unexamined ideological biases.

Nevertheless, the factual (or nuts-and-bolts) book has been the standard approach for over three decades. These books have been the most widely adopted despite criticisms that they make government and politics appear too pat, too neat, too good. All of this seemed to come unstuck after 1965, when American governments (federal, state, and local) proved they too could fail. The Vietnam War was a debacle despite the best efforts of our military establishment, which had for two hundred years known only victory. The other war, against poverty, not only stalled in the ghettoes but proved that equality did not exist in the U.S. and that there was little governments were able or willing to do about it.

Experience with the failure of government brought on a series of thesis books, in which the authors took an explicit theoretical or ideological position and argued it through a variety of selected everyday political experiences. From this vantage point the system can be logically and thoroughly criticized as well as described. But these books have produced another kind of frustration, a sinking sensation that they are spawning a generation of sophisticates—students who are opinionated but not educated. For many teachers, thesis books have served mainly to instill new respect for the standard nuts-and-bolts books.

Since 1959, when I began teaching American government, I have gone through the annual ritual of search, adoption, and apology. Apparently my frustration went deeper than that of most of my colleagues, since I went to the extreme of publishing a lengthy review essay covering the entire modern era of political science teaching, from Woodrow Wilson through the early 1960s. I set some very high standards in that essay—so high indeed that writing a text of my own was inevitably going to be a sobering experience. Now that I have completed the book I can report a renewed appreciation for the persistent flaws in all previous texts. These flaws bear witness to the magnitude of the task. No intellectual task is more challenging than the presentation of an entire area of organized knowledge to a novice.

Given the magnitude of the task, it was sorely tempting to adopt the path of the fact book—to take refuge in objectivity. Leonard Bernstein caught the problem very well by asking one of his characters in *Wonderful Town* to explain Moby Dick. She replied, "Well, it's about a whale." Her reply caught everything and nothing—a fate which is likely to befall anyone who parades facts about government as government itself. On the other hand, it occurs to me that the underlying character of our problem may begin to reveal itself if we admit that government, rather than Moby Dick, is a story about a whale. The whale may lead to an entirely new direction for American government, or at least to a few new angles on an old direction.

The whale is one of the most persistent metaphors in the history of political thought. The first great masterpiece of political theory in the English language is *Leviathan*, by Thomas Hobbes. Leviathan is an aquatic monster with origins traceable at least to the Old Testament. In the Book of Job, Leviathan is a symbol of evil ultimately defeated by the power of good. For Hobbes, Leviathan was the appropriate metaphor for the political order, "the commonwealth"; Leviathan was for Hobbes "the multitude . . . united in one person . . . to which we owe, under the immortal God our peace and defence." Judging only by the full title of his work—*Leviathan, or the Matter, Forme and Power of a Commonwealth Ecclesticall and Civil*—Hobbes chose this symbol because of the great power of the beast, like the state, to do evil as well as good.

The frontispiece for the original 1651 edition depicts a peaceful medieval town being watched over by a giant of a human being. This giant is crowned, with scepter in one hand and sword in the other—clearly a guardian of some sort. A closer look shows that the giant's arms and torso are composed of thousands of tiny people. From a distance these individuals are indistinguishable parts of the skin, giving the impression of armor or scales. The bottom half of the page, surrounding the title, author, and publisher, is a series of prints of articles or symbols of state: castle walls, cannon, spears, muskets, cavalry, and—yes—a council of elders and a cathedral.

The great beast Leviathan is not just a fact; yet it is not, and was not intended to be, merely a symbol. Leviathan is a fact and a judgment combined. Government, the ultimate rendering of Leviathan, is the center of all political authority (abstractly speaking, the state); political authority can incorporate everything in society, touching every person and every institution with evil or good. We come to love our government as we can love any great beast upon whom we rely for "peace and defence." We may be able to look upon the beast with scientific objectivity. But science and objectivity go far beyond, "Well, government is about a great beast." We may scientifically dissect the beast, examine its limbs and organs, put it back together again, and try to explain its actions on the basis of its parts. But we lose the beast entirely if we, in our objectivity, fail to recognize all along its corporate capacity for good and evil.

According to this view, government, as a beast, is a thing apart from us. We do not create it by contracts; it did not emerge as a response to our wishes or according to the conditions set down by some agreements we have made with each other. Our actions may influence the beast. We may even make a contract with it; but such a contract is made only after the beast already exists and only according to conditions laid down by the beast or by violence. Mythology and political theory aside, government exists. It may incorporate us all, but it is not us in any corporeal sense. We are creatures of our parents; government is a creature of our history. We hover near it; we create myths about its benevolence; but according to this view, government, or political authority, existed before there was a political community, and government is something we are born into and must contend with: First there was conquest. Then there was government. Then we began to make contracts with it or about it.

Here, fortunately, the metaphor of the whale begins to break down. Unlike the beast, government can take on different forms according to persistent social preferences. These forms are substantial, and changes in them produce substantial consequences. The forms are what revolutions are fought for and great heroes die for. The idea of the social contract is a benevolent myth contrived to reassure us, against our own direct experience, that government was made by us and is therefore good. But *forms* of government are or may be contractual, whether entered into by violence or by peaceful means. Through the manipulation of forms we seek to answer Hobbes and all other absolutists. We attempt to withhold our obedience until we can give shape to a more kindly Leviathan, rather than merely taking whatever swims along.

Who will have the final word? Hobbes would counsel us to give unquestioned obedience to the absolute ruler because we would find even more distasteful the consequences of having no ruler at all. We answer with constitutionalism, representative government, and due process of law—efforts to bind the ruler before binding ourselves, although Hobbes would tell us the ruler cannot be bound. Hobbes also would tell us sovereignty is "indivisible," but we proceed to divide it with federalism, the separation of powers, and civil liberties. He would tell us that in a duly constituted commonwealth, conquest, by definition, is complete. We answer with incomplete conquest.

Incomplete conquest is first of all an expression of a fact, for in fact no conquest has yet been complete. Incomplete conquest is also an expression of a hope, for we hope complete conquest will never come to pass. Incomplete conquest is a calculated risk, for, as Hobbes himself would have said, as long as conquest is incomplete, our "peace and defence" are in peril. We can have at best a love-hate relationship with government. The beast wallows among us, and we hover close. The beast is so large and so thick-skinned that it may roll over upon us at any time. We hover close, wherever we happen to find ourselves, knowing the beast cannot lie still. Will it roll upon us, leading us to call it evil, or will it roll upon others and appear to us "by its nature" good?

This view of government may appear novel, but only for a lack of recent usage in the United States. The idea of "the state" as separate from individuals is not new. Putting government rather than politics at the center of concern is not new. Giving government a history separate from any social contract is not new. One very important consequence of this point of view is that it leads to a focus on government rather than politics, and to a definition of political science as the study of control rather than the study of power. It leads us to ask what governs far more frequently than who governs.

Another extremely important result of this point of view is its stress on *form*. In this volume form will become the most important single political fact. We will study it in order to discover purpose. We will see that it expresses purpose and puts limits on purpose. We will see that in government, as in art, form is a method ensuring the fulfillment of purpose.

Some may say this is a view without the people at the center, therefore a view without hope or faith; but they would be quite wrong. Hope is simply not placed on the natural benevolence of rulers; faith is not placed upon the myth of social contract or consent. Hope is built upon the forms of government and upon the idea that there can be bad and good forms according to human contrivance. Form gives us a criterion: *Our particular forms of government and politics ought to correspond to political reality.* If the correspondence between the two is poor, this does not mean the forms are meaningless at all. It means that the political activity is illegitimate and should be changed. When government officials depart from forms, they depart from their authority to rule. Consent is something we can withhold as well as give. Government is defined by its legitimacy. But governments can be illegitimate as well; and usually we can sense the illegitimacy by recognizing the incongruencies between the forms and the realities.

This point of view permeates everything in the book. Each chapter is filled with nuts and bolts, because it takes nuts and bolts to describe forms. But the book seeks to discourage taking facts at face value. No fact should be fully understandable without the argument that places it. The reader should not try merely to memorize a fact; each fact is there to be contended with. And since I have tried to intrude myself everywhere, the reader will constantly have to contend with me.

ACKNOWLEDGMENTS

A profession can be known by its introductory books, because they inevitably synthesize part of what is available in the professional literature. Texts can easily be worse, but rarely better, than the ideas and the research in the journals, books, and dissertations of the field. If American government texts are frustrating, it is due largely to lack of consensus rather than lack of research or knowledge. In economics, where strong consensus does exist, the major text is a paragon of theory and facts, written by a winner of one of the first Nobel Prizes given for economics. In politics and government, many are called but few are chosen, because we have not yet reached a state of readiness in the art to accept one approach above all others. Nevertheless, one cannot undertake to write a text in government and politics without being impressed with the profession's honest endeavor and prodigious effort to contribute to knowledge. My footnotes offer ample evidence of the contribution of academic political science to my book, and I am pleased to acknowledge that fact. The individual footnotes should be regarded with care by all serious readers; in the aggregate, they can be taken as testimony from at least one author that the field of political science is very much alive and well.

Certain individuals within the field warrant special recognition for having read and commented upon all or parts of the manuscript. First among these is Alan Stone (Rutgers University), who worked tirelessly, creatively, and loyally through two full drafts. No single chapter has escaped his influence. Others who have read and commented on the entire first draft are: Sotirios Barber (University of South Florida), George J. Graham, Jr. (Vanderbilt University), Roger Marz (Oakland University), Edward V. Schneier (City University of New York), and Helen Sawyer (Memphis State University). Professors Barber and Sawyer also read certain portions of the second draft. William Collins read the second draft and wrote a brilliant commentary. On certain occasions I sought additional specialized expertise for a particular chapter from Isaac Kramnick and David Resnick (Cornell University), Mojmir Povolny (Lawrence University), Randall Ripley (Ohio State University), and Rose and Jeremiah Stamler (Northwestern University). Each of these colleagues will surely recognize some important places in the final version where their suggestions saved me from severe embarrassment.

The publisher submitted the second draft to more than thirty readers, chosen by the editor and several members of his field staff. Their comments, amounting to a large volume, gave me the kind of reality check an author desperately needs after months of isolation. While several of these individuals have chosen to remain anonymous, the following have agreed to break cover and give permission to acknowledge their contribution: Gottlieb J. Baer (American River College), F. Lee Harrell (Mt. San Antonio College), Fritz Nova (Villanova University), Albert E. Scott (Diablo Valley College), Jerry L. Yeric (North Texas State University), Harold E. Damerow (Union College), Marvin Weinbaum (University of Illinois, Urbana), Michael Drissman (Macomb County Community College), Floyd Stoner (Marquette University), Gilbert E. Scharfenberger (Salem State College), T. F. Thompson (St. Petersburg Junior College), Martin Sutton (Bucks County Community College), Robert Shanley (University of Massachusetts), Norman L. Zucker (University of Rhode Island), Oliver Walters (University of Wyoming), Parris N. Glendening (University of Maryland), Christopher A. Leu (California State University, Northridge), Michael Margolis (University of Pittsburgh), Abraham Holtzman (North Carolina State University, Raleigh), Jack L. Noragon (Cleveland State

University), Lawrence Longley (Lawrence University), Eric Elliott (Hillsborough Community College), Thomas Keating (Arizona State University), Stephen H. Polansky (College of San Mateo), Beverly Cigler (Wayne State University).

Since a textbook is so much more of a production than any other type of book, I have relied heavily upon people whose profession is production. And since I work almost entirely off the dictaphone, even the typists had to be unusually gifted. Paula Wissing typed a large portion of the first draft in Paris under less than ideal conditions. Ruth Black, Lois Livermore, Karen Sprole, and Mark Mizruchi all made significant contributions to the manuscript, proving definitively that the products of American schooling can spell. I am also grateful to Richard Joslyn and Richard Bensel, Cornell University graduate students at the time of writing the book, for some extremely valuable professional research.

But all of those who contributed to the production of the book will understand if I single out from among their company six people who were absolutely indispensable. Gertrude Fitzpatrick contributed in a variety of ways, but most importantly she helped keep the project alive while I was in Europe. Ardis (Tuk) Pesaresi typed and corrected an enormous proportion of the final version of the manuscript; and, perhaps of greater importance, she administered my office and most of my professional life. Judy Bleicher, copy editor extraordinaire, and Jo-Anne Naples, copy editor and photo researcher, were paid by the publisher but actually worked for me with a care and diligence and imaginativeness that can never be fully compensated in merely monetary terms. Stephen Rapley, the publisher's designer, took a manuscript of unproven artistic value and converted it into a volume worthy of admiration for its own sake. Last as well as first in all matters of production, administration, and editing is Ray Ashton. Ray is an unexcelled member of his own profession and a great complement to ours.

Among my many institutional entanglements of the past decade, I am particularly indebted to Cornell University, not only for helping me secure leave funds so soon after my return in 1972 but also for recognizing the importance of such a project to Cornell and to the profession at large. Cornell deserves still further thanks for having provided me with a course like Government 111 and a long tradition of superb students who enroll in it each year. By a strange bureaucratic quirk, the course number was changed from Government 101 (and will someday be changed back to Government 101); many generations of Cornell students who recognize Government 101 will understand why a professor can be grateful to a course and a course tradition. I also want to thank the University of North Carolina for a visiting professorship at a time when I needed to return to the introductory course after a gap of six years. The UNC students were the first to hear these ideas, and I hope their education did not suffer too much from my own. There is also the invaluable Centre Universitaire International in Paris, a place of great hospitality for visiting scholars. The academic year 1973/74 was my second visit there, and this book is the second book I completed there.

Finally, I have my family to thank, and it is a most substantial thanks. My wife continues to be my constant safeguard against sham and humbug. My children have, more or less good-naturedly, suffered through many months of life with an author whose ambitions exceeded his abilities. We have been more like a theater family than an academic family, making our moves and taking our trips in relation to the phases of the book. A special acknowledgment is due my parents, whose pride in having a scholar in the family has always been a challenge worth trying to deserve. I am only sorry my father died so shortly before publication. I think he would have liked this book. Raising a family of six children during the depression and the war taught him about conquest, which he passed along to us as justice.

T. J. L.
East Hill
Ithaca, New York

Contents

Chapter 7	Getting the People to Consent: The Public in Groups, in Opinions, and in Electorates	209

Chapter 16

Prospects of Conquest:

With Liberty and Justice for Some 691

Chapter 1   Conquest:
The Problem
of Government

If what is right may ever be violated, it is
for the getting of a kingdom; in all other
things keep faith.
Cicero

Government is our second most important problem. It is
superseded only by survival itself.

To survive, people must control nature. Then they must
turn almost immediately to the problem of living with each
other. Some say this happens because human beings are
innately good and prefer to live in society. Some say it is
because human beings are innately bad and must associate
with each other because the consequences of going it alone
are so much worse. But human nature is hardly the essential
problem if in either case we end up living our lives regularly
in association with others. People who are innately bad may
govern themselves differently from people who are innately
good. But government—not human nature—seems to be the
thing people have in common, and it seems to be what people
do least well for themselves.

We need not look far for evidence of the enormous success of our species on earth. There were probably five million *Homo sapiens* on earth at the beginning of recorded history. Now we are approaching four billion. In less than half a century there will be from six to eight billion. Our enterprise, economic and sexual, has been prodigious. When we move from survival to government, however, the progress between antiquity and modernity becomes depressing. In the economic realm, no one would think of rejecting the automobile for the horse and buggy, or reintroducing piecework labor in preference to mass production. Yet, every time a modern nation faces a crisis, it tends to select some form of primitive government. Since twentieth century societies have resorted to primitive forms of government—totalitarianism or terror in some form—more frequently than nineteenth century or eighteenth century societies, an argument could be made that the line of development in government is retrograde, directly contrary to the line of development in economics, technology, science, and sports. It is when we turn to government that we most feel the sting of truth in an observation popularly attributed to Konrad Lorenz: "Man appears to be the missing link between anthropoid apes and human beings."

Of all the indications of our lack of progress in dealing with the problem of government, war is the most damning. War is, almost by definition, the result of the failure of governments to cope with social problems. Yet war has become an institution. Modern societies have made tremendous progress in the art of war. A large number of our scientific and technological breakthroughs are attributable to the need to win wars. Wars were once fought for limited objectives, ending when one side determined that the costs were too high to continue. This means that wars among nations one, two, or three centuries ago were more civilized than twentieth century wars, which are almost a throwback to primitive times in that they involve virtually total commitment to conflict; almost no cost is too great to bear.

These frequent returns to totalitarianism and war are also an indication of the failure of political theory, as well as political practice, since each throwback to primitive means of government involves a breakdown in our effort to impose consciousness and conscience on our actions. The golden age of political theory in the West is generally associated with Socrates, Plato, and Aristotle, all of whom lived in Greece more than three centuries before the beginning of the Christian era. It is unpleasant to think that we cannot improve upon the "ancient" Greeks. It is even less encouraging to note that their superior understanding depended, at least in part, upon the leisure for learning and for self-government provided by slave labor.

Citizenship is no longer severely restricted, and slavery no longer exists. Most people are educated, if not learned, and awareness of the problem of government is probably more widely distributed now than ever before. Yet governments continue to turn primitive. Does this mean that the prospect of good government diminishes as citizenship expands? Is political and governmental understanding impossible in big societies and mass democracies? Will the rulers in such "big democracies" as the United States always disregard good principles and prefer war, totalitarianism, and other primitive solutions whenever they face a crisis?

Not even a tentative answer to these questions is possible without a thorough exploration of how at least one large population governs itself. Even the best of answers will not change the fact that government is our second most important problem. But without trying to understand government and to get a few tentative answers, we can only make our situation worse. Government is, for each of us, a matter of life and death.

GOVERNMENT: WHAT KIND OF A PROBLEM IS IT?

Though government is inescapably a matter of life and death, it means different things to different people. Each individual is free to choose any part of it as the defining element. This is what analysis in any field is all about—simplifying a problem by characterizing it in terms of what seem to be its essential and inescapable features. Much of the confusion in political discourse arises from the fact that different definitions of government are involved but are not made explicit. People may think they are arguing across a great ideological chasm when they are simply not communicating. They are, as Shaw might say, separated by a common language, where the words are all in English but the terms of reference are very different.

To avoid this possibility, two initial steps are most desirable—the identification of an approach to a problem and at least a brief analysis of its relationship to alternative approaches. Three distinctly different approaches will be identified: (1) government as politics, the prevailing definition in political science today; (2) government and politics as a product or "epiphenomenon" of social forces—the point of view that prevails in Europe, where the best-known school of thought is Marxism; (3) government as the institutionalization of conquest. If the prevailing American approach is a "politics of government," the third approach is a "government of politics." Since this approach is the one adopted for this book, it will be introduced first and then others will be briefly contrasted and compared with it.

Conquest: The Problem of Government

3

"Armed Prophets Have Conquered and Unarmed Ones Failed"[1]

Of all the possible defining characteristics of government, the one that seems least avoidable is *conquest.* Conquest in its most ancient as well as its most modern usage refers to "the action of gaining by force of arms; acquisition by war; subjugation of a country . . . by vanquishing; gaining of victory."[2] Conquest is not government; but conquest precedes government, and government is inconceivable without conquest. Conquest means bringing a territory and its population under control. This usually implies military action, seizure, the elimination of dissidents, and the claiming of that territory in the name of some higher authority. The means may be infinite, but the actions amount to the same thing—bringing territory and population under control. Government emerges out of the cold remains of conquest.

Sometimes territories and populations are conquered more than once. Imperialistic powers conquer and reconquer weaker nations. A colony is just a conquered weaker nation. Revolution is another form of conquest, where the replacement of one conqueror by another takes place through internal war entirely within the same population and territory.[3] One disillusioned guerrilla observed that "all revolutions degenerate into governments."[4]

By whatever form, conquest comes first, and government follows. Government can best be considered the *institutionalization of conquest.* From the standpoint of our definition, the essential, the primordial purpose of government is *to maintain conquest.* And when a government is unable to maintain conquest, it is almost certain to be replaced eventually by another government. Conquest is, therefore, something that never ends. It only changes form. Beginning with the original occupation of virgin territory, conquest continues from generation to generation because there are more people or because the composition or attitudes of the population may change, requiring new methods of control.

Control is the essential ingredient. It is perfectly possible to conceive of and to speak of "free government." But *free* is an adjective, not an absolute state of being. In a free government, government comes first, and free may or may not apply as a characteristic of that particular government. Except as a wandering people, we do not begin free. Our beginning as a community of people is after conquest, and we gain our freedom in relation to

---

[1]Niccolo Machiavelli, *The Prince and the Discourses,* with an introduction by Max Lerner, trans. Luigi Ricci with rev. by E. R. P. Vincent and Christian E. Detmold (New York: Modern Library, 1940), p. 22.

[2]*The Compact Edition of the Oxford English Dictionary,* reproduced micrographically in 2 vols. (Oxford: Clarendon Press, 1971).

[3]Ted R. Gurr, *Why Men Rebel* (Princeton: Princeton University Press, 1970), p. 11.

[4]Quoted in Octavio Paz, "Twilight of Revolution," *Dissent,* Winter 1974, p. 59.

Conquest: The Problem of Government

what and who has conquered us. Thus *the institutionalization of conquest* is the definition of government in this volume.

By beginning here, we are at least on solid ground in the history of the modern nation-states of the West. In some instances, conquest may have come all at once, as with the territories in the New World. Or it may have occurred in stages, where a nation-state emerged only after generations of development from a series of regional conquests (fiefdoms) to the ultimate subordination of all the fiefdoms to a single national conqueror. But the history of each and every European nation-state is a long account of war and violence, ending only with the conquest of the entire territory, as that is defined by such natural boundaries as mountains and rivers and by such cultural boundaries as distinctive racial characteristics or linguistic or other cultural similarities.

The clumsy term *nation-state* is essential to understanding the link between conquest and government. "A nation-state is a state that has become largely identical with one people."[5] Not all states are composed of a single nation—a single group of people who share a culture, a language, and a common historical heritage. But most modern states *are* nation-states, and certainly the most highly integrated and effective states are the ones based on those common ties of a real nation.[6]

The universality of the relationship between conquest and government has been especially well described by the eminent historian of feudalism, Marc Bloch. As he puts it, although "general development . . . followed very different lines from country to country," it was "virtually universal in its fundamental features."[7] The "general development" was the process by which one monarch or baron gained control of the state by dominating all of his neighbors and developing such supremacy as to become the "political authority" and the most affluent among them (p. 421).

In France the national monarch had achieved almost everything necessary for a nation-state by the end of the tenth century: subordination of the regional courts to the royal courts, subordination of the church to the idea of the state, establishment of the power to exact military service from all subjects (pp. 422–423). In Germany, national unification came later; but each component of what became modern Germany, such as Prussia, was a product of conquest. National authority was ultimately established by the same means as elsewhere; the "suppression of the dukes" was accomplished with the help of the church, whose contingents

---

[5]Karl Deutsch, *Nationalism and Its Alternatives* (New York: Knopf, 1969), p. 19.

[6]Again, see Deutsch, *Nationalism and Its Alternatives,* especially chapter 1, for a fine introduction to the whole phenomenon.

[7]Marc Bloch, *Feudal Society,* trans. L. A. Manyon (Chicago: University of Chicago Press, 1961), p. 422. In this and the following paragraph, page references to this edition will be in parentheses rather than in footnotes.

"formed the largest and most stable part of the royal army" (p. 427). In England, despite its many counties and its long tradition of representation, a genuine unity within a single nation-state was established, again by conquest: "The war of conquest, and the harsh suppression of the subsequent rebellions removed from the scene the great native chiefs" (p. 429).

These original acts of conquest fell far short of absolute success. Yet, after conquest once established some semblance of a state, further acts of insubordination against authority occurred within that context: "The powerful kingship of the conquerors had not destroyed all other powers; but it had forced them to act, even when in opposition to it, only within the framework of the State" (p. 431). In this context we can now complete the Machiavelli observation with which we began this section:

> Thus it comes about that all armed prophets have conquered and unarmed ones failed; for . . . the character of peoples varies, and it is easy to persuade them of a thing, but difficult to keep them in that persuasion. And so it is necessary to order things so that when they no longer believe, they can be made to believe by force.[8]

The annals of every country are filled with accounts of one ruler overthrowing another. Occasionally even more profound changes have taken place, where the whole basis of authority was replaced, along with the ruler—from church to secular authority, from Catholic to Protestant authority, from absolute to limited monarchy, from divine to popular consent. But this only illustrates from another angle the intimate kinship between conquest (through revolution and otherwise) and the building of the modern nation-state.

When at last most of the violent insubordination of the dukes (or the corporate executives or the proletariat or the Indians) has disappeared, we then say that the state has established itself. Some call this "integration." Others call it "political stability." Still others call it "nation-building." But by any name it is the same. People come to recognize the authority of the state and agree (at best) that the state is good or (at least) that further resistance to the state is useless. At that point people allow themselves to say that they are ruled by authorized agents of the state. When conquest has gone so far as to stabilize the relationship between the conqueror and the people, we can say that the people are being governed. But here again we are only restating the kinship between conquest and

---

[8]Machiavelli, *The Prince*, p. 22. A word ought to be said about use of the concept *state*. "The state" is an abstraction equivalent to "the body politic," which refers to the entire civil power or the source of civil or temporal authority. It is distinguished from "the church," an abstraction for religious authority. One does not actually see the state but rather the apparatus of the state: government. Care should be taken to avoid confusing this abstraction with the American states in the federal system, even though the terminology ("State of Illinois") comes from the old abstraction.

government. And at this point it is worth reintroducing our definition of government as institutionalized conquest.

Two Other Approaches: Government as Politics and Government as Epiphenomenon

For the past three or more decades the prevailing tendency in political science has been to define government *as* politics; political science has probably made progress by defining government as an institution or arena in which people seek power. As Harold Lasswell put it in one of the most influential formulations, political science is the study of "who gets what, when, how."[9] An important variation on this is the definition of government as a product of the long process of political activity. According to this definition, the search for power is comprised of repeated behaviors over long periods of time, involving organization into groups, application of "rules of the game," and so on. Nevertheless, this definition, like Lasswell's, looks at government and sees politics.[10]

This view of government has prevailed for so long among political scientists and journalists that many will be astonished to learn that it is not the only possible definition of government. The "politics" or "process" approach—sometimes called "scientific" or "realistic"—was itself a reaction against a nineteenth century definition of government as something called "the state." This latter approach is now referred to as formalistic, inasmuch as it tended to define government as a product of formal authority vested in constitutions, laws, rights, offices, and legally defined institutions. These concepts were virtually banned from use in modern, scientific, or realistic political science.[11]

During the 1960s, a certain amount of discomfort with a purely politics definition crept back into the field, and the search was on for an improved definition of government, a definition that would take into account the failure of governments on a large scale to cope with cold war, equality, and other intensely sought social goals. One important variation on the politics definition of government was a "politics of democracy" formulation. This was employed by some important analysts of the United States and was eventually adopted by many students of developing countries. The concern here was to

<hr />

[9]Harold D. Lasswell, *Politics: Who Gets What, When, How?* (New York: McGraw–Hill, 1936).

[10]See especially Arthur F. Bentley, *The Process of Government* (Chicago: University of Chicago Press, 1908). For a good review of this entire political process approach, see Michael Weinstein, *Philosophy, Theory, and Method in Contemporary Political Thought* (Chicago: Scott, Foresman, 1971), especially chapter 5. See also George J. Graham, *Methodological Foundations for Political Analysis* (Waltham, Mass.: Xerox College Publishing, 1971), chapter 1.

[11]The most severe attack against formalism, and one of the most influential, will be found in Bentley, *The Process of Government*. For a good intellectual history, see Paul Kress, *Social Science and the Idea of Progress: The Ambiguous Legacy of Arthur F. Bentley* (Urbana: University of Illinois Press, 1970). The reader will note by now that I am to a large extent returning to the older formalism—though with a few twists.

focus upon those aspects of the political process, if any, that produced desirable ends, such as broader participation, greater representation, more government accountability, higher per capita income.[12]

As with all definitions there are advantages and disadvantages to the politics approach. It is objective, leading the observer to phenomena that can actually be observed and studied with some precision. But in order to do this, it must leave out many aspects of government that are of historic importance. Many have neglected policy while studying policy formulation; many others have neglected bureaucracy while studying administrative behavior; still others have studied voting without concerning themselves with the purpose of elections. And, although they proclaim their commitment to the observable and the measurable, the students of politics take *power* as their standard of political outcomes, a concept that is not susceptible to direct measurement.

The politics or realist approach adds something very powerful to political analysis, but it does not seem to me to be strong enough to warrant resolving the problem of government into a political process. It has been strengthened by adding the normative dimension, the "politics of democracy." However, this approach tends to give the impression that the most desirable values in the society have already been attained and properly distributed.[13]

According to the Marxist view, government is a product of history. More concretely, government is a product of the history of social classes and their relationships to one another. At any point in time government can be understood as the instrument of the dominant class. According to this view, politics, far from being at the center of things, is hardly important at all. Politics may be important during a revolution—which in the American politics approach is not even politics, but war. Otherwise, the Marxists would tend to say that politics is a cover for class domination. Politics tends to lull individuals into acceptance and consent. That is to say, politics, along with religion, tends to instill "false consciousness." They would argue that government should be closer

---

[12]Perhaps the earliest contemporary approach of this sort was that of William Riker, *Democracy in the United States* (New York: Macmillan, 1953); but the book was little noticed, probably because it appeared during the time when most people were heavily committed to a pure politics approach. Another good related approach will be found in Marian Irish and James Prothro, *The Politics of American Democracy,* 5th ed. (Englewood Cliffs, N.J.: Prentice-Hall, 1971).

[13]Robert Dahl was so frustrated over the misunderstanding engendered by his use of the term *pluralist democracy* that he issued the following disclaimer in the Preface to his *Democracy in the United States,* 2d ed. (Chicago: Rand-McNally, 1972): "I had too readily taken for granted the facility of readers to maintain consistently the distinction authorized by dictionary usage and ordinary language between democracy as (1) an ideal system and (2) a class of actual, concrete political systems to which the term is conventionally applied. . . . The relationship between the ideal and concrete systems . . . has long seemed to me both interesting and highly problematical and I had thought that the distinction contained in ordinary language would allow me to express myself unambiguously enough. I was wrong."

than politics to center stage in political analysis. And if government is an instrument of the dominant classes, politics is a sop to the masses.[14]

Marxism is a great antidote to overdoses of the American brand of political realism. It helps unmask those aspects of the political process that are nothing but reinforcements of the interests of corporate capitalism and of the varieties of entrenched power brokers. Too much of American political activity *is* a ritual of reinforcement. Too little of American political science analysis is critical, because so much of our modern political analysis is focused at such a low level of political behavior that it cannot place that behavior into its larger meanings.

Yet with all that analytic power, a Marxist definition of government is also riddled with problems. When the Marxist view prevails, it tends to become more of an official ideology and, worse still, to take on the character of a religion intolerant of alternative definitions of government. Why? Precisely because Marxism tends to view proponents of alternative definitions as agents of counterrevolution. Marxist theory is important to us precisely because it sees government as a matter of life and death; it is appealing also because it gives political analysis a role of historic importance. But unfortunately Marxism tends to treat other approaches not as competing but as wrong.

The debilitating problem with these approaches—the Marxist and the various American realist approaches—is that each is attempting to include as part of the definition of government a hypothesis or guess about how government works or who makes it work. No matter how scientific these approaches seem to be, each is violating a canon of science as long as it attempts to incorporate researchable hypotheses as part of its definition of the problem. It seems to me plainly wrong to begin with a definition which holds that government *is* what the dominant interests say. It seems to me equally wrong to begin with a definition which holds that government *is* whatever a political process of momentary alliances provides. Later investigation may confirm or deny one or both of these hypotheses. But hypotheses and guesses about what or who influences the government ought not to be sneaked in as part of the definition. We ought to begin with a definition of government for itself alone. This is why I have sought to define government in terms of the inescapable and primordial element of control, extending from original conquest through the most recent provision of Congress or decision of an agency or court.

---

[14]A brief but extremely useful introduction to a Marxist type of political science will be found in W. G. Runciman, *Social Science and Political Theory* (Cambridge: Cambridge University Press, 1971), chapter 3. One of the best efforts to place Marx and Marxism into the twentieth century pattern of political thought is that of Weinstein, *Philosophy, Theory, and Method in Contemporary Political Thought,* chapters 1 and 7. For a Marxist treatment of government, see Ralph Miliband, *The State in Capitalist Society* (New York: Basic Books, 1969).

Government: The Institutionalization of Conquest

All institutions in society exist to exert some kind of control over human beings. In fact, government would be impossible if nongovernmental institutions were not functioning well. (The contributions to conquest made by some of these nongovernmental forces will be assessed in chapter 3.) However, *government is the only institution in society whose manifest purpose is to maintain conquest through the exertion of controls.*[15] People often speak of the purpose of a business enterprise as profit; in the same sense it seems to me we can speak of the purpose of government as control.

Governments control by direct use of coercion—for example, when the policeman gives an order to get off the grass. Governments also use control indirectly by the provision of money or goods and services in ways strategically designed to influence the conduct of individuals. Granted, the goods and services provided by governments are as real as goods and services produced by private enterprises. But there is a difference nevertheless, inasmuch as governmental goods and services will be considered wasted unless their distribution reduces disorder or otherwise rechannels individual conduct toward directions defined as more desirable for the society.

In sum, nongovernmental control differs from governmental in at least two respects: (1) for governments, control is the prime function; in contrast, for a large business or a large church or even a crime syndicate, control is incidental to some other group goal, such as profit; (2) the control exerted by nongovernmental organizations is simply a fact; it is exercised or not—a lot of it or a little of it. In contrast, government control is not merely a matter of fact—it is either legitimate or illegitimate. That is to say, it is claimed that governmental control is the only good or necessary control in the society; moreover, governmental coercion even in its most assertive form is generally accepted in that light by the people. If people do not accept governmental control as derived from some higher source, their particular country is in for a new round of conquest either by colonization from the outside or by revolution from within.

Here we are not merely quibbling over a definition of an abstract phenomenon. These distinctions clarify the difference between what is public and what is private, between what to hold and what must be rendered unto Caesar. This is what the eminent Max Weber had

---

[15]Some readers will recognize that a great deal of controversy could be avoided by substituting *function* for purpose. Function captures the same phenomenon but is more objective, implying "it happens that way." I prefer the more controversial term precisely because *purpose* implies nature and intention, that governments are built for the purpose of control and those who govern are aware, one way or another, that the obligation of government is to maintain conquest.

in mind when he proposed that government was that institution in any human community which successfully claims within a given territory the monopoly of the *legitimate* use of physical force.[16] It would serve us well here to quote at length from a brilliant characterization of Weber's definition:

> 'But what,' asks Weber, 'is a "political" association? . . . What is a State? Sociologically, the State cannot be defined in terms of what it does. There is scarcely any task that some political association has not taken in hand, and there is no task that one could say has always been exclusive and peculiar to those associations which are designed as political. Ultimately, one can give a sociological definition of the modern state only in terms of the specific means peculiar to it, as to every political association, namely, the use of physical force. If the only institutions which existed did not know the use of violence, then the concept "State" would disappear, and there would emerge what could be designated "anarchy" in the specific sense of the word. A State is a human community which successfully claims within a given territory the monopoly of the legitimate use of physical force.'[17]

Is it harsh and ungenerous to define one's own government in terms of conquest and violence, coercion and control? Yes, of course it is. But since government is universally people's second most important problem, how could coping with the problem be pleasant? Life and death have their moments of individual triumph; but triumph is, by definition, the momentous exception to an otherwise grim reality. And there is a good deal of solace in the fact that the experiences with government in the United States are no worse than the experiences with governments in other countries. The pragmatist would say that our system of government and politics must be pretty sound because it works, and that it works even though we are one of the largest and most complex of societies. To a pragmatist, the job of political analysis is to describe, with some admiration, how the system works.

But in this case the pragmatist is quite wrong. Our system does not work. The pure and simple fact is that we make it work. We spend billions of dollars and endure great tensions to make it work. As good analysts we cannot rest on the fact that we do make it work. That is distinctly not enough. As long as government falls short of the ideals of its own founders and the claims of current leaders, there is room for detached analysis and intense political criticism.

---

[16]One source of Weber's discussion of the state and government will be found in A. N. Henderson and Talcott Parsons, eds. and trans., *Max Weber: The Theory of Social and Economic Organization* (New York: Oxford University Press, 1947).

[17]Runciman, *Social Science and Political Theory*, p. 35. See also Runciman's discussion of Weber, pp. 35–42.

AN OVERVIEW OF THE BOOK

Conquest is the criterion; yet incomplete conquest is the fact. Conquest will never be complete, because there is insufficient technology to control all behavior all of the time, and because too few people want complete conquest. People are ambivalent about conquest. They want a government powerful enough to conquer all and restrained enough not to. Thus, in the real world government resides in a contradiction. *The peril and the freedom of the individual are both directly related to the failure of government to fulfill its purpose.* This is but a beginning of analysis, not a counsel of despair. There is a lifetime of fascination for those who are able to watch government as it attempts to resolve or to displace its own contradictions.

Some will say this book represents a view held by conservatives. But it is also a view widely shared among persons who do not write books but who must contend at one time or another with a prison system, or a court, or a legislative committee, or a presidential order, or a unit of the National Guard, or a summons to testify before a regulatory commission, or a notice of eviction prior to having private property taken for a highway. It is the unarticulated view of the welfare mother. It is the emotionally articulated view of a businessman trying to get a permit from City Hall to haul garbage; and it is the unarticulated but consciously understood view of a state bar association when it designs its examinations in order to reject the candidacies of most of the examinees for admission to legal practice.

I share that view not because I am any more sentimental about the powerless or the poor than anyone else. I have taken no vows of poverty or of powerlessness. I share the view of the powerless mainly out of recognition that most of us are powerless all the time and all of us are powerless most of the time. Government is an institution; it is a force in history to which, most of the time, we submit. Every action and every agency of contemporary government is an expression of a fundamental prerequisite that all governments share; conquest, in some form or another, permeates everything about government. Conquest is the common factor, tying together into one system the behavior of courts and cops, teachers and senators, bureaucrats and technocrats, generals and attorneys general, presidents and pressure groups. It is thus the single criterion which will guide evaluation in each section of every chapter.

The book is divided into five parts: "Occupation," "Constitution," "Politics," "Government," and "Policy." Part I, "Occupation," is comprised of two chapters concerned with conquest in its most literal sense. This means cowboys and Indians, seizure of property, slavery, and the violence associated with each. It means schools and television, churches and folklore, spectator sports and the national anthem, and the subtleties—as influential as they are unnoticed—of contemporary social controls. We may like or dislike the ways our society controls us, but it would be impossible to imagine a society without successful occupation, up to a point, of our lands as well as our minds, occupation by authority that is supported with armies.

Part II, "Constitution," provides a look at the transition from literal conquest to government by legitimate authority. Some countries never make a complete transition; they operate either without a constitution or with a new one to suit the convenience of each new regime. A constitution provides for the actual structure of government, but it goes far beyond that to gain legitimacy for the controls exercised by that government. A constitution is a particular type of appeal to the people to get them to accept the right of the conquerors to be rulers. Some countries try to gain this legitimacy by appeals to religion, or heredity, or ideology, or fear. A constitutional government seeks legitimacy by placing limits upon itself—upon what it can do and how it will allow itself to use its power. Many narrow economic interests have been written into the United States Constitution. However, many principles, such as the separation of powers, can be explained only by commitments to restraint. Many provisions of the Constitution continue to exert a profound influence on our everyday lives.

Part III, "Politics," is of course concerned with the usual phenomena of public opinion, groups, parties, campaigns, and elections. Nevertheless, these are placed within the context of conquest. Rulers seek legitimacy through consent of the governed; consent is one of the limitations the Constitution places upon rulers. This is a calculated risk, because although the consent may enable the government to govern more effectively, it also opens up the system to a far broader range of influences upon the rulers and contradictions within the institutions of government. The powerful want participation because it may lead to strong citizen support for the regime. The powerless want participation because it may open opportunities to influence the regime and to establish new terms of conquest. Both sides want participation for the right reasons, but both could turn out to be wrong in practice. Opinions are the basis of consent, and individual opinions are aggregated into "public opinions" by polls, by organized groups, by parties, and by elections. Each process of aggregating public opinions distorts the original opinions of individuals. No matter how sincerely rulers wish to govern by consent, they can never be sure they have it.

Part IV, "Government," discusses the institutions of governing—Congress, the president, the bureaucracies in the executive branch, the independent agencies, the courts, the local governments, and the various police and military bodies. Stress will be upon the institutions of the national government but only because they are sufficient to show the reader how governing institutions work and how well or badly they respond to the many inconsistent demands made upon them. We build a representative assembly and expect it to represent widely while governing well. We have erected a gigantic administrative apparatus on the basis of the best principles of scientific business administration and industrial engineering. Although this is the only way we would ever have been able to cope with conquest on a large scale, this creates enormous problems, because we expect bureaucrats, as civil servants, to follow the demands of political superiors rather than the dictates of their own profession. One of the lasting problems of modern government is not the corruption of administrators but their integrity. The president and the federal appellate courts are expected to make the syntheses among the various demands for control and constraint, but their responsibilities are approaching a scale beyond human ability. This may be why no presidential candidates ever seem to be qualified. They are not and they cannot be.

Part V, "Policy," describes the most formal and official way by which governments express and communicate controls. Foreign policy comes first, because without successful foreign policy there can be no sovereign government to make domestic policies. Domestic policies are not the only means by which governments exert controls over their population, since there are many administrators, police, and other officials who have the authority to make decisions according to personal discretion rather than announced policy. However, the policies of a government, as published before action, are clearly the most important and the most desirable means by which governments can maintain conquest. And indeed, policy will be defined as conquest updated.

A final chapter steps outside the framework to ask how people react to being conquered when they come to the conclusion that the terms of conquest are not in their favor. The chapter recognizes three things about most political systems, including that of the United States. First, violent reactions against authority have erupted frequently. Second, regimes prefer to suppress or to buy off political violence; they are unlikely to change themselves voluntarily. Third, some important changes have taken place. But how, and with what consequences? Violence has never been given its due in the analysis of American politics. Yet it has been so frequent that the forms of political violence have been virtually institutionalized.

During this bicentennial era, citizens of the United States have much to celebrate. But they must appreciate the good in relation to the bad, the gains in relation to the costs, and the successes in relation to the failures; otherwise, they are not good citizens, only servile ones. If we can agree that there are political problems yet unsolved in the United States, then we ought to be able to agree further that lack of effort to understand them can only make things worse. If criticism undermines patriotism, then our problems are even more serious than I had imagined.

Part One
Occupation

New and hostile territory presented some common
problems to the conquerers of North and South America.
Both were remote from their mother countries. Slavery was
important; in North and South America Indians were
subjected to it, blacks were imported to it. But differences
were also great and go far to explain the disparities in
political institutions that eventually emerged. Conquest in
South America was dominated by conquistadors and the
church, while conquest in the North was dominated by
civilians and by economic principles that came to be
known as capitalism. Slavery, though universal, was very
different in the two regions. These early experiences have
left in their wake some profound and recurring social and
political problems which can be dealt with only by
continuing efforts at conquest. Society "reconquers" itself
generation after generation by inculcation of important
common values through religion, patriotism, education,
and popular culture. Government is one more of society's
efforts. Yet with all of the apparatus of control, conquest
of a large territory and population seems always
incomplete.

Chapter 2 Unwanted Continent: The Conquest of North America

The conquest of the North American continent is surely one of the great adventure stories of all time. North America is a land mass over twice as large as all of Europe. It is larger than the entire Western world or "Christendom," as that was defined at the time of Columbus. Most of the available territory was hostile; in the course of time the aborigines conspired with the environment to make life miserable for the explorers, the exploiters, and the settlers. Nearly 130 years after Columbus the continent was still hostile, if we can believe William Bradford, whose journal is our most important source of information on the original *Mayflower* crossing. Of the landing on Cape Cod he wrote:

> Being thus passed the vast ocean, and a sea of troubles before in their preparation . . . what could they see but a hideous and desolate wilderness, full of wild beasts and wild men—and what

multitudes of them they knew not. Neither could they, as it were, go up to the top of Pisgah to view from this wilderness a more goodly country to feed their hopes; for which way soever they turned their eyes (save upward to the heavens) they could have little solace. . . . For summer being done, all things stand upon them with a weatherbeaten face, and the whole country, full of woods and thickets, represented a wild and savage hue.[1]

THE AMERICAN STYLES OF CONQUEST

As we shall see, it is not surprising that the conquest of North America followed that of South America by more than a century. Settlements accompanied Columbus's second and third voyages to the Caribbean. The very real prospect of precious metals, better weather, and, most importantly, passage to the Pacific and the riches of Asia enticed the Spanish and Portuguese farther and farther into South America. The adventurer who provided the New World with its name, Amerigo Vespucci, was an explorer of *South* America. Occasional probes north of Columbus's discoveries in the Caribbean Islands revealed little worthy of exploitation. The fort at St. Augustine (in what is now called Florida) was not built until 1565, and St. Augustine was a northern extremity, not a beachhead for expansion northward.

South America: Conquest in the Grand Style

The Spanish-Portuguese conquest of South America did not merely precede the conquest of North America. It was far more auspicious. In 1493 Pope Alexander VI gave conquest recognition by dividing the world into Spanish and Portuguese zones; colonies followed almost immediately. Of still greater significance for the development of political traditions, Spanish and Portuguese conquest was conducted by military means under the close control of the monarchies back in Spain and Portugal. The two best-known expeditions are those of Hernán Cortés, who invaded Mexico with a band of around 600 in 1519, and Francisco Pizarro in Peru in 1531. Similar military expeditions followed, until by 1580 Spain and Portugal had the first fully established empires in the New World, covering a very substantial part of the Atlantic and Pacific coasts, plus large portions of the interior.[2]

The various Spanish settlements constituting the empire were considered the personal possession of the crown of Castile on the

---

[1]Quoted in Kate Caffrey, *The Mayflower* (New York: Stein & Day, 1974), p. 113.

[2]The leading scholarly treatment of the subject is J. H. Parry, *The Spanish Seaborne Empire* (London: Hutchinson, 1966), part 1. See also the readable account of Simon Collier, *From Cortes to Castro* (New York: Macmillan, 1974), chapter 1.

The landing of the
pilgrims, 1620.

theory that Columbus sailed as the personal agent of Isabella. Thus, the various settlers owed personal loyalty and homage to that crown. In turn, local Spanish overlords exercised control over the American Indians through a system known as *encomienda,* under which the latter were compelled to render labor service and tribute to their new masters.[3] Here we see already the fetus of the Latin American tradition of rule by *juntas* (military cliques) and *caudillos* (strong men) even after independence was attained and the state and church were to some extent separated. These Spanish and Portuguese *conquistadors* and their greedy followers were probably no more violent conquerors than the northern Europeans who took North America. All seized the land and claimed it for their home country. All dealt as conquerors with the aboriginals—clearing them from desirable territory by relocation, murder, slavery, or forced tribute. Yet, as we shall see, the different *means* by which these conquests were conducted made a great deal of difference in the eventual development of political traditions and institutions.

---

[3]See Stanley Stein and Barbara Stein, *The Colonial Heritage of Latin America* (New York: Oxford University Press, 1970), chapters 2 and 3; also Max Savelle, *Empires to Nations: Expansion in America, 1713–1824* (Minneapolis: University of Minnesota Press, 1974), chapter 2. Note especially the military and hierarchical character of all titles of agents in the countries, regions, and provinces of South America from the very beginning. Portuguese conquest and early colonial control were apparently somewhat less brutal than Spanish, but the pattern of military-clerical-royal dominance was apparently the same. See Collier, *From Cortes to Castro,* p. 4, and Savelle, *Empires to Nations,* p. 29.

Conquest in North America:
From Conquistadors to Capitalism

In the late sixteenth century, when South America's conquest was an established fact, the North American beachhead was still uncertain. This was particularly true of the central portion that was to become the United States. It was apparently considered more a barrier than a discovery. Without promise of gold or passage to India, this central portion would have to await new developments and new incentives. Very late in this first century after Columbus some effort was made to actually colonize and settle rather than exploit. But Sir Humphrey Gilbert's two abortive efforts in Newfoundland after 1583 and Sir Walter Raleigh's tragic expeditions to Roanoke Island off Virginia between 1585 and 1587 gave little indication that changes would come soon.

The second century after Columbus began as the first had ended. In 1606, twenty years after the failure of Roanoke, the Jamestown Colony was founded; but in 1625 it was dissolved because of financial failure, and Virginia became a crown colony. A twin settlement in what is now Maine survived only one winter. But actually hindsight helps us understand that the Jamestown expedition was a break with the past rather than a repetition of it. At least four very significant things had intervened in the twenty years between Roanoke Island and Jamestown: (1) new international relations, (2) the emergence of religious dissent, (3) the emergence of mercantilism, and (4) the development or discovery of capitalism.

1. James I, the first in the new line of Stuarts, replaced Elizabeth in 1603 in England. James put an end to the long and costly war with Spain and took serious measures to terminate English piracy of Spanish shipping. Such basic shifts in international relations meant that the conflicts of interest between and among the great national powers would have to be sublimated toward competition and away from war. Thanks to this vigorous competition and to the economic theory of mercantilism that guided the competitive strategies (see below), European civilization was extensively involved in every major territory of the world within a century after Columbus.

2. The concept of religious freedom in England may have begun to take hold when Henry VIII declared his own independence from Rome. But little of it was granted to smaller protestant sects, so religious dissenters began to look toward emigration as the solution. Some went to Holland in 1607–1608. But the Holland settlement had not quite reached 500 settlers by 1620 when a Puritan group of pilgrims chose the more hazardous American crossing. These dissenters were the first of thousands who eventually came to view North America as a place to settle rather than to exploit.

3. Mercantilism was only a theory, and a vaguely defined one at

that.[4] But its influence on conquest in North America was enormous, for mercantilism helped channel international political and religious conflict into economic competition. Mercantilists were concerned about the total wealth of the nation, and in their view prosperity for the nation depended upon favorable balances of trade with all other nations. An unfavorable balance of trade involves an excess of imports over exports, the difference being made up in payments of gold or some other precious commodity. Gold in the treasury was about the only reliable measure of prosperity, according to the mercantilists.

Colonies came to be viewed as another prerequisite of a prosperous nation; the theory held that one of the sure ways of protecting national resources was to establish and settle real colonies that would produce raw materials and buy goods produced in the mother country, all in a manner that would guarantee the favorable balance of trade. Each country and its colonies would constitute an exclusive system, in direct competition with other such colonial systems. Mercantilism was in no way inconsistent with the absolute monarchies which ruled in most European countries during the seventeenth century. In fact, many mercantilist policies relied upon medieval monarchical power for grants of exclusive privilege. For example, all territories acquired in the colonies by adventurers, explorers, and conquistadors were assumed to be the private domain of the king. This was as true of the British and French colonial outlook as it was of the Spanish and Portuguese.

In practice this gave each king the power to grant each expedition to the colonies an exclusive privilege to a certain enterprise, or to the acquisition of certain raw materials, or, more important, exclusive access to large tracts of land. In this manner, absolute monarchy and mercantilism worked hand in hand. Overseas enterprises could be sponsored by the king, and each adventurer could be encouraged to engage in the enterprise because of the exclusive guarantee of access. Mercantilism was as much a part of the original colonial system as was absolute monarchy, the church, and the military conquerors.[5]

4. All of the above factors had alerted England, Holland, and to a lesser extent France to the attractions of exploration and colonization for purposes other than quick profit in gold or the establish-

[4]The best introduction to mercantilism is C. H. Wilson, "Trade, Society and the State," in *The Cambridge Economic History of Europe,* ed. E. E. Rich and C. H. Wilson, vol. 4 (Cambridge: Cambridge University Press, 1960), pp. 487–575.

[5]Carl Friedrich, *Constitutional Government and Democracy,* 4th ed. (Waltham, Mass.: Blaisdell, 1968), pp. 93–100. J. P. Seeley, a British historian of the 1880s, agreed with this thesis but went on to observe that "the hope of attaining such splendid estates and enjoying the profits that were reaped from them constituted the greatest stimulus to commerce that had ever been known" but that the system of monopoly granted by monarchs to each adventurer and entrepreneur in the New World "made trade and war indistinguishable from each other." Seeley, *The Expansion of England* (Chicago: University of Chicago Press, 1971), pp. 88–90.

Varieties of conquest in America. *This page:* Conquest by terror. *Opposite page, clockwise from top left:* Conquest by treaty, conquest by ownership, conquest by contract, conquest by grace.

ment of way stations to the Orient. Henceforth America was going to be a place for long-range enterprise involving people in communities. Once this change of perspective took place, these countries began to look toward the unheralded middle of North America—the territory which became the United States about 180 years later. From that point on the incentives were there but the practical problems were still extremely difficult. Rulers could grant monopolies and provide the mercantilist incentives of exclusive access to certain large tracts of territory, but they could not necessarily provide human resources and money. Britain in the seventeenth century was not yet a wealthy country. Although economic reforms consistent with capitalist development, such as the joint stock company and the Bank of England, contributed greatly to the growth of Britain's wealth (as did a new encouragement of science), the New World also played a substantial role in enriching the country.

Capitalism was the answer. The capitalism involved in the conquest of North America is rudimentary and crude by twentieth century standards. Nevertheless, it possessed the essential ingredients. One basic element of the capitalist approach was of course the actual granting of the charter and exclusive privileges—the royal franchise—to certain territories. This was the mercantilist side, and it shows the extent to which capitalism had its origins in the state and mercantilism. Every modern corporation begins the same way, with the granting of the charter, even though only a few of these charters provide for some kind of a monopoly.[6] But the fact that these first royal charters were monopolies does not change the basis of the incorporation.

The other typically capitalistic aspect of colonization was the way in which these enterprises amassed sufficient wealth to carry out a risky venture, such as settling Virginia, for a profit. No single merchant could foot the bill for such a large and risky undertaking. Thus, merchants in central cities like London and Leyden would organize their scheme into a "joint stock company," advertise their venture among the merchants and other prospective investors, sell shares to each for the money to be used in the enterprise, and spread the profit and the risk proportionately among the shareholders.[7] There had been trading companies throughout the sixteenth century well prior to the sailing of the *Mayflower*. But these companies worked from direct royal grants of monopoly in which the grantee built up his own capital, traded his own goods and services, and took all of the risks himself.

---

[6]A good, brief description of corporations and their historical antecedents is John P. Davis, *Corporations,* vol. 2 (New York: Putnam, 1961).

[7]For a discussion of one example, see M. Epstein, *The Early History of the Levant Company* (London: George Routledge, 1908).

Apparently it was the Dutch after 1600 who introduced the innovation of selling shares and spreading investment and risk. This was quickly copied by rival enterprises and spread to many countries during the seventeenth century. To this day, the conventional designation of corporations in England is not *inc.,* as in the United States, but *ltd.* (referring to the "limited liability of the investors"). Perhaps even more to the point is the conventional French and Spanish designation of a corporation as *S.A.,* which is an abbreviation of *société anonyme,*[8] an "anonymous society."

These capitalistic enterprises were monarchical in their sponsorship and aristocratic in much of their leadership, and they inevitably had to depend upon armed force to defend their resources once these were established in North America. Nevertheless, it was their capitalistic character that gave the conquest of North America its special and distinctive character. Perhaps the most interesting and revealing case study of capitalistic methods of conquest is that of the immigration of the pilgrims. The first crossing on the *Mayflower* has been acclaimed most often for the tremendous courage of the passengers and for their great wisdom in having framed and signed the Mayflower Compact, admired by many as the first example in modern times of a contract among free individuals to institute a government. Of even greater practical importance, however, was the fact that the pilgrims, though of very modest means, were able to finance their voyages, not only the *Mayflower* voyage, but all the later voyages, by adopting the best available capitalistic principles.

In 1620 three companies were engaged in making connections between land in the United States and prospective European immigrants—the Virginia Company, the London Company, and the Plymouth Company. Their interests stretched virtually from what we now call Chesapeake Bay to Nova Scotia.[9] Collectively the leaders of these companies called themselves the Merchant Adventurers or the Dorchester Adventurers. The Mayflower group entered into a seven-year agreement with the Merchant Adventurers which provided the pilgrims with their means of crossing the Atlantic in return for the profits that might come from fishing. The story of their crossing is filled with financial and environmental catastrophes, but it did indeed work. In fact, it was probably the only available means by which people of modest resources could have undertaken such an enterprise.[10]

During the 1620s, following the first crossing, the pilgrims grew

[8]For readable accounts that place these developments within American history, see Oscar Handlin, *America—A History* (New York: Holt, Rinehart and Winston, 1968), p. 14; also John M. Blum et al., *The National Experience,* 2d ed. (New York: Harcourt, Brace & World, 1968), p. 21.

[9]Still a valuable source of information is George L. Beer, *The Origins of the British Colonial System* (New York: Macmillan, 1908).

[10]A good account of plans for the first crossing, and of the business and other arrangements, will be found in Caffrey, *The Mayflower,* pp. 48–88.

in number and the Merchant Adventurers declined in prosperity, due to the failure of too many of their investments.[11] In 1628 many of the prominent religious dissenters remaining in England bought shares in the now failing Adventurers, which by that time was called the New England Company. Their license with that company authorized them to settle in an area known as Massachusetts Bay, and a year later they reorganized the New England Company as the Massachusetts Bay Company and managed to get their new charter and their land grant confirmed directly by King James. Once they had gained control of the new company, these colonists voted to immigrate and to transfer the entire company to America. In that one action, they took an English corporation and converted it from a mere business board of directors in England to a government in Massachusetts. According to one account, "In one bold stroke, the

---

[11]Caffrey reports that the Virginia Company alone granted forty-four charters comparable to the Mayflower charter before 1624. Blum et al., *The National Experience*, p. 22, attributes the failure of the Adventurers to the single effort in 1623 to set up a farming and fishing settlement at Cape Ann.

Puritans won for themselves the opportunity to do in Massachusetts what Puritans for nearly a century had been yearning to do in England."[12]

In contrast to the South American conquest by conquistadors and caudillos, the pattern of conquest in the territory that became our original colonies was really dominated by civilians and capitalists. The fact that the Massachusetts Bay Colony was established by religious separatists only underscores the historic significance of capitalism. Capitalist enterprises could serve any purpose. They were available for the pursuit of purely economic goals but could equally well serve political and religious goals by providing economic muscle. To the English king, a charter for one of these companies provided the prospect of economic gain and the removal of citizens who were political problems. To the pilgrims, these capitalist enterprises meant sufficient economic base upon which to launch a pursuit of political freedom. Both interests were well served by the corporation and set the stage for the spectacular success of North American conquest, despite inauspicious beginnings and enormous odds. Spain resisted such capitalistic innovations as the joint stock company in the colonization of South America and in so doing influenced to a large extent the type of government which was to develop in that part of the New World.[13]

Some Consequences of Conquest: Our Brighter Side

A brief review of other differences between South and North American patterns of conquest will begin to show how significant these origins are for later political traditions and institutions. Conquests in South America seem to have been shaped by the following facts. The Spanish and Portuguese had hit upon the wanted part of the continent, where profits could be immediate. The adventurers were primarily military people with extremely close ties to the church and to the monarchies. Moreover, the monarchies could maintain a great deal of legal control because Spanish and Portuguese kings were still quite powerful and were able to hold on to their power through the discoveries of precious metals in the New World. They could also maintain their control to a greater extent not only because they were willing and able to reward their military leaders through the encomienda system but also because of the

---

[12]Blum et al., *The National Experience*, p. 22. The Puritans were a fundamentalist sect within the Church of England who were committed to completing the Reformation. They were not heretics but dissenters. The Plymouth settlers of 1620, who in America came to be known as Pilgrims, were a group of Separatists within Puritanism who despaired of ever reforming the Church of England and left for Holland in 1609. After ten years of freedom but hardship in Holland, they departed on the *Mayflower* in 1620. Additional significant Puritan immigration direct from England did not begin for another nine years, with formation of the Massachusetts Bay Company.

[13]Stein and Stein, *The Colonial Heritage of Latin America*, pp. 49 and 50.

strong ideological ties between the colonists and their home central governments.[14]

Conquest in North America emerged in a far different situation. Much of the physical environment was more hostile than South America, and there was little promise of immediate gain in the discovery of precious metals. Because of the rise of the middle classes in England—absent in the Iberian Peninsula—the English monarchs were unable to dominate colonization to the same degree as the Spanish and Portuguese monarchs. Their task was made all the more difficult by the fact that so much of the immigration was Protestant; but even when it was Catholic, motivations much more often arose out of dissent rather than out of loyal service to state or church. Thus, because of the apparent absence of precious metals in North America and the religious divergence between the English church and the settlers, the kings of England and Holland had little incentive to become strongly involved and little power to maintain control, whether through loyalty or surveillance.

There seems to be little controversy among professional researchers regarding the proposition that the style of the Spanish and Portuguese conquest in South America goes a long way toward explaining the pattern of backward economic structures and ruling class political conservatism prevalent among most countries in South America.[15] All the imperial countries expected to implant their own political institutions in their colonies.[16] But Spanish and Portuguese efforts proved most successful. Important aspects of that success are the rigid aristocratic social structures, through which land ownership and conspicuous consumption, rather than investment by ruling classes, were successfully implanted; and these were justified by the close relationship between church and state.

Although many specific factors eventually intervened to give each of the Latin American countries its own special character, their common experiences in conquest have given all of them a common political culture set apart from our own. Conservative upper classes are opposed by revolutionary attitudes; governments thus are generally unstable, and there is little experience of stable self-government; the tradition of opposition political parties is very weak; and the rigid, oligarchic governmental patterns seem to be capable of being changed only through coups d'etat.

---

[14]See Celso Furtado, *Economic Development of Latin America* (Cambridge: Cambridge University Press, 1970), chapter 2; and Stein and Stein, *The Colonial Heritage of Latin America.*

[15]No treatment of this kind can be made without acknowledging a great debt to the following: Stanley M. Elkins, *Slavery—A Problem in American Institutional and Intellectual Life* (Chicago: University of Chicago Press, 1959 and 1968); Herbert S. Klein, *Slavery in the Americas—A Comparative Study of Cuba and Virginia* (Chicago: University of Chicago Press, 1967); and Savelle, *Empires to Nations.* For a challenging discussion of the backwardness of Latin American capitalism see André Gunder Frank, *Capitalism and Underdevelopment in Latin America* (New York: Monthly Review Press, 1967).

[16]Savelle, *Empires to Nations,* p. 24.

The North American pattern of colonization and conquest shows up brilliantly in contrast to this, as diamonds on a black silk cloth. One aspect of this pattern, the original separation or autonomy of the North American settlers, meant that laws and customs of the motherland were often given a highly local coloration as they were freely adapted to meet local conditions. It was very probably for these reasons that the feudal and medieval social structures of Europe did not take root in North America.

A second feature of North American conquest was the very early establishment of political freedom as an important political value. Even though observed all too often in the breech, especially by some of the religious sects who imposed their own views on others as soon as they managed to found their own theocracy, political freedom was nevertheless commonly espoused and was in fact practiced eventually in the elevation of the "freeman" to a person with rights of access to politics and government. The earlier concept of political freedom was a far cry from our present expectations; yet the seed was planted then.

Part and parcel of this was the very early establishment of institutions of representative government. As already observed, the Massachusetts Bay Company became the Massachusetts Bay Colony; but this meant that the governing board became a representative body vis-a-vis the stockholders in the enterprise. *Freeman* was an established name in England for stockholder; it quickly became the name for voters in the colonies. The Mayflower Compact of 1620 was another expression of the early espousal of representative institutions.

But there are other experiences of the same sort, even if they were not recorded for all times in a famous document. In fact, the first legislature in America, the Virginia House of Burgesses, was established a year before the Mayflower Compact, when two representatives from each settled district in the Jamestown area were elected, by a vote of all men over the age of seventeen, to meet with the governor and council in one large building, the Jamestown Church. The Virginia House has been a continuing representative body at least since 1621, while in the Catholic colony of Maryland there was an independent assembly as early as 1654, although apparently it nearly took a local civil war to establish it. By 1643 there had already been one attempt to form an independent confederation, the New England Confederacy.

In 1660 New England, Virginia, and Maryland were already full-fledged commonwealths possessing most of the apparatus of the civilized life as developed up to that time, reproducing or attempting to improve on the institutions of the homeland, yet conscious of their peculiar interests and capable of defending themselves against any

Public Sale of Negroes,
By RICHARD CLAGETT.

On Tuesday, March 5th, 1833 at 1:00 P. M. the following Slaves will be sold at Potters Mart, in Charleston, S. C.

Miscellaneous Lots of Negroes, mostly house servants, some for field work.

Conditions: ½ cash, balance by bond, bearing interest from date of sale. Payable in one to two years to be secured by a mortgage of the Negroes, and appraised personal security. *Auctioneer will pay for the papers.*

A valuable Negro woman, accustomed to all kinds of house work. Is a good plain cook, and excellent dairy maid, washes and irons. She has four children, one a girl about 13 years of age, another 7, a boy about 5, and an infant 11 months old. 2 of the children will be sold with mother, the others separately, if it best suits the purchaser.

A very valuable Blacksmith, wife and daughters; the Smith is in the prime of life, and a perfect master at his trade. His wife about 27 years old, and his daughters 12 and 10 years old have been brought up as house servants, and as such are very valuable. Also for sale 2 likely young negro wenches, one of whom is 16 the other 13, both of whom have been taught and accustomed to the duties of house servants. The 16 year old wench has one eye.

A likely yellow girl about 17 or 18 years old, has been accustomed to all kinds of house and garden work. She is sold for no fault. Sound as a dollar.

House servants: The owner of a family described herein, would sell them for a good price only, they are offered for no fault whatever, but because they can be done without, and money is needed. He has been offered $1250. They consist of a man 30 to 33 years old, who has been raised in a genteel Virginia family as house servant, Carriage driver etc., in all which he excels. His wife a likely wench of 25 to 30 raised in like manner, as chamber maid, seamstress, nurse etc., their two children, girls of 12 and 4 or 5. They are bright mulattoes, of mild tractable dispositions, unassuming manners, and of genteel appearance and well worthy the notice of a gentleman of fortune needing such.

Also 14 Negro Wenches ranging from 16 to 25 years of age, all sound and capable of doing a good days work in the house or field.

foreign enemy. Utopia was still far off, but the essential nuclei of the American Republic were already formed.[17]

The early development of vigorous, free economic forms was another factor which contributed to the maturation of govern-

[17]Samuel E. Morison et al., *The Growth of the American Republic* (New York: Oxford University Press, 1969), p. 65.

ment in our country. For nearly three centuries America was wide open for entrepreneurs. For even longer than three centuries North America has been a Utopia for technical innovation, dabbling, experimentation, gimmickry, gadgetry, self-made and self-destroyed men. While Europe has had to endure revolutions, assassinations, and depositions and restorations to create a free-flowing economy, North America has been economically relatively free and liquid from the start.[18]

All of these features of the original patterns of conquest explain how it was possible for a young and dispersed society on the North American continent to carry off a successful rebellion in 1776, to gain its independence from foreign control, and to establish a vigorous political system without staging a revolution against its own population.

The Darker Side of Conquest

The darkest of the residues of conquest in all of the Americas was slavery. In South America Indians were subject either to the encomienda system or to debt peonage, or they were enslaved at the outset. African slaves were imported as early as the sixteenth century and made up a sizable population by the end of the seventeenth century.[19] There were white slaves as well. In North America prisoners and vagrants could be sold under the British Statute of Apprentices, and many prisoners of war and of politics were shipped abroad for auction at the block. For a long while the various categories of involuntary servitude were vague and shifting. Absolute and permanent slavery was for many years a status suffered by a small minority, but not all of those in the permanent condition were Africans.

Eventually, of course, the line between servant and slave and the line between black and white servitude became more and more pronounced until we finally developed our exclusively black slave system—the "peculiar institution."[20] Within a generation of the

[18]Arthur M. Schlesinger, *Colonial Merchants and the American Revolution* (New York: Atheneum, 1968), chapter 1; see especially p. 19. Economic historians generally agree that the restrictive navigation acts imposed by the English on the colonies in reality did little harm to freedom of commerce, notwithstanding the hue and cry raised about them. See, for example, Ross M. Robertson, *History of the American Economy,* 3rd ed. (New York: Harcourt Brace Jovanovich, 1973), p. 49.

[19]Stein and Stein, *The Colonial Heritage of Latin America,* chapter 2, and Furtado, *Economic Development of Latin America,* chapter 2. On the exploitation of Indians in South America, as well as Indians and blacks in North America, see John Hope Franklin, *From Slavery to Freedom,* 4th ed. (New York: Knopf, 1974), chapter 6.

[20]For a good and readable treatment of the conditions of labor in the colonies, see Handlin, *America,* especially pp. 16–19 and 62–65. Longer and more authoritative versions will be found in Elkins, *Slavery,* and in Klein, *Slavery in the Americas.* A popular account of some of the more salient features of slavery and its consequences will be found in Charles Silberman, *Crisis in Black and White* (New York: Random House, 1964). An excellent study of the influence of slavery on American political institutions is provided by Donald L. Robinson, *Slavery in the Structure of American Politics, 1765–1820* (New York: Harcourt Brace Jovanovich, 1971). See also Kenneth Stampp, *The Peculiar Institution: Slavery in the Ante-Bellum South* (New York: Knopf, 1956).

beginning of significant slave importation (1640–1660), slaves in North America, rather than improving their lot, had become chattel. (This term has the same origin as the term *cattle.*) Slaves in North America were not considered human beings at all but a species of living property—their survival depending completely upon economic value. As one Virginia judge put it, the condition of chattel slavery defines the slave "below the rank of human beings, not only politically, but physically and morally."[21]

Chattel slavery emerged gradually, probably as a result of a slow process of adjusting the situation of the African to fit the needs of conquest. A long series of state and local court decisions which treated the African as different from other human beings in the New World simply led to the establishment of what anthropologists would call a caste system. As slaves increased in number, legislatures had to deal with the problem and used these court precedents as guides to the framing of statutes to handle whole classes of cases. And legislatures, precisely because they were representative, were concerned predominantly with the most pressing economic problems of the day. They were free to decide how far they wanted to go; and where slavery was concerned, they went the whole distance—an ironic but direct consequence of the patterns and practices of North American conquest.

Also on the dark side of conquest in North America is the tradition of violence. Slavery was in itself a type of violence, but it became institutionalized as property. There were other more direct and open acts of violence, for example, those caused by the regular and widespread hostilities between white settlers and the Indians. Again, a large part of this tradition of violence is attributable to the original patterns of conquest. Bear in mind for a moment not only the attributes of conquest already identified but also the character of many of the settlers themselves.

There were the *adventurers* and the true *entrepreneurs.* These often tended to be sons of aristocrats and upper bourgeoisie who would ordinarily have turned to military or clerical careers in better times. Then there were *escapees*—not only religious dissenters but debtors seeking to escape creditors, political dissenters seeking to escape execution, and felons either expatriated by the government or seeking their own expatriation to avoid punishment.[22] And finally, there were the *intelligent poor.* Thanks to the indenture system, it was possible for even poor persons to come to the colonies, provided they were sufficiently sound of body and mind to serve a master for the requisite seven to ten years. This produced probably a more than usually vigorous and ambitious working class.

---

[21]Quoted in Klein, *Slavery in the Americas,* p. 39.

[22]See Abbott Smith, *Colonists in Bondage* (Chapel Hill: University of North Carolina Press, 1947), p. 3.

All of these types of settlers seem to have had one thing in common. They were persons who had so little regard for Old World institutions and customs that they were willing to take great risks to settle in the colonies. This was a grim solution made attractive only by the fact that the alternative of remaining at home was grimmer. Most of the settlers were also *rootless* as a result of their move. They had little appreciation or respect for European institutions. As one historian put it, they were "the moving Americans," and produced a culture of moving Americans.[23]

We have already had occasion to admire the individuality and venturesome and innovative nature of the typical North American settler; and it would be wrong not to appreciate the great advantages we have gained by the system of private property that we have developed. But all of these considerations serve only to emphasize still further the darker side—the tradition of violence. Each wave of the continuing expansion of the frontier involved a seizure of land and a forceful removal of the Indians. Frontier expansion was largely spontaneous; settlers simply moved continuously along trails toward unknown areas or destinations reported by earlier trappers and explorers. Groups of settlers staked out areas as yet unclaimed and subdivided them into parcels of private property, usually no larger than could be reasonably farmed and defended by single families. The success of a few settlers in an area would attract still others, until finally a substantial settlement would appear.

This was all well and good until the right to settle there was questioned by others, particularly Indians. Thus it was that the frontier and violence became synonymous; and because the pattern of settlement involved this relationship between conquest, property, and armed violence, we can speak of a culture or tradition of violence. The laws of property were probably applied in the conquest of colonial territories with a purity and viciousness previously unknown to the Western world and without the counterbalancing consideration of other laws or the values of other cultures.

Most Indians did have some concept of ownership, and this concept varied among the tribes; but none of these concepts even approached that of the European notion of ownership, particularly with regard to land. Generally the nomadic Indian tended to recognize private ownership only of movable property.[24] This left the Indian susceptible to the white settler in unexpected and ironic ways. If a settler could stake out an area to call his own and get other settlers in the area to accept that claim, and if all of them in

---

[23]George W. Pierson, *The Moving American* (New York: Knopf, 1973).

[24]This treatment of the Indian concept of property is based heavily upon Harold E. Driver, *Indians of North America*, 2d ed. (Chicago: University of Chicago Press, 1969), especially chapter 16.

Unwanted Continent: The Conquest of North America

35

Conquest of the West:
Military defense of
property.

ATTENTION!
INDIAN
FIGHTERS

Having been authorized by the Governor to raise a
Company of 100 day

U. S. VOL CAVALRY!

For immediate service against hostile Indians. I call upon all who wish to engage in such
service to call at my office and enroll their names immediately.

Pay and Rations the same as other U. S.
Volunteer Cavalry.

Parties furnishing their own horses will receive 40c per day, and rations for the same,
while in the service.
The Company will also be entitled to all horses and other plunder taken from the Indians.

Office first door East of Recorder's Office.

HAL SAYR.

Central City, Aug. 13, '64.

turn got their claims recognized by some public agency, each settler
gained a singular advantage.

The private interest in each individual claim was supported by a
gigantic system of morality and an effective and dedicated system of
government—with an army. Because of the property concept, an
attack on any settler was an attack on all settlers. No people fight
more effectively than when their basic morality is directly at issue,
and no single individual can ever engage the collective moralities of
others more effectively than when that individual's property is
being attacked. In this sense, property *was* theft. To seize a piece of

unoccupied domain and to call it property was to engage simultaneously the protection of the state and of one's fellow citizens.

What a formidable one-two punch against the Indians. As the opening quote of this chapter suggests, the Indians had something of a mystical attitude toward the land, respecting it in their own way just as much as the Europeans. But their notion did not focus itself on the subdivision of the pieces and the distribution of each piece to individuals or families within the common group.

Property, then, was one of the basic mechanisms of conquest, especially of the conquest of the West after the coastal beachhead was fully established. A system based upon our highly defined concept of private property is obviously like a system of interlocking alliances in international relations, where there is a solemn obligation to consider an attack upon any one member as an attack upon all members. It is no wonder that the relationship with the Indian was incessant, expansive, and violent.

Anthropologists have described this process fairly well. It began relatively peacefully in the East,[25] but eventually settlers began seizing land without bothering with formal treaties, or else they deliberately disregarded the provisions of formal treaties. Wherever the provocation was sufficient and Indians retaliated, the war escalated until the Indians were annihilated or were pushed on farther west. Then other settlers began to move westward in small parties, and the next round of property claims started. Initially this stage might be peaceful, with only a few campers and traders moving in at a time. But eventually there would always be another round of seizure, after which land would be claimed by the settlers as their rightful property by virtue of their conquest. A new expansion, a new settlement, a new retaliation, a new removal, another expansion, another settlement, another retaliation, another removal . . .

This process of conquering the West continued for more than a century and was not changed appreciably by passage of the Northwest Ordinance in 1787 by Congress, which guaranteed to Indians that their lands would not be taken without compensation, "except in just and lawful wars authorized by Congress."[26] Since no "just and lawful wars" were ever authorized by Congress, this guarantee was not worth the paper on which it was printed. And with settlers streaming into the Ohio Valley, the Illinois country, and all over what was then the Northwest, the national government had become the leader in name only.

Consequently, when Andrew Jackson, the old Indian fighter, took

[25]Dee Brown, *Bury My Heart at Wounded Knee* (New York: Holt, Rinehart and Winston, 1970), p. 3. For a good description of the process of conquest in the West, see Driver, *Indians of North America,* especially "Hagan's Drama," p. 481.
[26]Driver, *Indians of North America,* p. 484.

Conquest of the West:
Bounties for law and
order.

REWARD

($5,000.00)

Reward for the capture, dead or alive,
of one Wm. Wright, better known as

"BILLY THE KID"

Age, 18. Height, 5 feet, 3 inches.
Weight, 125 lbs. Light hair, blue
eyes and even features. He is
the leader of the worst band of
desperadoes the Territory has
ever had to deal with. The above
reward will be paid for his capture
or positive proof of his death.

JIM DALTON, Sheriff.

DEAD OR ALIVE!
"BILLY THE KID"

office as president, it should have been expected that one of his first
acts would be a request of Congress for legislation removing all of
the Indians to territory west of the Mississippi. In 1830 and 1834
Congress complied with legislation providing for the removal of all
Indians not only beyond the Mississippi but to that part of the

United States west of the Mississippi "not within the States of Missouri and Louisiana or the Territory of Arkansas." This legislation provided that all of the rest would be Indian country, where no white persons would be permitted to trade without a license. There also were provisions that no white person would be permitted to settle in this country and that military force would be employed to carry out the provisions of these Acts.[27]

This is "the way the West was won," more by property than by cowboys, more by civilians than by armies. Civilians went in first, then implicated armies through their claims of private property. As the territories were pacified and governments were properly instituted, property was also pacified—and has in turn become one of the great foundations of stability in American society and in politics. But let us not forget the principle of conquest, for, without that, there would be no West *or* property.

Yet conquest has not really ended, not here or in Latin America or in the older countries. It is said that there will always be an England, but not all the Irish, Manx, Cornish, or Welsh are particularly happy being a part of it. We now hear increasingly of Scottish nationalism. There is Basque nationalism squeezed between France and Spain. There are strong separatist feelings among the Bretons in France and strong French feeling among the Québecois in Canada. Even in the tiny canton of Jura in the small country of Switzerland there is a strong sense of separatism. The Soviet Union is itself a federation of separate republics, and these republics are more clearly separated along ethnic and linguistic lines than are Alabama from New York or California from Florida.

The problems of keeping society together are ever present in some form or another even when violence is not involved. From time to time political action seems to solve the problems of the society, but these solutions are never final. We continue to pay Indian claims, but we have not been able to "assimilate" Indians and many other subject peoples in our country.

It is the same in another sense with blacks. We have "solved" the problem of the status of blacks in our society three or four times in our history. First we "allowed" blacks to help with the original conquest of the territory by serving more or less cooperatively as slaves. We then solved the problem once again, with one of the bloodiest civil wars in world history, by putting an end to slavery—and again by integrating blacks into the society as a separate and exploited caste, which lasted more or less peacefully for two and

---

[27]Brown, *Bury My Heart at Wounded Knee*, pp. 5–7; and Driver, *Indians of North America*, pp. 483–486. The Acts of Congress were the Indian Removal Act of 1830, legalizing removal of all Indians east of the Mississippi to lands on the west; and the Indian Trade and Intercourse Act, expanding the Bureau of Indian Affairs, prohibiting the sale of intoxicants to Indians, and other matters. A very good chronology of Indian–white relationships, including congressional enactments, will be found in Driver, *Indians of North America*, pp. 481–483.

EXECUTION OF

JAMES P. CASEY & CHARLES CORA,

.... BY THE ....

Vigilance Committee of San Francisco, on Thursday, May 22nd, 1856, from the windows of their Rooms, in SACRAMENTO STREET, BETWEEN FRONT AND DAVIS.

JAMES P. CASEY AND CHARLES CORA,

Were hung by the Vigilance Committee at precisely twenty minutes after one o'clock—the former for the murder of James King of Wm., and the latter for the murder of Gen. William H. Richardson. Both persons had been tried before the Committee, and found guilty. A promise had been made to Casey that he should have a fair trial, and be permitted to speak ten minutes. These conditions had doubtlessly been observed. Casey was informed on Wednesday afternoon, that he had been condemned to be hung. While under the charge of the Vigilance Committee his spirit appeared to be unbroken. When awaken, after a sleep, he would frequently strike the floor with his hand cuffs, and swear fiercely at his fate. During the evening previous to his execution, the Right Rev. Bishop Allemany attended Casey, who had been educated in the Roman Catholic religion. During the night he was restless, and passed a portion of the time in pacing his room.

Cora attracted less attention, and conducted himself more quietly.

At eight o'clock, on Thursday morning, the General Committee was notified that Casey and Cora would be executed at half-past one, and ordered to appear under arms. During the morning preparations were made for the execution. Beams were run out over two of the windows of the Committee Room, and platforms about three feet square extending out under each beam. These platforms were supported next the house by hinges, and outside by ropes, extending up to the beams. Along the streets, for a considerable distance on each side of the place of execution, were ranged the Committee—more than three thousand in number—some on foot with muskets, and others on horseback with sabres. No outsiders were permitted to approach within a hundred yards. Beneath the place of execution were several cannon and caissons ready for use if necessary. The houses in the vicinity were covered with spectators, probably, not less than eight or ten thousand persons.

At a quarter past one o'clock Casey and Cora were brought out upon the platforms. The former was attended by the Rev. Father Gallagher. The arms of both were pinioned at the elbows. The noose was placed around Cora's neck, when he stepped upon the platform and stood firm as a statue, a white handkerchief being wrapped around his head. The noose was placed around Casey's neck, but at his request removed, while he had some three or four minutes conversation with his priest. He then came forward and addressed the people as follows:

"Gentlemen, Fellow Citizens :—I am not guilty of any crime. When I am dead, when I am laid in my grave, let no one dare traduce my character or asperse my memory. Let no man exult over me, or point to my grave as that of an assassin. I am guilty of no crime. I only acted as I was taught—according to my early education—to avenge an insult. Let not the Alta, the Chronicle, and the Globe, persecute my memory; let them no more proclaim me a murderer to the world. Let them not insult me after death. I have an aged mother in the Atlantic States, and I hope that she will never hear how I died. I trust she will never know I am executed on a charge of murder. I am not guilty of any such crime."

About this time Father Gallagher touched Casey, and said: "Pray to God to pardon you for your crime; pray God to save your soul."

Casey, after a moment's hesitation, spoke again:

"Oh, God, pardon and forgive me. Oh, my mother! my mother! I hope she will never hear of this. Oh, God! have mercy on my mother; comfort her in her affliction. Oh, God! have mercy on my soul! Oh, my God! my God! I am not guilty of murder—I did not intend to commit murder."

After he had concluded, the noose was again adjusted, his eyes bandaged, and, as he was about to step forward, he faltered, and was about to sink, when the arms of two men were extended and supported him to the fatal spot.

Both prisoners being prepared, the signal was given, and, at the same moment, the souls of James P. Casey and Charles Cora were launched into eternity; and their bodies became an inanimate mass of corruption. Neither of them struggled much, Casey showing the most physical suffering.

From the time the prisoners appeared at the window until the drop fell, the immense mass of people stood uncovered, and the utmost silence was maintained, not a shout being heard, or a loud word spoken. The bodies continued to hang for nearly an hour as they were executed. Although a great many persons were in sight at the time, awaiting the climax of the tragedy, there were many others scattered about town, who had supposed the affair would be postponed. The news spread rapidly through the city, and in ten minutes after the death of Casey, great numbers of men were to be seen rushing down Clay, and Washington, and Commercial streets, as though it were a matter of life and death to get a sight of the spectacle. The bodies were then taken down and handed over to the Coroner.

For sale at M. Ullmann's corner of Washington and Sansome street.

[TOWN TALK, PRINT.]

May 22nd 1856

Loaned by W. H. Myrick, Mayfield.

perhaps three generations. In the past twenty years we have begun to look for another "solution." If even the Civil War was "incomplete conquest," how can we ever expect final solutions?

CONQUEST AND TYRANNY

An objective review of American history is a sobering experience only because we have insisted upon believing that our history is clean and our national conscience is clear. To deny that there was and continues to be conquest in American history is to deny the existence of its results, and that is absurd. Idealism about our past is the beginning of mythology. Idealism about a future in which governments can be made with a compact and without a conquest is idealism wasted.

Some solace can still be found. So close in time and place are conquest and government that we should be astonished when we find any government that is not also a complete tyranny. Yet, the remarkable fact is that tyranny has not been the general condition under which Americans and citizens of many other countries have lived during the past three or four centuries. Tyranny does indeed remain the specific condition for many Americans. And even now, those of us who are not ourselves directly tyrannized may often tyrannize others or tolerate organized tyranny by businesses or governments. Nevertheless, while this offers little comfort to those specific individuals who are tyrannized, tyranny has never been the general condition, and tyranny is not a condition that fits comfortably into the American scheme of values. Because we seek to eliminate tyranny and violence as methods of solving social problems, we are caught in a dilemma. Each such effort can easily lead to more rather than less conquest, even though in other forms. As we have already said so often, conquest never ends; only the form changes. *But the form makes all the difference.*

This is what the study of government is all about—or should be. Is it possible to improvise governmental institutions that are able to conquer some undesirable trait in the society without at the same time eliminating individuality itself? Can we have our conquest and our individuality too? Can we "stoop to conquer" without stooping too low?

Chapter 3   Conquest and Government in Contemporary U.S.A.

The British Broadcasting Corporation has barred television showings of "Sesame Street," saying that the popular American children's program has "authoritarian aims." The BBC announcement refers to the program maker's aim to change children's behavior. "This sounds like indoctrination and a dangerous use of television," the report concluded.
New York Times, September 8, 1971.

Merely gaining effective control over China's 800,000,000 people . . . was an epic achievement. But Mao Tse-Tung's ambitions did not stop there . . . Mao wanted to do nothing less than transform the traditional Chinese peasant . . . into a new Maoist Man.
Time, July 12, 1971.

Some would say that the government has not yet succeeded in truly occupying this vast and complex land and that we continue to resort to very primitive means of conquest. These observers could cite the tremendous size of our urban police forces and the apparently hopeless fight against urban crime. (New York City's annual murder rate is nearly five times that of Tokyo, and the per capita rate of violent crimes in many other American cities exceeds that of New York.) They might mention the large number of instances in recent years when National Guard troops have been called up against local disorders. Earlier cases of lynch mobs and goon squads and neighborhood riots could also be used to illustrate their point.

Even more revealing would be the fact that more than 75 percent of all murders and other criminal assaults in the

Conquest and Government in Contemporary U.S.A.

United States involved persons *who were acquainted with each other.* "The United States may or may not be the land of the free, but it is certainly the home of the brave. . . . You are safer on the streets than at home; safer with a stranger than with a friend or relative."[1] There is much dispute over how to interpret any crime statistic, but one proposition is probably beyond contention: a tremendously high proportion of the most serious violence in the United States is actually *informal self-government being carried out through violent means.* When two people who already know each other have an altercation that ends up in serious injury or death for one of them, this altercation typically involves a disagreement that in other situations might be settled by a third party—a friend, a friendly policeman, the bartender, or a government agency or court. Thus the murder and assault statistics are higher in the United States than in other countries precisely because so many social conflicts are settled by direct confrontation rather than by such nonviolent means as mediation, compromise, politics, or government. Violent confrontations of this nature have been romanticized as duels, shoot-outs, and tournaments. But when a social settlement involves violence, this can only mean that the persons involved have failed to conquer themselves sufficiently.

In the United States, the pattern of conquest continues to include more of these primitive confrontations than is the case in many other civilized countries. Perhaps someday we too shall become civilized, and at that point we will witness a significant reduction in the crime statistics. It is difficult to anticipate a time when fewer social conflicts will be resolved with violence. One of the most pronounced features of the social life in low income neighborhoods in the United States—white and black—is the inability of the members of these groups to put any trust in institutions. As Suttles observes in his classic study of a West Side Chicago slum, "Addams area residents must literally memorize the personal character of one another without the benefit of general rules that would apply to whole categories of people."[2] A situation like this will always call for a great deal of *self*-government, literally speaking, and in the absence of accepted authority, intensely felt conflicts will almost systematically require some amount of direct violence for their settlement.

We do not have to go back very far in history to understand at least some of the important social conditions underlying the contemporary American resort to violence as a form of self-government. At the very time the American frontier officially closed

---

[1]These and other important crime statistics and analyses will be found in Norvall Morris and Gordon Hawkins, *The Honest Politician's Guide to Crime Control* (Chicago: University of Chicago Press, 1969), p. 57.

[2]Gerald Suttles, *The Social Order of the Slum* (Chicago: University of Chicago Press, 1968), p. 93.

Table 3.1		Populations of the United States		
	Year	Total	Percent Negro	Percent Urban
	1790	3,929,100	19	5
	1800	5,308,000	19	6
	1810	7,240,000	19	7
	1820	9,638,000	18	7
	1830	12,866,000	18	9
	1840	17,069,000	17	11
	1850	23,192,000	16	15
	1860	31,443,000	14	20
	1870	38,558,000	13	26
	1880	50,156,000	13	28
	1890	62,947,000	12	35
	1900	75,995,000	12	40
	1910	91,972,000	11	46
	1920	105,711,000	10	51
	1930	122,775,000	10	56
	1940	131,669,000	10	57
	1950	150,697,000	10	64
	1960	179,323,000	11	70
	1970	203,235,000	11	74

Data from *Statistical Abstract of the United States* (Washington, D.C.: Government Printing Office), 1962, p. 24; 1974, pp. 17 and 19.

in 1890, immigration had reached a peak. As the superintendent of the census observed following the decennial census of 1890: "Up to and including 1880 the country had a frontier settlement but at present the unsettled area has been so broken into by isolated bodies of settlement that there can hardly be said to be a frontier line. In the discussion of its extent, its Western movement, etc., it cannot, therefore, any longer have any place in the census report."[3] This meant that the pattern of absorption had to shift significantly from dispersion toward integration.

Table 3.2 shows that the long wave of immigration crested during the decade ending in 1890 but that the rate of immigration has not appreciably declined since that time. The rate varies from decade to decade according to general world conditions, but there has always been a heavy flow. The third column of Table 3.2 shows that the sources of immigration shifted suddenly and drastically at the turn

[3]This passage is quoted in one of the most important essays in American historical thought, "Problems in American History," by Frederick Jackson Turner (1893). In this essay Professor Turner set forth his famous "frontier hypothesis" by which he tried to explain American national character. Reprinted in full in Daniel Boorstin, ed., *An American Primer* (Chicago: University of Chicago Press, 1966), pp. 524–547. Above quote from p. 524.

Table 3.2

Immigration: From Old to New World, 1840–1970

Years	Total	Changes in Source of Immigrants: Number and Percent from Eastern and Southern Europe, 1860–1960	
		Number	Percent
1841–1850	1,713,000		
1851–1860	2,598,000		
1861–1870	2,315,000	33,628	1.4
1871–1880	2,812,000	201,889	7.2
1881–1890	5,247,000	958,413	18.3
1891–1900	3,688,000	1,915,486	51.9
1901–1910	8,795,000	6,225,981	70.8
1911–1920	5,736,000	3,379,126	58.9
1921–1930	4,107,000	1,193,830	29.0
1931–1940	528,000	143,095	27.1
1941–1950	1,035,000	104,256	10.0
1951–1960	2,515,000	310,464	12.3
1961–1970	3,321,000		

Data from *Statistical Abstract of the United States* (Washington, D.C.: Government Printing Office), 1962, p. 97; 1974, pp. 98–99. Also from *Associated Press Almanac* (New York: Almanac Publishing, 1973), p. 140; and from Samuel E. Morison et al., *The Growth of the American Republic,* vol. 2 (New York: Oxford University Press, 1969), p. 108.

of the century from northern to southern Europe and from western to eastern Europe. This meant a shift away from the dominant cultural strains that had already established themselves in the United States. The shift from British, Dutch, and Scandinavian to Slavic, Russian, and Mediterranean meant greater problems of alienation and adjustment for each new immigrant and greater problems of social integration for established communities. The cultural gap between the established and the new citizens was social, stylistic, political, ideological, and religious.

Table 3.3 gives a quick picture of the way the immigration of yesteryear continues to affect the population of the 1970s. While the overwhelming proportion of the population is now American-born and has English as the native tongue (column 2), most individuals still identify themselves in terms of their ethnic origins as some kind of "hyphenated American" (column 1). Table 3.3 actually understates the case because most of these "hyphenated Americans," including the Afro-Americans, now live in a few large metropolitan centers, where the English-Irish or "old stock" component comprises an even smaller proportion of the population. These various figures reveal at least some of the reasons violence is so often employed as a means of direct self-government in American cities. But if violence is more widespread in the United States—if

Table 3.3		Ethnic Origins of the U.S. Population in 1970		
	Major Groups		**Mother Tongues**	
	English	19,060,000	English	158,954,000
	German	19,961,000	German	4,809,000
	Irish	13,282,000	French	1,801,000
	Italian	7,239,000	Italian	3,147,000
	Polish	4,021,000	Polish	1,982,000
	Russian	2,152,000	Yiddish*	1,142,000
	Spanish, Latin American	7,648,000	Other	7,111,000
	Spanish, other	1,582,000	Not reported	3,506,000
	American-born blacks	20,000,000		
	All other	85,000,000		
	Not reported or don't know	17,635,000		

Data from *1972 World Almanac and Book of Facts* (New York: Newspaper Enterprise Association, 1972).

*As the Bureau of the Census puts it, "Since very few persons migrated from Russia since 1930 when two-thirds of the Russian-born Americans reported they had spoken Yiddish in their childhood, it is likely that most persons of Russian origin had a Jewish cultural heritage."

violence is so systematic that it comprises a "culture of violence"— so is the determination of American leaders and officials to put an end to it. They have not succeeded; the rates of violence seem to rise even as measures to reduce violence are increased. But continued efforts will be made, and past attempts to pacify our nation have given rise to many very sophisticated techniques of modern conquest—or re-conquest.

The American Image: Melting Pot or Tossed Salad?

One of the great symbols of American culture is the melting pot. We project our society in the image of a crucible, into which the various national elements of the world are melted and mixed and poured out as a new alloy, the true American. But that is more of an ideal than a fact. A more meaningful image may be the tossed salad. The varieties of ethnic and national subdivisions of our population are almost as impressive as they were at the turn of the century, when the first mass influx of non-European immigrants began (see Table 3.3). In the 1970s it is still meaningful to repeat the old adage that in New York City there are more Italians than in Naples, more Irish than in Dublin, more Jews than in Jerusalem. These differences of national origin are only part of the picture. Another part of it is the rich religious composition of the country. In 1971 there were at least 152 separate denominations and organized subdenominations in the United States, and this does not count many smaller sects that are active but unincorporated. Moreover, according to the data provided

Conquest and Government in Contemporary U.S.A.

by the *Statistical Abstract of the United States* (1974), 87 of these religious communities had membership of over 50,000 persons. These range from the unified churches like the Roman Catholics with estimated adherents of over 40,000,000 and the Southern Baptist Convention with over 12,000,000 to the Russian Orthodox Church with just over 55,000 and the Armenian Apostolic Church with a reported 125,000. Religion is an important subdivision in and of itself, and looms all the more important in political matters because religious identification tends to be distributed along ethnic and national lines, and the two tend to reinforce each other.

It would be too easy to walk away from a description of our tossed salad population with the impression that heterogeneity means only ethnic and religious variety. For instance, nearly 10 percent of all Americans in 1970 were over the age of sixty-five. This group is capable of considerable self-identification, as is that still larger segment of the population under the age of eighteen. There is also a historically important sectional subdivision of the population in which southerners are in many important respects different from nonsoutherners, westerners continue to look with some considerable distrust upon easterners, and small-town folk tend to look with distrust upon city slickers. These various subdivisions are in part a mere product of physical proximity and familiarity. But if one looks at the two centuries or more of economic history, one can find some important economic interests back of these sectional identifications, and these interests provide a basis for saying that sectional distinctions involve differences that are truly significant. For example, the Civil War is enough reason to suspect that financial and commercial differences between North and South are significant, as are the differences between the type of enterprise concentrated in the Middle West and the type of enterprise concentrated in the Southeast. In addition to these societal subdivisions, we now witness the renewed self-assertion of still another important identity group in our society in the emergence of the female consciousness.

Yet another important group of subdivisions—although many have argued that this is less important in the United States than in Europe—is based on income and class. No one would argue with the contention that people gain many of their attitudes from the occupations they hold and the amount of income they earn. In addition to that, different occupations enjoy different levels of status in the esteem of the American population, and these differences of status set people apart from one another. This explains in part the existence of working-class bars, middle-class cocktail lounges, working-class fraternal organizations, and upper-middle-class country clubs. Every generalization about different occupational groupings and their attitudes involves a good deal of exaggeration; but there is also a strong element of truth in each.

Although we have not discussed all the social subdivisions which

Conquest and Government in Contemporary U.S.A.

add to the texture of the complete tossed salad, the point is sufficiently clear. These divergent subgroups do exist in our society, do not seem to want to disappear completely, and do continue to provide a source of differences and of conflicts in social and political goals. Thanks to the many techniques of conquest to be covered in the remainder of this chapter, Americans of different walks of life do share many fundamental values, skills, and behavioral traits. For example, the decline of the number of foreign language newspapers published in the United States from a maximum of nearly 1,300 in 1914 to 400 today suggests that our institutions have succeeded in assimilating the new Americans, up to a point.[4] Nevertheless, 400 is a lot of foreign language newspapers in a melting pot society. And the decline from 1,300 was also during a period when *all* of the print media in the United States declined.[5]

The persistence of foreign language publishing in the United States is a small indication of the persistence of ethnic and national identifications. During periods of relative social tranquility one reads a great deal about assimilation and the weakening of these subcultural identifications. But somebody's consciousness is usually raised just in time to upset the applecart. During the past few years there has been an intensive rediscovery of consciousness among blacks, Indians, Spanish-speaking persons, and women. America's Jews have had their cycles of intensity, and one very long period of ethnic identification has followed the establishment of Israel as the "Jewish homeland." The consciousness of other groups will rise up at other times, usually with all of the exhilaration of a conversion, as though this sort of thing had never happened before.

These identifications are not superficial, even though they don't always take a strongly political form. So conscious have we become of the various sociological differences in our society that we have scrubbed the word *ethnic* clean of all of its negative connotations and applied it with neutral or quite positive connotations to every subcultural grouping in the United States, even including the white Anglo-Saxon Protestant original majority.[6] Once upon a time the slang reference WASP was a term of opprobrium. Now it is itself

---

[4]Reported in Robert L. Linebery and Ira Sharkansky, *Urban Politics and Public Policy* (New York: Harper & Row, 1971), p. 70. See also Michael Novak, *The Rise of the Unmeltable Ethnics* (New York: Macmillan, 1972).

[5]In 1910 maybe 700 cities and towns enjoyed the services of two or more competing daily newspapers; by the end of the 1960s this number had fallen to 64. More than 25 percent of the fifty states enjoyed no newspaper competition at all, and in many cities where there existed more than one newspaper, the same publisher held both, as well as a monopoly on competing radio and television stations. A wealth of data on these matters will be found in the annual editions of the *Ayer Directory of Publications* (Philadelphia: Ayer Press). See also *Statistical Abstract of the United States* (Washington, D.C.: Government Printing Office, 1974), p. 50.

[6]Earlier dictionary and customary usage of *ethnic* implied such things as heathen and pagan, with distinct overtones of racial inferiority. See, for example, the 1937 edition of the Funk and Wagnalls dictionary.

going to be a normal and emotionally neutral designation for one more "minority group."

Figures 3.1 through 3.3 should give some useful visual introduction to the problem of modern conquest. Figure 3.1 is an oversimplified version of the Marxist or "socioeconomic" model of society. It visualizes the society with one major type of distinction. It recognizes other cultural and social distinctions, but would argue either that these are subordinated to the one major socioeconomic basis or that in the long run there will be so much exploitation of the lower classes by the upper classes that the lower classes will set aside the various differences within their class in favor of a single socioeconomic definition of their problems. If and when there is sufficient economic exploitation, any society can become polarized around socioeconomic cleavages. But until that exploitation is severe, there is a great deal of room for other values to come into play, and there is ample evidence that these values have separated workers from each other as often as working-class status has brought workers together.

As we can see in Figure 3.2, the picture is quickly complicated by taking into account only a few additional bases (wedges) of social distinction within American society. Social class remains an important distinction; but upper- and lower-class lines are dissected by other social subdivisions to such an extent that they lose significance. Figure 3.2 suggests, quite properly, that a Catholic worker can be separated much farther from a Protestant or black worker than from an upper-class Catholic Wall Street executive. This is not to say that all Catholic workers will follow that pattern. Some will and some won't. The lines of cleavage here are especially complicated precisely because some Catholic workers will define themselves as workers while other Catholic workers will define themselves as Catholics, or as Irish, or as urban, or as some other subcategory not even identified here.

Only a very few of these important lines of cleavage can be represented in Figure 3.2.[7] It would be impossible to represent even a small proportion of all of the wedges of class and cultural distinction that separate people from each other in our society. But if all of the important cleavages were represented by additional wedges and additional diagonal lines, there would be nothing in the circle but a very dense cross-hatching, as in Figure 3.3. If the entire circle were thought of as a log, a large number of these social, economic, and cultural wedges would long ago have chopped the log into tiny pieces of kindling. Perhaps we should replace the melting pot as well as the tossed salad with the image of a tinderbox. In any

[7]For a fine treatment of this phenomenon, see E. E. Schattschneider, *The Semisovereign People* (New York: Holt, Rinehart and Winston, 1960), chapter 4.

Figure 3.1
Quasi-Marxist model of society, where all other cleavages are overshadowed by socioeconomic interests

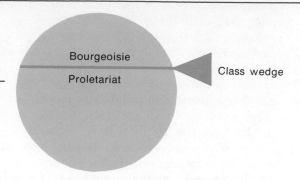

Figure 3.2
A few social cleavages in American society

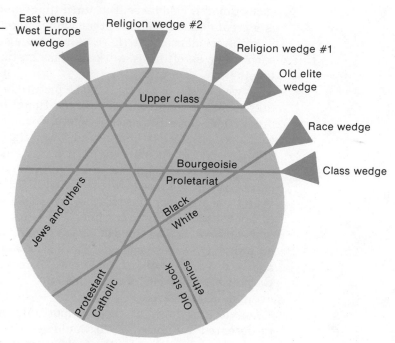

Figure 3.3
The "tinderbox society": A full representation of the social cleavages in a modern industrial society

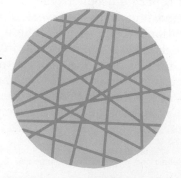

event, Figure 3.3 is not a very exaggerated representation of the society at large and the kind of problem that each generation must settle by some kind of re-conquest of the territory and the population.

CONQUERING AMERICA TODAY

Modern Conquest: The Control of Wants

It should be all the more evident by now that the problem of conquest never really disappears but merely changes form. During the original phase of conquest the main problem was simply to occupy the territory and survive. At some point in time after occupation was under way, the question motivating the most idealistic of those seeking freedom must have been: *How can we create a society in which all people get what they want?* On earth, that poses an impossible ideal, and among earthly societies it rather quickly becomes translated into the more practical question: *How can society produce individuals who want what they get?*

This is what all societies attempt to do, and success in this would virtually constitute the definition of *complete* conquest. One of the most fascinating statements of this kind of a solution is provided in Aldous Huxley's famous novel, *Brave New World*. In Huxley's new world motherhood is replaced by the chemical processes of birth. Children are not born; they are decanted. Scientists are able to produce individuals with different intellectual capacities and different wants by simply varying the temperature, gestation period, nutrition, and other conditions of fetuses in each of the bottles in the laboratory. If the society needs philosophers, philosophers can be produced by manipulating the various conditions in the bottle. If there are not enough soldiers or sanitation workers, these too can be produced by manipulating the various conditions, so that when the children grow to maturity they will be prepared for happy lives as soldiers or sanitation workers. In that manner, the society of the *Brave New World* can remain stable and yet allow individuals to fulfill themselves without coming into conflict with any other individuals. Our society may never try chemical motherhood even if the technology becomes available. However, our society does move as close to the Huxley solution as it can by attempting to produce individuals who are at least not too unhappy with what they get. This is not to argue that our society or any other modern society actually provides very much of what people really want. It is only to state that the task of any society is to provide for wants up to a point and then to deal in some systematic way with the unhappiness and disorder that may follow from falling short of complete success.

Without some modest success at producing individuals who want what they get, there would be no stable societies. It would be impossible to govern, because only a small proportion of the frustrations and conflicts in society can ever be settled by governmental means. People must adjust to their own limitations, or collective life in any form would become impossible. Thus, long before governments can solve anything, societies must already have produced individuals who are capable of doing at least two very important things:

1. Each and every individual must be capable of *governing himself or herself.* That is, all people must be able to pursue their own wants and at the same time to bring them into some kind of adjustment with the wants of others. Some have called this the development of "enlightened self-interest," and others have called it "superego." Either way it is self-government—government of the self.

2. The individual must be capable of *being governed.* That is, he or she must be able to understand rules, be willing to be guided by rules, and be willing to go some distance in accepting authority of some sort as necessary or worthwhile—or both.

This is a tall order. It is a task that is very probably a lot more difficult to fulfill than the task of original or primitive conquest even when the conditions of occupation are as arduous as those of Jamestown or Plymouth. It is an especially tall order because the necessary qualities must be taught. They do not come with birth. They must be learned by each individual, and the lessons necessarily change from one generation to the next.

There are many different names for this basic social process of producing individuals who want what they get or at least who are not too unhappy with what they get. Some have called it "the making of citizens," or citizen training, or civic education. More recently we have come to call it political socialization, which implies a long process of introducing each individual into the political culture, learning how to accept authority, and learning what is legitimate and what is not. Still others describe the process in more conventional terms, such as "learning good behavior," "learning the rules of the game," "learning the American way of life." There are negative names for the same process—indoctrination or propagandizing. For example, many Americans admire "Sesame Street" as a good approach to socialization, and at the same time British television officials call the program "indoctrination of authoritarian aims."[8] By any name it is the same. It is the conquest of modern

---

[8]The discipline of "political socialization" in the United States owes much of its inspiration to two sociologists. The first, writing early in this century, was Emile Durkheim, *Education and Sociology,* trans. Sherwood D. Fox (Glencoe, Ill.: Free Press, 1956); the other is Herbert Hyman, *Political Socialization* (New York: Free Press, 1959). See also Charles E. Merriam, *The Making of Citizens* (Chicago: University of Chicago Press, 1931); Fred Greenstein, *Children in Politics* (New Haven: Yale University Press, 1965); and Robert Weissberg, *Political Learning, Political Choice,*

society by modern techniques. There are many techniques, too many to treat each and every technique here. But it will serve our purpose just as well to single out a few of the most fundamental techniques of modern conquest and analyze them carefully. One of the most enrichening aspects of political education is learning to appreciate the fundamental significance of commonplace things.

Some Specific Techniques of Conquest:
The Seven Deadly Virtues

In Christian iconography, there are "seven deadly sins." Here we will follow the travesties of George Bernard Shaw and treat techniques of modern conquest as the "seven deadly virtues."[9] The "seven deadly virtues" are: (1) nationalism, (2) religion, (3) ownership, (4) popular culture, or folklore, (5) education, (6) participation, and (7) government. Our analysis of each of these techniques of modern conquest will of course be concerned largely with their employment as techniques of modern conquest in the United States. But in some form or another these are universal techniques. Every society finds it necessary either to invent them or to adapt them from other societies.

Nationalism   Nationalism is the widely shared belief that the people who occupy the same territory do have something in common. Nationalism is a belief in the nation. It is the belief that the entire nation is a single community. Nationalism is based upon myths about the origins and history of the people who comprise the nation. These myths are filled with the heroes, great deeds, and other indications of the ability and superiority of the ancestors and institutions of the people. The concept of *myth* as the basis of nationalism should not be misunderstood. A myth is not necessarily a falsehood. It is a belief that does not depend for its acceptance upon its truth or falseness. Many myths are of course based upon falsehood, but probably a larger number rest upon some events that actually did take place. The belief is a myth if it is retained due to its value to the believer. Thus it may well be true that the waters parted to let the Children of Israel through into the Promised Land. It may also be true that minorities are fully assimilated into the American culture. But both are myths inasmuch as they serve the purpose of elevating the attitudes of people toward themselves and toward their system.

The notion of a superior common mission or destiny is, in some

---

and Democratic Citizenship (Englewood Cliffs, N.J.: Prentice-Hall, 1974). For a comparative approach, see Annick Percheron, *L'univers politique des enfants* (Paris: Armand Colin, 1974).

[9]For a delightful and brief introduction to George Bernard Shaw's views of society see "Don Juan in Hell," a very long interlude in his very long play, *Man and Superman.*

form or another, involved in almost every nationalism. In some nations with long histories of defeat and occupation by foreign powers, pride in the ability to suffer and survive becomes a major nationalistic force. The history of Israel is a particularly good example of this. In any case, a special sense of separateness is expressed one way or another.

Patriotism is almost synonymous with nationalism, except that patriotism implies love of country in a somewhat more political sense. For example, many German refugees of the 1930s and 1940s continued to feel that Germany was the superior nation, although they were not supporters of the Nazi regime. *Chauvinism* and *jingoism* are references for extreme expressions of patriotism. Many American Legionnaires may be chauvinists in taking personally any criticism of the U.S.A. "America—love it or leave it" is a chauvinistic expression.

Nationalism arises out of loyalties toward family and tribe. But nationalism must also be a force strong enough to overcome and even to uproot any traditional tribal patterns that resist nationhood. Sometimes in new nations local loyalties are destroyed, or the national government attempts to destroy them. In other instances, nationalism emerges in a relatively comfortable relationship with local loyalties. But either way, nationalism demands loyalty to certain common myths, and these myths must be strong enough to encourage a high proportion of members of the nation to be willing to sacrifice something of themselves for the collectivity.[10]

It would be wrong to discuss nationalism without appreciating the

---

[10]Readable reviews of nationalism will be found in the following: Karl Deutsch, *Nationalism and Its Alternatives* (New York: Knopf, 1969); David J. Russo, *Families and Communities—A New View of American History* (Nashville: American Association for State and Local History, 1974); W. W. Rostow, *The Stages of Economic Growth* (Cambridge: Cambridge University Press, 1960), especially chapter 3.

price that is paid for it. Nationalism is indispensable, and it must be very strong if it is to provide a sufficient feeling of fellowship across millions of people. But that very strength, as a technique of conquest, has been one of the great problems of world conflict. Since nationalism encourages pride in one's own nation, it can also produce distrust and hatred of other nations. This may be a normal tendency, but it is often encouraged by rulers as a means of whipping up support for some very narrow economic interest. There will always be specific conflicts of interest between nations, but these conflicts are much more likely to escalate to total wars when they are backed by strong national myth. For example, American national leaders in the 1830s and 1840s wanted to obtain Texas and California, and they defined these aims as the "manifest destiny" of the nation. We used it once again in the 1890s to rationalize narrower goals in the Caribbean and in the Philippines. The U.S. joined with European nations in carving up Africa and other parts of the world under the patriotic call of "white man's burden." (See also chapter 15.)

Sadly enough, it is impossible to avoid seeing a connection between the rise of nationalism and the spread of large wars in the past three or four hundred years. Nevertheless, nationalism must be very profound if people are to live together in large aggregations. Perhaps a better understanding of nationalism can help produce some guidance toward a more enlightened use of it and guard against the conversion of healthy national feelings into vicious and dangerous snobbism. If national elites learn to ask how we can accomplish this we will then be in a position to reap the benefits of nationalism without having to pay a heavy price for it.

Religion Nationalism is not a well-articulated body of beliefs. Nationalistic beliefs tend to be a kind of fundamental common denominator; they must be vague and emotional to be effective. Religion as an instrument of conquest is very much a part of these beliefs, and religion reinforces nationalism, giving nationalism a special claim to the mysteries of nature and eternity. But religion is a separate factor; it is much more highly articulated and much more specific to actual behavior and morality. Religion is vital to conquest for at least three reasons.

First, as already suggested, religion is tremendously important in reinforcing nationalism. It varies from country to country, and in any case is not the only force back of national conquest. Otherwise, there would be only four or five great nations in the world, each coextensive with a major religious movement. But in most countries, particularly in the Western world, religion has been an all-important mode of conquering and integrating the population. For example, almost all movements to establish a strong nationalism were initiated by leaders who had a type of religious relationship with thousands of people. We tend to forget that the term *charisma* originally referred to the possession of *divine* powers in leadership.[11] One does not have to be a cynic to recognize that God is on everybody's side in war. Every armed force has its chaplains and holy men. This is not because religion is warlike but because all nations have religious feelings about their overall superiority and about the superiority of the cause that led them to war. A chaplain simply calls up these feelings and tries to evoke them among the squads and platoons. In our modern society, where so many traditional values have been broken down, religion may play an even more important role than before in gaining and maintaining legitimacy. Although church membership figures are unreliable, and church membership is not a perfect measure of the strength of religious ties, it is nevertheless significant that in the past thirty years church membership has kept pace with population growth. Public opinion polls indicate that well over 90 percent of the American population are willing to express identification with one of the major religions, and an even higher proportion assert a belief in God. Many students of society are impressed in addition by the commercial boom in religious artifacts.[12]

A second important function of religion in maintaining conquest is as a source of *ideology.* Ideology is a body of principles that justify behavior—especially the behavior of people who hold positions of power. Ideology contains myths and appeals to myths, but it is concerned with the specific and applicable principles of power that are drawn from nationalism, religion, history, sports, the economy, or anywhere else. President Eisenhower wanted to change the Pledge of Allegiance to include "under God" to associate himself more closely with religious leadership and to contrast this country with the atheistic Soviet Union. Since ideology and religion are not identical, there are many occasions when the prevailing ideology is antagonistic to the religious beliefs of one or more areas of the nation. Such antagonism may lead the dissenters to emigrate, as did the Puritans from England. But that "purifies" those who stay behind and serves further to underscore the political importance of religion. This is not intended to disparage religion. Religion can still be the source of revealed truth and can offer the direct and intrinsic sustenance that many millions of people believe it does. Our only

[11]A review of the role of charismatic leadership in national and lesser political movements will be found in Theodore Lowi, *The Politics of Disorder* (New York: Basic Books, 1971), chapter 2; see also the literature in the footnotes of that chapter.

[12]See Walter Lippmann, *The Public Philosophy* (New York: Mentor Books, 1956), for many insights into the need of national government for religion. Lippmann's outlook is extremely suggestive and very sound, except on the matter of his epectation that religious ties are weakening in the United States. Most indications are that religion may be changing form but is not changing extent. For excellent treatment of the contemporary phenomenon of religion, see John Blum et al., *National Experience: A History of the United States,* 2d ed. (New York: Harcourt Brace Jovanovich, 1968), pp. 836–837. See also various Roper and Gallup public opinion polls, published occasionally in the daily newspapers.

argument is that, *in addition,* religion is a prime force in maintaining the conquest of a nation. In fact, the closer the religion is to truth, the better it is likely to serve as an instrument of conquest, and the more likely the conquerors will attempt to use it as such.

Religion functions in conquest in a third way by setting limits upon wants. As suggested earlier, in modern democratic societies individuals are morally justified in having and pursuing their selfish wants. A democracy may not be characterized by equal conditions or equality of possessions or opportunities, but it certainly can be characterized as a society based upon the equality of all wants and interests. No interest is morally superior to any other. But with that kind of an outlook, society could easily be torn apart unless these wants were in some way or another restrained. We teach children very early to try to assess the consequences of their desires. "Do unto others as you would have them do unto you" is certainly a counsel of self-interest as well as of moral restraint. Among all the sources of self-restraint, it would be impossible to find one more important than religion.

An understanding of these three political functions of religion can help us appreciate how important religion is to politics, no matter what other purpose religion may serve in society. Some do not like this function of religion and denounce it as "the opiate of the masses" because it leads people to accept authority, to defer their wishes, and to accept their differences with their fellow humans. A lot can be said for that point of view, but a lot can also be said for the other point of view, which is that religion is an inevitable and indispensable force in politics wherever religion exists. We must develop our own views about this, but whatever our views may be, we cannot avoid an appreciation of the political significance of religion.

Religion has probably been all the more effective as an instrument of conquest in the United States precisely because of the historically clear separation of church and state. American leaders could draw upon religious principles without implicating themselves or the organized religion in question. Since religion was never as much a partisan matter in the United States as elsewhere, our citizens did not develop the distrust or the psychological defenses against religious appeals that many European citizens possessed. As de Tocqueville put it:

> When it connects itself with government . . . religion augments its authority over a few and forfeits the hope of reigning over all. . . . The Church cannot share the temporal power of the State without being the object of a portion of that animosity which the latter excites. . . . When religion clings to the interests of the world, it becomes almost as fragile a thing as the powers of earth.[13]

> If the Americans, who change the head of government once in four years, who elect new legislators every two years, and renew the State officers every twelve months . . . had not placed religion beyond their reach, where could it take firm hold in the ebb and flow of human opinions? . . . The American Clergy were the first to perceive this truth and to act in conformity with it. They saw that they must renounce their religious influence if they were to strive for political power. . . . In America religion is perhaps less powerful than it has been in certain periods and among certain nations; but its influence is more lasting. . . . Its circle is limited, but it pervades and holds it under undisputed control.[14]

Ownership   Property ownership is probably a less universal factor in national conquest than nationalism and religion. We can see this by pondering again the weakness of property values among many of the American Indians.[15] But of course property was absolutely vital in the original conquest of the United States, and is perhaps even more important in the maintenance of the national system in the twentieth century. Many social theorists vigorously deny there is any value to private ownership of property, many others proclaim its virtues, and probably a still larger number are neutral. But virtually all would agree that a wide distribution of property ownership is a conservative force in the society—that is, it is a preventive to disorder and revolution. Most would also agree that it is one important basis for the development of civic virtue, which can be defined as a willingness to do more than one's share for the community. All of this means that property, wherever it is widely shared and sought, is an instrument of conquest.

---

[13]Alexis de Tocqueville, *Democracy in America* vol. 1 (New York: Vintage Books, 1955), pp. 321–322.
[14]Ibid., vol. 2, p. 134.
[15]See also Karl Polanyi, *The Great Transformation* (Boston: Beacon Press, 1957), chapter 2.

Some of America's most practical statesmen have dreamed of creating an ideal polity around property ownership. It may have begun with Thomas Jefferson, who dreamed of a complete economy based upon a "sturdy yeomanry." The original definition of a yeoman was a man who possessed a small estate in lands—a freeholder of a class below the gentry who earned his own living by the use of his own hands on his own property. This was the Jeffersonian ideal, and it is still current today. It was certainly behind the nineteenth century federal government policy of giving up millions of acres of land from the public treasury to those persons who were willing to settle and improve the land, allowing them to call it their own after a period of residence. *Squatting* and *homesteading* were our names for it; this was a method of gaining property ownership encouraged by the government.

Industrialization has changed the meaning of property, but the value of property ownership does not seem to have weakened. For most people ownership can no longer mean the ownership of acreage for purposes of making a living. Thomas Jefferson would hardly recognize ownership today, despite the fact that it is our way of fulfilling his ideal. Ownership has come to mean possessing a mortgage on a house jointly with a finance company or bank, or possessing a certificate of stock indicating a tiny proportion of ownership in some large corporation. Nevertheless, these forms of possession do count as ownership, and most people who appreciate the function of property ownership are able to see that the new forms are equivalent to the old ones.

As we shall see in chapter 15, the federal government has adopted many policies that provide incentives to purchase homes rather than to rent them. Unions, too, encourage their members to own rather than to rent their homes. Companies encourage their clerks to buy shares of ownership in the firm. All of this is done because everyone seems to believe that ownership is virtuous in and of itself, involving a form of savings and a search for security. But in addition to all of those reasons, ownership has that value to the larger system we have been discussing here—establishing and maintaining conquest.

There is still another form which "modern property" takes. This is what we might call the *vested interest,* and it comes into operation whenever a person goes to work for a large company. Such companies of course encourage employees to look upon their employment as something more than a job—indeed, as a lifetime career of loyalty to and membership in the company. Workers are provided with retirement plans, career programs, and seniority privileges that mount up with each year of service. Most retirement plans are designed so that the individual will lose part of the retirement fund if he or she leaves the company prior to a certain period of time. Certain other privileges, such as stock options, flow from years of service. Each worker thus tends to develop an economic stake in the company. This means that employees own part of the company, conditional on their staying with that company. Whether one approves or disapproves of this type of property, it is clearly an instrument of conquest.

Leaders of some of the least privileged groups in our society have developed something of a renewed interest in the importance of ownership to their own group. As one black leader put it:

> Fulfillment and re-creation can never come through housing efforts which afford people no sense of investment in, nor ownership with control of, their immediate environment. Renters tend to be far less responsible than homeowners. Black people, in our urban ghettos, are a renter class, and hence the system tends inevitably to make them into irresponsible people.[16]

It has not been positively demonstrated that property has the effect hypothesized here. But an extremely large number of Ameri-

[16]Testimony of Dr. Mason Wright, Jr., Chairman of the National Conference on Black Power, before Senate Housing and Urban Affairs Subcommittee, 1967. See also Charles Reich, "The New Property," *Yale Law Journal* 13 (1964), 733–787.

can leaders believe that it does. For purposes of this book, we do agree that by and large the hypothesis is confirmed and that property is the important instrument of conquest these people think it is. This does not mean that every property owner is a peace-loving person with a fine and upstanding family. Recent studies do not confirm that close a relationship between home owning and good citizenship, or between non–home owning and juvenile delinquency, rioting, or other antisocial behaviors.[17]

Popular culture   A five-year-old once wrote the following story: "Abraham Lincoln was born in a log cabin, which he built with his own two hands."[18] This is popular culture at work. Heroes may earn their place in history by great deeds, but their value to the culture goes far beyond the deed itself. In the United States we take our heroes seriously. Heroes are a vital part of any folk culture, and perhaps the bigger the country the bigger the heroes. Or at least the more numerous the heroes. Heroes are only part of the fund of popular culture, whose function is to instill shared experiences and a common social conscience. Popular culture is an important medium through which the basic values of society, such as nationalism and religion, are spread. Through popular culture, individuals from very different backgrounds come to share common symbols, common aspirations, and common reactions to common challenges.

Popular culture was an important means of conquest long before there were media of mass communication, such as radio, television, and newspapers. Folk songs and folk tales have performed the same function for centuries. Each tale and each song and each performance arises out of a common environment and tends to reinforce that environment. Part of the special value and influence of popular culture is that its origins are highly spontaneous, but the distribution of popular culture is no longer left to chance. As one historian put it:

> Professional popular culture, the business of amusing and entertaining large numbers of common people, emerged in the United States during the first half of the 19th Century. After the War of 1812, many Americans expressed a need for native forms, symbols, and institutions that would assert the nation's cultural distinctiveness as clearly and emphatically as the War had reaffirmed its political independence. . . . New forces emerged demanding that "middling" Americans be able to shape the country in their own image. Besides political power and unhampered opportunities for economic and social mobility, they want-

[17]See, for example, C. R. Haw and H. D. McKay, *Juvenile Delinquency and Urban Areas* (Chicago: University of Chicago Press, 1969). For a general study of these values, especially the value that some lower working classes put upon property ownership, see E. H. Mizruchi, *Success and Opportunity* (New York: Free Press, 1964).

[18]H. Allen Smith, *Write Me a Poem, Baby!* (New York: Bantam Books, 1956), p. 19.

ed a "common man's culture" that glorified American democracy and
the average white man in contrast to European aristocracy and effete
"gentlemen."[19]

Some of the important expressions in the popular culture are
those of protest. Uncle Remus stories about Br'er Rabbit and his
enemies are stories about how the little guy wins out over the bully.
Slavery, trade union, and farmer folk songs are very often thinly
veiled attacks on the masters and the capitalists. Many movies
involve attacks on authority, making the boss or the officer look
ridiculous. Nevertheless, even protest is a conquering device inasmuch as it provides a basis for mass sharing, as well as mass
catharsis. If the common denominator is suffering or subjection to
bullying authority, that will help explain why a particular entertainment which speaks to the common problem is a success. But if
the entertainment is shared, and shared repeatedly, it becomes an
important integrating device. The most outstanding example in
American history may be the influence of gospel hymns on the
African slaves. Christianity was generally forbidden or discouraged
among the slaves and consequently became a channel through
which slaves expressed their protests as well as their hopes.
Following emancipation, the Christian religion became one of the
most important cultural factors in the development of the separate
black community, and at the same time it was already one of the

[19]Robert C. Toll, *Blacking Up—The Minstrel Show in 19th Century America* (New York: Oxford
University Press, 1974), pp. 3–4.

most important bases of culture sharing between American blacks and American whites.[20]

Twentieth century sophistication has not altered the pattern or importance of folk culture. If anything, folk culture is even more important because of its ease of passage through the modern media of mass communication. As media expert Marshall McLuhan has observed, television is particularly important in this respect because it provides its entire audience with the same patterns of response. Television entertainment is almost by definition "folk culture" to the extent that the behavior patterns we experience while watching television are uniform, highly simplified, and to a great degree predictable. This is absolutely essential to the production of the kind of common culture necessary for the maintenance of conquest. It starts early (in the United States the programs are attractive to children as early as the age of two), it must be simple, and it must insinuate the lessons rather than teach them directly and explicitly.[21]

"Sesame Street" is only a recent means of planning specifically for the introduction of children into the culture. But what it does by plan has long been done in television and elsewhere, less perhaps by plan, through situation comedies, soap operas, and other forms of family entertainment. Ponder for a moment the millions who have gotten their values regarding family life, consumption patterns, and ideals of authority through such programs as "Father Knows Best," "The Nelsons," "The Life of Riley," "The Dick Van Dyke Show," "All in the Family," and "Sanford and Son." The potency of this kind of instruction by example and insinuation can be appreciated by even the briefest review of war movies, especially those produced during World War II. Virtually the entire American population was mobilized against Germans and Japanese by films made for propaganda through entertainment.

Sports may be an even more lasting aspect of conquest through popular culture. The people involved in participatory sports learn to play by the rules, to give themselves to a larger cause, to gladly suffer pain or deprivation to attain victory. Participatory sport begins with the sandbox and the sandlot, but in the past generation it has become immensely and elaborately organized through little leagues, school teams, park districts, and so on. Even as we denounce the Russians for using sports for politics, we are deeply involved in the same activity ourselves. And it was all anticipated by the Romans and their "bread and circuses" for the masses.

---

[20]For attitudes and customs regarding conversion of slaves to Christianity, see Herbert S. Klein, *Slavery in the Americas: A Comparative Study of Cuba and Virginia* (Chicago: University of Chicago Press, 1967), pp. 87–126. For a brief review of American Negro churches in the twentieth century, see John Hope Franklin, *From Slavery to Freedom,* 4th ed. (New York: Knopf, 1974), pp. 424–433.

[21]Marshall McLuhan, *Understanding Media—The Extensions of Man* (New York: Signet Books, 1964), pp. 33, 159.

"The Battle of Waterloo was won on the playing fields of Eton." *Top:* Soviet athletes participate in a May Day celebration. *Bottom:* Class of 1915 West Point football team included Dwight David Eisenhower, Omar Bradley, James A. VanFleet and Joseph F. McNarney.

Indeed, spectator sport works almost as well as participatory sport when we look at it all from the standpoint of conquest.

There are an enormous number of other aspects of popular culture that could be brought into the analysis. Mass public education is one, but its importance requires that we treat it separately in the next section. The one final ingredient of popular culture that ought to be touched upon before leaving the reader to pursue an individual analysis is war, or rather, the "culture of war." Since war is a time of great individual sacrifice, it is also a time when most members of society experience the notion of restraint of selfish wants and of dedication to larger, socially defined causes. Therefore, the *lessons* of war are as important to the nonbelligerents (citizens) as the *acts* of war are to the generals. We dwell upon past wars and draw lessons from all of our wars not merely in order to learn how to fight the next war but in order to develop good character. This may look militaristic, and may have a militaristic side, but its primary function is character building. It is to our credit that very few of the great American heroes have been war heroes. Nevertheless, there are important character traits war has helped build—military heroism, for example.

During the years of the Vietnam War, the important medals for military heroism were awarded on an unprecedented scale. For example, 206 Congressional Medals of Honor were awarded during the undeclared Vietnam War, which involved 8.8 million personnel and 46,000 battle deaths. In contrast, during all of World War II, involving 16.4 million personnel and nearly 300,000 battle deaths, only twice as many Congressional Medals of Honor were awarded. (The medal was awarded to 124 World War I soldiers and to 131 Korean War soldiers.) Perhaps this was due to an unprecedented number of heroic exploits. But surely it had something to do with the unprecedented unpopularity of that war and with the involvement of an unprecedented proportion of blacks and Chicanos in combat.

How should we react to the fact that even commonplace TV shows and sports events, as well as the cultural attitudes which develop in times of war, can at any moment become instruments of conquest? Shall we eliminate "Sesame Street" or "Sanford and Son" because they contain propaganda? Shall we tolerate them only because the next shows may be worse? The question is merely a matter of taste, for we will never escape the effort itself to use popular culture to conquer. Our worst response would be to close our eyes and ears or to enclose ourselves in padded cells. The antidote to a propaganda-filled environment is a sophisticated, analytic mind, sensitive to the meaning of subtle as well as blatant symbols and appeals in commonplace entertainment. All communications, including this book, contain propaganda. But it is not wise to shrivel in distrust merely in order to avoid drowning in a sea of propaganda. The trick is to get into the water and stay on top of it rather than be swept under.

Education In the United States education is king. We believe in it for its own sake, and we invest billions of dollars in it. Until recently, few communities ever questioned the need for investment in school plants, school programs, and so on. The bullish market may be ending, but the faith is being kept nevertheless.

Faith in education is well-founded. Our billions of dollars invested in education have yielded superior skills, superior capacity and productivity, and a significant amount of social mobility. This is not to say that public education has helped every American child realize the American ideal of success. It does mean that education has made

Conquest and Government in Contemporary U.S.A.

it possible for most of the children of America to join the work force, and that is not easy in a highly mechanized economy. One observer described kindergarten as "academic boot camp." By that he meant that kindergarten children learned the student role, but in so doing they also learned "to go through the routines and to follow orders with unquestioning obedience, even when these make no sense to them." Much as the observer disliked all this, he did begrudgingly admit that such learning as one picks up in the school system is also a direct preparation for the bureaucratized and mechanized modern economy.[22]

As we shall see later on, most education policies in the United States are made at state and local levels. Therefore, each school system can in certain important ways be adapted to the economic and social needs of the region it serves, and it would be difficult for us to pick a representative sample of these adaptations. But at least twice in this century there have been national changes on a large scale in the curriculum of the public schools. These changes illustrate best the role of education and how it is consciously appreciated by American elites as an agent of conquest.

The most recent and most familiar of these was the reaction of the United States in the late 1950s and the 1960s to the embarrassment of Sputnik, the Soviet Union's triumphal first entry into space. This Soviet triumph gave rise to a feeling among many American policy makers that our pool of scientific and technical skills was much too small. Consequently, within two or three years there was an amazing reorganization of mathematics and the sciences throughout the country. These changes in the curriculum were a conscious and deliberate result of policies that were first adopted by corporate and intellectual leaders to produce a "specific, predetermined concept of science as seen by the developers of the project." These designs and policies were adopted very quickly throughout the United States and became the "new math" and "new science" that, within half a decade of Sputnik, dominated the curriculum throughout the country.[23]

To the parents and grandparents of contemporary students—to whom mathematical thinking, coding, and programming are *not* second nature—there was another curriculum change that was just as much a revolution for their day as the "new math" is for ours.

---

[22]Harry L. Gracey, "Learning the Student Role: Kindergarten as Academic Boot Camp," *The American Elementary School, A Case Study in Bureaucracy Ideology* (Report of research supported by grant #MH9135 from the National Institute of Mental Health). For a very good historical exposition of the value of education to the modern capitalist society, see Joel H. Spring, *Education and the Rise of the Corporate State* (Boston: Beacon Press, 1972).

[23]For a general review of curriculum changes during the 1960s and earlier, see Robert M. McClure, ed., *The Curriculum: Retrospect and Prospect,* the Seventieth Yearbook of the National Society for the Study of Education, part 1 (Chicago: University of Chicago Press, 1971), especially chapters 2 and 3. The quoted passage is by McClure, p. 69.

Here is the way the education revolution of the 1920s was described by an education historian:

> The curriculum leaders of that period were . . . influenced by the training program used in 1917–1918 for war-related occupations. With the greatly increased demand for skilled workers created by the war, apprentice training took too long to provide the numbers required. To solve this problem, the jobs actually performed by skilled workers were analyzed to identify the knowledge and skills involved. In most cases, the knowledge to be learned and the skills to be developed could be acquired by an average young adult in a few weeks of training. This suggested to educators the possibility of analyzing the activities which modern men carry on in order to identify the knowledge, skills and habits involved. The results of this analysis . . . would furnish essential contents of the school curriculum.[24]

Instances of careful curriculum design to produce students with desired skills go downward to the earliest levels of schooling and upward to the highest levels of graduate training. It should certainly be clear that the modern economy is inconceivable without a system of education that is consonant with it.

One of the most dramatic connections between the schooling system and the general economic system is to be found in the development of standardized examinations, which most Americans have been taking in one form or another for the past generation and more. Standardized tests are designed to select the sort of person that a given system needs. We could even say that the standardized test is part of a design to *produce* a desired student, since most school systems anticipate the standardized test and train their students to improve their performance on the test. For any system, a recruiting examination can be designed to eliminate all but the top 5 percent or 10 percent, or whatever is desired. The other 85 percent may appear to themselves or to others as ignorant or unqualified, and many of them are. But many are eliminated because they do not know the rules or customs involved in these kinds of examinations. Examinations could be designed that would virtually reverse the results, pushing the high achievers in this first type of examination toward the bottom of the new one. Use of examinations does not of course end with the initial recruitment from the school to the work force. Civil service competitive examinations are notorious for designing a job, then designing an exam for the job, and then fitting the person to the job.[25]

---

[24]McClure, *The Curriculum: Retrospect and Prospect*. The quoted passage is by Ralph W. Tyler, pp. 26–27.

[25]This is also true in private business. William H. Whyte of *Fortune* studied this along with other important facets of *The Organization Man* (New York: Simon & Schuster, 1956). He even gives the readers some hints on how to play the correct role on the examination in order to improve their score without actually knowing anything about being an executive.

It should come as no surprise to anyone that the education system is a reflection and a servant of the society. Early in this century, Durkheim observed rather matter-of-factly that education "consists of a methodical socialization of the younger generation" and that the education process "is above all the means by which society perpetually recreates the conditions of its very existence."[26] But it actually goes farther than this, because the educational system can also help establish a new order and a "new breed" of individuals whenever that is called for. Schools certainly helped the farmer in the transition during the late nineteenth century from an agricultural to an industrial economy. They were most certainly used by the Soviet Union to help mechanize their agriculture at a time when few peasants could understand a tractor, much less actually drive one. Neither the Soviet Union nor Communist China ever tried to make a secret of their interest in using the system of education as part of the overall process of creating the "new" member of society required by their new governing system. It is highly probable that we have made less elaborate use of the school system, but we are also a good deal less willing to admit that we are doing so.[27]

The schools serve society in another way by helping to regulate the size of the work force. Just as the schools must prepare each child for entry into the work force, the schools also have to help keep each child from entering, or being forced by parents or circumstanc-

---

[26]Durkheim, *Education and Sociology*, pp. 71 and 123.
[27]For an admission that we do so, and for a poignant look at the effects of our modern educational system on traditional rural communities, see Baker Brownell, *The Human Community* (New York: Harper & Bros., 1950).

es to enter, the work force until the child is ready and the economic opportunity is available. It is for this reason that most of the compulsory school attendance laws in the country followed the child labor laws. It appears that in the years during the late nineteenth century and the early twentieth century, as the number of qualified workers, clerks, and administrators increased, there developed a concern about labor surpluses. Out of this concern emerged the child labor laws setting age limits and working conditions in such a manner as automatically to reduce the available labor supply.[28]

The school system also shapes values along with skills and availability of workers. This is true not only at the very general level of patriotism, taste, and preference for entertainment. It is a good deal more specific. One careful study of elementary readers adopted for wide use in public school systems has revealed the extent to which the sexes are trained into different economic and social functions. It is clear to these researchers, and documented to a very plausible extent, that women choose inferior roles, service functions, and low-paying jobs, and that they tend to be quite happy with less pay for the same work, largely because their elementary schooling has prepared them for these preferences. This is part of what we meant earlier about learning to want what you get. Stories in these books of readings stress passivity, domesticity, incompetence, and dependence when the female is involved; and when the male is involved the stories tend to emphasize leadership, heroism, effectiveness, skill, and imagination.[29]

Happily, conquest through schooling seems to be least effective in spreading common political values and a uniform political ideology. Although schools contribute a great deal to a general sense of patriotism and probably help produce common approaches to political behavior, they seem to be fairly inefficient beyond the inculcation of these generalities.[30] The only general tendency that various studies of socialization have revealed is an early orientation toward authority, and the general development—at least in the United States—of a favorable attitude toward government and the political system.[31] The influence of schooling on political values declines in

---

[28]For the most thorough study of the relationship between the school system and the labor and education laws, see William M. Landes and Lewis C. Solmen, "Compulsory Schooling Legislation: An Economic Analysis of Law and Social Change in the 19th Century," *Journal of Economic History,* March 1972, pp. 64–91.

[29]What was probably the first important study along these lines was authored by several women and published under the auspices of a group called Women on Words and Images. See *Dick and Jane as Victims—Sex Stereotyping in Children's Readers* (Princeton, N.J., 1972), especially p. 75, for a summary of their findings.

[30]See, for example, David Easton and Jack Dennis, *Children in the Political System: Origins of Political Legitimacy* (New York: McGraw-Hill, 1969), especially around p. 399. For an excellent summary of all these patterns consult Michael Rush and Phillip Althoff, *An Introduction to Political Sociology* (London: Thomas Nelson and Sons, 1971).

[31]Schools are a good deal less successful in some other countries (for example, Colombia, Tanzania, and Uganda) according to studies by Professor Reading and by Professors Koff and Von der Muhl. These findings are reviewed in Rush and Althoff, *An Introduction to Political Sociology,* pp. 65–66.

effectiveness as it reaches toward more and more specific political attitudes. As children gain more information about their society and their government, their attitudes and their general respect for the system tend to vary tremendously, so that the overall pattern becomes unclear. Some children increase and others decrease in their reverence for authority. Some become more attached and some become less attached to such democratic values as tolerance for strangers and respect for majority rule.[32] One of the reasons the school curriculum is so blessedly ineffective in the inculcation of specific political attitudes is that the civics and social studies curriculum is so bland that it is hardly likely to affect even the most casual of students.[33]

This, despite television, advertising, folk culture, the work place, the peer group, and schooling of twelve to twenty years, conquest is still not complete by the time the school relinquishes its pupils and declares them adults. Differences among them remain. But the system of socialization is a success inasmuch as these differences are expressed within a bond of common culture and within a context of a general feeling that social institutions, including at least some political institutions, are legitimate. This is the context that formal schooling does help create; and we would be disastrously ill-advised to dispense with this function of schooling, no matter how distasteful the image of kindergarten as an "academic boot camp." If there is to be conquest, perhaps it is accomplished better through education than by its alternatives.

In any event, one very important analytic point should be clear by now. When analyzing and evaluating any social institution, we should bear in mind at all times that the relevant starting question is not *whether* there shall be conquest, but *what kind* of conquest, how, by whom, and for what. We remain free to complain that schools attempt to socialize too much and to humanize too little. We remain free to complain about methods used. But it is a foolish waste of time to compare present practices of conquest with some unknown, ideal system in which conquest supposedly does not take place at all.

Participation and cooptation   Dictionaries tend to belittle the term *cooptation* by defining it blandly to mean the addition of a person to a group or committee by the action of those who are already members. In the social sciences, however, the term takes on far greater importance, because it has come to refer to political

---

[32]Fred Greenstein, *Children in Politics* (New Haven: Yale University Press, 1965). For a study of the positive effect of higher education on democratic values, see Samuel Stouffer, *Communism, Conformity, and Civil Liberties* (New York: Doubleday, 1955); recent statistics of the same sort will be found in Lowi, *The Politics of Disorder,* chapter 5.

[33]Kenneth Langton and M. Kent Jennings, "Political Socialization and the High School Civics Curriculum in the U.S.," *American Political Science Review* 62 (1968), 866.

strategies with which elite groups manipulate the political environment by recruiting leaders of an opposition in order to weaken or eliminate the opposition. The term tends to have pejorative connotations because the classic situation is one in which individual opposition leaders become converted to the support of the system, eventually even becoming outspoken defenders of the system against the very "out-groups" from which they sprang. The elite usually offers something valuable to the coopted person, but very frequently membership in the elite is itself so valuable that it constitutes sufficient reward. Cooptation is used effectively by all stable regimes and most private groups and corporations.[34] It has probably been used with greatest effectiveness by colonizing powers in order to pacify native populations. The British and French civil service systems, for example, were very much a part of nineteenth century imperialism inasmuch as the imperial governments coopted large numbers of the most effective Indian and African leaders through well-paying and high status government jobs. These people in return existed as a symbol of the legitimacy of the British and French colonial regimes and were often used as explicit defenders of the policies of those regimes.

This is only a slightly exaggerated statement of what goes on every day in the world of political participation in the United States. Democratic theories stress participation as indispensable to democracy. There can be no "will of the people" without participation; participation is the only way citizens can gain proper political learning and a properly democratic character. John Stuart Mill, an eloquent spokesman for the participatory aspects of democracy, expressed it this way:

> A completely popular government is the only polity which can make any claim [to being the ideally best form of government]. It is preeminent in both the departments between which the excellence of a political constitution is divided. It is both more favorable to present good government, and promotes a better and higher form of national character, than any other polity whatsoever.[35]

There can be no questioning of the sincerity with which leaders and theorists in democracies espouse participation. Many of the historic expansions of the right to vote in the United States were due to a strong belief in the desirability of universal participation. This was probably most clearly true of the adoption of the Fifteenth Amendment, which added the freed slaves to the electorate. This action had

---

[34]A good, brief treatment of this phenomenon will be found in Alan Wolfe and Charles A. McCoy, *Political Analysis—An Unorthodox Approach* (New York: Crowell, 1972), p. 107. Cooptation does not of course always work in favor of the elite group. For perhaps the best general discussion of cooptation and its risks, see Philip Selznick, *TVA and the Grass Roots* (Berkeley: University of California Press, 1949).

[35]John Stuart Mill, *Considerations on Representative Government* (London: Basil Blackwell & Mott, 1948), pp. 141–151.

to be sincere and not merely a cynical act of cooptation, inasmuch as the overwhelming proportion of whites were antagonistic to blacks and felt no particular need to coopt them or their leaders.

The fact that we sincerely believe in participation does not alter its historic function as an instrument of conquest in the United States and elsewhere. Participation, like education and folk culture, is double-barreled. It is good in itself, and it is good for conquest. Take, for example, one statement about reasons other than the sincere belief in participation that would have led to an expansion of the electorate:

To assert that an indignant people wrested the right to vote from a reluctant government is a humorous inversion of the truth, an invention of persuasive politicians who sold the fable to the historians. It is impossible to explain the extension of the suffrage in terms that ignore the competition of the parties. The enlargement of the *practicing electorate* has been one of the principal labors of [two-party competition]. . . . In the search for new segments of the population that might be exploited profitably, the parties have kept the movement to liberalize the franchise well ahead of the demand.[36] (Italics are in the original.)

Every day we see evidence of the use of participation as a device for cooptation. For example, many may have wondered why youth between the ages of eighteen and twenty-one were given the right to vote just at the time when they were misbehaving at almost historic levels of noise and disorder. Many, of course, were in favor of reducing the age requirement to eighteen because they sincerely believed that the obligation to fight wars qualified a person to participate in elections as well. But another very important reason for lowering the voting age at this particular time was the need to assure the loyalty of the youth to the system—perhaps to make up for the incomplete socialization provided for them in the schools and perhaps to make up for the retrograde effects of an unpopular war. Even the most cursory review of the debate in Congress or the state legislatures regarding the ratification of the Twenty-sixth Amendment (1971) will reveal the strong preoccupation of the legislators with doing something to placate the youth and head off further disorder.

Another noteworthy example is the participatory provision of the War on Poverty during the 1960s. The whole purpose of "maximum feasible participation" was to get the poor, especially the newly emerging advocates for the poor, to collaborate with the government in the making of community decisions rather than to make their demands from the outside. There are different opinions as to whether the participatory aspects of the War on Poverty worked, but there would tend to be general agreement that participation was effective for a good while in reducing the alienation of many ghetto leaders.[37]

The most familiar example of cooptation might well be the phenomenon of ticket balancing. Most everyone knows that political party leaders try their best to select candidates for public office who "represent" each of the major minorities in city or state campaigns. In a well-organized party, this process of balancing selections in

---

[36]E. E. Schattschneider, *Party Government* (New York: Rinehart, 1942), p. 48.

[37]For a superb review of all of these issues, see J. David Greenstone and Paul E. Peterson, *Race and Authority in Urban Politics—Community Participation and the War on Poverty* (New York: Russell Sage Foundation, 1973). See also Frances Fox Piven and Richard A. Cloward, *Regulating the Poor: The Functions of Public Welfare* (New York: Random House, 1971) for a book which appreciates the cooptative aspects of the War on Poverty but which suggests a strategy for turning cooptation to the advantage of the poor. For a still more critical statement which attacks the War on Poverty as both cynical and self-defeating, see Theodore Lowi, *The End of Liberalism* (New York: Norton, 1969), chapter 8.

terms of ethnic and religious minorities extends even to the appointive as well as the elective posts. It is no coincidence that New York, the city with the longest history of bosses and machines, is also the city most systematic in its efforts to balance the selection of candidates for elective office and for appointments to high administrative positions.[38]

Once again in our discussion we have attempted to appreciate the political significance of commonplace things. An understanding of the political uses of participation does not lead us to a rejection of participation as a very desirable process in government. One can be in strongest accord with the position taken by such theorists as John Stuart Mill and still be able to appreciate participation as a useful instrument of conquest. After all, if there is to be conquest, participation is surely one of the more uplifting measures to employ. There are calculated risks on both sides. Rulers cynically trying to use participation to coopt support may find their powers seriously limited by a larger citizenry. Sincere efforts to improve the citizenry through participation may find the larger and inexperienced citizenry more susceptible to appeals by dictators for mass popular consent. But all government is a risk; we are only becoming more aware of what the specific risks are.

Government Government, the last of the seven deadly virtues, is at the same time dependent on and superior to all other instruments of conquest. It is superior because it can be the most efficient; it can be most efficient because it can be specific in its commands; and it can be specific because it can legitimately employ force. As we will have occasion to say more than once, government is the only institution in most modern societies whose primary purpose is to control. Control is exercised, for example, by every large corporation; but in such cases it is incidental to the profit motive. Control is intrinsic to government, not incidental. Government is composed of *institutions* which produce controls in the form of *policies.* These policies are passed on to *agents* and *agencies* of government, whose purpose it is to spend money and issue rules and orders aimed at the control of specific persons or their conduct.

The ability to change as well as maintain society is another aspect of government which adds to its superiority. Such changes have occurred only infrequently in the U.S., but the government's potential in this area is highly respected. Government in the U.S. has made corporations the key to our economic development. Govern-

---

[38]For a frank report on how bosses construct tickets, see the autobiography of the famous former boss of the Bronx, Edward J. Flynn, *You're the Boss* (New York: Viking Press, 1947). For statistical studies of the actual efforts to balance ethnic, religious, and other characteristics in the appointment of the top officials, see Theodore Lowi, *At the Pleasure of the Mayor* (New York: Free Press, 1964); and Marshall Langberg, "The Decline of Machine Politics" (Ph.D. diss., University of Chicago, 1973).

Table 3.4   Government and the Study of Government

This table is designed to provide direction for anyone who sees reason to fear government and who wishes to pursue the study of it. The second column contains no answers but is a listing of the political and governmental phenomena to be studied in each instance. In some instances, during certain eras, or in certain countries, there are actually no answers at all—or no acceptable answers.

What to Ask	What to Study
What methods are used to conquer?	Armed forces, war, foreign policy
What methods are used to maintain conquest?	Electoral process, the three branches, public policy, police
Why resort to deliberate control?	Classes, groups, the market, economic and political history
What limits and delimits conquest?	Constitutions, social institutions, party and group competition
How are directions and types of controls chosen?	Policy-making processes in legislatures, administrative agencies, polls
Who is in control, and how?	Elites in administrative agencies, armed forces, police forces, corporations, news media
How do they get consent to use government for control?	Elections, participation, legislatures, polls, precedent
What does it take to impose and remove controls?	Legislatures, court cases, political parties and elections, polls, agencies
What redress is there against bad controls?	Judiciary, legal system, political campaigning, rebellion, revolution, emigration
What if government control fails to maintain conquest?	Armed forces, war, foreign policy

ment has been behind the conversion of Americans from renters to owners. Government took us off feet and horses, put us on rails, then put us on rubber tires, and may soon be putting us back on rails, or on foot, again. Government has mobilized millions to fight wars. Government is collectivizing delivery of medical services, and governments have already brought about important changes in race relations.

Governments often fail. But governments never fail to coerce. This capacity to coerce engenders a fear of government, and in the twentieth century fear of government is associated with "conservatism." But if only conservatives hold this view, then only conservatives understand government; and John Stuart Mill *(On Liberty)*, Bertrand de Jouvenal *(On Power)*, and all constitutionalists are conservatives. Fear of government is one of the central themes in all political thought, and fear of government has made government one of the oldest subjects of study in the Western world.

*Conquest and Government
in Contemporary U.S.A.*

Part Two
Constitution

Everyone everywhere wants a constitution. Rulers want
one because subjects want one; the appearance of
having one may help routinize conquest. Subjects want
one because of the widely tested but never confirmed
hypothesis that a constitution might be a dependable
defense against tyranny. But can a constitution go farther
than providing legitimacy for rulers and false comfort for
subjects? Can it shape the pattern of conquest? Can it
prevent tyranny? Can forms and structures ever really
shape power? Or is it always the other way around? Is the
basic question: Who governs? Or is it: What governs?

Chapter 4   Legitimizing Conquest: Making a Constitution

We, therefore, the Representatives of the united States of America, in General Congress, Assembled, appealing to the Supreme Judge of the world for the rectitude of our intentions, do, in the Name and by Authority of the good People of these Colonies, solemnly publish and declare, That these United Colonies are, and of Right ought to be Free and Independent States; that they are Absolved from all Allegiance to the British Crown, and that all political connection between them and the State of Great Britain, is and ought to be totally dissolved; and that as Free and Independent States, they have full Power to levy War, conclude Peace, contract Alliances, establish Commerce, and to do all other Acts and Things which Independent States may of right do.
The Declaration of Independence, 1776.

The eloquence of the Declaration of Independence tended to overshadow the immense practical problems inherent in it. One of the lasting problems was the tremendous gap between "independent states" and "united states," which has not even yet been bridged entirely. Much of the history of the United States can be written as a struggle for barely enough national unity to survive as a nation.

ANTECEDENTS OF NATIONAL UNITY

Each of the American colonies had reached a fairly happy state of legitimate government well before the founding of the United States. The original charters accompanying the titles and land grants from the monarchy were broadly classified as either "royal" or "proprietary," but this masked the local autonomy the colonies enjoyed in developing their own particular characteristics. There were of course similarities arising out of common heritage. But within common cultural and political values were vast differences of economic interest and general perspective.

As might be expected, slavery was the major cause of cleavage among the colonies. Well before the emergence of a general national concept of America, slavery as a basic feature of the economy had already disappeared in most of the northern states and had become the essential foundation of the economy in the southern states. By the time of the war for independence, the geographical descriptions *North* and *South* clearly defined the free states and the slave states. Still other differences set specific colonies apart from each other. Among the slave states, Maryland became important for milling while neighboring Virginia became rich in tobacco. This alone could have given them different perspectives, since tobacco was very much an export crop while milling was oriented toward local and regional domestic markets. South Carolina fortunes came from rice and indigo. Then, too, each of the slave colonies was favored to different degrees by King Cotton, the crop that was most suitable for slave labor.

In the North the differences of economic interests were equally clear. New York was of course a center of trade and commerce but also a great state for truck farming and furs. The New England colonies were already engaging in manufacture and were especially adept in the conversion of wool into woolen cloth. Fishing and shipbuilding were also important industries in the north country. Under these circumstances it would have been perfectly logical for North America to go the same direction as South America, with each colony gaining its separateness and its independence as a country at different times and for different reasons. There was nothing natural or inevitable about the development of a concept of a single United States; it was going to be something the colonists would have to work toward.[1]

As has happened so often since the rise of modern colonialism, the British government eventually decided that the colonies ought to pay to help support the national debt, a large part of which had accumulated because of colonial policies and colonialist wars.

None of the actions taken by Great Britain against the colonies was unusually oppressive. The Stamp Act of 1765 is a good example. It was considered particularly oppressive only because it was the

---

[1]The incentives toward unity on a national scale have been so well covered by historians that they can receive only a brief treatment here. See, for example, Samuel E. Morison et al., *The Growth of the American Republic,* 6th ed., 2 vols. (New York: Oxford University Press, 1969), vol. 1, chapters 6–9.

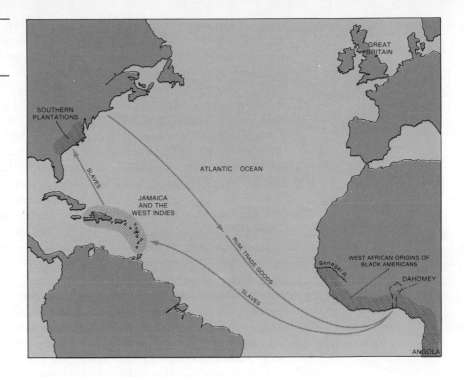

Figure 4.1
Antecedents of disunity: The triangular slave trade

GREAT BRITAIN

SOUTHERN PLANTATIONS

ATLANTIC OCEAN

SLAVES

JAMAICA AND THE WEST INDIES

RUM TRADE GOODS

WEST AFRICAN ORIGINS OF BLACK AMERICANS

Senegal R.

DAHOMEY

SLAVES

ANGOLA

first direct, internal tax ever laid on the colonies by Parliament.[2] The stamp in question was actually a revenue stamp which was to be bought and placed upon each of several types of merchandise, as we see regularly today on packages of cigarettes or bottles of whiskey. The reaction to this direct imposition of a not unreasonable revenue device began with the famous slogan "no taxation without representation" and became far more extreme than anyone had expected. It manifested itself not only in organized resistance but also in a very large reduction in the purchase of goods from England by the colonies. The Stamp Act lasted less than five months. The colonists celebrated its repeal, and things were never again to be the same. Colonists had tasted political victory, and the British, thanks largely to a combination of economic pressure and the political competition between Parliament and crown, could not resist additional interventions.

These pressures eventually led, among other things, to the infamous tax on tea and to a blunder that inflated this otherwise modest act to an event of historic proportion. It seems that the East

[2]The Revenue Act of 1764, also called the Sugar Act, was the first of these measures to raise revenues from the colonies, but it was a regular excise tax, simply upon goods that were of special relevance to the American colonies.

India Company, in financial trouble, sought and got from the crown a monopoly on the export of tea from Britain. In order to cut costs and to speed up the process of profit, the company eliminated the middle man—that is, it sold the tea directly in the colonies without going through existing local merchants. This, not the tax, seems to have been the main issue. In any case, the immediate outcome was the Boston Tea Party, which goaded the very jealous young King George beyond his level of equanimity. Within five months after the incident in Boston, the House of Commons had passed a whole series of Coercive Acts closing the port of Boston to commerce, changing the provincial government of Massachusetts, and eventually providing for the removal of accused persons to England for trial.

These Acts confirmed the worst criticisms of England and of colonialism that were being voiced by radicals such as Samuel Adams, Richard Henry Lee, and Christopher Gadsden. Each act of retaliation by England seemed to play into their hands. As Samuel Adams put it at the time of the Tea Party, every moment of calm "strengthens our opponents and weakens us."[3] This escalatory pattern, beginning early in 1774, eventually attracted larger and larger numbers of nonradicals and facilitated the shift from a focus on specific acts of oppression to the more general and abstract goals of representation and civil liberty.

It was perhaps the redefinition of specific acts of oppression into general goals of political democracy that made possible a movement toward nationalism. Early efforts to build regional or national concepts had failed. The Albany Congress in 1754, for example, had gotten nowhere despite the influential backing of such men as Benjamin Franklin. What had been lacking was the idea that could be shared nationally. The Boston Tea Party might affect Massachusetts; but "no taxation without representation" could be heard everywhere, and was.

The Declaration of Independence is a magnificent case study of the connection between selfish goals and broad ideals, between specific grievances and a national commitment to justice and individual freedom. It is a study of the dependence of each upon the other, and no one can read the text of it without feeling at once a connection between the everyday grievances of practical politics and the ideas of Locke, Rousseau, Jefferson, Paine, and Franklin.[4]

The Declaration of Independence is also a declaration of war. It was certainly the most unusual declaration of war ever written, because it was a treatise in political philosophy and statecraft. Yet for all that, it is an act of war, and as an act of war it was filled with

---

[3]Quoted in Morison, *The Growth of the American Republic,* vol. 1, p. 158. See also Alan Rogers, *Empire and Liberty* (Berkeley: University of California Press, 1974), especially chapters 7–9.
[4]For an excellent analysis see Carl Becker, *The Declaration of Independence* (New York: Knopf, 1922).

boasts, bluffs, and great hopes.[5] Thanks to the Declaration of Independence, the conduct of the war actually produced a great deal of national culture and common political ideals. But it did not produce an overwhelming amount of national unity. In addition to the separate tendencies of each colony, and the jealousies of each military contingent in having to yield to the single authority of General Washington, there were also the many loyalists who still held positions of power and influence throughout the nation. In effect we were waging a civil war as well as a war for independence. As late as the summer of 1782, nearly a year after the surrender of Cornwallis at Yorktown, General Washington was still finding it necessary to cajole and flatter his leaders and his men in order to keep up a common front. Without that, the victory would have been far less than satisfactory, since at the time of the peace conferences of 1783 the British still held New York, Charlestown, Savannah, Detroit, and a good deal of open country.

GOVERNMENT ACCORDING TO THE DECLARATION: THE ARTICLES OF CONFEDERATION

The new republic had been operating under the Articles of Confederation and Perpetual Union since November of 1777 even though it was not ratified by all of the new states until 1781. This document never gets the attention it deserves because it was our constitution for such a brief period. But it is particularly important because it, and not the Constitution of 1789, is truly indicative and expressive of the "Spirit of '76" and the Declaration of Independence.[6] As an expression of this spirit, the Articles of Confederation provides a basically negative approach. Everything about the provisions seems to insure that members of Congress would be little more than mere delegates or messengers from the state legislatures. Yet central government was based entirely in Congress—something we would perhaps call collective leadership today. But in addition, this was a Congress in which each state, regardless of its size, had the power to cast only a single vote. Delegates were chosen by state legislatures, salaries were to be paid by the state treasuries, and each delegate was subject to immediate recall by the state authorities.

Government without some kind of an executive power would have been extremely difficult to conduct, but that mattered very little,

---

[5]If Americans had really been so united and determined as the ringing phrases of the Declaration of Independence suggest, they would have achieved independence within a year. They already controlled 99 percent of the country; the English people were half-hearted in the war; and the difficulties of conquering a determined people three thousand miles overseas were enormous. Morison, *The Growth of the American Republic,* vol. 1, p. 177.

[6]For more on this period and on the Articles of Confederation, see Merrill Jensen, *The Articles of Confederation* (Madison: University of Wisconsin Press, 1940). The document itself appears as an appendix in the book.

since the national government under Congress was given so little power. Congress was provided with the power to declare war and to make peace, to make treaties and alliances, and to coin money and regulate trade with the Indians. Although Congress was given authority to appoint the senior officers, the United States Army was actually to be composed of the state militias. Congress was allowed to borrow money and issue currency, but the vital powers to levy taxes and to regulate commerce among the states were explicitly denied the national government. Congress became a supplicant, with a relationship to the states much like the contemporary relationship between the United Nations and its national members. As it turned out, the most unfortunate deprivation was that no power was given the central government to prevent one state from discriminating against other states in the quest for favorable foreign commerce.

The lack of unity evidenced in these provisions of the Articles of Confederation is especially significant inasmuch as the document was written during the years 1775 to 1777, at a time when the prospects and realities of war would have brought the colonies closer together than at any time before or after. The ideals of the Declaration of Independence and the revolution were not going to be sufficient to hold this nation together as an independent and single nation-state. Instead, the weaknesses inherent in the structure of government provided for in the Articles of Confederation discredited to some degree the idea of confederation and undermined the position of the revolutionary radicals who had been so important in the war. From almost the moment of armistice, moves were afoot to reform and strengthen the Articles of Confederation.

There was at this time great concern for the international position of the country. The democratic hunger would have to be satisfied in some way *after* a truly sovereign nation could be established. That sovereignty would require not complete unification but the establishment of enough independent *national* power to present a common front to the outside world. Apparently no leader really believed in a unified national system that would destroy the independent identity of the states. Such a belief would have required a complete overthrow of the Articles of Confederation and the elimination of virtually all of the radical leadership. But something just short of that had to be established, and the states would have to be more subject to the national government or the final result would be conquest by a foreign power. Confirmation of these concerns was not hard to find. Competition among the states was keen, and concessions created very confusing patterns on both sides of the Atlantic. At one point during the winter of 1786/87 when John Adams sought to negotiate a new treaty with the British covering disputes left over from the war, the British government answered that since the United States under the Articles of Confederation was unable to enforce existing treaties, the British could only negotiate with each of the thirteen states separately.[7]

During this same period the nationalists emerged. The great theoretical radicals and revolutionary leaders were replaced by the philosophic conservatives and the constitutionalists, and stress on abstract individual freedom was beginning to be replaced by stress upon the much more concrete notion of individual property rights.[8] By the fall of 1786, many state leaders were ready to respond favorably to an invitation extended by the Virginia Legislature to attend a conference of states at Annapolis to discuss the problem of trade among the states. All the states were invited to attend the Annapolis Convention, but only five states actually sent delegates. And only one positive thing came out of the convention. This was a carefully worded resolution calling upon Congress to send commissioners to Philadelphia at a later time "to devise such further provisions as shall appear to them necessary to render the Constitution of the Federal Government adequate to the agencies of the new Union."[9] This resolution had been drafted by young Alexander Hamilton, who had emerged as the leading conservative theorist. However, it should be emphasized that the capitalized *C* did not necessarily imply an intention to develop an entirely new constitution. As most readers are aware, older English, still under Teutonic influence, tended to capitalize most important nouns. Thus, the resolution was only referring to the desire to make an effort to improve and reform the Articles of Confederation.

Suspicion persisted, however, that the instigator of the Annapolis Convention, James Madison, and many of his associates had larger ends in view. It is quite possible that the Philadelphia Convention would never have happened at all, except for the intervention of a single event during the winter following Annapolis: Shays's Rebellion. Daniel Shays, a former army captain, was moved by angry farmers in the autumn of 1786 to lead them in a tax rebellion. Apparently, their objective was to prevent the local courts in western Massachusetts from meeting until after the next state election so that new judges might make less severe judgments on land burdened by tax debts. They were following the example of Rhode Islade, where previously the radicals had taken over the legislature and had so inflated the currency by printing large sums of cheap paper money that debtors were able to ease their way out of their heavy mortgages. Eventually, Shays's Rebellion failed and the

---

[7]Reported in Morison, *The Growth of the American Republic,* vol. 1, p. 243.

[8]For those who are interested in revolutions wherever they occur, this movement toward conservative leaders and conservative views in the United States tends to parallel and to confirm prevailing theories of revolution. Reaction or conservatism tends to be a second step following the initial success of the revolution. See, for example, Lyford P. Edwards, *The Natural History of Revolution* (Chicago: University of Chicago Press, 1970; originally published 1927). See also Crane Brinton, *The Anatomy of Revolution* (New York: Random House, Vintage, 1974).

[9]Quoted in Morison, *The Growth of the American Republic,* vol. 1, p. 244.

mobs were dispersed, but not before the government of the state of Massachusetts was deeply embarrassed.

The embarrassment spread nationally when Massachusetts appealed to Congress for assistance, and Congress found itself constitutionally unable to act at all. Shays's Rebellion converted the Philadelphia Convention into a bandwagon. State leaders throughout the colonies seized upon Philadelphia as the best available means of reform. Seven state legislatures appointed delegates to Philadelphia without even waiting for Congress to issue the call.

Figure 4.2
Slavery: The real
division of states at
Philadelphia

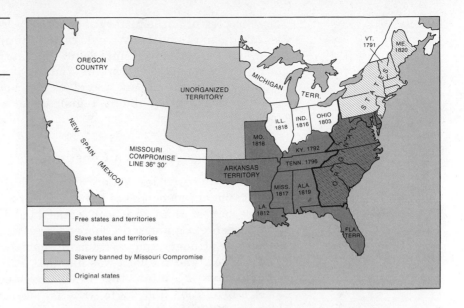

Then Congress quickly jumped on the bandwagon, adopting Hamilton's Annapolis resolution almost word for word. All of the states except Rhode Island eventually sent delegates to the opening of the Philadelphia Convention. And the absence of Rhode Island, with its radical legislature, was an indication of the issues that the delegates were going to face in Philadelphia.

THE SECOND REPUBLIC: CONQUEST OF THE STATES

The Constitution of the United States emerged out of failure, not success. The Articles of Confederation had failed on at least two counts: (1) no national sovereignty that was credible to the great and predatory nation-states of Europe was established, and (2) persons of property were insufficiently protected from the "leveling" efforts of debtors and the propertyless. The delegates converged upon Philadelphia during the hot summer of 1787, the Rhode Island and Massachusetts rebellions firmly fixed in their minds, determined to banish the twin specters of international embarrassment and domestic economic democracy.

The task in Philadelphia was essentially to create a new republic—either through reform of the Articles of Confederation or the writing of a new document. This is what we have called the Founding. It was actually the second founding, since we had already been governed as an independent nation under our first constitution for nearly fifteen years. But this is the more important of the two and should be studied with some care, because it is probably the most successful in the history of democracy.[10] This second founding is thus the most important single case study of the universal process by which rulers convert into legitimate authority the raw power acquired by conquest. A careful study of it will reveal the specific values and intentions, and therefore many of the realities, behind our own Constitution and the regime under which we are governed today.

On Foundings: What Is a Constitution?

Failure of the Articles of Confederation had proved that the step from national independence to national unity was going to require more conquest than had been anticipated by the Declaration of Independence. Conquest of independent states was going to require something stronger and vastly more sophisticated than force. This was an idea, and the idea was national legitimacy. Legitimacy is what leaders are attempting to achieve whenever they sit down after a revolution and try to write themselves a constitution. The term *constitution* merely refers to the makeup or composition of a thing. The state is composed of a government, and the government has a constitution of legislatures, courts, agencies, armies, budgets, and the various procedures and processes flowing through.

But to this objective definition of a constitution we add the *normative* idea of legitimacy. Thus, when we speak of the constitution of a government we speak of its makeup *and* of its moral character. At the time of any founding it is not enough to have a government with its agencies and agents. It is important that this government appear to be good. Since *appearing* to be good is not the same thing as *being* good, we speak of legitimacy rather than of goodness or of virtue in the vocabulary of government. Legitimacy is the next best thing to being good. Although legitimacy is a difficult concept, most readers have at least an instinct of what is involved. Legitimacy means more than popularity. It means more than that the people have not revolted. Legitimacy means widespread agreement that the government is based upon some higher scheme of values and can be defended as consistent with it. By the term *higher scheme of values* we mean here some notion of justice or absolute good that is beyond the immediate manipulation of the participants. That is, the person in power has to defend governmental action in terms of these values and is not free to change them for

---

[10]The Constitution was clearly the founding of the Second Republic. The Civil War and the three post–Civil War Amendments (XIII, XIV, and XV) so altered our system that it should be entitled the Third Republic. Many would say that the changes in the Constitution following 1937 deserve equal appreciation. Consequently, we could properly call ourselves the Fourth Republic, perhaps the Fifth, depending upon how the analysis is conducted. This is no mere academic exercise. It conveys a proper appreciation of the importance of the constitutional basis of government. (See also chapter 5.)

the sake of convenience. The source of these values may be religion, or philosophy, or folklore. But whatever their source, they must be big ideas with a history and a logic rather than little ideas that are improvised to fit the situation.

Our instinct also tells us that someone who calls a thing legitimate is actually conceding "that it is ethically suspect. . . . We appeal to the standard of legitimacy only when we know or suspect that our performance is less than ideal, that it requires defending."[11] But this is precisely why the concept of legitimacy is so important in politics. We know that every action involving the use of power requires elaborate justification, which means, conversely, that it is suspect. Those actions that can reasonably be defended *before they are undertaken* are at least legitimate, if not ideal. This minimal condition of virtue is a lot to ask of government. But when this condition is fulfilled, and the government is legitimate, people will in some important sense conquer themselves by submitting to government and by being content with the consequences. It is in this spirit that Max Weber defined government as that institution in society which possesses a monopoly of legitimate coercive power. Other institutions coerce, but none except government can cover their coercion in the shroud of legitimacy.[12]

The United States was not so well chosen by providence that it could sidestep these issues. As with any new nation, the founders had a limited number of choices of routes toward establishing legitimacy. For example, they could have proceeded to "discover" that their leader or leaders were descendants of God or some ancient kings. They could also have executed the original leaders of the revolution and staked out their legitimacy on the basis of that series of murders and the higher motives which required such action. Whatever those motives, they would have had to be drawn from a set of values high enough and imposing enough to give the second founding its legitimacy. Or, at least they could have tried it this way. They might later have taken the third route, or then again they might not have bothered.

The third route, the route chosen in the United States for the second founding, was not based on any inheritance of a tradition or upon any acts of violence through which the right of rule would be established. Instead, legitimacy was established by the very act of writing a constitution. This was an appeal to the basic rational faculties of the society. The essence of the attempt to achieve

[11]Wilson Carey McWilliams, "On Political Illegitimacy," *Public Policy,* Summer 1971, p. 431. This article is a brilliant treatment of the concept of legitimacy and illegitimacy. For a slightly different but equally challenging treatment of the concept, see Alan Wolfe and Charles McCoy, *Political Analysis—An Unorthodox Approach* (New York: Crowell, 1972), p. 71: "What makes a 'totalitarian' government different from a democratic one is not that its decisions are illegitimate, but that legitimacy is achieved in different ways."

[12]See Max Weber, *From Max Weber: Essays in Sociology,* ed. and trans. Hans Gerth and C. Wright Mills (New York: Oxford University Press, 1958), p. 78.

legitimacy through constitutionalism is an appeal to the self-interest of the citizen. Constitutionalism is a special approach to legitimacy in which the rulers agree to give up a certain amount of power in return for their right to utilize the rest. Thus a constitution is an effort to delimit power as well as to delegate it. It is an effort to convert the real and unquestioned power of rulers into procedures within which citizens may feel they have a better chance at defending themselves. If this effort to achieve legitimacy through constitutionalism does not work, the rulers may end up using raw power based upon some direct appeal to the heavens or to magic. But that does not stop us from recognizing that constitutionalism is a very real effort to achieve legitimacy in a very special way.

Some will continue to argue that our own Constitution is a very thin cover for the brute realities of national power, national elites, and entrenched economic and social interests. But that thin veneer makes all the difference. It makes all the difference to those in power if they can defend their interests and have their defenses accepted as legitimate. And it makes all the difference to the citizens, *if* the concessions made by the rulers are sufficient to protect the citizens from the completely arbitrary use of governmental power over them. All people must judge whether these concessions are sufficient; if they are not, perhaps they have the obligation to rebel.

The Founding: A Marriage of Interest and Principle

The fifty-five delegates convened in Philadelphia in May of 1787. The city itself seemed unaware that something of even modest importance was taking place; but most of the delegates were of a more sophisticated and self-conscious frame of mind. This was in fact an extraordinary gathering of men whose attainments in statecraft and philosophy were already so well recognized that their places in history were secure even without the opportunity of serving as one of the founders. For example, James Madison, at thirty-six years of age, Edmund Randolph, at thirty-four years of age, and James Wilson, at forty-five, were already notable as practitioners of law and writers of political theory. Alexander Hamilton was barely thirty years of age, but his reputation was already established by his role in the revolution and at the Annapolis Convention, and would grow in luster with his writings in support of the constitution *(The Federalist Papers)* and his role in the Washington administration. Benjamin Franklin and George Washington, two of the elder statesmen, obviously had a well-established place already carved out for themselves in history.

There were others whose accomplishments were impressive but whose convention roles were less notable for various reasons, including the fact that the debates were secret. Out of the fifty-five delegates, thirty-one were college graduates at a time when college attendance was quite unusual; two had been college presidents, three had been college professors, and many others had taught college at one time or another. Virtually all were experienced and learned, with substantial backgrounds in law, yet were young, vigorous, and eager to participate in any major event of state. Five delegates were under thirty; nearly one-third of all the delegates were under forty-five. Only four were past the age of sixty. What a contrast to state and national officialdom today.[13]

The backgrounds of the delegates are more difficult to read as indicators of how they brought their views and interests to bear upon the issues confronting the convention. Scholars have disagreed long and loud over these matters, grouping themselves roughly into two schools of thought, which we shall label the "enthusiasts" and the "sophisticates." No scholar holds strictly to either school; but juxtaposition of these two exaggerated positions will enhance our sensitivity toward the Constitution and what it has meant in the development of this country. The "enthusiasts" are those who tend to believe that the founders were divinely inspired, that their product is only slightly less sacred than the Bible, and that "the people" ratified the document in that spirit. The "sophisticates" view the founders as a loose conspiracy of property owners and speculators brought together to defend propertied interests against radical state legislators and "the people." According to these "sophisticates," the Constitution was a successful counterrevolution; lack of principle was not only obvious, but it served to confirm the general axiom that in politics economic self-interest comes first.

At first exposure, the weight of evidence clearly favors the "sophisticates." We can begin with the absence of so many of the revolutionary leaders from the convention. These included Sam Adams, George Clinton, Christopher Gadsden, and Patrick Henry, who were not even elected as delegates. Many others were or could have been elected but bolted the convention and became vocal Anti-Federalists in opposition to the Constitution as adopted in Philadelphia.

To this kind of impressionistic data should be added the research of Charles Beard. On the basis of his analysis of the economic backgrounds and property of the delegates, Beard argued that "the movement for the Constitution of the United States was originated and carried through principally by four groups of personalty [exchangeable personal property] interests which had been adverse-

---

[13]For good reading and for voluminous information on the delegates, see Charles A. Beard, *An Economic Interpretation of the Constitution of the United States* (New York: Macmillan, 1913; paperback, 1961); Forrest McDonald, *We the People—The Economic Origins of the Constitution* (Chicago: University of Chicago Press, 1958); Max Farrand, *The Framing of the Constitution of the United States* (New Haven: Yale University Press, 1912; abridged paperback, 1962); Clinton Rossiter, *1787: The Grand Convention* (New York: Macmillan, 1966); and Jackson J. Main, *The Anti-Federalists* (Chapel Hill: University of North Carolina Press, 1961).

ly affected under the Articles of Confederation: money, public
securities, manufactures, and trade and shipping."[14] The formation
of the Constitution, he argued, was brought about "by a small and
active group of men immediately interested through their personal
possessions in the outcome of their labors"; and national ratification
was led in each state by a similar group without the involvement of
the "propertyless mass" (p. 324). The formulation most to his
satisfaction was that the Constitution was supported by those
persons of wealth who were tied in mainly with what we would now
call the modern economy—"in short, capital as opposed to land" (p.
63). To Beard, his case was clinched by the fact that the Constitution took explicit action on such matters as prohibiting the states
from issuing paper money and from impairing the sacred obligation
of contracts. (For more on this, see the discussion of Article I later in
this chapter.)

   Strong though the case may be for a straight personal-interest
approach to the Constitution, it is far from flawless. A careful
review of the biographies of the Philadelphia delegates and as many
of the state ratification leaders as possible was done by Forrest
McDonald.[15] Where Beard had looked at backgrounds and then
made interpretations, McDonald tried to examine specific items in
the background of each delegate and match those items with the
specific positions that the delegates took on matters related to
provisions in the Constitution. McDonald's most devastating thrust

[14]Beard, *An Economic Interpretation of the Constitution of the United States*, p. 324. Henceforth
in this section citations from Beard will be put in parentheses following each reference.
[15]McDonald, *We the People*.

against Beard was the conclusion that while a goodly number of the pro-Constitution delegates (the Federalists) did in fact own securities of significant value, *so did a very large proportion of the delegates who ended up voting against adoption of the Constitution.*

There is actually no unbridgeable gap between these two authors nor between the two general schools of thought. They are simply emphasizing different aspects of one single, complex reality: the founders were attempting the conquest of the nation through a careful construction of the Constitution. *All* of the political leaders involved in the founding had a tremendous personal stake in maintaining and supporting the system. It was to a very large extent economic—they were quite troubled by the "leveling" of fortunes that was being attempted in some of the state legislatures. We would have to be amazed (1) if they did not have a stake in maintaining and supporting a government that would defend their interests, or (2) if they had a stake in the system but were self-consciously attempting to create a government that was inimical to their interests. It proves nothing to say that the founders had an interest. On the other hand, we are properly instructed if we are told that the interest that most of the delegates shared was a property interest. For some this meant the ownership of stocks whose values would deteriorate without a sound government; for others it actually meant landed wealth. A stable government with a credible national center was equally important for all. McDonald demonstrated that Beard had made a distinction without a difference.

The more general difference between the "enthusiasts" and the "sophisticates" remains, and about this we can be guided by the following proposition: although each delegate may have had his own personal stake to maintain, he had to consult a far larger range of values, because it was a constitution he was making and not merely a deal over a single, transitory piece of legislation. Constitution-making is an extremely complex mix of economic, ideological, and personal factors.[16] The "sophisticates" are unassailable in their argument that something primordial was going on and that political leaders were being influenced by it even when they were not aware of it. No amount of talk about good motives and high ideals can ever overshadow the fact that the Constitution was going to be a cover for conquest and that the delegates were there to see that the arrangements would be acceptable to them.

On the other hand, it is equally realistic to recognize that the selfish stake of the delegates could never be implemented directly and crassly; at the same time they had to gain the lasting support of the hundreds of thousands of citizens in 1787 who would have to

Legitimizing Conquest:
Making a Constitution

[16]For a "modern" interpretation of the founding, see John P. Roche, "The Founding Fathers: A Reform Caucus in Action," *American Political Science Review,* December 1961, pp. 799–816.

support ratification and the millions who would ultimately live peacefully by its terms. The argument of the "enthusiasts" is valid insofar as these new conquerors had to find some larger and more appealing basis upon which to legitimize their position. Many decisions that were vital to that period and became essential to the development of the future of this country can be understood only in terms of pure theory and ideals. Others are more a mixture of ideals and selfish interest, and purely selfish interest without any velvet cover explains still other provisions. But the important thing is that there are all three types of provisions and motivations, not the one or the other.

THE ALMOST PERFECT UNION: GREAT COMPROMISES, MODEST DECISIONS

The Greatest Compromise: Buying the South

The opening days of the convention were spent confirming the credentials of the delegates and establishing acceptable rules of structure and procedure for this deliberative body.[17] The first substantive issue came before the convention almost exactly two weeks after it opened, on May 29, 1787, when Edmund Randolph of Virginia offered a resolution proposing corrections and enlargements in the Articles of Confederation—which he later admitted was essentially a proposal for replacing that document with an entirely new one. This initial proposal by Randolph, which shows the strong influence of James Madison, provided for virtually every aspect of a new government, and eventually served as the bare form used by the delegates to construct the final Constitution.[18] However, the part of the Randolph resolution that immediately seized the delegates was the opening proposition that representation of the states in the national legislature ought to be based upon the proportion of the population of each state to the national population, or each state's proportion of revenue contribution, or both. He proposed a second branch of legislature to be elected by the members of the first branch. This was basically what came to be called the Virginia Plan. It was a plan thought to be favorable to the large states, since the states varied enormously in terms of size of population and amount of taxable wealth, and these larger states might thus have the advantage of greater representation.

---

[17]There was of course no verbatim record of the debates, as we now find in the Congressional Record, but we are fortunate to have had James Madison present at these deliberations, because he kept careful notes. These have been edited in four published volumes by Max Farrand, *The Records of the Federal Convention of 1787,* rev. ed., 4 vols. (New Haven: Yale University Press, 1966).

[18]Farrand, *The Framing of the Constitution of the United States,* abridged ed., p. 68.

As the convention was debating the Virginia Plan, additional delegates were arriving in Philadelphia and were beginning to mount some opposition. Eventually this was expressed in an alternative resolution, which came to be known as the New Jersey Plan. This new resolution did not oppose the Virginia Plan point for point. Quite the contrary. It concentrated upon some specific weaknesses in the Articles of Confederation and honestly aimed toward revision of that document rather than a radical replacement. The original proposal *did not* embody explicitly a provision for constituting the legislature in a way that would favor the small states and therefore oppose the Virginia Plan. The New Jersey Plan did offer a sufficient amount of opposition to require that both plans be sent back to committee, where they could be reworked into a common document. Despite the absence of an explicitly alternative principle of representation in the New Jersey Plan, it is nevertheless true that this question was uppermost in the minds of many of the delegates. As Benjamin Franklin (a member of the drafting committee) observed, until the question of proportional representation "came before us, our debates were carried on with great coolness and temper."[19]

The outcome of this debate was the so-called Connecticut Compromise, which provided for two branches of the legislature. The first branch was to be based upon the number of inhabitants in each state, with representatives apportioned accordingly. In the second branch of the legislature each state would have an equal vote. The remaining details of the composition of each branch were left to later drafting. One of the many compromises which made the Constitution possible, this has been called the *Great Compromise*.

All of this sounds a bit too neat, too easy, anticlimactic. And it is. There is a great deal more behind the Great Compromise, and if we leave the story as we have it here, we will only be contributing to the great American mythology. After all, the notion of a bicameral legislature was very much in the air in 1787; most of the states had been living with bicameral legislatures for years. The Philadelphia delegates might have gone straight to the adoption of such a legislature based upon two different principles of representation even without the dramatic interplay of conflict and compromise. Indeed, far more fundamental issues than the composition of the legislature had to be confronted before the Great Compromise could take place. We are of course talking primarily about slavery.

If the bicameral legislature was the Great Compromise, the agreements among the delegates about how to deal with slavery should be called the *Greatest Compromise*. As it turns out, most of the differences historians have described as differences between the *small* states and the *large* states were actually reflections of the fundamental distinction between *slave* and *nonslave* states. Over 90

[19]Ibid. p. 92.

percent of all slaves resided in five states, wherein they comprised 30 percent of the total population. In some places, slaves outnumbered the nonslave population by as much as ten to one. No constitution embodying any principle of national supremacy would ever be framed unless some basic decisions were made about the place of slavery in the general scheme. In the midst of debate over large versus small states, the Virginia Plan versus other approaches, note well Madison's observation: "The great danger to our general government *is the great Southern and Northern interests of the continent, being opposed to each other. Look to the votes in Congress, and most of them stand divided by the geography of the country, not according to the size of the states.*"[20] (Italics in original.) Madison hit upon the same point on several later occasions as different aspects of the legislature were being discussed. For example, on arguing against applying the principle of population to both branches, he observed that:

> It seemed now to be pretty well understood that the real difference of interests lay, not between the large & small but between the N. & Southn. States. The institution of slavery & its consequences formed the line of discrimination. There were 5 States on the South, 8 on the Northn. side of this line. Should a proportl. representation take place it was true, the N. side would still outnumber the other: but not in the same degree, at this time; and every day would tend towards an equilibrium.[21]

The delegates actually turned toward representation as a means of solving the problem of slavery, just as they hoped it would solve other problems, such as agrarian versus capitalistic economies or common man versus aristocracy. Here is a perfect instance of the interdependence rather than the inconsistency of ideological and economic factors, because the delegates truly believed in mixed principles of representation; yet at the same time the "mixed principles" of a preference for property in the Senate and a preference for population in the House would lead to a national government structure that would solve or postpone the uncompromisable difference between slave and free economies.[22]

Whether one looks at the outcome as a compromise or a sellout, the fact remains that the South was kept from seceding from the new union by the arrangement whereby the seats in the House of Representatives would be apportioned according to a "population" in which five slaves would count as three persons. They would not be allowed to vote, but the number of representatives would be

---

[20]Farrand, *The Records of the Federal Convention*, vol. 1, p. 476.
[21]Ibid., vol. 2, p. 10. See other references in vol. 1, pp. 486–487 and vol. 2, pp. 81–82.
[22]By far the best effort to put slavery in its proper place in the constitutional scheme is that of Donald Robinson, *Slavery in the Structure of American Politics, 1765–1820* (New York: Harcourt Brace Jovanovich, 1971).

Slave ship *Wildfire*, 1860.

apportioned accordingly nevertheless. This arrangement was supported by the slave states—which, incidentally, included some of the biggest and some of the smallest states of that time—but was also accepted by many delegates from nonslave states who so strongly supported the principle of property representation that they were glad to support property expressed in slaves as well as in land or money or stocks.

So few of the delegates opposed slavery as such, and so few intended to use the framing of the Constitution as the opportunity to abolish slavery, that the final arrangement about slavery probably required very little compromise. The concern was over *how much* the slaves would count rather than whether they would be recognized. The establishment of the three-fifths formula, which

Legitimizing Conquest: Making a Constitution

Madison recognized as essential to national unity, was accepted without a great deal of debate or compromise. The result was fundamental:

> It gave Constitutional sanction to the fact that the United States was composed of some persons who were "free" and others who were not. And it established the principle, new in republican theory, that a man who lived among slaves had a greater share in the election of representatives than the man who did not. With one stroke, despite the disclaimers of its advocates, it acknowledged slavery and rewarded slave owners. It is a measure of their adjustment to slavery that Americans in the 18th Century found this settlement natural and just.[23]

Once it was settled that the status of slavery would not be changed under the Constitution, it became possible to go on with other decisions that would not only reform the Articles of Confederation but would truly establish a national government. There would be ample room for compromise among economic interests, and there would be room for dealing with the less compromisable ideological questions of the best government for the United States. Slavery was of course enough in itself to confirm the argument that the Constitution is an economic document, for the economic value represented in slaves must have constituted a tremendously high proportion of the gross value of all capital goods in America.[24] However, the Constitution is much too complex for such a simple proposition. To say that constitutional recognition of the institution of slavery made possible the establishment of a national system of government is not to say that everything about that system concerned or was concerned with slavery. If slavery had not existed, we might well still have the same constitutional provisions except, of course, the three-fifths arrangement for counting slaves.

A New Document and a New Nation

There is no question but that the major accomplishment of the Philadelphia Convention was the conversion of the confederation into a federation. *National supremacy* is what this accomplishment should be called, not only because that was the term the delegates became willing to employ, but also because it helps to emphasize the very large step the delegates were taking away from the Articles of Confederation.

Actually, national supremacy was accomplished by several large steps rather than just one. The first of these steps was the decision

---

[23]Ibid., p. 201. For observation on the degree to which regard for property rights led many nonsoutherners to support slavery, see p. 206.

[24]For an elaborate effort to assess the capital value of slaves, see Robert W. Fogel and Stanley L. Engerman, *Time on the Cross* (Boston: Little, Brown, 1974).

The Ninth *PILLAR* erected !

" The Ratification of the Conventions of nine States, fhall be fufficient for the eftablifh-ment of this Conftitution, between the States fo ratifying the fame." *Art.* vii.

INCIPIENT MAGNI PROCEDERE MENSES.

that there would be a whole new document rather than a series of amendments to the Articles of Confederation. Many features of the original articles were retained, but they are minor in relation to the new elements. This was a calculated risk, leading to charges that the delegates were indeed staging a coup d'etat. But it was a risk few apparently hesitated taking. We have already observed that the opening resolution of the Convention presented the Virginia Plan, and that this was already a draft for a whole new document. As the new document emerged, one of the first explicit expressions of a commitment to national supremacy was the provision for ratification of the results of the Philadelphia Convention. (This became Article VII of the Constitution.) The delegates were very fearful of using the amending process provided under the Articles of Confederation to get their new provisions adopted, because it required that *every* single state legislature ratify amendments. Ultimately they decided to admit openly that their product was a new Constitution and proposed its adoption by the ratification by special state conventions in *any nine* of the thirteen states. This meant that nine states might commit the entire nation to an entirely new document. Based on the principle that there were certain national interests which overrode even a large majority, this method of ratification was clearly a stroke for national supremacy.

A second, and perhaps the most important, step toward national supremacy, was adoption of Article VI. Often called *the supremacy clause,* Article VI provides that all laws and treaties made "under the Authority of the United States" shall be superior to all laws adopted by any state or any subdivision. In addition, all state and local, as well as federal, officials in all the branches of government were required to take an oath to support the national Constitution. In other words, every action taken by the United States Congress would have to be applied within each state *as though the actions were in fact state law.* Note well that the supremacy clause required the states to respect treaties as well as statutes. This was a direct effort to keep the states from going off in their own separate ways in matters of international politics and economics.

Another important provision for national supremacy was put in Article I, which is known primarily for the direct powers it grants *to* the national government (Section 8). But in the same article are provisions that withdraw certain things *from* the states. For example, with one hand this article granted to Congress the power to coin and regulate money, to punish counterfeiting, and to regulate commerce, while with the other hand it restricted the power of the states in these same fields. In some areas the power of the federal government is exclusive, and in other areas the power is *concurrent,* inasmuch as the states retain and share some power to regulate commerce and to affect the currency by being able to charter banks, grant or deny corporate charters, grant or deny license to engage in a business or practice a trade, and regulate the quality of products or the conditions of labor. This issue of concurrent versus exclusive power has come up from time to time in our history; but wherever there is a direct conflict of laws between the federal and the state levels, the probability is that the issue will be resolved in favor of the federal level.[25]

Article IV is also concerned with national supremacy. It provides that each state must give "full faith and credit" to the official acts of all other states, and that the citizens of any one state are guaranteed the "privileges and immunities" of every other state, as though they are citizens of that state. These provisions for *comity* among all the states are extremely significant, for, without them, there would have been far less prospect of unobstructed national movement of persons and goods. However, since these two provisions were copied directly from the Articles of Confederation, we can be sure that the mere wiping away of obstructions by comity among the states would not in and of itself produce national unity *or* national supremacy. It took the other provisions of the Constitution to build positively toward this.

Finally, Article III creates a Supreme Court that can serve the needs of national unity as well as the needs for due process of law. In the first place, it is set up to be a supreme court "of the United States," and not merely the top court of the national government. "The federal judicial power was structured to enable the new national government to enforce its own laws . . . in a uniform way throughout the country. Thus national supremacy and uniformity were two of the main objectives of the jurisdictional clauses of

---

[25]The Supreme Court is then called upon to decide in each conflict whether a power is exclusive to the federal government, concurrent, or reserved exclusively to the states. This involves an additional concession to national power. For a discussion of these issues and the relevant cases, see C. H. Pritchett, *American Constitutional Issues* (New York: McGraw-Hill, 1962), chapter 17.

A symbol of our
association with ancient
Greece

Article III."[26] Another unifying aspect of the federal judiciary was
its jurisdiction over controversies between citizens of different
states. As we became a national market, we had to rely increasingly
upon the federal judiciary, because there was an increasing number
of cases involving "diversity of citizenship."

In all these matters, debate never seemed to occur on whether
there should be national supremacy, but only upon how to implement it. The discussion of national supremacy turned "less on its
general merits than on the force and extent of the particular terms
national & supreme."[27]

Securing Legitimacy: Restraints and Balances

Legitimacy required that for every provision for national power
there be a parallel provision extending the reassuring hand of
restraint on that power. In this sense the Constitution had to be just
as concerned as the Articles of Confederation with specific limitations of power and explicit statements of their application.

First among the provisions included for this purpose was the
doctrine of *expressed power.* The criterion of expressed power meant

---

[26]David Fellman, "Article III," *An American Primer,* ed. Daniel Boorstin (Chicago: University
of Chicago Press, 1966), vol. 1, p. 115.
[27]Farrand, *The Framing of the Constitution of the United States,* abridged ed., p. 73.

that the national government was to be able to exercise *only* those powers which were explicitly granted to it in the Constitution. All other conceivable powers were to be retained either by the states or the people. Article I, Section 8 contains a list of these expressed national powers, but at the same time it implies that what is not expressly granted there is not granted at all. Many will note that this same section concludes with something that looks like an escape clause; it states that Congress has the power "to make all laws which shall be necessary and proper for carrying into execution the foregoing powers." This was not intended as an escape route toward unlimited addition of new powers. Rather than a source of "invented powers," it was included as an indication to Congress that it could adopt whatever means seemed reasonable for carrying out the powers expressly granted to Congress.[28] The expansion of this *necessary and proper clause* into a source of new national powers is an exercise we have engaged in during the past two generations, but it is clearly not one specifically anticipated by the framers of the Constitution. The doctrine of expressed power was an absolutely indispensable means by which the states would be able to yield more power to the national government than they had been willing to yield under the Articles of Confederation.

The *separation of powers* was incorporated into the Constitution as yet another source of legitimacy. No principle of politics was more widely shared than the idea that power must be used to balance power. Very much a part of the general eighteenth century outlook, the notion of balancing power against power originated from Newtonian physics. Balancing power against power also became the basis for modern political economy as it was first and best expressed by Adam Smith in *The Wealth of Nations,* published, coincidentally, in 1776. Balance of power was elevated still higher in political theory by Montesquieu, who believed that separate departments of government were an indispensable defense against tyranny. Montesquieu's writings "were taken as political gospel" in Philadelphia.[29] The principle of the separation of powers is nowhere to be found explicitly in the Constitution. But it is clearly built upon Articles I, II, and III in the following manner: (1) provision of three separate and distinct departments or branches of government; (2) provision for very different methods of selection of the top personnel, so that each branch is based upon a different "constituency"—this is the idea of a "mixed regime" in which the personnel in each department are expected to develop very different interests and very different outlooks on how to govern; and (3) provision for "checks and balances" whereby each department is given some right to participate in the processes of each of the other

[28]*McCulloch* v. *Maryland,* 4 Wheaton 316 (1819).
[29]Farrand, *The Framing of the Constitution of the United States,* abridged ed., p. 49.

departments. Consequently, ours is not a system of separated powers but a system of "separated institutions sharing power."[30] A familiar example would be presidential veto power, which gives the president an opportunity to participate in the legislative process. Another example is the power of the Senate to approve presidential appointments to the top executive positions, offering Congress thereby its opportunity to extract information and other concessions from the executive branch.

Federalism is the other major means by which the national power was acceptably restrained and legitimacy won. This actually involved a relinquishment of state power enjoyed under the Articles of Confederation. Nevertheless, federalism did amount to a severe restraint, and federalism continues into the twentieth century to be probably the most effective restraint on national power. At the time of the founding, federalism was not a formal theory of governmental structure. It was more a result of the clear fact of the existence of separate and independent states. The founders knew only that they were striking a practical balance between the needs of a nation and the jealousies and fears of state governments. The very concept of federalism, the way the term is used today, was not in use until much later.[31] Nevertheless, all of the delegates seemed to agree that they were going to end up with a system of two sovereigns—the state and the nation—and that the competition between the two sovereigns was an effective limitation of the power of both. The absence of a concept for it only indicates the novelty of the arrangement.

Late in the convention the delegates made one final decision of relevance here. A motion was made to include a Bill of Rights in the Constitution. After a brief debate, in which hardly a word was said in its favor and only one speech was made against it, the delegates almost unanimously turned the motion down. The major argument at that time seemed to be that bills of rights should be adopted by the states since the federal government was to possess only the powers expressly granted to it.[32] Almost immediately following ratification, however, there was a movement to adopt a national bill of rights which resulted in the first ten amendments to the Constitution. These actions seemed to underscore one of the never-ending problems of government, which is to prove continually that it is sincere in its wish to restrain itself, to channel its powers, and to conquer no more than it must.

---

[30]Richard E. Neustadt, *Presidential Power* (New York: Wiley, 1960), p. 33.

[31]Farrand, *The Framing of the Constitution of the United States,* abridged ed., p. 69. See also William Riker, *Democracy in the United States* (New York: Macmillan, 1953), p. 306. Riker observes that not even the authors of *The Federalist Papers* had a word for it. *Federal* in their essays actually referred to the separate states, which they contrasted with the word *national.*

[32]Compare with Farrand, *The Framing of the Constitution of the United States,* abridged ed., pp. 185–186; see also Milton R. Konvitz, "The Bill of Rights: Amendments I–X," *An American Primer,* pp. 152–160.

The Pennsylvania Packet, *and Daily Advertiser.*

[Price Four-Pence.]   WEDNESDAY, September 19, 1787.   [No. 2690.]

WE, the People of the United States, in order to form a more perfect Union, establish Justice, insure domestic Tranquility, provide for the common Defence, promote the General Welfare, and secure the Blessings of Liberty to Ourselves and our Posterity, do ordain and establish this Constitution for the United States of America.

ARTICLE I.

Sect. 1. ALL legislative powers herein granted shall be vested in a Congress of the United States, which shall consist of a Senate and House of Representatives.

Sect. 2. The House of Representatives shall be composed of members chosen every second year by the people of the several states, and the electors in each state shall have the qualifications requisite for electors of the most numerous branch of the state legislature.

No person shall be a representative who shall not have attained to the age of twenty-five years, and been seven years a citizen of the United States, and who shall not, when elected, be an inhabitant of that state in which he shall be chosen.

Representatives and direct taxes shall be apportioned among the several states which may be included within this Union, according to their respective numbers, which shall be determined by adding to the whole number of free persons, including those bound to service for a term of years, and excluding Indians not taxed, three-fifths of all other persons. The actual enumeration shall be made within three years after the first meeting of the Congress of the United States, and within every subsequent term of ten years, in such manner as they shall by law direct. The number of representatives shall not exceed one for every thirty thousand, but each state shall have at least one representative; and until such enumeration shall be made, the state of New-Hampshire shall be entitled to chuse three, Massachusetts eight, Rhode-Island and Providence Plantations one, Connecticut five, New-York six, New-Jersey four, Pennsylvania eight, Delaware one, Maryland six, Virginia ten, North-Carolina five, South-Carolina five, and Georgia three.

When vacancies happen in the representation from any state, the Executive authority thereof shall issue writs of election to fill such vacancies.

The House of Representatives shall chuse their Speaker and other officers; and shall have the sole power of impeachment.

Sect. 3. The Senate of the United States shall be composed of two senators from each state, chosen by the legislature thereof, for six years; and each senator shall have one vote.

Immediately after they shall be assembled in consequence of the first election, they shall be divided as equally as may be into three classes. The seats of the senators of the first class shall be vacated at the expiration of the second year, of the second class at the expiration of the fourth year, and of the third class at the expiration of the sixth year, so that one-third may be chosen every second year; and if vacancies happen by resignation, or otherwise, during the recess of the Legislature of any state, the Executive thereof may make temporary appointments until the next meeting of the Legislature, which shall then fill such vacancies.

No person shall be a senator who shall not have attained to the age of thirty years, and been nine years a citizen of the United States, and who shall not, when elected, be an inhabitant of that state for which he shall be chosen.

The Vice-President of the United States shall be President of the senate, but shall have no vote, unless they be equally divided.

The Senate shall chuse their other officers, and also a President pro tempore, in the absence of the Vice-President, or when he shall exercise the office of President of the United States.

The Senate shall have the sole power to try all impeachments. When sitting for that purpose, they shall be on oath or affirmation. When the President of the United States is tried, the Chief Justice shall preside: And no person shall be convicted without the concurrence of two-thirds of the members present.

Judgment in cases of impeachment shall not extend further than to removal from office, and disqualification to hold and enjoy any office of honor, trust or profit under the United States; but the party convicted shall nevertheless be liable and subject to indictment, trial, judgment and punishment, according to law.

Sect. 4. The times, places and manner of holding elections for senators and representatives, shall be prescribed in each state by the legislature thereof; but the Congress may at any time by law make or alter such regulations, except as to the places of chusing Senators.

The Congress shall assemble at least once in every year, and such meeting shall be on the first Monday in December, unless they shall by law appoint a different day.

Sect. 5. Each house shall be the judge of the elections, returns and qualifications of its own members, and a majority of each shall constitute a quorum to do business; but a smaller number may adjourn from day to day, and may be authorised to compel the attendance of absent members, in such manner, and under such penalties as each house may provide.

Each house may determine the rules of its proceedings, punish its members for disorderly behaviour, and, with the concurrence of two-thirds, expel a member.

Each house shall keep a journal of its proceedings, and from time to time publish the same, excepting such parts as may in their judgment require secrecy; and the yeas and nays of the members of either house on any question shall, at the desire of one-fifth of those present, be entered on the

THE FINAL PRODUCT: AN INVENTORY OF ECONOMIC AND IDEOLOGICAL SOLUTIONS

These were the basic decisions: how to buy the support of the South, how to establish national supremacy, and how to gain national legitimacy through restraints. They provide a context within which we may now attempt some kind of meaningful review of the final document. Each article must be looked at with some care, and it is most important to read each provision at two levels. One level is the straightforward meaning of the words. But there is always a second level, always a deeper meaning. We may never be entirely certain what that meaning is, but we know it is there. We want to explore it not because of any antiquarian respect for the founders but because in founding a republic they solved problems that every republic has to face, including our own in the twentieth century. The closer we get to an understanding of the underlying meaning of our Constitution, the closer we will come to understanding how a complex country can be held together without resort, or too frequent resort, to tyranny.

The Preamble: The Balancing of Hope and Strategy

The preamble opens with "We the People of the United States." This is an expression of faith that government is better if the people ordain it, but it is also an act of political strategy, inasmuch as a great number of people were eventually going to have to ratify the document. Whether considered from the standpoint of strategy or as an expression of sincere faith, the preamble reflects the triumph of the average person. It reflects the triumph of the idea that all people have interests, that it is good to have interests, and that all interests are about equal, even if people are themselves not equal by talent or condition. Thus, the preamble proposes to "form a more perfect union" in order to secure defense, welfare, and liberty *"to ourselves and our posterity"* (italics added). In contrast to the Declaration of Independence, the Constitution appeals to the average person far more in terms of that person's self-interest than in terms of abstract principles of liberty or equality.

Article I: The "Pas de Trois" of Power, Representation, and Capitalism

Article I is by far the longest Article in the Constitution. Fortunately, it divides itself conveniently into three main parts, which will be dealt with here as though they were separate Articles. Sections 1–7 form a unit, with Section 8 and Sections 9–10, respectively, following.

Article I, Section 1

All legislative Powers herein granted shall be vested in a Congress of the United States, which shall consist of a Senate and House of Representatives.

Article I, Sections 1–7 The first seven sections provide for a Congress of two chambers; in the spirit of the separation of power each is given a different constituency. The original provisions anticipated a House of Representatives and a Senate that would be worlds apart, because the House members were given short terms and direct elections while the senators were given long terms with provisions for election not by the people but by the respective state legislatures.[33] The two chambers were brought closer together after

---

Legitimizing Conquest: Making a Constitution

[33]For the history of this change and an evaluation of its results, see Byron Daynes, "The Impact of the Direct Election of Senators on the Political System" (Ph.D. diss., University of Chicago, 1971).

1912 when the Constitution was changed to provide for direct election of senators. The purpose of all this was to provide for a vigorous representative assembly, yet one which was restrained by the fact that there were tensions and conflicts built into the system of relationships between House and Senate. Additional tension was introduced by providing that each chamber was to have control over its own members; however, this autonomy was limited by the power left to the states to control the "time, place and manner" by which their representatives would be elected.

Do these provisions make Article I an economic document? Those who answer yes are either basing their reply upon the three-fifths compromise over how to apportion the slave population, or they are engaging in circular reasoning. For, except for the three-fifths compromise, to call Article I an economic article is simply to assume that, since all the delegates had economic interests, there had to be an economic solution in there somewhere. On the face of it, the Article seems to be implementing the theoretical notion of balancing power against power. Section 7 strongly supports this interpretation inasmuch as it requires that all revenue bills originate in the House. The provision could only have emerged out of a strong theoretical or ideological consideration that the basic taxing powers belong to the House because the House is directly elected by the people and is much farther than the Senate from being a chamber of representatives of property.

Article I, Section 8

The Congress shall have Power to lay and collect Taxes . . . To borrow Money . . . To regulate Commerce . . . To coin Money . . . To constitute Tribunals inferior to the supreme Court . . . To declare War . . . To raise and support Armies . . . To make all Laws which shall be necessary and proper for carrying into Execution the Foregoing Powers, and all other Powers vested by this Constitution in the Government of the United States, or in any Department or Officer thereof.

Article I, Section 8   The decision to include Section 8 as part of Article I is probably a classic expression of the American view of constitutionalism and power. Section 8 provides for the general powers of the national government; yet it is included in the article concerned with representation. That is to say, the founders enumerated the *national* powers as powers of Congress, thus tying power and representation closer together than anyone might have expected. An appreciation of this vitally important part of the Constitution can be enhanced by beginning with paragraph 18 and reading backwards through the enumeration. As we have already observed, paragraph 18 is the *necessary and proper* clause—sometimes called the *elastic* clause. The position of this clause signifies that the seventeen enumerated powers were intended to be a source of strength to the national government, not a source of limitation. Each was to be used with utmost vigor, even though no new powers could be seized upon by the national government, except of course by constitutional amendment.[34]

---

[34]Controversy over the meaning of the "elastic clause" was probably settled for all time by Chief Justice John Marshall in one of the important constitutional cases in American history, *McCulloch* v. *Maryland*, 4 Wheaton 316 (1819). Chief Justice Marshall argued that so long as Congress was passing acts pursuant to one of the seventeen enumerated powers, then any means convenient to such an end were also legitimate. As he put it, any government "entrusted with

Section 8 is a case where economic motivation and pure theory were combined. While we cannot fully appreciate the economic forces back of Article I without Sections 9 and 10, some elements appear in Section 8. Granting taxing power to the national government (paragraph 1) was a direct remedy for ills in the Articles of Confederation. The requirement (also in paragraph 1) that all taxes must be uniform was included as an assurance to special interests that, for example, a "planner" would not be able to impose a 3 percent tobacco tax in tobacco-growing Virginia and a 1 percent tax in other states. On the other hand, the whole notion of enumerated powers is, as we have seen, an application of theory as well as an effective way to limit the national government. Moreover, mixing power and representation, by placing Section 8 in the Legislative Article, was an application of theory. This combining of economic interests, to gain selfish support, with representation and enumerated power, to gain general legitimacy, is an elegant solution to the problems of legitimizing conquest. It is political architecture second to none in world history.

Article I, Sections 9–10 These final sections of Article I are not merely preoccupied with economic problems but are unmistakably pro-property and pro-wealth in their inclinations. Section 9 is concerned primarily with an additional set of specific limitations against the national government, and some of these—such as guaranteeing habeas corpus and prohibiting Congress from passing bills of attainder and ex post facto laws—need not concern us here, except insofar as they were additional reasons the founders felt no need to add a bill of rights to the Constitution. More to the point here is that Congress was prohibited from giving preference to the ports of one state over those of another and that neither Congress nor the state legislatures could require American vessels to pay duties as they entered the ports of other states. This was all part of a vigorous effort to clear away the major obstructions to national commerce.

Section 10 concentrates primarily upon restrictions on the states, and all of this is immediately meaningful to anyone who recalls that many of the state legislatures in 1787 already had a well-earned reputation for radicalism. (State legislatures were notorious at that time in their willingness to cheapen currency and to weaken provisions in contracts for the paying of debts. States along the Atlantic coast had also been willing to place serious restrictions on commerce, as part of their effort to protect themselves at the expense of neighboring states. These are some of the grievances

---

**Article I, Section 9
[Some limitations on the federal government]**

[no suspension] of the Writ of Habeas Corpus . . . No Bill of Attainder or ex post facto Law shall be passed . . . No Tax or Duty . . . on Articles exported from any State. No preference . . . to the ports of one State over . . . another. . . . No Title of Nobility shall be granted . . .

**Article I, Section 10
[Some limitations on the states]**

No State shall enter into any Treaty . . . coin Money . . [or impair] the Obligation of Contracts. . . . or engage in War, unless actually invaded . . .

---

such ample powers . . . must also be entrusted with ample means for their execution." It was through this route that the national government could grow in pow*er* without necessarily taking on any new pow*ers* that were not already enumerated in Section 8.

that led to Annapolis and then to Philadelphia.) There are few absolutes in the Constitution, and most of them will be found here among the limitations expressed in Section 10 against state powers in matters of commerce. Section 10 explicitly and absolutely denies to the state legislatures the power to tax imports and exports; it also denies absolutely the power of the states to place any regulations or other burdens on any commerce other than that which takes place strictly within their own borders. Of even greater importance, Section 10 explicitly forbids the states to issue paper money or to provide for the payment of debts in any form except gold and silver coin. Finally, and of greatest importance, this section explicitly forbids the states to impair the obligation of contracts. This, as it turned out, was almost sufficient by itself as national protection for emerging capitalist enterprises. (For more on commerce powers, see chapter 5.)

Article II: Combining Monarch, Prime Minister, and Chief Clerk

All of the provisions of Article II, which establishes the office of president, are positively and vigorously favorable to national power but seem to arise far more out of theoretical than economic concerns. As Hamilton had put it from the beginning, the presidential article aimed toward "energy in the Executive" to provide for ways of overcoming the natural stalemate that was built into the bicameral legislature as well as into the separation of powers between the legislative and executive branches.[35]

Indirect election through a separate Electoral College was designed to give the president independence from the people and from Congress. (Although it has come under attack in recent years, the Electoral College was instrumental in preventing the decline of the separation of powers into a *fusion of powers,* which seems to occur wherever the legislature is responsible for electing the executive. Under these conditions, the legislature becomes the constituency of the chief executive. A fusion of powers system is worthy of admiration wherever it works, but if the theory calls for a separation of powers system, then something like an Electoral College is well-designed to serve it.)

In matters of national sovereignty, the president, like a monarch, is granted unconditional power to accept ambassadors of other countries; this amounts to the power to "recognize" other countries. He is also afforded the power to negotiate treaties, although acceptance of treaties requires Senate approval. Another sovereign power in the presidency is the unconditional right to grant reprieves and pardons, except in cases of impeachment. (For more on the

Article II

The executive Power shall be vested in a President of the United States. . . . [who shall be] Commander in Chief . . . have Power . . . to make Treaties . . . [and] appoint Ambassadors, . . . and all other Officers of the United States . . .

[35]See Hamilton's classic statement on the subject in *The Federalist,* No. 70.

significance of this, see chapter 11.) In addition, the president is given the power to appoint the major departmental personnel, the power to convene Congress in special session, and a very formidable, though far from absolute, power of veto over congressional enactments. All these features of the presidency favor separation and independence from the other branches as well as from the electorate.

Some might argue that by making the president strong enough to counterbalance Congress, the founders merely guaranteed governmental stalemate at the national level, thereby playing into the hands of the capitalists who wanted weak government. But that argument would be directly inconsistent with the general thrust of the economic interpretation, which is that the big interests *sought* the Constitution precisely to make a national government, including an energetic presidency, strong enough to defend economic interests from the unreliable and unpredictable states. It is closer to the truth to argue that Article II creates a neutral apparatus. The presidency has proven capable of being as vigorous or as passive as any occupant or political party has desired. That is the secret of its longevity. Unquestionably many, perhaps most, parties in power have favored capitalism. But they were not led to this position by the apparatus of the presidency. Quite the contrary. They sought control of the presidency and of the national government in order to use the apparatus to further their goals. The apparatus itself seems to have militated neither in favor of nor against any particular economic program.

Article III: Closing the Triangle

Article III, the judiciary article, might well have become a pure economic weapon, but it fell far short of that. The economic concerns of the founders were expressed in this article largely in the grant of power given the federal courts to deal with interstate disputes, especially in the commerce field. But, to repeat, while this was and is a matter of economic importance, the provisions do not go as far as the Constitution might have. Moreover, Article III expresses a great deal more concern for matters of national supremacy and international sovereignty than for domestic commerce and industry. For example, it goes into particular detail only on matters affecting ambassadors, disputes on the high seas, or disputes directly affecting foreign countries through their representatives or through citizens of the United States accused of treason. And it concerns itself with disputes involving two states or citizens of two different states.

The only other preoccupation in Article III is the role of the courts in the separation of powers. Judges are given lifetime appointments to protect them from interference from the other branches and then, in turn, are made susceptible to the other branches by provisions for presidential appointment of judges, senatorial approval of those appointments, and congressional power to create inferior federal courts and to change the jurisdiction of the federal courts.

No mention is made of judicial review in the Constitution, although it is generally felt to be implicit in the very existence of a written Constitution and in the power given directly to the federal courts over "all Cases . . . arising under this Constitution, the Laws of the United States and Treaties made, or which shall be made, under their Authority."[36] The Court eventually assumed and used judicial review in favor of property interests, but this was not foreordained by the original document. With or without judicial review, Article III seems to be an elegant expression of the separation of powers theory, which called for three separate and competing branches. All of this seems to outweigh, without being totally irrelevant to, the economic concerns of the founders or of their successors.

Articles IV–VII: Putting More Flesh on the Bones

The first three articles are without any question the most important among the original seven, or, for that matter, among the original seven and the twenty-six articles added as amendments between 1790 and 1971. They provide, in effect, the main body of our governmental structure. The rest add and subtract flesh and blood here and there. What follows is a brief review of the remaining articles of the original document.

Article IV   Article IV is supremely economic in form and purpose. Reference has already been made to the *full faith and credit* clause and the *privileges and immunities* clause as having had a tremendous amount to do with the effort to establish national supremacy. But back of these provisions was the undisguised intention to be sure that national supremacy included a national market for goods and travel. Section 2, which includes the privileges and immunities clause, also forbids one state to discriminate against the citizens of other states in favor of its own citizens. (This provision should be read also in the context of the interstate commerce power of Article I, Section 8 and in the context of Section 9, paragraph 6. It is for the Supreme Court to decide in each case when a state has gone too far with taxing or police statutes that burden interstate commerce. Nonetheless, the commerce power granted to the national government under these various articles and sections does operate as a

---

Article IV

Full Faith and Credit shall be given in each State to the public Acts . . . of every other State. . . . The Citizens of each State shall be entitled to all Privileges and Immunities of Citizens in the several States. . . .

---

[36]For a well-balanced treatment of this issue, see Alexander M. Bickel, *The Least Dangerous Branch* (Indianapolis: Bobbs-Merrill, 1962), chapter 1, especially pp. 15–16.

restriction on state power, in favor of a general effort to insure a free-flowing national economy.)[37] Section 2 also included the infamous provision regarding fugitive slaves, which obliged persons living in free states to capture escaped slaves and return them to their owners. Although repealed by the Thirteenth Amendment, this provision was certainly a promise to the South that it would not have to consider itself an economy isolated from the rest of the country.

There are two other sections of Article IV, and each makes it quite clear that national supremacy would assert itself largely in the economic realm, leaving most of everything else to the states. Section 3 concerns the admission of new states to the Union and provides existing states with the guarantee that no territory could be taken from any existing state without the consent of the state concerned. Section 4 sounds at first like an open invitation to the national government to intervene in the affairs of any states whenever it is the opinion of national officials that a state is depriving its citizens of a republican form of government. However, the provision has worked in exactly the opposite manner, thanks to the second part of that section, which states that the federal government can intervene in matters of domestic violence only when invited to by application of the legislature, by the state executive when the legislature is not in session, or pursuant to a federal court order. This has left the question of national intervention into local disorders almost completely to the discretion of local and state officials.

Article VI

All Debts contracted . . . before the Adoption of this Constitution, shall be . . . valid. . . . This Constitution, and the Laws of the United States . . . and all Treaties . . . shall be the supreme Law of the Land . . .

Article VI Here is another instance of an attempt to establish national supremacy for largely economic purposes. Article VI is most notable for its provision that national laws and treaties "shall be the supreme law of the land." However, this supremacy clause is the *second* paragraph of Article VI. The first paragraph concerns itself with the debts that were entered into under the Articles of Confederation, providing that all such debts were to be continued as valid under the new Constitution. The question of whether "all debts" included debts incurred by state governments during the revolution was left deliberately vague and unsettled. All of this was clearly a way of buying the loyalty, allegiance, and hopes of the new capitalist class, because all of the debts incurred by the national and state governments were being held in the form of commercial paper, traded on the market for speculative purposes. The matter of state debt was finally settled during the First Congress by legislation which provided for the complete assumption of all state debts. This

[37]For a bizarre but important application of this, see *Edwards* v. *California*, 314 U.S. 160 (1941).

was a major victory for holders of liquid wealth, especially for speculators.[38]

Despite the clearly economic motivation back of these arrangements, we would be making a very bad mistake if we interpreted too narrowly this act of insuring the loyalty and confidence of the new capitalists who held the bonds and notes representing the American debt. The issue here was more than merely making a deal for their loyalty. Since the overwhelming preoccupation of all of the leaders at that time was the establishment of a new nation whose sovereignty enjoyed the respect of all nations, it was imperative that all countries, especially France and England, strengthen their confidence in that new country. Could it be trusted in matters of trade, treaties, defense, credit? Repudiation of debts at the very outset—even if these debts did not directly affect many large European investors—would have made international treaties and international trade contracts far more difficult. Thus, even this strong economic preoccupation in Article VI is deeply colored by long-range considerations of international power and long-range concerns for the establishment of general domestic legitimacy. This should not be overlooked as we appreciate the short-range purchase of loyalty and regime support that is implicit in this article.

Article V

The Congress, whenever two thirds of both Houses shall deem it necessary, shall propose Amendments to this Constitution, or . . . shall call a Convention for proposing Amendments, which, in either Case, shall be valid . . . when ratified by the Legislatures of three fourths of the several States, or by Conventions in three fourths thereof . . .

Articles V and VII: Article V provides for the procedures by which the Constitution itself may be amended. These provisions are so difficult that Americans have availed themselves of this route to political change only sixteen times since 1791, when the first ten amendments were accepted at one time. Corwin and Peltason report that between 1789 and 1964 over 5,000 amendments were introduced in Congress but that only 29 were actually proposed and 23 ratified.[39] Since 1964, numerous efforts to amend the Constitution have produced just three new amendments, and the extremely low incidence of amendment is likely to continue. For those who need to find economic implications, it might be easy to argue that economic interest was served by the very difficulty of amending the Constitution. However, it must be borne in mind that the provision for amendment by three-fourths of the states under the Constitution is a great deal easier than the provision for amendment under the Articles of Confederation, which required the approval of *all the states.* Moreover, it should also be borne in mind that a great number of persons of every type of political persuasion will agree that constitutions ought to be very difficult to amend.

---

[38]For an account of this important issue and why it was resolved in favor of assumption of state debts, see Joseph Charles, *The Origins of the American Party System* (New York: Harper & Row, Torchbooks, 1961), pp. 7–36.

[39]E. S. Corwin and Jack W. Peltason, *Understanding the Constitution* (New York: Holt, Rinehart and Winston, 1964), p. 108.

There is a difference between changing the laws and changing the procedures by which the laws are adopted or implemented. There are good theoretical arguments, regardless of economic program, for not using the Constitution as a place to legislate. Many industrial countries have tried to cope with the fast pace of change by regularly changing the Constitution rather than by facing the issues head-on with specific policies. They have ample experience to confirm the proposition that the legitimacy of the regime can easily be brought into question by frequent manipulation of the Constitution.

Article VII was concerned with only one single event, ratification of the Constitution of 1787. Technically, this provision was unconstitutional, because it violated the provisions of the Articles of Confederation, which required that all amendments—which logically includes replacement of the entire document—would be submitted to the states, where approval by individual states would have to take place *in the state legislatures* (not in conventions). Ratification could be accomplished only by the *unanimous* concurrence of all the states. The legislatures in every state except Rhode Island eventually set up state conventions to consider ratification, and no one seemed to protest very loudly the extralegal character of the procedure.[40]

Perhaps the most significant fact about the entire period between May of 1787, when the Philadelphia Convention opened, and July 2, 1788, when the first nine states had ratified the Constitution, has not yet been mentioned. This was without any question the most active and productive period of creative political philosophy in the history of the United States, and it clearly rates as one of the most active periods of political philosophy since the establishment of the city-states in Ancient Greece. One of the most remarkable products of this period was of course the series of essays that ended up in a celebrated volume, *The Federalist.* Despite the historic importance and the eloquence of these essays, and despite the tremendous esteem with which they are treated today, these eighty-five essays were first published as letters addressed to the public in the newspapers of New York City between October 27, 1787, and the late summer of 1788. The authors of these papers were John Jay, Alexander Hamilton, and James Madison. The latter authored almost two-thirds of the total product. All of them wrote under the pseudonym Publius, and the question of exact authorship was a matter of some scholarly controversy until recent years. But Publius was not the only group of writers, and *The Federalist* was not the only philosophy being developed at the time. There were also a

[40]See, for example, Forrest McDonald, *We the People.*

number of *Anti*-Federalists who were writing essays of equal stature.[41]

This extraordinary philosophic creativity must rate as one of the most important characteristics of the whole period. It tends to suggest a general hypothesis that we ought to ponder long after we have settled for ourselves whether the founders were seeking their economic goals: *the higher the level of a political issue, the higher the level of political discourse.* That is to say, the bigger the universe within which the human being can see the problem, the bigger the human being. When we trivialize our problems, we run the risk of trivializing ourselves. Since the founders were able to appreciate the importance of their moment in history, they were led to elevate their sights toward extraordinary rather than ordinary expressions, and as a consequence both their writings and their accomplishments were historic. Granted, the founders were all part of a process of legitimizing conquest and solving their personal economic problems. But that is always true. The difference is that they placed their situation in the larger context. This is something our officialdom seem almost never able or willing to do today.

This is no call for admiration of eloquence and big ideas for their own sake. Only by taking the larger view of politics and placing it in the context of the history of conquest and control are we able to grapple with the contradictions inherent in the very idea of "self-government." Thanks to the enormous scope of the outlook of the founders, the United States has effectively met these contradictions and has enjoyed the longest stretch of stable and "near self-government" ever experienced by a large nation-state. To an extent, the United States has even defied Rousseau, who felt that self-government was not possible in principalities larger than a small canton or city-state. No one can claim that we have enjoyed precisely the democracy Rousseau had in mind—not everyone would want to have Rousseau's type of direct democracy in any case.

However, the United States has lived in rather close proximity to its own Constitution and can by virtue of that fact at least claim, with some plausibility, that as a country we have managed to maintain conquest over an immensely heterogeneous society without falling prey to tyranny. Such a claim is modest and is a long distance from the claim that America, and all Americans, enjoy democracy. Nevertheless, whatever it is that Americans enjoy, it is very far from absolute tyranny; and, considering what it takes to set aside the primordial needs of conquest, tyranny is probably the natural tendency of all governments. To resist it at all is something of a triumph.

---

[41]See, for example, the collected essays in John D. Lewis, ed., *Anti-Federalists versus Federalists: Selected Documents* (San Francisco: Chandler, 1967); and Morton Borden, ed., *The Anti-Federalist Papers* (East Lansing: Michigan State University Press, 1965).

Chapter 5   The Constitution and Contemporary Politics

... a constitution [is] intended to endure
for ages to come, and consequently, to
be adapted to the various crises of
human affairs. To have prescribed the
means by which government should, in
all future time, execute its powers, would
have been to change, entirely, the character of the instrument, and give it the
properties of a legal code. It would have
been an unwise attempt to provide, by
immutable rules, for exigencies which, if
foreseen at all, must have been seen
dimly, and which can best be provided
for as they occur.
John Marshall, Chief Justice (1819)

The Constitution has endured for almost two centuries. But in what form and with what result? It may have endured as a sacred text, etched in stone and stored under glass. It may have endured in a more lively form, but as an instrument of rule and rulers. Indeed it may even have endured as the instrument of restraint that it was supposed to be. Pursuit of these questions is possible only through a careful analysis of constitutional issues in the context of our own time. But this task is made exceedingly difficult by the fact that rulers have an interest in the answers. Anyone who holds power will eventually take pains to spread the impression that the affairs of government are being conducted strictly according to the Constitution. Granted, most leaders would prefer to go much further and—whenever possible—sincerely guide their actions by constitutional principle. But their personal interest in constitutionality must ultimately mask a great deal of reality. For example, every president has probably found it necessary from time to time to order his attorney general to "come in with reasons I can legally do what I propose to do, or come in with your resignation." There are times when we must accept Jonathan Swift's proposition that morality in general and a constitution in particular are "like a pair of breeches, which, though a cover for lewdness as well as nastiness, can easily be slipt down for the service of both."[1] Then there are other times when we feel that the Constitution is actually making a difference in the way power is used and government is conducted.

How shall we determine whether the Constitution is making a difference? What is a proper test of endurance? We must begin with a bold-faced admission that the Constitution must change, yet it must remain the same. It must change or else it will become irrelevant to existing problems—as though etched in stone. It must remain the same or it will be subject to manipulation to serve the needs of each power holder. No single criterion will serve in all cases. We must look at the current status of the Constitution and solicit the best available views on whether the Constitution has made a substantial difference in each instance to which it applies. By the time we have pursued our analysis of the durability of the Constitution we will also have touched upon every Amendment and almost every major provision of the contemporary Constitution. Only then may we begin to assess its value: Does it provide for a system of government to which we can enthusiastically give our consent?

WHERE THE CONSTITUTION COUNTS LEAST: SOVEREIGNTY

The inquiry might usefully begin with a selection of two dimensions of government where the Constitution counts for very little and was never expected to count for very much. An analysis of these dimensions will help define what should be expected from a constitution. The first of these is eminent domain. This defines the area where private property and conquest collide. The second area is, of course, war. This defines the place where the private individual and the conquerors of that individual finally come face to face.

Eminent Domain: Private Life and Public Plans

Eminent domain is a label for the ancient power of government to take private property for a public use. Most everyone is familiar

[1]Jonathan Swift, *A Tale of a Tub* (New York: Columbia University Press, 1930; originally published 1704), p. 15.

with this power. Public reference is constantly made to "condemnation" of a house or building to prepare for a highway, or "acquisition" of properties to assemble a site for an urban redevelopment project or an airport. These activities are taken for granted; they are accepted as a habitual and essential power of any government. But that is precisely why the significance of the power of eminent domain goes unappreciated.

In the legal tradition of the West, eminent domain is treated as inherent in sovereignty; "it requires no explicit constitutional recognition."[2] Beyond any doubt, therefore, any government, *or its agent,* may take private property and return it to the public domain; or it may take private property, return it temporarily to the public domain, and then turn it over to a different private owner for almost any purpose the government or its agent sees fit. This means that despite all the protections surrounding private property in our history, government may nevertheless reconquer any piece of property at any time. The conquest element is never absent from private property. Private property, as we have argued earlier, presupposes a successful conquest. Now we are arguing in addition that basically private property never loses its public character.

It is in this sense that eminent domain defines one of the boundaries of the notion of constitutionality. *Eminent domain is a power of government the Constitution is not free to withhold.* We should add immediately that our Constitution attempts to influence eminent domain power by prescribing *how* eminent domain should be used. In brief, the Fifth Amendment provides that the federal government shall not take property "without due process of law," and should not take property "without just compensation." But these provisions in no way reduce the power of eminent domain. And in practice the restrictions are extremely weak.

The requirement of just compensation is almost no restraint at all. First, the Fourteenth Amendment does not impose this restriction on the eminent domain power of the states. This means that states, local governments, public authorities, power companies, and so on are required only to provide due process, whatever that may mean. Second, *just compensation* has been defined as "fair market value," which means a price worked out in a voluntary transaction between a willing buyer and a willing seller. This means that just compensation is a myth as long as the seller is an involuntary participant.[3] This leaves us with due process as the only possible constitutional restraint on eminent domain, and that has come down to a very narrow question of whether the *purpose* for which land is seized is a public purpose. Once that public purpose is

[2]Herman Pritchett, *The American Constitution* (New York: McGraw-Hill, 1959), p. 658.
[3]Thomas and Julia Vitullo-Martin have provided a rare look at the myth of just compensation in Lowi et al., *Poliscide* (New York: Macmillan, 1975), chapters 10–11.

Tenants evicted from apartment building of Dr. Frederika Blankner Wednesday watch their belongings being carried outside.

Tribune Photo by Ray Gora

Will stay in street, says evicted woman

By Jon Van

AS MOVERS carted her possessions out the door, Frederika Blankner vowed that her seven-year fight with the city won't end with her eviction.

"They're putting me in the street," said the septuagenarian scholar and poet, "and I plan to stay in the street. I'll live where they put me."

Miss Blankner, who twice asked the U.S. Supreme Court to save her apartment building at 6043 S. Woodlawn Av. and was refused twice, lost again Wednesday before Circuit Judge Arthur L. Dunne, who refused to hear her case.

Miss Blankner, a 1922 Phi Beta Kappa graduate of the University of Chicago and a retired classics professor, has sought to prevent the city from taking her building under urban renewal laws. The site is included in plans to expand the University of Chicago campus.

"IT WAS all cut and dried in advance," she said of Judge Dunne's decision. "They started evicting my tenants the minute the judge said he wouldn't hear the case. The city's taking no chances of giving me due process. They'll bulldoze this place just as soon as they get everything out.

"My lawyer is trying to appeal the decision, but the city wants to get the building razed before he does appeal."

Miss Blankner said the city has offered to pay her less than a third of the building's actual value.

Tribune Photo by Ray Gora

Dr. Frederika Blankner (left), 74, stands outside her building at 6043-45 S. Woodlawn Av. Wednesday as sheriff's police evict the tenants. She vowed to continue her eight-year battle with the expanding University of Chicago to save her property.

Eminent domain in action.

established, the property owner has no prospect of stopping the seizure; he can only sue for a better price. In fact, he may not even be able to delay the seizure while the price is being bargained. Some agencies have the authority to seize and vacate the property, tear down the buildings, begin construction, and even arrest the owner for trespass. In this case all of the advantages are on the side of the government against the property owner.[4]

---

[4]Ibid. For a fascinating study of how these powers were used by Robert Moses to become one of the most powerful administrators in American history, see Robert Caro, *The Power Broker: Robert Moses, and the Fall of New York* (New York: Knopf, 1974), pp. 174, 182, 625–626, and 737.

In the past twenty-five years, the notion of "public purpose" has become so vague that it now means anything the legislature defines as a public purpose. In earlier times, the courts reserved this judgment for themselves; but in a succession of cases since World War II, especially those involving large public authorities like TVA and urban redevelopment, the courts have given up this power. In the decision handed down in *Berman* v. *Parker* (1954) the Supreme Court finally made quite explicit its willingness to accept anything the legislature says as sufficient assurance that a proposed seizure of property is for a public use.[5] This decision established two extremely important aspects of eminent domain. First, the Court recognized that it was the judgment of the legislature alone, without interference by the courts, that would define whether a given use was sufficiently public. Second, the Court went on to accept these seizures of property even where it was clear that the public agency intended to take it from one private owner and turn it over to a different private owner for a commercial use.[6] In effect the Court was pleading guilty to a charge one of the appellate judges had made in the *Berman* v. *Parker* case before it reached the Supreme Court for review: "If the government's power of seizure included everything that a commission determines to be in the interest of the urban redevelopment plan, the ascendancy of government over the individual right to property would be complete."[7]

Twenty years after the Supreme Court decision, the author of probably the most exhaustive study of land and its public developers ever made concluded that when the Supreme Court validated the Housing Acts of 1949 in *Berman* v. *Parker,* it

> extended the power of eminent domain, traditionally used in America only for government-built projects, so drastically that governments could now condemn land and turn it over to individuals —for them to build on it projects agreeable to government. . . . Here was power new in the annals of democracy. . . . "In my opinion," urban expert Charles Abrams was to say, "under present redevelopment laws, Macy's could condemn Gimbels—if Robert Moses [head of the urban redevelopment programs in New York City] gave the word."[8]

Here, then, we have truly the limiting case in "domestic" matters. Apparently, whenever a private power company or an authorized private developer in a redevelopment program determines that a piece of private property belongs back in the public domain, there is virtually no restraint. The individual property owner has the right to bargain over price, but he apparently has no right to a real

---

[5]Pritchett, *The American Constitution,* pp. 658–662. See also Benjamin Ginsberg, "Berman v. Parker: Congress, the Court, and the Public Purpose," *Polity* 4 (1971), 48–75.
[6]*Berman* v. *Parker,* 348 U.S. 26 (1954); for an extended discussion of the case and its holdings, see Ginsberg, "Berman v. Parker: Congress, the Court, and the Public Purpose."
[7]Caro, *The Power Broker,* p. 777.
[8]Ibid.

judicial determination of whether the public purpose is truly public; and he apparently has no right to the usual rules of evidence to determine if the price offered is a decent price. In this area we are left with only the hope that the agents who acquire land for the government are good people and will wish to treat us well. But this sentiment flies in the face of the basic assumption of the American Constitution, or, for that matter, any constitution.

War and the Constitution

War, they say, is hell. War is also tyranny. There was never any question about the slight degree of influence the Constitution was expected to have over the conduct of war. Here is the way Congressman Abraham Lincoln put the case over a dozen years before becoming president:

> Allow the President to invade a neighboring nation whenever he shall deem it necessary to repel an invasion, and you allow him to do so, whenever he may choose to say he deems it necessary for such purpose. . . . Study to see if you can fix any limit to his power in this respect. . . . If, today, he should choose to say he thinks it is necessary to invade Canada, to prevent the British from invading us, how could you stop him? You may say to him, "I see no probability of the British invading us" but he will say to you "Be silent; I see it, even if you don't."[9]

After a war is over, we slap the president's wrists for the liberties he may have taken with the Constitution during the war. But we slap him only after the war. One of the most dramatic examples is President Lincoln's suspension of the writ of habeas corpus in September of 1862. Another famous example is President Franklin Roosevelt's evacuation of West Coast Japanese to concentration camps after the bombing of Pearl Harbor. In the first case, the Supreme Court decided, in *Ex parte Milligan* (2 Wall. 2) that the president had no power to suspend habeas corpus for noncombatants. But the Court got around to this decision in 1866 after the war was over and an entirely different president was in office. In the second case, the Court decided in *Korematsu* v. *United States* (323 U.S. 214) that indeed the president did have constitutional power to order this evacuation. Three important dissents in that case did slap at the president, and in still another case in the same year, *Ex parte Enco* (323 U.S. 283), the Court held that those Japanese who were American citizens and whose loyalty had been established could not constitutionally be held in one of the so-called War Relocation

[9]Letter from Congressman Abraham Lincoln to W. H. Hernden, February 15, 1848. Quoted in Arthur Schlesinger, Jr., "Presidential War," *New York Times Magazine,* January 7, 1973, p. 12.

Centers. But these cases were handed down in 1944, when the centers were being broken up anyway.[10]

Nonetheless, there is a great deal about war that is very special in the United States because of the Constitution. It would be silly to insist that our Constitution prevents us from becoming a tyranny during war. Even the conduct of the undeclared Vietnam War was not substantially influenced by the Constitution. But at least this much can be argued: Although the Constitution had no appreciable direct effect on the conduct of the Vietnam War—only a president and his military advisers can choose to drop more explosives than in any prior war, including World War II—the Vietnam War had a very different effect at home because of the peculiarities of the Constitution.

The Constitution and Contemporary Politics

[10]See Clinton Rossiter, *The Supreme Court and the Commander-in-Chief* (Ithaca, N.Y.: Cornell University Press, 1951).

Two cases neatly bracket the main dimensions of constitutional concern and influence in questions of war in the United States. One of these is the decision by the president in 1970 to expand the Vietnam War into Cambodia—the so-called Cambodia incursion. The other is the draft and the scope of government power to require service during time of war. The Cambodia case concerns presidential power during war and whether any other institutions have any substantial constitutional power to limit the president. The draft issue and related cases raise an entirely different question, that of whether there is any limit to the power of government over the individual during time of war.

Cambodia and the separation of powers   In early May of 1970, President Nixon sent American forces into Cambodia as a bold and desperate strategy ostensibly to break the will of the Viet Cong and North Vietnamese. President Nixon made no effort to justify his action with the Constitution except to assert that it was "a valid exercise of his [my] constitutional authority as Commander-in-Chief to secure the safety of American forces."[11] He was saying essentially that our presence in Vietnam was sufficient justification for expansion of the war to include still another country. This was as clear an act of unilateral force as could be imagined. Nothing could have been more clearly outside constitutional provision. By definition, nothing could have been more tyrannical.

Yet perhaps the most important moment for the Constitution during the entire decade of the Vietnam War occurred directly in response to the Cambodia incursion. Immediately following the action, there occurred on the floor of the United States Senate a very rare debate. The debate arose over the Foreign Military Sales Act of 1970, but it centered on what came to be called the Cooper-Church Amendment to that act, which sought to prohibit the use of any of those funds or materiel provided for by the act in the conduct of any military activity in Cambodia either by the United States or by Cambodian or other personnel. Since the incursion had already taken place by that time, and since the president apparently had no intention of expanding the war in Cambodia, the amendment was not significant on its face. What was significant, and what will be significant for a good while to come, was the debate itself. During a period of six weeks between May 13 and June 30, 1970, over 3,000 pages of the *Congressional Record* were filled with arguments about the war. There was little about the wisdom of the war or the specific strategies involved in its pursuit. Most of the discussion actually centered upon the constitutionality of the war and the Cambodia action. To be specific, most of the debate centered upon the separation of powers and the question of the relationship between the

11Quoted in Schlesinger, "Presidential War," p. 26.

president and Congress in matters of war. For at least six weeks, the war in Vietnam became a domestic war for the revival of the Constitution.[12]

This debate demonstrates that constitutionality has a way of affecting the way people view war and the degree to which people appreciate their own rights. During the worst days of the Vietnam War, the Constitution tended to operate as a continual reminder that war converts democracies into tyrannies. The Constitution served as a criterion, a standard against which to measure the conduct of rulers during emergencies. This effect of the Constitution improved the possibility that rights would be not only restored but advanced following the war. One of the most eloquent statements of the relationship between war and the Constitution was made by Justice Robert Jackson in his dissent in the *Korematsu* case:

> Much is said of the danger to liberty from the Army program for deporting and detaining these citizens of Japanese extraction. But a judicial construction of the due process clause that will sustain this order is a far more subtle blow to liberty than the promulgation of the order itself. A military order, however unconstitutional, is not apt to last longer than the military emergency. . . . But once a judicial opinion rationalizes such an order to show that it conforms to the Constitution . . . the Court for all time has validated the principle of radical discrimination in criminal procedures and of transplanting American citizens. The principle lies about like a loaded weapon ready for the hand of any authority that can bring forward a plausible claim of urgent need.[13]

The Cooper-Church debate was not the only instance where war and constitutionality were recently intertwined. Another was the battle over the so-called Pentagon Papers. This raised the whole question of the constitutionality of keeping secrets from the American people, of punishing government employees for making those secrets public, and of the rights of the press to use such materials. An inexperienced federal judge issued a temporary injunction against the *New York Times*, but other papers disregarded it; and after a weekend of obedience the *Times* resumed publication of the documents which had been released by Daniel Ellsberg in order to reveal facts about the Vietnam War. In a six-to-three decision the Supreme Court held that the government had failed to show that publication of these particular documents would damage national security.[14] Reviewing the situation in 1973, a team of *London Sunday Times* reporters concluded that "the Pentagon Papers tipped the Nixon administration over the edge."[15]

---

[12]An extended series of excerpts from that debate will be found in Lowi and Ripley, eds., *Legislative Politics U.S.A.* (Boston: Little, Brown, 1973), chapter 1.

[13]*Korematsu* v. *United States,* 323 U.S. 214 (1944).

[14]*New York Times Company* v. *United States,* 403 U.S. 713 (1971).

[15]Quoted in William Manchester, *The Glory and the Dream* (Boston: Little, Brown, 1973), p. 1231.

War, the draft, and the individual   The constitutionality of drafting young persons into military service has not been an issue. That was settled in 1918 with apparent finality.[16] What did become an overriding constitutional issue all during the Vietnam War was the question of exemption for individuals if they are physically and mentally fit to serve. When can a person be excused from service on the grounds that his conscience will not allow him to fight? The issue of conscientious objection arises whenever there is a program of military conscription in the United States. But it arose with particular intensity and had outcomes of lasting importance during the Vietnam War.[17]

If you are a member of an established pacifist church such as the Quakers or the Jehovah's Witnesses, and can show membership well before receiving notice from your draft board, then the question of legally establishing the validity of your status as a conscientious objector is very simple. This was just about the only route to religious exemption until 1940; but these draft laws were probably in violation of the First Amendment, which prohibits laws that favor the establishment of a particular religion.[18] Revisions following 1940 made it easier to establish the sincerity of one's claim to pacifist status without being an established church member; even so, opposition to war had to be based upon "religious training and beliefs," and this still approached the "establishment" of a religion in violation of the First Amendment. In 1951, Congress came even closer to violating the First Amendment by explicitly defining "religious training and beliefs" to include "belief in relation to a Supreme Being" and to exclude moral codes that are merely "political, sociological, or philosophical."[19] Operating on this definition, the chief of the conscientious objector section of the Justice Department wrote an "advice letter" to the Selective Service Appeal Board of Kentucky, which was reviewing the case of boxing champion Muhammad Ali: "It seems clear that the teachings of the Nation of Islam preclude fighting for the United States not because of objections to participation in war in any form, but rather because of political and racial objections to policies of the United States as interpreted by Elijah Muhammad." (See chapter 15.)

Despite the very probable unconstitutionality of this provision, it was not successfully tested in the courts until 1965, when three young men sought conscientious objector status but refused to claim belief in a supreme being. They based their claim instead on "our democratic American culture, with its values derived from the

---

[16]*Selective Draft Law Cases,* 245 U.S. 366.

[17]According to the *New York Times,* July 25, 1970, in the single month of June 1970, 14,440 conscientious objector claims were officially filed.

[18]For an excellent treatment of these issues, see Henry J. Abraham, *Freedom and the Court* (New York: Oxford University Press, 1972), chapter 6.

[19]Section 456 (J), 50 App. USCA (1951).

Western religious and philosophical tradition."[20] In a momentous
decision, the Supreme Court accepted these claims and thereby
liberalized the 1951 provision to a point where it would be difficult
to deny that the Court had in fact overturned it completely. What
the Court had done was develop a whole new definition of religion
under the Constitution. The Court stopped short of a complete
rejection of the 1951 provision because the case could be disposed of
without going that far. But the issue was to come up again soon
thereafter. Some members of Congress who were greatly disturbed
by the court decision sought and got a new amendment to the draft
laws in 1967. They tried to solve the problem by eliminating any
reference to a supreme being but continued to include "religious
training and belief" and to exclude "essentially political, sociological, or philosophical views, or a merely personal moral code."
Consequently, claims for exemption continued to flow through the
draft boards into the courts and a major new test case was
inevitable.

The case finally came before the Supreme Court in 1970, arising
out of a draft case from early in the Vietnam War. Justice Black,
speaking for a five-man majority, rendered virtually all of the
religious provisions unconstitutional—without quite explicitly declaring them unconstitutional. He held that some politically or
sociologically based moral codes can be so firmly held as to be
considered religious within the meaning of the law. In a concurring
opinion, the ordinarily conservative Justice Harlan urged going the
full route, arguing that the 1967 provisions indeed violated the
First Amendment by discriminating in favor of religion as opposed

[20]*United States* v *Seeger*, 380 U.S. 163 (1965), as quoted in Abraham, *Freedom and the Court*,
p. 215.

to nonreligion.[21] Less than a year later the Court also disposed of the Ali case on the much more traditional grounds that Ali was clearly a member of an established pacifist church.[22]

These cases produced a two-fisted triumph for constitutionalism. First, they expanded the effective application of the First Amendment. There are still grave problems involved in any effort by the government to force citizens into the armed services. Nevertheless, the courts did virtually eliminate the idea that established religion, the very notion of religion itself, is the only basis for dissent against war in our society. Thus, the power of government to conscript citizens still stands, but the power of the citizen to object and to criticize the government in particular wars has been immensely strengthened. The second aspect of victory is a bit more abstract but perhaps equally important. These cases proved better than the most eloquent philosophic tract that war is tyranny, that war is an aberrant moment in the history of any country, and that decisions made under conditions of war must not be taken as precedent for situations during peacetime. Without the involvement of the Constitution, there would in all probability be no independent basis for the concept of tyranny. There would only be the brutal and ugly fact of tyranny without any systematic basis for recognizing it. Thus, although during war we lose the Constitution, war can be an opportunity for the triumph of constitutionalism itself.

FEDERALISM: WHERE THE CONSTITUTION COUNTS MOST

Federalism has counted for most because it provided the skeleton of government at the time of the founding. During the past two centuries much about government has changed, but the changes themselves have been shaped by the existence of the federal structure. The influence of the federal structure has been felt in at least three fundamental ways, and each warrants detailed assessment.

First, federalism operated for nearly a century and a half as a restraint upon the economic power of the national government because of the vastness of the powers federalism "reserved" to the states. Much of the history of American government has been written in terms of the effort to roll back these restraints, but there was no significant rollback until well after capitalism was mature enough to fend for itself.

Second, federalism created a second sovereignty, the state. This is

---

[21]*Welch* v. *U.S.,* 398 U.S. 333 (1970).
[22]*Clay* v. *U.S.,* 403 U.S. 698 (1971). For more details on the Cassius Clay/Muhammad Ali case, see chapter 16.

one of those commonplace facts whose significance is almost completely lost to sight because of its familiarity. Thanks to federalism, the states became the center of government in the United States. For the better part of two centuries, the overwhelming proportion of fundamental policies regulating the lives of citizens were made by the state legislatures, not by Congress.

Third, since the states were left to make the important policies, they were free to be different from each other. Federalism introduced tremendous variations in the rights of citizens, the roles of government, and the patterns of crime and punishment. Despite changes in many areas toward national uniformity, it continues to make a great deal of difference to citizens whether their crimes are committed in Missouri or Michigan, North Dakota or North Carolina.

There is a fourth dimension, but it should be reserved for inquiries into American jurisprudence. As the great British jurist A. V. Dicey put it, federalism produces legalism. It helps explain the extraordinary litigiousness of Americans, a characteristic observed by de Tocqueville in the 1830s. Legalism has, of course, been used many times by governments to cover up the unfair advantage that one class holds over another. But on many other occasions, the uncertainties of rights that are introduced by federalism have led to a greater concern for individual rights and a greater willingness to sue for those rights than one tends to find in other countries.[23]

From National Restraint to National Potential: Commerce Power

Although the Constitution was designed to eliminate the excesses of freedom the states enjoyed under the Articles of Confederation, the states apparently were willing to yield on this only on condition that the new Constitution severely restrain the national government as well as the states. The major vehicle for this restraint of national power became the commerce clause—something that was probably not entirely expected. Article I, Section 8 simply lists as one of the express powers of the national government the power "to regulate commerce with foreign nations, and among the several States and with the Indian tribes." This clause was a source of power as long as Congress sought to intervene in commerce only through subsidies, such as grants to encourage coastal shipping, or grants of land to railroad companies or to settlers. For almost the entire first century of government under the Constitution, intervention in commerce through various kinds of subsidies constituted the entire national economic program. (See Table 5.1, column 1.) However, as soon as the national government sought to interfere with commerce by

[23]See Pritchett, *The American Constitution*, p. 58.

Table 5.1   **The Federal System: Traditional Sources of Policy**

	1. Federal (Domestic)	2. States	3. Local Governments
	Internal improvements	Property law (including slavery)	?
	Subsidies (mainly to shipping)	Estates and inheritance law	
	Tariffs	Commerce law (ownership and exchange)	
	Public lands disposal	Family law (including morals)	
	Patents	Public health and quarantine law	
	Currency	Occupations and professions law	
		Education laws	
		General penal laws	
		Public works laws (including eminent domain)	
		Construction codes	
		Water and mineral resources law	
		Judiciary and criminal procedure laws	
		Electoral laws (including political parties)	
		Banking and credit laws	
		Insurance laws	
		Local government law	
		Civil service law	
		Tax liability	

regulating some of its conditions or its products or prices, the so-called commerce power began to cut the other way.

What *is* commerce? What kind of commerce qualifies as "among the several States" for purposes of federal regulation? Answers to these questions became essential. The courts came to define the phrase in question as equivalent to *interstate commerce,* and that narrowed the range of national power from all of commerce to only that part of commerce involved in actual movement across state lines. This meant that almost any effort of the federal government to regulate such problems as fraud, or the production of impure goods, or the use of child labor, or the existence of dangerous working conditions, was going to be unconstitutional, because it would require going into the work place itself before the goods began to move. Any effort to enter the actual factory was called *police power,* which is the name for the power reserved to the states to regulate the health, safety, and morals of its citizens. No such general power had been granted to the federal government.[24]

There was never any question about the power of the federal government to regulate certain kinds of businesses, such as the railroads, pipelines, and waterway navigation, because these things were intrinsically in interstate commerce. But well into the twentieth century, most of the other efforts of the federal government to regulate commerce had to be reached through subterfuge. In effect, Congress had only the power to say, "You may produce substandard goods in unhealthy working conditions at subsistence wages, but you may not pass these goods through interstate commerce." Even with this subterfuge only a few efforts passed the scrutiny of the courts. For example, the courts agreed Congress had power to keep sawed-off shotguns, kidnapped children, and adulterated and dangerous foods and drugs out of interstate commerce. But on the other hand, Congress did not have the power to prevent the movement in interstate commerce of goods made in factories that employed child labor. In general, before the New Deal the courts allowed Congress to use this subterfuge as long as the statute intended to protect and improve commerce. That is, they could do anything that most businessmen agreed was a good thing. But the courts found insufficient national power to do anything that might increase the costs or increase the difficulty of exchange in commerce. At one point, the Supreme Court found it necessary to face the inconsistency of its own position. When it declared unconstitutional the federal child labor act, the Court argued that lottery tickets, stolen goods, and impure foods were harmful in and of themselves, while goods produced by child labor "are of themselves harmless."[25] The weakness of this argument was almost universally understood, but it was not until twenty years later that the court decided to throw out all of this reasoning and start with a clean slate.

Eventually, changes in the national economy and in the status of American public opinion were too much for the Court to resist. It had become increasingly difficult to maintain the distinction implied by the term *interstate commerce,* because virtually every significant business was involved in interstate commerce, in terms of the goods it bought and the goods it produced and sold. The Court tried a variety of compromises to maintain the myth of interstate commerce before it finally gave way to an almost complete reversal of itself. The dam of restraint against national regulation of commerce broke in 1937 with the famous case of *National Labor*

---

[24]For a beginning student, the most efficient review of the cases and materials involved in the question of the commerce power will be found in Pritchett, *The American Constitution,* chapters 14, 15, and 32; see also Pritchett's companion volume, *American Constitutional Issues* (New York: McGraw-Hill, 1962).

[25]*Hammer* v. *Dagenhart,* 247 U.S. 251 (1918).

Relations Board v. *Jones and Laughlin Steel Corporation,*[26] where the Court upheld the Wagner Act and therefore the national government's effort to regulate a vast range of relations between labor and management. The Court has not completely abdicated its power to declare a congressional enactment in violation of the interstate commerce standard. Nevertheless, although the Court may scrutinize each case in which the charge is made that Congress has gone too far, it is very unlikely ever again to declare important congressional legislation unconstitutional on this basis.

For most of the period between the Civil War and 1937, the courts were not only invalidating federal efforts to regulate commerce but were also invalidating a large number of state laws in this area as well. Federal efforts were declared unconstitutional because they attempted to regulate *intra*state activity; state laws concerning that same intrastate activity were often declared unconstitutional because they impaired obligations of existing contracts or interfered with the rights of laborers to enter into contracts with employers or of buyers to enter into contracts with sellers. In constitutional law these decisions protecting commerce from federal and from state intervention are referred to as *substantive due process.* The courts were simply making a judgment in each regulatory effort as to whether the regulation was a *reasonable* way for a legislature to restrain business activity. This was an extremely significant judgment of due process to all "persons," including, therefore, corporations as well as real human beings.[27]

It is quite apparent from all this that the Constitution, through judicial application, was creating a no-man's-land, freeing the rising corporation from any and all governmental interference of federal *or* state governments. This is as close as the United States ever came to the ideal of the *laissez-faire* system of economics (see chapter 15). In this sense we can say that the Constitution, particularly the federal structure of the Constitution, contributed significantly to the development of the capitalist system. For our purposes here, this is a sufficient illustration of the importance of the Constitution in the everyday life of the country.

We now (and again later in chapter 15) must face the question of whether the Constitution is capable of favoring only capitalism and no other interests. No definitive case can be made, but a few points will help readers draw their own conclusions. First of all, it is clear that the commerce power after 1937 was expanded to allow the national government to intervene in almost any significant question affecting the economy. Congress has, in fact, used that power on several occasions to intervene in favor of interests other than capitalism and, at times, even in favor of some contradictory to

[26]301 U.S. 1 (1937).
[27]For a good discussion of this issue, see Pritchett, *The American Constitution,* chapter 32.

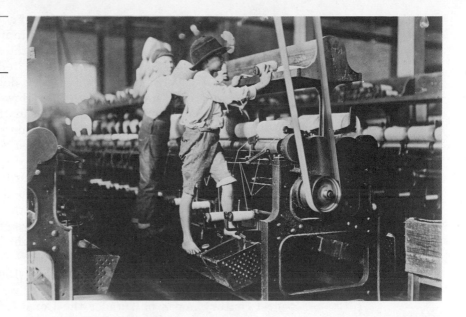

capitalism: the rights to organize unions and bargain collectively, credit and other protections to small businesses, aid to the elderly and other nonproductive persons, and aid to regions of the country that are inefficient from the strict point of view of economic rationality. Perhaps the most interesting intervention is the regulation of business and other institutions in favor of blacks and other minorities. The national government has no explicit power to deal with racial discrimination. It is appropriately ironic that one of the powers Congress has most effectively relied upon to improve the opportunities for minorities is the interstate commerce power, because it is through this power that Congress is now able to deal effectively with problems like discrimination in jobs and union membership.

In the next two sections of this chapter there will be additional illustrations of the capacity of the Constitution to favor interests other than the corporate or capital interest. These illustrations do not add up to a compelling case. But they do render extremely difficult any argument that the Constitution is purely a capitalist document. Life would be much easier for the social scientist if such a simple case could be made either way regarding such a complex phenomenon as constitutional government.

Divided We Stand

It is probably safe to say that one of the essential principles of constitutionalism is the goal of balancing the power at the center in order to leave room for freedom of movement at the periphery. It is also probably safe to say that no system of government has gone as far as the United States to arrange room in its Constitution for the periphery, which of course we call the states. Everyone describes the United States in these terms, as a federal system wherein the national government exercises only delegated powers, leaving the rest to the states or the people. However, few fully realize how far we have gone to institute this in the practical affairs of government, and even fewer fully appreciate its significance.

The federal arrangement in the Constitution did not merely produce two layers of government. It produced two sovereignties. Ponder the significance of that: two separate sources of law, two separate sources of legitimate control, two almost completely separate sets of institutions that govern. The consequences of this dual sovereignty are fundamental to our system, in theory and in practice. A brief look at what it has meant in practice will easily show us its significance in theory.

Table 5.1 deserves close attention (see p. 130). It is an inventory of the major types of public policies by which we were governed for the first century and a half under the Constitution. Certain changes since the 1930s can be noted, but they are not numerous enough to change the pattern. Only a glance is necessary to see that the principle of express powers has meant something quite real to the government of the United States. Note in column 1 that the role of the federal government was quite small in comparison to the state governments. Moreover, most of what the federal government did was in the realm of subsidies. During the first decade under the Constitution (1789–1800), the federal government did a few special things, such as creating the major executive departments, framing the treaties that would establish basic relationships with other countries, establishing control of the territories, constructing a system of currency and a national bank in which to control it. But after that, the most frequent federal public policy enactments concerned themselves with how to promote or to reward specific enterprises in the economy. Money was spent by the federal government to build a few highways, passes, and canals—activities well within its power to provide for post offices and post roads and to regulate commerce *among* the states—but relatively large sums of money were also spent to encourage the development or expansion of certain enterprises. Examples include monetary grants to the coastal shipping businesses and grants of land to railroad companies and settlers. These kinds of activities would not necessarily have doomed the federal government to minuscule size or infinitesimal influence. The bold plans of Alexander Hamilton for constructing a large industrial nation were based largely upon the techniques of public policy listed in column 1 of Table 5.1. His plan was written up in one of the most important state papers in American history,

Report on Manufactures, which he wrote and circulated while serving as Washington's secretary of treasury.[28]

The federal government had no laws on capitalism and needed none. It did have a few laws on commerce, mainly concerning foreign commerce or commerce around the ports. The federal government neither had nor needed laws on property or slavery. In the United States, slavery was simply a subdivision of state property law. Only one time, in 1850, did it even try to deal with slavery, and its effort to pass the Fugitive Slave Acts nearly tore national institutions apart. This suggests that the institutions of the national government were not all that capable of making fundamental social choices. National government was mainly good at helping private commerce husband and expand its resources. The American government, in its first 150 years, was clearly a limited government that would probably have been quite acceptable to even the most "strict constructionist" among the founders.

Tremendous contrast will be found in column 2 of Table 5.1. We can safely say that until the 1930s well over 90 percent of all the fundamental provisions of government in the United States were enacted by the state legislatures and carried out by agencies of the state governments. Even since the 1930s the change has only been a minor matter of degree. Despite the "Roosevelt revolution" my own guess would be that well over 80 percent of the fundamental decisions of government are still made by the states. The list in column 2 is far from complete; yet it makes quite clear that literally every aspect of life from cradle to grave is almost the exclusive province of state law. The fundamental institution of private property in the United States was, and still is today, a series of titles in the state property laws. Slavery was simply a matter of a few additional provisions in that property law; and the abolition of slavery required revision of state property laws. The practice of many important occupations is illegal, except as provided for in the state law. Try to acquire a child, by any means, and your behavior and your rights will be governed by state law. Try to educate your own child, or try to carry out a decision *not* to educate your own child, and your problem will be with the state law. Even though banking was established very early in our history as an area of federal power,[29] states were regulating banks and credit well before the national government got into the act; and most of the fundamental law governing our entire commercial civilization still re-

---

[28]An extensive excerpt of this report will be found in Theodore Lowi, ed., *Private Life and Public Order* (New York: Norton, 1968). For some good historical sources on early public policies, see Louis Hartz, *Economic Policy and Democratic Thought* (Cambridge, Mass.: Harvard University Press, 1948).

[29]The power of the federal government to establish banks was vigorously confirmed in *McCulloch* v.*Maryland,* 4 Wheaton 316 (1819).

Murder case
Legal flaw ends imprisonment

By Richard Phillips

SAMUEL SAIKIN, 54, a former Chicago businessman convicted in the slaying of an 18-year-old woman whose body was found on his Indiana farm, won a reprieve Tuesday from returning to prison to complete a 2-to-3-year sentence.

Federal District Judge Thomas R. McMillen ruled that even tho her body was found on the farm, state police who discovered it had used a defective search warrant, thus violating Saikin's constitutional protection from unreasonable search and seizure.

Saikin, who now lives in New Carlisle, Ind., had been imprisoned for 12 months, half of that time in the Cook County Jail while awaiting trial and half in Stateville Penitentiary before he was released on appeal.

Saikin, 55, was found innocent of murder in a September, 1969, Criminal Court trial here but guilty of obstruction of justice for concealing the death of Ella Jean Scott, also known as Mrs. Tina Mumma, a former secretary to Saikin, who owned the Biological Research Products Co., 243 W. Root St.

THE TRIAL WAS sparked by testimony by Saikin who charged that his son, Joel, then 25, had killed the girl, and by the son's accusation that his father had killed her. The killing allegedly took place in a far South Side warehouse of Saikin's firm. The girl for a time had been the son's girl friend.

Saikin appealed his conviction but it was upheld in 1971, by the Illinois Supreme Court, which also revoked his bond. Saikin went to Stateville prison in May, 1972, but was freed Nov. 20, 1972, as a result of a habeas corpus suit he filed in Federal Court.

McMillen then freed him on a $10,000 bond, ruling that a faulty warrant had led to the search and finding of the girl's body on his 20-acre farm in Chesterton, Ind.

Without the Constitution things could be worse: 2 news stories.

---

sides in the statute books of the states. State provision for our commercial civilization not only extends to banks and banking but also to most kinds of commercial exchange and to insurance, one of the most technically complex aspects of modern industrial civilization. So much have all of these matters of commerce been within the tradition of state regulation that when the Supreme Court decided that the national government ought to get into the act at least with regard to the insurance industry, Congress promptly enacted a statute explicitly turning this power back to the states.[30]

Government in the United States is so legitimate that much of what is contained in column 2 of Table 5.1 is not even thought of as government. People generally think of state governments as corrupt, unstable, and unimportant; yet even now their everyday lives are touched infinitely more by state government than by federal or by local governments. The state governments *created* capitalism in America, because capitalism is the sum total of laws providing for property ownership, property exchange, contracts, speculation, fraud, mortgages and other forms of credit, and the very legal essence of the corporation—its corporate charter or act of incorpora-

---

[30]*United States* v. *South-Eastern Underwriters Association*, 322 U.S. 533 (1944); for Congress's reaction see Walter F. Murphy, *Congress and the Court* (Chicago: University of Chicago Press, 1962), especially chapter 3.

Must have more latitude in fight against terror, says FBI chief

By Robert Enstad

Chicago Tribune Press Service

MONTREAL—FEDERAL BUREAU of Investigation Director Clarence Kelley said Saturday that the threat to national security posed by domestic terrorist groups makes it imperative that the FBI have some latitude in such investigations.

Tho he did not name the activities, he made reference to wiretaps, burglaries, and the opening of mail by the FBI in a speech to the meeting here of the American Bar Association.

"I think we are justifiably alarmed about the increase in the number of persons who are engaged in activities inimical to our country," Kelley told the lawyers. "Not only has their number increased in the last few years, but their proficiency has greatly increased.

"Faced with this threat—we [the FBI] must have a certain amount of latitude."

KELLEY POINTED out that the FBI has been accused of opening peoples' mail, committing burglaries, and of a general disregard for individual rights.

He said he would not discuss the mertis of such practices. But then he said investigations of national security matters must have their own rules.

"The rules applying to criminal investigation in this country cannot be transferred into and applied to our national security efforts," said Kelley. "If an individual's rights are violated by a law enforcement officer,

remedies are available. But there is no appeal, there is no such remedy for a terrorist's bomb.

"If our nation's ability to legitimately defend itself from destruction is lost, there are no appeals either."

KELLEY SAID his two years as FBI director have made him "acutely aware" of the dimension of intelligence activities, and the need to preserve certain techniques of intelligence.

He said rules could be legislated governing FBI activities, but these rules, he said, would hamper the agency in intelligence gathering.

"What rule-making authority does any government have over another nation?" Kelley asked. "And tho we may, in our country, cling tenaciously to moral and legal laws protecting human rights, other nations who may be hostile to us have no obligation to recognize such laws."

HE SAID disclosures of the FBI's intelligence activities have bene beneficial for the FBI, even tho they have spotlighted mistakes of the bureau.

"We have been shocked to find that the American people possess little knowledge of what the realities are in protecting the national security of our country," Kelley said.

"We erred in not adequately informing the American people of our national security role, of the vital importance of this role, and finally of the grave consequences that could result from our failure to fulfill this role."

tion, through which the corporation receives the benefits of limited liability. (A corporation is a fictitious person; it exists separately from all of the individuals who own shares of stock in it. When a corporation goes bankrupt, all of the assets of the corporation are of course distributed to the creditors. But the creditors cannot reach the personal property of the owners—that is, the stockholders—who are liable only for the amount of their shares in the corporation. Thus they have limited liability. In contrast, in a partnership, each partner is subject to unlimited liability. Not only is the personal fortune of each partner involved in the business, each partner can commit all the other partners by any one business action.)

In column 3 of Table 5.1 there is a question mark, which illustrates quite well the status of cities and other local governments under the Constitution. Basically, all are creatures of the

The Constitution and Contemporary Politics

137

states. In practice, they existed only as administrative conveniences for the states until the 1920s, when the states began giving the larger towns and cities "home rule"—the privilege to make some laws for themselves. Before the move toward home rule, cities made almost no fundamental policy choices for themselves. And even since the expansion of home rule, the sphere of policy made by cities is tiny in comparison to that of the states, which continue to make most of the laws. The local governments do have a certain amount of freedom to make exceptions and variations in those state laws according to local needs. For example, states make it illegal to operate a public conveyance for a fee (a taxi, for example); but each city can then proceed to grant the privilege to operate a taxi to a limited number of people. We call this a license—a sovereign's grant of a privilege to do something that is otherwise illegal. Licensing belongs to a category of public actions that include permits, franchises, entitlements, and "certificates of convenience and necessity." Each of these terms is used in different contexts, but they all amount to the same thing—the grant of a privilege to engage in some activity or to occupy some territory that is otherwise illegal. (See also chapter 15.)

Since cities were spared the need to make the fundamental social choices, they were able to develop political stability despite great social and economic instability. It is in this way that federalism served as the foundation for the development of our cities, especially our large cities. The urban political machine is simply one manifestation of political stability within social turmoil; and by all accounts the machine was made possible by the freedom of urban leaders to pass on the hard choices to the state legislatures while at the same time controlling the local distribution of privileges and variances within the context of state laws. This same pattern also helps explain why national politics remained stable despite the economic dynamism and social upheaval in the nation. In delegating the police power to the states, the Constitution saved the national government from burdens that might have proven too onerous in a country of continental size.

There is, beyond any reasonable doubt, evidence for the proposition that the Constitution has counted for a great deal in this area. But has it been an influence worthy of our admiration? There are always two sides to such a question, and both should be taken into account. Federalism helped keep the national government stable—but at the price of deferring for seventy-five years a confrontation on slavery. Yet one could say that if in 1787 there had been a confrontation instead of federalism the South might very well have carried out a complete secession, establishing a separate and permanent slaveholding nation.

Then, too, federalism helped provide for a smaller national government, maintaining more power closer to the people. This was especially important before modern communication made mileage irrelevant. But this very closeness to the people has operated as a barrier to social change. Nearly every national commitment requires an agonizingly slow battle in each resisting state—as the civil rights issue demonstrated. Just to emphasize this point, contemplate the problem of a revolutionary regime after it has staged a successful coup d'etat. If it is to carry out its revolutionary program and not simply sit ineffectually in Washington, the revolutionary regime will have to erase and rewrite thousands of pages of state statutes. This has led to the problem of variability in rights, crimes, and punishments, which requires separate treatment.

Federalism and Variability: A Matter of Death, and Life

Though each state has the right to choose its own controls, it would be inconceivable for any state to be silent on questions such as marriage and divorce, property, estates, and contracts. Nevertheless, the variations from state to state are tremendous. Some are humorous. A famous Rube Goldberg cartoon depicts the design of a moving van that would satisfy all of the state requirements. The center of the van is built like an accordion to accommodate variations in provisions for maximum length. Helium balloons are used to adjust the weight of the truck as it moves across state lines. It also has retractable wheels to be used in states that allow extra axles. It is, of course, a ridiculous-looking machine. Most variations are a good deal more serious, and some are shocking. Yet all of the variations are expressions of the spirit of constitutionalism in the United States. Let us review some of the most significant and extreme instances.

Crimes and punishment: Variations on a theme   Without much question, the most serious matter of variation among the states has been the provision for capital punishment. For example, before 1972, if you intended to be a murderer or rapist, it was very important to commit your crime in one of the nine states where there was no death penalty for any crime. These states (and the year in which they abolished capital punishment) were: Alaska (1957), Hawaii (1957), Iowa (1965), Maine (1887), Michigan (1947), Minnesota (1911), Oregon (1964), West Virginia (1965), and Wisconsin (1853). Five other states—New Mexico, New York, North Dakota, Rhode Island, and Vermont—had successively narrowed the application of the death penalty to a very small and unusual number of crimes, such as killing a prison officer, piracy, and treason. In all other states there was, until 1972, some provision for a death penalty. Nevertheless, it was important even among these states to select carefully the site of the crime. For example, Georgia provided the death penalty for castrating someone, or for advising a woman to have an abortion, or for robbing a grave. In Florida there were provisions for the death penalty in cases of discharging a machine gun in public, even if no one was actually hurt. In those states, as well as in others, the death penalty also applied for the more normal forms of capital crime, such as first degree murder, rape, and kidnapping. A cynic once said that morality is a matter of geography. It would disappoint him to know that he was guilty of serious understatement. In this context, the geography of immorality is a matter of death, and life.

On June 22, 1972, the Supreme Court decided that the variations in the laws and the implementation of capital punishment were too great to tolerate. In a historic five-four decision, the majority of the Court decided that capital punishment constituted a "cruel and unusual punishment" forbidden by the Eighth Amendment because the provisions are administered in such a discriminatory manner from state to state. The Court did not abolish capital punishment. The Court said only that inconsistencies in application were not tolerable.[31] Within two years of that decision, nearly thirty states had restored the death penalty, and over a hundred prisoners were back on Death Row awaiting the executioner. The provisions had been narrowed to a smaller number of crimes, and judges and juries had been given less discretion to select those among the guilty who would live and those who would die. But variations of death and life continue to exist among the states, and they will continue to exist in this area unless and until the Supreme Court decides that capital punishment in any and all circumstances constitutes a "cruel and unusual punishment."

Even if the Court does eliminate the inconsistencies of the uses and types of capital punishment by declaring it all unconstitutional, there will still be great disparities among the states in what is defined as a serious crime. In many ways this type of disparity may be more shocking than that involved in decisions on how severely to punish a crime that is universally considered a crime. For example, as indicated in Figure 5.1, if as late as 1970 you had the misfortune to be apprehended carrying marijuana in Alabama or Minnesota, your minimum sentence would be five years imprisonment, and your *maximum* sentence could be as high as twenty years. In Texas, although the minimum sentence was only two years, the maximum sentence could run to life imprisonment. A few years ago a night club stripper by the name of Candy Barr received a fifteen-year sentence in Texas, served four of those years, and was then paroled for the remainder. If she had been caught in New Jersey instead of Texas, she might very well have gone scot free, serving six months at the most.[32]

---

[31]*Furman* v. *Georgia,* 408 U.S. 238 (1972).

[32]Her case was reported in Lloyd Shearer, "Pot and Justice," *Parade Magazine,* March 7, 1971; see also *New York Times,* March 22, 1971.

Figure 5.1
State provisions on
marijuana as of 1970:
Prison terms for simple
possession of marijuana
(first offense)

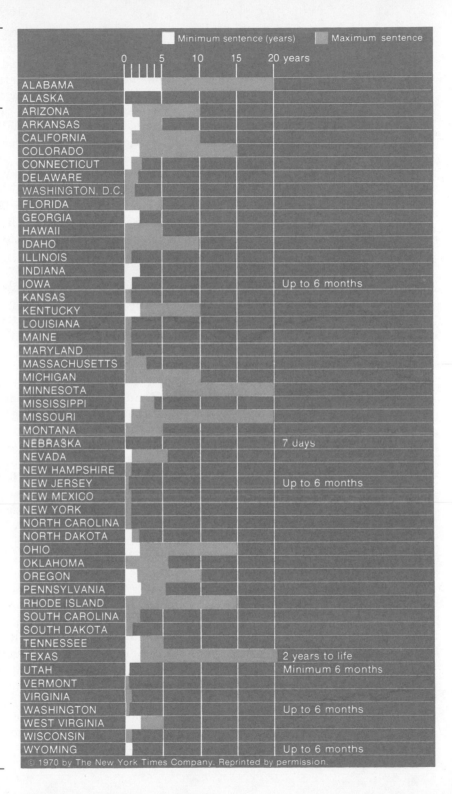

	Minimum sentence (years)	Maximum sentence

ALABAMA
ALASKA
ARIZONA
ARKANSAS
CALIFORNIA
COLORADO
CONNECTICUT
DELAWARE
WASHINGTON, D.C.
FLORIDA
GEORGIA
HAWAII
IDAHO
ILLINOIS
INDIANA
IOWA — Up to 6 months
KANSAS
KENTUCKY
LOUISIANA
MAINE
MARYLAND
MASSACHUSETTS
MICHIGAN
MINNESOTA
MISSISSIPPI
MISSOURI
MONTANA
NEBRASKA — 7 days
NEVADA
NEW HAMPSHIRE
NEW JERSEY — Up to 6 months
NEW MEXICO
NEW YORK
NORTH CAROLINA
NORTH DAKOTA
OHIO
OKLAHOMA
OREGON
PENNSYLVANIA
RHODE ISLAND
SOUTH CAROLINA
SOUTH DAKOTA
TENNESSEE
TEXAS — 2 years to life
UTAH — Minimum 6 months
VERMONT
VIRGINIA
WASHINGTON — Up to 6 months
WEST VIRGINIA
WISCONSIN
WYOMING — Up to 6 months

*The Constitution and
Contemporary Politics*

141

What indeed *is* a crime? *How serious* does misbehavior have to be before it is considered a crime meriting serious punishment? As the marijuana examples and Figure 5.1 suggest, the Constitution relegated these fundamental choices to the states; and the founders probably went along with this in full knowledge of the consequences. However, as the capital punishment decision indicates, some crimes and some rights have been "nationalized." That is to say, in some instances, discretion has been removed from communities and the states; in these cases variation among the states has, of course, been eliminated. But here, too, the Constitution has been profoundly influential. A review of the situation will show one view of constitutionalism pitted against another. This is the very kind of competition that helps maintain a healthy balance between a constitution that must change and a constitution that must remain the same.

Nationalization of crimes On a number of occasions in our history a crime has come to be considered so serious, or so far beyond the capacities of state and local authorities to deal with it, that Congress has nationalized it by making the punishment uniform throughout the country and by giving federal agencies and the federal courts immediate jurisdiction. One of the most sudden such nationalizations of a crime was in the instance of kidnapping. This followed the kidnap-murder of the Lindbergh child in 1932, when Congress provided that any kidnapping would be a crime by definition "in interstate commerce"—thereby involving the FBI as well as uniform punishment. National security is another area preempted by national law. During the Cold War of the 1950s, the Supreme Court held that states could not legislate on such subjects as sedition and espionage.[33]

Many other crimes have been nationalized, mainly in the area of interstate commerce. Early in this century Congress began passing laws establishing minimum standards of quality in agricultural products. This spread to other areas—purity in drugs and safety in cosmetics, for example. There is an abundance of national law on fraud, false advertising, abuse of the mails, abuse of credit, abuse of the currency (counterfeiting), and misrepresentation of securities. In addition to these, there are a few nationalized crimes that are not crimes of commerce but rather crimes that Congress has sought to reach through its commerce power. Production and sale of alcohol was banned for about a decade through a direct constitutional amendment, but many other crimes were nationalized without such drastic resort. For example, through the commerce power, Congress sought to control the use of sawed-off shotguns. Automobile theft was made a crime against the national government whenever the

[33]*Pennsylvania* v. *Nelson,* 350 U.S. 497 (1956).

stolen goods were passed across state lines. The same technical device was used to prevent the sale of colored oleomargarine and phosphorous matches.[34]

In this area, where we are concerned with the question of what is a crime and who declares what it is, it seems quite clear that the Constitution was influential in a very fundamental but also in a very particular way—the way of capitalism, or perhaps better yet, the way of a commercial civilization. The general tendency, as illustrated by the examples cited, was to nationalize a few of those crimes that seemed too heavily to burden the passage of goods or to cut too strongly into trade in well-established commodities or into business practices. A still more important example might be the entire area of trade regulation under the Federal Trade Commission. This commission was set up to concern itself with any and every conceivable type of business competition that might tend to burden commerce. It is altogether consistent with the Constitution that such crimes would be nationalized while the crimes that might involve the death penalty or long jail sentences were left to the discretion of each state. (For more on these policies, particularly trade policies, see chapters 15 and 16.)

Nationalization of rights Although by now the Constitution may appear to protect only the freedom of commerce, this is not entirely true. There is the "other side" of crime, which concerns the rights an accused person enjoys prior to any punishment he or she may receive if found guilty. As recently as the 1950s, variations in the definition of a crime and in the amount of punishment provided for each crime were matched by extreme variations in the procedural rights available to the accused persons. This variation in rights from state to state was perfectly in accord with the Constitution as it stood until the late 1950s, and this fact can be considered one of the gravest shortcomings of the Constitution. Indeed, although attributable more to Supreme Court interpretation than to explicit provisions in the Constitution, two levels of citizenship—not one— could be, and were, justified on the basis of the Constitution. The question here is whether the rights and privileges embodied in the Bill of Rights were intended to protect citizens against injustices that might befall them because of state actions or whether they were to be protected only from injustices which resulted from the actions of the federal government and its agencies. Even here the Court held that federalism was the thing; thus the Bill of Rights was only intended to protect persons as citizens of the United States and not of the state in which they might reside.[35] Even something as

---

[34]For a review of this crazy-quilt pattern, see Philip Kurland, *Politics, the Constitution, and the Warren Court* (Chicago: University of Chicago Press, 1970), chapter 3.
[35]*Barron* v. *Baltimore*, 7 Peters 243 (1833).

apparently fundamental as due process of law under the Fifth Amendment depended strictly upon the extent to which a state constitution and the state laws made provision for it. It was not something that you possessed wherever you went and wherever you lived in this country.

The Fourteenth Amendment was framed meticulously to apply due process to individual citizens regardless of the state in which they resided. However, it was never clear whether the Fourteenth Amendment incorporated the *entire* Bill of Rights or only the relevant due process aspects of those first ten Amendments. Consequently, the Supreme Court allowed many quite shocking anomalies to exist. For example, the California constitution has never provided its citizens with the right to a grand jury. Instead, the prosecuting attorney may present his own "bill of information," testifying that in the opinion of the prosecuting attorney sufficient grounds exist for carrying out the trial. In the test case, *Hurtado* v. *California,* the accused was duly convicted under such a system and was sentenced to be hanged. In a seven–one decision, the Supreme Court rejected the condemned man's appeal on the grounds that although the bill of information did replace the grand jury process, this replacement did not deprive him of any of his rights in the California courts. That is to say, the Fourteenth Amendment did not incorporate the right of grand jury indictment directly from the Bill of Rights into the protections that individuals enjoy in their capacity as state citizens.[36] This position of the Court was reaffirmed sixteen years later when the Court concluded that even the right to the twelve-person jury in the trial following indictment was not part of the due process of law as applied by the Fourteenth Amendment to the states.[37]

Another important provision of the Bill of Rights is the right not to be tried twice for the same crime—the practice known as *double jeopardy.* Until quite recently, Supreme Court rulings extended no such protection against state action unless the state constitution itself granted that right. Frank Palko was indicted by a Connecticut grand jury for first degree murder, but the trial jury convicted him of second degree murder and he was given a life sentence. The state of Connecticut appealed, arguing that the trial judge had committed an error. The higher state court ordered a new trial, in which Palko was convicted of first degree murder and was sentenced to death. The Supreme Court upheld the conviction. If Palko had lived in another state, where double jeopardy was prohibited, he would certainly have escaped execution. But in 1937 the Supreme Court refused to include elimination of double jeopardy as part of the Bill of Rights to be applied nationally, regardless of residence.[38]

[36]*Hurtado* v. *California,* 110 U.S. 516 (1884).
[37]*Maxwell* v. *Dow,* 176 U.S. 581 (1900).
[38]*Palko* v. *Connecticut,* 302 U.S. 319 (1937).

There are many other rights of this kind which citizens enjoyed in relation to the national government but could not claim in their capacity as citizens of a state: the right to abstain from self-incrimination, protection against unreasonable search and seizure, the right to keep and bear arms, the right to compel the appearance of witnesses on behalf of the accused in a trial, the right to a jury trial in civil cases, and the protection against excessive bail and cruel and unusual punishment.[39] For nearly a quarter century following the Palko case, there was no clear definition of the rights that citizens of every state enjoyed by virtue of incorporation from the Bill of Rights into the Fourteenth Amendment. The only certainty was that virtually all of the First Amendment was incorporated under the Fourteenth Amendment. Beyond that, the situation seemed to depend upon the membership of the Supreme Court and the opinion of a majority of the justices as to whether a given right was or was not "of the essence of a scheme of ordered liberty . . . so rooted in the traditions and conscience of our people as to be ranked as fundamental."[40] These are eloquent words, but they offered little guidance to defense attorneys and little solace to a person accused of committing a crime in the wrong state.

All of this began to change in the 1960s at the height of the influence of the chief justice at that time, Earl Warren. This is called the *Warren Era* or the *Warren Court.* There was a burst of activity reinterpreting the Fourteenth Amendment and the degree to which it incorporated the Bill of Rights as part of the rights a citizen enjoyed regardless of the state in which he lived. In 1961 unreasonable search and seizure was incorporated; in 1962 cruel and unusual punishment was brought in. In 1963—one of the most important of these decisions—the Court decided to include the right to counsel in *all* criminal cases, whether capital or noncapital cases.[41] In 1964 the Court actually reversed earlier decisions that had excluded self-incrimination from the Fourteenth Amendment, saying in part:

> The Fourteenth Amendment secures against state invasion the same privilege that the Fifth Amendment guarantees against federal infringement—the right of the person to remain silent unless he chooses to speak in the unfettered exercise of his own free will, and to suffer no penalty . . . for such silence.[42]

In 1965 the Court decided to include the provisions of the Sixth Amendment, which guarantees that the accused will have the right to confront all witnesses. In 1967 the Court went even further to

---

[39]For the clearest and most comprehensive review of the rights that were and were not incorporated under the Fourteenth Amendment, see Abraham, *Freedom and the Court,* chapter 3.
[40]Justice Cardozo for the majority in *Palko* v. *Connecticut,* p. 327.
[41]*Gideon* v. *Wainwright,* 372 U.S. 335 (1963). This is generally considered the most important "incorporation decision" since the Palko case.
[42]*Malloy* v. *Hogan,* 378 U.S. 1 (1964).

rule that the accused also has the right to compel the appearance of favorable witnesses as well as adverse witnesses. In 1966, the Court at long last decided that the right to trial by an impartial jury was also to be included as part of the Fourteenth Amendment, and this had the effect of seriously regulating the conduct of county prosecuting attorneys, bailiffs, and other officers who had it within their power to make comments to juries aimed at prejudicing the outcome of jury deliberations. The right to a speedy trial was included in 1967, as was the right to a jury trial in all criminal cases in 1968. Finally, in 1969, the Court came full circle by including double jeopardy[43] and thereby explicitly overruling the Palko case, which had been the beginning of the long and arduous case-by-case route from the Bill of Rights to the Fourteenth Amendment.

Virtually all of the provisions of the Bill of Rights are now applied to the states through the Fourteenth Amendment. Step by step, the Court has essentially overruled everything back to *Barron* v. *Baltimore* (see footnote 35 of this chapter). But only as of 1969 or 1970 can we say that the distinction established in that 1833 case has been rendered irrelevant by the passage of the Fourteenth Amendment; it took us about one hundred years to truly nationalize due process of law. Note clearly what has happened. The constitutional provisions for a federal structure continue to influence contemporary politics and government very strongly, but in a special way: *Crimes and punishments are permitted by the Constitution to vary from state to state, while procedures for dealing with crimes, and with those accused of crimes, have been nationalized.* State laws may make birth control, voluntary abortion, homosexuality between consenting adults, or operating a store on Sunday a crime; in other states no controls on these behaviors may exist at all.

Two things are clear about the pattern. First, it is a direct and explicit result of our Constitution. The crimes in question are on the books in a particular state because they reflect prevailing notions of morality in that state, and they will change when the distribution of values changes in that state. Second, despite specific instances of crimes that should not be crimes, or actions we feel should be made crimes, the pattern of variation we have found is a remarkable thing in a country like ours. It flies directly in the face of the otherwise national tendencies in our economy. In a country where a mass market is important, where large corporations deal with each other across many states, and where people move from state to state every month by the millions, we would tend to expect the reverse of what we are getting. We would tend to expect national uniformity in the laws and state-by-state variation in procedural standards. That is, it would be most convenient for all of us if we knew exactly how to behave in each state; and it would be very convenient to the

[43]*Benton* v. *Maryland*, 395 U.S. 784 (1969).

elite of each state and community if they could deal with "criminals" and the "criminal element" as they wished. Thus, however much our constitutional forms may accommodate or actually serve national capitalism, there are many other instances where the constitutional structure has its influence in ways that are either antagonistic to capitalism or do not distinguish one type of economic system from another.

Many will argue that even where the Constitution is not serving an economic establishment, it is serving or defending other established social or political interests. For example, a federalism that allows capital punishment amounts to the defense of a criminal justice system that executes murderers and rapists who are poor and black, while white, especially middle-class, murderers and rapists get life sentences and actually serve only a few years. For another example, protection of the obligation of contracts is only effective for those who understand contracts or have the freedom to determine which contracts are worthy of entering into—the educated middle and upper classes. All this is true. A constitution that fails to protect prevailing interests is inconceivable—almost by definition.

All the more significant, then, are any instances where the Constitution works universalistically—where it provides defense for the powerless as well as the powerful. The right to counsel for all criminal defendants, for example, cannot be understood in any other terms. We have already cited numerous instances, and there are still others. One vital area especially worthy of note here is freedom of religion. The notion of an established religion seems remote in the United States, but it is remote in large part because of constitutional provisions against it which uphold the freedom of the individual to exercise religious beliefs or not to espouse any at all. Prior to 1940 there were very few "free exercise" cases. But since 1940 there has been a whole line of fundamentally important cases concerning this part of the Constitution, and the overwhelming preponderance of these cases has been in favor of the odd sect and the individual practitioner, as opposed to the convenience of the state or city governments or the conventional religious groupings. In fact, some of the earlier cases denying freedom of conscience have been explicitly overturned in recent years.[44]

We have barely scratched the surface of a thorough investigation into the modern influence of the established constitutional structure in the United States. On balance it is possible to find that the influence of the Constitution on the everyday affairs of government and politics has been significant and positive—if one begins with the assumption that people in established positions will not volun-

[44]The best review of all of these cases will be found in Abraham, *Freedom and the Court*, chapter 6 and Tables I–II.

Portraits of three great American radicals. *Left:* Carrie Nation, fanatical proponent of the Prohibition Amendment. *Right:* Clarence Earl Gideon, whose Supreme Court case extended the right to counsel. *Bottom:* Rosa Parks, who broke the first racial barriers in Montgomery, Alabama.

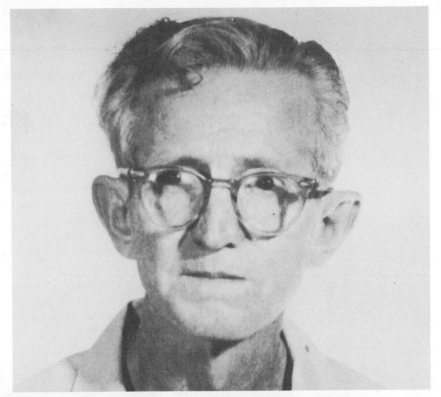

tarily yield anything. From that standpoint, the influences attributable to the Constitution represent a stupendous achievement.[45]

CHANGING THE CONSTITUTION BY AMENDMENT: WHAT, WHEN, AND HOW

Notwithstanding any good influences that may have come of it, the Constitution is forever a matter of some unrest in the United States. One possible measure of the universality of the constitutional structure could be the frequency with which drastic amendments are sought by members of established interests groups. A few significant examples of amendments sought by entrenched interests in the past couple of decades are: the proposal to limit the treaty-making power of the national government, the proposal to impose a 25 percent ceiling on the income tax, another proposal to repeal the income tax, a proposal to restore the right of public schools to hold prayers, and several proposals to reduce the jurisdiction of the federal courts in the area of state and local criminal procedure. A host of examples can be found in the area of women's rights; these movements have consistently been led by upper-middle-class women.

Why indeed should most constitutional change come through the route of judicial interpretation? Would it not be better to channel these changes through the political branches? There are four ways the people can amend the Constitution, and these multiple routes were implanted in Article V as "an easy, regular and Constitutional way" because the Congress "may abuse their power and refuse their consent on that very account . . . to admit to amendments to correct the source of the abuse."[46] All of these routes, which are illustrated in Figure 5.2, are "closer to the people" than a Supreme Court. Yet the results almost suggest that the Constitution was not intended to be changed through any one of these methods. In all the years since ratification in 1789, only twenty-six amendments have been passed. Since 1791, after passage of the Bill of Rights (the first ten amendments), only sixteen have been passed, and two of these—the prohibition amendments—cancel each other out, for all practical purposes leaving only fourteen. A mere eleven amendments have

---

[45]For an argument by a very responsible and very knowledgeable scholar that we have gone too far in the direction of nationalizing rights in favor of criminals and dissenters, see Philip Kurland, especially pp. 81ff. For other treatments of political change and the role of the Constitution and the courts in that change, see Alexander Bickel, *The Least Dangerous Branch* (Indianapolis: Bobbs-Merrill, 1962); Clement Vose, *Constitutional Change* (Boston: Heath, 1973); and, for anyone who doubts that we have made progress in the effective application of the Bill of Rights, consult Leonard Levy, *Legacy of Suppression* (Cambridge, Mass.: Harvard University Press, Belknap Press, 1960).

[46]The observation was made by Colonel Mason early during the Constitutional Convention on June 11. See Max Farrand, *The Records of the Federal Convention of 1787*, rev. ed., 4 vols. (New Haven: Yale University Press, 1966), vol. 1, pp. 202–203.

Figure 5.2
Amending the
Constitution: Four
possible routes

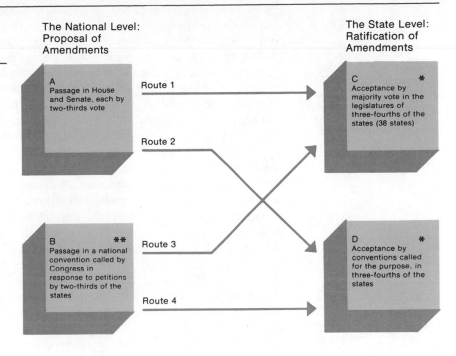

The National Level: Proposal of Amendments

The State Level: Ratification of Amendments

A
Passage in House and Senate, each by two-thirds vote

Route 1

Route 2

B **
Passage in a national convention called by Congress in response to petitions by two-thirds of the states

Route 3

Route 4

C *
Acceptance by majority vote in the legislatures of three-fourths of the states (38 states)

D *
Acceptance by conventions called for the purpose, in three-fourths of the states

*Congress chooses the mode of ratification. In each amendment proposal Congress has the power to provide for the mode of ratification, the time limit for consideration by the states, and probably other conditions of ratification.

**This mode of proposal has never been employed, so that amendment routes 3 and 4 have never been attempted.

been adopted in the entire century since the passage of the Civil War amendments—nine in effect, due to the cancellation of the two prohibition amendments. This cannot be explained on the basis of the adequacy of the Constitution or on the basis of the satisfaction of Americans with their Constitution. As already reported, the people have tried on at least 5,000 occasions between 1789 and 1964 to amend the Constitution. Yet through 1964, Congress had only officially proposed 29, and only 23 were finally ratified. In the tumultuous decade after 1965, a grand total of 2,504 constitutional amendments were introduced into Congress. Of those, only 9 came anywhere close to receiving the two-thirds vote. Two were passed and eventually became the Twenty-fifth and Twenty-sixth Amendments. The Equal Rights Amendment may possibly have become the Twenty-seventh by the time this book is published.

It is obviously very difficult to pass an amendment to the Constitution. After all, a proposal for an amendment can be killed by only 34 senators *or* 146 members of the House. If the necessary

The Constitution and Contemporary Politics

two-thirds vote does go through Congress and a formal proposal is made, the proposal can still be killed by the refusal or inability of only 13 state legislatures to ratify the proposal. The tremendous difference between the number of amendments proposed and the number actually adopted is ample measure of the difficulty. But there is another reason why so few amendments are adopted. Only a limited number of changes needed by the society can be made through the Constitution. People persist in trying to use the Constitution to solve a variety of problems, but only a special kind of change ever seems to succeed. A review of the actual amendments will give us some insight into what the conditions of constitutional change are. That, in turn, will tell us a great deal about our Constitution and about constitutionalism in general.

Only a brief look at Tables 5.2 and 5.3 is necessary to perceive and appreciate the main criteria of constitutional amendment in the United States. Five of the sixteen amendments adopted since 1791 are directly concerned with the expansion of the electorate (Table 5.2). This, of course, was made necessary by the fact that the founders were unable to establish a national electorate with uniform voting qualifications and decided instead to stay away from this hot issue. They provided in Article I, Section 2 that eligibility to vote in a national election would be the same as "the Qualification requisite for Electors of the most numerous branch of the State Legislature." This meant that any expansion of the national electorate, for whatever reason and by whatever motivation, would require a constitutional amendment. That does not mean these amendments would pass simply because they were proposed; nor does it mean that amendments to the Constitution would be limited to this area simply because it was an area that required change by constitutional amendment. Nevertheless, five of the sixteen were in this area. Table 5.3 shows that six more of the sixteen amendments

Table 5.2	Amending the Constitution to Expand the Electorate		
	Amendment and Purpose	**Year Proposed**	**Year Adopted**
	XV Extended voting rights to all races	1869	1870
	XIX Extended voting rights to women	1919	1920
	XXIII Extended voting rights to residents of the District of Columbia	1960	1961
	XXIV Extended voting rights to all classes by abolition of poll taxes	1962	1964
	XXVI Extended voting rights to citizens aged 18 and over	1971	1971*

*The Twenty-sixth Amendment holds the record for speed of adoption. It was proposed on April 23, 1971, and finally adopted on July 5, 1971. The only other adoption time that comes close is the Prohibition Repealer (XXI), proposed February 20, 1933, and adopted December 5, 1933.

Table 5.3	**Amending the Constitution to Change the Relationship between Elected Offices and the Electorate**		
	Amendment and Purpose	**Year Proposed**	**Year Adopted**
	XII Separated ballot for vice-president in the Electoral College	1803	1804
	XIV (Part 1) Provided a national definition of citizenship*	1866	1868
	XVII Provided direct election of senators	1912	1913
	XX Eliminated "Lame Duck" session of Congress	1932	1933
	XXII Limited presidential term	1947	1951
	XXV Presidential succession in case of disability	1965	1967

*In defining citizenship, the Fourteenth Amendment actually provided all the necessary constitutional basis for expanding the electorate to include all races, women, and residents of the District of Columbia. Only the "eighteen-year-olds amendment" should have been necessary, since that changed the definition of citizenship. The fact that additional amendments were required following the Fourteenth suggests that, at least in the United States, voting is not considered an inherent right of citizenship. We have, perhaps without fully thinking through the implications, defined voting in effect as a privilege rather than a right. (See also chapter 7.)

are also electoral in nature, although not concerned directly with voting rights. Instead, these amendments are concerned with the elective offices themselves or with the relationship between elective offices and the electorate. Table 5.4 provides the third and final category of amendments. Three of the sixteen since 1791 have sought to expand or to delimit the powers of the national or state governments. The Fourteenth Amendment is included in this table as well as in Table 5.3 because it seeks not only to define citizenship, but also to make clear that this definition meant that citizenship included with the right to vote also all the rights of the Bill of Rights, as has already been mentioned.

Let us now review the pattern. First, the Constitution has been amended very few times in its 180-year history. This infrequency can be appreciated if compared to the typical state constitution, which grows steadily by amendments year by year. Second, among these scant few amendments, only one has sought directly to deal with some substantive social problem. This is, of course, the prohibition amendment (XVIII), and it is the only amendment ever to be directly repealed. Only two other amendments can be said to have had the effect of legislation—the Thirteenth Amendment, which abolished slavery, and the Sixteenth Amendment, which established the power to levy an income tax. However, in both of these instances the legislative effect was incidental to the direct effort, which was to reduce the power of the states as well as expand the power of the national government. The only direct effect of the

Table 5.4

Amending the Constitution to Expand or Limit the Power of Government

Amendment and Purpose		Year Proposed	Year Adopted
XI	Limited jurisdiction of federal courts over suits involving the states	1794	1798
XIII	Eliminated slavery, eliminated right of states to allow property in persons	1865*	1865*
XIV	(Part 2) Applied due process of Bill of Rights to the states	1866	1868
XVI	Established national power to tax incomes	1909	1913

*The Thirteenth Amendment was proposed January 31, 1865, and adopted less than a year later on December 18, 1865.

Thirteenth Amendment, for example, was to wipe out all of the state laws dealing with blacks as though they were property. Section 2 of that amendment clearly implies that no legislation was directly intended where it states, "Congress shall have power to enforce this Article by appropriate legislation." As for the Sixteenth Amendment, it is certainly true that income tax legislation followed immediately; nonetheless the amendment concerns itself strictly with the establishment of the power of Congress to enact such legislation. Thus, prohibition is the only clear act of legislation by amendment.

There have been a large number of other efforts to legislate by constitutional amendments. For example, proposals have been made for amendments to eliminate child labor, to establish women's rights to jobs, to eliminate any and all unreasonable discrimination, to provide for a ceiling on the amount of income taxation. However, all of these efforts except prohibition have either failed or have been obviated by accomplishment of the same goals through the normal legislative and judicial channels. Finally, the overwhelming proportion (eleven of sixteen, or eleven of fourteen, depending on how you count the prohibition amendment and its repealer) have concerned themselves with the composition of government, the makeup of the electorate, or the relationship between the two. Some of these have been trivial or highly specialized. Others have been far-reaching. Either way, this is what most of constitutional change has been about.

If a constitution is by definition the makeup or composition of a thing, our Constitution is certainly a good illustration of this definition, which has been used as a rigid criterion in the course of the amendment process. Even those who would prefer more changes than we have accomplished would have to agree that there is great

300 DOLLARS
REWARD!

RUNAWAY from John S. Doak on the 21st inst., two NEGRO MEN; LOGAN 45 years of age, bald-headed, one or more crooked fingers; DAN 21 years old, six feet high. Both black.
I will pay ONE HUNDRED DOLLARS for the apprehension and delivery of LOGAN, or to have him confined so that I can get him.
I will also pay TWO HUNDRED DOLLARS for the apprehension of DAN, or to have him confined so that I can get him.
                                    JOHN S. DOAKE,
Springfield, Mo., April 24th, 1857,

wisdom in this particular criterion. The purpose of a constitution is to establish a structure within which government and politics can take place. The purpose of a constitution is to enable legislation to take place rather than to set forth the legislation within the structure itself. And the major purpose of amending the Constitution is to change it sufficiently to have a structure that appears usable and relevant—that is, legitimate—to each generation.

For those whose hopes for change center on the Constitution, it must be emphasized that this route to social change is and always will be extremely limited. Through a constitution it is possible to establish a working structure of government; and through a constitution it is possible to establish basic rights of citizens with regard to governments and with regard to each other. Once these things have been accomplished, where else is there to go with the constitution? How many new rights are there to establish?

Further reflection would suggest that the real problem beyond the

*The Constitution and
Contemporary Politics*

original constitutional establishment of rights is how to extend rights *which exist in theory* to those persons and classes of persons who do not already enjoy them in practice. The extension of rights in the real world will always be much more a matter of legislation than of constitutional amendment. The Constitution can have a real influence on everyday life inasmuch as a right or a procedure set forth in the Constitution can become a *cause of action* in the hands of an otherwise powerless person (see chapter 13 for a detailed discussion of this). But whether that person's cause of action will have any effect will still depend upon the ordinary workings of courts and legislatures rather than any basic change in the Constitution. Property is an excellent example. Property is one of the most fundamental and well-established rights in the United States; but it is well-established not because it is recognized in so many words in the Constitution but because courts and legislatures have made it a crime for one person to take away or trespass upon the property of another. A constitution is good if it produces the *cause of action* that leads to good legislation, good case law, appropriate police behavior.

This is indeed a great deal to require of a constitution. First of all, a constitution cannot enforce itself. It cannot be better than the political culture in which it exists; it cannot be better than all of the laws, agencies, and courts that attempt by legislation and implementation to realize constitutional goals. For example, the Constitution of the German Weimar Republic of the 1920s was said to be the most enlightened in history; yet it became little more than a smooth skid toward the dictatorship of Adolph Hitler. A constitution cannot eliminate power and the powerful. Yet it may be the only dependable defense that the powerless have against the powerful. As long as power seeks legitimacy by setting limits upon itself in a constitution, there is some hope for the powerless. Consider that we are dealing with a natural tendency toward tyranny whenever conquest is the essential issue. Consider that all of the important weapons of violence are in the hands of governments and that most of the mechanisms for creating legitimacy and manipulating the symbols of legitimacy are available first and foremost to the tyrant. The constitution is an embodiment of a few substantial victories over the tyrant.

A constitution can do no more than that. But if its few victories are substantial, it may contribute to politics on a scale large enough and public enough to transform the tyranny into a responsible form of government: incomplete conquest without chaos. The sphere of incomplete conquest is large or small, dynamic or disorderly, mainly according to the vigor and the forms of a nation's politics. Politics is made possible by an enlightened constitution, and an effective constitution depends upon a vigorous, broadly based politics. The constitution and the politics of a nation are one long continuum.

Time and again we will see that the one cannot be understood without the other. In a constitution the ultimate criterion is justice. In the world of action, justice itself can never amount to more than politics raised to a higher level of aspiration. But what is aspiration? In the political system, aspiration is defined and delimited very largely by a constitution.

Part Three
Politics

If conquest were ever complete, there would be no
politics. Politics depends upon incomplete conquest;
and politics, once it becomes an organized part of society,
probably prevents complete conquest. But what are the
forms of politics, and are some forms better antidotes to
conquest than others? Can there be democratic politics?
To what extent do interest groups and parties—the
American forms of politics—produce desired responses
from government? "Organized politics" may be an
inconsistency in terms. Is organized politics an effective
force for democratizing conquest, or is organized politics
conquest in another form?

Chapter 6   Incomplete Conquest: Politics

The latent causes of faction are thus
sown in the nature of man. . . . So strong
is this propensity of mankind to fall into
mutual animosities that where no substantial occasion presents itself the
most frivolous and fanciful distinctions
have been sufficient. . . . But the most
common and durable source of factions
has been the various and unequal distribution of property.
James Madison, 1787

Complete conquest is almost inconceivable. There will probably always be a sphere of social life we call freedom—the
absence of imposed order. When the sphere grows large, some
call it anarchy—absence of rule, a condition of lawlessness.
By whatever name, it is an area of individuality and of peril.
Individuality is the source of politics. Politics is a means of
coping with the conflicts that human differences produce.
Physical violence is another way of coping with conflict;
throughout history physical violence has apparently been the
most frequently employed means of coping with conflict. This
is why life outside the state has been defined as one of
"continual fear, and danger of violent death" where life is
"solitary, poor, nasty, brutish, and short."[1] As a way of coping
with differences outside the state, politics is a much rarer
experience, "something to be valued almost as a pearl beyond
price in the history of the human condition."[2]

Incomplete Conquest: Politics

[1]Thomas Hobbes, *Leviathan* (New York: Macmillan, 1947), p. 82.
[2]Bernard Crick, *In Defense of Politics* (Baltimore: Penguin Books, 1964), p. 17.

Politics is not a synonym for freedom. Politics is beyond anyone who is not free, but it is a particular use of freedom. Politics is impossible to define precisely, because it can refer to the entire life of citizens in relation to their state or community. Despite many differences of stress among political scientists, however, it is possible at least to say that politics refers to all human efforts to resolve conflict nonviolently by constructing laws or controls, or otherwise extending conquest.[3]

Politics is, therefore, a contradictory phenomenon, like almost everything else in the history of government. Since politics arises out of incomplete conquest yet seeks to extend conquest, it has a dual nature. On the one hand, it seeks to impose solutions to conflict, thereby extending conquest. On the other hand, politics tends to thwart complete conquest by reinforcing human differences. In the Western world especially, politics is embraced to the extent that it is thought to be a means of selecting social controls while at the same time reinforcing the desire and the ability to remain otherwise free. In this context, democracy takes on a special meaning. *Democracy is that predisposition to accept incomplete conquest as a positive virtue.* This approach to politics will be sustained throughout the volume, and it will suffice as long as the reader remains alert to three prejudices inherent in it:

1. Politics will be confined to the realm of conquest and government. Politics exists, of course, in every realm of human endeavor, including churches, businesses, schools and universities; but in the context of the government of a large nation-state, these phenomena are trivial, and we will not concern ourselves with them, except perhaps for an occasional example.

2. By defining politics in relation to conquest, we are in effect saying that government is more important than politics, that the test of politics is whether it shapes and influences what governments do, and that therefore governments should be the central focus with politics at the margins. Sometimes these margins are substantial, but they are, nonetheless, margins.

3. This approach accepts politics as *purposive* action. It brings to the very center of attention the actual, substantive differences which lead people to engage in politics. Politics is not defined simply as a process. Politics *is* the interests and demands that motivate people. Moreover, all interests will be treated as equal. All interests *are* equal, though individuals and opportunities are not. This formulation will gall anyone who feels that some interests have higher moral claim than others; but the traditional American

---

[3]For a good treatment of the problem of trying to define politics, and for some excellent distinctions among approaches to the study of politics, see George J. Graham, Jr., *Methodological Foundations for Political Analysis* (Waltham, Mass.: Xerox College Publishing, 1971), chapters 1 and 2.

democratic answer would be, "Let the political process determine that."[4]

THE INTERESTS

If politics begins with freedom to pursue differences, differences in politics are expressed as interests. The *interest* is the unit of action. In government, certain interests become embodied in laws, decrees, orders, rules, and constitutions. These are the successful interests. In politics, all interests are encompassed; some are simply not as successful as others.

A Practical Classification

The number and variety of interests in the United States will defy any description. Even reduced to the narrower field of "organized interests," the numbers are astronomical—beyond conception. A quick count from the Yellow Pages of the Ithaca telephone directory produced the following list of *formally* organized groups, with telephone numbers and headquarters:

> Civic and business . . . 30
> Trade unions . . . 11
> Church . . . 48
> Church-related . . . 96
> Social service . . . 15
> Fraternities and sororities . . . 60
> Social clubs . . . 8
> Fraternal organizations . . . 6
> Political organizations . . . 3
> PTAs . . . 18

This listing does not include professional organizations of lawyers, doctors, and businessmen or officialdom, whose government agencies certainly qualify as organized interests. The population of the Ithaca metropolitan area in 1970 was less than 75,000. Imagine the situation in larger cities and suburbs.

In order to proceed with an analysis of these interests, some method of classification is required. The system we will use is based upon a few of the objective attributes of human beings that are most likely to be translated into interests. Table 6.1 presents the general

---

[4]Ultimately some values are recognized as having a higher moral claim, but these are the First Amendment freedoms thought to be essential for the pursuit of all *other* interests, among which there are no moral distinctions. For probably the first formulation of the "preferred position" of the interests embodied in the First Amendment, see Justice Stone in *United States* v. *Carolene Products Company*, 304 U.S. 144 (1938). A good discussion will be found in Herman Pritchett, *The American Constitution* (New York: McGraw-Hill, 1959), pp. 393–396.

Table 6.1	The Interests: A Classification		
	Big Interests	**Special Interests**	**Strategic Interests**
	Mass	Sector	Services
	Class	Trade	Conduits
	Section	Occupation	Processes
	Race	Neighborhood	Channels
	Ethnicity	Cause	Authorities
	Religion	Sect	Elites
	Age		
	Sex		
	Armed Forces Experience		
	Consumerism		
	Environment		

categories of interest groups founded on this basis. If, for example, an individual is a wage earner in the sub-$10,000 income bracket, that fact is likely to be a matter of considerable *interest* to that individual; and this wage earner's interest in economic status is likely to be quite different from that of a corporate executive whose salary exceeds $50,000 per year.[5] The socioeconomic status of the individual is not the only politically relevant attribute of that person, but its undeniable importance warrants putting it in a separate category of interests, which may be called *class* or *class consciousness.*

Socioeconomic status, or class, is included in column 1 with several other big interests—attributes shared by very large numbers of people in any country. No one would disagree with the proposition that all those listed in this column are very basic attributes. However, not all individuals in each category will feel an equal consciousness of a specific attribute or will rate it as high in their own scheme of interests as other members of the same category might. Each such difference in priorities is a source of interests and is activated as an interest from time to time according to changes in the environment, efforts by leaders to intensify the consciousness of that difference, or other external influences. Many Marxists continue to argue that, due to economic exploitation, socioeconomic class *ought* to be the most intensely shared interest among all workers, regardless of other interests they do not share as a class. Workers who hold other interests higher than their socioeconomic status are thus considered to be expressing "false con-

---

[5]There is a voluminous literature attempting to analyze how socioeconomic status expresses itself in politically relevant interests. For a good brief discussion of these issues and a review of some of the classic studies, see W. G. Runciman, *Social Science and Political Theory* (Cambridge: Cambridge University Press, 1971), chapter 5.

sciousness." If that is the case, the data on public opinion in the United States reveal that a great deal of false consciousness is being expressed.[6] On the other hand, as the initial quote from James Madison suggests, you do not have to be a Marxist to rate economic status as very significant among all the possible interests.

In all three columns of Table 6.1, the same principle of classification is applied. The attributes listed are those that social science and common sense agree are important in the formation of interest groups. All along, the major assumption is that people share these attributes with at least a few other people, that they are aware or become aware of these important attributes, and that eventually something happens to activate these attributes as interests. The conversion of attributes into interests is one of the most fundamental aspects of any political process. If we knew exactly how and when this sort of thing happens, one of the central problems of political research would be solved.

The Big Interests: Masses and Classes

Distinguishing big interests from special interests involves a largely subjective judgment. However, the important instances of this distinction are not all that difficult or controversial. For example, most everyone would recognize the distinction between a religion, broadly defined, and a sect. Christianity might be considered, therefore, a big interest; but Christianity is in turn composed of literally dozens of Christian sects ranging from very populous ones like the Baptist denomination to a variety of small but intense subdivisions within the Baptist church, as well as other denominational divisions and subdivisions. Another important example is what the social scientist has come to call ethnicity. All "hyphenated Americans" are members of this very large category of ethnicity; on the other hand it is well-known that Italians comprise a more specialized type of ethnic group that has an identity separate from the Irish, or the Poles, or other ethnic groupings. Thus, very often the specialized interest is a subdivision or a sub-subdivision of some big interest rather than simply a separate attribute that is associated with a smaller number of people.

Among all of the big interests, *masses* and *classes* have been considered the most important. Sociologically, a *mass* can be defined as all the people who are engaging in some conventionally designated activity. Consumers are such a mass. Football spectators comprise another mass. The United States has sometimes been called a mass society because observers have felt that more and more of our time is spent in such activities, where the thing we

---

Incomplete Conquest: Politics

[6]See, for example, Bernard Hennessy, *Public Opinion* (Belmont, Calif.: Wadsworth, 1965), chapter 13.

share with other people does not involve much mutual identification and interaction. A *class* is usually defined as all those people who bear about the same basic relationship to the economic system or the market. The term *proletariat* refers to that very vague but very large stratum of people in an industrial society who work for wages. More specific definitions of economic classes rely upon distinctions in annual income, type of occupation, education, or some combination of these "indicators."[7]

Once a few of these big interests have been defined, it is impossible not to be impressed with their political potential. Many historians believe that masses and classes *actually explain history.* And there is a great deal of documentation in favor of the proposition that when a whole economic class, or a religious or racial segment of the society, is mobilized, this is the dawning of a new historical era. On the other hand, big interests are so large and diffuse throughout society that they are usually very difficult to mobilize politically. They have of course been mobilized, but it usually takes great provocation, such as a war, a revolution, or a sudden economic depression.

These mobilizations have been relatively infrequent in the United States. Although one aspect of the explanation for this infrequency may be that our economic classes or sectional aggregates or religious groupings have been less dissatisfied than in other industrial nations, federalism is another important aspect. Economic class dissatisfaction in one or two states may not occur at precisely the same time as dissatisfaction in the other states. Much of the energy of class mobilization in that instance would be contained within state boundaries and would focus itself on the respective state capitals rather than on Washington.

The so-called Madisonian formula states this principle. The best way, according to Madison, of controlling the "mischiefs of faction" (his word for interest groups) is to be sure that there are so many factions that no one or no one combination of them can ever achieve a national majority:

The influence of factious leaders may kindle the flame within their particular States but will be unable to spread a general conflagration throughout the other States. . . . A rage for paper money, for an abolition of debts, for an equal division of property, *or for any other improp-*

---

[7]Max Weber has done the best job of bringing Karl Marx into the twentieth century; see his definitions in *From Max Weber: Essays in Sociology,* ed. and trans. Hans Gerth and C. Wright Mills (New York: Oxford University Press, 1958). Translations of these considerations into actual economic class strata in American society will be found in a variety of places. See, for example, S. M. Lipset, *Political Man* (New York: Doubleday, 1960), especially chapters 4–5 and 7–9. See also Angus Campbell et al., *The American Voter* (New York: Wiley, 1960). Campbell and his associates at the University of Michigan have probably done more than any other single group to reduce the study of social class to terms that are susceptible to political analysis. A very large proportion of the most significant work in this area during the 1960s and 1970s was either done by this group or drawn from the data collected under their supervision at the University of Michigan's Survey Research Center.

er or wicked project, will be less apt to pervade the whole body of the Union than a particular member of it, in the same proportion as such a malady is more likely to taint a particular county or district than an entire State. In the *extent* and *proper structure* of the Union, therefore, we behold a Republic remedy for the diseases most incident to Republican government.[8] (Italics added.)

The two dimensions of Madison's argument are apparent in the italicized phrases. First, all interests or factions are seeking goals that are contrary to the public interest; they are thus a problem in need of a solution. Second, since suppression of these interests would be a cure that is worse than the disease, the only acceptable solution is to make the country so large and to cut it up into so many separate pieces that all the factions will remain too diffuse and too weak to impose their will upon the rest.

Business   Quite clearly the politics of business in our day is occupied primarily by sectors or special industries, or by trade associations representing the one or the other. For this reason there is a tendency among political scientists to see the Chamber of Commerce or the National Association of Manufacturers as paper tigers whenever they try to organize the entire business class, or bourgeoisie, of the nation.[9] However, this is a very short-sighted view based upon case histories drawn from the last forty years or so, when business has indeed been fighting against a retreat in the face of efforts to change its status as the dominant class. The pressure for these retreats has arisen as a reaction to the immensely successful nineteenth century political victories by business. The property laws treated in earlier chapters are certainly evidence of business success in politics. The considerable political cohesion within the bourgeoisie during that earlier period is evidenced in the gains made on virtually all those matters that are fundamental to capitalism, such as incorporation, banking, contract law, and the discouragement of trade unions.

Business was also successful at the national level, first by fighting off efforts to legislate against business interests and then by gaining legislation advantageous to business as a class. For example, although business groups failed to stop antitrust legislation, business did succeed in the passage of an act establishing the Federal Trade Commission, which was an approach to trade regulation that was almost a direct antidote to antitrust laws.[10] Business may have failed to stop the passage of an act creating a progressive income tax, but the degree to which the income tax structure favors

---

[8]Final paragraphs of *Federalist* No. 10.

[9]See, for example, a classic essay on the NAM by Richard W. Gable, "NAM: Influential Lobby or Kiss of Death?" *Journal of Politics* 15 (1953), 253–273. See also Raymond A. Bauer et al., *American Business and Public Policy* (Chicago: Aldine-Atherton, 1972), especially part 4.

[10]Gabriel Kolko, *The Triumph of Conservatism* (New York: Free Press, 1963).

business and commerce in the United States is quite well known.

There are at least three reasons why business so infrequently speaks as a class in the politics of our era. First, business is indeed more pluralistic now than ever before. The economy is much more specialized and differentiated; membership within each specialized interest within the business class is often more intensely felt than membership in the business community at large.[11] For example, the independent druggists or grocers or clothiers may hate the big discount stores far more than they hate the unions.

The second reason is in past success. As a class, business had achieved its major gains in the nineteenth century; the fundamental needs of business are already deeply imbedded in our laws and values. When we speak of ourselves as a business civilization or a capitalist system, we should understand that this means that the terms of conquest of our government are themselves very largely of a commercial nature. The job of business as a class is to keep things from happening. It has been argued by some that the real test of the business elite is not to be found in the study of policy decisions but rather in the study of the phenomenon they prefer to call policy *nondecisions*. The nondecision today is actually a successful effort to keep from reviewing an actual decision that was made at some earlier time.[12]

The third reason is the lack of cohesiveness of the class antagonists to business. The needs of agriculture, labor, the nonwhite races, the youth, the aging, and women are quite frequently antagonistic to business. To the extent that each of these interests finds it difficult to mobilize, business is saved from mobilizing as a class to defend itself. As we shall see, the Madisonian formula works very effectively against the mobilization of most of these interests.

Agriculture The political history of agriculture is an almost unbroken history of frustration. After the Civil War, agriculture in the United States was commercialized; that is to say, most farms became an investment represented by mortgages that had to be paid off, and most crops were grown for the purpose of being sold for cash on the market rather than for direct consumption by the farmer. One of the responses to this commercialization was a widespread effort to politicize agriculture, because commercialization never

---

[11]For the best treatments of this highly pluralistic aspect of business, see David Truman, *The Governmental Process: Political Interests and Public Opinion* (New York: Knopf, 1951); for an economist's view of the same, see John Kenneth Galbraith, *American Capitalism: The Concept of Countervailing Power* (Boston: Houghton Mifflin, 1952). See also Galbraith's more recent formulation in *Economics and the Public Purpose* (Boston: Houghton Mifflin, 1973), p. 108.

[12]Peter Bachrach and Morton Baratz, "The Two Faces of Power," *American Political Science Review*, December 1962, pp. 947–952.

The symbolic uses of power: Farm constituents dramatize their interests.

worked as well for agriculture as for industry and commerce.[13] The road into the twentieth century is paved with the vain efforts of agriculture to mobilize itself as one single and cohesive big interest. Important examples include the Grange, the Farmers Alliance, and the People's Party.[14]

As it turns out, agriculture is not a class in the same sense as business and labor in the United States. It is a big interest, but it cuts across class interests rather than paralleling them. There are, in fact, deep divisions of economic classes within agriculture; this is the major reason why agriculture has so rarely been able to cohere as one single big interest. In our day, the National Farmers' Union has attempted to speak for all the subsistence farmers and low-income commercial farmers. It carries on a program of encouraging cooperatives and fighting corporate farming and other forces that threaten the small farmer. But it finds itself in opposition to some of the most powerful farm interests in the country, and its appeals

[13]For the best brief treatment of the economics of agriculture and the factors leading to politicization, see Walter Adams, ed., *The Structure of American Industry,* 4th ed. (New York: Macmillan, 1971), chapter 1. See also Grant McConnell, *The Decline of Agrarian Democracy* (Berkeley: University of California Press, 1953).

[14]Sources include Solon J. Buck, *The Granger Movement* (Cambridge, Mass.: Harvard University Press, 1913); John D. Hicks, *The Populist Revolt* (Minneapolis: University of Minnesota Press, 1930); and McConnell, *The Decline of Agrarian Democracy.*

Incomplete Conquest: Politics

have been limited to only a few types of commodities in a limited geographic area of the United States.

The higher-income farmers—those who have succeeded in making the transition to commercial farming—belong to several types of farm organizations. The famous American Farm Bureau Federation claims to speak for all of agriculture. But the AFBF is a federation of state Farm Bureau organizations and spends as much time trying to keep these together as it does speaking effectively to the outside world. As a matter of fact, it has concerned itself with only a few specific issues rather than with the whole range of problems in agriculture. "The American Farm Bureau Federation, with a tinge of arrogance, asserts that it is the voice of the farmer. A powerful voice it is indeed, but it speaks principally for the corn and cotton farmer."[15] The AFBF has always fallen far short of integrating agriculture into one single big interest.

The only time in our history when we can truly say that agriculture managed to organize and to cohere as a single movement would be during the populist period of the 1880s and early 1890s. For that brief period it succeeded in dominating the political agenda of the national government and of the two major political parties. But it began to crumble as an effectual interest group as soon as the political parties, especially the Democratic Party, began to adopt most of the agriculture program. By the end of the 1890s there was no nationwide agriculture movement left. The Grange remained in certain midwestern states, and the AFBF emerged after 1914. What was left after the 1890s was a large number of special interests organized around each of the major commodities. Agriculture politics today is dominated by the activities of these special interests. Each is concerned with a small segment of the whole; none makes any effort to deal directly for all of agriculture.

Labor Labor is by definition and by common sense a basic economic class. But from the standpoint of political mobilization and cohesion, how much of a class is it? The National Labor Union tried to organize labor into a proletariat in the 1870s but lasted only long enough to dramatize the needs of labor. The Knights of Labor formed at about the same time, lasted longer, and came closer to success. However, this group also failed eventually, largely because the leadership could find no way to instill class consciousness and solidarity among laborers in all the various cities across the country. Other groups, notably the Molly McGuires, tried to take the leadership by militant action and violence. This seemed to work no better than peaceful action.[16]

---

[15]V. O. Key, *Politics, Parties, and Pressure Groups*, 5th ed. (New York: Crowell, 1964), p. 33. This volume is generally the best source for quick and accurate characterizations of most of the important traditional interest groups in the United States.

[16]The best study of these efforts will be found in John Laslett, *Labor and the Left* (New York: Basic Books, 1970).

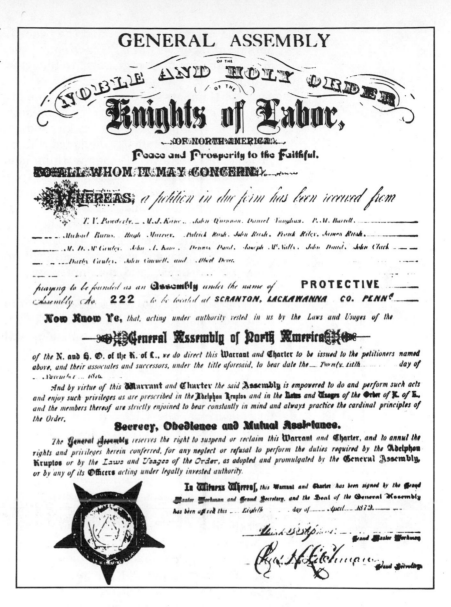

The rise of organized labor in the United States really began with the formation of the American Federation of Labor under the leadership of Samuel Gompers. Gompers's success, however, is attributable largely to his rejection of the concept of labor as a class. He directly and explicitly rejected class consciousness, political radicalism, anticapitalism, socialism, and all other available sources for a class appeal to labor in the United States. He turned instead toward a moderate reform position he called *business unionism,* which continues to characterize the AFL position today.

Business unionism actually begins with recognition of the validity of the capitalist system and the peaceful and cooperative membership of labor within it. This is one of the strongest confirmations of the witticism of George Bernard Shaw, that trade unionism is the "capitalism of the proletariat." The other important aspect of the secret of Gompers's successful technique in organizing labor was his strategy of building on craft unionism rather than industrial unionism. Gompers was not against industrial unionism in principle; in fact, he explicitly accepted the mine workers and their jurisdiction over all craftsmen working near the mines and opposed the ouster of another industrial union from the AFL, the Brewery Workers.[17] Yet neither Gompers nor his successors took any initiatives to organize industrial workers, while taking every sort of initiative to organize the skilled trades. As one expert put it in 1918, "The Federation remains, with the striking exceptions of the miners' and garment workers' organizations, mainly the organizations of the upper and medium strata among the native wage earners."[18]

These very limitations of the AFL eventually gave rise to a second effort to speak for labor as a class. The CIO had at first been a Committee on Industrial Organizations within the AFL but eventually split off because its principle of spreading identity consciousness to all workers regardless of skill, ethnic group, or working condition was alien to the traditional craft unions in the AFL. After its separate formation in 1935, as the Congress of Industrial Organizations, the CIO enjoyed a series of spectacular successes organizing workers in the mass production plants. But it has never come near the goal of reaching all of the laborers in the United States.[19]

In 1955 the two organizations merged to become the AFL-CIO; and yet this gigantic organization has never managed to solve the problems of cohesion that would make it a "House of Labor" in opposition to a "House of Capital." On many issues, such as international trade and tariffs, there is confusion and indecision in labor, leading to a mad scramble of every union leader for himself and his own union.[20] Even on the issue of labor-management relations and collective bargaining, labor has not been a solid front since the passage of the Wagner Act in the 1930s.[21] Indeed, according to one observer, "The fact is, there is not, and perhaps never has been, a labor 'movement' in this country. There is—and has been, at least since the days of the Depression—an inharmoni-

[17]See J. David Greenstone, *Labor in American Politics* (New York: Knopf, 1969), especially p. 23.
[18]Ibid., p. 24.
[19]Art Preis, *Labor's Giant Step* (New York: Pioneer Press, 1964).
[20]Bauer et al., *American Business and Public Policy*, chapter 22.
[21]For the story of Taft-Hartley and labor's incohesiveness in that intensive struggle, see Stephen K. Bailey and Howard Samuel, *Congress at Work* (New York: Henry Holt, 1952), chapter 15. See also Alan McAdams, *Power and Politics in Labor Legislation* (New York: Columbia University Press, 1964).

The assembly line: Are the interests of labor and capital contradictory?

ous group of autonomous unions capped with a purposely weak and ineffective superstructure, the parent federation."[22]

Labor has probably sought more intensely and ambitiously than business or agriculture to organize itself as a single class. There have been more labor militants than business or agriculture militants. And labor has been more willing to seek alliances with a single political party—even though it has never tried seriously to form a national labor party.[23] Nevertheless, labor is not, and has not been, a cohesive class organized in opposition to other big interests or, indeed, organized to further its own big interest. Labor as a class in the United States may be an especially significant illustration of the Madisonian formula. There is now and probably always has been a great deal of working-class consciousness in our country. The working class has many heroes, many theorists, and ample provocation in the ruthless march toward boring and routine work. But our working-class awareness simply has been cut through and pulled apart in all sorts of contrary directions by overlapping memberships, sectional and racial jealousies, the separation of skills from crafts, and religious conflict. In the 1880s no one would have been able to predict the outcome of a struggle for dominance between the socialist version of capitalism and the Madisonian version of a continental republic. The dispersion and incohesive nature of the labor movement suggest that Madison, not Marx, is having the last word. And the programs, ideologies, and strategies of contemporary unions range so greatly and conflict with each other so frequently that it may take some cataclysmic event to bring about real labor consciousness in the United States.

Some Other Big Interests

Labor, agriculture, and business are all aspects of one type of big interest—class. We have presented a more or less detailed discussion of these specific interests. Unfortunately, space does not permit us more than a brief look at some of the other big interests. Even a brief look, however, will provide a sense of their magnitude.

Religion   Among each of the three great Western religions in the United States, there have always been certain groups that claim to speak for the entire aggregate. Many of these groups are capable of a good deal more political solidarity than the groups identified immediately above that have claimed to speak for an entire economic class. There may be many reasons for this, but surely one of the most important is that issues involving the major religions almost

---

[22]The conclusion of McAdams in *Power and Politics in Labor Legislation,* p. 277, on the basis of his study of the Landrum-Griffin Act of 1959.

[23]A thorough account of this relationship between labor and the Democratic Party will be found in Greenstone, *Labor and American Politics.*

never get on the national agenda. As our review of the sources of public policy in chapter 5 showed, virtually all of the policies of most fundamental concern to the churches are made by the state legislatures. Moreover, these policies are either administered by state agencies or are delegated to local governments. Thus, the Big Three religions must be organized in the states and in the major cities if they are to have any regular influence on such matters as marriage, adoption, education, health and welfare, and parole. Rarely do the spokesmen for all of the major religions get together and speak as a single voice for religion as such. In fact, there are many issues on which they fight among themselves with great intensity. But each major religious grouping is frequently quite cohesive on the issues that most affect its adherents. Perhaps someday their solidarity will enable them to expend more energy on such social issues as race relations and the alleviation of poverty.

The veterans   There were nearly 29,000,000 veterans at the end of 1971. They constitute a substantial portion of the population and are represented by several of the most vocal organizations in the country. Often these groups differ with each other, but there are several major issues on which they are capable of speaking with a single voice. Each of these organizations emphasizes the importance of patriotism and the proper upbringing of American youth, flag etiquette, and other matters of public conduct. There are also several basic economic issues on which these groups are quite cohesive, even as they compete vigorously with each other for membership. The leading veterans' groups are the American Legion, the Veterans of Foreign Wars, the Disabled American Veterans, and the Amvets. When it comes to such important economic issues as veterans' retirement benefits, hospitalization benefits, insurance, special mortgages, and most of the provisions of the so-called GI Bill, these groups are cooperative and mutually reinforcing. Thanks to their support for and success in obtaining "veterans preference"—a system of adding points to the scores of veterans on the Civil Service Commission entrance examinations—the United States civil service, especially the Post Office, has almost become a United States veterans' service. Taking all of these achievements into consideration, veterans' organizations may have produced a political record better than that of groups speaking for any other big interest.[24]

Race   Since the beginning of the twentieth century there have been groups speaking effectively for all blacks. Yet rarely was there any attempt to create a real solidarity among all blacks, or to raise the level of black consciousness. There were a few efforts of that

[24]Davis Ross, *Preparing for Ulysses* (New York: Columbia University Press, 1969).

sort, most notably Marcus Garvey's movement in the 1920s; but most of the group effort on behalf of blacks has been for a segment of the black community a good deal smaller than the total. The most outstanding of these traditional groups, of course, has been the NAACP. It was joined somewhat later by the Urban League. Many black leaders, such as A. Philip Randolph, Bayard Rustin, and Martin Luther King, had very large and diffuse followings throughout the black community even though each had only a small organizational base. From their relatively narrow bases, the contribution of these individuals and groups to the welfare and to the consciousness of blacks has been almost immeasurable. Nevertheless, for purposes of political analysis it should be noted that these leaders were *speaking for* the large racial aggregate rather than actually *representing* or *organizing* a significant segment of that aggregate.[25]

The emergence of Martin Luther King and the Montgomery bus boycott in 1956 were the beginnings of new efforts to reach and to mobilize the entire black community as well as to speak for it or organize just a small segment of it. The effort began in the South, due largely to the fact that racial outrages were more explicit there. The credibility of such efforts surely was spread by the sit-ins, the marches, and the less planned and more violent ghetto riots. But none of these conditions would have produced a lasting mobilization of the race without effective *theory*—effective statements of the collective purpose, of the nature of black identity, and of the goals of the race at large. This side of racial organization probably began with the seasoned Congress of Racial Equality (CORE) and reached special heights of respect, good press, and effective organization with Martin Luther King's Southern Christian Leadership Conference (SCLC). It was followed by a succession of steps involving new organizations, some with more intensified special demands and others with greater concern for separatist theories and the need for separate identity. One such group which exercised a tremendous amount of initial influence in this transition, despite its narrow base in the South, was the Student Nonviolent Coordinating Committee (SNCC). Another such group concerned with a separate place for black power and black identity was the Nation of Islam (popularly known as the Black Muslims). Even the Black Panthers, probably the smallest of the splinter groups, managed to exert a considerable amount of influence on black and white society before the police and the FBI suppressed it.[26]

---

[25]Among the many books on blacks in America perhaps the best brief survey will be found in Eli Ginzberg and Alfred Eichner, *The Troublesome Presence* (New York: Free Press, 1964). One of the best cases of the single individual who can touch the entire mass of followers without organizing any of them is to be found in Malcolm X, with the assistance of Alex Haley, *The Autobiography of Malcolm X* (New York: Grove Press, 1965).

[26]A good review of these groups and their strategies and tactics will be found in Harold L. Wolman and Norman C. Thomas, "Black Interests, Black Groups, and Black Influence in the Federal Policy Process," *Journal of Politics*, November 1970.

Interest group access: Whitney Young, executive secretary of the National Urban League, and A. Philip Randolph, president of the Sleeping Car Porters Union, meet with President Johnson to discuss civil rights legislation.

From a larger perspective, the emergence of new groups of the latter sort amounts to a serious fragmentation. This same problem exists within virtually every big interest, but it is probably more serious here. Wage laborers have certainly been threatened historically with exploitation; however, the exploitation of wage laborers is on an individual-to-individual basis, with "class exploitation" being simply the result of the large-scale exploitation of individuals. In contrast, blacks have been exploited *as a collectivity,* as a group. Yet, it has nevertheless proven extremely difficult to create an awareness of race and of this collective exploitation among a very large proportion of individual blacks. Many blacks will express their support for famous black leaders, but how many of them are truly conscious of how much they share with others of their race and how many of them are willing to be mobilized and to expend any of their scarce resources on collective goals is quite another question. Support is one thing. Sharing, in the full sense of consciousness and membership, is quite another.

Recent movements Still other widely shared attributes are mobilized from time to time as big interests. During the 1960s there was a good deal of this sort of mobilization, which has been identified by sympathizers and opponents alike as "turmoil." General familiarity with these recent movements reduces our need for lengthy coverage. The emergence of women to consciousness of their position in society already seems to have caused something of a

Incomplete Conquest: Politics

social revolution even if an elaborate political program is never adopted in their behalf. As we mentioned earlier, by the time this book is published, women may have achieved their second constitutional amendment—the Equal Rights Amendment—which would prevent the United States or the state governments from making laws that discriminate on the basis of sex. Groups such as the National Organization for Women (NOW, formed in 1966) have been extremely effective on bread-and-butter issues of concern to women. But these groups have fallen far short of reaching the entire aggregate of women. Most of the leadership and the activists in the organizations that speak for women are middle- to upper-middle-class.[27]

From time to time we have seen the emergence of organizations and individuals who speak effectively for the most important mass, consumers. Ralph Nader, for example, has exerted enormous influence on behalf of consumers; yet Nader has never sought to create a mass consumers' organization. Apparently his books, articles, and appearances before congressional committees have been so well-prepared and have hit the mark so well on widely shared problems that Nader's small staff of hardworking, low-paid investigators ("Nader's Raiders") has sufficed without organizing a large movement.[28] The movements for population control and protection of the environment have each resulted as responses to mass sentiment triggered by one or more research reports published in some eloquent and widely marketed book.[29] Every once in a while there are other such cases where large aggregates of individuals are mobilized into big interests.

Political scientists make a mistake by not studying these movements with more care, because errors of great theoretical and practical significance can be made about these phenomena. On each such occasion the society and its government are taken almost completely by surprise; yet there is hardly a conceivable mass aggregate that has not been mobilized into a big interest at least once before. For example, the emergence of black consciousness was celebrated as if it were the first and only source of deliverance for the Negro race in America when actually it is, perhaps, the third such movement in the past century. Because the society is unpre-

[27]An excellent account of the development and significance of the feminist movement is by Alice Rossi, "Women: The Terms of Liberation," *Dissent,* November/December 1970, pp. 531–541. The most thorough account of the sources and strategies of the women's movement thus far is by Jo Freeman, *The Politics of Women's Liberation* (New York: David McKay, 1975).

[28]Among the many influential publications of Nader and his Raiders, probably the first was the most important: Ralph Nader, *Unsafe at Any Speed* (New York: Grossman, 1965). See also Mark Nadel, *The Politics of Consumer Protection* (Indianapolis: Bobbs-Merrill, 1971). For a study of another large interest, the aged, see Sheldon Messinger, "Organizational Transformation: A Case Study of a Declining Social Movement," *American Sociological Review* 20 (1955), 3–10.

[29]For example, Paul Erlich, *The Population Bomb* (New York: Ballantine, 1968). For a review of the literature concerned with the impact of these movements on governments, see Paul Sabatier, "Social Movements and Regulatory Agencies," *Policy Sciences,* Fall 1975 (forthcoming).

pared, its power structure tends to react to each movement with a
kind of siege mentality. The appeals that are necessary to convert a
large aggregate into a mobilized big interest will inevitably sound
threatening to existing institutions. Without a sense of history and
an appreciation of the recurrence of broad social movements, the
police tend to be activated, suppression tends to be justified, and the
sense of crisis is allowed to set our terms of public discourse.
Similarly, the lack of appreciation for the repetitiveness of social
movements tends to lead to the assumption that once the movement

Incomplete Conquest: Politics

is mobilized it will remain mobilized. Then, when it declines, as it inevitably does, there is great disappointment on the part of the sympathizers and a sense of relief on the part of the opposition, as though everything will thereafter return to the permanent status quo.[30] The disappointed sympathizers are led to the conclusion that the decline of their movement is evidence of the corruption of the society or the vanity of efforts to reform the society, or to the more specific notion that there was a conspiracy to kill the movement or its leaders.[31]

A broader view, a view that incorporates many of these efforts and places them in some kind of historical context, would lead to a slightly more balanced conclusion. This view would of course have to begin with a concession that established leaders will use every device in the books, legal and illegal, to prevent the mobilization of big interests or to avoid responding to the massive demands that big interests are likely to make when mobilized. It would also have to recognize that a big interest is exceedingly difficult to mobilize under any circumstances. Then, too, this broader, more historical view would have to take into account the fact that the most important and durable influences of the big interests often occur *while they are in the process of formation* rather than after a leadership group has been organized. Our most recent example of this is probably the Women's Liberation movement, which has brought a veritable revolution in sex, morality, and political leadership even during a period when many women's groups were still worrying over the identity and nature of the central leadership organization.[32]

Finally, care should be taken not to espouse too enthusiastically the principle that the big interests should be easier to organize or that the system ought to be more helpful and responsive to them. In the first place, the leaders of big interests must necessarily simplify their appeals to the indeterminate thousands or millions who share the unifying attribute which may be able to mobilize them; this always amounts to a misrepresentation and distortion of the real opinions of the members. In the second place, if the system were more responsive, it might choose to respond to just the wrong big interest. There is a certain wisdom in the Madisonian idea that all majorities are tyrannical. At least we can say that skepticism should precede responsiveness.

---

[30]For the cyclical quality of these movements, and the significance of it, see Marver Bernstein, *Regulating Business by Independent Commission* (Princeton: Princeton University Press, 1955).
[31]See, for example, the essays by Robert Paul Wolff and Herbert Marcuse in Wolff et al., *A Critique of Pure Tolerance* (Boston: Beacon Press, 1969).
[32]For a review of the difficulties of staging a movement, and for an identification of some of the classics in the literature, see Theodore Lowi, *The Politics of Disorder* (New York: Basic Books, 1971), chapters 1 and 2. See also Freeman, *The Politics of Women's Liberation.*

The Special Interests

Most of the types of special interests listed in column 2 of Table 6.1 are self-explanatory—sector, trade, occupation, neighborhood, cause, and sect. Some may not be familiar with *sector,* which in economics is usually a synonym for a basic industry, such as steel or textiles or utilities. *Trade* is sometimes used synonymously with sector, and at other times it refers to a commercial grouping, such as dry goods, or druggists, or people in the shoe business. It is sometimes used also to refer to a well-established occupation, in the sense of something one learns as an apprentice or in a trade school. Both of these examples serve as good illustrations of a special interest. By *cause*—the only other term which might be confusing—we usually mean a group organized to pursue a purpose that is not directly relevant to the economic positions or statuses of the members. For example, the American League to Abolish Capital Punishment is composed of members who are very unlikely ever to be hanged.[33]

These are the specialized subdivisions of society that are the typical basis for what are variously labeled special interests, pressure groups, or interest groups. All three of these labels are accurate. Seen together, they tell us a little something about ourselves. These terms imply that we are of two minds about special interests. We concede the right of individuals to organize and to pursue their own interests within such organizations; yet we cannot fully accommodate ourselves to the idea that special interests gain special privileges. That ambivalence colors all treatments of group interests and group politics.

Some of the better known special interest groups—for example, the American Petroleum Institute and the American Association of Newspaper Publishers—are composed of only a few hundred businesses and individuals who happen to occupy that sector or trade in the economy. Medicine is another narrowly defined activity or trade, as is typography; but the American Medical Association and the International Typographers Union, with their few thousands of members, have a long and impressive history of service to their members and of influence upon local, state, and national politics.[34] The small size of the typical specialized interest group is compensated for by cohesion. All the great size and great wealth in the world is no good to a group unless it has the ability to pull its members

---

[33]A very good treatment of groups that pursue special or general causes will be found in E. E. Schattschneider, *The Semi-sovereign People* (New York: Holt, Rinehart and Winston, 1960), chapter 2.

[34]The best history of the AMA, although dated, is Oliver Garceau, *The Political Life of the AMA* (Cambridge, Mass.: Harvard University Press, 1941). The ITU is a subject of one of the classic studies in sociology, *Union Democracy,* by S. M. Lipset, Martin Trow, and James Coleman (Glencoe, Ill.: Free Press, 1956).

Table 6.2   The Organized Interests: A Few Notable Washington Examples

Big Interests	Special Interests	Strategic Interests	General Cause Groups	Special Cause Groups
Chamber of Commerce, U.S.A.	American Bankers Association	Air Line Pilots Association	National Conference of Christians and Jews	Zero Population Growth, Inc.
Water Resources Congress	American Hot-Dip Galvanizers Association	Association of Oil Pipe Lines	Izaak Walton League	Zionist Organization
American Farm Bureau Federation	City of Philadelphia, Washington, D.C., office	Building and Construction Trades Department of AFL-CIO	Americans for Democratic Action	Federation of the Blind
National Federation of Business and Professional Women's Clubs	National Cotton Council	National Association of Real Estate Investment Trusts	John Birch Society	National Society, Daughters of the American Revolution
National Council on the Aging	Dairy Industry Committee	American Association of State, County and Municipal Employees		Diabetes Association
AFL-CIO	Disabled American Veterans	American Postal Workers		National Abortion Rights Action League
	Hawaiian Sugar Planters Association	Brotherhood of Locomotive Engineers	These two columns are extensions of columns 1 and 2, respectively. They are comprised of groups acting on behalf of interests other than their own.	
	Poultry and Egg Institute of America	Communications Workers of America		
	National Association of Retail Druggists			
	United Steelworkers			
	United Mineworkers			

Information from Washington, D.C., Yellow Pages; other examples are in the text.

together and to speak through its leadership as a single voice. Cohesion, the ultimate requirement, is the object of the tiny leadership group at the top of each of these organizations with its secretariat to maintain the office, print the newsletter, run the addressograph, etc.[35] Cohesion is the means by which size and wealth and any other resources are transferred into political power. It would take an entire book to identify the major special interest groups and their resources and activities.[36] In order to provide some sense of the range and variety of the most politically interesting groups, a tiny proportion are presented in Table 6.2.

A good example from among the largest and most notable of the special interests would be the National Association of Home Build-

---

[35]The classic study of organization in interest groups, especially concerning the natural tendency of interest groups toward oligarchy, is Robert Michels, *Political Parties,* trans. Eden and Cedar Paul (New York: Dover, 1959; first English translation published 1915).

[36]The most valiant effort to do this is by David Truman, *The Governmental Process.* A somewhat more recent effort is Harmon Zeigler, *Interest Groups in American Society* (Englewood Cliffs, N.J.: Prentice-Hall, 1964).

ers. This is one of the largest and certainly one of the richest special interest groups in the country. It will have vocal representation any time housing legislation is proposed in Congress, in the state legislatures, in the local or suburban city councils, or in any of the relevant administrative agencies, especially those that operate in the national Department of Housing and Urban Development. But the establishment of housing policy is not at all an everyday affair. Therefore, the headquarters of the NAHB spends the greatest proportion of its time serving the needs of its own members. Sociologists might call this *organization maintenance.* Only by these services can this organization be certain that it is ready and has sufficient cohesion to fight the political battles when they occur.[37]

Another good example, precisely because it is obscure in comparison to the NAHB, is the Porcelain Enamel Institute. Obscure indeed, but its members include General Electric and Westinghouse as well as many very small firms engaged in the production or processing of enamel-covered metals. This is an energetic trade association. Its involvements in politics are probably even more infrequent than those of the NAHB, but when it has acted as an interest group it has shown results. One of its triumphs, for example, has been its success in maintaining among all public housing agencies a building code specification against the use of plastic bathtubs and sinks.

It is no coincidence that trade associations parallel the rise of big industry in the United States. The growth of trade associations began in the late nineteenth century, when businesses had grown to the point where further success depended more upon market stability than upon market competition. (American business had five-year plans long before the Soviet government.) About this same time, federal and state laws were attempting to make many anticompetitive devices illegal. It had become illegal to reduce competition by agreements to buy out competitors (monopolies). It had become illegal to reduce competition by agreeing to exchange stock or directors or both (trusts). It had become illegal to apportion sales or geographic areas among competitors (pools). But it was *not* illegal for these competitors to form trade associations in order to control unethical practices or to share information on new technologies, on standardizing weights and sizes of items, or even on upcoming political issues. It was not necessarily illegal to pool research funds or to cooperate on advertising. Trade associations could and did do these things, engaging in political activity only infrequently. (The

---

[37]A general theory concerning the problems of building an organization and maintaining it will be found in Mancur Olson, *The Logic of Collective Action* (New York: Schocken Books, 1968). Olson also applies his theory very effectively to the problems of maintaining organization in the trade unions (chapter 3). Another good study of the internal life of groups will be found in Bauer et al., *American Business and Public Policy,* chapters 21–24.

forms of this political activity are treated in the next section of this chapter.)

Virtually every business is a member of at least one trade association in addition to other interest groups. We can almost define a sector as any business activity represented by a trade association! The last systematic census of trade associations was taken in 1940. At that time there were at least 12,000, of which more than 25 percent were national or international in scope.[38] We do not know the exact number today, but it is difficult to imagine that trade associations have declined in number or in importance. Trade unions are not appreciably different from business trade associations. The AFL-CIO is a big interest, but it is in turn composed of dozens of specialized interests, a few of which are listed in Table 6.2. Many of these unions work directly on Congress and government agencies without bothering to go through AFL-CIO headquarters at all. And like the business trade associations, much of the work of unions is internal, having little to do with politics or pressure group action. Most of the time of the union headquarters staff is spent on highly bureaucratic activity. They must keep careful records of all disputes and grievances; they must study closely the productivity and profits of management. They are constantly involved in job classification and reclassification. They must scrutinize the contract under which they are operating to see that its provisions are fulfilled by its own members as well as by management.

Even the most dramatic aspect of union life, the strike, is political in only the remotest sense of the word. In the normal case, the strike in the United States is a means of changing the terms of collective bargaining (see chapter 16). And as soon as the dramatic moments of bargaining and striking and contract signing are over, the rest of the contract period involves more of the bureaucratic burdens and a good deal less of the public and political activity. Politics may require steady vigilance, but it also requires only irregular and infrequent action. It is no wonder that the typical union delegates this activity to a special unit or relies upon the lobbyists of the AFL-CIO. It is also no wonder that the parent organization, AFL-CIO—the big interest—has great difficulty mobilizing unions when the moment comes for union-wide action.

The principles and patterns of organization in agriculture are highly comparable to those of business and labor. The major difference is that the sector that defines the most important special interests within agriculture is the *commodity*.[39] The farmers and a

---

[38]Donald C. Blaisdell, *American Democracy under Pressure* (New York: Ronald Press, 1957), p. 59. See also Temporary National Economic Commission, *Trade Associations Survey,* Monograph 18 (Washington, D.C.: Government Printing Office, 1941).

[39]For a good account of the commodity basis of agriculture organization, see McConnell, *The Decline of Agrarian Democracy.* See also Murray Benedict, *Farm Policies in the United States, 1790–1950* (New York: Twentieth Century Fund, 1953).

Organized interests: The
tip of the iceberg? An
excerpt from the
Washington, D.C., Yellow
Pages.

Associations

A Better Chance 1028ConnAvNW -------
A-C Pipe Producers Association
                    1875ConnAvNW-
AAR ------See Association of American Railroads
AARP--See American Association Of Retired Persons
A D A 1424 16thNw --------------
AFL-CIO Appalachian Council
                    1730 RI AvNW-
AFSCME Va Public Employees Council 30
        7617LittleRiverTrnpk Annandale-
AIM--------See Action For Independent Maturity
ALTA Legislative Reporting Service
                    1019 19thStNW-
A M V E T S 1710 RI AvNw -----------
AMVETS National Service Foundation
                    1710 RI AvNW-
ANACS
    P O Box 87 - Ben Franklin Station
        1329 E StNW ------------------
AOPA 7315WisAv Beth --------------
AOPA Service Corporation 5100WiscAvNw -
APPA Inc 3022 14thNe --------------
APRS-R 1730PaAvNW --------------
ASPO 1523 L StNW-----------------
A & T State University Alumni Assn
                    1810 15thNw-
Academy of Model Aeronautics
                    806 15thNw-
Academy Of Model Aviation
                    806 15thStNW-
Accrediting Commission for Business Schools
                    1730 M Nw-
Accuracy In Media Inc 777 14thStNW ---
ACTION FOR INDEPENDENT MATURITY
                    1909 K StNW-
Ad Hoc Committee Defense Of Life Inc
                    NatlPressBldg-

Allied Lines Rating Organization Of The D C
                    WoodwrdBg-
Almas Temple Aaonms 260 3½thStNE ---
America the Beautiful Fund 1501 H Nw --
AMERICAN ACADEMY OF CHILD
    PSYCHIATRY 1800 R StNW--------
AMERICAN ACADEMY OF ENVIRONMENTAL
    ENGINEERS 14211TravilahRd Rockvl-
American Academy Of Family Physicians
                    470L'EnfantPlz E SW-
AMERICAN ACUPUNCTURE COLLEGE
    Dr Della G Walker
    A Non Profit Organization
    Acupuncture Treatment - Theory -
    Practice
        147GranbySt NorfolkVa
    From DC And Va Suburban Telephones
    No Charge To Calling Party
    Ask Operator For ----------
American Advertising Federation
                    1225ConnAvNw
American Alliance For Health Physical Education
    And Recreation 1201 16thNW -------
American Annals Of The Deaf
                    5034WisAvNW-
American Anthropological Assn
                    1703 NH AvNw-
American Arbitration Association
                    1212 16thStNW-
American Arbitration Association-Public Sector
    Education 1212 16thStNW----------
American Assembly Of Collegiate Schools Of
    Business 1755MassAvNW -----------
AMERICAN ASSOCIATION FOR HIGHER
    EDUCATION 1DupontCirNW --------
American Assn For The Advancement Of Science
                    1515MassAvNW
American Association Of Advertising Agencies
                    1730 M StNW-

few basic processors of each commodity tend to organize around the needs of that commodity within the principal region or regions where it is produced. These various and numerous commodity organizations exist quite separately from one another and often compete against each other. They "seldom unite for legislative purposes."[40] Individual members of the commodity organizations may also be members of other farm groups, such as the American Farm Bureau Federation (AFBF), but as often as not the commodity organizations are thorns in the sides of the big agricultural associations. Farmers also organize in cooperatives in order to control the markets for their products. Locally these cooperatives operate like small business trade associations. In turn they form into potent national parent groupings, such as the National Cooperative Milk Producers Federation. Other groups follow the pattern of the AFBF and build upon the counties, where most of the state and national administration of government programs takes place. The National Association of Soil Conservation Districts, the Association of Land Grant Colleges and Universities, and the National Association of County Agricultural Agents are examples of very different agriculture groups organized along very similar lines.[41]

---

[40]Key, *Politics, Parties, and Pressure Groups*, p. 40.
[41]Grant McConnell, *Private Power and American Democracy* (New York: Knopf, 1966), chapter 7. See also Harmon Zeigler, *The Florida Milk Commission Changes Minimum Prices* (Tuscaloosa: University of Alabama Press, 1963).

Many special interest groups, like the American League to Abolish Capital Punishment, are not economically oriented at all. Some of these are *self-interested,* of course, but noneconomic—for example, the many organizations of churches. Another type of group would be the American Association of University Professors (AAUP), which is composed of people whose commitment to free speech and civil liberties is extremely strong but who are also concerned with defending the ability of their members to earn a decent living. In contrast, there are groups like the American Civil Liberties Union (ACLU), whose members are people who will probably never get into trouble for using their right to free speech but who are committed to strong judicial and political protections of the unpopular speeches that might be made by others. ACLU thus comes close to being a pure case of a "special cause" group. Other such groups have worked hard to eliminate child labor. There have been groups to get us into, and out of, the United Nations. There are groups to legalize marijuana, abortion, and prostitution whose members have little, if any, selfish personal interest in the outcome.

It is of course extremely difficult in many specific instances to determine whether a particular group is motivated by unselfish or selfish causes. At least it can be said that most groups are likely to be most effective when they combine broad causes with personal causes. This has already been true of many groups, such as ethnic and religious groups. Some of the most important advances in American law have been made by Jehovah's Witnesses, Jews, blacks, and Italians, whose religious organizations and antidefamation leagues have fought for larger causes even as they were fighting for the very personal interests of their members. It is important to note that in our effort to be sophisticated and objective about politics and conquest, we should not underestimate the political potency of unselfish causes.

Strategic Interests and Strategic Groups

Strategic groups are special interest groups so sensitively located that they tend to have an intensely strong self-consciousness and a comparatively high level of status and power. For these reasons they deserve to be singled out, although organizationally they are indistinguishable from most other special interest groups. The idea of a strategic interest can be dramatically portrayed by the impact of a single airplane hijacking. One person in one airplane or with one threat can bring the entire industry to a standstill. An example of the numerous strategic groups in our society is the Teamsters Union. It sits astride the neck of the bottle that is the entire transportation industry, and its opportunity to exert influence has not gone unnoticed in the transport industry or in government. This is probably why the federal government under Attorney General

Strategic interests:
Federal troops move the
mail when postal workers
go on strike.

Robert F. Kennedy declared war on Jimmy Hoffa, the head of the
Teamsters Union at that time, rather than on some other equally
controversial labor leader.[42] Another important example would be
the building trades unions, which many people in business and in
local government feel, with considerable justification, enjoy a
stranglehold position in many cities. Their influence on industry
and on the cost of labor is generated from the vital position of
skilled trades throughout the rest of the urban economy.[43]

Other strategically placed occupations whose unions have been
noted for special identity-consciousness and solidarity include the
railroad workers, the communications workers, and the transit
workers. There are many strategic occupations outside the area of
wage labor. The county, state, and national associations of doctors
have enjoyed tremendous sway in all matters concerning themselves. There is also the large and very sensitive area of public
employment. In the past twenty years or so, there has been a
significant increase in the degree to which public school teachers,
police, firefighters, and sanitation workers have organized themselves in order to exert direct influence over politics and the
economy in the cities and states.

These services, conduits, and channels are strategic because so

---

[42]For the best account of this declaration of war, see Victor Navasky, *Kennedy Justice* (New
York: Atheneum, 1971), especially chapter 9. For Kennedy's own account and justification, see
Robert F. Kennedy, *The Pursuit of Justice* (New York: Harper & Row, 1964), especially chapter 1.

[43]For an evaluation of the building trade unions by the main consumers of their services, see
Fortune, December 1968 and October 1970.

many other economic and social functions must depend on them, must go through them, or must gain their cooperation. For this reason there has generally been a tendency to treat them distinctly in public policy. We expect a special responsibility from these strategic groups, even though we don't always get it. For example, it is unlikely that the Teamsters have been more corrupt or more self-indulgent than other unions; yet they have come in for a far higher share of public scrutiny than most unions or other groups.

In order to head off some of the special influence—some would call it blackmail—of these strategically located groups, we generally try to convert the functions they perform into public functions. This comes closer to guaranteeing us that these services will be performed and these channels will be kept open, because very few public employees have the right to strike. Cities have a long history of public ownership of local transit facilities, for example, despite the preference in the United States for private enterprise. Electricity and other power sources are treated to the special status of "utilities," whenever they are not owned outright by the public. This is for the same reason. And whether the function is public or private, there is a tendency in these areas to restrict the right to strike. In fact, the eighty-day "cooling off" period under the Taft-Hartley Act was fairly clearly provided in order to deal with these strategic functions and channels in our society. Under the Taft-Hartley Act and also under war and emergency powers, the president can forcibly terminate a strike or seize and operate the industry or service in question if in his judgment these actions are necessary to meet a national emergency.

If there is going to be an increase in the number of strategic channels, functions, and conduits in our society, there is also likely to be a decrease in the political and economic rights that these occupations will enjoy. If these restrictions are already the case for thousands of communications workers, construction workers, public service workers, and transport workers, one can begin to imagine how many additional persons and groups will be affected when the nation becomes even more highly interdependent, thanks to the computer and other aspects of electronic communication. In fact, it will probably soon be possible for a very small group of computer experts to bring an entire banking system to a halt. They will not need picket lines or very much planning to do the job. Will their right to political action be even more restricted than all strategic workers who have come before? Will the public have or exert the right to keep the conduits and channels open?[44]

We cannot adequately deal with these kinds of questions here. We

[44]For a fascinating scenario, see the novel by Kurt Vonnegut, *Player Piano,* new ed. (New York: Holt, Rinehart and Winston, 1966).

ask them only to emphasize the intimate relationship between groups and politics, and groups and rights. This situation seems even more complicated after an identification and analysis of the strategies that these groups employ in their effort to transfer their resources into political power.

STRATEGY: THE SEARCH FOR POWER

Historically *strategy* was a term associated with acts of government, especially military government. The *strategos* was an Athenian unit of government headed by a *strategia,* who was in effect a military commander-in-chief elected by a show of hands of the citizens. The term has now come to cover any and all types of maneuver oriented toward a goal. But when we are in the context of interest groups seeking political power, it is good to recall the original definition. The political strategy of an interest group refers to all those actions oriented toward summoning and utilizing the resources of the group for purposes of influencing government.

Actually the strategies available to any group are very limited in number and variety. Since there is no established way to classify strategies, we will employ a very permissive classification here: going public, lobbying, establishing access, going partisan, using the courts, and using bribery. Surely this does not exhaust all the possibilities, and very often in the real world one of these strategies blends into another, but these distinctions among strategies will be useful in our effort to identify and assess the ways groups go about maximizing their power.[45]

Going Public

Going public means attempting to mobilize the widest possible favorable climate of opinion. Many groups consider it imperative to maintain a favorable climate of opinion at all times, even when a specific campaign of influence is not being cooked up. Increases in this kind of strategy since the birth of modern advertising shortly before World War I led one of the leading political analysts of the 1930s to make a distinction between the "old lobby" of group representatives around Congress and the "new lobby" of public relations men addressing the public at large.[46]

The American Medical Association has been one of the most spectacular and effective users of public strategies to build up a

---

[45]The best general treatment of strategies among interest groups will be found in Truman, *The Governmental Process,* chapters 8–15. See also Schattschneider, *The Semi-sovereign People,* and Ziegler, *The Florida Milk Commission Changes Minimum Prices.*

[46]E. Pendleton Herring, *Group Representation before Congress* (New York: McGraw-Hill, 1936), pp. 30 and 59.

Could America run out of electricity?

America depends on electricity. Our need for electricity actually doubles about every 10 or 12 years.

Can we keep meeting this need year after year?

It depends on what we do in the next few years.

We have the technology to make all the electricity we need. About 85% of our electricity is made simply by boiling water to make steam to turn a turbine.

But it takes fuel to boil water. Coal. Oil. Gas. Uranium. And now some of our fuels are in short supply. Oil and natural gas, for example.

OIL COAL WATER URANIUM GAS

Almost any fuel can make electricity.

We have to continue the search for new oil and gas reserves. But we can't depend on them alone. Many experts believe we have already found most of the oil and gas that will ever be found in the U.S.

We are going to have to rely more and more on our resources that are in ample supply.

Coal and nuclear fuel, for example.

We are going to have to build more nuclear power plants. And new, more efficient coal-burning power plants.

General Electric has been working to do both. Since the first nuclear plant 18 years ago, GE has been working with utilities building nuclear power plants across the country and around the world. GE has also designed power plants that will squeeze more electricity out of every lump of coal.

Someday, our electricity may come from the sun.

But we have to use this electricity and all our resources wisely. And continue to look for new ways to make electricity.

Because America depends too much on electricity to ever run out.

Progress for People.

GENERAL ⓖⒺ ELECTRIC

---

specific campaign for or against a given policy issue.[47] More subtle but nevertheless effective uses of public strategies have been associated for many years with some of the largest business corporations and business groups in the country. One of the most ubiquitous forms is institutional advertising. A casual scanning of the most important mass circulation magazines will provide innu-

---

[47]For a careful study of these techniques and how they are employed by the AMA as well as other organizations, see Stanley Kelley, *Professional Public Relations and Political Power* (Baltimore: Johns Hopkins Press, 1956). More recent coverage will be found in Raymond Tatalovich, "After Medicare: Political Determinants of Social Change in the American Medical Association" (Ph.D. diss., University of Chicago, 1971).

merable examples. Automobile and steel companies are regularly buying expensive and well-designed ads to show how much they are doing to protect the environment or to provide more creature comforts. One of the most notable examples is the long series of very expensive ads produced for the Container Corporation of America. Most of each ad is devoted to a beautiful painting and a quotation from some famous philosopher or scientist about progress or social change or revolution. The company simply associates itself with these sentiments. The purpose is to create and maintain a strongly positive association in the community at large in hopes that the favorable feelings can be drawn upon as needed for specific political campaigns later on.[48]

Going public is not a strategy limited to business or upper-middle-class professional groups. Quite the contrary, it can sometimes be the only method available to a group which lacks the resources or the access to choose other political strategies. Strikes by unions are often used as a political weapon. A strike is very often employed simply to reinforce the credibility of union strength; memory of a recent strike may last through several contract periods. A strike will also be resorted to on occasion in hopes that the government will be forced to intervene and impose a settlement. Strikes may cause a great deal of anti-union feeling in the public at large, but at the same time they can very well impress a very wide segment of the wage-earning community as to the power and effectiveness of organizations which represent them or hope someday to do so.[49] Any group will at times toy with the idea of going public to enhance or expand its political position. But our examples here are sufficient to suggest the risks and the costs of this kind of strategy.

Lobbying

To adhere more closely to the language of the Constitution, this strategy should be called petitioning; but somehow, as early as the 1870s, lobbying became the common term. Lobbying is now an officially accepted designation for the act of petitioning legislators. The Federal Regulation of Lobbying Act—which is actually Title III of the Legislative Reorganization Act of 1946—defines the lobbyist rather than lobbying itself: "Any person who shall engage himself for pay or any consideration for the purpose of attempting to

---

[48]For an excellent study of the risks of going public, see Andrew Hacker, "Pressure Politics in Pennsylvania: The Truckers versus the Railroads," in *The Uses of Power,* ed. Alan F. Westin (New York: Harcourt, Brace & World, 1962).

[49]For an excellent account of the American labor movement and why it did not develop a full and sophisticated theory of the strike as a political weapon, see Marcus G. Raskin, *Being and Doing* (New York: Random House, 1971), chapter 3. For an account of some occasions where the strike was used effectively for political purposes in the United States, see Greenstone, *Labor in American Politics,* especially chapters 2–3; see also chapter 11 for an evaluation of the problems of labor in a fully industrialized society.

influence the passage or defeat of any legislation of the Congress of
the United States." The provision goes on to require that each such
person register with the clerk of the House of Representatives and
the secretary of the Senate. (Registered lobbyists and their groups
are regularly reported in the *Congressional Quarterly,* an indispensable source of research on policy making and lobbying in the
United States.)

This implies that the American public tends to consider lobbying
a problem in need of some kind of regulation. Since the First
Amendment guarantees the right of speech and petition, organized
efforts to influence legislators or administrators cannot be prevented or even seriously limited. The regulation of lobbying must rely
upon publicity only. The assumption is that if persons have to reveal
their activity, they will limit and regulate themselves. We require
lobbyists to register and to report their expenditures and their
clientele. We would probably go further if we thought the First
Amendment would allow it. But in *United States* v. *Rumely,* 345
U.S. 41 (1953), the Supreme Court held that Congress could not
regulate groups or lobbyists if they were trying to influence public
opinion in general rather than to persuade Congress directly. This
meant that ads in *Fortune* against "creeping socialism," or the
printing and distribution of millions of newsletters and circulars
against national health insurance or guaranteed wages would not
be considered lobbying, and would therefore not come under the
regulations of the act of 1946.

As defined in the 1946 act and as understood in everyday political
life, lobbying is activity that takes place in lobbies and other public
meeting places. It can involve intimate relationships; but in thou-

sands of instances lobbying simply involves a great deal of energetic activity on the part of someone speaking in behalf of an interest. The lobbyist badgers and buttonholes the legislator or administrator or committee staff with facts about the pertinent issues and the public support concerning those issues. The lobbyist is thus often useful in acquainting members of Congress with new facts or new slants. In turn, the sophisticated member of Congress is usually quite dubious about any claims lobbyists might make for the amount of support or the size of the group they represent.[50] Lobbying has an undeserved reputation for effectiveness. This is probably because there is a tendency to confuse lobbying with one or more of the other strategies of group participation in the political process. As observed earlier, lobbying is quite a sporadic activity for most of the big trade associations and unions. Many of these groups do maintain a paid lobbyist in Washington and in the state capitals, but the pattern is very uneven and very difficult to generalize. The instances of great effectiveness or of great corruption—we have had many of these since the Watergate exposures—have contributed to the reputation of lobbying and to our efforts to regulate the lobbyist. But more perspective is needed.

Table 6.3 provides a statistical impression of the very uneven and unstable business of lobbying. These figures are based upon a study of lobbyists published by Lester Milbrath in 1963.[51] Perhaps the single most indicative figure in Table 6.3 is the first one, which does not appear in the Milbrath book. About three years following the completion of Milbrath's interviews, I attempted to conduct a follow-up interview with these same lobbyists. To my great surprise, well over one-third of the 114 lobbyists in the original study had left Washington without a trace. They had left no forwarding address, and since local post offices maintain forwarding information for at least eighteen months, it seemed fairly certain that these people had not remained in Washington for very long beyond the time they were first interviewed. Perhaps still more significant is the fact that many of their Washington addresses were apartments or residential hotels rather than standard offices in the center city. All of this suggests that their involvement as Washington lobbyists was short and specialized. Lobbyists simply do not constitute a separate and stable industry in Washington, nor do they belong to some larger political community in Washington. They seem to be sent there to do a specific job and to return to the hinterlands once that job is completed.

[50]The best direct look at lobbying tactics will be found in the numerous case histories that political scientists and journalists have published over the years. A good collection of such cases is Bailey and Samuel, *Congress at Work*. A more recent collection is that of John Bibby and Roger Davidson, *On Capitol Hill*, 2d ed. (Hinsdale, Ill.: Dryden Press, 1972).

[51]Lester W. Milbrath, *The Washington Lobbyist* (Chicago: Rand-McNally, 1963). Although his data are now well over a decade old, the situation does not appear to have changed appreciably since that time.

Table 6.3

The Washington Lobbyists: Profile of an Unstable Industry

Is lobbying a stable industry?
35% had left Washington, with no forwarding address,
3 years or less after interview.

Is lobbying a profession?
70% were actual salaried lobbyists
29% lobbied on a fee or fee and expense basis

49% depended upon lobbying for 95% or more of their total yearly income
26% depended upon lobbying for 50-95% of their total yearly income
23% depended upon lobbying for less than 50% of their total yearly income

Are lobbyists seasoned politicians?
78% had no previous Capitol Hill experience prior to becoming lobbyists
43% had no direct government experience at all

Are lobbyists card-carrying members of the groups they represent?
53% yes
47% no

From Lester W. Milbrath, *The Washington Lobbyist* (Chicago: Rand-McNally, 1963); however, the interpretation here is novel; Milbrath would not necessarily agree in every respect.

Other figures in the table suggest that even the people who continue to function as lobbyists for more than a couple of years do not build much of a stable industry. Nearly half of all the lobbyists interviewed by Milbrath received income for work other than lobbying, and nearly a quarter of the lobbyists earned more than half their annual income from work other than lobbying. Many of them had no relationship to the group they represented except the fee or salary they received. An even larger number, 47 percent, could not even claim membership in the group whose interests they spoke for before congressional committees or administrative agencies. Another very surprising fact is that 74 percent had attempted to engage in lobbying without any prior knowledge of Congress, and 40 percent had had no direct experience with governments at all.

Here is the picture presented by these figures. When groups send their own loyal members to lobby for them, they are sending dedicated people with very little knowledge or experience regarding Washington and national politics. When groups choose to use more influential lobbyists, they pick people with a considerable amount of knowledge and political experience, politicians or Washington career lawyers, for example, who have no close relationship, if any, to the group itself. This latter factor may be one of the sources of misgivings about lobbying in the United States. Lurking somewhere in our subconscious is probably a sense that the most influential lobbyists care only for income and not for the interests they are there to represent. Americans are very tolerant about

Table 6.4	Washington Lawyer-Lobbyists: A Selection of Notables, Their Public Experience, and Their Specialties	
	Former Public Office	**Firm and Specialty**
William P. Rogers	Nixon Secretary of State Eisenhower Attorney General	Rogers and Wells—antitrust, international bankruptcy, insurance tax law, securities
Clark Clifford	Johnson Secretary of Defense	Clifford, Warnke et al.—general practice for such clients as Time, duPont, GE, ITT, ABC, Standard Oil
Mortimer Caplin	Kennedy Commissioner of Internal Revenue Service	Caplin and Drysdale—federal tax practice, corporations, securities, antitrust
Sheldon Cohen	Johnson Commissioner of Internal Revenue Service	Cohen and Uretz—federal tax practice and appeals
Lee C. White	Johnson Chairman of Federal Power Commission	White, Fine and Ambrose—federal power law
Bruce Clubb	Johnson and Nixon Commissioner of U.S. Tariff Commission	Baker and McKenzie—international trade and taxation
Abe Fortas	Roosevelt Securities Exchange Commission, Johnson Justice of the Supreme Court	Fortas and Kaven—securities law, trade regulation, corporate law (see also Table 6.8)
Charles Murphy Joseph Goldman	Truman and Johnson members of Civil Aeronautics Board	Partners in Morison, Murphy et al.—aviation law, securities, federal trade
Lawrence Silberman	Nixon Undersecretary of Labor	Steptoe and Johnson—labor law, securities, antitrust, insurance

interests but may not be comfortable unless each interest is represented by someone who really identifies with it. Yet there are the two kinds of communities of lobbyists. One is the amateur, the bird of passage. The other is the experienced but uncommitted professional; it is this latter type who gives lobbying its reputation.

Lobbying is of course only one small part of what the professional lobbyists do in Washington.[52] Very few of those who live permanently in Washington are full-time lobbyists. A very large number of them, particularly the highest paid and most prominent, are practicing lawyers who may occasionally take on the role of lobbyist for one or two clients (see Table 6.4). Much of their work is honest professional representation before courts and administrative agencies. And a lot of their work involves simply providing access to these governmental bodies for clients, an activity which is often confused with lobbying.

[52]This is certainly not exclusively a Washington phenomenon. Even though the discussion and the illustrations here are drawn from Washington, the practices are probably identical in all of the state capitals and probably around the city halls of the country as well.

Access

Access is often the outcome of successful lobbying, but access and lobbying ought not to be confused. The fact is that many interest groups resort to lobbying only when they have no access and insufficient time to develop it. Lobbying is an effort to communicate information and influence to a leader independent of the lobbyist. Access is a more intimate relationship involving close mutual identification rather than mere communication. Despite all this apparent intimacy, access is nevertheless a strategy. Many people come to have access by inheritance or an effortless process of proximity to power. But for the normal run of interest groups, access is the result of a decision to take the time and effort to cultivate belongingness within the inner councils. This often requires the sacrifice of short-run influence. For example, many of the most important organized commodity interests in agriculture devote far more of their time in the constituencies cultivating state agriculture schools and county agents than they do in Washington buttonholing members of Congress or bureaucrats. This way they have a chance of electing a "corn congressman" or a "wheat senator" who can exercise influence *in* the appropriate legislative committee rather than merely *on* that committee with petitions and dinner parties.

Figure 6.1 provides three sketches of the access pattern as this has been classically developed in agriculture. Each pattern is almost literally a triangular shape, with one point in a program in the executive branch, another point in a Senate or House legislative committee or subcommittee, and the third point in some highly stable and well-organized grass-roots interest group. Each point in this triangular relationship is mutually supporting. Each is indispensable to the other. But this is something that requires years to build. For example, the location of one point of the pattern in a legislative committee or subcommittee requires that at least one member of that committee or subcommittee build up very high seniority. This requires well over ten years of continuous service on a committee that is relevant to the interest in question (see chapter 11).[53]

It has often been said that agriculture "writes its own ticket." This is only a slightly exaggerated account of the history of agriculture legislation during the past forty years. The access pattern that has made this possible has also enabled agriculture politics to work in a virtual public opinion vacuum. It is no paradox that agriculture can manage to maintain high price supports even during inflationary periods. It is no paradox that tobacco farmers have continued to get their special supports even after tobacco has

[53]For more on these triangular access patterns, see Theodore Lowi, *The End of Liberalism* (New York: Norton, 1969), chapter 4.

**Figure 6.1
Triangular trade in
agricultural politics**

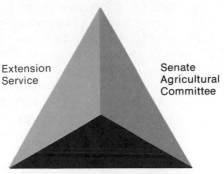

Extension
Service

Senate
Agricultural
Committee

American Farm Bureau Federation;
National Association of Land
Grant Colleges and Universities

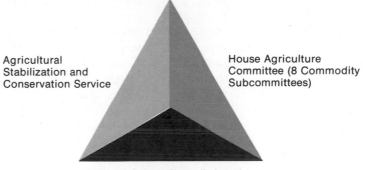

Agricultural
Stabilization and
Conservation Service

House Agriculture
Committee (8 Commodity
Subcommittees)

National Cotton Council; American
Wool Growers Association

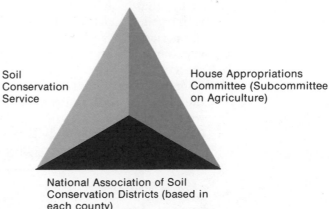

Soil
Conservation
Service

House Appropriations
Committee (Subcommittee
on Agriculture)

KEY

Program or Agency

Group Support

Special
Congressional
Access Point

National Association of Soil
Conservation Districts (based in
each county)

been declared hazardous to health. There are far fewer instances of successful access in labor politics. This may be due to the relative recency of labor's emergence into national politics. It may be due to some residual class consciousness or fear of social rejection. Or it may be due to faith in the efficacy of other political strategies.

The access strategy is not played universally among all business interests. But outside the field of agriculture, the classic cases of access politics will probably be found in business relationships to defense and military programs. The *military-industrial complex* is a popular label for access politics in this area of public policy. President Eisenhower formulated this notion in his farewell address, and almost immediately it became a weapon of criticism against many of Eisenhower's strongest supporters. Over four years before that farewell address, a subcommittee of the House Armed Services Committee conducted a survey of the postmilitary careers of retired armed forces officers above the rank of major. This survey disclosed that more than 1,400 officers, including 261 at the rank of general or its equivalent in the navy, left the armed forces for employment by one of the hundred leading defense contractors.[54]

Figure 6.2 provides three examples of the triangular access pattern among major defense agencies. A more concrete example of the actual interchange of personnel would be the General Dynamics Corporation of a scant few years ago when it was headed by a former secretary of the army (Frank Pace) and staffed at the top by 187 Pentagon retirees, including 27 generals and admirals. These access strategies beginning in the mid-1950s obviously paid off handsomely. By the end of fiscal year 1972 (June 30, 1972) General Dynamics ranked third among the top ten defense contractors, with government contracts amounting to $1,289,167,000.

Although federal law provides for a two-year period following retirement from active duty before military retirees can return to Washington as direct representatives of a private industry, there is no law that prohibits them from taking gainful employment. These retiring military officials simply stay out of direct contact during the period covered by law, but are in the meantime free to take the very same jobs in private industry they had held at a high level in the Pentagon—for example, research director, development supervisor, designer, comptroller, systems analyst. This access pattern in the military-industrial complex also flows in the opposite direction, with many civilians coming from Wall Street and the major industries to take top civilian positions in military and defense agencies. The typical secretary of defense has been a man like

---

[54]A challenging treatment of this will be found in Jack Raymond, *Power at the Pentagon* (New York: Harper & Row, 1964). See also Leonard Riessman, "Life Careers, Power and the Professions," *American Sociological Review,* April 1956, pp. 215–221. For a broad interpretation of the meaning of this interchange of personnel, see C. Wright Mills, *The Power Elite* (New York: Oxford University Press, 1956).

Figure 6.2
Triangular trade in
defense

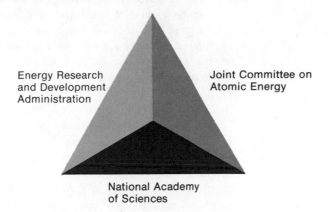

Energy Research
and Development
Administration

Joint Committee on
Atomic Energy

National Academy
of Sciences

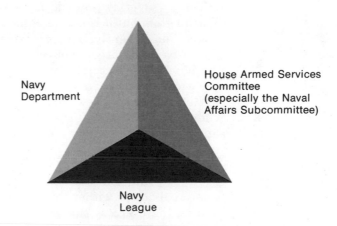

Navy
Department

House Armed Services
Committee
(especially the Naval
Affairs Subcommittee)

Navy
League

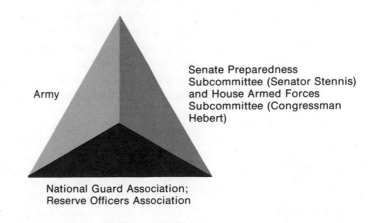

Army

Senate Preparedness
Subcommittee (Senator Stennis)
and House Armed Forces
Subcommittee (Congressman
Hebert)

National Guard Association;
Reserve Officers Association

KEY

Department or Agency

Group Support

Special
Congressional
Access Point

Charles Wilson of General Electric, Neil McElroy of Proctor and Gamble, or Robert McNamara of Ford Motor Company.[55]

In spite of all the interchange of personnel underlying the access strategy in the defense policy areas, the mainstay of access politics in most other areas is not the civilian who takes the government job or the government official who retires to a civilian job but the professional influence peddler. Influence peddling is simply a bad name for a typical function being performed in Washington (and in the state capitals) by retired members of Congress or lawyers of long and high standing in the political community. A standard joke about retiring and defeated Congressmen is, "They never go back to Pocatello." It is well known that the senior partnerships of the top law firms in Washington are heavily populated with former government officials. Many of them practice law before the very commissions on which they once served as a commissioner or executive director (refer again to Table 6.4).[56]

These "superlawyers" do indeed enjoy a great deal of access in Washington, but it is not necessarily transferable to each and every client. Consequently, the access strategy can end up simply being an expensive and rather ineffective form of lobbying. That is to say, many groups and corporations operate as though they are buying the exclusive services of a high-access influence peddler when they are only getting a few moments of time as one of many political clients. The name of the superlawyer may gain the necessary appointments to see the influential officials, and this can be important. But often this gives the interest groups a false sense of confidence in their own strategy when the access they have gained is, in fact, only nominal. On the other hand, once a group has gained some real access, either through a superlawyer or through its own efforts, these access channels are likely to be guarded extremely carefully. This real access can even limit the willingness of these interests to engage in more public forms of politics, for fear that the publicity might destroy the access. For example, during the anti-ballistic missile (ABM) debate in 1969/70 the top ABM contractors sought to avoid open lobbying in favor of the ABM for fear that their interest in the contracts would be revealed. At least three of the top twelve defense contractors (Motorola, GE, and Lockheed) became members of a front organization called, significantly, the

---

[55]Ibid.; also Raymond, *Power at the Pentagon*. For more recent and more critical insights, see Richard J. Barnet, *The Economy of Death* (New York: Atheneum, 1969); and Adam Yarmolinsky, *The Military Establishment* (New York: Harper & Row, 1971). It is enjoyable to trace out these access patterns for oneself. All one need do is consult the *Government Organization Manual*, locate the current occupants of high government office, and then check out their backgrounds in *Who's Who in America*.

[56]There is an excellent review of this in Sheldon Zalaznick, "The Small World of Big Washington Lawyers," *Fortune*, September 1969. A more recent treatment will be found in Joseph C. Goulden, *The Superlawyers* (New York: Weybright and Talley, 1972).

American Security Council and quietly helped finance the ABM lobby through the ASC.[57]

Going Partisan

Many interest groups travel the partisan route for short distances by appearing before the platform committees and the nominations committees of the presidential conventions of the two major parties. Sometimes this can be effective, as in the case of Alben Barkley in 1952, whose campaign for the Democratic presidential nomination was vetoed by a coalition of spokesmen for important trade unions. Other groups try partisanship at local levels, seeking to influence the nomination or election of legislators, or seeking to get existing legislators to commit themselves on some important public policy. But very few groups have gone the full partisan route of associating themselves completely with one political party. A few important unions have gone this direction; this has been an effective and an enthusiastically embraced strategy on the part of the United Auto Workers, and as one would expect, the strategy has worked for them especially well in Michigan, the automobile capital of the world.[58]

By far the most common example of the partisanship strategy is the interest group financial contribution to a party or an election candidate. Since this so easily crosses the threshhold of unfair advantage or outright bribery, efforts have been made to regulate the strategy. Laws seek to prevent contributions to political campaigns by corporations; laws seek to limit severely the ability of trade union treasuries to cough up funds for campaigns. In 1971 Congress sought to go farther than ever to curb abuses in campaign financing by legislation designed to force disclosure and publication of all campaign contributions regardless of the source. The Federal Election Campaign Act of 1971 requires that each campaign committee or candidate itemize the full name and address, occupation, and principle business of each person who contributes more than $100. These provisions seem to have been effective up to a point, because publicity regarding these practices can be severely punitive. Beyond that, their effectiveness can be measured in the rather large number of indictments and resignations, and even in a few convictions, in the aftermath of Watergate. Watergate can be said to have begun with campaign abuses, and these would have constituted a scandal of almost historic proportions even if Nixon's

---

[57]*Congressional Quarterly Weekly Reports,* January 1970, p. 70. Another example would be the subdued role of duPont and other giant corporations in the battle over international trade in the late 1950s and early 1960s. For that story see Bauer et al., *American Business and Public Policy.* At the end of this chapter there will be more commentary on how the adoption of one strategy can limit the freedom to adopt other strategies.

[58]The leading study of labor and the partisanship strategy is that of Greenstone, *Labor and American Politics.*

Table 6.5		Interest Group Support of Party Campaigns: A Survey of Thirteen Selected Trade Associations			
		Amount Contributed			
	Year	Republicans	Democrats	Miscellaneous	Total
	1972	$3,324,583+	$339,950+	$32,206	$3,696,740+
	1968	1,132,982+	136,106	11,967	1,281,055+
	1964	200,310	225,790	4,618	468,218
	1960	425,710	63,255	2,500	493,465
	1956	741,189	8,000	2,725	751,914

Data from Herbert E. Alexander, *Money and Politics* (Washington, D.C.: Public Affairs Press, 1972), p. 329. (Current reports on contributions will be found regularly in the *Congressional Quarterly* and the *National Journal*.)

The trade associations selected were American Bar Association, American Medical Association, American Petroleum Institute, American Iron and Steel Institute, Association of American Railroads, Business Advisory Council, Chiefs of Foreign Missions and Special Missions, Manufacturing Chemists Association, National Association of Electric Companies, National Association of Manufacturers, National Association of Real Estate Boards, National Coal Association, and Chamber of Commerce of the United States. In this table Alexander put a + next to some figures for which there were problems of verification but indicated that these figures are the minimal known amounts and that actual amounts probably exceed them (p. 139).

presidential tapes had never revealed criminal conspiracies or illegal wiretaps.[59]

The force of the Watergate scandals may keep interest group actions under control for a while. The pressure on interest groups to give money for campaigns may be relieved by recent legislation as well. The 1972 act in combination with the Revenue Act of 1971 provides tax breaks for political contributions up to $50 for single and $100 for joint returns, plus the right to assign $1 of taxes to the political party of one's choice. In November of 1974 these acts were amended to provide federal assistance of up to $20,000,000 for the presidential campaigns of the candidates of the two major parties plus substantial matching grants for candidates in presidential primaries. It is unlikely, however, that interest group partisanship through campaign contributions will disappear. Table 6.5 is based upon reported campaign contributions of thirteen trade associations to political parties, candidates, and campaign committees. The table shows not only that these contributions have always been substantial but also that all groups and corporations tend to hedge their bets by giving fairly substantial support to both major parties; the Democrats gain or lose depending upon their prospects of gaining or retaining the presidency.

What this illustrates is that for these interest groups, although

[59]Some of these abuses were being revealed and prosecuted two and three years after the Watergate scandal broke open. See, for example, Michael C. Jensen, "How 3M Got Tangled Up in Politics," *New York Times,* March 9, 1975.

they clearly prefer Republicans, going partisan really is something of a bipartisan matter; and bipartisan strategy really means that they are giving campaign contributions *in order to buy access.* This is true of a great number of groups—not just those included in the statistics in Table 6.5—and it means that interest groups will find a means of giving contributions to parties or campaigns whenever it appears that their contributions may provide an opportunity to maintain or improve access after the election is over. It is unlikely that any group or combination of groups can buy an election. But groups can buy the elected, and there will never be a dependable remedy for this. Ultimately we have to depend upon the good character of the elected. That may not offer a great deal of solace.

Using the Courts

Interest groups turn to litigation when access is lacking and when satisfaction with the government in general or with a specific government program is running particularly low. An interest group can use the courts either by suing directly, by financing suits brought by individuals, or by filing a companion brief as *amicus curiae,* literally "friend of the court." The most significant contemporary illustrations of this strategy will probably be found in the history of the NAACP, a group which virtually existed in order to use litigation in the pursuit of political goals. The NAACP was resorting to litigation years before it turned to lobbying. In fact, litigation had to be used for blacks in order to clear paths to lobbying and other strategies that had not been considered appropriate for them.[60]

Business groups are probably the most frequent users of the courts because there is such a wide variety of governmental action which may be questioned on technical or narrowly legal bases. There are mountains of public law involving business litigation in such areas as tax law, antitrust law, regulations involving truck transportation, or TV advertising. Often an individual business takes the initiative; often it is brought to court against its will by virtue of initiatives taken by other businesses or by the government acting as plaintiff. (One of the less frequent but most spectacular areas of business litigation is antitrust. In a recent case between Control Data and IBM, the stakes were valued at more than one hundred million dollars.) The major corporations and trade associations pay tremendous amounts of money each year in retainer fees for the most prestigious law firms in Washington. Admittedly some of this is to ensure access. But the great part of it is to ensure that

---

[60]A classic study of litigation as a political strategy is that of Clement Vose, "Litigation as a Form of Pressure Group Activity," *Annals of the American Academy of Political and Social Science* 319 (1958). Also, see his book *Caucasions Only: The Supreme Court, the NAACP, and the Restrictive Covenant Cases* (Berkeley: University of California Press, 1959).

Table 6.6   Arnold & Porter: A Washington Law Firm and Its Clients

Allis-Chalmers Mfg. Co. (139)

American Baseball League

American Brands, Inc. (74)

American Council of Learned Societies

American Farm Lines

American Home Products Corp. (87)

American Safety Razor Co.

American Trading & Production Corp.

Bank of America

Bi-Lo, Inc.

Bohemian National Cemetery Assoc.

Braniff Airways, Inc.

Center for Auto Safety

Chesebrough-Pond's, Inc. (376)

Chocolat Tobler American Corp.

Chris-Craft Industries, Inc. (792)

Clark Oil & Refining Corp. (368)

The Coca-Cola Co. (67)

Commissioner of Baseball

Common Cause

Confederation Internationale des Fabricants de Tapis et Tissus d'Ameublement (Switzerland)

Cresca, Inc.

Crown Cork & Seal Co., Inc. (256)

Democratic National Committee

District of Columbia Psychological Assoc.

El Salto, South America (Guatemala)

Electronic Industries Assoc.

Embassy of Switzerland

Fairchild Camera & Instrument Corp. (425)

Federated Department Stores, Inc.

Federation of British Carpet Manufacturers (United Kingdom)

First Security National Bank & Trust Co. (Lexington, Ky.)

Florida East Coast Railway Co.

Gulf & Western Industries, Inc. (65)

Gulf Life Holding Co.

Hoffmann-Laroche, Inc.

R. A. Holman & Co., Inc.

HRH Construction Corp.

Institute for Policy Studies

Insurance & Securities, Inc.

Koppers Co., Inc. (209)

Kroger Co.

Lamar Life Broadcasting Co. (WLBT-TV)

Lawyers Co-op Publishing Co.

Lever Brother Co. (214)

Ling-Temco-Vought Inc. (15)

Madison National Bank (Washington, D.C.)

Martin Marietta Corp. (130)

National Retail Merchants Assoc.

National Council of American Importers, Floor Covering Committee

North American Research and Development Co. (Narisco)

Northwest Industries, Inc. (232)

Philip Morris, Inc. (123)

Playboy Magazine

Recording Industry Assoc. of America, Inc.

Rockwell-Standard Corp. (North American Rockwell) (35)

Neil Sheehan (*New York Times*)

State Farm Mutual Automobile Insurance Co.

Swiss Cheese Union (Switzerland)

Tobacco Institute, Inc.

Tropical Gas Co., Inc.

Unimed, Inc.

George R. Whitten Jr., Inc.

Xerox Corp. (60)

From Jonathan Cotton, "Washington Pressures," *National Journal,* January 8, 1972, p. 46. Arnold & Porter declined to provide a list of clients, but enterprising reporters gleaned this list from public records and interviews. Each person, corporation, or group retained the firm for legal work in recent years. A number in parentheses indicates a company's rank if it was listed among *Fortune's* top 1,000 corporations in terms of 1970 sales. The firm was formerly Arnold, Fortas and Porter before Fortas joined the Supreme Court. For Fortas's activities after he left the court, see Table 6.4.

the best and most experienced lawyers will be ready to represent the corporation in court or before the commissioners of an administrative agency.

    Table 6.6 represents only one law firm, and not the largest, in Washington. The firm of Arnold and Porter (formerly Arnold,

Fortas and Porter, prior to the departure of Fortas for a brief stint on the Supreme Court) is an especially interesting illustration. It is famous for a large number of liberal Democratic and antibusiness clients, but at the same time it represents a star-studded roster of ordinary giant corporations and trade associations. And make no mistake about it. These corporate clients are as willing as the ideological clients to use litigation whenever they perceive it to be appropriate as an additional strategy in the search for power.

Bribery

Personal favor is a tactic which may ultimately become involved in any political strategy. There are innumerable descriptions of this political tactic that stress the giving and taking of favors as an essential and ubiquitous feature. "Give-and-take," "pulling and hauling," "mutual back scratching," and "bargaining and compromise" all convey a sense that in politics you give a little to gain more. Patronage, for example, means not only the distribution of jobs; it should be understood to mean any and all efforts to patronize. Consequently, the line between politics and corruption, between legitimate and illegitimate compromise, will always be difficult to draw clearly and impossible to draw permanently.

We know that illegal favor—bribery—is extensive in our society. We simply do not know its extent. And by its very nature, we are unlikely to find out. Some say it is declining and an occasional scandal like Watergate is proof to them that we are exposing it and rooting it out. Others would insist that it is not declining and would tend to use the same example as their evidence![61] While it is impossible to resolve the dispute between optimists and pessimists, it is possible to say a few things about bribery that might keep the entire issue in context.

First, bribery is probably used more often to sustain friends than to convert opposition.[62] An offer of a bribe to a member of the opposition is extremely risky; the offer itself could be exposed, or it could be accepted with nothing given in return. The briber would certainly not bring suit for breach of contract.

Second, the offer of a bribe is frequently seen as evidence of weakness. This is a quite justifiable attitude. Since bribery is risky, it would tend to be used only when all other tactics had been tried and found wanting. Thus the offer of a bribe could be counterproductive.

---

[61]Either side will find a parade of examples in Robert N. Winter-Berger, *The Washington Pay-off* (New York: Dell Publishing, 1972). The Watergate documents provide another source of information, although it is limited largely to bribery and other forms of dishonesty in campaigns only and not in the legislative or administrative processes.

[62]Key, *Politics, Parties, and Pressure Groups*, pp. 137–138.

Third, bribery and other forms of corruption are not limited to the political realm but are facts of life in all realms of social activity. For example, department stores must build into their cost structure a factor of at least 10 percent for losses each year due to shoplifting and to thefts in various other forms.[63] These department stores must of course keep corruption down as far as possible. But they cannot even try to eradicate it, because all of the security forces and television surveillance and bag checking required for an effective program would discourage the overwhelming majority of honest customers from doing business in the store.

Fourth and finally, bribery is probably limited to the narrowest of political issues, such as who gets the subsidy, who gets the bridge, how much of a tax break can I get, whether this case can be settled before it gets to the commission. The bigger the issue—the broader the scope of conflict, the larger the number of participants, the more publicity—the less likely that bribery will be employed as a strategic tactic. With a big issue, the stakes are definitely big enough to make people want to use bribery; however, there would be too many people to bribe, too much uncertainty, and too many advantages to be gained by the opposition from exposing the briber.

There are, therefore, a few reassuring things to be said about politics in response to even the most pessimistic estimate of the extent of bribery. And, while there is no real solution to this kind of a problem in a society composed of normal human beings, we have been able to identify at least two responses to it. One is to try to keep the political issues big and public. In reviewing the founding, we had occasion to observe how big issues can bring out the best in people. Now we can see also that big issues can help to suppress their worst tendencies. The second perceivable antidote to bribery can be found in the behavior of the department store manager who must decide how to run a good store despite corruption. The same decision must be faced in politics—how to govern well despite the fact that many participants are giving and accepting bribes.

Groups, Strategies, and the Consent to Govern

Organized interests are the most important political resource in our society. But an intelligent survey of the strategies available to groups is bound to raise questions about whether the economic and membership resources of a group can really be translated into political terms. What indeed is lost in the translation? Not only are the available strategies limited in number and variety. Sometimes these strategies are interconnected, and at other times one strategy may be inconsistent with other strategies. For example, a group

---

[63]One student of corruption in private industry estimates that business losses due to theft have been climbing up to 25 percent. Mark Lipman, *Stealing: How America's Employees Are Stealing Their Companies Blind* (New York: Harper Magazine Press, 1970).

that is lacking in access must either go public or resort to lobbying, litigation, partisanship, or bribery. But if the group chooses to turn to litigation to make up for its lack of access, the group will probably be acting unwisely if it also resorts to active political campaigning during the course of the litigation.

Access and litigation both require quiet skill and long cultivation. Access is of course even more sensitive than litigation; once access is gained, there is a strong temptation not to engage in any other strategies at all for fear it might be lost. Even when strategies are not inconsistent, the switch from one to the other nevertheless involves cost and risks. A group with considerable access may for some reason decide to go public; but the stakes must be awfully large, because it clearly risks the severing of the more confidential lines of communication. It risks losing the upper-class Washington lawyers, or it risks alienating the older leadership that is comfortable with back rooms and quiet restaurants. For example, when a group like the NAACP, which was primarily in the business of going to court, turns to lobbying, it not only risks compromising its favorable position with the courts; it also risks losing credit and respect with its supporters if its lobbying effort does not succeed.

Choice of strategy has moral implications. If a group chooses to improve its access, it must be prepared to keep many of its actions secret from its own membership. Many people in mass membership organizations are alienated by any sense that important things are being kept from them, and many leaders in such groups simply refuse to try to improve access precisely because it sounds too uppercrust, involves too much secrecy, too much role playing. Other leaders will not under any circumstances resort to bribery. Many old and high-status interest groups will not resort to lobbying because it seems vulgar or requires too much personal publicity, or both. Other groups actually prefer to go public or to use lobbying, despite the risks, because to them these strategies seem the only honest way to play politics.

Finally, very frequently the choice of strategy is dictated by problems internal to the group. For example, some interest groups go public in hopes that the public campaign on a given issue may excite their own membership and increase the cohesiveness of the group. This revival spirit of the Protestant churches is certainly not lost on public relations experts. Other groups turn to the cultivation of access in order to avoid revealing to their own membership the commitments they are making. Leaders of other groups turn to litigation because they lack a large group membership but have enough resources to hope for a larger political impact through a broad court ruling. Success in legal action may then encourage greater membership, opening a larger number of options for political strategies.

This gives rise to a still larger and more significant point. If interest group leaders are constantly picking strategies for the purpose of building their resources as well as using them, then they are constantly uncertain about the real character of opinion among their members, the cohesiveness of their members, and the true value of their group resources for political purposes. And if the group leaders themselves are in the dark about these matters, then government officials are even more in the dark, because the political strategies of these interest groups are intended in part to mislead government officials. In turn this means that governments and political leaders in the twentieth century are farther and farther removed from their constituencies at the very time when they would especially hope to be guided by, or at least popular with, constituent opinion. The ideal of government by consent has emerged at a time when it is less and less possible to gain knowledge of the opinions that comprise consent.

How can conquest be maintained on the basis of a maximum of consent when there is a vast public but no identifiable public opinion? We cannot construct public opinion *or* consent by adding up group demands and group leadership strategies. Can we gain the requisite knowledge of the public by leaving groups and going directly to the public itself?

Chapter 7　Getting the People to Consent: The Public in Groups, in Opinions, and in Electorates

We hold these truths to be self-evident, that all men are created equal, that they are endowed by their Creator with certain unalienable Rights, that among these are Life, Liberty and the pursuit of Happiness.—That to secure these rights, Governments are instituted among Men, deriving their just powers from the consent of the governed.
The Declaration of Independence, 1776

The medium is the message.
Marshall McLuhan, 1964

Getting the People to Consent: The Public in Groups, in Opinions, and in Electorates

One of our most treasured beliefs is that the free expression of individual self-interest will produce a government of minimum force and maximum legitimacy. This happy connection is called *consent*—the thing without which the drapes of government fall aside to reveal the everlasting reality of conquest. Government by consent is, of course, a myth. A myth, it will be recalled, is a belief that does not depend upon truth to be accepted. A myth may be based upon truth, but not necessarily. A myth can be close to or far from the truth. How far from the truth is the American myth of consent?

THEORIES OF CONSENT IN THE UNITED STATES: THE OLD AND THE NEW

From the very beginning in the United States, interest and consent were tied closely together. The Declaration of Independence rings with the phrase "pursuit of Happiness." What is this but a rhetorical expression of the notion of interest? An interest, after all, can be defined as anything which, when acquired, may produce more happiness. Note in the quotation which introduces this chapter that the sentence immediately following expression of the right to pursue happiness declares that the very purpose of governments is to ensure the pursuit of happiness (interests) and that governments may justify themselves only in terms of their success in maintaining this right. Indeed, the Declaration bases the right of revolution on these considerations.

The founders of the Constitution, a decade later, were generally a more conservative lot than the framers of the Declaration of Independence. Although they too espoused the myth of consent, and although they too based consent upon the pursuit of interests, their approach was a good deal more sober. One could say it was a good deal more honest; it was certainly a good deal more elitist. According to their view, a good constitution encourages multitudes of interests in order to be sure that all interests will regulate each other. As long as there are many interests, no one interest can ever constitute a majority in order to tyrannize the other interests. The assumption of the founders was that the competition among interests would lead individual interests to neutralize each other or at least leave in doubt the actual shape of public opinion on many issues.

This kind of competition could thus enable the government to operate independently of interests and government officials to develop competence in the ways of government. Their thought was that such an arrangement would also encourage all competing factions and groups to support the government as the only dependable defense against each other. This theory of consent is called Madisonian because it was expressed so clearly in Madison's famous essay, *Federalist,* No. 10 (see especially the opening quotation for chapter 6). But it goes far beyond Madison. It is deeply embedded in the Constitution itself, and it must have been accepted by a wide variety of thoughtful persons at the time.

It is largely on this basis that the Federalists preferred a republic to a democracy. They defined a republic as "a government in which a scheme of representation takes place."[1] It was their belief that such a republic would help control the effects ("mischiefs") of interests in

---

[1]All quotations here clarifying the views of the Federalists are taken from Madison's essay, *Federalist,* No. 10.

Accommodation of interests.

at least two ways: (1) it would help enlarge individual views "by passing them through the medium of a chosen body of citizens"; and (2) it would contribute toward ensuring that the chosen body of representatives would be composed of a higher proportion of people "whose wisdom may best discern the true interest of their country." These representatives would thus tend to produce government "more consonant of the public good than if pronounced by the people themselves."

This was a plausible theory for one very important reason. Consent, or, as we would call it today, the "public interest," in the older theory was not defined simply as the summation of all individual interests. Consent was something granted independently of the specific interests themselves. That is to say, the people were expected to have an interest in giving consent *independent of their individual interests.* In fact, individual and group interests were defined as contrary to the public interest: "The regulation of these various interfering interests forms the principle task of modern legislation." The coupling of consent with regulation is an essential feature of the older theory of consent. Government and interests were not the same thing. Factions and groups would agree to give their consent to be governed if they were unable to impose their will upon each other.[2]

Getting the People to Consent: The Public in Groups, in Opinions, and in Electorates

[2]For a longer treatment of this view and its relationship to the modern American theory of consent, see Theodore Lowi, "Interest Groups and the Consent to Govern: Getting the People out, for What?" *Annals of the American Academy of Political and Social Science,* May 1974, pp. 86–100.

In the twentieth century the United States has witnessed a very substantial change in the theory of consent. The new theory continues to stress interests, but we have come to see interests as virtuous rather than as mischievous. Moreover, the theory of consent now requires that interests be accommodated rather than regulated. The new theory of consent is best defined by two of America's most distinguished political scientists, David Truman and Robert Dahl. Truman initiated his treatment of interests with Madison's definition of an interest group:

> A number of citizens, whether amounting to a majority or minority of the whole, who are united and actuated by some common impulse of passion, or of interest, *adverse to the rights of other citizens, or to the permanent and aggregate interests of the community.* [Italics added.]

Yet while continuity was thus established between the new and the old definition of interests, the contrast in attitude toward the phenomenon of interests was defined by Truman's elimination of that part of the definition printed in italics.[3] Dahl went on to establish a good deal more explicitly the place of interests in the larger political process according to the new approach:

> I define the normal American political process as one in which there is high probability that an active and legitimate group in the population can make itself heard effectively at some crucial state in the process of decision. . . . When I say a group is heard "effectively" I mean more than the simple fact that it makes a noise; I mean that one or more officials are not only ready to listen to the noise, but expect to suffer in some significant way if they do not placate the group, its leaders, or its most vociferous members.[4]

There are at least three basic aspects of this shift in perspective. First, according to the new theory, no interest is adverse to the public interest unless it involves a violation of law. Second, all interests must have about equal status. No moral ordering among them is possible. No choice among interests can be made except through the process by which interests with the best resources or most effective strategies win out. Third, government must gain consent by going out and discovering the real interests in society and then accommodating those interests by a judicious selection of public policies.

Leaving aside the important issue of the morality of such a perspective for the moment, we can say at the very outset that consent based upon accommodation to interests is a standard far more difficult to fulfill than consent under the older theory, which is based upon the independence of government from interests. The

---

[3]David B. Truman, *The Governmental Process* (New York: Knopf, 1951), p. 4.
[4]Robert A. Dahl, *A Preface to Democratic Theory* (Chicago: University of Chicago Press, 1956), p. 145.

new concept of consent, based upon actual accommodation, means that elites must concern themselves with getting knowledge about specific demands that are being made. This requires detailed information about interests before policies are made, and it also requires detailed information from interests afterwards to determine whether the advantages and disadvantages in each policy have been equitably distributed. (The term *equitably* is not intended to have any philosophic value, nor should it be thought to imply any objective or absolute criterion. A distribution is equitable if the spokesmen for the various interests report that the distribution is equitable. That is all part of the contemporary notion of consent by accommodation to interests.)

If such a theory of consent by accommodation proves to be impossible, this will not mean that every politician is by nature a deceiver. Most politicians probably accept the theory of consent by accommodation and go on to spend an enormous amount of time and money trying to gain the political knowledge sufficient to be guided by the people. This chapter will be filled with such instances. There is a great deal more evidence to suggest that the most powerful political leaders in the United States prefer to operate on the basis of broad consent *even when they could get what they want without it.* The magnificent dream, "government by the people," may have helped keep conquest incomplete. But those who have translated this into "government by consent of all those who have an interest" should try to examine the implications. The specter of Machiavelli and his advice to the Prince to use deceit when necessary hovers over all efforts to maintain consent, because the distance short of real accommodation to interests must be filled with deceit. Sufficient accommodation to interests requires political knowledge on a scale almost beyond belief.

One way to assess the modern theory of consent and its prospects of being fulfilled is to examine the major sources of political knowledge, which are identified in Table 7.1. To what extent is our theory of consent a myth? Perhaps there is a better way to put the same question: How substantial a myth is the modern theory of consent?

INTEREST GROUPS AND POLITICAL KNOWLEDGE: CONSENT, BUT FOR WHAT?

Despite the explosion of electronic technology and the revolution in scientific polling, the task of learning about the relevant opinions and interests of the public is growing more and more difficult. This is due partly to the scale of modern life and partly to the revolutionary expansion in expectations that leaders will in fact subscribe to the modern theory of consent. As recently as fifty years ago, getting

Table 7.1	Major Sources of Political Consent and Political Knowledge
Source	**Rationale**
Interest groups	Go to organized interests. This is an efficient source because the opinions are more intense and more relevant to the key issues of the day and because groups can energetically support the regime as well as inform it.
Mass behavior	Observe how the people behave and reconstruct their interests from their actions. For example, declining demand may tell more about public opinion than a consumer survey; and "white flite" will tell more about racial attitudes than sample surveys or interviews with group leaders. There are many regularities in mass behavior, and each pattern expresses a real opinion. But how does one interpret this behavior?
Public opinion	Go ask the public what it wants. Behavior is ambiguous, or by the time leaders read the behavior it is too late to act on the knowledge. But methods are constantly being improved, and some of the results in the forecasting of future behavior are most impressive.
Elections	Let the public speak through its choice among candidates. Weaknesses inherent in each of the other sources of political knowledge have made elections all the more important. Elections are the only source of official consent, and elections can distinguish among candidates who represent different interests. But what kind of additional knowledge is really produced? Can elections guide leaders to accommodations of interest in matters of government between elections?

the opinions of many segments of the public was still a matter of direct experience. When entertainers or politicians sought knowledge and popular support, the measure of their success was the applause and cheers of actual crowds in actual meeting places. The Lincoln-Douglas debates were seven confrontations before audiences in cornfields and courthouse squares during the parched summer and autumn of 1858. Slightly over one hundred years later, the Kennedy-Nixon debates took place on three separate evenings before fewer than a dozen reporters and television technicians in a parched studio that might as well have been on the moon. Public response was not capable of being experienced at all. This tremendously increased distance between leaders and followers is one of the outstanding features of modern society.

Politicians have probably turned to groups as a source of political information for as long as groups have existed. But, as we have already seen, groups assume a much larger and more legitimate place in our scheme of consent today, and politicians are more likely than ever to rely on group information in making their decisions and in justifying the decisions they make. Yet even the most superficial exposure to the strategies of group politics will suggest that group information about opinions is highly distorted. Some of the distortion comes from deliberate misrepresentation; groups claim to speak for followings far larger than their membership, and they tend to give a false impression about the cohesiveness and uniformity of interests among their members.

Distortion, however, goes far beyond deliberate misrepresentation. It should be emphasized here once again that distortion refers to any changing or twisting from the natural state. Not all distortion is deliberate, and not all deliberate distortion—as in modern art—misrepresents. There are at least three types of distortion that are actually built into the nature of group organization itself and are not a matter of accident or of strategy. Interest groups cannot be placed into any theory of consent until these distortions are understood. A brief treatment of these quite commonplace types of distortions will suffice.[5]

Distortion I: To Organize Is to Distort

Anyone who has ever been called upon to name his or her favorite composer or to redecorate a living room will know something of the discomfort of organization and the distortions inherent in it. To organize, the individual must establish some priorities. But the expression of those priorities requires the subordination of some interests as well as the elevation of others. Moreover, the expression of priorities communicates some part of the individual's character and personality to others. The problem of priority ranking and the distortion of individual values becomes especially acute in politics. As we shall see later, almost every public issue expressed as a yes-and-no alternative is a distortion. When it comes to taking a stand on issues or joining a group, any choice the individual makes is likely to misrepresent certain of that individual's priorities or specific values.

In modern societies, few persons are known except through the choices they make and the roles they play. So much has this become the case that modern social science tends to define the human being as a bundle of roles and interests. One is known as a Democrat, or a lawyer, or a Protestant, or a liberal, or a swinger, or a square. Few individuals are familiar with each other across several of these roles. This has its advantages in everyday life and in social science analysis. Nevertheless, the approach does involve distortion, since interests and roles are not people, and people cannot be fully reconstructed from the roles they play and the interests they hold. Perhaps this is the reason so much of the fiction and popular sociology of the day concerns itself with problems of community, communication, and "getting to know" one another. Perhaps the trouble with contemporary people is not that they are "one-dimensional" but that they are "multi-dimensional." Since we cannot be known as whole persons, we oversimplify ourselves with every action we take and every choice we communicate.

[5]A somewhat longer treatment will be found in Lowi, "Interests Groups and the Consent to Govern."

Distortion II: The Distorting Effect of Collective Life

Distortions of even greater proportion are involved when individuals try to combine their priority schedules in order to organize collectively. This particular source of distortion is almost completely beyond solution through social science research; as we shall see later in this chapter, public opinion polling tends to give us negative knowledge about group membership, leading us to distrust any claim leaders might make for the consistency or cohesion of interests among the members. Even when only a husband and wife are involved in a joint effort to buy or remodel a house, small differences between their individual priority schedules can create great conflict, unless each is willing to suppress some of the differences and to accept the priority schedule of the other to some degree. Each individual added to a collective endeavor tends to increase the complexity of collective action and the potential for distortion at something like an exponential rate.

To put this in as conventional a mode as possible, collective life requires the suppression of minority interests. This is inherent in organization and is intrinsic to group politics. Except for small groups, where consensus on a single priority schedule might be reached, members of a group must establish a few choices in priorities and then act as though these were the priorities of the corporate group itself. The more committed the group is to action, the more likely it is that the members will employ methods of decision that will establish a majority position and thus legitimize the suppression of persistent dissenters. Nearly all political groups operate on this basis of "democratic centralism," even if they do not intend to use violence to enforce the established position. There are many excellent studies on interest group processes which reveal the extent and nature of suppression of minority membership views. One of the most effective explications can be found in David Truman's classic work, where he refers to the phenomenon as "the democratic mold."[6]

From the standpoint of the society at large, suppression of minorities within groups is an extremely important and valuable form of social control. *In order to engage effectively in politics, groups must first conquer their own members.* This means that much of society's own need for conquest is done *for society* by the very groups seeking to exert influence over the government. Whatever value this has for the society, it must necessarily influence our understanding of democracy and of government based on consent; opinions expressed in groups cannot be taken as *public* opinions. If they

---

[6]Truman, *The Governmental Process,* chapter 5. This line of inquiry was probably first opened up by Robert Michels, *Political Parties,* trans. Eden and Cedar Paul (New York: Dover, 1959; first published in English 1915).

DELETED

)

The CIA also makes considerable use of forged documents.*
During the mid-1960s, for instance, the agency learned that a certain West African country was about to recognize the People's
Republic of China and that the local government intended to force
the withdrawal of the diplomatic representatives of Nationalist
China. This was considered to be contrary to American foreign-
policy aims, so the CIA went into action. (

DELETED

)

The Pentagon Papers have revealed some other examples of CIA
propaganda and disinformation activities. One top-secret document written in 1954 by Colonel Edward Lansdale, then an agency
operator, describes an effort involving North Vietnamese astrol-
ogers hired to write predictions about the coming disasters which
would befall certain Vietminh leaders and their undertakings, and
the success and unity which awaited the South.

Lansdale also mentioned that personnel under his control

are accepted as public opinions by government officials, then our
form of government by consent is to that degree different from what
it claims to be.

Distortion III: The Illogic of Collective Action

The first two types of distortion are the result of actual suppression—real world suppression dictated by the pressing need to make
choices. The individual suppresses lower priority items in order to
pursue higher ones and in the process misrepresents himself. The
group makes a choice only by suppressing its minority members. In
contrast, the third type of distortion is an artifact of collective life
itself. It lies in the logic, or illogic, of collective life rather than in
the behavior of the members. This type of distortion is referred to

technically as the *welfare function,* explored most originally and prominently by Kenneth Arrow.[7]

There is a highly technical method of demonstrating the anomalies of logic introduced by collective decision making, but for our purposes here a very homely example provided by Herman Kahn will suffice. As Kahn relates the parable, a committee was sent to the local butcher shop to buy meat for a large picnic. The butcher informed the committee that only chicken and beef were available in sufficient quantity for their picnic. After some discussion, the committee informed the butcher of their decision to buy chicken. However, while the committee was deliberating, the butcher had discovered that there was also turkey available in sufficient quantity. This meant that the committee had to go back into deliberation. They then returned to the butcher and reported that since there was turkey, they had decided they no longer wanted the chicken but would take the beef![8] This strange and anomalous process of collective decision making occurs more frequently than is generally realized.

Another good example from the public realm is congressional behavior during the late 1950s on the civil rights issue. There seem to have been a majority in favor of civil rights legislation and also a majority in favor of federal aid to public education. However, when the two issues were put together as a single legislative proposal, both went down in defeat.[9] This kind of peculiar outcome can happen, and does frequently happen, because many members of a majority may support the majority position very weakly while having an alternative they prefer, which they will pursue as soon as there is an opportunity.

Groups attempt to adjust to the instabilities inherent in their decision-making processes by delegating more and more choices to the central leadership of the group. Members may continue to vote on important choices; however, the decision on what choices shall be submitted to a vote tends to be made by the central oligarchy. This means that a few people, sometimes no more than three or four, are left with the all-important function of setting the agenda for the group. These decisions are made on the basis of the instincts and intuitions of the leaders regarding the real interests of their members. But if this is the way the group maintains consistency in the presentation of its interests to government, it amounts to exchanging one kind of distortion for another. If the group is really run by its members, it runs the risk of inconsistency from issue to

[7]Arrow's work on the welfare function earned for him a Nobel Prize in economics. See his book, *Social Choice and Individual Values* (New York: Wiley, 1951).

[8]Herman Kahn, *On Thermonuclear War,* 2d ed. (Princeton: Princeton University Press, 1961), pp. 121–122.

[9]I thank my colleague Professor Helen Sawyer for this worthy suggestion. Details of those issues can be found in H. Douglas Price, "Race, Religion, the Rules Committee," in *The Uses of Power,* ed. Alan F. Westin (New York: Harcourt, Brace & World, 1962).

issue. If it seeks to avoid inconsistency, it must delegate control over the agenda to the leadership, and this delegated authority necessarily implies a distortion in the representation of the interests of the group. Indeed, in his analysis of the welfare function, Arrow has shown "that our intuitive criteria for a democratic decision cannot in fact be satisfied unless we are prepared under certain conditions to accept a social ordering which is either 'imposed' or 'dictatorial.'"[10]

Distortions and Conquest

Obviously the distortion inherent in group life exists as a terrifying contradiction in the contemporary theory of consent based on accommodation to group opinions. Politicians and political scientists have tried to live with that contradiction by making one or more of the following assumptions:

1. Since groups are voluntary associations, the members are usually so homogeneous that leaders can gain good impressions of their real interests.

2. In a free society there will always be several alternative groups, so that minorities suppressed in one group may join or form another in order to pursue their interests elsewhere.

3. Competition among groups for members will prevent the leaders of any one group from straying too far away from the real interests of its members.

4. There are ways of getting knowledge about group members without depending entirely upon statements of group leaders.

5. Most group members don't have strong and clear interests anyway.

These assumptions might be confirmed by proper investigation. However, left uninvestigated, they produce the beliefs that myths are made of. No matter what assumptions are made, distortion of opinions in the group process is not likely to disappear. The more social science improves, the more distortion we are likely to discover through good sample survey methods, and the more we will discover group positions being simply asserted by group leaders. This means that we will have to adjust our theories of consent to the realities of the group process rather than assume that the group process is consistent with our theories of consent. Until that adjustment is made, politics in the United States will continue to take place on the edge of a credibility gap.

Even as our political leaders are making claims that their actions are based upon public support, they are showing increasing distress over the validity of information they get from group leaders.

Getting the People to Consent: The Public in Groups, in Opinions, and in Electorates

[10]W. G. Runciman, *Social Science and Political Theory* (Cambridge: Cambridge University Press, 1972), p. 133.

Politicians in our country are constantly searching for knowledge about public opinions that is more reliable than the reports they get from leaders of individual groups. Candidates for public office are spending increasingly higher proportions of their precious campaign funds to conduct surveys of potential voters. They use the resulting knowledge to help them decide whether to run for office and on what kinds of appeals they should base their candidacy. National politicians are also relying increasingly on information gained from nationwide polls. Lyndon Johnson was noted for carrying the latest results of Gallup or Roper in his hip pocket; and he began to withdraw from politics as the polls reported losses of public support.

Most of the evidence suggests that modern politicians continue to espouse the theory of consent based upon accommodation (or popular support) but that they operate in tremendous ignorance of the real interests of the public while constantly engaged in an effort to reduce that ignorance. While they have not rejected the support they get from group leaders, American politicians have long since abandoned reliance upon these individual representatives of groups for real political knowledge. Increasingly, they have gone directly to the public, either to observe that sphinx or to coax her to speak. Alas, going directly to the public for political knowledge does not necessarily lighten the burden of ignorance. Direct study of public opinion often changes the form of the ignorance rather than producing better political knowledge. This may be the reason the concept of a credibility gap has developed *along with* improved methods of, and vastly more expenditure for, studying public opinion.

OBSERVING THE SPHINX: RECONSTRUCTING PUBLIC OPINION FROM MASS BEHAVIOR

The term *credibility gap* is an expression indicating the distrust citizens feel toward the testimony of their leadership. But there are two sides to every gap, and on the other side of the credibility gap the leadership is usually equally distrustful of the testimony gained from and about citizens. As we shall see, politicians are turning increasingly toward approaches that are thought to be scientific. However, there have long been other approaches to the study of public opinion that require neither polling nor reliance upon the testimony of group leaders. Every leader develops a few instincts about how to interpret public opinion; in fact, an ability to read opinions from behavior has to be fairly well developed or the conduct of public affairs or business would be close to impossible. A few examples will suffice to show how certain regularities of behavior can, in the hands of imaginative observers, produce dependable knowledge about public thinking.

Some may be surprised to learn that there are many regularities in mass behavior and that we possess a great deal of knowledge about that behavior. There would be no banking, and therefore no modern industrial capitalism, for example, without the knowledge that depositors will withdraw their money at different times and that not everyone will decide to withdraw all deposits at the same time. It is on the basis of this regularity that we have in the past hundred or so years developed fractional reserve banking. Any basic economics textbook will describe fractional reserve banking and its importance to the modern economy. In brief, regularities of the behavior of depositors enable bankers to loan out as much as 80 percent of each deposit. Each of these loans creates new deposits, which in turn can be loaned out at the level of about 80 percent. This pattern is what gives a capitalistic economy much of its liquid wealth. Bankers could probably loan out more than 80 percent of existing deposits; however, federal and state laws tend to set the limit at around 80 percent for fear that we do not know as much about mass investing behavior as we think we do.

While there may be more dependable regularities in the realm of knowledge of consumer activities, there are nevertheless some regularities of behavior that reveal knowledge directly relevant to politics. In the past twenty years we have been carefully studying patterns of behavior in race relations in order to discover how to deal with this immense problem in the United States. The "white flite" from the central cities in response to the influx of blacks has been a standard indicator of white racial opinions. Changes in white reaction as middle-class blacks move toward the suburbs is also a behavior pattern that indicates shadings in the opinions of whites towards blacks. Inevitably, analysts will tend to use a ghetto riot as data for interpreting the prevailing and changing opinions inside the black community. Similarly, the spread of drug usage and the rebellion against conventional modes of dress and sexual behavior have been taken as data indicative of the changing opinions among the new generation.

Perhaps the behavior most closely watched by politicians is economic behavior that may be indicative of changing political opinions. Traditionally it is assumed that the business cycle is associated with changes in public opinion and that these changes will ultimately express themselves in voting behavior. The most important theory in this area is that people will vote against the party in office during a downward turn in the business cycle and will support the people in office during the upswings of the business cycle.

Louis Bean is probably the most famous exponent of the

method of reconstructing opinions from regular economic events.[11] On many occasions Bean made better predictions about the changes in public opinion than the pollsters. His most spectacular success was in the 1948 presidential election, when he predicted Truman's victory and virtually all of the nationwide pollsters predicted Dewey would win. Bean's successes extended all the way back to 1936, when the *Literary Digest* was virtually laughed out of business because it predicted a landslide for Alf Landon against Franklin Roosevelt on the basis of a very extensive postcard poll of the electorate.

Academic political scientists have developed a more systematic approach to the same problem by studying the relationship between voting behavior and certain economic indicators in each district. Basically, the method is to correlate the aggregate election results in each district or county with selected aggregate population characteristics in each of the same districts. By such methods we can hope to learn certain things about the meaning of an election. We might learn that the middle classes are increasingly conservative; we might learn that the working classes have turned more conservative in response to racial appeals; or we might learn that it was an ethnic or religious factor rather than an economic issue that had been uppermost in the minds of people in many districts. Systematic analysis of the relationship between voting behavior and important social characteristics is one area where political science has made some of its most important contributions to political knowledge.[12]

In many ways the regularities of mass behavior do provide the most dependable sources of knowledge about mass opinions. When people are buying certain products or voting for certain candidates, they are making choices that reveal real opinions rather than imaginary opinions or misrepresented opinions. But unfortunately, there is a tremendous limitation on the extent to which we can rely upon mass behavior to produce knowledge of public opinions. First of all, there are only certain areas in which regularities may exist at all. In the second place, we often need knowledge of opinions on issues for which the regularities have not had time to develop. For example, politicians needed to know more about the public attitude

---

[11]Louis Bean, *How to Predict Elections* (New York: Knopf, 1948).

[12]See especially the following two volumes: V. O. Key, *Politics, Parties, and Pressure Groups,* 5th ed. (New York: Crowell, 1964), especially the middle chapters on campaigns and elections; and V. O. Key, *Southern Politics* (New York: Knopf, 1949), especially chapters 2–12, which are devoted to each of the southern states. The effort to reconstruct public opinions from a systematic analysis of election returns and population statistics goes back to the turn of the century from work first done by the national Bureau of the Census. This approach was pursued by many scholars in the United States and in Europe for years before the materials were picked up and used by politicians. For an account of these developments, see Richard Jensen, "American Election Analysis," in *Politics and the Social Sciences,* ed. S. M. Lipset (New York: Oxford University Press, 1969), pp. 230–232. There will be more on these approaches later in this chapter.

toward anti-ballistic missiles just at a time when behaviors were beginning to change. When the time came to locate the anti-ballistic missile sites, the Department of Defense got all kinds of surprisingly intense and well-organized community protests.

It should be remembered, after all, that one of the main functions of modern law is to *impose* regularity in areas of social life where too little regularity exists. This is precisely why politicians are so desirous of better political knowledge. They would sincerely like to know better how people will react to controls, so as to be able to legislate controls which are more likely to be accepted. Thus, the desire to govern with popular approval, or consent, is not only sincerely felt among modern politicians; it is also very realistic politics.[13] As has already been mentioned, however, most of the time politicians will need political knowledge precisely in those areas of public life where there are no regularities of mass behavior to interpret. The sphinx does not speak without some coaxing.

COAXING THE SPHINX: BUILDING PUBLIC OPINION FROM INDIVIDUAL OPINIONS

Leaders in a democracy probably share one dream: rapport with the people. Though they often abuse it, they all seem to accept as a privilege the obligation to go to the people, to mingle with them, to shake their hands, to get the feel of the crowd. And they do not seem to be deterred by the risk that these experiences can be misleading. The sphinx so often speaks with a forked tongue, even when the methods of study are quite systematic. Mistaken decisions based upon results obtained by the most systematic efforts to gain knowledge of the people are frequent and costly. One of the most famous instances of the unreliability of data of this sort was the disastrous decision made by Ford Motor Company, while Robert McNamara was the chief executive, to introduce an entirely new car, the Edsel. The polls had told them that there was a place in the market for a new class of car above the "working-class" Pontiac and Dodge—"the car for the young executive on the way up." The buying public later told them an entirely different story.[14]

Thus even leaders in private industry, who spend more than politicians on opinion research, can get the wrong guidance from polls. The trouble is, political and business leaders feel they may be more viciously criticized if they make their decisions without trying systematically to study public opinions. This is why there will

[13]For an excellent treatment of the congruency between political realism and the sincere desire for consent, see Carl Friedrich, *Constitutional Government and Democracy* (Boston: Ginn, 1950), especially chapter 14.

[14]The story is reported entertainingly in Martin Mayer, *Madison Avenue U.S.A.* (New York: Harper & Bros., 1958), chapter 7.

Who speaks for labor? Chocolate workers demonstrate against their own union leaders in Hershey, Pennsylvania.

always be a love-hate relationship between politicians and the study of public opinion.[15]

The approaches to the study of public opinion divide conveniently into two fairly distinct types—the impressionistic and the scientistic. These are in no way inconsistent, and the intelligent politician tends to employ more than one. Limitations on choice are usually financial. There are of course some prejudices in these as in all matters of strategy. For example, conservatives have probably tended to distrust scientistic approaches more than liberals. Big city politicians may have a bit more faith in the accuracy of polling or of reports by group spokesmen, while politicians from small towns probably have more confidence in their own personal approaches to the people, even after they have moved to larger constituencies. Above all, politicians with some background in college psychology or sociology are much more likely to put their faith in sample survey methods.

<hr />

[15]For good cases reporting on the use of polling and other methods, see Aaron Wildavsky, "The Intelligent Citizen's Guide to the Abuses of Statistics: The Kennedy Document and the Catholic Vote," in *Politics and Social Life,* ed. Nelson Polsby et al. (Boston: Houghton Mifflin, 1963), pp. 825–844. In that same collection, see Senator Jacob Javits, "How I Used a Poll in Campaigning for Congress," pp. 845–847. For a good study with some criticisms concerning what can happen when politicians do not make use of public opinion data available to them, see Nelson Polsby, "Toward an Explanation of McCarthyism," in the same collection, pp. 809–824.

Impressionistic Approaches to the Sphinx

The personal approach Traditional ways of getting knowledge from the sphinx will never be obsolete. For most politicians, intuition may still be their most important source of knowledge; and when they have been reelected several times, their confidence in their own intuition is likely to grow. When personal intuition is not felt to be sufficient, many politicians turn first to the intuition of their friends rather than directly to some kind of polling. This has been one of the primary functions of the cronies around presidents of the United States. It is but a short step from these practices to reliance upon individuals who represent specific groups. However, the individuals most heavily relied upon are those who are also close and trusted friends of the politician. Turning to these people is far different from taking a census of all of the representatives of all the various groups in the constituency.[16]

There are, of course, many advantages to this approach. It is quick and efficient, not expensive, and it may be no more misleading than more expensive approaches. But the disadvantage is that personal intuition and the intuition of cronies may close off awareness of unpleasant information, or may limit the awareness of the leader regarding entirely new issues. Thus the traditional type of politician may be very well informed on the issues that interest him and may be operating completely in the dark on a whole variety of other things.

Selective or impressionistic polling Whenever politicians lack confidence in the intuition of their immediate associates, and especially whenever they come to distrust the reports they are getting from group advocates, they may then turn to crude and limited, but still effective, forms of polling. Old-line journalists as well as politicians find selective polling a favorite method. They deliberately and self-consciously select ordinary citizens drawn from different walks of life—such as three middle-class Catholics, a Baptist taxi driver, two Methodist merchants, three Jewish housewives, four hard hats, and two black laborers—in an effort to reconstruct meaningful distributions of an entire constituency. Some will call it luck; nevertheless, many politicians and professional students of public opinion have been successful with such methods. For example, in 1948 Samuel Lubell outwitted the national pollsters by these very impressionistic and slipshod methods. On the other hand, most politicians seek to expand on this toward more

---

[16]For a very good treatment of the "attentive publics" around major politicians and how their opinions are used as a gauge of those of the larger public, see Richard Neustadt, *Presidential Power* (New York: Wiley, 1960), especially chapters 4 and 5.

systematic approaches as soon as they can afford to. They are all too aware of the fact that we hear of the spectacular successes of the intuitive approach, such as Lubell's, while we do not hear about the failures.

Bellwether districts[17] Another approach lies somewhere between selective polling and systematic random sample polling. It involves the selection of one or more towns or districts that have been assumed to be microcosms of the whole population or have been found according to past studies to be good predictors of attitudes of larger segments of the population. These microcosms or predictor districts are selected after careful study of past elections. Then they are studied with intense care, with the expectation that the opinions located within them can, for certain purposes, be taken as the opinions of the population at large. This is typically the method used by the major television networks on election night. Their expert staff people have spent months prior to November selecting important districts—especially districts on the East Coast, where the polls close an hour to three hours earlier than the rest of the country, giving the forecasters a head start. They then enter into a large computer the past history of voting in those districts, coupled with other information about the opinions and the economic and social character of the residents and their precincts. As the

[17]Bellwether originally was the leading sheep on whose neck the bell was hung. Eventually it came to mean any cue or indication for where the flock was going to go.

voting results begin to flow in from these districts on election day, the computer is able to quickly compare these results with prior elections and then make some fairly precise predictions about the outcome of the current election.

The exact character of the information entered into the computer, and the exact methods of weighting and comparing results in order to make these election forecasts are closely guarded trade secrets. Nevertheless, it is possible to evaluate the contribution this approach makes to political knowledge.[18] First, this method seems to work primarily when there is an election, and when the contests in the election are between a limited number of candidates. Second, generally it works well only when the analysis takes place very close to the actual day of the election. Finally, all of this may be useful as a form of entertainment, but the lasting political knowledge to be gained from it is limited. No matter how accurately it forecasts elections, this method is not particularly useful for telling us what specific opinions people are holding, why those opinions are held, and in what respects they might be changing.

The Scientistic Method and Public Opinion

The ever increasing difficulty of getting reliable political knowledge eventually produced the demand for a major new industry: *public opinion polling.* Polling is a poor substitute for direct experience with an audience or neighborhood, but it is an immense improvement over traditional and intuitive approaches to large populations. The industry grew mainly out of the field of merchandising and advertising. Improvements in the techniques of survey design and analysis were made during World War II, especially through the development of experts on the creation and analysis of propaganda; but most of the breakthroughs in modern polling were commercial in origin.[19]

It is impossible to provide a dependable estimate of the amount of money spent annually for sample survey research on opinions in the business or political world. Although figures are available on certain public polling agencies, such as the Gallup and Roper Polls, one expert has estimated that as much as 98 percent of the polling that is done each year is conducted privately, is reported confidentially to the clients alone, and never reaches the public at all.[20] It should also be emphasized that many companies, advertising agencies, and political party organizations conduct their own polling

---

[18]For a good evaluation of these and other methods see Nelson Polsby and Aaron Wildavsky, *Presidential Elections,* 2d ed. (New York: Scribner, 1968), pp. 155–157.

[19]For a readable account, see Mayer, *Madison Avenue U.S.A.*

[20]Oliver A. Quayle III, president of Oliver Quayle and Company, a well-known survey firm, before the subcommittee on libraries of the House Committee on Administration, September 1972, as quoted in the *Congressional Quarterly Almanac,* 1972, p. 660.

18. Are you satisfied or dissatisfied with the President's policy on taxes?

Satisfied.	33-1
Dissatisfied	2*
Don't know	3

   *A. IF"DISSATISFIED": Why?

34-

19. Are you satisfied or dissatisfied with President Truman's policy on helping European countries recover from the war?

Satisfied.	35-1
Dissatisfied	2*
Don't know	3

   *A. IF "DISSATISFIED": Why?

36-

20. (HAND RESPONDENT CARD) Here are some big questions that have been in the news-- would you please look down this list and tell me which of these things President Truman is for, and which ones he is against?

	For	Against	DK	No Position
Immediate cuts in our income taxes . . .	37-1	2	3	4
Getting rid of Communists in the government	38-1	2	3	4
Taft-Hartley Bill to regulate labor unions	39-1	2	3	4
Going easy on the Nazis.	40-1	2	3	4
Getting manufacturers to keep prices down	41-1	2	3	4
Giving in to Russia.	42-1	2	3	4

21. Do you consider yourself a Democrat or Republican, or do you favor some other party?

Democrat	43-1
Republican	2
Independent, vote for man. . .	3
Other party (specify).	R
Don't know	4

44-X

operations and are not clients of anyone else. It is generally believed, however, that increasing millions of dollars are spent on business and political polls, and the expectation seems to be that the growth of the polling industry will continue.

As early as the presidential elections of 1892 and 1896 attempts had been made to conduct polls to obtain political information. Moreover, the knowledge of random sampling and interviewing was well enough developed at that time to make systematic polling a viable method of producing political knowledge. Nevertheless, the practice of political polling did not establish itself and begin to spread until well after 1936. The low esteem in which polling was

Part Three: Politics

SURVEY 4209   -40-   DECKS 06-07

100.   ASK IF "INDEPENDENT," "OTHER," OR NO PREFERENCE:

       Do you think of yourself as closer to the Republican or to the Democratic party?

                                        Republican . . (ASK A) . . 1   71-9
                                        Democratic . . (ASK B) . . 2
                                        Neither   . . . (ASK C) . . 3

                                                                       BEGIN DECK 07

       A.   IF CLOSER TO REPUBLICAN: Was there ever a time when you thought of yourself
            as closer to the Democratic party instead of the Republican party?

                                        Yes . . . . (ASK [1]) . . . 1   07/9
                                        No, never (GO TO Q. 101). . 2

HAND
CARD   [1] IF YES TO A: When did you change?
V
                                        ENTER "PARTY CHANGE"   ┌──┬──┐   08-09/99
                                        CODE NO. FROM CARD V;   │ │ │
                                        THEN GO TO Q. 101   └──┴──┘

       B.   IF CLOSER TO DEMOCRATIC: Was there ever a time when you thought of yourself
            as closer to the Republican party instead of the Democratic party?

                                        Yes . . . . (ASK [2]) . . . 1   10/9
                                        No, never (GO TO Q. 101). . 2

HAND
CARD   [2] IF YES TO B: When did you change?
V
                                        ENTER "PARTY CHANGE"   ┌──┬──┐   11-12/99
                                        CODE NO. FROM CARD V;   │ │ │
                                        THEN GO TO Q. 101   └──┴──┘

       C.   IF CLOSER TO NEITHER: Was there ever a time when you thought of yourself as a
            Democrat or as a Republican? (IF YES: Which?)

                                        Yes, Republican (ASK [3]) . 1   13/9
                                        Yes, Democrat   (ASK [3]) . 2
                                        No, never (GO TO Q. 101) . 3

HAND
CARD   [3]   IF YES, REPUBLICAN OR DEMOCRAT: When did you change? (IF CHANGED MORE
V   THAN ONCE, PROBE FOR MOST RECENT CHANGE.)

                                        ENTER "PARTY CHANGE"   ┌──┬──┐   14-15/99
                                        CODE NO. FROM CARD V;   │ │ │
                                                                └──┴──┘

101.   We hear a lot of talk these days about liberals and conservatives. I'm going to
       show you a seven-point scale on which the political views that people might hold
       are arranged from extremely liberal--point 1--to extremely conservative--point 7.
       Where would you place yourself on this scale?

                                        1) Extremely liberal 1   16/9
HAND   2) Liberal 2
CARD   3) Slightly liberal. 3
W   4) Moderate, middle of the road. . . 4
                                        5) Slightly conservative 5
                                        6) Conservative. 6
                                        7) Extremely conservative. 7
                                                   Don't know 8

held in the earlier period is indicated by a letter sent to the editor of
an Indianapolis newspaper: "Polling the voters before the election is
an infamous, contemptible conspiracy in this glorious, free republic."[21]

At first, polling for political opinions was strictly "piggyback,"
involving merely the addition of a few politically relevant questions
to polls that were otherwise oriented toward commercial information. For example, in 1937 the young Gallup organization (officially
the American Institute of Public Opinion) began to ask members of

Getting the People to
Consent: The Public in
Groups, in Opinions, and in
Electorates

229

[21]Jensen, "American Election Analysis," pp. 228-229.

its sample group whether they favored labor unions or not. By 1940 there was enough demand for political information from polls to encourage the design of surveys explicitly for the production of political information. The first important political poll was conducted by Paul Lazarsfeld, who had, until that time, been a leading market researcher. Although his first political poll was conducted on only one county, the study used methods of interviewing and sample selection that were so far in advance of others in use at the time that it set most of the precedents for the political surveys that were to follow in great numbers.[22] The first nationwide systematic sample survey of public opinion was conducted by the National Opinion Research Center during the presidential election of 1944. In 1948 the Survey Research Center of the University of Michigan initiated its long series of national election surveys. By then this approach was well established among academicians and politicians who needed to use this type of political information, and the capacity for producing such information had been institutionalized.[23]

Apparently polling did not begin to develop as an important technique in politics in the United States until there was a political demand for it. At the turn of the century, as we shall see, the political parties were still very strong in most of the wards, counties, and states. It was only as the political parties weakened and the candidates were thrown upon their own initiatives and personal organizations that the need for political knowledge produced the conditions upon which the polling industry is based. Knowledge is not always power, but when some kinds of knowledge are eventually perceived as sources of power, then they become valuable. This seems to be what happened with political polling. Political scientists and other academic persons who are interested in polling and in learning about political behavior in society are not themselves power oriented, nor are they necessarily interested in serving political elites. Nevertheless, it is undeniable that the increasing need in the political world for political knowledge loosened up the purse strings of the great foundations and of many government agencies. During the 1950s a flow of foundation and

---

[22]This concession to the historic importance of that study was made by one of Lazarsfeld's competitors, Angus Campbell, in Campbell et al., *The American Voter* (New York: Wiley, 1960), pp. 14–15. The Lazarsfeld study was based on a central assumption that voting is a choice very much like choosing between two products in a department store. Eventually Lazarsfeld found this was a poor assumption; it led to large-scale revision in the notions of social psychologists and political scientists about the character of political opinions and political decisions. On this point, see Runciman, *Social Science and Political Theory*, p. 89. See also Peter Rossi, "Four Landmarks in Voting Research," in *American Voting Behavior*, ed. Eugene Burdick et al. (New York: Free Press, 1959). The results of Lazarsfeld's first study were published in Lazarsfeld et al., *The People's Choice* (New York: Duell, Sloan & Pearce, 1944).

[23]There are several important academically based public opinion survey institutions as well as several independent commercial organizations that do political and commercial polling on contract for clients. A review of these organizations, coupled with a useful history of polling, will be found in Bernard Hennessy, *Public Opinion* (Belmont, Calif.: Wadsworth, 1965), chapter 3.

government grants for public opinion projects brought about a "behavioral revolution" in political science.[24]

There is a significant reason why it is better to call polling scientistic rather than scientific. Most of the people involved in the polling industry try their sincere best to employ the principles of science and are as careful as possible to translate these principles into the best available techniques of random sampling, interviewing, and data analysis. However, the important thing about the approach is that it must *resemble* science and the people who produce it and utilize it must have *faith* that it is a science or comes close to being a science. And for the consumer or client the point here is not whether all or part of this industry *is* science but whether the conduct of the surveys is done in such a way as to increase the credibility of these materials as political knowledge. Since the producers and the users of this knowledge are far removed from direct experience against which they can check the findings, the findings will not be accepted and acted upon unless the users can *believe in them*. In this sense, the story of the "behavioral revolution" in political science is an important chapter in the contemporary history of American politics.

Polling: An Evaluation

No treatment of political knowledge would be complete without an evaluation of some of the actual data produced by systematic polling, how these data are used, and what effect they have on the users. Only after such an evaluation can we begin to appreciate the place of this new kind of knowledge in the political system at large.

It is necessary to say at the very outset that polling data will predict elections far more frequently than any alternative type or source of political information. Statements based on polling data are not limited to gross generalities about one candidate being ahead of another or one type of opinion outnumbering another. These data allow the analyst to get fairly close to actual percentage differences among contenders; the data are also sensitive enough to pick up changes in percentage differences from one week or one month to the next; these data can, more importantly, pinpoint the different socioeconomic and regional characteristics that may or may not underlie political opinions.

Table 7.2 shows that the major national polling organizations have been quite accurate for several major elections, and have been getting more and more accurate all the time. The record of the three

[24]David B. Truman, "The Impact on Political Science of the Revolution in the Behavioral Sciences," in *Brookings Institution, Research Frontiers in Politics and Government* (Washington, D.C.: The Brookings Institution, 1955), pp. 202–231. Professor Truman will not necessarily agree that the political need for information was a causal factor back of the "behavioral revolution," but he does indeed provide a good deal of useful information on the subject.

Table 7.2

The Pollsters and Their Record, 1952–1972

	Predictions			
	Harris	Gallup	Roper	Actual Outcome
1972				
Nixon	59%	59%	No	60.8%
McGovern	35	36	polling	38
			done	
1968				
Nixon	40%	44%	No	43.4%
Humphrey	37	31	polling	42.7
Wallace	16	20	done	13.5
1964				
Johnson	64%	64%	67%*	61.1%
Goldwater	36	36	28	38.5
1960				
Kennedy	49%	51%	47%	49.5%
Nixon	41	49	49	49.3
1956				
Eisenhower	Not	51%	57%	58%
Stevenson	ascer-	41	38	42
	tained			
1952				
Eisenhower	47.4%**	51%	49%	55.4%
Stevenson	42.3	49	37	44.4

Data from published press releases, courtesy of Louis Harris and Associates, American Institute of Public Opinion (Gallup Poll), and the Roper Organization, Inc.
*Polling done in August.
**Reported by Crossley.

major polling organizations during the past six presidential elections shows that in no case was the prediction of victory given to the wrong candidate. In most cases their actual percentage prediction was very close to the mark. Even in 1948, when the polls were deeply embarrassed by almost uniformly predicting a Dewey victory over Truman, they were not very far off. For example, Gallup predicted 44.5 percent for Truman, and Truman actually received 49.9 percent. Although the failure to predict the winner embarrassed Gallup, the actual percentage error was not all that great. As a matter of fact, in the six presidential and congressional elections between 1950 and 1960, the Gallup Poll averaged an error of less than 1 percent between what it predicted and the actual percentage that each candidate received. These predictions were made on the basis of random samples of no more than 2,500 respondents. Since the total national voting population was more than sixty million, these estimates become tremendously impressive.[25]

For many, Table 7.3 may be even more dramatic. Note how consistently the statewide polls captured the voting pattern in each state. Many of these statewide polls worked from very small

[25]Hennessy, *Public Opinion*, p. 70.

Table 7.3   The Polls: Their Record in 1964

	Johnson	Goldwater	Undecided or Not Saying	Actual Popular Vote Percentages	
				Johnson	Goldwater
Nationwide Polls					
Gallup	61	32	7	61.4	38.6
Gallup (after allocating undecided vote)	64	36	—	61.4	38.6
Harris	62	33	—	61.4	38.6
Harris (after allocating undecided vote)	64	36	—	61.4	38.6
Statewide Polls					
Hal Dunleavy (California)	58	37	5	59.8	40.2
California, by Mervin D. Field	60	34	6	59.8	40.2
Arizona, for the *Phoenix Gazette*	46	45	9	49.7	50.3
Albuquerque Journal, by the University of New Mexico (New Mexico)	51.5	25.4	23.1	59.1	40.9
Tennessee, by John Kraft for the Democratic Party	49	35	16	55.5	44.5
United Press (Oklahoma)	53.1	32.2	15.7	55.8	44.2
Texas, by Joe Belden	61	34	5	62.9	37.1
Chicago Sun-Times (Illinois)	62.63	37.37	—	59.5	40.5
Indianapolis Star (Indiana)	51.5	38.1	10.4	56.1	43.9
Oliver Quayle, for the Democratic Party (Indiana)	51	36	13	56.1	43.9
Minnesota, by the *Minneapolis Star and Tribune*	67	29	4	64	36
Detroit News (Michigan)	68	23	9	67.7	32.3
Iowa, by the *Des Moines Sunday Register*	57	37	6	61.9	38.1
Denver Post (Colorado)	64	31	5	61.5	38.5
Denver Post (after allocating undecided vote)	66.2	33.8	—	61.5	38.5
Denver Post (Wyoming)	68	31	1	56.4	43.5
South Dakota, by the *Sioux Falls Argus Leader, Aberdeen American News,* and *Watertown Public Opinion*	45	49	6	55.7	44.3
New York Daily News (New York)	74.5	25.5	—	68.2	31.8
Portland Sunday Telegram (Maine)	56	18	26	68.8	31.2

Data from William C. Selover, "How the Polls Fared," in *Political Opinion and Electoral Behavior,* ed. Edward Dreyer and Walter Rosenbaum (Belmont, Calif.: Wadsworth, 1966), pp. 19–22.

samples and did not have the skilled staff to probe responses for accuracy and honesty. Yet, in state after state, the estimates made from the samples came close to the actual election results.

This ability to predict elections by projecting estimates from small samples to enormous populations validates the methods used in studying public opinions. It validates the principles of random sampling. It validates the methods of interviewing. It validates the statistical tests in the data analysis. And it strongly supports, without completely validating, the "model of behavior" by which social scientists attempt to predict voting behavior on the basis of characteristics other than simply the reports of individuals as to how they intend to vote.

Indeed, the scholars at the University of Michigan's Survey Research Center were able to predict the behavior of more than 85 percent of the electorate, while in contrast, only 75 percent of the votes of the respondents were consistent with their earlier expressed intentions. This means that the pollsters are able to predict the behavior of voters *better than the voters can predict their own behavior.*[26] This is made possible by that "model of behavior" in which assumptions are made that habit plus the position of the respondent in the social structure will go far toward determining how that respondent will make political choices and shape political opinions. The influence of these so-called correlates seems to be far greater than most respondents are aware of, at least in the United States.[27]

These validated methods, coupled with a simple but powerful "model of behavior," have led to insights and knowledge far beyond the mere prediction of the next electoral decision. For most academic social scientists, and even for many political practitioners, prediction of the electoral outcome is merely a test of the methods rather than an end in itself. The question here is less one of the polling accuracy than of the conditions under which important voting decisions are made. For example, when and under what conditions do individuals vote according to their pocketbook, and when do they vote according to the color of their skin or their emotional feelings toward the candidate? How strong is habit in political opinions, as compared to campaign appeals or recent politically relevant events? How responsive are voters to changes in recent economic conditions? In general, how class-conscious are voters? Once we free ourselves of the need merely to predict

[26]Campbell et al., *The American Voter,* p. 74.

[27]The actual methods of this kind of correlational analysis do not need to be presented here. However, interested students might want to go back to some of the actual published studies to get a better acquaintance with the analyses, for example, Campbell, *The American Voter.* But after all is said and done, the analytic approaches are usually quite simple, especially with the help of a computer.

elections, we begin to find extremely important uses for the data drawn from public opinion polling. [28]

In spite of all this analytic power, there are nevertheless some important disadvantages inherent in the polling approach to political knowledge. The most popularly cited but least serious disadvantage of polling is the "bandwagon effect," whereby reports of the results of polls may influence the average voter to vote for whomever he or she thinks will be the victorious candidate. There is no dependable evidence that this actually happens, but there have occasionally been proposals to prohibit election night predictions of outcomes based upon polls and bellwether districts until after all the polls on the far West Coast are closed, in case there is such a bandwagon effect. Other disadvantages are a good deal more potential and substantial. The two most serious of these are the illusion of central tendency and the illusion of saliency.

The illusion of central tendency   There is a fairly well-established assumption that in most stable countries, especially the United States, opinions, like weights and heights and scholastic aptitude scores, are "normally distributed." As illustrated in Figure 7.1, the assumption of normality is graphically realized in a bell-shaped curve. This means that if the members of a sample are asked an opinion question and allowed to choose from five or six different responses, their responses will be more heavily distributed toward the center, or moderate, position. This can be represented by simply drawing a bar chart in which the height of each bar represents the proportion of the sample who chose each reponse. When the midpoints of each bar are connected, the resulting line then resembles a bell-shaped curve. In Figure 7.1 the proposition with which members of the sample group were asked to agree or disagree is very general, but even if a more particular issue were concerned, such as "The government ought to help everyone get a job," the hypothesis is that most respondents would still tend toward the moderate disagree or moderate agree positions.

The trouble is, this normal distribution is not necessarily a true description of every issue on which Americans have opinions. Moreover, it would be quite astonishing if any sample drawn in the United States would tend toward the center on all of the great issues. On at least a few issues, opinions are likely to be distributed more as represented in Figure 7.2. This is called a bimodal distribution, where the population is said to be "polarized." For example, opinions on the question of abortion during early pregnancy were

[28]It would be impossible to list even the important articles and books based upon sample survey data on public opinion. In addition to the sources already cited in this chapter, see V. O. Key, *Public Opinion and American Democracy* (New York: Knopf, 1961). For a more recent survey of surveys, see Robert A. Dahl, *Democracy in the United States,* 2d ed. (Chicago: Rand-McNally, 1972).

Figure 7.1
The assumption of centrality can be visualized as a bell-shaped curve. When asked to express their attitudes toward this moderately controversial proposition, members of a hypothetical sample group might respond as illustrated by this bell-shaped distribution.

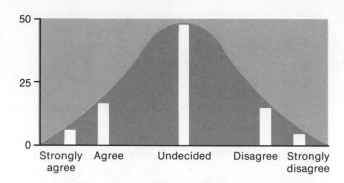

Proposition:
Business has become too big in the United States.

Percentage of members of hypothetical sample group who chose each response.

Figure 7.2
A polarized population can be visualized as a bimodal distribution. When asked to express their attitudes toward this highly controversial proposition, members of a hypothetical sample group might respond as illustrated in this bimodal distribution.

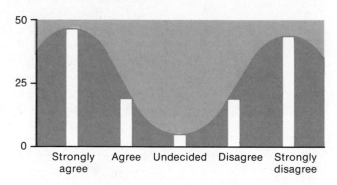

Proposition:
During the first several weeks of pregnancy, the mother ought to have the last word on abortion.

Percentage of members of hypothetical sample group who chose each response.

highly polarized in the 1960s. Admittedly, in a stable society during stable times, there may not be many issues distributed this way, but there are very likely to be some. Yet, the effect of polling is to suppress much of this polarization, and thereby to perpetuate the illusion of central tendency among politicians.

This illusion of a central tendency can be produced by asking questions so general in scope that only a foolhardy person or a militant activist would answer by choosing one of the extreme responses. For example, a respondent usually has only five or six choices of response to such questions as: "Do you favor busing?" or "Should we spend more money on law and order?" or "Has business become too big in America?" For most respondents there are many considerations to be taken into account before they check off a response. The necessity of making such a response forces each respondent to engage in a kind of internal dialogue. No matter which response is finally checked, it does not truly represent the respondent's views; it has been oversimplified to fit an item on the questionnaire; that is to say, it is only reported "on balance" after all of the contingencies and exceptions have been considered and suppressed. Thus, a great number of moderate responses are not moderate at all but rather are the result of a balance among extreme feelings within the response.

This might best be exemplified by the responses of two very different persons asked to agree or disagree with the statement that businesses have become too big. One respondent may wish to disagree in the extreme, not because of a feeling that big business is good but rather on the principle that big business can be more easily nationalized than a very large number of small businesses. The second respondent may very well be strongly pro-business yet may hate monopolies as the enemy of good business. Both of these types of respondents may end up choosing a moderate or "it all depends" response to the question; yet in both instances the moderate attitude expressed to the interviewer or on the questionnaire is an artifact of the alternatives provided by the poll and not a description of the true opinion of the respondent. Inasmuch as central tendency gives the appearance of consensus, then clearly in a large number of instances, the consensuses reported in opinion polls are artificial. They are neither false nor contrived by the pollsters, nor are they the result of persuasiveness of political campaigns. Rather, they are a result of the mixing of very unlike opinions through the mechanical limits of the responses available to respondents.

It might be argued that responsible polling organizations can avoid producing the appearance of consensus by providing a larger number of responses and by asking a larger number of questions on the specific issues rather than one or two very general questions about issues as complex as law and order or big business or liberalism versus conservatism. But even that does not stop the users of this type of data from deriving central tendencies. This is partly because they want to find these central tendencies, which to them are the essence of a moderate society. They produce these illusions statistically, as follows. Political candidates or officeholders are faced with a morass of information about the opinions of the electorate. They see responses to a whole gamut of questions from racial integration or the rights of police to stop and search suspects to raising or lowering taxes or amnesty for Vietnam deserters. They proceed to summarize the various results, hoping to find some general patterns of opinions, such as "tending toward the right," or "generally holding to the Democratic line."

Such summaries may in fact help predict votes in the next election. However, they also can do a certain amount of violence to the actual findings. Note in Figure 7.3 how this is possible. If the responses to each of several issues are cumulated in order to produce

Figure 7.3
Artificial consensus: The shape of several issues treated together in a "typology." When asked to express their attitudes toward the five propositions listed here, members of a hypothetical sample group might respond to these separate propositions as charted. The cumulated result of charting attitudes on several issues, as in this case, is likely to be a bell-shaped curve of central tendency even if the actual opinions on each of the individual issues are in a polarized or bimodal distribution.

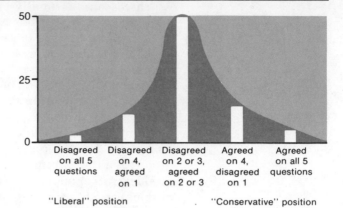

Percentage of members of hypothetical sample group who chose each pattern of response.

| Disagreed on all 5 questions | Disagreed on 4, agreed on 1 | Disagreed on 2 or 3, agreed on 2 or 3 | Agreed on 4, disagreed on 1 | Agreed on all 5 questions |

"Liberal" position   "Conservative" position

Law and order–related propositions:
a. Racially integrated neighborhoods will not solve urban violence problems.
b. Local police need more support.
c. Those accused of crimes receive more protection than victims of crimes.
d. Stop-and-frisk powers are necessary for local police.
e. Detention without bail for repeated offenders would help prevent crime.

a distribution of liberal versus conservative opinions, the result is likely to be a bell-shaped curve of central tendency *even if opinions on each of the individual issues are actually distributed in a polarized or bimodal distribution.* That is to say, even if the distribution of opinions on each of the single issues should look exactly like Figure 7.2, the result of cumulating all of the issues in order to simplify candidate positions would nevertheless look like Figure 7.3. What is happening here is that *the extremes are eliminated statistically.*

On each issue there may be a very large number of respondents who respond at the extremes. However, there will be very few respondents who respond consistently at the extremes on all issues posed in the survey. These are the ideologues and the college professors who are concerned about being clear and consistent, or who may have a particularly intense dedication to all of the subjects covered in the questionnaire. But virtually everyone else in the survey may have strong feelings about one or two of the issues and no hard and fast opinion about all of the others. When you start cumulating these results, you will find that the "extremes" will drop to a small proportion of the total, because there will be so few who strongly disagree or strongly agree with all of the propositions. Thus, a central tendency is produced.

The effect of this tendency on politicians can be very important. First, it tends to make them centrists, no matter what their inclinations might otherwise be. Second, it tends to lead them to

Dissatisfaction can arise
from unexpected sources:
Grey Panthers fight age
discrimination.

distrust or to suppress reports of polarized distributions of opinion in the society. As a consequence of these two influences, most candidates feel the urge and the justification to avoid any clear positions and to move always toward the center and toward their opposition in the campaigns. If candidates are sure that the electorate is highly concentrated in the center, it will obviously be irrational for them to behave otherwise than to move themselves toward the center, and toward the other candidates. Picture the bell-shaped curve as a space filled with people. Any candidates who move a step or two to the left or right of center might feel themselves sliding down the slope of the population toward a very sparsely occupied area.[29]

Some may feel that it is a virtue if the polls do influence politicians toward the center in this way. They may feel that this functions to eliminate any tendencies among American politicians toward extremism. This is a chimera—a creature only of the imagination. The extremes we are talking about here are not revolutionary extremes but only the somewhat more intense attitudes toward fundamental issues and conventional methods of government. Politicians who are constantly tending toward the center because the polls tell them that is the position where they can

*Getting the People to
Consent: The Public in
Groups, in Opinions, and in
Electorates*

[29]The most systematic statement of this behavioral tendency among politicians will be found in Anthony Downs, *An Economic Theory of Democracy* (New York: Harper & Bros., 1957).

establish and maintain popularity are simply muddying the water of political choice. Moreover, they are actually creating more of a central tendency than is otherwise likely to exist by providing the voters with so few clear alternatives. The center, therefore, has become a very conservative place for politicians to locate themselves; yet it often appears to them as the only rational place to be.

On the other hand, if a sufficient number of politicians suddenly should make the opposite assumption—that the electorate is sufficiently polarized to make clear statements of position an effective political strategy—it might very possibly turn out that the electorate would not abandon these bold politicians. The point here is that politicians are unlikely to quit sticking to each other like barnacles as long as the polls are thought to be reporting real central tendencies on all matters.

The illusion of saliency The *Oxford English Dictionary* defines saliency as "the quality of leaping up . . . or projecting beyond." Salient interests are those that stand out beyond other interests; in our context the term *salient* will be used to refer to those interests that are of more than ordinary concern to the respondents in a survey or to voters in the electorate. When politicians, social scientists, journalists, and others assume something is important to the public which in fact is not, they create an illusion of saliency. This illusion can be fostered by polls in spite of the most careful controls over sampling, interviewing, coding, and data analysis. In fact, the illusion of saliency is strengthened by virtue of the extra credibility that scientization has given survey results. If the designers of a survey include questions on twenty subjects they or their politician clients feel to be of potential importance, *this survey will produce twenty issues.* If by definition an issue is any public problem on which a significant number of people disagree, then also by definition each of the twenty questions will produce an issue.

The responses may be sincere, but the cumulative impression is false, inasmuch as a high proportion of the respondents may not have seriously concerned themselves with some of these so-called issues until actually confronted with questions about them on the questionnaire or by the interviewer. Many respondents feel that nonresponse would reveal their ignorance or that it would be rude not to answer. It is nearly impossible to discover what proportion of people feel obliged to answer even when they have never given a survey question serious forethought. Worse, we will probably never be able to determine specifically which members of a sample give improvised responses and which do not. That is the heart of the problem. It is rare for more than 10 percent of a sample to report that they have no opinion on a given question; yet, it is difficult to imagine that as many as 90 percent of the responses on any sample survey are the responses of individuals who have found twenty or more questions about public policies salient!

One of the baneful effects of the illusion of saliency is that politicians move between two extremes, from a politics of no issues to a politics of too many issues, in which each issue is skimmed over or trivialized. On the one hand, there are all too many cases where our representatives in Congress defend their institution by citing all the things they worked on during the past session while at the same time apparently not perceiving that they neglected in part or altogether the one or two truly salient issues of the day. When politicians are preparing a major state or national campaign, on the other hand, they seem to feel obliged to prepare position papers on virtually every conceivable issue, as though each elected member of Congress will have to be president of the United States or the world's first omnicompetent politician.

A related, and perhaps still more important, aspect of the influence of polling is the absence of reporting on some issues that may indeed be deeply salient in the electorate. After all, there is a limited amount of space on any questionnaire, and the design and processing of the questionnaire takes too much time to be able to account for the latest development in issues. Surveys could be run more frequently; and questions could be left open-ended to give each respondent a chance to define for the interviewer the actual issues that are salient to him or her. But each of these alternatives represents a tremendous increase in the cost of getting direct knowledge of public opinions. (The cost of a single interview on a responsible sample survey is running toward a minimum of $100.)

It is quite clear that the public opinion survey industry has become one of the media of mass communications. A few major national polling organizations, along with the three major television networks, a scant few national newspapers, and two or three international and national news syndicates comprise a strategic sector of the economy in their ability to create information and biases among electorates and among politicians. As we have seen here, very often the biases and illusions are unintentional; sometimes they are unavoidable features of the very nature of the sample survey procedure. Nevertheless, polling is capable of setting political agendas, of artificially putting irrelevant items on them, and of artificially keeping items off them.

Public Opinion and the Functions of Ignorance

Many will be distressed to find public opinion analyzed in terms of limited knowledge, distorted messages, shortsighted analysts, and deluded politicians. Yet, it would have been a great deal more pessimistic to argue, as many have, that public opinion does not really exist and that knowledge about it can never be improved.[30] Instead, the argument here has been that widely distributed public opinions do exist and that our efforts to reduce our ignorance of the public have some good and some bad effects on politicians. On the negative side there is the possibility that once politicians realize their ignorance they become cynical, because all politicians know they have a good deal of flexibility in picking and choosing the interests they will "represent." One of the worst expressions of this kind of political cynicism is the blatant claim to public opinion support politicians sometimes make on the basis of completely unfounded or biased reports drawn from their constituencies.[31]

On the optimistic side, as long as politicians know they are operating mostly on the basis of ignorance, they may be somewhat more uncertain than otherwise about their power and their legitimacy. This uncertainty provides something of a modest opportunity for the powerless, inasmuch as it may make politicians more accountable. One of the more hopeful signs is the ability of responsible survey research to produce "negative knowledge." This is knowledge that pierces through irresponsible claims to public support. Such negative knowledge makes citizens less gullible, politicians less deceitful, and survey research more important to the future of American politics.

Where, then, are we in the history of self-government when we tie conquest to consent, consent to mass interests, and mass interests back to elite ignorance? To say the least, the ship of state has loose moorings. But the modern state is tied to popular consent by more than crude and ambiguous expressions of public opinion. *Doubts about the value of knowledge of public opinion have enhanced the importance of elections in modern politics.*

POLITICAL KNOWLEDGE, CONSENT, AND THE ELECTORAL PROCESS: ELECT, ELECTOR, ELECTORATE, ELECTION, ELECTED . . .

It is estimated that in 1972 Americans spent nearly one-half billion dollars on elections. This was up 25 percent over 1968, and there is no reason to expect election expenditures to go down. Exact amounts can never be known because some important expenditures are illegal and others simply get lost in the thousands of spontaneous efforts made to gain nomination and election. But these astronomical figures are not altogether surprising when one considers that as

---

[30]See Hennessy, *Public Opinion,* chapter 5, for a good discussion of the history of public opinion and how the term has been used in theory and in empirical research.

[31]The best analyses of this aspect of political ignorance are those of Lewis A. Dexter; for example, consult his classic "The Representative and His District," *Human Organization* 16 (1947), 2–13.

many as a half million elective offices had to be filled in November of 1972, and a very high proportion of these were involved in some kind of pre-electoral nominating campaign even before the election campaign.[32] Undoubtedly the satisfactions provided by elections must be special if the country is willing to sustain such heavy and regular investment.

One might assume that it is the purpose of elections to express to the elected the will of the people concerning fundamental issues in society. This type of revealed meaning would go a long way toward justifying the tremendous expense of elections. Yet the meaning of an election is almost inherently unclear, except perhaps in instances where candidates are exclusively associated with only one or two issues.

Figure 7.4 portrays the issue orientation of a number of very enthusiastic Nixon supporters—defined as those who felt extremely happy with Nixon's stand on at least thirteen of twenty possible positions he took during his campaign in 1972. Note how it was possible for these supporters to agree with him on thirteen of twenty issues and with *each other* on as few as six of the twenty. Then take into account other segments of the population made up of individuals who felt intensely enough about only one or two issues to prefer Nixon to McGovern but who still did not agree with the Nixon supporters as defined above on more than those one or two issues. This suggests that even victories in strongly issue-oriented campaigns do not necessarily convey a clear meaning. Talk of "mandates from the people" is usually a rhetorical effort by an elected person to rally public support. Thus, although some elections can produce genuine and clear information about the will of the people, this is not a sufficiently dependable result to justify the enormous investment in elections. The electoral process must exist for purposes other than or beyond the production of political knowledge.

Every analyst has his own argument about the purposes of elections. But no argument is worthy of consideration if it arises only out of personal reflection. Reflection must be based upon direct examination of the electoral process. And although some understanding of the purpose of elections can be gained from an examination of actual election statistics, we must get behind those statistics, because they may tell us too much about specific elections and not enough about the nature of elections. We must search for the purpose of elections in the *forms and structures* of elections; this is the only way to see what it is that elections are *designed* to do. The following paragraphs are literally a glossary of concepts essential to an understanding of the actual electoral processes. They may help

[32]For a discussion of these figures and the methods by which estimates can be made, see Herbert Alexander, *Money in Politics* (Washington, D.C.: Public Affairs Press, 1972).

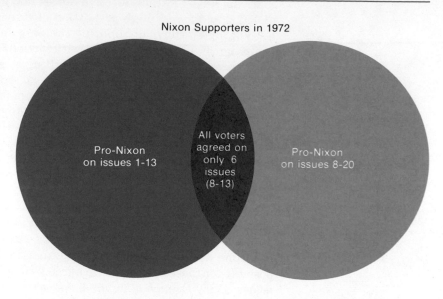

Figure 7.4
How much meaning can be drawn from a landslide election? An unclear result of a campaign "on the issues." The most enthusiastic Nixon supporters in 1972 could have disagreed with each other on a majority of twenty specific issues identified in the campaign for election, as indicated in this illustration.

Pro-Nixon on issues 1-13

All voters agreed on only 6 issues (8-13)

Pro-Nixon on issues 8-20

locate the place of the electoral process in the larger scheme of government.

Elect

Election as a separate and distinctive part of government is not so very old: "There have been kings, revolutions, constitutions, and bureaucracies since time immemorial, but the mass voter is something quite recent."[33] To *elect,* according to the *Oxford English Dictionary,* is to "pick out," to "choose among," as from a group of alternatives. The notion of making a choice by *voting* is actually the third definition listed, an indication of the relative recency of voting as an important feature of government. Popular elections and mass voting seem everywhere to follow rather than to precede the development of representative government.

In the electoral process, one thing comes even prior to the voter himself, and that is the principle of election: *Who* is going to have to submit to election? The American answer to this has been severely orthodox during most of its history, because the requirement of election was applied not only to chief executives and legislators but also to many other kinds of officials. Until perhaps forty years ago, the typical ballot submitted to the voter on election day contained the names of hundreds of candidates for fifty or sixty different types

[33]Friedrich, *Constitutional Government and Democracy,* p. 284.

of offices. The ideal seems to have been a government staffed almost entirely by elected officials.

This extraordinary situation has been changed in favor of shorter ballots, fewer elective offices, and somewhat longer terms of office. However, the theory back of all this has not changed appreciably, and it is not likely to. Election is supposed to achieve accountability. If citizens can periodically give and withhold their consent through voting, those in power are more likely to conduct themselves responsibly. The frequency of elections, the length of the term of office, the size of the district, the number of constituents in the district, the manner of election, and the conditions of candidate and voter eligibility may vary enormously from one state to another. But the theory does not seem to. Consent is given and consent can be withheld.

Consent is necessarily broad; it is virtually a license without guidelines to govern for the full length of the term of office. Responsibility is supposed to arise out of the fear of not being re-elected. There is also the hope that through a career of elective office the politician will develop good character and be encouraged to seek to be responsible even beyond the expectations of the voters. This is a noble theory, but it is only a theory. There is voluminous literature on virtually every aspect of this issue, yet disagreements are still extensive. These disagreements spill over from academia into the political process itself. Optimism or pessimism about the virtues of the electoral process goes a long way toward defining the general political ideology of thoughtful people.[34]

Elector

The concept of elector, or voter, is not as simple as popular lore would have it. Who is qualified to be an elector? How many are there to be, and how shall they be allowed to express themselves by their vote? The term *voter* is a legal definition which varies according to the particular statute in which it is contained. Voting and universal suffrage are often thought to be one and the same aspect of democratic government. But actually, universal suffrage is literally impossible. Even where support for voting is strongest, there are limits at least in terms of minimum age, and also usually in terms of sanity. Criminals and former criminals are often denied the right to vote. Literacy is a widely accepted limitation on eligibility to be a voter; and residency is widely considered a reasonable restriction, despite the fact that millions of otherwise qualified persons are excluded as a consequence. Property ownership was once felt to be

[34]For a general treatment of these issues and their relation to representative government, see Friedrich, *Constitutional Government and Democracy,* especially chapters 14–16. See also Harold Gosnell, *Democracy: Threshold of Freedom* (New York: Ronald Press, 1948); and Douglas Rae, *The Political Consequences of Electoral Laws* (New Haven: Yale University Press, 1967).

an essential qualification, and there are probably many sincere conservatives who continue to feel that the only truly responsible voter is a property holder.

Voting is also severely limited by restrictions even on those who are qualified voters. Until recent years, qualified voters were required to pay a poll tax in order to vote in many southern states. This was eliminated by constitutional amendment, but other even more effective barriers have remained. Most effective is the requirement of registration. One must think ahead and go through the bureaucratic routines in order to become a registered voter, or all the best intentions of citizenship in the world go for naught. This is a particular problem in the United States because of all the movement from one county or state to another. Thus the requirement of a specified period of residence in an area before registration can take place is often a problem here, as well as pure ignorance on the part of many citizens as to where to go and what to do in order to get on the voter rolls. Yet another restraint on voting that is strongly biased against the working classes rather than against the entire electorate is the American practice of holding elections on regular working days. Many union contracts and state laws provide for released time to vote; nevertheless, it is a great nuisance to have to vote on a regular working day, if only because voting places can be extremely crowded during rush hours.

It would be impossible to estimate the actual number of persons who are nonvoters because of these restrictions rather than because they are apathetic. It has been estimated that between five and eight million voters are rendered unable to vote due to residency requirements alone. Liberalization of state residency requirements has tended to reduce that number toward the lower side, but it is still a shockingly large number.[35] It is almost certain that a far larger number of voters are interfered with by the sheer bureaucratic business of registration. This would mean that the nonvoter is a much more ambiguous and much less problematic category than civic complaints about nonvoting would lead us to believe. It is true that a turnout of only 63 percent of the estimated voting population in the 1972 presidential election is very low in comparison to turnouts in European elections. But when we look at the formal restrictions on voting, most of the difference can be explained without resort to notions of apathy or dissatisfaction or bad citizenship.

However, these various formal definitions of and restrictions on the voter produce another kind of conclusion, which is that voting is considered more a privilege than a right. Note in addition to the variations in definitions of the voter that the two most important

[35]These figures are reported in *Congress and the Nation* (Washington, D.C.: Congressional Quarterly, 1969), vol. 2 (1965–1968), p. 437.

synonyms for voting are *suffrage* and *franchise.* The *Oxford English Dictionary* defines the term *suffrage* as a liturgical concept having to do with prayers, especially prayers for the souls of the departed. It also refers to the giving of help or assistance in response to prayers. Not until the third definition do we reach the notion of voting, and at this point it is quite clear that voting is historically understood in the context of a plea made or assistance given in response to a plea. The fourth definition of suffrage refers to the expression of approval, but clearly this notion of approval is deeply imbedded in the context of pleading; that is, suffrage connotes a privilege granted in response to a plea.

The other synonym, *franchise,* is in many ways more interesting. Its definition includes three notions—freedom, immunity, and privilege. Franchise, like license, implies a privilege to do something that is otherwise illegal. Franchise is thought to be a privilege or "an exceptional right" granted by a sovereign to any deserving person. Thus, when the word *franchise* was used as a synonym for *the vote,* some notion of privilege was clearly intended.

The obvious ambivalence in all of this complicates our understanding and interpretation of voting in particular and of the electoral process in general. Voting seems, then, to be both a right *and* a privilege, so that the ambivalence we may feel about the concept is an ambivalence that inheres out there in the real world and not merely in our definitions. Since voting is something that people have had to seize from the sovereign, voting appears to be a right. On the other hand, since voting is very heavily regulated and is allowed to vary according to the whims of the legislature, it is either a very limited right or a very extensive privilege. If all of this produces confusion in the mind of the reader, that confusion is itself a privilege inasmuch as it is shared with many of the great figures in the history of political philosophy.

Electorate

The term *electorate* has come to mean the mere population of voters. But in origin it meant the *dominion* of the electors; that is to say, it meant the elector defined in the larger context of what he uses his voting power *for.* Consequently, the best definition of the electorate is *the electoral process and the system of electoral representation based upon it.* This definition includes all of the electors, the size and shape of the districts in which they have electoral power, and the type of relationship the electors have with the people they elect.[36] Some have called these latter factors "electoral geometry" or "electoral engineering." But by any name we are talking about

*Getting the People to
Consent: The Public in
Groups, in Opinions, and in
Electorates*

247

[36]A great deal more on this relationship will be found in chapters 9 and 10 on Congress and representative government.

aspects of the electorate which are of vital importance to the
political system. As Marshall McLuhan would put it, the structure
of the electorate is a medium that profoundly shapes the electoral
message.

The art and craft of designing electorates   The most dramatic
portrayal of the significance of the shape of electorates is the
American version of electoral engineering which we call *gerrymandering* in honor of a district in Massachusetts designed by Governor
Elbridge Gerry at the beginning of the nineteenth century. Since
the district had the shape of the salamander, it quickly came to be
labeled a "gerrymander"; and since its wildly convoluted shape
seemed to typify the widespread practice of forming districts with
distorted boundaries, the usage of the term spread. Gerrymandering
continued into the early 1960s. For example, one congressional
district in Brooklyn was drawn almost precisely in the shape of a
dragon—which made possible the election of a Republican in a

decidedly Democratic area of New York City. Another was long and narrow and had a total of 51 sides in Brooklyn, as well as an entire second part across the Narrows on Staten Island.

The strategy of gerrymandering in New York and elsewhere was to draw district lines in such a way as to pull together into a single district enough voters of a given persuasion to have them count as a majority rather than let them be spread too thinly across several districts. Another widely adopted strategy is just the opposite—to design a district deliberately to spread voters of a given persuasion so thinly that they do *not* constitute an important political force.

Reformers in the United States have constantly complained about abuses of electoral engineering and have often brought suits to force legislators to do a better job. Until 1962 the Supreme Court constantly sought to avoid these issues, arguing that they were "political questions" that should be left for settlement to the normal political process.[37] In 1962, in a historic decision, the Supreme Court reversed itself, deciding that henceforth disputes over electoral engineering should be adjudicated.[38] Within a few years following that decision, the federal courts virtually redrew the electoral map of the United States. They applied the principle of "one man–one vote" to congressional electorates and all the way down to city council districts. The rule was that representative government could not take place equitably as long as districts were of vastly unequal size. In the opinion of the courts, the voter in a district with 500,000 other voters was valued very differently from a voter in a district of only 300,000 other voters.[39]

However, even though the courts did bring about a reapportionment revolution, they did not eliminate electoral engineering—nor would it be possible to do so. The courts are able to deal with only the shape and size of electorates. They cannot reach and control many of the "political questions" that are involved when legislatures draw districts. It is quite obvious that a clever legislator can draw up a district to meet judicial requirements of equality and at the same time place district lines in such a manner as to ensure that blacks will elect only one representative rather than two, or that Republicans in a city will elect at least two rather than none. All that is necessary is a study of the racial and economic characteristics of neighborhoods in a certain area, and then an application of the political rule that no district should contain more than 30 or 40

---

[37]Until 1962 the leading case was *Colgrove* v. *Green*, 328 U.S. 549 (1946).

[38]*Baker* v. *Carr*, 369 U.S. 186 (1962). A comprehensive review will be found in Philippa Strum, *The Supreme Court and "Political Questions"* (University, Ala.: University of Alabama Press, 1974), chapter 3.

[39]For a brief and sober discussion of this whole line of cases, see Philip Kurland, *Politics, the Constitution and the Warren Court* (Chicago: University of Chicago Press, 1970), p. 83. For an insight into the implications of the requirement of drawing districts with electorates of equal size in a reasonable geographic area, see Stuart Nagel, "Simplified Bi-partisan Computer Redistricting," *Stanford Law Review* 17 (1965), 863.

percent of any characteristic of party or race or economics that the legislator seeks to keep under control.

Opportunities for this kind of gerrymandering will continue to exist, and we will have this kind of problem as long as we continue to have an electoral system in which electorates are allowed to elect only one representative from each district. This is called the single-member constituency system, and we use it for almost every election to any representative assembly in the United States. Of course we would have no problem of electoral engineering if we shifted to the multiple-member constituency system, where all candidates are elected at large from the whole state or the whole city and each voter is given the number of votes equivalent to the number of seats to be filled. Then every representative represents the entire electorate of that state or city rather than an artificially carved district with an artificially defined electorate. That sounds like a very good solution, but it raises almost as many problems as it solves.

We will have occasion to look at some of the problems of multiple-member constituency systems in our discussion of Congress. Suffice it to say here that there are several different kinds of electoral processes that European legislatures have adopted to deal with multiple-member systems. One of these is called proportional representation. Another is called list voting. And there are variations on each of these. Some of the problems that are incurred in either of these systems can be indicated by two fairly well-established characteristics of multiple-member district systems. One of these is that there is a tendency to encourage several parties rather than two. The other is that the multiple-member district system, especially list voting, strengthens the hand of political parties.

Neither of these consequences would be considered a "problem" by many people. The point is that each method of defining an electorate and granting it powers has important consequences for the political process. Even among people who uniformly agree on the desirability of democratic government, there will be differences on what kind of an electoral system to have; and they will tend to take their positions in terms of which system will produce the greatest amount of results they value. The courts were always right when they argued that the electoral process is a political question.[40]

The size of the electorate   Size of legislative districts is one of the knottiest problems in the entire field of elections despite the fact that it is easy to characterize. Every decision about size affects

[40]Good assessments of these issues will be found in Friedrich, *Constitutional Government and Democracy,* chapters 14–16; Rae, *The Political Consequences of Electoral Laws;* and Maurice Duverger, *Political Parties* (New York: Wiley, 1954).

almost everything else about the electoral process, and a great deal about government as well. The size of the district affects the relative weight of each vote and the ability of the elected representative to gain useful knowledge about the district. The problem of size of districts is all the more knotty because it influences the actual size of the legislature. As James Madison put it in *Federalist* 55, "no political problem is less susceptible of a precise solution than that which relates to the number most convenient for representative legislatures; nor is there any point on which the policy of the several States is more at variance."

Those who are concerned mostly about the ability of legislatures to do their work will generally favor a smaller legislature and therefore be committed by definition to electoral districts of very large size. Those who are concerned with the ability of the elected officials to gain knowledge about their districts will tend to stress districts of smaller size and be willing to let the resulting enlargement of the legislature take care of itself. This is a fundamental problem of constitutional theory about which knowledge of electorates and voting will be no guide. Each person must decide what values ought to be protected.

Election

It is impossible in a brief treatment to do justice to election, the one concept that rounds out all the rest. Only three aspects of this complex matter can be covered here. The first of these has to do with the actual definition of winning. The second has to do with whether the voter is given power to choose candidates or can only choose delegates who will in turn make the actual choice. The third aspect is the frequency and regularity with which these options are placed before the voter.

Who wins? One of our basic political axioms is: The majority rules. Yet we rarely obey it. And we rarely obey it for the simple reason that in most districts it would be impossible to require majority rule without being prepared to hold more than one election for the same office. If there are only two candidates in a contest, of course, the candidate with the most votes will not only win but will win with a majority of all the votes cast. However, what happens if there are more than two candidates for the same office, or if the election is close between two candidates and there is a small but sufficient number of blank ballots? We could finesse the latter case by defining majority to mean the majority of those voting. But what of the former instance? If in that case we insist upon majority rule, we would have to provide for a "primary" election and then for a second or "run-off" election between the two candidates receiving the largest number of votes in the "primary." (A discussion of this

will be found in chapter 8.) It should be noted here that we call the process of nominating by election the *primary*. This is actually a misnomer, suggesting that the nomination is the first election and the November election is the second. Actually, in many states, especially in the South, the primary itself consists of two elections, the first round and then the runoff between the two leading candidates.

Except for our nominating procedures, the American electoral process rests upon a serious modification of majority rule—despite our habit of calling it majority rule. Our provision for victory is in fact quite a permissive one, which should be called *plurality rule*. This simply means that no matter how many candidates are running for a particular office, and no matter how small the actual vote for the leading candidate, that candidate with the largest number of votes is declared the victor. Thus in an equally divided three-way race, victory could go to a candidate who received barely more than 30 percent of the vote. It is quite conceivable, in a race involving several candidates, for the victorious candidate to receive little more than 10 percent of the vote. This plurality system is a significant departure from true majority rule and should be judged accordingly. The disadvantages are patently clear. The major advantage is that plurality rule is a great deal easier to get than absolute majority rule. This underscores our point that the primary purpose of elections is consent; a nation's officialdom is most fortunate if citizens are willing to accept plurality in place of majority rule.

What kind of choice does the elector have?   The problem of majority rule is frequently solved by taking the power of direct choice away from voters, leaving them with only indirect choice. This identifies two different types of electoral power, direct election and indirect election, and the United States has had considerable experience with both types.

The most significant example of indirect election is the method of electing the president of the United States. The voters in their respective states are given the power only of voting for a small group of representatives, people the Constitution calls "electors." These electors form an Electoral College, which is assembled in respective state capitals on the first Monday after the second Wednesday in December of presidential election years.

In these gatherings, which of course take place after the popular, at-large presidential elections, the electors cast their ballots directly for their preferred presidential candidate. They are in no way bound by the Constitution to vote for the candidate selected by the voters in their state; they are not even obliged during the campaign to pledge how they will vote. However, the original design was completely perverted by political parties as early as 1800, when parties were able to choose electors who agreed to pledge their vote, if elected, to the presidential candidate of the party's choice.

The founders had designed the Electoral College in order to ensure that presidential elections would be indirect and that the presidential constituency would be no larger than a state, rather than the nation at large. They got their indirect election, but through the parties rather than through the separate institution of an Electoral College, which does only the parties' bidding. The founders also got their smaller constituency, because the one important influence of the Electoral College has been to keep a national electorate from developing. More will be said of this later, but it should be pointed out here that since the party with the most popular votes in a state wins all the electors, the state has remained the key unit in presidential elections. Consequently, the presidential election is comprised of fifty indirect elections.

For over a century the United States Senate was also an example of indirect election. This was changed by the Seventeenth Amendment (1913) which abolished the selection of senators by state legislatures in favor of direct election on a statewide basis. Since that time, all members of both houses of the United States Congress, as well as all members of state and local legislatures, are directly elected. The only exceptions are, of course, those members appointed for brief periods to fill unexpired terms.

Getting the People to Consent: The Public in Groups, in Opinions, and in Electorates

253

The preference for direct election in the United States is patently clear. But there are many reasonable people who are concerned about the consequences of direct election, and their considerations should not be overlooked in any serious evaluation of the electoral process. One of the most articulate among them was Alexis de Tocqueville, who was struck by the "vulgar demeanor" of the members of the House of Representatives. When he compared members of the House to members of the Senate, he was led to the conclusion that the difference between them was attributable to direct election in the one case and indirect election in the other. Tocqueville then concluded that "the time must come when the American Republics will be obliged more frequently to introduce the plan of election by an elected body into their system of representation or run the risk of perishing miserably among the shoals of democracy."[41]

Political scientists who have studied these matters tend to doubt the dire consequences predicted for direct election by such classic observers. In fact, there is so little concern about these consequences that few political scientists have looked seriously into the issue for many years. Fortunately, two recent studies get at least part of the issue evaluated. In one of these, all of the presidential elections of the past century were replayed, applying to each a set of rules providing for direct election of the president.[42] It was determined thus that direct election would have made almost no difference to the outcome of presidential elections during most of the twentieth century—although prior to the twentieth century a few elections would have had different outcomes. In the second study, an exhaustive analysis was made of the members of the United States Senate and their behavior before and after the introduction of direct election.[43] It was found that the impact of the switch was very slight. There was certainly no evidence to support Tocqueville's dire prediction that direct election would bring down the stature of that august body.

The decision to have direct rather than indirect elections may sometimes make a difference in the outcome of elections. What little evidence has been collected suggests that appearances are more important than expectations of likely consequences in the trend toward direct elections in the United States. This may help to explain why the march toward universal suffrage has been accompanied by a march toward virtual elimination of indirect election of

---

[41]Alexis de Tocqueville, *Democracy in America,* vol. 1, trans. Phillips Bradley (New York: Knopf, Vintage, 1954), p. 212. Other more contemporary expressions of concern will be found in Walter Lippmann, *The Public Philosophy* (Boston: Little, Brown, 1955); and José Ortega y Gasset, *The Revolt of the Masses* (New York: Norton, 1932).

[42]Carlton Sterling, "The Political Implications of Alternative Systems of Electing the President of the United States" (Ph.D. diss., University of Chicago, 1970).

[43]Byron Daynes, "The Impact of the Direct Election of Senators on the Political System" (Ph.D. diss., University of Chicago, 1971).

Do the people vote with
knowledge, or just with
regularity?

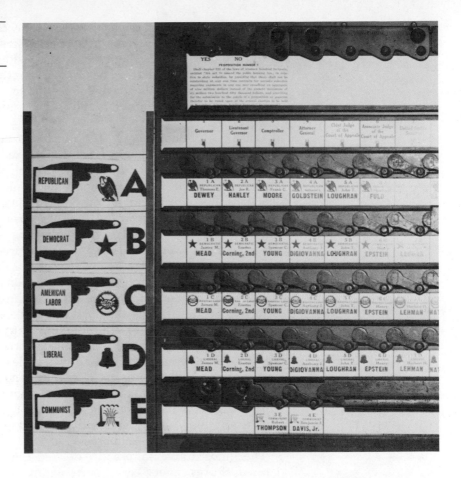

governmental officeholders in the United States. It is almost certain
that in the coming decade the Electoral College will go the same
route and be overturned in favor of a direct, national election of the
president, although undoubtedly many will continue to express
the fear that this will bring on the risk of too much "mass
democracy."[44]

When can the electors exercise their right (or privilege)?
Periodicity is a clumsy word that refers to two very important
features of any electoral process. The first of these features is the
frequency with which elections are held; the second is their regularity. Not so very long ago the preference in the United States was

---

*Getting the People to
Consent: The Public in
Groups, in Opinions, and in
Electorates*

[44]One's concern here depends heavily upon the definition of such terms as *vulgar*, or
responsible, or *of higher stature*. For example, one study reports that appointed and
indirectly elected municipal officers make more responsible decisions than directly elected
municipal officers. But a lot of that rides on a definition. See Robert Crain, Elihu Katz, and
Donald Rosenthal, *The Politics of Community Conflict* (Indianapolis: Bobbs-Merrill, 1969). This is
obviously an area which deserves a great deal more research than political scientists have given it.

almost universally in favor of annual election for all legislators; even for chief executives the general sentiment favored terms limited to two years. The amount of consideration and discussion devoted to the subject of the proper length of terms of office is largely relative to the degree of satisfaction Americans receive from their governments, but the issue is always a very sensitive one.[45]

Completely independent of that issue is the question of whether these elections should take place on a fixed and regular basis or whether they should occur whenever the need arises. The constitutional principle of fixed and regular terms of office, and thus regular elections, has never been seriously questioned in the United States. But many other democratic countries prefer irregular elections, which are usually called by the governing party. Many observers feel that the power to call elections at unpredictable and irregular times is an essential requirement for responsible party government; the feeling is that the irregularity of elections keeps parties on their toes, requiring that they remain well organized at all times. They also believe that this is the only way to be sure that the elections will concern themselves with the important issues of the day. Their argument would be that when the electoral period is fixed far in advance, many issues may have grown stale by the time the election occurs and elected officials may feel they can rest easy in the interim period. These arguments have obviously not been convincing in the United States, but they do emphasize the significance of the choice Americans made many generations ago and have, by mere habit and repetition, ceased to appreciate.

The almost universal practice of fixed and regular elections in the United States underscores once again our argument that the primary purpose of the electoral process in the United States is to provide consent rather than to produce political knowledge. If the main concern for elections was to have them produce knowledge about issues and choices, then surely there would be a great deal more agitation in favor of the power to call elections at the time an important issue needs to be settled. There would be more agitation against the single-member district system. There would be more nostalgia in favor of annual elections. There would almost certainly be more debate dedicated to the development of new mechanisms of electoral practice that might produce more political knowledge. In our electoral system no effort whatsoever has been made to design the forms and structures which would produce mandates. Our system allows candidates to claim they have a mandate after the election is over. But all they really have is consent.

---

[45]See, for example, *Federalist,* 52 and 53, where Madison felt he had to argue very strongly against demands for *one*-year terms for members of the House.

OPINIONS, ELECTIONS, CONSENT, AND CONQUEST

In the case of democracy versus conquest, the verdict may never be in. It is clear enough that democracy must rely upon elections to limit the tyrant. But it is not at all clear that elections will, in any form, be able to do the job. Our examination of the forms and structures of our electoral process has revealed that the purpose of election is to give consent in return for accountability. It has also become clear that consent *is* given. But is accountability gained in return? Elections, especially in the United States, provide elected officials with two, four, or six years of unlimited participation in government. Each elected official may pay in the end by "electoral punishment"—defeat at the polls—if he or she misbehaves in some noticeable and unacceptable way. The point the jury must ponder, however, is whether the prospect of electoral punishment provides sufficient sanction. If not, is there an electoral design that would strengthen this sanction? Is there a public opinion by which the official can guide accountability even in instances where he or she wishes sincerely to be accountable? It seems necessary to admit that elections, considered in and of themselves, do not fulfill their own expectations. On the other hand, the jury must continue to sit; the arguments are not yet complete. Thus far, we have only been able to look at public opinion, the electoral process, and what the electoral process is designed to do. Further judgment must await evidence on how the elected officials behave once they are in office.

The electoral process is something like Jacob's Ladder. It is cut off at the bottom from public opinion in its fullest sense, and it is cut off at the top from the actual conduct of officials once they have gained consent. Once representatives are elected to an assembly, for example, they find themselves in a collective body and must immediately contend with each other rather than with their home constituency. This catches them in a web of contradictions. If they are to contend with their colleagues, they must be prepared to disregard their followers in the short run, hoping that in the long run they might reach some favorable accord with them.

Nor is that the end of it. The representatives must also concern themselves with their collectivity as an institution; that is to say, the elected representatives do not merely assemble as a collection of individuals but rather as a governmental institution with its own structures, its own rules, and its own rights, all of which are independent of the individual legislator and the electorates and voters. The representatives must be concerned with this matter, because if this institution is incapable of making important governmental decisions, then there is no good reason for their participation in government in the first place. If, on the other hand, this institution is capable of formulating effective governmental policy,

Getting the People to Consent: The Public in Groups, in Opinions, and in Electorates

then it will necessarily develop a life of its own independent of any one crop of representatives and independent of transitory modes of public opinion.

Thus, we can speak of consent as the purpose and place of elections in the larger governmental system. But the full meaning of that notion, and the actual prospect of consent working as a limitation on tyranny, requires consideration in the larger context of representative government. The question of whether elections effectively express public opinion is an aspect of *representation*— one part of the duality that we call representative government. The other part of that duality is *government,* and its demands are quite inconsistent with the demands of representation. It is as an integral part of this contradiction that the electoral process must now be studied.

But before we can do that, we must consider one additional aspect of politics: political parties and the party system. Political parties have, in the past two centuries, become something of a bridge between the electoral process and representative government. Political parties have become part of both representation and governing; what parties do affects both. Once parties have been drawn into consideration, we can then begin to take on the bigger problem— government itself.

Chapter 8   Political Parties:
Can Government
Be Governed?

Let me warn you in the most solemn manner against the baneful effects of the spirit of party generally. This spirit . . . exists under different shapes in all government, more or less stifled, controlled, or repressed; but in those of the popular form it is seen in its greatest rankness and is truly their worst enemy.
George Washington, Farewell Address, 1796

The spirit and force of party has in America been as essential to the action of the machinery of government as steam is to a locomotive engine.
Lord Bryce, 1888

Political parties created democracy and . . . modern democracy is unthinkable save in terms of the parties.
E. E. Schattschneider, 1942

In the Carnavalet Museum in Paris, there are under glass a number of displays of documents from the French Revolution, including the journal of Louis XVI lying open at July 14, 1789 (Bastille Day). On that evening, King Louis had written a single phrase in his diary, *rien à signaler;* his perception of what had occurred on the day the Revolution began was that there was "nothing to note."

Many absolute monarchs, before and since Louis XVI, have had good reason to lament the absence of reliable political knowledge, and more, the absence of an orderly and peaceful process of acquiring and relinquishing governmental power. But would anything have made any difference at the time of the deposition and execution of Louis XVI? Can governments ever be governed except by the whim of rulers or the whip of revolution? We answer with elections, because elections are supposed to provide the people's guideline to conquest. But even according to postrevolutionary theory, elections are insufficient. Elections may produce good character in politics, but character alone is not a sufficient restraint on conquest in countries where aristocracies have been rejected.

Political Parties: Can Government Be Governed?

Elections have maintained their importance in our approach to governing the governors largely because elections have produced political parties; political parties are supposed to provide a meaningful connection between elections and accountable officials. Yet there has to be a lot of blind faith in this, because it is impossible to document beyond reasonable doubt the argument that political parties focus the electoral sanctions so specifically that power holders are brought regularly into line with the "will of the people." Consequently, Americans have been very ambivalent about political parties.

The opening quotations represent a great deal of the actual story of political parties and their status in American history. George Washington began with a stern warning; Lord Bryce at midpassage observed that, for better or worse, parties had become an indispensable part of the American governing scheme; and for our own day Schattschneider tells us that the whole development was clearly for the better. Each may represent the dominant view of the period in which the author was writing; but all three views coexist today among different groups of people and as an unresolved ambivalence in the minds of millions of individuals.

Washington's original fears seem to have been well-founded. He was not even out of office before the Federalists and Republicans had organized and recruited virtually every member of Congress to the one party or the other. And by 1798, with the enactment of the Alien and Sedition laws, we witnessed a historic instance of one party (what Madison had called a "majority") seeking to tyrannize over all other interests. The Sedition Act made it a crime to publish or say anything that might tend to defame or to bring into disrepute either the president or the Congress. Under this law twenty-five men, including several Republican newspaper editors, were arrested and ten were actually convicted.[1] Another strong confirmation of Washington's fears was the quick and dramatic way in which parties transformed the Electoral College by controlling the selection of electors to such an extent that each pledged to vote for a particular presidential candidate and, almost without exception between 1800 and 1972, cast their votes according to their party pledge. This practice almost completely subverted the purpose of the Electoral College. The electors were supposed to report to their respective state capitals about five weeks following the presidential election and to exercise their individual judgment among the outstanding presidential candidates. Thanks to party pledging, the

---

[1]For a readable account, see Daniel Sisson, *The American Revolution of 1800* (New York: Knopf, 1974), chapters 6–8. For the story of the development of political parties in the new nation, see Joseph Charles, *The Origins of the American Party System* (New York: Harper & Row, Harper Torchbooks, 1961). See also William N. Chambers, *Political Parties in a New Nation* (New York: Oxford University Press, 1963).

electors became errand boys and might as well have mailed in their ballots.

In the first case it could be argued, however, that the Republicans under Jefferson were able to capitalize on such mistakes; they succeeded in gaining control of the presidency and Congress in 1800 and simply allowed the sedition provisions to expire. The Sedition Act was the first and last time the majority political party tried directly to suppress the opposition party—until Nixon's Committee to Re-Elect the President tried it in 1972. As for the second example, many might say that the subversion of the Electoral College was a necessary part of the general democratization of the presidency. If that is the case, this example actually supports Schattschneider's position rather than Washington's. But that depends very much on each individual's personal point of view.

All of this leaves the concepts of conquest and incomplete conquest in a thicket of possibilities from which they can be freed only by the most arduous analysis. Once again, analysis must begin with definitions, because the definition of certain key concepts is the only way we can identify the *forms and structures* of the major political parties in the United States. Once this has been done, it will be possible to inquire into the purposes of our political parties and, finally, into the impact they have had on our system of government. Only then will we be able to go a step farther in our speculation on whether any government can be governed in terms other than the whims of the governors.

WHAT IS A POLITICAL PARTY?

Political parties as we know them today in the United States developed along with the spread of suffrage and have little meaning outside that context. *Party* was one of several names associated with organizing to influence elections. Considering the variety of terms available, adoption of the neutral concept of *political party*—rather than *cabal* or *conspiracy*, for instance—is probably evidence of acceptance of the actual practice of organizing to influence elections, although it was probably a great deal later into the nineteenth century before parties became a significant part of the theory of democracy.[2]

Parties belong to a species of the genus *political organization*, which includes interest groups, revolutionary groups, and protest groups as well. In the United States, scholars usually distinguish

[2]E. E. Schattschneider, *Party Government* (New York: Holt, Rinehart and Winston, 1942), chapter 1; and Austin Ranney and Willmoore Kendall, *Democracy and the American Party System* (New York: Harcourt, Brace, 1956), especially chapters 5 and 6.

Figure 8.1
Forms of organized
political action,
conventional and radical

Cognitive Purpose or "Manifest Function"	Relationship to the State	Recognized (protected)	Unrecognized (illegal or unprotected)
	Personnel	**Conventional political parties** election strategies theory of consent	**Revolutionary parties** radical strategies theory of transformation
	Ideology	**Third and protest parties** non-participatory strategies theory of education	**Utopian social movements** cathartic strategies theory of improvization
	Policies	**Interest or pressure groups** bargaining strategies theory of net gain	**Rebellious groups and parties** radical strategies theory of redemption

Each box contains two types of information. First is the name of the party, group or association most generally employed. Second, there are phrases briefly describing the typical strategies or outlooks (theories, roughly speaking) of each type of party or group. Take, for example, conventional political parties. They appear in the upper left-hand box because parties are defined generally as legal organizations concerned with controlling government by controlling the personnel of government. Their strategies are generally electoral, and their general outlook is that government control can be determined through debate, majority rule, compromise, and so on. The parties that appear in the upper right-hand box are also concerned with the personnel of government, but since their strategy is to make a fundamental (radical) change in government itself (transformation), they are likely to use disruption and seizure rather than consent as political strategies. Each box should be read in this manner.

between parties and interest groups on the basis of *policies versus personnel*. According to this view, interest groups are oriented toward the policies of the existing government, accepting it as it is and attempting to shape its decisions. In contrast, parties are believed to seek control of the government itself; control of elections is a means to that end simply because elections determine the top personnel.

Figure 8.1 puts all of this into a larger context. On the left, or vertical, axis are the terms of the distinction between parties and interest groups—*personnel* and *policy. Ideology* is interposed be-

tween these two terms in order to account for some groups whose members may use party election strategies but are willing to sacrifice winning elections to the furtherance of their program. We cannot, however, leave the matter there because there is another dimension entirely, portrayed by the distinction made across the horizontal axis. As indicated on this axis, experience in the United States and many other countries reveals that the government does not always choose to recognize some parties and groups, treating them actually as illegal, or defining them as not worthy of the protections afforded by the Constitution.

Political parties and interest groups have been so important that we are forced to spend most of our discussion on them and to sacrifice appropriate treatment of the other cases. But as we do so, it would be wrong to overlook the fact that political parties and interest groups comprise only about one-third of all the possible experiences. We might assert that the dominance of these two types of political action in the United States is due to a strong tradition of political freedom and stability which allows us to embrace many parties and groupings that might in some other nation have been suppressed. Yet there have certainly been many social movements and revolutionary groups which state and local police, private police, and federal troops have ruthlessly suppressed before they could grow into a significant factor in our politics.[3]

Figure 8.1 is not simply a convenient set of designations. The scheme does indicate certain important dynamic relationships; there is simply no appropriate place in this book for dealing with them (though part of the scheme is mentioned in chapter 16). For example, it is worth pondering what happens to a "revolutionary party" if suddenly its status is changed and it becomes a legally recognized party. This can cause an internal crisis of considerable proportion, as when a European Communist party suddenly finds that the government no longer opposes it. Another example of the dynamic relationships among these categories is the interest group whose leaders decide to engage in electoral action as though it were a political party. Immediately it must decentralize itself toward all of the districts in which it seeks to run candidates. It can no longer limit its activities to collecting funds and representing the group's interests at city hall or in Washington. One of the most fascinating problems is that of the so-called social movement, which is in a constant state of crisis over whether to develop into a political party

---

[3]A few very significant examples of this will be found in Richard Rubenstein, *Rebels in Eden: Mass Political Violence in the United States* (Boston: Little, Brown, 1970); for more recent and dramatic examples, it is only necessary to refer to the 1974–1975 Congressional Hearings and the *New York Times* for numerous revelations of infiltration and subversion of tiny radical groups by FBI and CIA agents. See also chapter 16.

What is a political party? A party may be defined in terms of its purpose and in terms of the methods used to attain its purpose. A political party is first of all an organized attempt to get power. Power is here defined as control of the government. That is the objective of party organization. The fact that the party aims at control of the government as a whole distinguishes it from pressure groups. The fact that the major party bids for power at all distinguishes it from minor parties whose interest in power is too remote to have a determinative effect on their behavior. . . .

Whatever else the parties may be, they are not associations of the voters who support the party candidates. . . .

As a matter of fact, membership in a political party has none of the usual characteristics of membership in an association. In most states the party has no control over its own membership. Any legal voter may on his own initiative and by his own declaration execute legal formalities before a duly designated public official making himself a registered member of the party. The party as such is not consulted. It does not accept the application; it does not vote the applicant into the association; it may not reject the application; and, finally, there is usually no recognized and authoritative procedure by which the party may expel a member.

Moreover, the member assumes no obligations to the party. He takes no oath prescribed by the party. He does not subscribe to a declaration of party principles and does not sign articles of incorporation. He does not pay membership dues, is not liable for the debts of the party, and has no equity in its property. He has no duties whatever to perform as a condition of membership. He is not required to solicit votes, is not required to participate in the campaign, need not attend party rallies, and need not vote for the party candidates. In fact, he need not vote at all. If he wishes to leave the party he does not resign. He does not even notify the party. He merely goes to the proper public authorities to register with another party. Membership in a political party is therefore highly unreal because the party has no control over its own membership and the member has no obligations to the party. . . .

The party is divided into two entities: (1) an organized group of insiders who have effective control of the party, and (2) a mass of passive "members" who seem to have very little to say about it.

From E. E. Schattschneider, *Party Government* (1942)

or an interest group, or to remain outside of the state by becoming a revolutionary or rebellious grouping.[4]

As already noted, the electoral process becomes an intrinsic part of the strategies employed by conventional political parties in their efforts to gain control of government. It is the only route toward that and which at the same time provides acceptable status under existing laws as well as adequate police power. There is no other process of sufficient scale to affect the personnel of government. Such groups often do employ other strategies when there is a chance of gain; it is not inconceivable for parties to adopt strong ideological

[4]This particular phenomenon is discussed at length in Theodore Lowi, *The Politics of Disorder* (New York: Basic Books, 1971), chapters 1 and 2.

positions or engage in ordinary interest group lobbying between elections. Nevertheless, the electoral process is the defining characteristic of political parties in the United States.

Party Organization in the United States: Where Structure Is Function

Parties and elections are so intertwined that the very structure of parties is shaped by the electoral process. As the sociologist might put it, here is a case where function *is* structure and structure *is* function. *Parties in the United States are the organizational aspect of the electoral process.* Parties were formed because there were elections to run; parties monopolize the electoral process, and they take their organizational shape from the fact that elections are taking place.[5]

Party structure follows a single rule: For every election district there has to be some kind of party unit. Now it is true that some parties are not successful enough to be represented in every state and county; there are times when good strategy requires the concentration of effort in areas where there is chance of winning. But for most of the history of the United States, the two major parties have offered candidates in the overwhelming proportion of districts in the United States at all levels, and this makes the American political party system one of the oldest political institutions in the history of democracy.[6]

In contrast to European party systems we have no strong notion of party membership and required participation; nonetheless, there is more structure to the party organizations in the United States than popular lore would have one believe. By almost universal practice, the party organization in each election district is a committee. The best-known examples are at the national level—the Democratic National Committee and the Republican National Committee. Each of the two major parties also has a state committee, or state central committee, because the state is the most important electoral district in the United States. Even the presidential elections are conducted at the state level, where the contest is fought over which candidate will receive a plurality of the popular vote and 100 percent of the electoral vote in each state.

[5]For some superb accounts of how modern parties begin in legislatures but develop by moving out from there into the districts, see Wilford Binkley, *President and Congress* (New York: Knopf, 1947); E. E. Schattschneider, *Party Government;* and Maurice Duverger, *Political Parties: Their Organization and Activities in the Modern State,* 1st ed., trans. Barbara and Robert North (New York: Wiley, 1954).

[6]For figures on the extent of party organization in the counties and other districts, consult Walter Dean Burnham, *Presidential Ballots, 1836–1892* (Baltimore: Johns Hopkins Press, 1955). For a good review of the 1896–1936 presidential elections, during which the two major parties restricted themselves to only certain regions of the United States and did not offer candidates in other regions, see E. E. Schattschneider, *The Semisovereign People* (New York: Holt, Rinehart and Winston, 1960), chapter 5.

Below the state level the situation varies a bit. Almost without exception the parties have county committees. In some cities the parties try to organize committees at a city level; but more frequently the county (which includes most cities anyway) and the ward are the important levels around which parties attempt to organize committees. But there are other practices as well. Each congressional district, each state senate district, and each district in which judges are elected qualifies as a unit around which parties might set up committees.

The formal organization of a party in New York County (Manhattan) of New York State is illustrated in Figure 8.2.[7]

---

[7]It happens that the historically famous Democratic Organization of New York County is named Tammany Hall, after the place where the county committee headquarters used to be. This does not, however, make it any less typical of party organization.

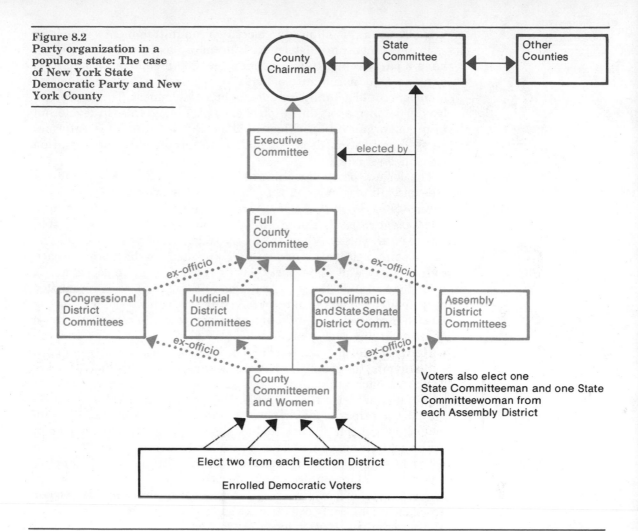

Figure 8.2
Party organization in a populous state: The case of New York State Democratic Party and New York County

Although this is an organization in a populous county in a populous state, it differs from any other city or county of smaller size only in its larger number of districts around which committees are organized—a smaller county or city would probably not have a judicial or a congressional district committee. In the case of this particular party, there is a single election for all committeemen and committeewomen in the county. All serve on the full county committee, and then each also serves on the district committees whose boundaries include their residence.

That is to say, each county committeeperson is a member of the full county committee and is ex officio a member of all of the relevant district committees. Each of these district committees can be very large. If each and every precinct (containing between 300

*Political Parties: Can
Government Be Governed?*

and 600 voters) is allowed to elect two committee members (one of each sex), then any district with as many as 30,000 voters could have a party committee of as many as 200 members. It is hard to imagine that a committee made up of such a large number of members could actually conduct any party business. This is precisely why the formal organization of each party tends also to develop an informal organization (illustrated in Figure 8.3). This informal party organization does not make the formal party organization meaningless, however.

The formal party structure as displayed in Figure 8.2 paints a true picture of parties in the United States, which are a *series of layerings of committees with overlapping boundaries and interlocking memberships.* The large size of committees gives parties most of the regular workers they are likely to get from year to year. The overlapping boundaries and interlocking memberships provide each county party and state party with a good deal more coordination than they would otherwise get. Each district and each committee may tend to go its separate way; there are few "bosses" in the United States who have the authority or power to coordinate these districts in any highly predictable way.

However, the districts tend to coordinate themselves up to a point. For example, the committees in two separate assembly districts may disregard each other in the matter of making respective nominations for candidates for assembly. But the two districts in question may belong to the *same* congressional district or state senate district or judicial district, and as a consequence they are forced to act as a single group for the more inclusive nominations. There is a lot of incentive to "hang together" if the alternative is "hanging separately." Many observers of American parties, especially foreign observers, have been struck by the absence of unifying ideology or program among party organizations in the United States. The secret of their ability to stay together despite the absence of common program must be found in these overlapping jurisdictions.

Informal organization is not the same as hidden organization. It is simply a result of the fact that party leaders have made use of those parts of the formal organization that have proven convenient and effective. Informal organization usually consists of (1) regular reliance upon one or two committee levels, allowing the other levels to atrophy, and (2) reliance upon the executive committees of those levels to make the effective decisions, utilizing the larger committees only for the more formal or symbolic occasions. Note therefore in Figure 8.3 that all the layers disappear except the ward (or assembly district), the county, and the state; note also that the main operation at each of those levels resides in the small executive committee rather than the full and unwieldy committee.

There are variations on the lowest level that becomes the "base of the party." The determination of this base level usually has depend-

Figure 8.3
Informal organization
of a party

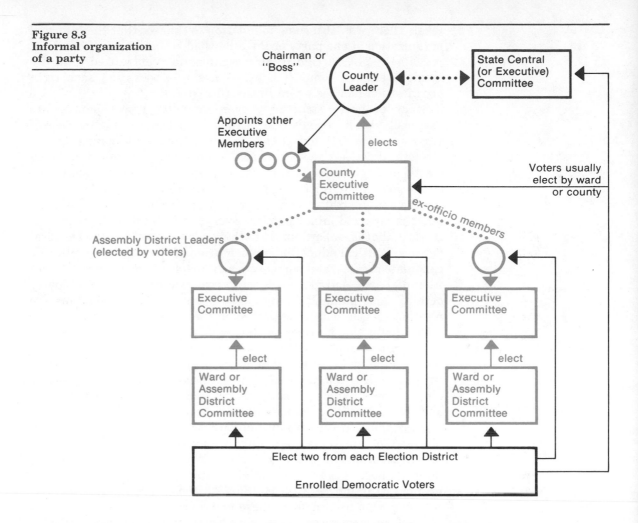

ed upon the frequency of elections and the importance of a particular post to the party. Therefore, the ward is very often the base of the political party, because for many decades members of the city council were elected from wards each year and these postions were essential to the control of city hall. The county became an important level of party organization because of the judicial and district attorney positions that could be controlled.

In any event, the development of this concentrated power in the executive committees gave rise to charges of "bossism." Those charges were often well-founded, but in very few parties could a boss be truly an autocrat. The position of the boss depended largely upon having a solid majority of support in his executive committee. That was true at the ward level, at the county level, and at the state

Political Parties: Can Government Be Governed?

level. There was also some foundation to charges that the informal organization of one party or the other had become a "machine." But *machine* implies a tightly knit organization centralized toward a single executive committee under a single boss, and such tight organization has been rare in the United States.[8]

Study of party structures, even in states where parties are extremely weak, reveals clearly that the overwhelming purpose of parties in the United States is controlling and managing the electoral process. The specific goal of each party is to win as many elections as possible. Taken together, the major parties share the single goal of administering the electoral process, in fact monopolizing the administration of the electoral process to the exclusion of all other groups and minor parties. Everything else done by parties is tactical, that is, subordinated to the goal of controlling the electoral process. Political education, presentation of the issues, simplifying candidate choices, and personalizing impersonal government are all part of party activity. But these are latent functions of party activity—not planned or anticipated consequences—and thus are not the essential aspect of parties in the United States.[9]

The distinction between the formal and the informal organization is a very real and meaningful one in this regard. Each corresponds to one of the two different dimensions of party activity: *the nominating process* and *the electoral process.* These are the two processes or dimensions to which all party tactics and strategies are dedicated, and the real or functional distinction between formal and informal organization is precisely parallel to these two dimensions. Electoral processes or functions are mainly carried out by the formal organization. Nominating processes or functions are carried out by the informal party organization. Nominating processes will come first in our discussion because nomination comes first in the political schedule. Our treatment of these two processes in this chapter will be brief, since many aspects of each are more meaningfully included in an analysis of the workings of the presidency and Congress (see chapters 9 through 11).

Party Structure and the Nominating Process

The entire electoral process, including nominations, is regulated by the laws of each state. According to most state laws, anyone can run as a candidate in any election as long as the minimum age and other

---

[8]There are many good portraits of bosses but few convincing descriptions of machines or ordinary political parties. Some of the best descriptions, though somewhat out of date now, will be found in Schattschneider, *Party Government,* and Duverger, *Political Parties.* The best contemporaneous treatment of party structure will be found in Frank Sorauf, *Party Politics in America,* 2d ed. (Boston: Little, Brown, 1973), parts 1 and 2.

[9]For the best explication of the distinction between purpose, or manifest functions, and latent functions, see Robert Merton, *Social Theory and Social Structure* (Glencoe, Ill.: Free Press, 1957), especially p. 71, where Merton illustrates this distinction with a superb analysis of Tammany Hall and other traditional machines.

Table 8.1   **How State Nominating Laws Favor Parties and Discourage Independents: The Case of New York**

| Office Sought | Number of Signatures Required for Nominating Petitions | |
	Party Designation*	Independent Nomination
Statewide	5% of enrolled members	12,000 (at least 50 in each county)
Citywide	5,000	7,500
County or borough	2,500	5,000
Municipal government, Congress, or State Senate	750	3,000
State Assembly	350	1,500

*Successful party candidates are merely designated and must still go on to face a primary election, while successful independents go directly onto the November ballot. Nonetheless, it is clear that the independent route is much more arduous. For example, there were 3.6 million enrolled Democrats in New York in 1975, meaning that a Democratic candidate for the regular party nomination for governor would have to get about 18,000 signatures. This party candidate would have associated party members around the state to help get signatures from habitual signers. But the independent would not have such help; furthermore, some of his or her signatures would have to come from every county in the state. All of this makes the 12,000 far harder to get.

objective criteria are observed. However, the laws in most states are written quite deliberately to make independent candidacies extremely difficult. Table 8.1 is a sketch of some of the difficulties in the state of New York. New York is more strict than some states and more lenient than others; however, in virtually all instances a distinction is made between party candidacies and independent candidacies, with the advantage going to party candidacies, in much the same way as diagramed in the table.[10]

There are other ways in which states attempt to discourage independent candidacies in favor of party candidacies. For example, state laws often provide for a period of only six weeks in which to collect the requisite number of signatures on petitions for nomination, which is ample time for a party candidate but a very severe restriction on independents. Sometimes the law requires that candidates not only have a minimum number of signatures but that they be distributed among each of the counties of the state or each of the precincts within the district. This is especially rough on those candidates who have a strong following in one section and would like to use the campaign itself to gain publicity in other areas. Many states require candidates to post a modest amount of money—a

[10]A systematic study of these provisions in all of the fifty states will be found in Henry Goldstein, "Paths to Power" (M.A. thesis, Cornell University, 1975). For a good insight into the importance of these electoral laws and how they can be used to maintain the monopoly position of the parties, see Justin Feldman, "How Tammany Holds Power," *National Municipal Review*, July 1950. See also "Legal Obstacles to Minority Party Success," *Yale Law Journal* 57 (1948), 1276.

Political Parties: Can Government Be Governed?

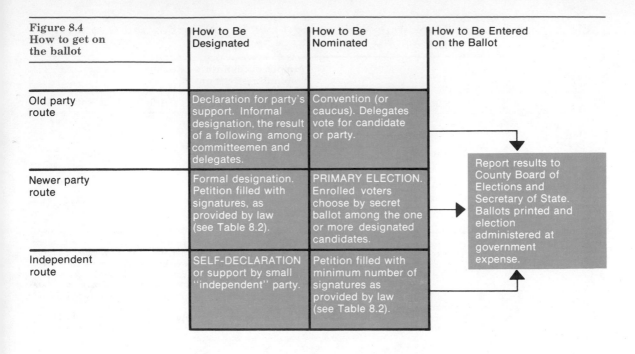

Figure 8.4 How to get on the ballot	How to Be Designated	How to Be Nominated	How to Be Entered on the Ballot
Old party route	Declaration for party's support. Informal designation, the result of a following among committeemen and delegates.	Convention (or caucus). Delegates vote for candidate or party.	Report results to County Board of Elections and Secretary of State. Ballots printed and election administered at government expense.
Newer party route	Formal designation. Petition filled with signatures, as provided by law (see Table 8.2).	PRIMARY ELECTION. Enrolled voters choose by secret ballot among the one or more designated candidates.	
Independent route	SELF-DECLARATION or support by small "independent" party.	Petition filled with minimum number of signatures as provided by law (see Table 8.2).	

bond—which is forfeited by any candidate who receives less than a prescribed minimum percentage of the vote. The purpose of this type of provision is to discourage casual and frivolous candidacies, but clearly it is another instance where the law discriminates against independents and in favor of the party route to the ballot.

Figure 8.4 is a sketch of the most important routes available to persons seeking to be candidates for elective office—and further confirmation that the independent route is the most difficult one. In addition, it tends to show more clearly how these three routes to candidacy for elective office are available under different conditions. The difficulty of the independent route is only one factor involved in a person's choice of route. The independent route is sometimes chosen by people who are basically antagonistic to party politics. For them, the difficulties are irrelevant. This route is also taken by persons who decide on their candidacy too late to meet the legal requirements for a party nomination. (After all, in most states it is necessary to be an enrolled voter of the party well prior to the time when petitions for formal designation as a primary candidate must be signed.) And once in a while, a regularly enrolled party member will choose an independent route if it is his or her assessment that success in politics is thereby accelerated.

Within the context of party politics, the nominating process—whether by the old or the new route indicated in Figure 8.4—is the toughest of all party jobs. When more than one person wants the nomination as the candidate for a particular office, the choice of which person shall be nominated involves friends and associates within the same organization—usually of about equal (even if equally *low*) qualification. In comparison to that kind of decision, the election campaign is almost a joy and a relief, because there the fight is against strangers, declared adversaries.

Winnowing out aspirants and settling upon a single candidate to compete in an election is a profoundly important responsibility of each party. The two basic procedures for this, identified in Figure 8.4 as primaries and conventions (which may be called caucuses when party members gather in small districts or in legislatures to choose nominees), come at the end of a long process. In the course of this process party leaders try ardently to avoid contested nominations, which are exceedingly costly both in dollars and in the exposure of dirty linen. Contested nominations also make it difficult for the party to plan carefully for the election campaign.

A contested nomination is more costly than a contested election because nomination is particularly personal. Members of the same party tend to know more about each other and may reveal vital information if the contest hangs on a few votes. The dollar costs are also higher because rich contributors may alienate part of the party no matter what they do, and in turn the contest may alienate them. And each candidate in a contested primary or convention must bear a heavy personal obligation to each contributor, whether the candidate wins or loses. The party organization tends to lose either way because there are few large donors, and they may use up their available political capital long before the election campaign has begun.

Consequently, there is a widespread, though unconfessed, practice of requiring each candidate for a nomination to make large personal contributions to the party in return for the party's designation as the regular candidate for the nomination. In the big cities, the party's regular designation for a judgeship may cost the candidate the equivalent of one or two times his annual salary—and there is no guarantee he will win the election simply because he gets the nomination. This practice of virtually selling nominations is quite widespread, although documentation is naturally difficult to get. It obviously militates heavily against candidates from low income occupations and families, even though party leaders occasionally make an exception and allow the candidate to make party contributions after being elected to office. Either way, one can easily begin to see why the party organizations detest the prospect of numerous contests for nominations.

Campaign finance reform laws adopted during the years 1970 to 1974 have attempted to clean up the nominating processes of the parties at the national level. They have put a limit on the amount of

Views from the inside and from the outside: Scenes from the 1968 Democratic Convention.

contributions from individuals and political committees, and they now provide for federal matching funds for candidates seeking the presidential nomination as well as for parties after they have decided which candidate to choose. However, to qualify for matching funds during the nominating process, a candidate must be able to raise a minimum of $100,000, spread throughout at least twenty states. In all, each candidate is allowed to spend up to $10,000,000 for preconvention campaigning, plus $2,000,000 for fund raising. If there are five candidates, as is almost certain to be the case for any party which is not already in the White House, this means that at least $50,000,000 of money available to the party will have been spent by individual candidates before the campaign for election is even begun. The resources available to the party are thus wasted before the enemy is met.

The second concern about contested nominations is for the impact that the nominations will have on the elections to follow. When party leaders are in effective control of the organization and are thereby able to keep to a minimum the number of contested nominations, they can carefully plan the overall ticket for maximum impact. Traditionally called ticket balancing, this is a strategy whereby the selection of nominees with different religious, ethnic, and regional backgrounds gives the party effective rapport with a maximum number of segments of the electorate.

Where a local electorate is highly heterogeneous, it has been traditional to balance the ticket with proportional numbers of Protestants, Catholics, and Jews. With the rise of black power, rational party leaders now try to divide the Protestant proportion between blacks and whites. Sometimes balance can be achieved only with a person of mixed heritage. The late Clinton Rossiter once constructed an ideal running mate for anyone on the national presidential ticket: a black nun from Mississippi who is a member of the CIO. Yet, this kind of rational campaign strategy is not possible unless party leaders control the nomination process, and they cannot control it if they have to contend with large numbers of contested nominations.

Although the nominating process can thus exhaust financial resources and interfere with rational party campaigning, the contested primary is currently considered a sign of healthy politics. This may be the case, but the price of health comes fairly high. The implicit weakening of a party's control over nominations means that the party is less able to provide full racial and ethnic representation. It can also contribute mightily to corruption, because candidates for all offices except the presidency must rely mainly upon themselves and their friends to invest in the preelection campaigning for nominations.

Primaries, the most important procedure for party nominations, vary according to whether participation in them is "closed" or

National party politics is an accumulation of local politics.

"open," and this has a considerable effect on their conduct and outcome. In a closed primary participation is limited to persons who have declared their party affiliation by enrolling in the party of their choice months prior to the primary election; the final date for enrollment is usually the previous November, except for persons who become eligible voters after that time. In an open primary a person declares party affiliation only on the actual day of the primary election itself, usually by going to the polling place and asking for the ballot of a particular party.

Closed primaries are obviously much easier for the party leadership to control. Open primaries can be extremely volatile, because voters can decide whether they are Democrats or Republicans during the campaign period itself. There are instances where it is widely believed that thousands of adherents of one party will "raid" the primary of the other party in order to influence the nomination of the one candidate who will run the weakest race against their own preferred candidate. This is one of the charges that the Democrats hurled against the Committee to Re-Elect the President in the 1972 campaign—that the Committee's agents were acting illegally and unethically to encourage the nomination of the weakest Democrat to run against President Nixon.[11]

Party Structure and Elections

Although party leaders dread contested primaries at open conventions, they nevertheless get a lot of free publicity from them. Often they are able to make electoral virtue out of nominating necessity. This is especially true of national nominating conventions, which are worth millions in free national publicity. In fact, the party in the White House often has to face the problem that an uncontested convention does not have the entertainment value of a suspenseful outcome. In recent years parties have adjusted well enough to this difficulty. The 1972 Republican Presidential Nominating Convention brought the art of convention ritual to new and higher levels and kept network TV ratings high despite the fact that Richard Nixon was clearly going to be the nominee.[12]

[11]Carl Bernstein and Bob Woodward, *All the President's Men* (New York: Simon & Schuster, 1974) pp. 127–142.

[12]For an assessment of the effect of primary battles on electoral outcomes at state and local levels, see Andrew Hacker, "Does a Divisive Primary Harm a Candidate's Election Chances?" *American Political Science Review* 59 (1956), 105–110; and Sorauf, *Party Politics in America*, chapters 9–10. See also V. O. Key, "The Direct Primary and Party Structure," *American Political Science Review* 48 (1954), 24. Key argues that the system of nominating candidates by primaries contributes to the domination of a given area by a single party. He observes that the primary attracts the most prestigious and dynamic personalities of the area and uses up a great proportion of the available political money as well. Key probably overstates the case, inasmuch as he also shows in other of his own writings that the system of nomination by primary elections was first instituted in the South, which was already dominated by a single party. Nevertheless, his analysis is fascinating and suggestive. For the history of primaries see V. O. Key, *American State Politics: An Introduction* (New York: Knopf, 1956), chapter 6.

The actual electoral period begins immediately after the nominations of candidates have been settled. And it is a time of glory for the formal party organization, which includes all of the committees heretofore described and a whole variety of special committees, reform clubs, and fragmentary political activities for which there is no appropriate label.[13] Many observers have reported on a "coattail effect" in American politics, whereby the candidates at the top of a ticket have such appeal that they help pull other candidates to victory.[14] Undoubtedly there occasionally is a coattail effect. In 1952 General Eisenhower probably had some very long coattails in many states. The reverse phenomenon is probably more often the case, however. The top of the ticket tends to depend very heavily on the bottom of the ticket, because the candidates for obscure offices have the friends among committee members and in individual neighborhoods who will turn out to vote and bring others with them.

This is not meant to deny the importance of the new media of communications. Candidates and parties do not spend hundreds of millions of dollars on advertising and programing in television, radio, and newspapers for the sheer pleasure of it all.[15] However, it seems fairly clear that the main influence of this newer means of campaigning has largely been to sever the top of the ticket from the rest. In the resultant "ticket splitting" voters rely upon their habits and traditions to guide them in their choice of local candidates and then depart from those traditions in their selection of the more exposed candidates at the top of the ticket about whom there is more specific information. Thus nationwide and statewide campaigning through the major media of mass communications has had a definite effect on politics in the United States; however, the newly emerging patterns at those upper levels should not be allowed to overshadow the great stability and continuity of party politics at the lower levels.[16]

There is ample evidence in Table 8.2 of the continuing effectiveness of local political party activity despite the vicissitudes in national politics since World War II. During that period party affiliations of American adults have remained amazingly stable. Democratic affiliations swelled a bit in 1964, but the long line of development is stable. Between 45 and 50 percent of all American adults call themselves Democrats and tend to remain Democrats over long periods of time and across large varieties of voting choices.

---

[13]Sorauf, *Party Politics in America;* see also James Q. Wilson, *The Amateur Democrat* (Chicago: University of Chicago Press, 1962).

[14]The most elaborate argument for a coattail theory will be found in Malcolm Moos, *Politics, President and Coattails* (Baltimore: Johns Hopkins Press, 1952).

[15]One of the most fascinating studies of the orientation of national campaigners toward modern advertising techniques and mass communications technology is Joe McGinnis, *The Selling of the President, 1968* (New York: Pocket Books, 1969).

[16]See especially Walter Dean Burnham, "The Changing Shape of the American Political Universe," *American Political Science Review,* March 1965, p. 7.

Table 8.2   **Party Identification, 1952–1972**

Party Identification of Each Respondent	Oct. 1952	Oct. 1954	Oct. 1956	Oct. 1958	Oct. 1960	Nov. 1962	Oct. 1964	Nov. 1966	Nov. 1968	Nov. 1970	Nov. 1972
Strong Democrat	22%	22%	21%	23%	21%	23%	26%	18%	20%	20%	15%
Weak Democrat	25	25	23	24	25	23	25	27	25	23	26
Independent, leaning Dem.	10	9	7	7	8	8	9	9	10	10	11
Independent	5	7	9	8	8	8	8	12	11	13	13
Independent, leaning Rep.	7	6	8	4	7	6	6	7	9	8	10
Weak Republican	14	14	14	16	13	16	13	15	14	15	13
Strong Republican	13	13	15	13	14	12	11	10	10	10	10
Apolitical, don't know	4	4	3	5	4	4	2	2	1	1	2
Total number of respondents	1,614	1,139	1,772	1,269	3,021	1,289	1,571	1,291	1,553	1,802	2,249

Data from Center for Political Studies, Institute for Social Research, University of Michigan.

Similarly, between 25 and 30 percent of all American adults consider themselves Republicans in the same terms. These results of survey research are consistently confirmed in voting behavior. Between 50 and 60 percent of all Americans who declare their party for purposes of participating in primary elections are Democrats, while Republican enrollments are consistently below the 40 percent level.[17]

This pattern helps explain some of the more puzzling aspects of American politics. The harder the leading candidates work, the more things seem to remain the same. Astronomical expenditures on presidential elections have served to differentiate only the presidential election from the rest. We have witnessed great extremes in voting outcomes at the national level, including three very significant turnovers in party control of the presidency since World War II. But during that same period, elections continued to produce results at all other levels that are consistent with the figures in Table 8.2.

A look at Table 8.3 and Figure 8.5 reveals that even the landslide victory of Eisenhower in 1952 gave him only a very bare majority of less than 52 percent in the House and only 50 percent in the Senate; and that lasted merely until the next election, 1956, when a Democratic majority was returned. In view of these circumstances, Eisenhower's own success is a tribute to his personality, but it tends strongly to confirm the stable and continuous relationship between voters and the local party affiliations. His second victory in 1956 was an even more decisive personal triumph than 1952; yet he was

Political Parties: Can Government Be Governed?

[17]See Clinton Rossiter, *Parties and Politics in America* (Ithaca, N.Y.: Cornell University Press, 1960), chapter 3.

Table 8.3

Parties and the Electorate: The Stability of Local Partisanship and the Resistance of Local Parties to National Campaigns

| | Democratic Percentage of: | | |
	Popular Vote for President	House Seats	Senate Seats
1948	49.6	61	56
1950		54	51
1952	44.5	48	50
1954		54	50
1956	42.0	54	51
1958		69	65
1960	49.7	60	65
1962		58	67
1964	61.1	68	68
1966		57	64
1968	43.4	56	57
1970		59	54
1972	39.0	56	57

unable to budge local support for Democratic House and Senate candidates. The most recent instance of this divergence is the massive victory of President Nixon in 1972, which was accompanied by the continuation of decisive Democratic majorities in the House and in the Senate.

In summary, three of the five presidential elections between 1952 and 1972—1956, 1968, and 1972—have been completely at odds with the House and Senate elections of the same period. In contrast, that situation did not occur a single time in the previous hundred years. It is the presidential electorate that has changed. It has become more volatile, focusing more and more intensely upon personalities and idiosyncrasies. The situation in the electorate *below* the presidential level continues to be highly stable, composed of parties, strong party affiliations, tradition, habit, and an occasional issue or charismatic personality.

All of this suggests that the voting behavior of Americans is to a great extent a party phenomenon. It is habit backed up by the regular reinforcement of local institutions and traditions. Although individual "campaigns" occasionally sway significant numbers of people by appealing to specific personalities or specific issues, the overwhelming tendency of campaigning is to activate and reactivate electorates, reinforcing their habits and tendencies rather than

Figure 8.5
The Democratic
percentage of the
two-party vote for the
President and the House,
1900–1972. This figure
shows how the two rise
and fall together, but with
the Democrats never
falling as far in House
elections as in
presidential elections.

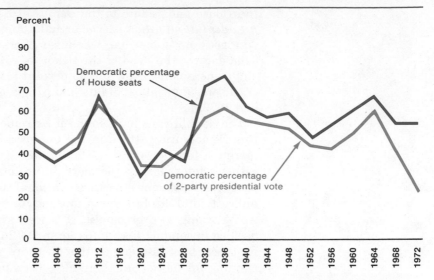

Figure reprinted from V. O. Key, *Politics, Parties and Pressure Groups*, 5th ed. (New York: Crowell, 1964), p. 557. Some variation is masked by giving House results every four years to parallel presidential elections.

converting them to new ones.[18] These stable voting patterns can change, but such changes are so infrequent that they are used to identify the opening and closing of major political epochs in our history. Most observers agree that there have been significant realignments of voters between the two major parties no more than five times in the entire history of the United States since 1789.[19]

There should be no sense of mystery about this kind of stability. In fact, it might be harder to explain the situation if there were greater voter volatility at the local level. Party organizations, even where they are weak and unable to control their members, are very much an institutionalized part of most local communities in the United States.[20] In Figure 8.5, the comparison of presidential and congressional voting suggests how this expresses itself. The present party structure in the United States, weak and ineffectual as it may appear to be, sets a kind of floor and ceiling on the behavior of the electorate. This seems to give a standard 50 percent of all seats in

[18]These effects were first studied carefully in Bernard Berelson, Paul Lazarsfeld, and William McPhee, *Voting* (Chicago: University of Chicago Press, 1954). Studies of the psychological dimensions of voting and partisan stability were pioneered by the Survey Research Center of the University of Michigan; see especially Angus Campbell et al., *The American Voter* (New York: Wiley, 1960).

[19]Walter Dean Burnham, *Critical Elections and the Mainsprings of American Politics* (New York: Norton, 1970); also V. O. Key, "A Theory of Critical Elections," *Journal of Politics*, February 1955, pp. 3–18.

[20]See, for example, the effect of party organization and local campaigning in one middle-sized, fairly typical American city in Berelson et al., *Voting*.

Political Parties: Can Government Be Governed?

the House and Senate to the Democratic Party *no matter what the presidential situation is.* The actual number of seats the Democrats win goes up somewhat whenever there is a strong Democratic candidate at the head of the ticket, but it does not go more than a slight increment below the 50 percent mark even when the Democratic presidential candidate and campaign are a fiasco, as in 1956 and 1972.

The Republicans have found it extremely difficult to break down this Democratic pattern in the Congress, largely because it is not merely a few decisions on candidates that have to be changed but rather a much larger and more diffuse attachment to some kind of party institution or structure. National campaigners recognize this difficulty and are beginning to come to the conclusion that it is not worth trying to overcome it. It is well known that Richard Nixon decided to conduct his campaign in 1972 through the Committee to Re-Elect the President as though there were no other candidates running for office. But there have been precedents for this kind of behavior in several presidential campaigns since 1952. There were, for example, the very important Volunteers for Stevenson in 1952 and 1956, the Citizens for Eisenhower during the same period, and the Citizens for Kennedy and Johnson in 1960.

Parties are, therefore, a formative part of the American system of politics and government. They occupy a place in each community to channel the electorate even when they have no power to guide it. At the most exposed and volatile political level—the presidency—the electorate still tends to support one of the parties for eight to twelve years before switching to another. Trends of congressional support tend to run between thirty years and half a century, as is indicated in Table 8.4. Here we see that the Republicans were ascendant well over 70 percent of the time in the seventy years from 1861 to 1931,

Table 8.4	**Partisan Control of the Houses of Congress, 1861–1931 and 1931–1971**			
	Number of Congresses* in Which Each Party Held the Majority of Seats			
	House of Representatives		**Senate**	
	Democrats	**Republicans**	**Democrats**	**Republicans**
1861–1931 (37th–71st Congress)	12	23	5	30
1931–1971 (72nd–92nd Congress)	19	2	18	3

*A "Congress" is the actual two-year period between elections for the entire House and one-third of the Senate. Thus, for example, between 1861 and 1931 there were 35 Congresses, and the Democrats held majorities in the House for 12 and in the Senate for 5.

while the Democrats have been ascendant over 90 percent of the time since 1931.[21]

Many would argue that the institution of parties, despite the influence identified above, is nevertheless a reflection of other social forces rather than an independent force all its own—for example, that the Democratic Party only became an independent influence after being shaped by urban and working-class forces. This is a sophisticated approach which is not to be discounted. But our figures and others like them suggest that party, though influenced by socioeconomic factors, is an independent force. Note in Figures 8.6 and 8.7 how even the most sophisticated measures of socioeconomic status of the voters will predict far less of the vote than the simple question, "How did you vote last time?" This is not intended to suggest that socioeconomic forces have been irrelevant in the development of parties in United States politics; nor is it to suggest that these socioeconomic forces are irrelevant to contemporary parties. But it does seem to show that parties function independently of the social forces. Parties become a convenience for the electorate; as we shall see later in this chapter, parties often serve as a substitute for social class conflict in politics.

Parties do not exist in isolation. All of the aspects of parties, their relationships to each other, and their functions in elections are interrelated in what is called a *party system*. This system is a whole, and its consequences for the larger body politic can be assessed without reference to the individual contributions that the parties themselves might be making—the party system is a factor independent of individual party activities in the conquest of a nation.

American third parties Although most of our political history has been dominated by the idea and the ideal of a two-party system, the real situation is more complicated. The two-party system, with its various third parties, is to be distinguished on the one hand from a one-party system (of which more is said below) and on the other hand from a multi-party system—a system of three or more parties in which each party is large enough to elect some important legislators and other officials but no party is anywhere near a majority size.[22] In the United States the two major parties do occupy most of the electoral space, but there have been many third parties whose place in the system must be taken into account before a proper assessment of the "American two-party system" can be made.

There have been many occasions when a third party has been a formidable force in our politics. The Populists and the Progressives of the late nineteenth century and early twentieth century are

[21]Frank Sorauf, *Party Politics in America*, 1st ed. (Boston: Little, Brown, 1968), p. 135.
[22]For a review of many systems, see Duverger, *Political Parties*.

**Figure 8.6
The relationship between
socioeconomic status and
voting**

Family income,
county by county

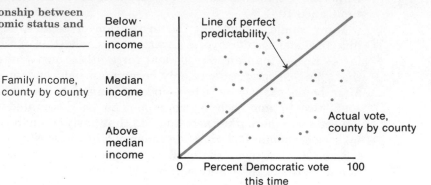

**Figure 8.7
The relationship between
voting in the last election
and the next election**

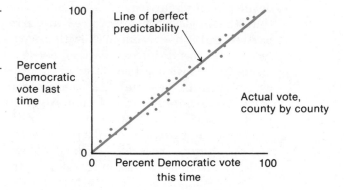

These figures are hypothetical and are intended to give a clear picture of the relationships. The distance between each point and the slanted line is a measure of the "error" that would be produced by trying to predict actual voting from knowledge of immediate income (Figure 8.6) or knowledge of how each voter or each district voted last time (Figure 8.7). Note that the average distance between the points and the line in Figure 8.6 is far greater than the average distance between the points and the line in Figure 8.7. Using actual election data, and taking New York State as a single case, the relationship between the aggregate vote for Congress in 1966 and 1968 produced a product-moment correlation coefficient of .88. This high correlation was obtained despite the decline from strong Democratic voting in 1964–1966 to a Republican victory for President in 1968.

recent examples. Contemporaneous examples include the American Labor Party, the Liberal Party, and the Conservative Party, all of the State of New York; the Farmer-Labor Party in Minnesota; the Dixiecratic Party in the Deep South states; and George Wallace's American Independent Party of the Deep South and Border states in the late 1960s. Still other minor parties have exerted an important influence over our political ideas even when they did not enjoy as large an electoral base as the ones mentioned here. This was especially true of the Socialists before World War I; toward the end of his life, perennial Socialist presidential candidate Norman

Table 8.5	**Minor Parties in 1972**[*]

Total votes cast for president, all minor parties, was 1,063,400, or 18 percent of the total vote; there were no electoral votes.

American	Less Federal Taxes
America First	Libertarian
American Independent (Schmitz)	La Raza Unida
Action Party	Liberty Union
Conservative (Schmitz)	Prohibition
Concerned and Capable	National Democratic
Communist	Peace and Freedom
Constitutional	People over Politics
Concerned Voters Voice	People's (Spock)
Free Liberation	Protest, Progress, Dignity
Freedom and Liberty	Socialist
George Wallace	Socialist Labor
Human Rights	Socialist Workers
Independent American	Taxpayers
Independent Conservative	Tenants Rights
Independents for Congress	Taxpayers to Stop Taxes
Industrial Government	Taxation with Representation
Liberal	Universal

[*]These parties offered candidates in one or more states on a separate line on the ballot. From *Congressional Quarterly Weekly Report,* March 10, 1973, p. 531; *Congressional Quarterly Almanac,* 1972, p. 1013.

Thomas observed that he had quit running for president because the New Deal had stolen and adopted most of the Socialist program.

Even though some third parties have had an important influence, they have nevertheless enjoyed limited careers in American politics. Table 8.5 is a listing of all of the third or minor parties which offered candidates in one or more states in 1972. Cumulatively they received around 18 percent of the total vote and none of the electoral votes for president; most of them disappeared immediately after the election. Even the occasional successful third party has tended to have a short career, due to either the drift of its members toward one of the major parties or the direct absorption of the party and its leadership into a major party.

One of the main problems with our third parties has been that their electoral support is severely limited to one or two regions of the country. The very large Populist and Progressive Parties had a great influence on national politics; nevertheless, they were based in only the middle western and southern states. The Progressive Party polled 1,157,172 votes for Henry Wallace's presidential race against Harry Truman and Thomas Dewey in 1948, but nearly half

Political Parties: Can Government Be Governed?

285

(510,000) was provided by New York State alone. The American Independent Party received nearly 10,000,000 popular votes and 45 electoral votes in 1968—the most ever polled by a third party candidate for president; however, George Wallace's popular vote was concentrated in the Deep South, and all of his electoral votes came from that area.

The limited career of each of the third parties in the United States tends to emphasize the importance of the two major parties in the system.[23] But this phenomenon of two dominant parties in such a heterogeneous nation does call for some explanation, inadequate as that explanation is likely to be. Why, for example, has no third party been able to escape its regional confines?[24] Part of the reason is that third parties are more homogeneous in the composition of their memberships and are purer in their ideological and programmatic content. Minor parties are usually a response to some specific challenge, as was true even of the Republican Party in the 1850s. Unless a single issue becomes the dominating issue of the age—as was the case with slavery and the Republican Party in the 1850s—third parties must either change their nature and give up their primary ideological or programmatic component in order to appeal to a larger region and population, or they remain small and tend to decline. Thus there is a self-limiting feature to minor parties.

History itself is another factor. After nearly two centuries, Americans simply prefer to identify with one of the two major parties. Even in the past generation, when party identifications were thought to be weakening, fewer than 10 percent of the population insisted that they were independent of the two major parties. Now it is true that the notion of "independent" here is ambiguous. For example, in sample survey research, the question on party identification is usually followed up with another, such as, "Do you think of yourself as an independent tending toward the Democratic Party or toward the Republican Party?" Generally, those who respond, "Independent leaning toward the Democratic Party" are indistinguishable from those who report themselves as "weak Democrats." We can therefore disagree upon the size of the nonaffiliated population in the United States. However, it is quite clear that the overwhelming proportion of the electorate will declare an affiliation for one of the two major parties, and a few will profess to no party affiliation at all. Membership or affiliation in one

---

[23]A good guide to literature on third and other minor parties will be found in V. O. Key, *Politics, Parties, and Pressure Groups*, 5th ed. (New York: Crowell, 1964), chapter 10.

[24]There is of course one major exception to the rule that third or minor parties either die or remain minor. This is the Republican Party, which began its career as a third party in 1854. However, these were the most critical years in the entire history of our republic, and the Republican Party became the second party within two years after the presidential election of 1856. See Charles O. Jones, *The Republican Party in American Politics* (New York: Macmillan, 1965), especially chapter 1.

Campaigning: Will the
mass media ever replace
the human touch?

of the minor parties is thought by most Americans to be a "wasted vote."[25]

Some have gone further to argue that this preference for one of the two major parties is not the cause, but the effect, and that the cause of the two-party system really must be found in the laws and rules governing the electoral system. The most intriguing theory along these lines is that the two-party system was caused by the single-member district, plurality system of elections. It does seem fairly clear that the single-member system places an enormously high premium on going after a majority of votes in an election. That, in turn, discriminates against third parties because of their ideological or programmatic purity. The argument is that eventually the tendencies toward fragmentation among minority parties are overcome in the single-member system, since the various factions must make up their differences within one of the two major parties in order to get 50 percent or more of the votes.[26] The trouble is that the same forces in the single-member system that discourage third parties *can also discourage second parties.* That is to say, if one party consistently gets a majority in a certain district, even the

[25]For a good recent discussion of these matters, see Joyce Gelb and Marian L. Palley, *Tradition and Change in American Party Politics* (New York: Crowell, 1975), chapter 1 and p. 305.

[26]The two scholars most prominently identified with this theory are Schattschneider, *Party Government,* and Duverger, *Political Parties.*

affiliation with the second party comes to be considered a wasted vote.

This actually gets us somewhat closer to an explanation of the type of party system we have had in the United States. For most of the period between 1900 and 1956, it would be quite inaccurate to say without qualification that Americans lived under a two-party system. It is far more precise to say that during that time the United States had a two-party system at the *national* level which was produced by two sectionally based one-party systems. In the southern states the Democratic Party dominated to such an extent that in vast numbers of elections the Democratic candidates ran without opposition. The same situation prevailed for the Republican Party in the Northeast and also in many states in the Midwest. Even in those few states with two-party systems, there were seldom really competitive elections except at the statewide level. For example, New York was a highly competitive two-party state during the entire period; however, the Democratic Party was overwhelmingly dominant in New York City while the Republicans ran consistently without opposition in most of the "upstate counties."

This pattern of a one-party system at lower levels and a two-party system at some higher levels was reinforced, if not caused, by the single-member system of elections, but it was also extremely compatible with the dominant interests in each of the sections of the country. Whenever one party consistently elected its own candidates, it could attract the economic and political support of the most important interests; together, the dominant party and the dominant interests could, and did, suppress weaker interests. Included among the latter in all sections of the country were the interests of workers and lower status ethnic groups, since they tended to present problems that the party leadership could not easily accommodate without too much conflict with the sustaining dominant interests. At the *national* level during most of this century, therefore, the two parties differed fairly distinctly from each other inasmuch as the economic interests of the North and the South differed.

Change in this pattern had already begun by 1936, but the full impact of it was not felt until 1956, when President Eisenhower literally opened up the South to Republican voting. In the North the change came about more or less naturally with the emergence of organized labor inside the Democratic Party; it was accelerated in the South by the passage and application of national voting rights laws. Since 1964 the Republican Party has been a consistently important force throughout the South; the Democratic Party was by that time already a consistent force in many areas of the North.

This spread of the two parties into all states put to an end the prospect that a single economic interest would dominate a single political party. But that was never really the case anyway. A look at the more recent situation will show that there was always a strong *organizational* element which was independent of economic interests and could contend on an independent basis with business leaders. Even after the Republican Party had moved into all of the southern states and had begun to attract many important conservative agricultural and business interests, very few established Democratic leaders or activists switched to the Republican Party; most stuck doggedly to the old party and the old ways of doing things. Southern Republicans tended to pick up new and hitherto unaffiliated elements rather than chip off significant parts of the old. They even failed to make important and lasting inroads among black voters, despite the racist backgrounds of most southern Democratic candidates. Everywhere decisions to switch parties have been so infrequent as to rate front page newspaper coverage when they occur.

The proposition that political parties may be heavily influenced by economic interests but are not the indistinguishable political wings of specific economic interests tends thus to be confirmed. Parties are an organizational phenomenon, and there are regular and significant reinforcements for their essential nature. There were few switches during the dramatic developments of the past generation because party membership was the only way to maintain chairmanships of the important standing committees in Congress and access to the nominating and electoral machinery for the presidency. When political professionals spend twenty or more years building up seniority in Congress or access to the presidency, they are likely to require overwhelming provocation before disassociating themselves from the existing party organization.

As a result, the two major parties in the United States are always to a great extent out of alignment with the most important socioeconomic interests. Economic and political relationships are constantly in a state of readjustment. Parties are basically electoral organizations, and the requirements of electoral support and of economic interests are not always parallel and mutually reinforcing. Party alignments with economic interests become even more problematic in districts and states where two or more parties are seriously competing with each other; and the number of states with serious competition has indeed grown in the most recent decades.

During that same period when the two major parties began to extend their organizations to all regions and states, interests became increasingly organized in groups. As indicated in Figure 8.1, the primary strategy of any interest group is not to become a political party and directly control electoral personnel but rather to take those officials as they are and develop influential lines of access to them. To this extent, interest groups have become a channel for the primary interests of the country *alternative to the political parties.* Wherever parties are in competition and electoral outcomes are uncertain, the rational strategy for any organized interest is to cultivate access to both parties. This can be done by alliances and friendships. More probably, it is done by monetary contributions to parties, in order to reward friends and punish enemies. Organized labor is quite explicit about this, in fact. The purpose is to buy and maintain access to both parties, so that the influence process can work efficiently regardless of the outcome of elections.[27]

In summary, at least two things have conspired in the United States to keep the role of minor parties down, to keep the two major parties from fragmenting into a multi-party system, and at the same time to keep the two major parties out of alignment with the dominant economic interests. The first of these is electoral competition itself. The fight to get support sufficient to win a majority of the votes forces each of the parties in a two-party system to seek economic and social support far beyond the one or two interests that may dominate on economic terms but do not have a vast popular following. The second of these is the stake that each party has in control of the government or the personnel of government. Even if a political party leadership wanted to be bought out by an economic group, it would have nothing to sell unless it had a reputation for electing significant numbers of people to important offices. But if it is to maintain that reputation, it must be prepared to sacrifice some short-range economic gains. Thus, while no single argument can explain why we have a two-party system, we are able to appreciate at least some of the reasons it maintains itself once it is established.

The two-party system and what it means to be one of the two parties   Having begun with a look at third parties, we may now be better able to appreciate the two-party system and what it means to be one of the two major components of it. One of the most commonplace statements about the American two-party system is that the parties try to be all things to all people. We have already noted that candidates generally prefer not to distinguish themselves very clearly from their opponents, but rather to stay close to the "central tendency" (see chapter 7). Even in the late 1960s, when our society seemed to be more polarized than ever before in this century, in campaign after campaign the Republican candidate stood forthrightly for "law and order" while the Democratic candidate claimed equally forthrightly to favor "law and order—with justice." On foreign policy, the Democratic candidates argued for "peace in Vietnam," while the Republicans asserted just as strongly that they stood for "peace—but with honor." A sharp chisel could hardly have separated the barnacles from each other on specific issues.

---

[27]For a good discussion of this pattern, and of the extent to which the major business interests enjoy direct access to both parties, see Kenneth Prewitt and Alan Stone, *The Ruling Elites* (New York: Harper & Row, 1973), especially chapters 2–5.

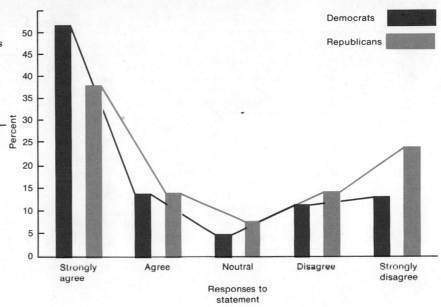

Figure 8.8
Opinions are polarized *within* parties, and not between them: Responses to the statement, "The government in Washington ought to see to it that everybody who wants to work can find a job."

Data from Center for Political Studies, Institute for Social Research, University of Michigan, 1964. Figure from Theodore Lowi, "Party, Policy, and Constitution in America," in *The American Party Systems*, ed. William Chambers and Walter Dean Burnham (New York: Oxford University Press, 1967).

Being all things to all people makes the parties look more or less like Figure 8.8. Note how there is a bar of proportionate height for each of the parties on each of the responses to an important policy question. This seems to indicate that party candidates have espoused such indistinguishable points of view that the electorate responds proportionately, no matter what the party affiliation. A closer look at Figure 8.8., however, will reveal something else that is not quite so commonplace about the two parties. Note that opinions are distributed bimodally *within both parties.* When two parties in a two-party system attempt to be all things to all people, they do in fact tend to absorb the conflicts of opinion that exist in the society, so that wherever opinion is bimodally distributed, it is likely to be that way inside both of the parties.

Table 8.6 shows that Figure 8.8, which is based on the single question about the government's obligation to give everybody a job, is typical of many of the important issues of the day. Although there is, of course, some degree of variation, these figures suggest that the most important policy issues of the day tend to be fought out *within the parties* rather than between them. In its appeal to the electorate, each of the parties tries to accommodate itself to the differences of interest among its active members; as we found with interest

Political Parties: Can Government Be Governed?

Table 8.6
Opinions Are Polarized Within, Not Between, Parties, Even among Strong Party Identifiers and Precinct Leaders

Issues and Opinions	Party Identifiers*		Precinct Leaders**	
	Strong Democrats	Strong Republicans	Democrats	Republicans
Federal provision for low-cost medical care				
For	74%	35.6%	76%	28%
Uncertain	2.3	8.1	4	11
Against	14.8	39.6	15	53
Federal aid to education				
For		10.1		
Uncertain	4.8	1.3		
Against	34.4	72.5		
Foreign aid to countries regardless of their attitude toward Communism				
For			59	37
Uncertain			4	8
Against			22	35

*Data from Center for Political Studies, Institute for Social Research, University of Michigan, 1968. For additional data from the same survey, see Frank Sorauf, *Party Politics in America,* 1st ed. (Boston: Little, Brown, 1968), pp. 160–163.
**Data from Samuel J. Eldersveld, *Political Parties: A Behavioral Analysis* (Chicago: Rand-McNally, 1964), pp. 186–205. See also Theodore Lowi, "Party, Policy and Constitution in America," in *The American Party Systems,* ed. William Chambers and Walter Deal Burnham (New York: Oxford University Press, 1967), p. 260.

groups, so with political parties, the leadership must conquer its own minorities before it can hope to conquer the government. The wide range of interests within the Democratic Party are represented by such leading conservative figures as Senators Eastland, Stennis, Talmadge, and Allen, along with Senators Humphrey, Mondale, Bayh, and McGovern, all politicians more inclined to advocate change. A similar spectrum exists within the Republican Party, as represented by such conservatives as Gerald Ford, Barry Goldwater, John Tower, and Ronald Reagan, and politicians with a far more liberal outlook, like Jacob Javits and Mark Hatfield.[28]

[28]Samuel Lubell, one of the most sensitive and imaginative analysts of American politics, was early to appreciate this pattern of working out issues within parties rather than between parties. He has suggested that this works with particular intensity within the *majority party,* where lies, in his view, the key to political conflict in any given period of time. He was probably correct in saying that this internal pattern is more intense within the majority party, but the same tendency should not be overlooked in the other party as well. See Samuel Lubell, *The Future of American Politics* (New York: Doubleday, 1956), p. 212.

Although it is generally agreed that parties differ very little from each other on particular issues, there is also a widely shared sense that the two major parties do differ from each other *in general*. If this is true—and I feel it is—we are not necessarily involved in a paradox. On the contrary, this becomes one of the most important insights into the significance of our party system within the larger scheme of government. It should be recalled from the previous chapter that an "illusion of central tendency" can be created wherever several specific issues are lumped together and analyzed simultaneously. Even when the distribution of opinions on each issue is polarized, this polarization can be masked statistically, because, as was indicated, very few people feel consistently negative or positive on all ten, or twenty, or thirty issues about which opinions can be expressed.

Now let us add political parties to this picture. Each party is constantly collecting bundles of separate issues and taking a stand on all of them simultaneously; that is the essence of party campaigning. But note the result of this in Figure 8.9, where the attitudes of the Democrats have been charted separately from those of the Republicans. Again, there were few whose answers were 100 percent positive or 100 percent negative on the six issues included in this study. However, there were some who did answer in this extremely consistent way; nearly all whose answers were 100 percent positive were Democrats, and all whose responses were 100 percent negative were Republicans. As we saw in Figure 7.3, when opinions were distributed for the sample as a whole, both "tails" of the distribution were reduced. When Republicans and Democrats were distributed separately, the left tail of the Republican and the right tail of the Democratic distribution tended to wither. Figure 8.9 demonstrates the actual statistical results, showing how it is indeed possible for parties to differ from each other *in general* without differing appreciably from each other *in particular*.[29]

The Functions of Parties in the American Scheme of Government

Data on the party system reveal at least three regular tendencies: (1) Parties in the two-party system in the United States have attempted to be all things to all people. (2) In the process of making that attempt, the two parties tend to become internally polarized, absorbing significant numbers of people with opposing attitudes on each and every issue. (3) Although the two parties do not differ much on specific issues, they do differ from each other in general;

[29]These patterns and arguments are pursued through the entire history of American political parties in Theodore Lowi, "Party, Policy, and Constitution in America," in *The American Party Systems,* ed. William Chambers and Walter Dean Burnham (New York: Oxford University Press, 1967), pp. 238–276.

Figure 8.9
Tweedledum and
Tweedledee? Not true.
When party respondents
are compared on several
issues at one time, a clear
difference between the
two parties emerges.

Y = Yea
N = Nay
NA = No Answer

Democrats

Republicans

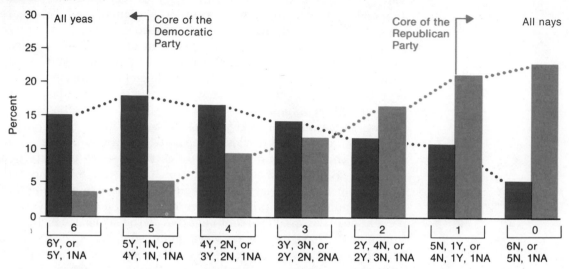

For this 1964 sample, Democrats and Republicans were separated. Each individual was categorized by the proportion of yea and nay answers to each of the six domestic issues. They were then grouped into seven categories. When the issues were grouped, few respondents consistently answered yea or nay. Democrats more consistently answered yea; Republicans, nay. The weight of the two parties was distinctly separated in the results.

Data from Center for Political Studies, Institute for Social Research, University of Michigan, 1964. Figure from Theodore Lowi, "Party, Policy, and Constitution in America," in *The American Party Systems*, ed. William Chambers and Walter Dean Burnham (New York: Oxford University Press, 1967).

this gives people a *sense* of a difference between the two parties even when they cannot articulate what that difference is. Ours is a very peculiar party system, and its impact on the larger governmental system follows accordingly.

Study of the history of parties in the United States tends to support the following propositions about the impact or "functions" of our party system: The party system regulates conflict over control of the regime. Parties organize disagreement but do not determine outcomes; in other words, our two-party system is not a "responsible party system." Competing parties tend to disperse or decentralize power—relative to what the distribution of power would otherwise have been. The two-party system tends to soften or displace class conflict.

Each of these functions will be discussed in turn. At this point, the reader should perhaps be reminded that the concept of *function* refers to a regular impact that an institution has on the larger system. This concept is chosen because it can capture the idea of a regular contribution without implying that such a contribution is intended. As party leaders and candidates go about the only business that is important to them—getting elected—their strategies and activities produce the consequences that our listing here is trying to describe. In order to dramatize the difference between intended consequences (goals) and unintended consequences (functions), let me suggest that it is this difference which makes it possible to dislike the pettiness and frailty of most politicians and to admire the system they have created and maintained.

Regulation of conflict   The party system regulates conflict over control of the regime. This statement is so fundamental that it serves literally to define the party system. The struggle over personnel of government is ritualized by the party. The parties convert political conflict into political competition, with its rules, regularities, and, most important, the practice whereby losers will accept the outcome and will allow the winners to occupy powerful offices. The importance of this function cannot be overemphasized. The reader should recall that in almost every election there is a tremendous amount at stake. Those who are elected to occupy the high offices of government can literally write their own version of conquest into law. It is a remarkable accomplishment in any country to regularize this conflict over control of the regime. Emphasis on our two-party system should not overshadow comparable functions in the party systems of other countries. Parties in a stable multi-party system also perform this same function, and even a one-party system, if it provides real competition over nominations, can do the same.[30]

Organization of disagreement   In addition to regularizing the contest for the personnel of government, the parties play an extremely important role in organizing the agenda of public policy. This does not mean that the parties take a position on the items of the agenda; it has already been shown that they are rarely able to do that, and rarely try. Rather, parties organize disagreement by *agreeing on what to disagree about.* This is one of the most difficult and creative processes in the entire political system. Once a problem is well defined, it is far less difficult to make decisions. It would be impossible for assemblies or electorates, which rely on voting, to play a role in decision making unless they possessed this capacity to agree on what to disagree about.

We tend too often to assume, completely without foundation, that issues naturally have two sides. The fact is that most collective life

[30]See, for example, V. O. Key, *Southern Politics* (New York: Knopf, 1949).

tends to make problems more complex. Nothing about an "issue" is natural except, perhaps, the underlying problem; and a natural problem does not become a public problem until there has been a great deal of definition. The parties are able to do that even when they are unable to take an organized stand on one side or the other.[31]

Dispersion of power A system of competing parties tends toward the dispersion of power. Political parties are not directly responsible for creating democracy, but they have been responsible for adulterating old elites with new elements and for pulling the power centers more toward the peripheries. For example, in one peaceful generation between 1800 and 1828, party politics broke apart forever the monopoly of the original American aristocracy.[32] To say that parties in the United States have *decentralized* the distribution of power may sound a bit paradoxical, considering the oligarchic leadership structure in the urban machine, the seniority system in Congress, and the "smoke-filled room" atmosphere of party nominations for the presidency until recent years.

Yet party competition, despite the preferences of party leaders, has kept political power from becoming more and more concentrated *in the state*—that is, in the apparatus of government bureaucracies, executives, and corporations. Although we cannot know what the distribution of power would have been without party competition, we do have the indications of the opening up of elite recruitment, as observed earlier. Another bit of telling evidence in favor of the proposition that the party system functions to decentralize things is the maintenance of federalism. Parties organize at state and local levels and are thus already decentralized in relation to the large national government. In addition, leadership in both parties in Congress have preferred to establish national programs that recognize and reinforce the federal system. Parties are organized in districts up to the state level, and party leaders tend to be fearful of any new programs that would weaken those lines of organization. The Social Security system is a good example; the party leaders opted for a system of state unemployment and old-age packages rather than a unified national approach.[33]

---

[31]"Agreeing on what to disagree about" is another one of those very important formulations of Carl Friedrich. See, for example, *The New Belief in the Common Man* (Boston: Little, Brown, 1942), p. 171.

[32]For some data on this subject, see Lowi, "Party, Policy, and Constitution in America," p. 243; also William Chambers, *The Democrats, 1789–1964* (Princeton: Van Nostrand, 1964), p. 28; and Schattschneider, *Party Government*, p. 152. This effect can be better observed at state and local levels. For data on these developments during the nineteenth century see Robert A. Dahl, *Who Governs?* (New Haven: Yale University Press, 1961); also Gabriel Almond, "Plutocracy and Politics in New York City" (Ph.D. diss., University of Chicago, 1939).

[33]This entire argument has been made best by Morton Grodzins, "Party and Government in the United States," *Political Parties U.S.A.,* ed. Robert A. Goldwin (Chicago: Rand McNally, 1964), p. 102; see also Morton Grodzins, "American Political Parties and the American System," *Western Political Quarterly* 13 (1960), 974–998.

Grass roots in the Black Belt: A voting place in Peachtree, Alabama, after the Civil Rights Act of 1965.

Another aspect of parties tending toward the dispersion of power is their contribution to the *democratization of the executive branch.* Most observers will tend to agree that this has been a major effect of the parties even though they may disagree among themselves as to whether it has been an entirely good thing. We need only cite here the way in which the parties transformed the Electoral College through the practice of pledging the elector candidates to support the nominee of the party. This subverted the original purpose of the Electoral College and contributed directly to giving the presidency a popular base in the electorate, outside the national capital, outside Congress, and even outside the state legislatures. Parties further democratized the presidency by providing for candidate nomination in national conventions, beginning in the 1830s. This practice surely broke the grip of the East Coast on the presidency and eliminated the custom of congressional nomination of presidential candidates as well.

Most people have considerable misgivings about the contribution the American party system has made to the "spoils system." Yet this too is a part of its tendency to disperse power. As soon as the political parties controlled the national executive, they proceeded to fill offices with loyal party workers. Government by patronage may or may not have produced havoc; but most certainly it democratized the composition of the federal service a century before this was conceivable in Europe.[34]

[34]For a good, brief history, see Herbert Kaufman, "The Growth of the Federal Personnel System," in *The Federal Government Service,* 2d ed., ed. Wallace Sayre (Englewood Cliffs, N.J.: Prentice-Hall, 1965); chapter 1. See also James L. Grant, "The Administration of Politics" (Ph.D. diss., University of Chicago, 1970).

In all fairness to the political science literature, I should report still another area in which the two-party system effects a dispersion of power—*expansion of the electorate.* Many political scientists believe that this has been a regular function of the American party system, but I am constrained to concur only in small part, dissenting in large part. One well-known political scientist has observed: "The enlargement of the practicing electorate has been one of the principal labors of the parties, a truly notable achievement for which the parties have never been properly credited."[35]

But the facts of party life in a great number of American cities and in the southern states throughout most of the twentieth century show little evidence that parties, even under stress of great competition, have taken initiatives to expand electorates in any significant way. Most of the important expansions of the electorate are attributable to the elimination of legal restrictions on voters and the passing of civil rights laws that made it a crime to interfere with voting. These laws were passed in legislatures dominated by the parties, but the obligation to change the laws came from constitutional amendments and Supreme Court decisions.

In partial attenuation of the record of parties in the electorate, one can at least say that although two parties in a vigorous two-party system do not seek to expand the electorate, a new party emerging as the second party does tend to have an exhilarating impact on the electorate. The argument proposing the expansion of the electorate as a significant function of the party system is based too heavily on the nineteenth century, when the parties and the party system were emerging. By the end of the nineteenth century the tendency seems to have been almost the reverse.[36]

Softening of class conflict   Almost everything about the history of parties in the United States tends to confirm the proposition that the two-party system softens class conflict. Here is another function that we can like or dislike intensely even as we agree it is happening. There is necessarily some development of classes and class consciousness in any large industrial nation like the United States. Nevertheless, every effort to build upon the class consciousness of the workers as a proletariat has been foiled, even if not deliberately, by the fact that the two existing parties do not provide channels of communication consistent with class cleavages. Both major parties have been comfortable with workers; both have made efforts at different points in time to attract workers, just as both parties have made efforts to maintain strong ties to the middle and upper classes and corporations. It might be useful to look once again

---

[35]Schattschneider, *Party Government,* p. 48.
[36]For a statistical demonstration of the difference between a system with an emerging second party and a system with established parties, see Lowi, "Party, Policy, and Constitution in America," pp. 250–252.

at the distribution of opinions within the two parties, as that picture is sketched in Figure 8.8 and Table 8.6. As long as the opinions of a significant portion of each party resemble the opinions dominant in the other party, there is little prospect of either major party seeking to base itself heavily in any one class.

AMERICAN PARTIES—A BALANCE SHEET

There may be some value in repeating that the so-called functions of the party system are not the *goals* of the system or of either party in it. They are called *functions* because they are thought to be regular consequences which flow, without intention, from the pursuit of the only goal of parties, which is to control governments by winning elections. Once we have established that these functions do flow regularly from normal party activity—and I think the voluminous literature on political parties will support each of the above propositions—we can go a step further to make some speculative conclusions about the place of our party system in our larger scheme of government. I do not suggest that these conclusions are truths to be committed to memory as some kind of political catechism. I do suggest that they flow logically from reflection on the functions of the party system and that, if proven true, must necessarily shape our vision of and our outlook on incomplete conquest.

The conclusion that comes most immediately to mind is that the two-party system *produces automatic majorities.* It is quite obvious that when the two parties occupy almost all of the political space, the party candidate with the most votes not only has a plurality but has, or is very close to having, an absolute majority. This ability to produce automatic majorities is a very significant advantage for government, inasmuch as those who occupy the elective offices have a clearer "right" or "mandate" drawn from the electorate.

There is, however, something very peculiar about these automatic majorities. The two-party system in the United States tends to produce *artificial majorities.* That is to say, the majorities provided to most candidates are not clearly representative of any meaningful aggregate of voters, in terms of social class, section of the country, ethnic grouping, or anything else. Majorities produced by the American two-party system are simply numerical majorities; they usually have no political content whatsoever.[37] This is simply a direct extension of the earlier notion that parties soften class conflict. The significance of these numerical majorities is that although issues flow through parties and party leaders decide which issues get on the agenda for debate at what time, the force and

[37]As far as I am able to determine, the notion of artificial majorities was formulated by William Riker in *Democracy in the United States* (New York: Macmillan, 1953), pp. 108–109.

consensus for final public policy decisions are rarely provided by the parties themselves.

The next step in our argument here must be that there are no "responsible parties" in our kind of two-party system. By definition, responsible parties are parties which present programs to the electorate and which eventually discipline party members in the legislature to support those promises when they come up as bills. Many parties in multi-party systems, and even some in two-party systems, approximate this ideal of responsibility. American parties come nowhere near this, and there is little likelihood that responsible parties will ever develop in the United States.[38]

We need not be too pessimistic. Something may be lost in "irresponsible parties," but something may also be gained. One gain we should consider is the stability of the regime. One of the most important ways that our party system contributes to the stability of the regime is a direct result of party irresponsibility. A two-party system separated from classes and producing artificial majorities tends also to *detach issues from regimes.* In our system, the government does not stand or fall on the outcome of a vote in the legislature, even when the issue is a fundamental one on which the government has taken a strong stand. The government does not have to put its future on the line in a vote of confidence. It is extremely rare for people to question the legitimacy of the regime and to look toward a radical solution even when the government or the party in power has failed to provide action on a whole series of popular demands. Parties in a two-party system have gained consent from the electorate to govern for a period of time prescribed in the Constitution, and this consent is not accompanied by any provisos or contingencies. This fact has contributed enormously to the stability and the institutional conservatism of the American political system.[39]

A balance sheet drawn from all of the various observed and imputed consequences of the two-party system in the United States leads almost unavoidably to a single conclusion that our party system is extremely well designed for conquest in a modern industrial state. It provides an orderly process of exchanging power among intensely competing interests. It acts somewhat like a buffer between masses and regimes. Yet it provides all of the appearances

---

[38]The classic statement in favor of the development of responsible parties is by the American Political Science Association in *Toward a More Responsible Two-Party System,* an *American Political Science Review* supplement to the September 1950 issue. For two objections, see Julius Turner, "Responsible Parties: A Dissent from the Floor," *American Political Science Review,* March 1951, pp. 143–152; and Edward C. Banfield, "In Defense of the American Party System," in *Political Parties U.S.A.,* pp. 22–39.

[39]One of the best essays on institutional conservatism of parties in the United States is that of Samuel P. Huntington, "Political Modernization? American versus Europe," *World Politics,* April 1966, p. 378.

of consent, committing the minorities as well as the majorities to the support of the government during its tenure of office.

Quite clearly the party system does not provide for consent according to the "new theory" of consent (see chapter 7). Ironically, considering the fear of parties shared by most of the founders, modern parties come much closer to fulfilling the older ideal of consent, based on the notion of *regulated interests.* This puts modern parties at variance with the modern myth of consent even though modern politicians and political scientists continue to embrace it.

What ought to change? If we try to make parties more responsible, they are that much more likely to yield to the interest with the highest bid. There is already too much of this kind of tendency, as can easily be seen in the unholy patterns of party finance. Up until this point in time it has at least been possible to say that the efforts of the large corporations or large unions to buy out one of the parties have been adulterated by the need of each of the parties to reach out toward opposing interests. If parties did become "responsible," we would continually have to ask: To whom, for what?

Compared to some abstract ideal of democracy, government with two-party politics does not show up very well. But of course ideal government is an inconsistency in terms. Government itself is an expression of the weaknesses of people in society; ideal government would have to be either no government at all or a government of such absolute efficiency as to leave no freedom of individual maneuver at all. Once a political party system becomes an acceptable mode of conducting politics and all sides to intense political conflict are able to accept the victory of someone else, parties as an institution become a means for reducing the absoluteness of government without destroying all capacity of government to maintain conquest. Although the party system must be judged in terms of the primordial requirement of maintaining conquest, we may not, for all that, be able to express great admiration for parties or party systems. Nonetheless, if a party system provides a regular, even if modest, departure from absolute tyranny, then it should not be judged too harshly.

Part Four
Government

To state the purpose of governmental institutions is to restate the definition of conquest. Government is conquest institutionalized, and the key problem of government is getting the people to obey. Although governments are prepared to use any available means of coercion to ensure obedience, these will be to no avail unless most people are already prepared to obey; that is, the government must be legitimate. However, most democracies have sought legitimacy in ways that produce contradictions in government.

The principle of limited power and the principle of representation require that legislatures be highly representative of the people and at the same time capable of making timely and appropriate decisions. These principles also require that the bureaucracy be a highly professional organization as well as highly responsive to the specific demands of the politicians. They require a judiciary which can set severe limits on the power of the government's branches, regardless of demands for more government on the part of the executive, the legislative body, or popular majorities. Our governing institutions are so constructed that both our freedom and our peril rest upon the inability of government to fulfill its prime tasks.

Chapter 9   Getting the People to Obey: The First Branch

American politicians consider the legislature the first branch because it is an ideal place for maximum interaction with a minimum of action. This is no frivolous matter. Since government must command obedience, government is, by definition, the place where politics ends.[1] Politicians are ordinarily moderate sorts who would rather talk about a problem until it goes away than legislate a mandatory solution. To command obedience and to punish disobedience goes against the grain of political life. In the United States even the vocabulary of coercion has been changed; we now speak of "policies" to offer ourselves reassurance that governmental acts are temporary and conditional. This may paint a picture of what we would like government to be, but we should never forget that *policy* shares etymological roots with *police*. From the standpoint of simple longevity, the legislature is the last

---

[1]For many, it may be comfortable to imagine that "politics" is going on all the time. It should be emphasized, however, that there are two types of politics. The first type involves efforts to bring government to a closer fit with someone's preferences. The second type begins when someone's preferences have been governmentalized, and coercion begins; and this politics is comprised of reactions to coercion.

branch. We look to it as the first branch because in the past two centuries it has been holding out to us a solution to the problem of tyranny that has always been presented by other, more ancient governing powers, such as kings, generals, priests, presidents, and administrators.

A representative government is a concrete expression of the hope that at least one institution of government may keep politics alive as long as possible before the command of obedience must take effect. This has been the American expectation for far more than two centuries, despite many disappointments with the state legislatures and with Congress. Perhaps the most important single provocation for the American Rebellion was "no taxation without representation." King George's taxes were not unusual or oppressive; but by the time of their imposition the sentiment for representative government was so strong that, without it, *any* policy would have been considered oppressive.[2]

A HISTORY OF ASSEMBLIES

The Revolutionary Age of the late eighteenth century was very much an age of the commoner. The assembly, or legislature, as a means of expressing the interests of commoners, was fixed upon as one of the goals of revolution. Yet the assembly was in no way an invention of the American or the French Revolution. Assemblies had been around in one form or another for several centuries before the emergence of the idea that the common man deserved representation. The eighteenth century seized upon an already well-developed institution and attempted to bend it toward the service of new ideals. Assemblies were primarily the invention of monarchs, and in the hands of monarchs the assembly was an effective instrument of conquest. The calling of assemblies "was necessary because the undeveloped state of central administrative systems and the absence of effective means of coercion rendered the collection of [extraordinary war taxes] impossible without local cooperation."[3]

From the standpoint of the monarchy, the main purpose of the assembly was to gain support from the hinterlands, primarily to wage war, and to have some assurance that the message of military needs was spread sufficiently in the countryside. But once an assembly was called into being, the members might naturally be expected to proceed to act as ambassadors on their own behalf to try to extract concessions from the monarchy in return for the consent

---

[2]For more on this point see Merrill Jensen, "Democracy and the American Revolution," *Huntington Library Quarterly* 20 (1957), 321–341. See also Lyford Edwards, *The Natural History of Revolution* (Chicago: University of Chicago Press, 1927), p. 117.

[3]Carl Friedrich, *Constitutional Government and Democracy* (Boston: Ginn, 1950), p. 274.

and money the monarch so badly needed. Consequently, the assembly ultimately became a place where regional barons, and eventually the rising merchant classes, or bourgeoisie, could state their case against the monarch or the agents of the monarch. Although invented as an instrument of conquest, the assembly slowly became the institution which led to the downfall of the feudal societies and the old absolute monarchies. It was the essence of antifeudalism. It was a place where, contrary to feudal custom, a whole gamut of economic, administrative, and military decisions were made by contract—in short, where politics was possible. The assembly was neither a democratic nor a representative body. However, well before the age of the common man it had already become an institution where interests of a great variety could attach themselves. This was the beginning of modern politics.[4]

Clearly, the institution of representative government began with assemblies whose primary task was *getting obedience through consent.* This function of an assembly has never disappeared; it has simply been joined by new functions in order to accommodate the institution to new demands. Once the assembly became a place where a variety of country aristocracy could meet one another, share interests, and perhaps plot against the monarchy, the assembly became a parliament—a place where people got together to talk about issues important to themselves (French: *parler,* "to talk"). And once being a member began to signify status and power, it became important to know what interests were represented in such an assembly, and by whom. Before the rise of the assembly the only way population could be represented was through a monarch. Writing at the very time of the emergence of mature representative assemblies, the great political theorist Thomas Hobbes insisted that "a multitude of men, are made one person, when they are by one man, or by one person, represented" (*Leviathan,* 1647). The idea of a *representative* assembly was truly a revolutionary addition to the theory, and eventually the practice, of government. Last of all in this development came the emergence of the assembly as a *legislature*—an assembly with the power to make laws. As we shall see, this was probably the most important turn in the long struggle between the people and absolute monarchy. Many things had to happen before the assembly could become a legislative assembly.

Assemblies in the United States—the state legislatures and the United States Congress—provide some of the best early examples of mature assemblies, assemblies that are at one and the same time parliaments, representative assemblies, and legislatures. From the

---

[4]For an appreciation of the place of the assembly in the crumbling of feudal society, see Marc Bloch, *Feudal Society,* trans. L. A. Manyon (Chicago: University of Chicago Press, 1961): "It was assuredly no accident that the representative system, in the very aristocratic form of the English Parliament, the French 'Estates', the *Stand* of Germany, and the Spanish *Cortes* originated in states which were only just emerging from the feudal stage and still bore its imprint" (p. 452).

moment of their origin, American legislative institutions were all of
these. Taken together all of these separate dimensions of the
assembly define representative government; they must be looked at
separately to be appreciated.

Representative government is an extraordinarily complex phenomenon, not because it has a long history, but because it combines
inconsistent and contradictory expectations. The most efficient way
to govern is to have a single, responsible individual presiding over a

well-organized bureaucracy; commands generate from the center and are implemented at the periphery through a direct "chain of command." The concept of representative government introduces exceptions to the rule of efficient government. Every ounce of representation introduced into a well-organized scheme of central government is likely to produce a pound of inefficiency. There is no ideal or fixed balance between a desired amount of representation and a desired amount of efficacious government. Each generation tends to make its own decision, perhaps more by accident than by design, as to how much of each there is going to be. Each change in the balance between representative government and efficient government will tend to create a new procedure or a new layer or a new practice in the assembly. In the period since the Vietnam War and the Watergate scandal, there seems to be a tendency away from executive-centered government toward more representative government. However the balance is struck for the new political generation, the governmental situation will be that much more complicated.[5]

Reasonable observers will always disagree on the proper definition of the first branch. But surely an analysis of the separate aspects of representative government must precede any comprehensive understanding or definition of what it is. And throughout our analysis, we must be guided by the ultimate question: Can a democratic ideal be translated into real institutions that can make any difference to conquest?

CONGRESS AS AN ASSEMBLY

Congress is not one but two assemblies.[6] There are "bicameral" assemblies in many countries, but it is rare outside of the United States to find true bicameralism, where both houses or chambers are equally meaningful parts of the government. Bicameralism was already something of a habit in the United States prior to the Constitution. Though the arrangement for dual assemblies is considered one of the great compromises in the Constitution, it was not drawn out of thin air. For example, Article I, Section 2 assumed that most assemblies in the state were bicameral when it based the qualification for voting in the national elections upon the provisions of each state for voting for "the most numerous branch of the State Legislature."

---

[5] This interplay between representation and government will crop up regularly in this and the next chapter. For more detailed argument along these lines, see Lowi, introductory essay, in Theodore Lowi and Randall Ripley, eds., *Legislative Politics U.S.A.* (Boston: Little, Brown, 1973); also Friedrich, *Constitutional Government and Democracy,* especially chapters 14–16.

[6] The use of Congress as a single example for a case study of representative government is discussed briefly at the end of this chapter.

Wherever there is bicameralism there tends to be an assumption that each chamber will be based on a different principle of composition in order to place additional checks and balances on arbitrary uses of power.[7] However, a less clearly articulated but even more fundamental purpose underlies the principle of mixed composition—to have an assembly which is a place where all kinds of interests will find a means of expression. In bicameralism we have perhaps the most concrete manifestation of the idea that modern government is based upon equality of interests, interests without moral ordering. The assembly is the place where these interests interact in an open market situation.

The U.S. House of Representatives and the Senate, of course, constitute our bicameral assembly. The House, sometimes deprecatingly called the "lower house," is composed of 435 interest-bearing members. Until 1913, federal statutes permitted the House to increase its membership in response to each increase in the population, as reported in the official decennial census. In 1929, Congress passed a law setting an absolute limit of 435 members, the size it had attained in 1913. Since that time, the states have had to *reapportion* members from states with declining populations to states with increasing populations. The Senate is at present composed of 100 members, 2 from each state; and it will continue to grow by twos if new states are added. Senators enjoy consistently higher prestige than members of the House, probably due to the higher visibility and larger constituency of most senators. (Some members of the House are elected at large, but only where the state population is very small, or where, temporarily, the state legislature is unable to reapportion.) It is unheard of for a senator to resign in order to run for the House, but the reverse situation occurs quite frequently.

From the beginning the expectation was that the House would be the people's assembly. Even the practice of providing for single-member districts was adopted in the spirit of having a people's assembly. Though it may appear to many to be absurd today, there was good reason in the nineteenth century to believe that districts sparse and homogeneous in population could produce representatives that bore a strong resemblance to the actual distributions of opinions in the district. As we have seen already, the Senate was designed so that its members would be more attuned to the interests of property.

Despite all this, the Senate has turned out to be on the average more oriented toward the modern problems of an industrial-urban society than the House. This shift is mainly due to economic and

[7]Considerations back of our own two chambers are discussed in chapter 4. See also the *Federalist Papers* dedicated to this subject, especially numbers 62 and 63.

social developments which have given almost every senator at least one major urban-industrial center to worry about, while many members of the House continue to come from districts heavily composed of rural, suburban, or other nonindustrial interests. For example, during the Ninety-second Congress (1971–1972), Senator Hugh Scott, Republican Minority Leader from Pennsylvania, voted with the "conservative coalition" 62 percent of the time; eight of the thirteen Pennsylvania Republicans in the House had higher conservative support scores. Scott's Republican colleague from Pennsylvania, Senator Richard Schweiker, voted with the conservative coalition only 35 percent of the time, which was lower than all of the thirteen Republican House members. Charles Percy, Senate Republican from Illinois, had a score of 31 percent, which was lower than all eleven Illinois Republican House members—whose combined scores averaged 74.3 percent.[8]

There will be ample opportunity to inspect the behavior of members of Congress. The important point here is that the composition of the membership of the assembly is an important political criterion *in and of itself,* without regard to the terms and conditions of election or the behavior of individual members of either chamber. This phenomenon of the overall or aggregate composition of an assembly can be called sociological representation, or symbolic representation. It is to be contrasted with mechanical or behavioral representation, where the question is whether the representatives conduct themselves in accord with the wishes of their constituents. The presence or absence of certain social characteristics in the assembly is taken as an important criterion of status and worth in the community.

Indeed, concern for the so-called fairness of the proportion of women, blacks, and ethnic minorities in the legislature (and of course elsewhere in the government) seems to intensify as the country grows more sophisticated. This does not necessarily mean that influence is in any way proportional to the weight of a given social characteristic in the assembly; nevertheless, it is rare to find a social grouping whose members do not feel shortchanged if someone like themselves is not a member of the assembly.[9]

---

[8]The "conservative coalition" is a voting alliance of Republicans and southern Democrats against northern Democrats in Congress. This index of votes is compiled on an annual basis by *Congressional Quarterly* and is generally considered a good indication of conservatives versus liberals. See *Congressional Quarterly Almanac,* 1972, pp. 65–70. For a good discussion of this phenomenon, and a great deal of data on the behavior of senators and members of the House, see L. A. Froman, *Congressmen and Their Constituencies* (Chicago: Rand-McNally, 1963).

[9]There is a large body of literature on the "recruitment of elites," probably inspired by a series of small monographs done in the early 1950s under the leadership of Harold Lasswell, *The Comparative Study of Elites* (Stanford: Hoover Institute, various dates). A very good survey of the entire literature on elites will be found in Kenneth Prewitt and Alan Stone, *The Ruling Elites: Elite Theory, Power, and American Democracy* (New York: Harper & Row, 1973). See also Andrew Hacker, "The Elected and the Annointed: Two American Elites," *American Political Science Review,* September 1961.

Getting the People to Obey:
The First Branch

Table 9.1

Religious Affiliation of the Members of the House and Senate, 1973

Religion	House			Senate		
	D	R	Total	D	R	Total
Protestant	146	149	295	41	33	74
Catholic	69	31	100	10	4	14
Jewish	10	2	12	1	1	2
Other*	11	9	20	6	4	10
None	3	2	5	0	0	0
Total	239	193	432	58	42	100

Data from *Congressional Quarterly Weekly Report,* January 6, 1973, p. 13.
*"Other" includes Mormon, Greek Orthodox, Unitarian, Quaker, Adventists.

Table 9.2

Blacks and Women in Congress, 1947–1972

Congress	Senate		House	
	Blacks	Women	Blacks	Women
93rd (1971–1972)	1	0	15	14
92nd	1	2	12	13
91st	1	1	9	10
90th	1	1	5	11
89th	0	2	6	10
88th	0	2	5	11
87th	0	2	4	17
86th	0	1	4	16
85th	0	1	4	15
84th	0	1	3	16
83rd	0	3	2	12
82nd	0	1	2	10
81st	0	1	2	9
80th (1947–1948)	0	1	2	7

Data from *Congressional Quarterly Almanac,* 1972, pp. 1035–1036.

A Brief Sociology of Congress

Preoccupation with social and symbolic representation has produced a host of statistics on the House and Senate members. For example, Table 9.1 presents data on the religious affiliations of members of the House and Senate in 1973. As should be expected, both chambers are overwhelmingly Protestant—although that statistic masks the fact that the Protestant category was, as of 1973, composed of more than fifteen different sects. Actually the most distinct minori-

Table 9.3

Occupational Backgrounds of the Members of the House and Senate, 1973

Occupation	House			Senate		
	D	R	Total	D	R	Total
Agriculture	14	24	38	4	7	11
Business or banking	72	83	155	12	10	22
Education	41	18	59	7	3	10
Engineering	1	1	2	2	0	2
Journalism	16	7	23	4	1	5
Labor leader	3	0	3	0	0	0
Law	137	84	221	42	26	68
Law enforcement	1	1	2	0	0	0
Medicine	3	2	5	1	0	1
Public service/ politics	201	152	353	55	42	97
Minister	2	2	4	0	0	0
Scientist	2	0	2	0	0	0
Veteran	175	142	317	42	31	73

Data from *Congressional Quarterly Weekly Report*, January 6, 1973, p. 3.

ty in Table 9.1, as well as in most of American politics, is the minority of those who possess no religious affiliation at all. Perhaps there is some solace in the fact that people who profess no religious affiliation apparently do continue to have political rights in the United States.

The results of a study of the racial and sexual composition of the two chambers in the years 1947 to 1972 are shown in Table 9.2. Blacks and women have made some modest strides in the past decade, although in neither case is the proportion of their membership in Congress comparable to the proportion of their membership in the population at large. Until the racial and sexual composition of Congress comes closer to the actual distributions in the population at large, there is likely to continue to be a considerable amount of clamor for reform; but at that time, as now, only a careful assessment of the actual policy decisions of the national government will reveal whether blacks and women are properly treated in our society.

Occupational backgrounds of members of Congress are a matter of continual interest. A fair, though incomplete, mix of occupations, as identified in 1973, is presented in Table 9.3, which is drawn from studies made by the semi-official *Congressional Quarterly.* These are not cumulative figures, because individual members can pursue more than one occupation during their lifetime. Some of the more interesting figures are those on the extremely low and the extreme-

Getting the People to Obey: The First Branch

ly high side. There are, for example, almost no scientists or educators now (nor have there ever been) serving in the House or Senate, despite the fact that science and education are two of the largest industries in the United States. In contrast, people with backgrounds in agriculture and related occupations have contributed a very high proportion of the membership in the past, but their number has declined proportionally to the decline of those industries in the economic system. Forty-nine members of Congress reported agriculture as their occupation but were really in business or banking related to agriculture. Most members of Congress, whatever their claim for occupational background, have strong ties to business and industry. This is particularly true of those who give law as their occupation.[10]

Three very important types of social characteristics are not reported in Tables 9.1 to 9.3. The first of these is the ethnic group category—minority groups other than blacks. It is extremely difficult to find reliable statistics on ethnic or national origin, despite the fact that most candidates attempt to capitalize on any special ethnic characteristics they possess. The problem is especially complex among older ethnic groups, where the senator or member of the House may be from the third or fourth generation of the group in the United States. It is, however, probably fair to say that a single ethnic group must be extremely heavily concentrated within a district before the representative in Congress for that district is likely to be drawn from that group. One study demonstrated that it would be to the advantage of anyone intent on pursuing a career in Congress to be "a late-middle-aged male lawyer whose father was of the professional or managerial class; a native-born 'White,' or—if he cannot avoid being an immigrant—a product of Northwestern or Central Europe or Canada, rather than of Eastern or Southern Europe, Latin America, Africa or Asia."[11]

The presence or absence of an upper-class background of old and hereditary wealth among members of Congress is also not surveyed in Tables 9.1 to 9.3. The upper-class group, in fact, is underrepresented in Congress, especially when one considers the wealth and status of these people. This is probably due to the fact that the upper classes do not need to engage directly in electoral politics to prove their standing to themselves or to the rest of their community. Congress is attractive to people and groups usually called "upwardly mobile." Old wealth is old wealth in large part because of economic and political influence in an earlier generation. Many members of the upper classes would consider it a reduction in status if they or their children decided to enter into the rough-and-tumble atmosphere of electoral politics.

---

[10]More will be said later about the significance of the law profession.
[11]Marian D. Irish and James Prothro, *The Politics of American Democracy,* 5th ed. (Englewood Cliffs, N.J.: Prentice-Hall, 1971), p. 352.

The third missing category is poverty; but even if we could get figures on the number of our congressional representatives who originated in poverty, we could be fairly sure that they would also constitute a highly underrepresented group. Some would argue that this is due to the fact that poor people do not identify with each other and do not give preference to other poor people if and when they go to the polls to select their leadership. This line of argument could lead to the conclusion that inadequate representation of the poor in the national legislature is not a significant or dangerous factor. An alternative explanation would be that the poor are inadequately represented because they are too far removed from local institutions, too weakly attached to basic political values, and too lacking in self-esteem and social status, as well as knowledge, to reach beyond their neighborhoods. This type of explanation leads to a much more unsettling conclusion about the significance of under-representation of the poor.

The purpose of this review of sociological representation in Congress is not to predict where the stress for reform will come from. Its purpose is to underscore the significance of the national assembly as a source of political symbolism. The maintenance of conquest requires that there be some degree of correspondence between a few important social characteristics in the legislature and the same characteristics in the society at large. Traditionally, Americans have stressed religious, racial, and sectional characteristics in their nominations for public office and in the overall composition of assemblies. To a large number of observers, including non-Marxists, symbolic representation is cynical; it tends to instill "false consciousness" and diverts people from the concrete economic and social interests with which governments should be concerned. Nevertheless, stress on the symbolic composition of the national legislature and other elite positions in politics seems to have worked. Congress, as an assemblage of individual members, has contributed to the political stability of the United States.[12]

CONGRESS AS A PARLIAMENT

As has already been mentioned, the derivation of the name *Parlement* (cognate: *Parliament*) from the French *parler* ("to talk") is indicative of one activity the French felt was essential to their

---

[12]For a non-Marxist appreciation of the effectiveness of racial consciousness in masking and blunting the strong class antagonisms, see V. O. Key, *Southern Politics* (New York: Knopf, 1949); Key's analysis is filled with the importance of instilling racial fear into the lower classes in the South as an antidote to populist class radicalism. See also C. Vann Woodward, *The Strange Career of Jim Crow* (New York: Oxford University Press, 1955). For a study of the importance of various kinds of symbols in politics, see Murray Edelman, *The Symbolic Uses of Politics* (Urbana: University of Illinois Press, 1964). However, the classic treatment of the importance of "sociological representation" will be found in Gaetano Mosca, *The Ruling Class*, trans. Hannah D. Kahn (New York: McGraw-Hill, 1939).

national assembly. Although we do not give our assembly the name which implies talking, talk in Congress is not merely a personal predilection of the members; talk is literally built into the structure of the institution. Probably the most important single condition favoring talk in the Congress is the fact that each member of the House and Senate is elected completely independently of all other members. In each chamber each member is equal to all other members by virtue of the fact that membership is determined entirely by election from districts defined as equal. Each member owes responsibility only to the district and not to a party, to a list, or to other candidates running at the same time. This fact of equal districts is universally recognized and respected in Congress, so much so that a tradition of mutual assistance has grown up. One of the very strong, though unwritten, rules of Congress provides that each member of Congress should be helped in any effort to gain reelection, regardless of party, as long as that member has been a conscientious and respectful member.[13]

Another important support in Congress for the parliamentary function is enshrined in the Constitution itself. This is a provision that senators and representatives "shall in all cases except Treason, Felony, and Breech of the Peace be privileged from Arrest during their Attendance at the Session of their respective Houses, and in going to and returning from the same; and for any Speech or Debate in either House, they shall not be questioned in any other place" (Article I, Section 6). This has freed members of Congress from fear of libel and slander suits or arrests on grounds of incitement to riot for anything they may say while doing congressional business. Supreme Court decisions have extended this immunity to activities of members of Congress in their capacity as members of committees—such as investigatory committees of the Watergate type. Such protections are extended even when Congress is not in session, as long as the activities can be shown to relate to congressional business. Members of Congress, according to Article I, can be disciplined only by their fellow members.

There are additional indications of the degree to which Congress protects and fosters the freedom of its members to speak out on all issues. One of these is the size of the verbatim record of all talk on the floor of Congress. For most of our history this has been printed and published in the *Congressional Record,* and the amount of talk so recorded is almost inconceivable to the neophyte. For example, talk in the first session of the Ninety-second Congress (which includes only the calendar year 1971) fills thirty-six volumes, plus a whole volume for the index and another volume for a digest of the

---

[13]For example, one of the most important factors in distributing assignments to standing committees is whether the assignment will help the member in a bid for reelection. For a description and assessment of this tradition, see Nicholas A. Masters, "Committee Assignment," reprinted in Nelson Polsby, *Congressional Behavior* (New York: Random House, 1971), p. 165.

daily record. The thirty-six volumes add up to nearly 48,000 pages, double column, small print.

Some observers will express concern that public and published debate converts free talk into guarded rhetoric. They will argue that a parliamentary assembly cannot do its job except behind closed doors. That argument cannot be lightly dismissed; nevertheless, the choice in the United States has been in favor of public talk and published debate. In defense of this choice it can be said that secrecy and the need for confidence is satisfied in the lobbies, in party caucuses prior to debate on the floor, and in the standing committees where compromises over the drafting of bills can take place behind closed doors. Moreover, the rules of Congress also protect the members from mistakes made on the floor in public debate. Each member has the privilege of changing the remarks recorded by the stenographers before these remarks are published in the *Congressional Record.* Thus, even though the legislators may blunder in speaking before their colleagues and the people in the galleries, they are at least given the opportunity to change the record of their remarks and later deny that they ever made them.[14]

Reference so far has been to only one kind of talk—debate. This is the essence of parliamentary talk, but there is still another type of talk—deliberation. Debate tends to take place on the floor. Deliber-

[14]The various views on the value of publicity and the value of talk will be found in Bertram Gross, *The Legislative Struggle* (New York: McGraw-Hill, 1953), p. 365; and Carl Friedrich, *Constitutional Government and Democracy*, p. 363.

ation is a very different kind of talk and takes place in a very different place—in committees and subcommittees. A great deal more will have to be said about this distinction later; but it is important to note here that the distinction between the two types of talk clearly and concretely illustrates that talk in Congress, although very much protected and encouraged, is nevertheless severely restricted. If Congress were only a parliamentary assembly, then there could be no restrictions on talk, and all of the members would be on a completely equal plane. However, since Congress does also function as a representative and legislative assembly, it must channel talk in directions that may produce governmental decisions. Thus, as we shall see in various contexts, access to the floor for purposes of engaging in parliamentary talk is tightly controlled by the chair and the party and committee leadership. One must gain recognition in order to talk, and that recognition tends to be allocated according to whether the person is a member of the committee whose bill is being discussed, according to party and seniority, and according to many more subtle social factors that so often make one member "more equal" than others. Deliberative talk inside committees and subcommittees is also restricted, very often according to seniority.

Despite all these restrictions, talk is well enough protected in both chambers—even more carefully in the Senate than in the House—to produce meaningful debate on important legislative issues. The value of talk cannot be assessed in isolation. Without talk in Congress, there would probably in the long run be less willingness in the population to obey the laws. On the other hand, the more talk we get, the fewer laws Congress will be able to pass and the less capable Congress will be of participating with the executive and the courts in the actual government of the country. The parliamentary dimension can, therefore, be evaluated only in terms of all of the dimensions and functions of Congress.

CONGRESS AS A REPRESENTATIVE ASSEMBLY

Representation quite literally means to present again, to bring or present something to someone else, or to describe something in words or pictures in order to present an image of something or someone. These original usages of the term had nothing to do with the contemporary idea of one person speaking for and being responsible to other persons. Even after there were well-developed assemblies, the notion of representation in this sense was apparently not important. There might have been a notion of sociological representation, as described in the earlier section; but it did not

involve the idea of representatives' responsibility to their constituents.[15]

In the modern definition, the representatives stand in the place of their constituents, but they are also expected to speak for their constituents as though they were their agents. This is probably the most important reason there are so many lawyers in Congress and in the state legislatures of the United States. It would be neither surprising nor necessarily bad if *all* the members of Congress were lawyers. It is, after all, the profession of lawyers to *speak for* an individual or group (a commonplace synonym for *lawyer* is *mouthpiece*). Basic to the practice of law is the notion of agent and principal. It must be emphasized immediately that the lawyer's relation to a client is very different from the relationship between a single representative and as many as 300,000 clients in a district. A single client usually has a single set of interests and gives a designated agent some fairly explicit instructions—buy this house, write that contract, execute that will.

In contrast, there are many thousands of interests in a single district, and the representative has a good deal of freedom to choose which messages to hear and which interests to pursue.[16] Moreover, the agent is usually chosen by the client, whereas the representative to Congress or a state legislature has to win an election to

[15]See Hanna Pitkin, "Introduction," in *Representation,* ed. Hanna Pitkin (New York: Atherton Press, 1969), pp. 1–23. One of Pitkin's most interesting examples of the early notion of representation is that of the Pope and the College of Cardinals, who were spoken of as representing the persons of Christ and the Apostles, but were not thought of as actual agents speaking for them. The Pope and the Cardinals "stood for" but did not necessarily "speak for" Christ and the Apostles (p. 2).

[16]See especially Lewis A. Dexter, "The Representative and His District," reprinted in *Legislative Politics U.S.A.,* pp. 175–184.

achieve that status.[17] Very few people really believe that a representative of a large district can act like an agent of a single client. This is why we depend so heavily upon elections. It is through the electoral process that we try to provide incentives and sanctions designed to make representatives more accountable to their constituents. As we have already seen, the theory is that election makes officials vulnerable to a far wider range of district interests than they would otherwise be; vulnerability forces the candidates to engage in "search behavior," seeking maximum knowledge of the people and the interests in their districts.

While this theory of elections can never be fully confirmed, there is evidence that it is effective some of the time for all representatives and all of the time for some representatives. We know, for example, that virtually all members of Congress engage in search behavior. Although it is impossible to get an accurate count on the number of letters received by members of Congress, it is possible to get some sense of the scale of communications between these legislators and their districts by the annual record of letters sent out from their offices.[18] In 1938, members of the two houses of Congress sent out 24 million pieces of mail. Twenty years later, by the end of the Eisenhower administration, members of Congress were sending out 85 million pieces of mail per year. By the end of the Kennedy administration in 1963, the annual rate was 119 million pieces of mail. Since 1966, the yearly average has been running around 180 million.[19]

Responding to Constituency Pressure

We can get a fairly clear picture of how representation affects the actual work of representatives and their staff in Table 9.4. It shows that well over a quarter of the time of individual members of the House and nearly two-thirds of the time of their staff members is devoted to constituency service. This is not merely a matter of writing and mailing letters; the lot of these legislators would be a much happier one if that were the case. Review of any single business day in the life of an individual member of the House will

---

[17]Gaetano Mosca, in *The Ruling Class* (especially pp. 153–158), has used this as the central distinction in his arguments about the myth of representation in government. As far as he is concerned, it is not possible to think of a representative as an agent as long as the constituents have so little role in actually picking out the person they want. There are many contemporary polemics charging that members of Congress represent only the wealthier members of the district, or that the wealthier members of a district do the choosing. Recent examples include Drew Pearson and Jack Anderson, *The Case against Congress* (New York: Simon & Schuster, 1968); Mark Green, et al., *Who Runs Congress?* (New York: Bantam Books, 1972); and Robert Winter-Berger, *The Washington Pay-off* (New York: Dell Publishing, 1972).

[18]This record is kept by the House and Senate post offices because of the "franking privilege," which entitles members of Congress to send out business mail free of postage. Their signature goes where the stamp is usually found.

[19]Other figures on mail and other types of district communications will be found in *Guide to the Congress of the United States* (Washington: Congressional Quarterly Service, 1971), pp. 519–550.

Table 9.4   **The Work of Representatives and Their Staff**

	Hours per Week (Average)	Percentage of Time in Each Activity
The Representative		
Legislative work	38.0	64.6
In committee	(11.1)	(18.9)
Other	(26.9)	(45.7)
Constituency service	16.3	27.6
Education/publicity	4.6	7.8
The Staff		
Legislative support	30.8	14.3
Constituency service	142.1	65.5
Education/publicity	22.4	10.3
Other	21.4	9.9

Data from John S. Saloma, *Congress and the New Politics* (Boston: Little, Brown, 1969), pp. 184–185. Compare with Roger Davidson, *The Role of the Congressman* (New York: Pegasus, 1969), pp. 97–109.

turn up the inordinate amounts of time spent with constituents or colleagues in Congress or in the executive branch carrying constituency messages. These messages range from minor patronage matters, such as getting an appointment to a military academy or a special bill for a respectable immigrant, to attempting to influence a decision made by a regulatory commission.[20]

Members of the national legislature from districts east of the Mississippi River run into special pressure from their constituents precisely because of the closer proximity of their districts to Washington. Many of them belong to a mythical group derisively called the "Tuesday-Thursday Club" in reference to the allegation that they spend only Tuesday through Thursday on legislative business, relaxing at home on long weekends. One congressman gave the following response to this kind of claim:

> Problems of world peace and international tension pale into insignificance beside some personal problem of many constituents. People knock the Tuesday-to-Thursday group. I agree that it is a problem. I would be very happy if I didn't live so close to Washington . . . I go to my district on weekends and I hold office hours every Friday evening. . . . This life is no picnic no matter what some people think.[21]

[20]See, for example, John Bibby and Roger Davidson, *On Capitol Hill* (Hinsdale, Ill.: Dryden Press, 1972), chapter 3.

[21]Quoted in Charles L. Clapp, *The Congressman: His Work as He Sees It* (Washington: Brookings Institution, 1963), pp. 68–69. See also Kenneth Olson, "The Service Function of the United States Congress," in *Congress: The First Branch,* ed. Alfred de Grazia (Washington: American Enterprise Institute, 1966). For a classic statement of the problems and prospects of being in Congress, see Clem Miller, *Member of the House* (New York: Scribner, 1962).

Getting the People to Obey: The First Branch

We must ask, however, whether all of these constituency communications and constituency services reflect an actual effort to represent the district. A good case could be made that all of this action is simply a cover for the realities of an independent congressional existence. Despite a great deal of research in this area, the record is not entirely clear. Tables 9.5 and 9.6, drawn from one of the most important studies of constituency influence, will enable us to make at least a few reasonable statements about the relationship between representatives and their districts in the United States.

Table 9.5 demonstrates fairly clearly that whether Democrats come from metropolitan or rural districts makes a good deal of difference in how they vote. In recent years, metropolitan Democrats have disagreed with rural Democrats on nearly half of all the roll call votes. The metropolitan-rural factor has been considerably less divisive among Republicans, but this kind of district influence clearly has been extremely significant for members of both parties. We cannot know from these statistics the specific kind of interest that each of the legislators attempted to represent in these votes; but we can reasonably infer that the agricultural or metropolitan character of the district meant something very important to most representatives.

In many ways, Table 9.6 is more dramatic. At one level it proves only what most observers have known without the help of any statistical analysis of roll call votes. Sectional and racial interests in the South have had a tremendous influence on the behavior of Democratic members of the House from southern states. The party

Table 9.5 **Influence of the Constituency on the Member of Congress: Metropolitan versus Rural Districts**

Year	Total Roll Calls	Democrats		Republicans	
		Split Roll Calls	Percent Split	Split Roll Calls	Percent Split
1921	56	10	17.9	13	23.2
1930–1931	29	9	31.0	8	27.6
1937	85	29	34.1	5	5.9
1944	56	28	50.0	16	28.6
1948	67	22	32.8	21	31.3
1953	58	30	51.7	16	27.9
1959	79	40	50.6	11	13.9
1964	90	46	51.1	21	23.3

Data from Edward V. Schneier and Julius Turner, *Party and Constituency: Pressures on Congress* (Baltimore: Johns Hopkins Press, 1970), p. 111.

Some members of Congress represent rural districts, some metropolitan. How often does that difference lead members of the same party to disagree with each other on a roll call vote? "Significant disagreement" is defined statistically to mean that the odds were 100 to 1 against these split decisions occurring by chance alone. (This is the "chi square test.") That being the case, we are allowed to say that the metropolitan-rural factor may have caused the split votes.

Table 9.6	Where Constituency Interest Is Strong: Race versus Party Loyalty among Northern and Southern Democrats		
		Party Regularity	
	Year	Northern Democrats	Southern Democrats
	1921	81.2	88.9
	1930–1931	83.8	92.9
	1937	82.8	79.3
	1944	88.5	70.5
	1948	78.2	70.2
	1953	76.1	71.6
	1959	84.0	70.2
	1964	82.4	55.7
	1972	70.0	34.0

Data from Edward V. Schneier and Julius Turner, *Party and Constituency: Pressures on Congress* (Baltimore: Johns Hopkins Press, 1970), p. 173; and *Congressional Quarterly Almanac, 1972*, pp. 60–61.

"Party regularity" (also referred to as party support scores or party unity scores) is defined as the proportion of all roll call votes on which individual members voted with the position taken by a *majority* of the members of their party. All the individual member scores are averaged here. In the 1920s and early 1930s the Democratic Party was very much a southern party, and the majority position was compatible to most southern Democrats. After World War II the center of gravity of the party shifted, and southerners who no longer agreed with the majority in their party had to choose between the party and the constituency. By the end of the 1960s they were choosing home over party more than 60 percent of the time.

regularity of southern Democrats has declined from an all-time high of over 90 percent, because southern Democrats once controlled the Democratic Party and then lost that control to the northern Democrats during the 1930s. From that time on, southern Democrats were unable to keep sectional and racial issues from the agenda and were forced increasingly to dissent from the Democratic Party line. These dissents are partly due to the fact the southern Democrats are generally more conservative on racial and many economic issues; but their departure from the northern Democrats is also due to the fact that even the more liberally inclined southerners in Congress feel they had better go along with the conservatism of their districts or face defeat in the next election. In one study it was discovered that on matters of foreign policy and social welfare legislation, the voters in southern districts did not seek a great deal of information and were not particularly aware of the behavior of their representatives in Congress. However, on civil rights issues the voters had a great deal of knowledge on the behavior of their representatives, and the representatives were forced to behave almost like "instructed delegates."[22]

[22]For a report on this research, see Warren Miller and Donald Stokes, "Constituency Influence in Congress," *American Political Science Review*, March 1963.

Taken together, Tables 9.5 and 9.6 suggest quite strongly that no member of the House is immune to constituency pressures. Representatives may have a good deal of flexibility and choice about the interests to which they will be most susceptible, but among these interests are usually two or three issues on which constituency opinion is so pronounced that the representatives will feel it is very risky to exercise any freedom of choice. For example, no member of Congress from a wheat or cotton or tobacco district will wish to exercise a great deal of independence on relevant agriculture legislation. In the first place, it is unlikely that a member of Congress elected from such a district would want to exercise very much independence; but if a legislator ever did have an urge to exercise independence, that person would probably do everything possible to suppress the urge. Then there are the so-called oil states, such as Oklahoma, Texas, and California, as well as other states which have strong hopes that oil will be found in their offshore territories. Senators and members of the House from such states are likely to be leading advocates of oil interests and usually do not hesitate to vote accordingly.

More specifically, the congressional career of former Senator J. William Fulbright serves well to illustrate the complexities of representation. Senator Fulbright's independence and courage comprised a large part of the history of foreign policy during the 1960s. His vision helped frame some of the most important international cultural policies of the entire postwar period, including the scholarships and fellowships named in his honor. However, this same senator signed the Southern Manifesto of 1956, in which he joined with other southerners in denouncing the Supreme Court for the civil rights decisions that took authority away from the states. In the late 1950s and early 1960s, Senator Fulbright also took the lead in legislation serving the natural gas interests, in which his state, Arkansas, was deeply involved. In the mid-1960s, Senator Fulbright went even further than his Arkansas colleague, Congressman Wilbur Mills, in pushing for increased depletion allowances for Arkansas aluminum interests, an effort which was denounced as an attempt to open up a "grab bag."

Senator Fulbright should not be too quickly denounced. His concessions to his district only prove that districts count for a great deal even to those members of Congress with great independence and foresight. The influence of constituencies seems to be so pervasive in the United States that the House and the Senate have developed a variety of devices to permit members to disguise their positions or avoid taking positions wherever their obligations to their party or the leadership might conflict with important interests in their districts. Of course, a member may only be seeking to hide a crass sellout. But there are other, more justifiable reasons to play hide-and-seek with the district. For example, a member may have to agree to give up a regional office of the Commerce Department one year in exchange for a harbor project later on; but this member naturally finds it preferable to suppress knowledge of the give until proof of the take can be shown. Or another legislator from a strong union district may have to vote in favor of some tighter labor regulations in order to bargain effectively for other votes to raise the minimum wage, but this legislator always faces the unhappy prospect that the local unions may fail to appreciate the connection between the two issues. In many other instances, the member may simply feel, as did Edmund Burke, that it is more essential to seek what the district needs rather than to pursue what the district may want.[23]

Avoiding Constituency Pressure

In any or all of these instances, the member will almost certainly wish to minimize the risk of electoral defeat for having felt the obligation to vote contrary to the interests of the district. The first, and until recently the most frequent, form of escape has been to camouflage actual voting positions on the final passage of important legislation. There are three ways to cast votes in Congress: voice vote; vote by division, or by lining up and passing in front of a "teller" for a head count but no identification of who voted yea and who voted nay; and vote by calling roll, where each member's vote is identified in the *Congressional Record* as a yea or a nay. Obviously a voice or teller vote is preferable whenever a member of Congress wishes to avoid publicly revealing a position.

The voice and teller methods of voting may decline in frequency now that there are electronic methods of casting roll call votes. Legislators can no longer use the excuse that calling the roll is too time-consuming, and this might make it increasingly difficult for them to hide their real positions. But there are other ways to hide the vote, and these are likely to be employed more frequently as voting by voice or division declines. One of the methods of hiding a real position from the public is to vote both ways on the same subject. This is actually possible in Congress, because more than one vote is usually required on the same bill during the course of its passage or failure. For example, a member of Congress who is against a certain bill which may be favored by important people in the home district can try first to kill the bill by voting against it on an important procedural motion. Procedural motions are usually very complicated, and they are often not even carefully covered by the best journalists.

The following hypothetical situation illustrates one way this

[23]Edmund Burke's most important single statement on the obligations of the representative will be found in his "Speech to the Electors of Bristol," 1744.

complication can be used to a legislator's advantage. Let us say that Senator Historic is from an important agriculture state but is nevertheless opposed to the annual rivers and harbors bill because he has come to the conclusion that this kind of legislation—popularly known as "pork barrel legislation"—is no longer the proper way to deal with flood control and the environment. Senator Historic also knows that his vote against such a bill would be very unpopular in many areas of his state. Thus, he may try to kill the legislation with a motion to table it or a motion to recommit the bill to its standing committee. In the U.S. Congress, given the limited amount of time there is to deal with thousands of bills and motions, a successful tabling or recommittal motion effectively kills the bill for the rest of the session, and sometimes for the entire two-year period of a Congress. Yet, since these procedural motions are not well understood by the public, Senator Historic can try first to kill the pork barrel bill without much risk of sacrificing the favor of his constituents; then, if that fails, he can later vote in favor of final passage when his position is more likely to be identified by his constituents.

Of course, one of the most effective ways to avoid the pressure of representation is to be absent at the time an embarrassing roll call vote will take place. As a member of the House and later of the Senate, John F. Kennedy was often criticized for his absenteeism at significant moments. And there are many worse offenders. But among all of the ways to play hide-and-seek with the district, probably the most effective and the most frequently used is the method of *pseudo-legislation*. Now, to appreciate pseudo-legislation, one must bear in mind the fact that any member of the House and Senate may introduce a bill on any subject at any time Congress is in session. There may be a slight inconvenience in drafting the bill or in printing it up in proper form. Otherwise, however, introduction of a bill involves the very simple and easy matter of handing it over to the clerk, who then goes through the ritual of giving the bill a "first reading," before dropping it into the "hopper." Eventually the bill is referred to the relevant standing committee; and in a high proportion of instances, the standing committee also operates as the graveyard.

Every legislator enjoys denouncing committees for murdering thousands of legislative proposals and other motions every year. For example, in the Ninety-first Congress (1969–1971), 29,040 bills were introduced in the Senate and House, and only 2,250 were reported back to the floor by the committees. The rest died without any further action. Despite all the public denunciation of this apparent inefficiency, committees are relied upon by members of Congress to save them from their own folly. Committees, and their willingness to operate as graveyards, make pseudo-legislation possible.

Later we will trace the process through which a bill goes to become law. At this point it is more important to ask how and why a bill becomes a bill. Some bills are introduced in order to give a specific interest group the satisfaction of thinking that the legislator is working arduously on their behalf. Sometimes, too, bills are introduced with the more serious intention of "scaring the wits out of" some administrative agency by giving the impression that a concerted attack on the agency might follow. Usually nothing happens after that. Other bills are introduced in order to test, as trial balloons, member opinion or public opinion; often this type of pseudo-legislation becomes a serious legislative effort in some later session. Many hundreds of bills are introduced merely in order to provide the impression that legislators are hard-working fellows. All of this pseudo-legislation is an expression of the seriousness with which each legislator takes the representative role, even while trying to escape it temporarily.[24]

Private Bills

One final example of congressional powers which provide members with opportunities to engage in representation is Congress's power to pass *private bills*. A private bill is a proposal to grant relief or a special privilege or exemption to a named person; this is distinguished from a *public bill,* which deals with general rules and with

[24]For an excellent review of "why a bill becomes a bill," see Gross, *The Legislative Struggle,* chapter 9.

Any member can
introduce a bill at almost
any time.

"THE SENATOR FROM ILLINOIS PRESENTS THE FOLLOWING BILL."

categories of behavior, people, and institutions. Most private
bills—over 75 percent of all private bills introduced—are concerned
with providing some kind of relief for foreign nationals who cannot
get permanent visas to the United States because the immigration
quota for their country is filled, or because of some irregularity
about their particular situation. Many of the private bills dealing
with immigration seek to prevent the deportation of foreign nationals already residing in the United States. In the Ninetieth Congress
(1967–1968), for example, 7,293 such private bills were introduced,

of which 218 were passed. Some would argue that such a tremendous divergence between the number introduced and the number passed is indicative of additional pseudo-legislation. That is perhaps true; but legislators are generally quite serious about introducing these bills even if they make no campaign to get their colleagues to vote for them.

Another important category of private bills involves claims of individual citizens for some kind of monetary relief because of an injury they allegedly received from a public action, or because of some meritorious act (such as an invention) that went unrewarded. About 2,000 such private bills are introduced during each session of Congress, and about 20 percent of these become law. All told, between 25 and 35 percent of all laws passed by the United States Congress involve private bills. This is alarming, especially when one considers that the privilege of introducing private bills can be very heavily abused. Yet, it is impossible to imagine members of Congress giving up this privilege.

A private bill is one of the easiest, cheapest, and most effective forms of patronage available to individual members of Congress. The mere introduction of a single private immigration bill is likely to earn the permanent gratitude of the applicant and his extended family and neighbors, all of whom may already be citizens and thus eligible to vote in the next election. The title of a typical private bill is "For the Relief of . . . ," with the name of the supplicant supplied. That kind of recognition alone possesses a considerable amount of value, even when the bill has no chance of passage. And if the member reintroduces such a bill several times in a succession of Congresses, the chances of passage go up considerably. Meanwhile, word is bound to get around that the representative in Congress is willing to work hard for constituents.

Little harm may be done by private bills. On the other hand, no general good is accomplished either. Private bills are not yet government, but rather an effort to manipulate government for specific privileges. They are an indispensable part of the process by which individual members of Congress seek to fulfill their role as representatives.[25] This is yet another reminder that representation and government are not the same thing but rather are inconsistent with each other.

CONGRESS AS A LEGISLATURE

Legislating was the latest function to develop in assemblies, because there first had to be a revolution in the concept of law itself. *Legis* means law; *legislator* is the bringer of law; *legislature* is the

[25]For further information on private bills, consult *Guide to the Congress of the United States*, pp. 329–351.

power that makes law. Until modern times, these ideas were beyond conception. Law made in and by legislatures is *positive law*—law made self-consciously to fit an occasion, law made by talk and changed by talk as situations change.

The importance of positive law can be appreciated only in relation to other kinds of law. In times past the most important law was divine law. In this context, law was not thought of as a thing made; it was a thing discovered and handed down. There was mystery in the law—mystery about its source, mystery about its meaning, and even mystery about its significance. All law, including positive law, has to appeal to some kind of higher authority if obedience is to be assured. Divine law appealed to divine sources, inspirational sources. Obedience was based upon the sharing of mystical experiences, coupled with fear and the sense of immortality. The Ten Commandments were good laws whether divinely inspired or not. But the important fact here is that the *appeal* to the people was put in divine terms and prospects of obedience were thus increased. In contrast, a contemporary Moses would probably claim "majority support for the Ten Commandments" even if the Commandments *had* been received from God rather than from Congress.

Before there can be an assembly operating as a real legislature, the law has to be demystified. It must come to be accepted as a human creation and must draw its authority from appeals other than the divine. One important type of law which provided some linkage between divine law and positive law was judge-made law. In Anglo-Saxon countries this is called *common law.* It existed in one form or another all over Europe. Common law did not mean law by or for the common man. Common law meant the law common to the realm.[26]

Common law—law made by judges—is closer to divine law than to positive law inasmuch as judges claimed to discover it rather than to formulate it. As judges traveled their circuits and decided cases, they allowed themselves to be guided by previous cases, which were treated as precedents. The Latin phrase is *stare decisis* ("to stand on decided matters"). Judges were never quite explicit about these precedents—to state the precedent explicitly as a rule to be applied to future cases would have been legislating. Since common law was expected to emerge out of the wisdom of the community, the judges had to go through the motions of "discovering" that wisdom. The appeal to authority in judge-made law was the appeal to the mystical notion of the community, even though the voice of the community was not necessarily thought of as the voice of God. One scholar described these ancient legal systems in the following manner:

> When a case arises for which no valid law can be adduced, then the lawful men or doomsmen will make new law in the belief that what they are making is good old law, not indeed expressly handed-down, but tacitly existent. They do not, therefore, create the law; they 'discover it'. Any particular judgment in court, which we regard as a particular inference from a general established legal rule, was to a medieval mind in no way distinguishable from the legislative activity of the community; in both cases a law hidden but already existing is discovered, not created. There is, in the Middle Ages, no such thing as 'the first application of a legal rule'. Law is old; new law is a contradiction in terms.[27]

Positive law did not emerge suddenly or in full form. It grew with the rise of national conquerors, with absolute monarchy, and with the search for bases of authority and legitimacy other than God and nature. This distinction between legitimacy based upon a mystical source and legitimacy based upon popular consensus or majority was so large and so fundamental that centuries were required for its full development: "[When law] was looked upon as the expression of the will of the people, it could no longer be considered as declaring what had always been the law. . . . It was only then that statutory law became a validly different kind of law from the existing customary law."[28]

---

[26]See Frederick Pollack and F. W. Maitland, *The History of English Law,* vol. 1 (Cambridge: Cambridge University Press, 1899), pp. 176–178.

[27]Quoted in Peter Stein, *Regulae Iuris* (Edinburgh: University Press of Aberdeen, 1966), p. 5. This passage is a description of early Germanic law, but it could just as easily have been a description of the English common law. See also Sir Matthew Hale, *The History of the Common Law of England* (Chicago: University of Chicago Press, 1971; first published in 1713), especially editor's introduction and chapter 1.

[28]Stein, *Regulae Iuris,* p. 21.

Roman law may have been earliest to develop in this regard because Roman conquerors needed explicit and relevant controls for each of the countries that came under the authority of the Empire. Our Anglo-Saxon positive law developed much later, but it, too, was associated with the emergence of the right of thirteenth and fourteenth century kings to issue new edicts without bothering to present them as the "restoration of 'good old laws.'"[29] From there, law by statute made in legislatures, based upon the new myth of the common man and popular consent, was simply one more step. It may or may not be a paradox to some that the right of legislatures to make law depended upon the establishment of the right of absolute monarchs and other conquerors to make law.

It is only with the power to make law that an assembly can make the enormous advance to its place as a serious instrument of government. Yet the power and function of legislation drastically alters the structure of assemblies. The legislative functions seem to be the most imperialistic of all of the functions that have attached themselves to assemblies. The legislative function virtually destroys the ideal of equality and equal access among the members. From the moment assemblies assert legislative power, they move farther and farther away from the picture painted earlier of organizational equality, free and protected talk, and pure representation toward the division of labor, hierarchy, and rules that establish inequalities among members and put severe limits upon talk. It should not be difficult to understand how it is possible for human institutions to combine inconsistent ideals. To legislate, it is necessary to decide. To decide, it is necessary at some point to stop talking in order to vote; and it is necessary to override minority views if the vote is to produce an authoritative result. If this is to be done regularly, year in and year out, it is bound to have an overwhelming effect on the assembly as an institution.

This, it seems to me, is the best way to understand any legislative institution, especially the U.S. Congress, which, despite its failings, continues to be closer to the center of real government than possibly any other national assembly in the world. Every state in the United States has a legislature with its own unique history, deserving careful study for its own sake. But the study of Congress, as a single case, is sufficient, because *Congress is an almost perfect study of how any assembly grows away from the ideal of a representative assembly as it becomes a legislative assembly.*

It should be clear by now that Congress would be incomparably different from what it is today if it did not possess the power to make laws. Without that power, it would be unimportant. Its effort to be important as a governing institution is what transforms it, but the

[29]Ibid., p. 24.

transformation does not preclude the parliamentary and representative features we have discussed. They are there and they are constantly competing for dominance. The reality of Congress is the interaction among these elements. Although the legislative function is dominant, it is constantly being influenced by parliamentary and representative tendencies.

Chapter 10   Congress: Making Law

It may now be possible to appreciate the full significance of the simple phrase *making law.* Positive law demystified government and opened government to participation by representative assemblies. But in the process, government was made infinitely more complicated. Representative government is complex because of the scale and publicity of participation and because of the immense number of procedures necessary to enable so many people to participate. It is infinitely complex because it is open to interests. *In a system of representative government, any interest can become a law.*[1]

Why do certain natural resources enjoy the special privilege of a "depletion allowance" in the federal tax law when other natural resources do not? Why is tobacco subsidized even after it has been declared a health hazard? When legislatures participate in the making of positive law, morali-

---

[1]One of the great critics of representative government, Gaetano Mosca, observed toward the end of his long and distinguished career that representative government is "the most complex and delicate type of political organization that has so far been seen in world history." Gaetano Mosca, *The Ruling Class*, trans. Hannah D. Kahn (New York: McGraw-Hill, 1939), p. 389. As if to emphasize the complexity of representative government, Mosca made a most remarkable confession later in the same chapter (p. 491): "Fifty years ago the author of this volume opened his career as a writer with a book which . . . sought to lay bare some of the . . . defects of parliamentarism. Today advancing years have made him more cautious in judgment and, he might venture to say, more balanced."

ty is a matter of proximity. And when any interest can become a law, legality is a matter of opportunity. In such a system, no interest is secure unless it is embodied in law. This makes government a magnet, a center of gravity, even for those who are on principle antagonistic to the idea of a growing government. Although power holders seek power, it is often the powerless who seek an enlarged government. When any interest can become a law, everyone wants more of it. Everyone wants more law, because conquest through law can be made very specific. Interests that become law displace the cost of conquest upon all the other interests which have not become law.

Yet "making law" is something of a miracle, because those who have succeeded in legislating their interests are not particularly interested in cooperating with those who have not. For the thousands of active interests that gravitate toward the legislature at any given point in time, there must be elaborate methods for enabling the interests to live together and enabling the legislature to deal with one of them at a time. Conquest through positive laws made in legislatures will always involve elaborately collective decision making. No interest can bind society unless it has become a law in competition with other interests. Such competition among interests in collective decision making gives rise to a procedural madhouse.

Once law is accepted as something that is made rather than discovered, almost everyone comes to agree that making law is something that should, if possible, be done in an assembly. But the power to make laws does something not altogether admirable to the assembly. In order to participate seriously in making laws and therefore to share in the conduct of government, the assembly must first relinquish the standard of equality among its members. It must relinquish much, though not all, of its commitments to full representation and maximum talk. It must divide up the labor and the agenda in order to deliberate upon demands, one at a time.

Although periodic elections keep assemblies from becoming completely hierarchical, Congress is nevertheless far more organized than it would like to admit. We are thus brought face to face with the most important reason for the complexity of representative government—the mixing of the inconsistent functions of representation and government. Congress's processes can be appreciated best if the facts about that institution are seen in the context of a constant tension between equality and hierarchy, between the demand for more representation and the requirements of participating in government. This is a classic expression of incomplete conquest in modern dress. Congress cannot fully do its job if it sincerely attempts to keep faith with the ideals of representation. "Representative government" is an inconsistency in terms. More of one value necessarily means less of the other.

As a consequence, Congress cannot stand still. For example, when Congress accepts presidential leadership, it gains greatly in efficiency by having a program all prepared, as well as a means of disciplining members. Yet almost inevitably a reaction sets in, expressed in terms of a "reassertion of legislative power." At other times, greater ability to make laws is gained by strengthening party leadership within Congress. This, too, inevitably brings about a reaction justified as a reassertion of the power of the members against the tyranny of the Speaker or the organization. At other times the members react against too much efficiency gained in committee power, and again the rhetoric includes such terms as *tyranny* and *dictatorship of the institution over the members.* We have been witnessing at least two such reactions in the aftermath of Vietnam and Watergate—reassertion of Congress against presidential leadership, and reassertion of the members of Congress against the committee system. But such reassertions do not last long before old structures are restored or new ones are invented.[2]

There are at least five basic dimensions to congressional organization. Four are hierarchical, and the fifth exists largely to support the other four.

---

[2]Other legislatures, in Europe or in the American states, organized themselves in ways quite different from the United States Congress. However, their structures can also be best understood as a response to the problem of governing. Where more of the government takes place in the executive branch, parliamentary participation will be less and legislative structure will be less pronounced. On the other hand, legislatures that participate heavily in government can afford less of a committee structure if their party system is strong and operative. There are many ways to deal with the inconsistency between representation and government, but it has to be dealt with; it cannot be flanked.

1. Party organization, which includes the elected congressional leadership structure. It is the oldest hierarchy in Congress and was once (but is no longer) the most important.

2. The committee system, which long ago became the most important organizational feature. It is also the most tightly hierarchical of the five dimensions, and consequently it has also been the most maligned. In its committee system, Congress has probably gone farther toward hierarchy than any other legislative assembly in the world.

3. The staff, which includes the staff of individual members and of the committees. For reasons of space this subject will not be treated in our examination of Congress. The staff is a fact that needs none of the description or assessment that the other dimensions need. Its growth and size has not been very dramatic since the 1940s, but its absolute size and its solid professionalism have given rise to concern among many serious observers that the staff is making Congress a miniature version of the executive branch. This is definitely an aspect of the basic contradiction, but it is not a problem which deserves a great deal of direct attention here.[3]

4. The executive, especially the White House, in its capacity as official and unoffical legislative participant. Nothing has contributed more to Congress's ability to make law than the president's program and the president's legislative leadership. And nothing except the committee system has pushed Congress more toward hierarchy and the division of labor, whether in yielding to presidential leadership or in organizing to defend itself against presidential leadership.

5. The rules, most of which exist in order to defend and protect the congressional hierarchies, especially the committee system. Where the rules do not defend hierarchy, they limit talk. What, after all, is debate? It is a highly formalized and controlled form of talk. Controlling talk is, therefore, an important component of establishing a hierarchy.

CONGRESS'S OLDEST HIERARCHY: POLITICAL PARTIES

The Constitution makes only one provision for the conduct of business in Congress. Article I gives each chamber a presiding officer. The Senate is presided over by the president of the Senate, an office held ex officio by the vice-president of the United States.[4] The Constitution allows the Senate to elect a president pro tempore

---

[3]For a full treatment, see Kenneth Kofmehl, *Professional Staffs of Congress* (Lafayette, Ind.: Purdue University Press, 1962).

[4]*Ex officio* means that one office is filled by virtue of some other office already held.

(temporary president) to serve in the absence of the vice-president. The Constitution provides the House of Representatives with a Speaker, who is to be elected by the entire membership.

Everything else has been improvised, and not always consciously. This is underscored by the fact that members of the House and Senate met their first needs for organization with political parties, the very arrangement most feared by the original leaders of the new republic. Before Washington was out of office, the members of Congress had organized themselves into two political parties, and for the first century or more of the republic, there was literally a party government in Congress.

The Importance of Parties

Perhaps the most concrete illustration of the importance of parties in the first century of congressional history is the conversion of the presiding offices into party offices. The president of the Senate became partisan along with the Electoral College and the presidential nominating process. Once the parties took over these two functions, the vice-president became a person who was either a leader in his party or a captive and tool of the party leaders in the presidency or in the Senate. The vice-president must now frequently preside over a Senate in which his own party is in the minority. This has been true of fourteen of the twenty-four years between 1952 and 1976, which may be a great thing for minority rights but also an indication of the decline of political parties. Prior to the 1930s this situation was extremely rare. The Speakership in the House has been a partisan office for probably as long. The significance of the party basis of these two offices can best be appreciated by comparing them to the presiding officers in European national assemblies, which are usually quite distinctly *non*partisan. In Great Britain, for example, where the House of Commons is very tightly controlled by political parties, the Speaker is treated more like a chief judge than a legislator.[5]

For most of the period between 1800 and 1910, the parties were the most important hierarchy in Congress. This was especially true in the House, where legislative life centered on the Speaker. As long as the Speaker had the support of a clear majority of his party, he possessed a variety of quite formidable powers. These included, of course, the very valuable power of recognition, which meant the Speaker controlled access to the floor for purposes of engaging in debate. In addition, the Speaker was chairman of the all-powerful

---

[5]Between 1914 and 1962, there were only four contested elections for Speaker in the House of Commons. The Speaker is elected by members of the majority party, but he may be reelected time and again, if he wishes, even when party control changes. In return for this, he must give up party relations; usually he is provided with a constituency where he can be reelected without a contest. Samuel Beer et al., *Patterns of Government* (New York: Random House, 1962), p. 126.

**Figure 10.1
Majority party structure
in the House of
Representatives**

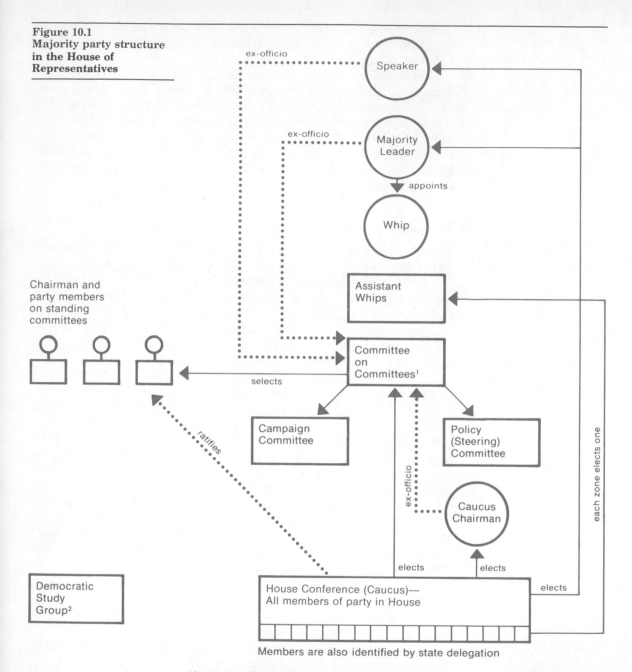

My thanks to Randall Ripley for help on this figure.
[1]Includes Democratic members of the Ways and Means Committee, plus Speaker, majority leader, and caucus chairman, as broken lines denote. For the House Republicans and for both parties in the Senate, the Committee on Committees is a special elected body rather than an ex-officio one. Some additional differences between Democrats and Republicans are in the text.
[2]Republicans have a similar group, the Wednesday Club. These two groups attempt to serve as self-conscious, policy-oriented voting blocs. The Democratic Study Group is the larger and is thought to be the more effective of the two.

Rules Committee, which, then as now, controlled the timing of legislation and the conditions under which it was to be debated; as chairman of the Committee on Committees for his party, the Speaker also controlled the selection and transfer of committee members as well as the selection of committee chairmen. The minority leader enjoyed similar powers for the lesser of the two parties.

In the Senate, despite the greater freedom enjoyed by the members, party was still an important hierarchy. The very permissiveness of Senate rules probably encouraged the Senate still further to rely on its party leaders. Even now (and this was more the case before 1911) the conduct of Senate business depends heavily upon daily agreements between the majority leader and the minority leader on what bill shall be discussed, who shall be allowed recognition for debate, and how tightly debate should be controlled for purposes of amending proposed legislation.

Members of Congress staged a revolt against party hierarchy in 1910. Called the "revolt against the Speaker," it deprived the Speaker of membership in the Rules Committee and the power to make committee assignments and select committee chairmen. However, the reaction was at bottom against party control, and it seems to have worked, because party control has not been as significant since that time. Even in this weaker state, however, the party system in Congress continues to be an important force in the House and the Senate, as indicated in Figures 10.1 and 10.2. While these figures exaggerate the hierarchical features of the parties to a certain extent and oversimplify the relationships among party officials, they do illustrate some important aspects of congressional parties.

At the beginning of each new Congress, the members of each party (traditionally called the caucus or conference) in the House elect their leader. The elected leader of the majority party is later proposed to the whole House and elected to the position of Speaker, with voting along straight party lines. The House majority caucus also elects its majority leader. The minority party goes through the same process. If at a later point it becomes the majority party, its minority leader steps up to the job of Speaker. These House leaders proceed to appoint the other party functionaries, the most important appointments being those of majority whip and minority whip. Each party has a Committee on Committees, whose all-important job is to assign freshman legislators to standing committees and to deal with the requests of incumbent members for transfers from one committee to another. As we shall soon see, the whip system is the center of everyday party activities in the House and Senate.

Committee assignment is of course the most important decision the parties make, but this happens only at the beginning of each Congress and is not available as a regular resource for the leader-

Figure 10.2
**Majority party structure
in the U.S. Senate**

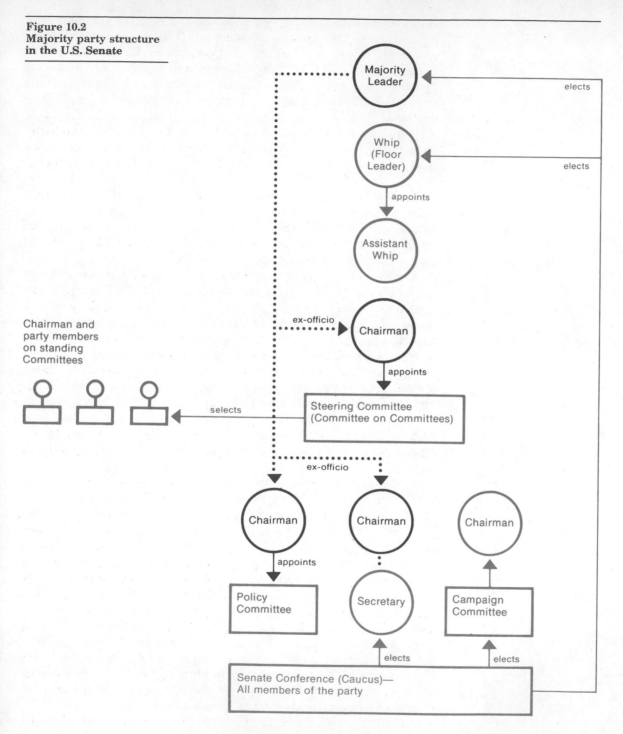

My thanks to Randall Ripley for help on this figure.

ship. These Committees on Committees are also probably not as responsive to the party leadership as would be necessary to make committee assignment a truly valuable tool of the leadership. The Democratic members of the Ways and Means Committee, who serve as the ex officio Committee on Committees, are elected from their respective regional zones and are more likely to be responsive to the House members from that zone. The House Republican Committee on Committees officially consists of one representative from each state that sends a Republican to Congress; but since a subcommittee is appointed from this large group by the House Republican leader to serve as the real Committee on Committees, this smaller group is likely to be more responsive to the Republican leadership. In either case, however, the big decisions are made at the beginning of each Congress and cannot be manipulated later on when important votes are at issue.

Since the Senate rules provide only very loose structure, the Senate Democrats have tried to centralize party structure by making the majority leader chairman of all party committees, including the Committee on Committees. (For the Senate Democrats, this is called the Steering Committee, but it is not to be confused with the Steering Committees in the House, which are policy committees.) The Senate Republicans elect a different person to each chairmanship. However, although the Democrats thus appear to be more centralized, this really varies with the character of the majority leader, since the Democratic conference must ratify all of his appointments. Under Lyndon Johnson, the Democrats were quite centralized. Under Mike Mansfield, general opinion holds that the Democrats are far less centralized.[6]

Party Discipline

Although the party organization in the two chambers is intended to improve the reelection opportunities of the individual party members, Table 10.1 presents some evidence to suggest that the parties remain a substantial and meaningful institution within Congress. The average member typically votes with the majority of his party on over 80 percent of the roll call votes. Even committee chairmen are "regulars" on the average, despite all that has been said of their independence and conservatism.

---

[6]Good treatments of these features will be found in L. A. Froman, *The Congressional Process* (Boston: Little, Brown, 1967), pp. 169–182; see also Randall Ripley, "The Party Whip Organizations in the U.S. House of Representatives," *American Political Science Review*, September 1964, pp. 561–576. For a good popular account of the potential of the Senate Democrats for centralization, see Rowland Evans and Robert Novak, *Lyndon B. Johnson: The Exercise of Power* (New York: New American Library, 1966), pp. 88–118. See also John G. Steward, "Two Strategies of Leadership: Johnson and Mansfield," in *Congressional Behavior,* ed. Nelson Polsby (New York: Random House, 1971), p. 61.

Table 10.1

Party Regularity in Floor Voting, House of Representatives, 1935–1970 (Percentage of Votes with Majority of Own Party)

Congress	Democrats			Republicans		
	Floor Leader	Committee Leaders[1]	All Democrats	Floor Leader	Committee Leaders[2]	All Republicans
74th	94	87	83	93	84	84
75th	84	81	79	91	84	85
76th	88	85	83	95	84	88
77th	86	83	82	89	86	86
78th	85	80	80	93	86	86
79th	96	81	82	89	83	83
80th	89	79	82	97	91	88
81st	91	77	81	93	84	84
82nd	95	75	81	89	86	82
83rd	89	79	79	94	87	87
84th	96	82	84	87	79	81
85th	93	75	80	81	78	79
86th	95	75	81	88	80	81
87th	98	84	87	87	81	82
88th	96	84	87	87	83	84
89th	97	79	85	88	87	85
90th	96	84	83	86	85	84
91st	94	83	82	87	85	84
Average (mean)	92	81	82	90	84	84

From Randall Ripley, "Party Leaders and Standing Committees in the House of Representatives," a working paper for the House Select Committee on Committees, 93rd Congress (Washington, D.C.: Government Printing Office, 1973), p. 4. Figures for the Senate run roughly parallel at a somewhat lower level—70 to 75 percent party loyalty.

[1]These are committee chairmen for all Congresses but the 80th and 83rd, for which ranking minority members are used.

[2]These are ranking minority members for all Congresses but the 80th and 83rd, for which chairmen are used.

Table 10.2 shows, however, that although party regularity has remained fairly pronounced, party *discipline* is no longer what it used to be. Around the turn of the century, party discipline remained so effective that the leaders of both parties could line up large majorities on specific roll call votes. This is called a "party vote," and it means that at least 90 percent of one party is voting in opposition to 90 percent of the other party. Not since 1948 have the party leaders been able to discipline their members on as many as 10 percent of the roll call votes. The rest of the time, the leaders consider themselves lucky if they can summon up a bare majority on a divisive vote. In fact, since 1965, over 10 percent of the

Table 10.2

The Decline of Party Discipline: Proportion of Party Votes Cast in Selected Sessions of the U.S. House of Representatives, 1921–1967

Session of Congress	Percentage of "Party Votes"	
	When 90% of Democrats Opposed 90% of Republicans	When over 50% of Democrats Opposed over 50% of Republicans
1897–1901	50*	—
1921	28.6	66.1
1930–1931	31.0	65.5
1933	22.5	64.7
1937	11.8	61.6
1944	10.7	55.4
1948	16.4	44.4
1950	6.4	47.5
1953	7.0	52.1
1959	8.0	55.2
1963	7.6	48.8
1964	6.2	54.9
1965	2.8	52.2
1966	1.6	41.5
1967	3.3	36.3

Data from Julius Turner and Edward Schneier, *Party and Constituency: Pressures on Congress,* rev. ed. (Baltimore: Johns Hopkins Press, 1970), pp. 17 and 37.
*The first figure is an average for the three sessions, in which, Turner and Schneier report, "better than half" were party votes.

members of the House vote more often with the other party than with their own party.[7]

How can there be so much regularity (Table 10.1) and so little discipline (Table 10.2)? In the first place, a great deal of the regularity comes from identifications and habits built up in the local districts. When representatives come to Congress, most of them make it a point to vote with the party except when they feel a specific obligation not to. In the second place, regularity is not very difficult on a very large number of roll call votes, inasmuch as the majorities of both parties are *on the same side* over 60 percent of the time. Figure 10.3 shows that the majorities of both parties have agreed with each other over 50 percent of the time since 1953, with the exception of a two- or three-year period during the Kennedy administration. Observers who approve of this type of agreement

Congress: Making Law

[7] Julius Turner and Edward V. Schneier, *Party and Constituency: Pressures on Congress,* rev. ed. (Baltimore: Johns Hopkins Press, 1970), p. 36.

Figure 10.3
Proportion of all roll
call votes on which the
majorities of both parties
were on the same side
(bipartisanship)

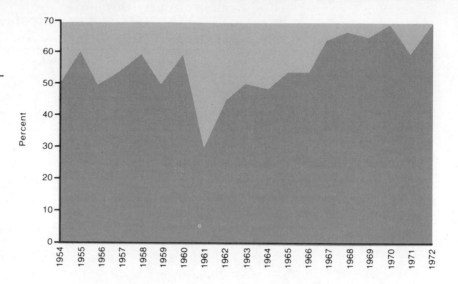

across party lines euphemistically refer to the practice as bipartisanship. Rarely do they stop to consider the fact that it is almost
the opposite of party responsibility. In any event, this helps to
account for the maintenance of party regularity even as party
discipline continues to drop.

The real test of party organization in Congress is whether the
leaders are able to bring out party votes on *particular* roll calls
when there is a great deal at stake and the party leadership and the
president have made a commitment to the outcome of the vote.
From this perspective, the 80 percent figure for party regularity
does not look so impressive; and the declining figures shown in
Table 10.2 begin to glare out as a strong indication that party
organization has weakened considerably.

Although party organization has weakened, party leaders do have
several means of maintaining party power. For example, they can
create some debts among members by helping to bring about
favorable committee assignments. Leaders in the Senate gained a
new lease on the power of assignment during the 1950s, thanks to
Majority Leader Lyndon Johnson's imagination. The "Johnson
rule," now observed with some consistency in both parties in the
Senate, provided that no senator could receive an assignment to a
second major committee until all senators had received consideration for a major committee assignment. This gave Senate party
leaders additional leeway to use their personal discretion. However,
the problem with committee assignment and transfer is that once

the decision is made, the assignment cannot be taken back. Thus, although the Johnson rule probably helped delay the decline of parties in the Senate, it could not have brought about any revolution. (A Johnson rule would not make sense in the House because members serve on only one major committee at any time.)

A more regularly effective resource in the hands of party leaders is their control over access to the floor. Clearly, the allocation of time to speak and the scheduling of bills are of great interest to every member of the House and Senate. Access to the floor is a weapon that can be turned on and off on any particular day, and it can be used against recalcitrant committees. The only committee impervious to this kind of party influence is a committee whose leadership is not interested in getting any legislation passed.

Some additional influence accrues to party leaders through the whip system. Between twelve and twenty assistant and regional whips are selected by state and zone delegations to operate at the direction of the majority (or minority) leader. The whip system is primarily a communications network. Whips take polls of the membership in order to learn their intentions on specific legislative issues. This information is invaluable to the party leadership in two respects. First, the leadership can learn whether there exists sufficient support to allow an issue to come to a vote. It is a poor legislative leader who does not know the amount and nature of his support. Johnson and his cohort in the House, Speaker Rayburn, used this part of the whip system most effectively between 1952 and 1962, when the two of them were never mistaken on any roll call by more than a few votes.[8]

Leaders also use the whips to discreetly convey their wishes and plans to the members. Only in rare extremes is actual pressure exerted on a member. But well before such pressure is needed, many votes can be influenced by simple provision of information about how other members intend to vote. Through the same system, the party leaders can keep fairly good records of who owes what to whom. Such records are essential for effective logrolling. Logrolling, it may be recalled, results in a coalition of members who may have nothing in common. Their only agreement is to support each other—"you support me on roll call X, and I'll support you on any roll call of your choice; just tell me when and how to vote." Hundreds of these logrolling contracts are made in any session of Congress, and some system is needed to see that the contracts are kept. Members of Congress prefer to logroll with members of their own party, and the whip system helps keep the record.

But of all the influences that maintain some clarity of party lines in Congress, the president, or the presidency, is probably the most

[8]Ripley reports, in "The Party Whip Organization in the U.S. House of Representatives," that in 1962 and 1963 House Democratic whip polls were on the average 90 percent accurate.

Table 10.3		Support Given the President by Members of His Own Party (PP) and of the Opposition Party (OP) on Roll Calls on Which the President's Position Was Known			
		Percent Senate		Percent House	
	Year	PP	OP	PP	OP
	1954	73	38	71	44
	1955	72	56	60	53
	1956	72	39	72	52
	1957	69	51	54	49
	1958	67	44	58	55
	1959	72	38	68	40
	1960	66	43	69	44
	1961	65	36	73	37
	1962	63	39	72	42
	1963	63	44	72	32
	1964	61	45	74	38
	1965	64	48	74	41
	1966	57	43	63	37
	1967	61	53	69	46
	1968	48	47	64	51
	1969	66	47	57	48
	1970	60	45	66	53
	1971	64	40	72	47
	1972	66	44	64	47

These figures are average presidential support scores, compiled as follows. All roll calls on which the president took a position are identified. Each member received a score according to the proportion of times he or she voted with or against the president's position. Averages of all member scores for Senate and House, respectively, were then computed.

important. The details of presidential legislative leadership will be covered later. The point at issue here is the degree to which the presidency is a touchstone of party discipline in Congress.[9] When a particular roll call involves a bill that is part of the president's program, the parties are farther apart from one another than under any other set of conditions. As Table 10.3 indicates, except for 1968, when the power of the president was at an all-time low—leading to the decision of President Johnson not to seek reelection—members of the president's party supported the president's position well over 60 percent of the time, while the opposition party members supported him between 40 and 50 percent of the time. This gives any

[9]For an excellent inside look at how presidents influence votes in Congress, particularly along party lines, see Lyndon Johnson's memoirs, *The Vantage Point* (New York: Holt, Rinehart and Winston, 1971), especially chapter 19; it is reprinted in Theodore Lowi and Randall Ripley, *Legislative Politics U.S.A.* (Boston: Little, Brown, 1973), pp. 237–254.

president the support he needs to get most of his program passed
without at the same time compromising the parties in their effort to
create distinct legislative records.

With vigorous presidential involvement in the legislative process,
congressional party leaders could probably go farther toward influencing members on specific legislation, even though they might
never produce responsible parties along the lines of the parties in
the British House of Commons. One reason the presidential parties
have not encouraged such strong involvement is probably their
strong preference for representation. Leaders consistently restrain
themselves in their use of available resources which might at any
time threaten the reelection of a party member in an individual
district. Party leaders have great respect for the differences among
districts from which their members are elected, something that
would be impossible to find in countries with strong party traditions. British party leaders, for example, would prefer to search out
a new district for a member rather than let him abandon the party
position merely in order to gain reelection.

In Congress, whenever members feel a conflict between the
demands of the leadership and the demands of their districts, they
simply go to the leader and ask for release from their obligation to
support the party in the specific case in question. In some instances
these individuals will say, "Let me plan to vote the other way unless
you find that my vote is absolutely indispensable." Or an alternative

approach might be, "You can depend on my vote, but please release me as soon as you find you have enough votes to win without mine." Obviously these arrangements work poorly unless the whips are providing the leadership with good information. But even when the information is perfect, it will not result in clearer party discipline and differentiation if the leaders are willing to release party members from their obligation to support the party except where the divisions are very close and one or two votes can make all the difference. Thus, even with the most vigorous presidential support, American parties are not likely to achieve real clarity and discipline as long as party leaders have more respect for representation than for party responsibility.

There are of course some reasons why American parties could never achieve true European party government even if they decided to seek it. Each of the parties has its campaign committees in Congress, but they have little independent money and cannot in any case easily use it to reward supporters and punish dissenters. Most importantly, the party leadership in Congress lacks the power to prevent dissident members from using the party label. This would be inconceivable in a European party situation; to them it is quite bizarre that anyone in the United States can use the name of any party simply by going through some minor enrollment procedures. If national party leaders wanted to change this, they would have to change the law in every state in the United States. For all these reasons, the British must think us rather quaint for using a term like *whip,* since it arises out of a British tradition in which certain party officers called whips could bring actual disciplinary action against recalcitrant members.

Political parties are not pretty, and in the United States they are not widely admired. However the advantages of a modest amount of party discipline might be appreciated in the wake of Watergate. The worst abuses of Watergate were really the result of efforts by the president to avoid relying on his party. He depended on functionaries who were personally loyal only to him, not the leaders of his party, to undermine the opposite party and its leading candidate. In the post-Watergate period we have witnessed a more assertive Congress. But during the same period there has also been a reassertion in Congress of political parties against the committee system and against the presidency.

In 1975, for the first time in recent decades, we witnessed a dramatic reassertion of power by the Democratic Party caucus (or conference) in the House of Representatives. Every committee chairman was brought up for review; some chairmen were actually deposed without regard for the seniority system, and others had to make a variety of promises and amends as conditions for retaining their positions. This was very simply one more expression of the discomfort the members feel living with the inconsistent demands of their dual responsibilities to representation and government. The period of adjustment in the 1970s may tend more toward party dominance than anyone could have anticipated a few years ago. In the meantime, the committee system is still the most important hierarchy, even if it is suffering somewhat in the post-Watergate period.

THE COMMITTEE SYSTEM: ORGANIZATIONAL CORE OF THE MODERN CONGRESS

Political parties may draw some justification from democratic theory for cutting down on the freedom of individual legislators. The committee system can make no such claim; yet it is our most fundamental commitment for congressional organization and against member individuality and freedom. The committee system provides Congress with a strict division of labor. When it is coupled with the principle of seniority, the result is a series of extremely tight hierarchies of privilege and power. This may be an efficient way for 435 House members and 100 senators to conduct business, but the committee system changes the whole meaning of making law in a representative assembly.

History of the Committee System

Congress got along with almost no standing legislative committees for the first twenty-five years of government under the Constitution. The House got along with three during the first decade. Agriculture, Interstate and Foreign Commerce, and Ways and Means were established in 1795. Another committee was added in 1805 and two more in 1808; four were added between 1813 and 1816. The Senate created no standing legislative committees whatsoever until 1816, when in a single year that august chamber revolutionized itself with the establishment of eleven standing committees.

By the end of 1816, the Senate had its eleven standing committees, and the House had ten. Other standing committees were added on an average of five or six every decade, until by the end of the century there were over sixty standing committees in the House and seventy in the Senate. Efforts to reform the system and cut the number of committees were unavailing until after World War II, when the Legislative Reorganization Act of 1946 streamlined things by cutting the number of committees down from over one hundred in each chamber to nineteen in the House and fifteen in the Senate. Very few new committees have been added since 1946, but something else of almost equal significance has happened. There has been a marked increase in the number of *subcommittees* within

Table 10.4   Committees in Senate and House, 1975

Senate Committees	House Committees	Jurisdiction
Standing Committees		
Aeronautics and Space Sciences 6D, 4R; no subcommittees	*Science and Technology* 25D, 12R; 7 subcommittees	NASA; NSF; scientific and military aspects of space; Bureau of Standards
Agriculture and Forestry 9D, 5R; 6 subcommittees	*Agriculture* 29D, 14R; 10 subcommittees	Agriculture Department; agricultural credit, rural electrification, etc.
Appropriations 16D, 10R; 15 subcommittees	*Appropriations* 37D, 18R; 13 subcommittees	All appropriations for support of government; adjournment resolutions
Armed Services 10D, 6R; 9 subcommittees	*Armed Services* 27D, 13R; 7 subcommittees	Pentagon; Panama Canal and the Canal Zone; weapons research; stockpiling
Banking, Housing and Urban Affairs 8D, 5R; 7 subcommittees	*Banking, Currency and Housing* 29D, 14R; 9 subcommittees	Federal Reserve; HUD; government finance except taxation
Budget 10D, 6R; no subcommittees	*Budget* 17D, 8R; no subcommittees	Established 1974; no legislative authority; studies effect on budget of existing and proposed legislation, effect of tax on budget, etc.
Commerce 12D, 6R; 13 subcommittees	*Interstate and Foreign Commerce* 29D, 14R; 6 subcommittees	Commerce Department; communications and power transmission (FCC, FPC)
District of Columbia 4D, 3R; no subcommittees	*District of Columbia* 17D, 8R; 5 subcommittees	All matters relating to the municipal affairs of the District
Foreign Relations 10D, 7R; 9 subcommittees	*International Relations* 25D, 12R; 10 subcommittees	State Department; treaties (Senate); diplomatic corps; UN; Red Cross
Government Operations 9D, 5R; 5 subcommittees	*Government Operations* 29D, 14R; 7 subcommittees	Reorganization of the executive branch; intergovernmental relations
Interior and Insular Affairs 9D, 5R; 7 subcommittees	*Interior and Insular Affairs* 29D, 14R; 7 subcommittees	Interior Department; Indian Affairs; possessions and public lands
Judiciary 9D, 6R; 15 subcommittees	*Judiciary* 23D, 12R; 7 subcommittees	Courts and judges; immigration; House apportionment; patents; claims against United States
Labor and Public Welfare 9D, 6R; 11 subcommittees	*Education and Labor* 27D, 13R; 8 subcommittees	Health, Education and Welfare; Labor Department; medical care and welfare, except social security
Post Office and Civil Service 5D, 4R; 3 subcommittees	*Post Office and Civil Service* 19D, 9R; 6 subcommittees	Post Office and Civil Service; Census; National Archives
Public Works 9D, 5R; 8 subcommittees	*Public Works and Transportation* 27D, 13R; 6 subcommittees	Public buildings and roads; flood control; rivers and harbors; water power; water pollution
Rules and Administration 5D, 3R; 7 subcommittees	*House Administration* 17D, 8R; 11 subcommittees	Management services for each chamber and for Library of Congress and Smithsonian Institution

Table 10.4 (continued)

Senate Committees	House Committees	Jurisdiction
Veterans Affairs 5D, 4R; 4 subcommittees	*Veterans Affairs* 19D, 9R; 5 subcommittees	Veterans Administration; veterans hospitals, education, GI Bill
Finance 11D, 7R; 11 subcommittees	*Ways and Means* 25D 12R; 6 subcommittees	Taxes; tariffs; import quotas; social security; Treasury Department
	Merchant Marine and Fisheries 27D, 13R; 5 subcommittees	Coast Guard; Coast and Geodetic Survey; Canal Zone (see also Senate Commerce)
	Rules 11D, 5R; no subcommittees	
	Small Business 25D, 12R; 6 subcommittees	Problems of small business; participation of small business in government contracts
	Standards of Official Conduct 6D, 6R; no subcommittees	Establish and enforce standards of conduct for members of the House
Standing Joint Committees *Atomic Energy* 5SD, 9HD, 4SR, 4HR; 6 subcommittees	*Printing* 2SD, 2HD, 1SR, 1HR; no subcommittees	These committees appear in two columns only in the interest of conserving space. They are *joint* committees, not committees of either the House or the Senate.
Budget Control 9SD, 9HD, 7SR, 7HR; no subcommittees	*Defense Production* 3SD, 3HD, 2SR, 2HR; no subcommittees	
Congressional Operations 3SD, 3HD, 2SR, 2HR; no subcommittees	*Economic* 6SD, 6HD, 4SR, 4HR; 9 subcommittees	
Library 3SD, 3HD, 2SR, 2HR; no subcommittees	*Internal Revenue Taxation* 3SD, 3HD, 2SR, 2HR; no subcommittees	
Select and Special Committees Senate in 1973: 7	House in 1975: 5	Important examples in 1975 include Select Committee on Aging and Select Committee on Intelligence.

From Commerce Clearing House, Inc., *Congressional Index,* 1974–75; and Senate and House Rules.
Abbreviations are: D, Democrats; R, Republicans; SD, Senate Democrats; HD, House Democrats; SR, Senate Republicans; HR, House Republicans. The number of subcommittees refers only to the number of *standing* subcommittees; there are many additional select and ad hoc subcommittees, especially in standing committees that have no standing subcommittees.

each of the standing committees. From the standpoint of congressional organization, the proliferation of subcommittees has almost the same meaning as the earlier growth of committees.[10]

During the past one and a half centuries, there has apparently been no period when members of Congress felt they could meet their

[10]George Goodwin, *The Little Legislatures* (Amherst: University of Massachusetts Press, 1970).

legislative obligations without using, expanding, and generally strengthening the committee system. As the national government expanded, Congress expanded its committee structure. Table 10.5 presents the essential features of the committee system, which indicate quite clearly the intention of Congress to be a continuing body, an organized body, a body that is able to perform regular tasks.

The first three features shown in Table 10.5 are inherent in the system as it has been operating for the entire century and a half. Moreover, they have been officially recognized and sanctioned in the rules of the House and the Senate. Even the most important reform in the history of the committee system—the 1946 Legislative Reorganization Act—mainly strengthened the committee system. Granted, it drastically cut the number of committees, but the bulk of it was concerned with shoring up the committee structure by clarifying the jurisdiction of each committee. This was done by careful definition of each committee's jurisdiction in an actual rule enacted into law, as well as by a reiteration of the historic power of each committee over one or more executive agencies. The fourth and fifth features of the committee system shown in Table 10.5 are as important as the first three and should be set apart only because they are not officially recognized in the rules of Congress. All five

---

Table 10.5	The Committee System: Five Fundamental Features

1. Each committee is a standing committee. It is set up in the official rules to be permanent. It has a fixed membership, officers, rules of its own, a staff, offices, and above all, a jurisdiction that is recognized by all other committees and, usually, by the leadership.

2. The jurisdiction of each standing committee is designed according to the actual *subject matter* of basic legislation. Except for the House Rules Committee, all the important committees are organized to receive proposals for legislation and to process them into official bills. There is no way for a legislative proposal to escape committee processing.

3. The subject matter or jurisdiction usually parallels that of a major department or agency in the executive branch. There are important exceptions, such as Ways and Means (House), Finance (Senate), Appropriations (House and Senate), Rules (House), Internal Security (House), Expenditures (Senate); but by and large the division of labor is designed self-consciously to parallel executive branch organization.

4. Each committee is unique, sui generis. No committee is a microcosm of the whole body; no effort is made to compose the membership of any committee so that it is representative of the total House or Senate membership; and no one ever tries to suggest that the committees are or should be "little legislatures." Each committee is deliberately *un*representative. Members with a special interest in the subject matter of a committee are expected to seek and gain membership on it.

5. Each committee is a tight, absolute, vertical hierarchy based on *seniority.* Seniority is a committee phenomenon, determined by years of continuous service on a *committee,* not by years of service in the House or Senate.

taken together clearly illustrate that Congress has never had any intention of operating as a flat assembly made up of equal representatives.

Many would argue that this was inevitable, that *some* kind of committee system was necessary if Congress was to participate seriously in government. An assembly without a capacity to do legislative work would have been an assembly purely for ceremonial functions. However, the argument for the inevitability of our particular committee system is not plausible. The British House of Commons has an effective committee system which has nevertheless avoided the rigidifying commitment to permanent standing committees. The French National Assembly does actually employ a version of standing committees, but these committees are fewer in number, broader in jurisdiction, and considerably more flexible about work and about seniority. There have to be other reasons we have our particular system.

Perhaps the most important reason is the separation of powers. Congress either had to equip itself to deal with the executive branch departments, or it had to face the prospect of not dealing much at all. This certainly goes far toward explaining why the 1816 House and Senate had already begun to organize themselves by standing committees whose lines of jurisdiction paralleled those of executive branch departments. It has been said that the original Ways and Means Committee was created in the mid-1790s as an effort by the House to defend itself against the vigorous secretary of treasury, Alexander Hamilton. This kind of a relationship has become a tradition, feeding a general American distrust of "bureaucracy." In contrast, in Great Britain and France (at least in this century) strong parliaments have been part of a *fusion of powers system* which produced a different influence on the assembly, as well as a different set of problems for it.

Another factor that helps explain our committee system can be found in the type of public policy the federal government was producing in the formative years between 1800 and 1900. As reported at length in chapter 5, the primary output of the United States Congress during that entire period was composed of various subsidies and bounties—distributive policies. These policies were so readily adaptable for patronage that members of Congress were willing and able to engage in the administration as well as the authorization of these programs. It is most probably for this reason that Woodrow Wilson, as a political science professor in the 1880s, complained that "Congressional government is committee government."[11]

---

[11] For a series of brilliant thrusts against "the imperious authority of the standing committees," see Woodrow Wilson, *Constitutional Government in the United States* (New York: Columbia University Press, 1908); reprinted in Lowi and Ripley, *Legislative Politics U.S.A.*, pp. 98–105. (The opening quote of this chapter is taken from this passage.)

Congress: Making Law

355

Seniority

One more aspect of the committee system which has militated very
strongly in favor of maintaining all its magnificent rigidity is the
investment current members of Congress already have in the
system as it is. It is difficult to imagine a majority of members of
either chamber eager to change a system in which they may already
have ten to fifteen years invested in obtaining a committee rank
high enough to gain essential influence.

None of this, however, adequately explains the extent to which
seniority is employed as the major criterion of promotion and
ranking. Seniority is, of course, a universal phenomenon. The
promotion of a younger executive "over the heads" of senior persons

is almost always a newsworthy event, usually the occasion for multiple resignations.[12] However, two facts make Congress's system of seniority stand out from all the rest. First, Congress is supposed to be a representative assembly and should thus express a weaker rather than a stronger preference for the rigid rank ordering of seniority; yet, congressional seniority is more prominent than the seniority patterns in armies, government agencies, businesses, or foundations. Second, seniority is not an institution-wide phenomenon in Congress; that is, seniority means years of *continuous service on a committee.*

General parliamentary seniority counts for little except when two members apply to transfer to the same committee. Once on a committee, continuous committee service has been the sole criterion of promotion, to such an extent that if two members of the same party were appointed the same year, the first sworn in would be the senior person, even if the difference in length of service were only a matter of minutes. An interesting recent case of this is Senator Hubert Humphrey. In 1964 Humphrey left his high-ranking position in the Senate to serve as vice-president. When he was reelected to the Senate in 1970 he became the *junior* senator from Minnesota. His prestige gave him preferment among freshmen for assignment to the Foreign Relations Committee, but he entered as the low-ranking member of that committee. This rigid pattern is especially bizarre in the Senate, which has managed to escape so many of the other rules that confine the House.

Part of the explanation may be found in the fact that seniority did not become such an important formula in Congress until after 1910 and the "revolt against the Speaker." Before 1910, the party leadership in House and Senate enjoyed considerable discretion in the assignment of members to committees and in the promotion of members to committee chairmanships. In those days there were frequent instances where preferment was given without regard to the order of seniority ranking. Within a decade following the Speaker revolt, these "violations of the seniority rule"—for indeed by the 1920s it had become a rule—had dropped toward zero. According to one study, between 1925 and 1959 there were only two departures from seniority even in the matter of removing committee members following the loss of seats by their party. Committee seats are apportioned between the two major parties in the House and the Senate according to the relative size of the party delegations. Therefore, when a party loses seats in the general election, it must relinquish some of its committee posts. Between 1925 and

---

[12]The story of Dwight Eisenhower's promotion early in World War II is a very significant one from this standpoint.

1970, there were *no departures* from seniority in the selection of chairmen.[13]

With seniority as the criterion of selection and promotion, committees could more or less govern themselves without intervention by party and parliamentary leaders, because if assignment, promotion, and removal were automatic, party leaders would lack an effective weapon of control of the committees. Party leaders have been able to live with the system probably because committee chairmen have as much party loyalty as the average member. But the seniority formula has deprived the party leaders of important means of disciplining votes on specific issues.

Seniority may not last forever as the sole criterion of selection. It is stressed here not only because it remains important but also because it emphasizes the significance of hierarchical organization in the United States Congress. Congress lived with parties and committees for a century. When parties were overthrown in the early part of this century, Congress did not opt for a flatter and more representative system of organization; instead it overthrew one of its hierarchies by throwing itself more fully into the arms of the other.

The Johnson rule has very probably softened the seniority system permanently in the Senate. Changes in the rules during the period 1971 to 1973 may also function to soften the seniority system in the

[13]Nelson Polsby et al., "The Growth of the Seniority System in the U.S. House of Representatives," *American Political Science Review,* September 1969, pp. 787–806. On the Senate, see Barbara Hinckley, *The Seniority System in Congress* (Bloomington: Indiana University Press, 1971).

House. Those reforms returned to the caucus of each party the power to approve *by secret ballot* the recommendations of their Committees on Committees for new assignments, for transfers, and for elevation to committee chairmanships. During the first year of operation of these new rules, only one challenge was made against a chairman, and this was an unsuccessful effort to unseat a highly conservative chairman of the House Committee on the District of Columbia.

All of the twenty-one chairmen of standing committees in the House in 1973 remained by virtue of their seniority ranking and were approved by the caucus by large margins. However, in 1975, thanks probably to the Watergate embarrassments and the unusually large influx of freshman House members, these new rules suddenly made a great deal of difference. For the first time in the twentieth century, the Democratic caucus vacated the seniority rule and unseated three very senior members of extremely powerful committees—the Armed Services Committee, the Agriculture Committee, and the Banking and Currency Committee. A fourth chairman barely escaped removal, and all of the other chairmen were put on notice that they could no longer assume that seniority was sufficient.

Eventually these recalcitrant freshmen will either be defeated for reelection or will age in their offices and perhaps soften in their attitudes toward seniority according to the process described so eloquently by Woodrow Wilson in the quotation that opened this chapter. But the "rebellion of 1975" will last as an ever-present threat to the defenders of the committee system and will serve as an ever-present reminder to outside observers that nothing is permanent even in the United States Congress as long as members are trying to make the best of the contradictions inherent in representative government.

PUTTING REPRESENTATION IN ITS PLACE: THE RULES

It is virtually inconceivable for an assembly to espouse the ideal of equality and freedom to such an extent that it rejects the entire notion of parliamentary procedure. Yet, for nearly a century the House and Senate operated on the basis only of rulings from the chair. Precedents from one period to another were relied upon for guidance, but they were not considered determinative. Parliamentary order seemed to depend more upon the power of the chairman and majority party than it did upon the relevance and applicability of procedural rules. Congress was entering its second century before any effort was made to oblige members to attend sessions, to answer roll calls or quorum calls, to make speeches relevant to the bill before the chamber, or to establish orders of priority among motions and other business.[14]

In the late 1880s and 1890s the House began to formulate some effective parliamentary rules to reduce the casual nature, or frequent chaos, of legislative activity. The Senate did not adopt rules at that time but continued to operate by a set of very general parliamentary rules laid down by Thomas Jefferson while vice-president (and president of the Senate)—*Jefferson's Manual*. Although most of the Senate's business continued to be conducted by "unanimous consent," we shall soon see that the Senate has not managed to get along without rules.

There seems to be no coincidence that a concern for parliamentary rules emerged in the 1890s and continued from that time on with frequent additions and revisions of the rules. The Interstate Commerce Act, adopted in 1887, and the Sherman Antitrust Act, adopted in 1892, were the first important steps by the national government to intervene systematically in the economy through regulation of the conduct of business. Here again we find a very close relationship between the effort to govern and the requirement that Congress keep the process of talking and representation under control. Each important round of expanded national government seems to have been accompanied by important adjustments in the rules by which Congress conducted its business.

For example, important changes occurred following 1910 and again in 1917, when even the Senate made a vain effort to control its highly permissive floor operation by adopting its first "cloture rule," permitting a majority to set a time limit on debate over a given bill. This first effort to control Senate debate turned out to be meaningless. It provided that two-thirds of those senators present could close debate; however, the cloture rule did not apply to the motions to *call up* the bill. This meant that debate on the bill could be closed but debate on the motion to debate the bill could not be closed. It was not until 1949 that the cloture rule was adjusted to cover these procedural motions, but in return for that concession, the reformers had to agree to require that two-thirds of the entire membership (an absolute majority), rather than two-thirds of those present, would be required to close the debate. This was changed early in 1975 to an absolute majority of three-fifths—60 votes to close debate. Nevertheless, although the Senate has managed to go far in protecting the freedom of members on the floor, it has not avoided other types of rules, as we shall see.[15]

---

[14]The best contemporary appreciations of the rules and their importance are Bertram Gross, *The Legislative Struggle* (New York: McGraw-Hill, 1953); and Froman, *The Congressional Process.*

[15]On the cloture rule, see Raymond E. Wolfinger, "Filibusters: Majority Rule, Presidential Leadership, and Senate Norms," in *Readings on Congress,* ed. Raymond E. Wolfinger (Englewood Cliffs, N.J.: Prentice-Hall, 1971).

Filibuster: Senators rest during the civil rights debate of 1964, while some colleagues use their rights under the cloture rule to talk almost endlessly.

All of this should suggest that the rules are a fundamental aspect of legislative institutions, especially the United States Congress. All of the major rules of the House and Senate were serious responses to some kind of problem of governing, and each rule should be understood within that larger context. No rule is neutral. Each rule serves some interest and was probably drafted deliberately for that purpose. The fact that the purpose of a rule may have been forgotten years after its adoption should not be allowed to overshadow the probable origins of the rule; forgetting the original purpose contributes to the effectiveness of those in whose favor the rule is biased.[16] Table 10.6 is an outline of the most important rules in Congress. While just a partial listing, the impression it conveys can be strengthened by a closer and more detailed look at all of the rules.

First, deliberation is quite clearly committee business. Even if an executive agency or commission has already deliberated for months, and even when their proposals take the form of drafts of legislation, these proposals do not become bona fide bills until a committee—usually one in each chamber—has also had an opportunity to deliberate on them. Everyone must wait until this committee process has taken place (or try a discharge petition, discussed below and in Table 10.6). Many will wait forever. For example, in the

[16]For probably the best specific case study of how certain rules have worked consistently in favor of interests, in this case southern racial conservative interests, see Howard Shuman, "Senate Rules and the Civil Rights Bill: A Case Study," *American Political Science Review,* December 1957, pp. 955–975.

Table 10.6   The Rules—A Selection, with Comments

Rules	Comments
DELIBERATION	
1. Most of the rules of each chamber, especially since 1946, define the jurisdictions of the standing committees, one rule for each.	1. Leadership power over committees is limited since chair no longer has much discretion on where to assign a bill.
2. All proposals are read over and referred immediately to committee.	2. Committee can be bypassed only when bill has already been passed by the other chamber.
3. Public bills cannot go to calendar until reported out of committee.	3. Again, the exception is when the bill has already been passed by other chamber.
4. Committees may be given power to subpoena witnesses and compel testimony, as a type of grand jury and as part of power of deliberation on bills.	4. Limitation: Committee questions must have a legislative purpose when citizens other than administrators of agencies and departments are subpoenaed.
5. Bills remain in committee until the committee is ready to report them out.	5. This power of life and death over bills is mainly a result of the great difficulty of discharging bills from committee.
6. Discharge and Calendar Wednesday are the only two meaningful exceptions to the power of a committee to retain and deliberate on bills as long as it chooses.	6. House: Discharge petition must be signed by an absolute majority (218); then the bill goes on calendar, after which it can only be debated on the second or fourth Mondays of the month. Senate: Looks easy, but is not. Petitions require a simple majority, but a motion to discharge is subject to four different opportunities to debate. Thus a cloture (two-thirds) might have to be involved four times. Calendar Wednesday is even more cumbersome.[1]

Eighty-eighth Congress (1963–1964), 11 percent of the bills introduced were eventually reported out of committee back to the calendars. In the Ninety-first Congress (1969–1971), less than 8 percent of all of the introduced bills were reported out of committee. Most of the favored bills were introduced in the first place by the administration or by important members of the congressional leadership or the actual committee whose jurisdiction covered the bill. But no matter who introduced the bill, it had to come through the committees.

This protection of the committee system is as much a part of the Senate rules as of the House rules. With the establishment of the Rules Committee, however, the House has provided for additional protection of committee deliberation. Although this committee exists mainly to control debate, it formulates its debate-controlling rules in cooperation with committee chairmen. Important committees, such as Ways and Means, usually get preferential treatment, such as "closed rule," which limits debate and the opportunity to amend bills on the floor (see Table 10.6). This makes the House floor more orderly than such a large body would otherwise be.

Table 10.6 (continued)

Rules	Comments
DEBATE	
1. Rule and tradition give unlimited power of recognition to the presiding officer, especially the Speaker of the House.	1. Senate presiding officers try to play down this power, attempting to work through agreements between majority and minority committee leaders.
2. While in session, Congress must meet every day except Sunday.	2. There rarely are sessions on Saturday or Sunday, thanks to adjournment Thursday nights by unanimous consent, in violation of Congress's own rule. But the threat by the leadership to meet weekends is a powerful discouragement of casual and dilatory actions.
3. To encourage talk, House rules allow the House to adjourn into "Committee of the Whole House on the State of the Union."	3. Quorum is 100 instead of 218, and rules governing debate are less strict than formal House rules.
4. In House and Senate actual debate time is controlled by the committee responsible for handling the bill.	4. The "floor managers" are the chairman and the top ranking minority member of the committee whose bill is up for debate; or they can designate another committee member as floor manager.
5. House rules set severe limits on the power of a member to offer amendments to bills. Policed by Rules Committee and chair, Senate sets no serious limit on right of senators to offer amendments and to speak for them.	5. Even in the Senate, however, there is a long distance between offering an amendment and getting it adopted as part of the bill. Amendments not agreed to in advance by the bill's sponsors have an extremely low probability of acceptance.
6. When the House becomes the House again, it hears the Report of the Committee of the Whole. Amendments rejected by the Committee of the Whole cannot be reconsidered, and debate on the bill is usually closed very quickly. The Senate allows amendments at any time.	6. Senate rules require germaneness, but "unless someone makes a point of order that a rule is being violated, the rules of the Senate may be violated at will."[2]

[1] In the House, between 1923 and 1962, 344 discharge petitions were submitted; 18 were actually discharged, but only 2 of these ever became law. Calendar Wednesday is available mainly for unprivileged bills; in any case, committees are called alphabetically, and a whole session may pass before the eager member has a crack at the committee where the bill is stalled. Moreover, adjournment is a nondebatable motion, and the chamber can be quickly adjourned to kill the long-awaited Wednesday.

[2] L. A. Froman, *The Congressional Process* (Boston: Little, Brown, 1967), p. 112.

Since the Rules Committee is also a standing committee organized according to the five features listed in Table 10.5, its leadership can get itself out of tune with the House majority. When that happens, this committee becomes a great obstruction because it controls so much of the activity of other committees. In the early 1960s, the Rules Committee had apparently reached such a state, and the Democrats eventually rebelled against it. In 1961, the Speaker engineered an expansion of the committee from twelve to fifteen members. The three new members, two Democrats and one Republican, were selected in such a manner as to liberalize the Rules Committee majority. Moreover, in 1965, the House adopted a rule granting itself permission to take up a bill without a Rules Committee action if the Rules Committee has delayed for longer

Congress:
Making Law

than twenty-one days. These actions have probably reduced the Rules Committee's powers but have not appreciably reduced its importance.[17]

Procedures for Passing a Bill

An understanding of the procedures for passing a bill serves to emphasize still further how strongly congressional rules are oriented toward supporting the committee system (see Figure 10.4). The rules first of all require that each bill be placed on a calendar, which is Congress's name for its agenda. There are several calendars, to indicate the status as well as the stature of bills; and some bills, though favorably reported by committee, may stay on a calendar through one or both sessions of Congress, while others go on the calendar and off to the floor for debate after only a brief wait. In both chambers, the actual week's business is drawn from the calendar according to decisions made by *party* leaders on the majority and minority side, through consultation with appropriate committee chairmen, the White House, and leaders from the other chamber. Usually an actual program of floor activities is posted on Friday for the following week, so that members may plan accordingly.

In the House this is frankly called a whip notice. In the more informal Senate a more elaborate scheduling apparatus is used— perhaps because the Senate has no Rules Committee. During the years of Democratic Party domination, the Democratic Policy Committee, headed by the Senate majority leader, has arranged the weekly schedule, taking pains of course to consult the minority leader. As stressed earlier, the arrangement of the agenda— agreeing on what to disagree about—is preeminently a party activity. This is recognized in the rules by the provision in both chambers that the power of recognition is in the hands of the presiding officer. Usually the chair knows the purpose for which the member rises well in advance of the occasion. Spontaneous efforts to gain recognition are often foiled. It is not unknown for Speakers to ask, "For what purpose does the gentleman rise?" before deciding whether to grant recognition.

Nevertheless, although rule and precedent give the parties power over scheduling and agenda, and although so much of the legislation originates in the White House, action on the floor—once it is finally allowed to take place—is determined more by committee than by party *or* presidential influence. In the House, most of the substantive debate takes place in a parliamentary situation called Committee of the Whole House (see Table 10.6); but virtually all of

---

[17]For a good examination of the traditional Rules Committee, see James A. Robinson, *The House Rules Committee* (Indianapolis: Bobbs-Merrill, 1963).

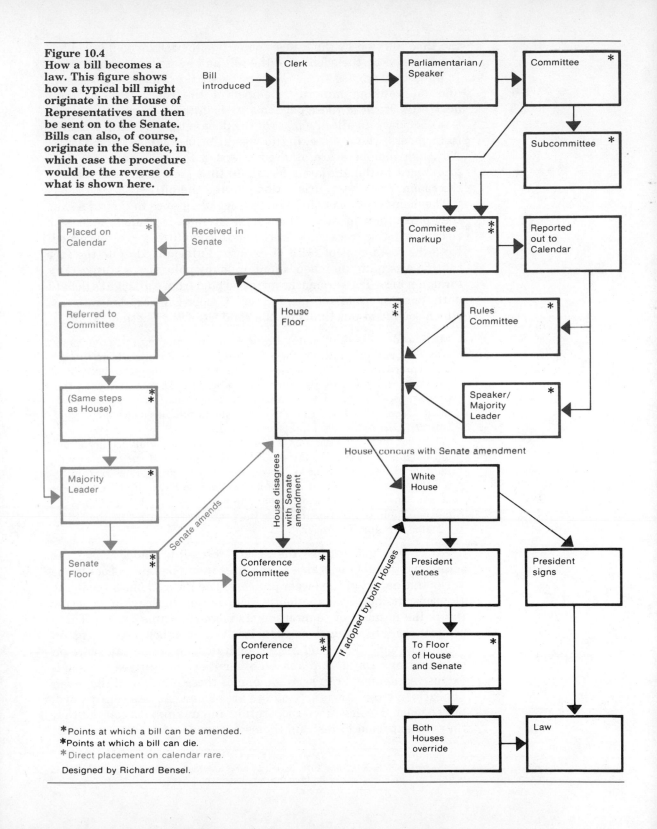

Figure 10.4
How a bill becomes a law. This figure shows how a typical bill might originate in the House of Representatives and then be sent on to the Senate. Bills can also, of course, originate in the Senate, in which case the procedure would be the reverse of what is shown here.

Bill introduced

Clerk

Parliamentarian/ Speaker

Committee *

Subcommittee *

Committee markup **

Reported out to Calendar

Placed on Calendar *

Received in Senate

Referred to Committee

House Floor **

Rules Committee *

Speaker/ Majority Leader *

(Same steps as House) **

Majority Leader *

House concurs with Senate amendment

Senate amends

House disagrees with Senate amendment

White House

Senate Floor **

Conference Committee *

President vetoes

President signs

If adopted by both Houses

Conference report **

To Floor of House and Senate *

Both Houses override

Law

*Points at which a bill can be amended.
**Points at which a bill can die.
*Direct placement on calendar rare.

Designed by Richard Bensel.

the time allotted by the Rules Committee for debate on a given bill is controlled by the sponsor of the bill and by its leading opponent. In almost every case, these two persons are the committee chairman and the ranking minority member of the committee—or their designees. Each of these participants is granted by rule and tradition the power to allocate most of the debate time in small amounts to members who are seeking to speak for or against the measure. Although members are allowed to speak for or against any bill, preference in the allocation of debate time goes to the members of the committee whose jurisdiction covered the bill.

The members do not stand and pledge allegiance to the rules, but they prove their loyalty whenever an attempt is made to bypass or circumvent the rules, especially where committees are concerned. Note the testament of faith of Senator Fulbright, despite the fact that he was quite an independent on many policy issues, especially foreign policy. These remarks are excerpted from Fulbright's debate with Senator Dole on the famous Cooper-Church Amendment, which sought to put limits on the conduct of the Vietnam War:

> Mr. President [of the Senate], I cannot say any more than I have as to why the Senator's amendment is inappropriate. It departs from the usual procedure. . . . One of the important parts of the procedures of the Senate is following the committee procedure. In fact, following the proper procedure is very relevant to our democratic form of government. One does not override the established procedures of a body like this and still reach any kind of result.
>
> I do not blame the Senator, in view of his brief attendance here, for not having learned all of the proper procedures. . . . If the Senator will read the rules of the Senate, he will see each committee has certain jurisdictions. The Senator can make any motion he wants to. Of course he can. That does not mean we have to accept it. . . . I am going to move to table the motion, because the procedure proposed by the Senator is highly improper.[18]

All of this underscores the severe restraints under which the individual member operates. Committee influence on the floor is one very large aspect of the larger problem. The Rules Committee in the House is another. Still another is a rule in the House which severely limits the number of committees its members can serve on. Three committees are exclusive; that is, if a member is serving on Appropriations, Ways and Means, or Rules, he or she can serve on only that one committee and no other. Ten committees are semiexclusive; members can serve on one of these plus one of the seven nonexclusive committees. Senators are somewhat less constrained, but so much depends upon cooperation and unanimous consent that they are expected to restrain themselves even where the restraints

[18]*Congressional Record*, June 1970; quoted in Lowi and Ripley, *Legislative Politics U.S.A.*, p. 57, along with a lengthy excerpt from this very important debate.

are not imposed upon them. For example, senators as well as members of the House are expected to identify with their committee assignments and to specialize in those fields. It is not considered good form to enter too frequently into subject areas beyond one's committee specialties.[19]

There is some room for individuality in Congress, but the dilemma is eternal. If members had all of the freedom and dignity their high office and the theory of representation accord them, their institution would decline in power to such a degree that the office would be less exalted, eventually hardly worth having. No one can say that Congress has worked out the best solution to the dilemma of the member. Committees, seniority, severe rules, specialization, and strict control of time are all heavy costs. These are part of the price Congress has paid in order to maintain itself as a major participant in government. Whether the price is right is a matter of individual judgment.

PRESIDENT AND CONGRESS

For all of its power compared to other assemblies in the world, Congress has nevertheless been unable to cope with its governmental responsibilities without increasing reliance upon the White House to provide it with legislative work and to help it do its work. For many, the emergence of the White House as the key to lawmaking is the most damning evidence that Congress has organized itself too much and in the wrong way. Others feel that the pronounced executive role in lawmaking is a gain for the legislative branch. In either case, it is true that the overwhelming proportion of important bills originate in the agencies and departments of the executive branch even though they are subjected to a considerable amount of deliberation later on by the congressional committees. When committees hold their hearings on bills, a great number of witnesses are from the agency where the bill originated. Many of the interest group witnesses have already submitted briefs on the subject to the agency. Very frequently, the proposal from the executive branch is already so mature as legislation that the main job of the congressional committees is to create by their debate of the proposed legislation a record of legislative intent that may influence later interpretation of the statute when the same executive agencies receive it as law and have to implement it.

---

[19]Donald Matthews, *U.S. Senators and Their World* (Chapel Hill: University of North Carolina Press, 1960), especially his treatment of the "folkways" of the Senate. For good studies of the prospects and problems of being an individualist, see Ralph Huitt, "The Outsider in the Senate: An Alternative Role," *American Political Science Review*, September 1961, p. 566; see also Huitt, "The Morse Committee Assignment Controversy: A Study in Senate Norms," *American Political Science Review*, June 1957.

Liberals for many years celebrated this rise of presidential power because (1) they believed it would make Congress more efficient, and (2) to them the president, rather than Congress, represented the only truly national majority.[20] Even before Watergate a serious reconsideration of these views was beginning to take place. Watergate simply brought them into critical focus. However, Congress is not likely to move very far from its dependence on presidential initiative in the production of legislative work or from its reliance on presidential discipline to help forge voting majorities on roll calls.

The president's political resources are not only rich but are quite suitable for vigorous legislative involvement. His influence with and access to the vast bureaucracy allow him to call for information and expertise quickly and continuously. The president also has far better access than Congress to public opinion; although there are limits to how often he can campaign for legislation, he can fairly quickly build a public opinion backfire against Congress.[21] The president's veto power is another factor in favor of strong legislative influence, and the threat of its use can be more effective than its actual use.

But the greatest of all the president's advantages is probably the

[20]See, for example, James MacGregor Burns, *Deadlock of Democracy* (Englewood Cliffs, N.J.: Prentice-Hall, 1963). For the best counterattack, see Willmoore Kendall, "The Two Majorities," *Midwest Journal of Political Science*, November 1960, pp. 317–345.

[21]There are, however, special conditions when members of Congress perceive that they can buck presidential power with impunity. See chapter 11 for a more detailed assessment of these resources and their limitations.

universal expectation that legislative initiative will flow from him. This phenomenon of regular presidential involvement in the legislative process can accurately be called the "institutionalization of the strong presidency." Historians have tended to reserve the notion of the strong president for those few who were known for vigorous engagement and competition with Congress. Yet since World War II, every president has either chosen the role of strong president or has had the role thrust upon him.[22] There has, consequently, been a steady and impressive growth of communication between the two branches.

There has probably always been someone in the White House responsible for legislative liaison. However, in recent years, White House staff performing such functions has expanded, and staff status in the White House has grown immensely. Lawrence O'Brien, who was one of the inner circle around John Kennedy and Lyndon Johnson, was primarily a legislative liaison officer. Before O'Brien there was Bryce Harlow for President Eisenhower. And some of Nixon's closest and best-known aides, such as Ehrlichman and Laird, were relied upon heavily for legislative strategy. The institutionalization of the president's legislative role can also be seen in the emergence over the past twenty years of the Office of Management and Budget (formerly Bureau of the Budget) as a place where legislative proposals of administrative agencies are collected and cleared for inclusion or exclusion in the president's program.[23]

The consequences of this institutionalization of the strong presidency for the behavior of individual members of Congress should not come as any surprise. *Members of the House and the Senate have come to the point where they conduct their affairs and govern their decisions to a great extent in terms of presidential actions.* This does not mean that individual members of Congress or Congress itself rubber stamps legislation initiated by the president. What it does mean is that legislative behavior is less strictly organized along party lines and more organized along pro-president and anti-president, or what the British would call government and opposition. But there is a difference, in that the American version is not altogether parallel to parties, as is the British.

Tables 10.3 and 10.7 suggest that the parties tend to depend upon the president as a basis for their own alignments and divisions. Table 10.3 shows that the parties are much more clearly differentiated from each other on bills where the president's position is

[22]Probably the first to recognize the institutionalization of the strong presidency was Richard E. Neustadt. See his two classic articles: "Presidency and Legislation: The Growth of Central Clearance," *American Political Science Review,* September 1954, pp. 641–671; and "Presidency and Legislation: Planning the President's Program," *American Political Science Review,* December 1955.

[23]Neustadt, "Presidency and Legislation: Planning the President's Program." See also chapters 11 and 12 for treatments of the Office of Management and Budget in various contexts.

Table 10.7   **Republican Voting on Vetoed Bills, 1973**

Bill and Chamber	Vote on Original Passage		Vote to Override Veto	
	Republican Voting	Percent Supporting Nixon Position	Republican Voting	Percent Supporting Nixon Position
Vocational Rehabilitation Act (Senate)	35–2	5	10–31	76
Water-Sewer Program (House)	105–48	31	24–161	87
OMB Confirmation (Senate)	16–17	52	14–22	61
OMB Confirmation (House)	20–164	89	18–167	90
Cambodia Bombing Halt (House)	63–120	66	53–133	72

From Randall Ripley, *Congress—Process and Policy* (New York: Norton, 1975), p. 125. In both houses, "OMB Confirmation" was a bill requiring Senate confirmation of the director and deputy director of the Office of Management and Budget, as with other cabinet and top political appointments.

known. Table 10.7 shows that the president can activate party support even when party members are clearly inclined to vote the other direction. Note how much higher the percentage of Republican support for Nixon was in the vote to support his veto than in the original vote. All of these figures suggest that the presidency is the touchstone, or center of gravity, of legislative conduct.

Review of the entire congressional situation, however, will oppose any conclusion that the president and the presidency completely control legislative action. Committees continue to dominate legislative deliberation and to control the floor, regardless of the source of the bill. Party leaders continue to control the scheduling on virtually all procedural motions. Parties are especially important to the president because it is quite clear that presidential legislative power tends to flow most strongly along party lines. A president who ignores these facts does so at great risk.

One other aspect of the relationship between the president and Congress has been overlooked by presidents and either overlooked or misrepresented by most scholars. *Presidential power does not rise at the expense of congressional power.* Political scientists and historians have been much too impressed with Congress's docility during the famous "100 days" after Franklin Roosevelt took office in 1933. They have too easily taken that experience and let it lead them into a general conclusion that congressional power goes down as presidential power goes up.

In order to investigate president-Congress relationships, we undertook a study some years ago of the degree to which bills that come from committee are changed by various amendments on the floor of the House and Senate. We felt that the power or creativity of the floor could be measured by the extent to which amendments to change bills in significant ways are offered during the course of debate. What we found after studying hundreds of bills is that *a strong president tends to enhance floor activity at the expense of committee power.* Thus, it is not Congress that declines in response to presidential power but the committee structure, which gives way to a more assertive parliamentary Congress.

We found, for example, that during the sixteen years between the Eighty-first and Eighty-eighth Congresses, the amendment of bills on the floor of Congress was at least 10 percent more frequent under such strong presidents as Kennedy and Johnson than under a weaker president, such as Eisenhower. Counting only the most controversial efforts to amend—amendments offered by nonmembers of committees which were supported by a minimum of fifty senators or two hundred House members—we found that floor action was around 60 percent more frequent under strong presidents than under weak presidents. This occurred despite the fact that President Eisenhower was more permissive, even inviting Congress to amend his budget requests. And it occurred despite the fact that the Democrats controlled Congress for two of the eight Eisenhower years, during which time one would have supposed that Congress would have been more rather than less assertive. "Part of the tragedy of the strong, independent President literature has been that it encouraged Presidents to believe that their strength can and should be exercised independently of Congress."[24] Watergate proves, if nothing else, that Congress is as powerful as its assertions can make it.

PUTTING IT ALL TOGETHER: A CASE STUDY OF LAWMAKING

The case history to be recounted here is the State and Local Fiscal Assistance Act of 1972. Its nickname was the "Revenue Sharing Act," and its official name, after passage, became Public Law 92-512. It was a major element of the domestic program of Richard Nixon's first administration and an ideal case through which to tie together the various loose ends in our discussion of congressional structure.[25] No single case of congressional action is representative of all actions, of course. However, for an initial exposure to congressional dynamics, one good story tells enough about all the rest.

Revenue sharing was not new in 1972. It had been around in one

---

[24]Peri Arnold and L. John Roos, "Toward a Theory of Congressional-Executive Relations," *Review of Politics*, July 1974, p. 429. For some related and confirming data see the same article, p. 428.

[25]A more detailed account of the Revenue Sharing Act, plus an exhaustive analysis of congressional behavior, will be found in Joseph Penbera, "A Test of the Lowi Arenas of Power Policy Approach: The Case of the State and Local Fiscal Assistance Act of 1972" (Ph.D. diss., American University, 1974).

•It is unlawful for a child to solicit money on the street for any purpose whatever. It is therefore unlawful for children to solicit donations for UNICEF. (190–10)

•It is unlawful to let your homing pigeons loose in the 7th Ward, but not in any other ward.

•In the city of Chicago it is an offense punishable by a $50 fine for a person to ride in an elevator and wear a hatpin the point of which protrudes more than one-half inch "beyond the crown of the hat in, upon, or through which such pin is worn."

•It is unlawful to "utter lewd or filthy words, sing any song the words of which are suggestive of indecency or immorality, or to make any obscene gesture in the presence of other persons." Remember that.

•It is unlawful for a sidewalk newspaper stand to sell any publication "except daily newspapers printed and published in the city."

•It is unlawful to wash windows in such a way that you get water on the sidewalk between 7 am and 7 pm during the months from May 1 to October 1.

•It is unlawful to play hopscotch or skip rope on the sidewalk without a permit.

•It is unlawful to skate in the street.

•It is unlawful to "indecently exhibit" a stud horse. Horses and cows are required to mate only "in some enclosed place out of public view."

•It is unlawful to play a musical instrument on the beach, or to display a flag there, without a permit.

•It is unlawful to take a cigaret butt out of a public ashtray with intent to resell it.

•It is unlawful for a liquor licensee to give away popcorn or pretzels.

•In a section labeled "promotion of marriage", the ordinances of the city of Chicago deem it unlawful for anyone to take money for arranging a marriage.

•It is unlawful to build a car showroom within two hundred feet of a church.

•It is unlawful to give away a cigaret within one hundred feet of a school building.

•It is unlawful to sell fruit of different sizes in the same container. The Board of Health is required to inspect every fruit, vegetable, or berry sold within the city of Chicago.

•It is unlawful to tell fortunes in the park.

•According to city ordinance 99, subsection 9, "All weeds . . . are hereby declared to be a public nuisance."

form or another at least since the Morrill Act of 1862, which provided the land grants that helped build the gigantic state university systems. The 1972 act is novel, however, in that it works through unconditional rebates of taxes to the states rather than grants for specific purposes, which are usually called categoric aid. (Some familiar examples of categoric aid are federal aid to education, to the unemployed, for public housing and urban renewal, and for agricultural extension.) Revenue sharing was first seriously proposed by two leading Kennedy economists. President Johnson became interested, and in 1964 he appointed a Task Force on General Revenue Sharing, which boldly proposed returning to the states an actual proportion of federal revenue each year, with no strings attached. Two important Senate Democrats, Muskie and

Humphrey, submitted bills favoring the plan. When President Nixon took office in 1969, revenue sharing was not only very much alive, it had captured the support of many conservatives. Consequently, President Nixon included the proposal in his very first State of the Union Message in 1969 and went on to make it "part of the President's program," calling revenue sharing a "turning point in the federal system."

Almost immediately thereafter, bills were drafted for President Nixon and were submitted to Congress. The most important of these proposals originated in the Senate and eventually was given the title S. 2483. The companion bill in the House was entitled H.R. 4182. Since revenues were involved in the proposals, they were assigned to the Committee on Ways and Means in the House and to the Finance Committee in the Senate. House action was required first, because revenues were involved, and thus the task fell to the chairman of the Ways and Means Committee, Wilbur Mills, who at that time was still considered one of the most formidable members of Congress.

Mills made no secret of his opposition, publicly confessing that he was going to delay committee action until he could "kill the idea once and for all." Committee delay took care of the bill for the year, but Nixon forces persisted, including it once again in the 1970 State of the Union Message. Bills were not reintroduced until November of 1970, perhaps because of the 1970 congressional elections. But Chairman Mills chose once again to sit on the issue, waiting until April of 1971 to announce that hearings would be held the following June—over seven months after bills had been reintroduced and nearly eighteen months after the president's first proposals.

The White House had been active during this period and had lined up a great deal of impressive support. Nixon handed over the position of chief legislative liaison to a skillful assistant secretary of the treasury, who lined up the support of leaders of most of the professional associations of state and local officials. These included the National Governor's Conference, National Legislative Conference, National Association of Counties, National Society of State Legislators, International City Managers Association, and U.S. Conference of Mayors. During this time the president met several times with Chairman Mills. Clearly presidential power was not merely a matter of making demands and enjoying congressional obedience.

Hearings were finally held during June of 1971, on H.R. 4187 (the new number for substantially the same bill as H.R. 4182, introduced during the previous Congress). This was an administration bill which had been changed in ways that seriously, but vainly, sought to meet some of Mills's objections. Mills even announced that the hearings would be used to "expose the dangers and weaknesses of the revenue sharing concept and to kill the bill." Among the witnesses, the proponents outweighed the opponents. Spokesmen for the aforementioned organizations were joined by the mayors of several cities hard-pressed to bring in revenue adequate to fund their governments.

Well before the hearings were completed there were rumors that the chairman was changing his position. In addition to the impressive parade of witnesses favoring revenue sharing, there was also the fact that President Nixon had met with Mills over twenty times privately on this issue. It was apparently no surprise when the chairman finally made his switch, although no one was quite sure what it was going to mean. From the end of the hearings in late June until the end of the session in December, the Ways and Means Committee worked over the bill in closed sessions. The president finally managed to get from Chairman Mills a concession that in 1972 revenue sharing would be his committee's first order of business.

Once again, in 1972, revenue sharing was prominent in the State of the Union Message; but by this time there had been so many compromises written into H.R. 14370 (the new number) that the bill came to be known as the "Committee Bill" and "Mr. Mills's Bill." Some of the changes in the bill were important but quite technical. In brief, the committee had shifted President Nixon's bill in at least three significant ways: (1) two-thirds rather than one-third of the total money would go to local governments rather than to the states, (2) the sharing formula would weigh the population factor more heavily and would thus redistribute more of the funds toward the states with the largest and most dependent populations, and (3) cities would be restricted slightly toward uses defined as "priority" instead of being given the money unconditionally.

The Rules Committee granted the bill a "closed rule" barring all floor amendments and limiting debate to eight hours. In fact, the only serious opposition to the bill was on a procedural point that the bill had wrongly bypassed the Appropriations Committee. The objection was raised by George Mahon, chairman of the Appropriations Committee, who chose to make his fight against the closed rule rather than against the bill itself. However, the rule—entitled House Resolution 996—was adopted by a vote of 223 to 185 on June 21, 1972. A last-minute motion to recommit the bill was rejected 241 to 157, and the next day the House passed H.R. 14370 without amending the committee bill, by a roll call vote of 275 to 122.

The bill was sent to the Senate and referred immediately to the Senate Finance Committee, which insisted on holding its own hearings. For the six days of hearings spread over the period of June 29 to July 26, witnesses were about equally divided pro and con. As usual in revenue bills, the focus was on amending the House version rather than killing the bill. The key witness was the new secretary of the treasury, George Schultz, who favored H.R. 14370 in general while pursuing several specific changes in the hope of bringing the bill back toward the original administration version. Organized

A typical bill as
introduced in the House
of Representatives.

94TH CONGRESS
1ST SESSION

H. R. 7912

IN THE HOUSE OF REPRESENTATIVES

JUNE 16, 1975

Mr. HALL introduced the following bill; which was referred to the Committee on Ways and Means

A BILL

To amend the Internal Revenue Code of 1954 to increase the exemption for purposes of the Federal estate tax, to increase the estate tax marital deduction, and to provide an alternate method of valuing certain real property for estate tax purposes.

1   *Be it enacted by the Senate and House of Representa-*

2   *tives of the United States of America in Congress assembled,*

3   That (a) section 2052 of the Internal Revenue Code of

4   1954 (relating to exemption for purposes of the Federal

5   estate tax) is amended by striking out "$60,000" and

6   inserting in lieu thereof "$200,000",

I—O

labor continued to oppose revenue sharing, but by this time opposition had been abandoned by almost everybody else. On August 16, 1972, the Senate Finance Committee reported out a bill also substantially different from the House version, modified to favor the Nixon position somewhat more. (As with Ways and Means, the "mark-up sessions" on the bill were almost all private and closed sessions.)

Action was then interrupted by the summer presidential nominating conventions and was not resumed until early September, after the Labor Day recess. As usual, floor action was more open and creative in the Senate. Thirty amendments were offered on the floor—ten times as many as were offered in the House—although only a few relatively minor amendments were adopted. All efforts to restore the House version failed, so that when the Senate did pass the bill by an overwhelming 64 votes to 20 on September 12, there remained a very large problem for the Conference Committee (the all-important committee made up of members from both House and Senate which functions to allow both chambers to draft identical bills for passage).[26]

House and Senate conferees met almost immediately following Senate passage and by September 25 managed to iron out differences between the two versions. One of their compromises is a good illustration of what these two great chambers often have to do in order to coexist. The biggest difference in the two versions was in the formula for how to allocate the funds, with the Senate formula favoring city and rural aid and the House version bending more toward the larger states. The Conference Committee Report—that is, the final version to be presented in identical form to the House and the Senate—provided that *both* formulas were to be included and that each state could choose the one most advantageous to it. No wonder they say a camel is a race horse designed by a committee.

On October 12, 1972, three months short of four years after President Nixon's first revenue sharing proposal, the House adopted the Conference Report by a vote of 265 to 10. However, in an unusual move, the House amended the Conference Committee bill to prevent states from using revenue sharing funds to meet the dollar-matching requirements of federal welfare programs. This move could have cost the program still another year, except for Senate action to adopt the House proviso. The Senate adopted this final version by a vote of 59 to 19. On October 20, President Nixon signed the State and Local Fiscal Assistance Act of 1972. But to what extent was this a presidential program after all? The act differed significantly from his original plan, and it had taken him nearly four years to get it. True, it had come from the White House, and executive lobbying had helped turn Mills around. But for Mills's switch the president had had to pay a heavy price, and that price is a measure of the creative role that Congress played in the framing of this legislation.

Congressional influence had primarily been committee influence. However, the floor, especially the Senate floor, had once again proven its ability to count heavily in the making of laws. Party leadership had also come into the picture, as usual in the role of conduit rather than user of discipline. Chairman Mills had kept his party colleagues informed by consultation on the bill with the party leadership. But little effort seems to have been made to keep members in line for voting. In this particular instance that would not have been necessary anyway, because there seems to have been

[26]See David Vogler, *The Third House* (Evanston: Northwestern University Press, 1971).

broad consensus for revenue sharing in some form. The final form bears the heavy stamp of presidential planning. On the other hand, Congress proved that there is almost always room for legislative creativity. Yet the question remains: Will this creativity always require four years to express itself?

THE EFFECT OF THE LEGISLATIVE ASSEMBLY ON ITS MEMBERS

The assembly's struggle to cope with governing has its effect on the individual members as well as on the organizational structure of the institution. This is simply another dimension of the contradictory relationship between representing and governing. The effect of the legislative function on the membership can be summed up in a single word—*careerism.* Most of the data on the membership tend to point in the same direction, indicating that during the past century or so, Congress has declined as a place for amateurs and has become an institution filled with individuals who intend to make their careers as legislators.[27]

As late as the 1840s, the average length of service in the House was less than two years, and the average length of service in the Senate was less than four years. This meant that many members were resigning before their terms of office were over in order to seek opportunities in other governmental or private careers. And it also meant a very large proportion of members were defeated for reelection. By the end of the 1960s the average length of service for members of the House was nearly ten years, and the average length of service for senators was nearly twelve. Another indication of the change can be found in the eagerness of House members and senators to seek reelection. In the 1880s, after full post–Civil War national stability had been restored, around 40 percent of the Senate members and around 60 percent of the House members had been elected to those posts more than once. During the 1960s, well over 60 percent of the Senate was composed of reelected members, and well over 90 percent of the House was composed of such seasoned persons.

Other data help complete the picture of careerism, giving the impression that the way of life in the House and Senate has also become more and more professionalized. For example, members

[27]See Carl Friedrich, *Constitutional Government and Democracy,* 4th ed. (Waltham, Mass.: Blaisdell, 1968); Theodore Lowi, "Introduction," in *Legislative Politics U.S.A.;* Samuel P. Huntington, "Congressional Responses to the Twentieth Century," in *The Congress and America's Future,* ed. David Truman (Englewood Cliffs, N.J.: Prentice-Hall, 1965), chapter 1; Nelson Polsby, "The Institutionalization of the House of Representatives," *American Political Science Review,* March 1968, p. 144; and H. Douglas Price, "The Congressional Career—Then and Now," in *Congressional Behavior,* ed. Nelson Polsby (New York: Random House, 1971). Huntington has referred to the phenomenon of careerism as "insulation." Polsby has called it "institutionalization."

The congressman and his constituency: Illinois Senator Adlai Stevenson III with his friend and supporter, Mayor Daley, "Boss" of the Chicago Democratic organization.

tend to remain on the committees to which they were originally assigned. They specialize in the work of those committees and tend to project their reputations outward from their committees. They are in large part tied to their committees by the seniority rule, which identifies seniority in terms of continuous service on the committee rather than general length of tenure in the House or Senate. Then, too, the respect of other members for the knowledge of their colleagues in their areas of committee specialization tends to reinforce the seniority principle.

Finally, one of the most dramatic indications of careerism and professionalization can be found in the fact that it now takes virtually a lifetime career in the House to become a legislative leader. This is in tremendous contrast to the other branches, where there are many hundreds of top level administrators and judges who have enjoyed careers in other areas before moving laterally into high office. This is truly ironic, considering that the legislature ought to be the place where the rate of turnover is sufficient to respond to the fast pace of change in society at large.

Even as recently as 1900 a member of the House could hope to become Speaker after ten years of service. But abruptly with the beginning of the new century, the situation changed. Since 1903 there have been twelve Speakers, and only one of these, the famous John Bankhead, had served fewer than *twenty years* in the House prior to his elevation to the Speakership. Only two of the Speakers went on to other, perhaps higher, offices—Garner to four years as vice-president (1932–1936), and Gillett to ten years in the Senate (1924–1934). For all of the other Speakers, the House was a career from start to finish.

This careerism has expressed itself in virtually all of the other top leadership positions in the past generation. Not only have these leaders clocked long service in their chambers; they have also gone through a period of orderly apprenticeship and promotion through lesser offices prior to reaching the top ones. According to Barbara Hinckley, between 1949 and 1966, there were sixty-seven cases of leadership change. In sixty-one of these, the House voted to elevate an existing leader to the next higher rung. Serious and contested departures from routine promotion actually occurred only twice.[28] This is careerism in the extreme. Seniority is important; but in the election of general party and parliamentary posts, where committee seniority is not involved, the members consistently choose people in the orderly line of promotion, as one would expect in a far more hierarchically organized institution.

Any member who wants to be influential in Congress must plan a career in Congress. The first two or three terms in the House and most of the first term in the Senate involve parliamentary education, specialization, making friends. But since most members of the House and Senate are over forty at the start of their legislative careers, they reach something of a critical point in their lives just as they begin to approach the point of real influence in Congress. This is especially critical for members of the House, which is less exalted than the Senate as a culmination of one's career. House members confront a "fourth term crisis," when they must either strike out for the Senate or the governorship, or concentrate exclusively on cultivating true influence and recognition in Congress.[29] Once this decision has been made, the goals are survival, longevity, institutional loyalty; and the rewards tend to follow accordingly.

Consequently, one rarely finds a member of the House or Senate accepting higher office in the administration or in business. In recent years, one can name Truman, Nixon, Kennedy, Johnson,

[28]Hinckley, *The Seniority System in Congress*, p. 97. For a still more intensive analysis of the same phenomenon, see Robert L. Peabody, "Party Leadership Change in the U.S. House of Representatives," in *New Perspectives on the House of Representatives*, ed. Robert L. Peabody and Nelson Polsby (Chicago: Rand-McNally, 1969), pp. 359–391.

[29]See Huntington, "Congressional Responses to the Twentieth Century," p. 11; another good treatment of the "protégé-apprentice" system is Richard Fenno, "The Internal Distribution of Influence: The House," in *The Congress and America's Future*, p. 71.

Goldwater, Miller, Humphrey, McGovern, Eagleton, and Ford who were willing to throw over their congressional investment for a nomination for president or vice-president. But these are a very small number of all the members of Congress between 1944 and 1974, and in each instance the risk involved the very top offices in the American political hierarchy. In contrast, it should be noted that Melvin Laird was the only member of Congress to join the Nixon cabinet, and Stuart Udall was the only member of Congress to join the Kennedy administration. In fact, among the top seventy-five leaders in the Kennedy administration, President Kennedy, Vice-president Johnson, and former Congressman Stuart Udall were the *only* three ever to have served in the House or Senate. Most executive branch appointees with congressional experience are former congressional staffers or defeated congressmen who are taken care of with a patronage appointment.

The very intense and elaborate career commitment necessitated by the organization of the House and Senate of course guarantees a great deal of institutional loyalty. But too often this loyalty insulates Congress from its constituencies and from the other institutions of government. Congress is not as dynamically interconnected with the society as a representative institution ought to be. What else can be said about the fact that members of Congress are serving an *average* of over five terms? What other argument can be made against the fact that, whereas in 1897 there were thirty-four congressmen of two terms or less for every one who had served ten terms, in the 1960s, for each ten-term member of Congress there were not even two members who had served two terms or less? What other response is there to the fact that 90 percent of all congressional incumbents are reelected? Congress has become a Jacob's Ladder, suspended from the ground and from the heavens by its own doing. Congress is truly a "separated power." But is this really the kind of separation of powers the founders intended?

SUMMING UP:
CONGRESS AS A SYSTEM OF CONTROLS

Although Congress is a Jacob's Ladder, it is nevertheless a ladder worth climbing. Things could be worse. Congress could have become, as is true of many of its sister institutions in the world, a "treadmill to oblivion."[30] Congress is without any question an important part of the scheme of government. Whether or not all of its flaws and problems flowed inescapably from the effort to partici-

---

[30]This magnificent phrase was the title of Fred Allen's autobiography (Boston: Little, Brown, 1954). Allen was a great vaudeville radio comedian who failed to make the transition to television.

Table 10.8	Congress: Weapons of Control

1. Statutes
   Public laws: Authorization acts
   Public laws: Revenue acts
   Public laws: Appropriations acts
   Private legislation

2. Oversight of administration
   Hearings
   Investigation
   Supervision (congressional lobbying)

3. Oversight of citizens (committee as grand jury)
   Hearings
   Investigation

4. Advise and consent (Senate)

5. Debate

6. Direct committee government (public works)

7. Congressional veto

The four types of statutes are listed here only to provide the proper perspectives. Each has received some treatment elsewhere, in chapter 9 or 10. The distinction between hearings and investigations is easy to make in principle but hard to maintain in practice. *Hearings* are held on an existing bill or package of bills; *investigations* are held on a general problem area, with the hope that legislative proposals will emerge.

pate effectively in government, it is difficult to argue that less effort on the part of Congress to participate in government would be preferable in order to provide a more representative assembly. For Congress has not merely staked a claim to participation in real government by occasionally writing laws and amending presidential proposals. Congress has drawn to itself several additional weapons of control through which it has been able to participate more effectively in the maintenance of conquest in the United States. Some of these weapons would be unavailable to Congress if it were not organized in its peculiar way. Table 10.8 is an outline of the primary weapons of control available to Congress. Few need lengthy treatment to be appreciated.

Statutes While the statute (item 1 of the table) is the only positive power given Congress by the Constitution,[31] it should be understood that all laws are made by, and only by, Congress.

Making law is Congress's most important weapon of control for at least two reasons. First, a law is the broadest and most legitimate method of control of our society. Second, it is the source or basis of the other weapons. In everyday political affairs the other weapons may appear to be more important. Congress contributes to this

[31]The Constitution also distinguishes revenue statutes by requiring that bills of such nature originate in the House. The only other weapon provided by the Constitution is to the Senate, which can use its power to approve top presidential appointments and to adopt treaties (advise and consent) as weapons of control in the broader sense.

impression by passing laws of such vagueness that agency and departmental heads often end up doing the real lawmaking, leaving to Congress the function of looking over bureaucratic shoulders and kibitzing. Many observers have concluded that this latter function is Congress's only real opportunity to engage in the act of governing; but this conclusion should be avoided, for, if Congress lets the lawmaking pass to administrators, the other weapons will eventually atrophy as well.[32]

Oversight Nevertheless, Congress does maintain considerable power of "oversight" even when the statutes give administrators clear guidelines. Committee members delight in being able to call or visit an agency which falls under the jurisdiction of their committee and get trembling cooperation on an appointment or a contract for a constituent. This "supervision," or congressional lobbying, is not nearly as significant, however, as the power of Congress and its committees to subpoena witnesses and compel testimony. The courts have allowed Congress to interpret oversight powers quite broadly when the witnesses are administrators. Administrators have a public trust and are obliged to respond at length to members of Congress, from whom the trust was received. Most programs and agencies receive some kind of scrutiny every year during the course of hearings on appropriations. This is an occasion when Congress— more specifically the relevant subcommittee of the House or Senate Appropriations Committee—can examine the past behavior of bureaucrats as well as the budget for money being requested.[33]

An important distinction should be made between hearings and investigations. In both, the committee usually possesses the authority to subpoena witnesses, take oaths, cross-examine, compel testimony on pain of contempt, and bring criminal charges for perjury. However, the hearing is a process concerned with a specific bill or proposal; each committee may choose to hold hearings for any bill referred to it, and the questions usually revolve around the building of a record with regard to that bill. The investigation requires a specific authorization by Congress for a standing committee or a special committee to examine a broad area or problem in order to come up later with proposals for legislation.

It is with the investigatory weapon that problems begin to emerge. As long as the committee limits itself to administrative witnesses in its hearings or its investigations, it has sufficient claim to its authority. Where citizens are witnesses before committees, the Supreme Court has required that each question must be shown to

---

[32]The consequences of delegating broad legislative powers from Congress to the Executive are discussed in Theodore Lowi, *The End of Liberalism* (New York: Norton, 1969).

[33]Richard Fenno, *The Power of the Purse* (Boston: Little, Brown, 1966). For an assessment of how it looks from the other end, see Aaron Wildavsky, *The Politics of the Budgetary Process* (Boston: Little, Brown, 1964).

serve a "legislative purpose" before the witness is required to respond.[34] If the committee seeks to investigate wrongdoing under a statute rather than investigate the implementation of the statutes by the administrators, the committee has suddenly converted itself into a combination grand jury and trial court and as such appears to threaten the rights of citizens. With this realization we may suddenly become less interested in maintaining Congress's power and more interested in limiting that power to strictly legislative purposes.

Probably the most important twentieth century example of the use of congressional power of hearings and investigations was the House Committee on Un-American Activities (popularly called HUAC). It was abolished in 1974, after thirty years as a standing committee to investigate questions of loyalty and security. Loyalty and security are extremely vague concepts for which almost any question could be defended as serving a legislative purpose. For years the committee badgered private citizens and administrators about their activities twenty or more years prior to the time of the hearing. Often the questions concerned themselves with the beliefs and associations of witnesses rather than with activities that might seriously have affected national security.

More often than not, the committee already had the answers to the questions, gained from extralegal access to FBI files, but went on to ask the questions in order to enter them onto the public record. Whenever a witness refused to answer, on the grounds that any answer might tend to be self-incriminating, the committee would denounce that witness as a "Fifth Amendment Communist."[35] Because so many of the questions of the committee concerned political beliefs and associations that are protected by the First Amendment, there was apparently a widespread concern in Congress about abuses of civil liberties. Although no one ever succeeded in establishing the principle that the First Amendment protects citizens against questions by congressional committees, this concern was eventually expressed in the abolition of the committee.[36]

However, HUAC did not exceed its authority any further than did the Senate Select Committee to Investigate the 1972 Presidential Campaign Activities (the so-called Ervin Committee), which was set up in 1973 to conduct the now historic Watergate investigation. The Ervin committee was not a standing committee but a select committee set up specifically to investigate a general problem. Although its authority rested upon a Senate resolution charging the committee

---

[34]*McGrain* v. *Daugherty*, 273 U.S. 135 (1927).

[35]The Supreme Court sought to protect witnesses at congressional investigations by extending to them the rights of the Fifth Amendment, which were designed to protect persons from being witnesses against themselves in court cases where they were defendants. *Blau* v. *U.S.*, 340 U.S. 159 (1950), and *Barenblatt* v. *U.S.*, 360 U.S. 109 (1959).

[36]For more on the problem, see chapter 13 on *Stamler* v. *Mitchell*.

with the responsibility to produce new legislation on "the electoral process by which the President of the United States is chosen," the committee did not long stay within the framework. Instead, the chairman and the more vocal members of his committee proclaimed almost from the start that their job was not to explore new legislation on campaign finance and campaign ethics but to "expose wrongdoing," to "bring out all the truth," and to "alert the public."

These tasks, however laudable they may sound, are strictly unconstitutional, if Supreme Court decisions beginning in the 1920s with *McGrain* v. *Daugherty* have any meaning. Virtually every question asked of the Watergate witnesses by the committee or the counsels of the committee that could have eventually related to criminal charges was an infringement on the rights of the witnesses. There is a difference between the excesses committed by HUAC and those committed by the Ervin Committee or by earlier committees to investigate problems in the drug industry or problems of monopoly. HUAC was investigating beliefs and associations on which the First Amendment provides that "Congress shall make no law." Although a very large difference, it should not overshadow abuses of power by any committee.[37]

To all of these concerns one might respond that Congress must have the power to bring before its committees powerful administrators and knowledgeable citizens to testify on matters that require legislation. When a committee seeks to expose wrongdoing under the statutes, as well as to gain information necessary to amend the statutes, where should its power stop? It should be quite clear that the power of "oversight" is at its greatest over administrators. However, as soon as the administrator reaches a point before the committee where his answers may involve him in criminal charges, the administrator has the same rights as any citizen. These rights should not be denied merely to alert the public or to expose for the sake of exposure.

It is very difficult to determine when the cause of good legislation is served by congressional investigation of private citizens. Those who hated the HUAC investigations of the 1950s seem generally to have approved the Ervin investigations of the 1970s. Yet all the rough treatment of witnesses produced very little legislation. Moreover, in both instances, the committee already had most of the information and was using the public interrogation of witnesses mainly to enter the information onto the public record. Clearly the investigatory process mainly serves the political interests of those who control the investigation. But since this weapon is inevitably

[37]For a catalogue of abuses, see Telford Taylor, *Grand Inquest* (New York: Simon & Schuster, 1955).

going to be used, we should try to understand it as a weapon of control, rather than as a neutral instrument of deliberation, and try to surround it with as many limits and guidelines as possible.

Why cooperate when a congressional committee seeks to govern by using investigatory weapons without providing all the rights available to citizens before courts? One important reason is that the risks of cooperating with the committee are often a great deal less than the risks of standing on one's rights and not cooperating. Noncooperation in a public and highly popular investigation runs an extremely high risk of disgrace—that is, conviction in the court of public opinion. In contrast, cooperation, especially in the spirit of contrition, can mean safety from social jeopardy and often leads to exoneration or probation in later criminal procedures.

Probably the most famous case of cooperation was that of Whitaker Chambers, who had been a Communist Party member in the 1930s, apparently a rather active Communist. By making a clean breast of his "evil ways" in 1946 and 1947 before HUAC, he eventually went scot free, later publishing a best-selling book *(Witness)* and ending his life in comfort. His adversary, Alger Hiss, who did not cooperate, was eventually convicted of perjury and sent to prison. The outcome could have been very different if Hiss had not insisted upon being a "hostile witness." Incidentally, the man who "cracked the case" and rose through it to great political prominence was a young California congressman, Richard Nixon. Perhaps the men around President Nixon in the Watergate scandal had learned their lesson from the Hiss case and President Nixon's frequent reference to it, because those who cooperated with the Ervin Committee received extremely light sentences, if any at all.

Advise and consent The other weapons of control are not so difficult to describe or so problematic to use. The Senate has a constitutional grant of power to advise and consent—to approve treaties and presidential appointments. Since the power to approve involves the power to disapprove, it also involves the power to amend or to set conditions. The Senate has been known to avail itself of its treaty power and appointment power, but given all the complaints about presidential encroachment heard on Capitol Hill, it is a wonder that this weaponry is used so infrequently. A few recent cases, such as the eventual exposure and rejection of Richard Kleindienst, nominee for attorney general, and Patrick Gray, nominee for director of the FBI, during the Nixon administration, served to remind all future presidents that this power is significant. Presidents are usually so fearful of the Senate's authority to set conditions on treaties that they generally attempt to pursue the same purposes through "executive agreements," which have the effect of treaties but do not have to run the gamut of advice and

consent in the Senate.[38] However, executive agreements can be abrogated by the mere passage of a congressional resolution to that effect. Indeed, if the Senate has lacked influence over foreign affairs, this cannot be because it lacks the weaponry.

Debate   The value to Congress of the three remaining weapons listed in Table 10.8 should not be taken lightly, although they will

[38]The similarities and differences between executive agreements and treaties will be taken up in chapter 14.

be given only a brief review here. Debate is, of course, part of the legislative process, but it is quite an effective instrument of direct control when great issues are treated in meaningful ways. As early as the 1880s Woodrow Wilson lamented the decline of debate because it can be such a great method of educating citizens. Debate, even without eloquent speeches, is still important, because it can produce a record of legislative intent that can have great influence over administrative conduct. One of the best examples of debate used for this purpose is the six weeks of debate over the Cooper-Church Amendment seeking to halt aid to Laos.

Direct committee government   Item 6 of Table 10.8, direct committee government, refers to the practice of delegating certain congressional powers from the Congress at large to one of its committees. Either chamber can grant a committee power to approve a proposed agency project without having to return to Congress for authorization and appropriation. This is usually described as a requirement that the agency and the committee "come into agreement," but it is actually a delegation of congressional power to a committee. The device was in especially wide use during the 1950s and early 1960s, when so much money was being spent on defense and space public works. This was Congress's way of guaranteeing itself a role in handing out some of the choicest projects.[39]

Congressional veto   Finally, there is the congressional veto. Existing laws grant power to the president to reorganize executive agencies on condition that the reorganization plan be submitted to Congress. Congress may then veto or alter the plan by joint resolution. However, if Congress takes no action within sixty days, the plan can be considered law and put into effect. Although the congressional veto seems to be an extra safeguard against executive discretion, some consider it a delegation of still greater power to the president, because Congress has only sixty days to change the reorganization plan to suit itself. But whether this is a sign of congressional weakness or congressional strength, there is some doubt as to whether this veto can be used in areas other than administrative reorganization. An interesting constitutional question is involved, since the legislative veto reverses the constitutional relationship between president and Congress, where it is the legislature which proposes and the executive who has the power to veto.

---

[39]Comments on this weapon will be found in Richard Neustadt, "Politicians and Bureaucrats," in *The Congress and America's Future;* see also Raymond Dawson, "Congressional Innovation and Intervention in Defense Policy: Legislative Authorization of Weapons Systems," *American Political Science Review,* March 1962, pp. 42–57.

Draining Away Legislative Potential

Looking back over these weapons, it is clear enough that they comprise a formidable arsenal—but for what? On closer inspection it becomes necessary at least to ponder the possibility that Congress is good at governing in almost every way except the way originally intended—making laws. Congress fritters away much of its real power on private bills, cheap pork barrel legislation, and individual self-advancement. Congress allows even more of its legislative potential to drain away whenever it passes statutes that are extremely vague in their intention and severely lacking in guidelines to the administrators. The courts no longer review congressional legislation for whether there is too broad a "delegation of power"—that is, to determine whether Congress has violated the principle of the separation of powers by abdicating the legislative function to the administrative branch. This means that the courts have decided to allow Congress to commit legislative suicide if it so wishes.[40] When Congress delegates so much of its decision-making power to administrators, it *must* rely upon its other weapons if it is to maintain its serious participation in governing. Will this work?

As each new budget year approaches, Congress can rely upon its powers of oversight by using the appropriations hearings as a method of substantive review of the programs. Although this particular weapon is relied upon more than any other, most of its value as a weapon capable of providing real influence in policy decisions turns out on further inspection to be a myth. Most of these hearings are lost in the details rather than the policies of the agency.[41] So unsatisfactory is the process of committee oversight of administrators that there has been continual talk in recent years of the possibility of requiring annual *authorization* to go along with annual appropriation. (This practice of Congress not only gives broad delegations of power to agencies and departments but also gives a no-time-limit authorization with no automatic or routine way by which the programs come back before the relevant standing committees.)

Annual authorization is, however, unlikely to be adopted except in specific instances.[42] The appropriations process is already an annual affair, and experience with it ought to be sufficient to cast doubt upon the prospect that legislative oversight of administration will ever make up glaring weaknesses in original legislation.

---

[40]A brilliant new treatment of this problem will be found in Sotirios Barber, *The Constitution and the Delegation of Congressional Power* (Chicago: University of Chicago Press, 1975). For an appeal to the courts to revive the practice of reviewing the constitutionality of delegated legislative power, see Lowi, *The End of Liberalism,* especially chapter 10.

[41]Compare with Wildavsky, *The Politics of the Budgetary Process.* For a popular review of some of the limitations on the Congress's power of the purse, see Timothy Ingram, "The Billions in the White House Basement," *Washington Monthly,* January 1972.

[42]John S. Saloma, *Congress and the New Politics* (Boston: Little, Brown, 1969), pp. 145–153.

Reforms in 1974 leading to the establishment of new budget committees in the Senate and in the House reflect upon the weaknesses of the established methods of oversight without necessarily promising any fundamental improvements. One hopeful part of the reform is that the new budget procedures call for full debate twice each year in the House and in the Senate on budgetary issues. It is too early to tell what effect these procedures will have. We can only join with one of the most optimistic appraisals of the new budget procedures in Congress by saying, "It can't hurt."[43]

Yet, no one who follows the printed record of testimony in committee hearings held for the purpose of reviewing agency and departmental policies can read many pages before finding out that the concerns of committees are very particularistic. It is rare for a committee to engage in deliberation on a grand scale. Committees conduct their most serious business in private, and the committee membership is distinctly unrepresentative of the larger body. Perspective is deliberately narrow and specialized. Committees often become special advocates for the agencies under their supervision. We may speak of committees as "little legislatures" only in the sense that they deal in little things. If Congress intends to participate in governing, making law is inescapable. It cannot delegate large chunks of its legislative power to administrative agencies and hope to gain it back in bits and pieces through oversight *or* instructive debate. Even these very worthy weapons of congressional participation in government will atrophy and disappear if Congress ceases to assert itself clearly as a legislative body.

It is foolish to imagine that Congress can altogether stem the flow of governmental power toward the executive branch. But it is even more foolish to imagine that Congress can maintain an effective influence on executive government by yielding to that flow, encouraging it, swimming with it. We can call Congress's attitude of submission by the technical term *delegation of power.* We can defend it as constitutional (indeed that is the prevailing attitude of the Supreme Court). And we can justify it by the argument that Congress is unable to deal with the complex modern world except by taking full advantage of the expertise in administrative agencies.

But whatever we call it, congressional cooperation with the executive branch that takes the form of habitually vague and ill-considered statutes and that relies on administrators to make the real policy decisions could lead us directly, though by a different route, back to the very "tyranny of the executive" and "taxation without representation" for which the original republic founded in 1776 was supposed to be an answer. If Congress intends to maintain its role in governing, it must look to its lawmaking; that is the source and foundation of real representative government.

[43]Eileen Shanahan, *New York Times,* April 20, 1975.

Chapter 11 Instrumentation of Control: The Presidency

The tyranny of the legislature is really the danger most to be feared, and will continue to be so for many years to come. The tyranny of the executive power will come in its turn, but at a more distant period.
Thomas Jefferson, 1789

For the existing requirements of American foreign policy we have hobbled the President by too niggardly a grant of power.
Senator J. William Fulbright, 1961

Our country has come far toward the concentration in its national Executive of unchecked power over foreign relations. . . . So far has this process advanced that . . . it is no longer accurate to characterize our Government . . . as one of separated powers checked and balanced against each other.
Senator J. William Fulbright, 1970

These are exceedingly difficult times for studying the office of president. President Nixon's resignation, unprecedented in American history, rendered inoperative a very large body of conventional wisdom on the presidency and executive power. No new consensus among presidential experts has had time to develop. Pre-1973 treatments strike the eye and the ear as downright quaint. In 1965, the distinguished political scientist James MacGregor Burns observed that if Lord Bryce had been alive in the 1960s he would almost certainly have revised his famous essay of the late nineteenth century, "Why Great Men Are Never Chosen President," and would now have entitled it "Why Great Men *Are* Chosen President."[1] As recently as 1971, the equally distinguished Robert K. Carr could still quote with approval Clinton Rossiter's famous 1950s characterization of the functions and roles of

[1]James M. Burns, *Presidential Government* (Boston: Houghton Mifflin, 1965), p. 295.

Table 11.1	The Post-Roosevelt Model of the President

Presidential Roles Drawn from the Constitution
1. Chief of state, representing the American people as a nation.
2. Chief executive, managing the government's executive branch.
3. Commander-in-chief, first in command of the nation's armed forces.
4. Chief diplomat, whose primacy in foreign affairs has been recognized since the time of President Washington, in spite of the Senate's power to advise and consent on treaties.
5. Chief legislator, with an important role in determining the legislative agenda of Congress.

Presidential Functions Added by Custom and Usage
1. Voice of the party.
2. Voice of the people.
3. Protector of the peace.
4. Manager of prosperity.
5. World leader.

Based on Clinton Rossiter, *The American Presidency* (New York: Harcourt, Brace, 1956), pp. 4–25.

the president, shown in Table 11.1.[2] All of these references were removed from the 1974 edition of the same work.

The characterizations are not factually incorrect; their optimism simply seems excessive in the context of the 1970s. This optimism had arisen with big government, beginning perhaps with Woodrow Wilson, certainly with Franklin Roosevelt. The only way to cope with the problem of big government was by expanding the presidency. The more power in the chief executive's hands, the more he could do—and the more *good* he could do. One could have argued that the bigger the job the more *evil* that could be accomplished as well; but no people were making such an argument. If they had, they would have been drowned out by the noises of the friends of presidential power, who considered the president the true representative of the national majority.[3] For them the problem was how to make him powerful enough to carry out the mandate.

For example, in 1937, one of the most famous studies of the presidency ever done opened its report with the appeal, "The President needs help."[4] And in 1959, far and away the most sophisticated and the most widely read presidential analyst could open his major work: "My theme is personal power and its politics: What it is, how to get it, how to keep it, how to use it. My interest is in what a President can do to make his own will felt within his own Administration; what he can do, as one man among many to carry

[2]Robert K. Carr et al., *Essentials of American Democracy* (New York: Holt, Rinehart and Winston, 1971); see chapter 14, especially p. 288.
[3]Robert A. Dahl, *Preface to Democratic Theory* (Chicago: University of Chicago Press, 1956); see especially the references and commentary on this work in Willmoore Kendall, "The Two Majorities," *Midwest Journal of Political Science*, November 1960.
[4]*Report of the President's Committee on Administrative Management* (Washington, D.C.: Government Printing Office, 1937).

his own choices through that maze of personalities and institutions called the Government of the United States."[5]

Dissenters from this faith were disregarded as conservatives until 1973, when almost overnight the dissent became the majority opinion. Presidential mystique began to take on some of the character of the *Fellowship of the Ring*. In that fantasy, the ring gave the bearer great powers, but it also had an insidious influence upon him, making him increasingly evil, wanting more and more to do evil things the longer he wore the ring. Many sought the ring for its powers; yet everyone feared it and sought to destroy whoever possessed it.[6]

Questioning conventional wisdom is a healthy sign, especially where power is concerned. And the shrinking esteem for the presidency may yet bring that gigantic office back toward a closer approximation of its constitutional dimensions. At least this gives us a starting point, enabling us to focus on those features of the presidency that are least likely to change. Some of the features define the *purpose* or *purposes* of the presidency while others define its *sources* and *resources*. Since neither purposes nor resources change appreciably, except over a period of decades, we have here a sound basis for exploring continuity and change. For even when variations between presidents are dramatic, the permanent changes are likely to be marginal. And if the unchanging features arise out of a constitutional definition of this office—as most of them do—then we will also have some dependable criteria for judging presidential conduct.

THE PRESIDENT: PURPOSE AND POWERS

Despite the consensus of the past half century that the presidency ought to be a large and growing institution, there has been considerable confusion about the purposes and powers of that office. Bigness for what? Power for what? Control, but on the basis of what kind of authority?

Article II, called "the most loosely drawn chapter" of the Constitution,[7] encourages confusion. Section 1 of Article II states only that the "Executive Power shall be vested in a President of the United States of America." The remainder of that long first section concerns itself with the terms of office of the president and vice-

---

[5]Richard E. Neustadt, *Presidential Power* (New York: Wiley, 1960), p. vii.

[6]This trilogy by J. R. R. Tolkien should be read primarily for its pure and joyous entertainment. However, morality and political philosophy are inherent in the dramatic aspects of the story. Tolkien is of course not unique in his view that the possession of power is likely to have a corrupting influence on the possessor.

[7]E. S. Corwin, *The President: Office and Powers* (New York: New York University Press, 1957). First published in 1940, this remains the definitive work on the constitutional basis of the presidency.

president, the qualifications for office, the manner of election and succession, and the oath of office. Sections 2 and 3 provide for the formal powers of the president, but nowhere is the Constitution clear on what purposes those powers are expected to serve. The fourth and final section of Article II provides for impeachment. The only explicit statement of the purpose of the office comes near the end of a list of provisions for powers and duties: "he shall take care that the Laws be faithfully executed." The Constitution does specify other purposes elsewhere in the document, but these are stated as obligations of the national *government,* not as obligations or purposes of the president or the executive branch.

The looseness of Article II, coupled with the vagueness of its relationship to the general delegation of powers to the national government, has given rise to a variety of outrageous claims for the office of president. The following description exemplifies the pre-Watergate outlook, as expressed by an important counselor to the president:

> He vetoed minor bills that he did not like, impounded appropriated funds that he did not need, ignored restrictive amendments that he found unconstitutional and improvised executive action for bills that would not pass.
> He did not feel obligated to risk unnecessary delay and possible defeat by sending every important international agreement to the Senate for approval as a formal, long-termed treaty. Nor did he follow Eisenhower's precedent of seeking Congressional resolutions of approval for major foreign policy initiatives. He dispatched personal and

official advisers on important missions abroad. . . . He invoked the claim of executive privilege to prevent Congressional investigators from harassing State and Defense Department civil servants.[8]

It turns out that the counselor in question was not John Ehrlichman defending Richard Nixon but was in fact Theodore Sorenson speaking for President Kennedy.

When the shoe was on the foot of the other party in the 1970s, President Nixon proclaimed his right *to proceed without congressional authorization or even consultation* to invade Cambodia, to bomb Laos, and to engage in saturation bombing of North Vietnam at the risk of total war. Nixon had claimed his power was inherent in his responsibilities as commander-in-chief "to defend the security of our American men."[9] Kennedy adherents did not like this, but they had prepared the way for it.[10] In spite of differences among the various observers, pre-Watergate opinion seems to have been that the presidency could (and perhaps should) be as large as a president could make it. As President Kennedy put the case, "The Constitution is a very wise document. It permits the President to assume just about as much power as he is capable of handling. . . . I believe that the President should use whatever power is necessary to do the job unless it is expressly forbidden by the Constitution."[11] In the wake of Watergate the consensus among political scientists, journalists, and presidents and their staffs has weakened enough to allow once again the posing of an old question: Does the president have *prerogative?* Prerogative is a sovereign right to act without limit, hindrance, or interference. Is this the way our presidency is defined in the Constitution?

Presidents Kennedy, Johnson, and Nixon would probably have answered that question strongly in the affirmative. Historically, the answer would probably have been negative. Article II obliges the president to see that the laws are faithfully executed but provides for the powers of the national government in the *legislative* article—Article I, Section 8. This would suggest that the presidency was expected to be an agent of the government rather than the government itself. It means that the office was not to be the crown (the government itself), even though most assuredly its occupant was to operate as the head of state. Inquiry into the purpose and form of the presidency requires separating the office into its two main dimensions—foreign and domestic.

---

[8]Theodore C. Sorenson, *Kennedy* (New York: Harper & Row, 1965), p. 347.

[9]President Nixon asserted this on several occasions, including his address to the nation of April 30, 1970, and his press conference of May 8, 1970.

[10]For an example of the reaction of Kennedy people to Nixon uses of "their" presidency, see the eloquent plea for constitutional proportion by Arthur Schlesinger, Jr., "Presidential War," *New York Times Magazine,* January 7, 1973, p. 12.

[11]Quoted in James MacGregor Burns, *John Kennedy: A Political Profile* (New York: Harcourt, Brace, 1959), p. 275.

Presidential Purposes and International Powers

The most important presidential powers are those that equip the president to deal with other countries. In the list of formal presidential powers in the Constitution, there are apparently only two upon which no limitations are placed. One of these is the power to "receive Ambassadors and other public ministers" (Article II, Section 3). The other is the "power to grant reprieves and pardons for Offences against the United States, except in Cases of impeachment" (Article II, Section 2). These are given further form by a third provision which establishes a single rather than multiple head of the executive branch. (There was a great deal of controversy among convention delegates over this issue, many fearing that a single chief executive would indeed combine too many elements of the kingship the Revolution had opposed; the decision in favor of a single chief executive was an extremely significant one.)

These three provisions go far toward defining the form and nature of presidential power. The power to "recognize" other countries and to seek recognition for the United States among other countries gives the president the power to accept, or not to accept, the claim of a ruling group in another country that it is indeed in control of its territory and population, that it has the right to commit that population, write contracts for it, and claim territory or defend territory against encroachment by ruling groups of other countries. The power to grant pardons, reprieves, and amnesties involves the power of life and death over all individuals who may be a threat to the internal order and security of the United States, whether or not it is used on as large a scale as it was by President Andrew Johnson, who in 1868 declared full amnesty to all participants in "the Late Rebellion," except those charged with treason or felonies.[12] This power of life and death over individual criminals or political dissenters helps elevate the president to the level of earlier conquerors and kings. It reinforces the image of the president as a person before whom supplicants come to make their pleas.

By investing these three powers in the presidency, the founders obviously intended to use that office to some extent as a personification of national sovereignty. But that still does not answer the question of whether there is prerogative in the presidency—whether these elements of sovereignty allow the president to draw still other powers to himself. Other provisions of the Constitution may help answer this question. Actually, the Constitution seems to stop far short of making the presidency a sovereign office, because it grants no other powers without accompanying them with strong limitations. For example, the president is indeed commander-in-

---

[12]A good review of amnesty will be found in Julius Duscha, "Should There Be Amnesty for the War Resistors?" *New York Times Magazine,* December 24, 1972, p. 7.

The international
presidency: A historic
meeting of East and West,
as President Nixon and
Red Chinese Premier
Chou En-lai open up their
two countries to
diplomacy.

chief, but he can command only on the basis of a declaration of war
made by Congress. The president is given the power to make
treaties with other nations and to appoint ambassadors, but in
neither case can he do so without the "advice and consent" of
two-thirds of the Senate.

Much has been made of the right of the president, recognized by
the Supreme Court, to use executive agreements instead of treaties
to establish relationships with other countries. It is also true that
executive agreements are equivalent to treaties, yet do not have to
be approved by the Senate.[13] However, the overwhelming proportion of executive agreements are actually carried out under direct
authorization of some statute or joint resolution passed by Congress. Even agreements made just prior to the beginning of World
War II, such as Lend-Lease and Mutual Aid, were carried out in
direct furtherance of legislation. The deal made between President
Roosevelt and the British in 1940, whereby we exchanged "50
over-aged destroyers" for a ninety-nine–year lease on certain British bases, is one of several exceptions. But the exceptions are all
extraordinary situations that tend to prove the rule that the

[13]*United States* v. *Pink*, 315 U.S. 203 (1942). See also chapter 14.

president, even in international affairs, generally operates within a legal framework. Many years ago one observer noted that the rise of national power and the pressure on the president to act decisively led to the acquisition of increased power in the hands of *Congress* at the expense of the Senate, because the president must operate under statutory authorization and budgetary appropriations rather than on the authority of a treaty.[14] But none of this suggests that the president has inherent power, or prerogative.

During the 1960s and early 1970s the powers of the presidency seem to have been extended to a large degree. Presidents Johnson and Nixon used their executive authority on a scale unprecedented in a period without a national emergency. The Gulf of Tonkin Resolution of 1965 was not a declaration of war, and the Viet Cong were probably not going to invade our shores. Yet Congress gave its authorization to the president to use all national resources to prosecute the war according to his personal judgment. During this period the government centered around the executive branch as never before. Apparently this new system of presidential power had existed long enough to provide the basis for widespread belief that presidents do have prerogative.

President Nixon's advisers thought so little of the Tonkin Resolution that they cooperated fully with Congress in the move to rescind it in 1970, despite the appearance that its revocation narrowed the power of the president. The president's top legal adviser, William Rehnquist—whom President Nixon later appointed to the Supreme Court as a "strict constructionist"—testified that the president's unilateral and unannounced invasion of Cambodia was no more than a "valid exercise of his constitutional authority as Commander-in-Chief to secure the safety of American forces."[15] This was a claim to inherent power inasmuch as Rehnquist was arguing that the existence of one position in the international system—such as having troops already in the field—was always justification for the next step.

Presidents Johnson and Nixon did get by with their claim to unlimited power to carry out international obligations. But their actions created enormous tensions throughout the country. President Johnson's stock in his own political party began to fall with his personal involvement in Vietnam. He was the first president ever to claim inherent authority to take unilateral action except when the nation was threatened by some kind of imminent danger. He was also the first president in modern times to have to face rejection for renomination by his own party. Presidents Johnson and Nixon claimed inherent authority to take unilateral action, but both were forced to misrepresent the political and military situation in South-

[14]Corwin, *The President*, p. 217.
[15]Quoted in Schlesinger, "Presidential War," p. 12.

east Asia in order to make their claims stick. It is distinctly possible that the tension in these cases, which mounted directly with the presidential claim to emergency powers, contributed to bringing the presidency back toward some proportionate relationship to the other branches—something of a confirmation of the separation of powers.

Yet there is little ground for optimism that a balanced separation of powers can be maintained where foreign rather than domestic national security is at issue. In such cases, neither the courts nor Congress have seen fit to intervene until the presidential action at issue was an accomplished fact. President Truman, for example, had no authority from Congress to order American troops to Korea. President Eisenhower also had no authority when he dispatched troops to Lebanon in 1958. President Kennedy had no legislative authority when he ordered troop mobilization during the Berlin crisis of 1961; his authority was equally questionable when he committed combat forces to Southeast Asia and ordered a naval quarantine of Cuba, both in 1962. Nor did President Johnson have any authority until after the fact when he continually escalated the Vietnam War between 1965 and 1968. When President Johnson dispatched the marines to the Dominican Republic, this act was justified only on the basis of our traditional control of the Caribbean. No further mention needs to be made of President Nixon's "incursions" into Cambodia and Laos. And despite the new, assertive mood of Congress after Watergate, President Ford received almost universal approval for his unilateral action invading Cambodian territory to rescue the U.S. supply vessel, the *Mayaguez*.

All of these actions were taken without formal authority. They were taken in the name of necessity, which presidents seem always to claim whenever they take unilateral action. But that is another way of claiming inherent powers for the presidency. Thus, we end this inquiry where we began. Separation of powers provides a continual state of tension in United States foreign policy. Perhaps our greatest concern in all of this should be to keep this tension alive, because if it subsides the resolution will almost inevitably be in favor of presidential government.

History, not logic, will finally answer the question of whether there is prerogative in the presidency. Nonetheless, certain logical conclusions can be made about the effects of certain types of presidential behavior in the sphere of foreign policy. Surely the main purpose of the presidency in the international dimension is to establish and maintain credibility—a reputation for power and action that is respected by any other country whose interests may be in conflict with ours. When a president steers a course independent of Congress and of the Constitution on the basis of the claim to prerogative, greater flexibility and speed of reaction may be gained; but long-run credibility may not. Presidential credibility depends heavily upon popular support, which in turn depends upon support

Provisions of War Powers Act of 1973

● Stated that the President could commit U.S. Armed forces to hostilities . . . only pursuant to a declaration of war, specific statutory authorization or a national emergency created by an attack upon the United States, its territories or possessions, or its armed forces.

● Urged the President "in every possible instance" to consult with Congress before committing U.S. forces to hostilities or to situations where hostilities might be imminent, and to consult Congress regularly after such a commitment.

● Required the President to report in writing within 48 hours to the speaker of the House and president pro tempore of the Senate on any commitment or substantial enlargement of U.S. combat forces abroad, except for deployments related solely to supply, replacement, repair or training; required supplementary reports at least every six months while such forces were being engaged.

● Authorized the speaker of the House and the president pro tempore of the Senate to reconvene Congress if it was not in session to consider the President's report.

● Required the termination of a troop commitment within 60 days after the President's initial report was submitted, unless Congress declared war, specifically authorized continuation of the commitment, or was physically unable to convene as a result of an armed attack upon the United States; allowed the 60-day period to be extended for up to 30 days if the President determined and certified to Congress that unavoidable military necessity respecting the safety of U.S. forces required their continued use in bringing about a prompt disengagement.

● Allowed Congress, at any time U.S. forces were engaged in hostilities without a declaration of war or specific congressional authorization, by concurrent resolution to direct the President to disengage such troops.

● Set up congressional priority procedures for consideration of any resolution or bill introduced pursuant to the provisions of the resolution.

● Provided that, if any provision of the resolution was declared invalid, the remainder of the resolution would not affected.

Following is the text of a letter sent May 15, 1975 by President Ford formally notifying Congress in compliance with the War Powers Resolution of 1973, of his actions in ordering the rescue of crew members aboard the freighter *Mayaguez*. The letter was addressed to the Speaker of the House of Representatives, Carl Albert.

Dear Mr. Speaker:
On 12 May 1975, I was advised that the S.S. Mayaguez, a merchant vessel of United States registry on route from Hong Kong to Thailand with a U.S. citizen crew, was fired upon, stopped, boarded and seized by Cambodian naval patrol boats. . . . In accordance with my desire that the Congress be informed on this matter and taking note of Section 4 (A) (1) of the War Powers Resolution, I wish to report to you that at about 6:20 A.M., 13 May, pursuant to my instructions to prevent the movement of the Mayaguez into a mainland port, U.S. aircraft fired warning shots across the bow of the ship and gave visual signals to small craft approaching the ship. Subsequently . . . I directed the United States armed forces to isolate the island and interdict any movement between the ship or the island and the mainland, and to prevent movement of the ship itself. . . . This operation was ordered and conducted pursuant to the President's constitutional executive power and his authority as Commander in Chief of the United States armed forces.
Sincerely,
Gerald R. Ford

N.Y. Times, Washington, May 15—Along with the general mood of euphoria in Congress over the success of the operation in the Gulf of Siam, there was mild criticism from some Senators and Representatives that President Ford should have complied more explicitly with the law requiring him to "consult with Congress" in advance of military operations.

Can Congress, by
statutory action, limit the
power of the president to
commit American forces
abroad?

in Congress. It may depend even more upon a general sense of the rightness of the specific actions involved; and that, in turn, depends in part upon whether there is full justification for them. Each time a president acts without these supports, particularly without clear constitutional sanction, he is literally engaging in a mini coup d'etat. The Viet Cong and the North Vietnamese may have appreciated and used our system to better effect than Presidents Johnson and Nixon by stalling the war, stalling the peace talks, and deliberately provoking United States retaliation. Both presidents were in a strong sense casualties of that war inasmuch as at least part of their failure to survive can be attributed to their disregard for constitutional forms.

The Domestic Presidency: Powers and Purposes

The main purpose of the domestic presidency is not unrelated to that of the international presidency. In domestic matters, the president must secure obedience; as agent of the national government, the president is charged with doing everything that is "necessary and proper" to see that the laws are faithfully executed. But here again, the Constitution has put power into tension with form. It is very difficult for the president to do what is necessary and at the same time be proper about it.

Article IV, Section 4, of the Constitution directs the national government to protect every state "against Invasion . . . and against domestic Violence," and Congress has made this explicitly a presidential power through statutes directing the commander-in-chief to discharge the obligations of Article IV.[16] These arrangements make the president the true chief executive, because they put him in command of the armed forces as well as of the administrators in the executive branch. This underscores, if underscoring is needed, the essentially military background of all domestic government.

The Constitution does require the national government to wait for requests by the state legislature, or the governor when the legislature is not in session, before ordering troops to stop the rioting in any state or to enforce the laws. However, this limitation is not absolute for two reasons. First, many governors and mayors prefer to make the request for troops in order to throw the responsibility of deciding whether to use forceful suppression upon the national government. Second, the president may in fact use troops without a specific state's request if it becomes necessary in order to enforce a federal judicial order or to protect federally guaranteed civil rights that state authorities are unable or unwill-

[16]These statutes are contained mainly in Title 10 of the United States Code, Sections 331, 332, and 333.

ing to protect.[17] The most famous instance of this was probably during the Pullman strike of 1894, when President Cleveland dispatched federal troops to break the strike on the grounds that the troops were needed in order to enforce federal court injunctions against the American Railway Union. But regardless of whether there are limitations on the president, the power of the domestic presidency stems from this military foundation.

In a well-ordered society like our own, the military axe does not frequently have to be taken in hand in order to maintain civilian rule. Consequently, we view the president in his civilian role and tend to miss the military underpinnings of the office. Yet there could be no prospect of civilian rule unless the government held an overwhelming monopoly of all of the available instruments of violence. With this perspective in mind, we can proceed to look at the civilian aspects of presidential powers.

The Constitution makes the president the civilian chief executive through the cumulative impact of several provisions in Article II. Section 1 vests "the Executive Power" in the president, a single person. This is as important in the domestic as in the international dimension. Next, the president is given the power to appoint the principal executive officers and to require each of them to give him written opinions on subjects relating to the duties of their departments. This helps establish his authority over these officers and departments. Two additional grants give him great authority in the legislative process—the provision that he deliver legislative messages to Congress and the provision giving him the power to veto congressional enactments. These powers constitute the foundation for what President Truman once called, with a little exaggeration, "the most powerful office in the history of the world."

Appointment and removal power Although the domestic dimension of the presidency has less claim to prerogative than the international dimension, that has not stopped presidents from occasionally making such claims. The strongest argument against any notion of prerogative in the domestic presidency is that none of the domestic powers are absolute. Each of the powers is accompanied by a very distinct limitation. The appointment power requires approval by two-thirds of the senators. The Constitution is silent on removal power, but the courts have filled this silence with a series of decisions that leave the president power to remove top officials without hindrance but that also leave Congress with power to set conditions by statutes limiting such removal wherever they see fit to do so. Congress limits the presidential removal power largely by setting specific terms of office within which the appointee can be

[17]The best study covering all aspects of the domestic uses of the military is that of Adam Yarmolinsky, *The Military Establishment* (New York: Harper & Row, 1971).

removed by the president only following specific charges, hearings, or reviews. Thus, while Congress cannot tell the president whom to appoint, Congress nevertheless has a tremendous amount of influence over the character of the appointee and that appointee's security in the job.[18] The presidential power to deliver legislative messages to Congress is accompanied by a power to call either or both chambers into special session. The president cannot, however, require Congress to enact anything. Moreover, his veto may be, and frequently is, overridden by a two-thirds vote of both chambers.

Emergency power   Attempts to go beyond these limits and constraints tend to arise over "emergency power"—the power that may be inherent in any head of state to set the country back on course if in his opinion it has temporarily gotten off. In effect, such an attempt by a president is an effort to draw domestic power from the international powers vested in the presidency.[19] Congress has very frequently granted the president specific emergency powers, to such an extent that the president rarely needs to make a claim of inherent powers. In 1952 President Truman unsuccessfully attempted to seize the steel mills on the basis of the inherent powers of his office. His actions were declared unconstitutional largely on the grounds that he should have relied on statutory authorization

*Instrumentation
of Control:
The Presidency*

[18]See Corwin, *The President,* p. 87.
[19]This nice distinction between pow*er* and pow*ers* is used to good effect in Neustadt, *Presidential Power,* chapter 3, note 1.

made available to him through enactments by Congress during World War II and still operative in 1952.[20]

One student of emergency power reports that there are at least two hundred laws that give the president virtually unlimited power in particular situations defined in the law or by him as a crisis. For example, in an emergency situation the president has the power to requisition any ship owned by a citizen or seize a foreign ship, if he "finds it to be necessary to the national defense." President Nixon used statutory authority to declare a national emergency in 1970, calling out troops to deliver the mail during a postal strike. In 1968 President Johnson invoked statutory emergency powers to restrict the amount of American capital that could be invested abroad in order to fight unfavorable balances of trade.[21] In all of these instances the president's power is available to him under *explicit statutory authorization.* This authorization can be removed any time Congress sees fit, and Congress has occasionally seen fit to do so. Thus the area of "emergency power" does not involve any presidential prerogative on the domestic side, even though a cooperative Congress helps make it unnecessary for the president to make a claim to prerogative.

Power to impound funds   The claims to presidential prerogative have a second source, however. This is the power of the president to impound funds appropriated by Congress. At least since President Truman, presidents have occasionally refused to spend money on programs authorized and funded by Congress. For example, Congress in the late 1940s appropriated economic aid to Spain, hoping this would make our relations with Spain cordial enough to gain permission to build strategic air bases in that country. President Truman was against this move, and he simply refused to make available the appropriated funds; he successfully held out against congressional complaints for over two years until our general policy toward Spain had changed.

Truman's action is insignificant in comparison with President Nixon's impoundment of over a billion dollars in congressional appropriations intended for major health programs. This constituted more than one-fifth of the entire 1973 budget for the health segment of the Department of Health, Education and Welfare. Nevertheless, the Truman action was one of several precedents for the Nixon action. There was a tremendous amount of partisan complaining about President Nixon's action; but many of the same critical Democrats had probably been silent in 1961, when

---

[20]*Youngstown Sheet and Tube Company* v. *Sawyer,* 343 U.S. 579 (1952).

[21]These and other examples will be found in a book published by the Office of Emergency Preparedness (Washington, D.C.: Government Printing Office, n.d.), mentioned in an excellent review article by K. W. Clawson, *Washington Post,* September 5, 1971.

The limits of executive privilege: Aides delivering the Nixon tapes to Congress, following *U.S. v. Nixon* in 1974.

President Kennedy impounded 780 million dollars which was in excess of his budget request for B-52 and B-70 bombers.

By what authority can a president impound funds, especially when the impounding of the funds sabotages a program which Congress intends to have carried out? Nixon did this with health funds. And so did Kennedy in his decision to withhold moneys appropriated for schools or libraries from segregated school systems. Legal opinion on this subject probably remains in agreement with a study published in 1962, which concluded that "the President has no general statutory authority to impound appropriated funds for reasons other than economy and efficiency of operation . . . nor can the President validly claim such authority as derived from the duty 'to take care that the laws are faithfully executed.'"[22] For example, if the president judges that a congressional program would tend to support segregated schools, his obligation would be to veto the legislation rather than to wait and impound funds aimed at those schools. Any other position would in fact give the president "retroactive veto power" based upon his personal opinion of the constitutionality or desirability of any provision in a statute.[23]

The Impoundment Control Act of 1974 was designed to circumscribe the president's ability to impound funds appropriated by

[22]Robert E. Goosetree, "The Power of the President to Impound Appropriated Funds," *American University Law Review*, January 1962; reprinted in Aaron Wildavsky, ed., *The Presidency* (Boston: Little, Brown, 1969), p. 727.
[23]Ibid.

Congress. It provides, among other things, that the president must spend appropriated funds unless both houses consent to impoundment within forty-five days of a presidential request. But in a way Congress's action is almost an admission that the president is going to continue impounding funds from time to time. It will be difficult to determine what all this means until we have acquired a few years of experience under the new act.

Executive privilege   A third area where executive prerogative is sometimes claimed is "executive privilege," which has been invoked in regard to information sought by Congress, the courts, or any other institution with a right to know. There is indeed something quite substantial to a chief executive's claim of executive privilege. A chief executive cannot get good advice if his closest advisers stand a chance of exposure. The members of inner councils cannot be frank with one another; they cannot consider those impossible alternatives that help define the reasonable ones. They cannot afford to give advice that turns out later not to be heeded, or if heeded turns out to be wrong. Without some definition of privileged communications there would be nothing but constant hedging and ambiguity in the inner councils of government.

The question is, how far can executive privilege be extended? Can it be used as a source of additional presidential power? The claim to executive privilege became President Nixon's final weapon of defense. He tried to use it as a blanket to cover a variety of actions that many others had alleged were either unconstitutional or criminal. If his claim had been sustained, Congress would have been unable to subpoena the White House tapes and other documents deemed essential to the impeachment proceedings of the House Judiciary Committee. The Supreme Court rejected President Nixon's broad claim that executive privilege immunized him from congressional subpoenas. This broke down all remaining barriers to the president's removal, and he resigned before the impeachment process could be completed. However, the Court narrowed the doctrine of executive privilege *only* where the congressional demand was for information involving criminal charges. Otherwise, the Court left the president with a very strong basis for refusing to account to Congress for his actions. In fact, the doctrine of executive privilege may be stronger as a result of the Supreme Court decision, because it clarified the situation and gave it judicial sanction.[24]

Executive privilege does support very considerably the institution of a strong presidency. Yet the president is subject to as much restraint as Congress is able and willing to bring to bear upon him. In all of its worst and its best features, the presidency is a democratic institution. The president does not derive pow*ers* or all

[24]*U.S.* v. *Nixon,* 418 U.S. 683 (1973).

United States v. Richard M. Nixon

. . . In support of his claim of absolute privilege, the President's counsel urges two grounds. . . . The first ground is the valid need for protection of communications between high government officials and those who advise and assist them in the performance of their manifold duties. . . . The second ground asserted by the President's counsel in support of the claim of absolute privilege rests on the doctrine of separation of powers. . . . Neither the doctrine of separation of powers, nor the need for confidentiality of high level communications, without more, can sustain an absolute unqualified Presidential privilege of immunity from judicial process under all circumstances. The President's need for complete candor and objectivity from advisers calls for great deference from the courts. However, when the privilege depends solely on the broad, undifferentiated claim of public interest in the confidentiality of such conversations, a confrontation with other values arises. Absent a claim of need to protect military, diplomatic or sensitive national security secrets, we find it difficult to accept the argument that even the very important interest in confidentiality of Presidential communications is significantly diminished by production of such material for in camera inspection (in the judge's chambers) with all the protection that a District Court will be obliged to provide.

The impediment that an absolute, unqualified privilege would place in the way of the primary constitutional duty of the judicial branch to do justice in criminal prosecutions would plainly conflict with the function of the courts under Art. III.

that much power from a popular base. We will see time and time again that most of the real power of the presidency comes from the powers granted by the Constitution and laws. *The popular sources and resources of the presidency are important not because they give the president power but because (1) they give him consent, and (2) they shape what he will want to use his powers for.* This is precisely what makes the presidency a democratic institution. It is tied to no hierarchy; it derives from no established ruling classes or cultures or regions or family connections; it is built upward from political coalitions rather than backward toward inheritance from original conquerors or superior classes.

This does not mean that the office or the occupant is free from and uninfluenced by the most powerful members of the society. It simply means that the process of selecting the president is the broadest and most popular selection process known among large nations. It may indeed turn out that the dictates of achieving the presidency are so extensive and so demanding that only those persons who belong to the top economic interests and favorite classes have a chance. But that only helps define where the important influences may come from; it does not disprove the contention that the sources and resources of the presidency are democratic. The arrangements for the nomination and election of the president have made the presidency something almost unique in the annals of government. The popular sources of the presidency rank second only to constitutional and statutory provisions as shapers of the office and of those who occupy it.

THE PRESIDENT: SOURCES AND POWER

Although the founders were acutely aware of the problem, the Constitution is conspicuously silent on the *selection* of qualified candidates for the office of president. The Constitution merely specifies that the voters are to pick candidates for an Electoral College. According to the Constitution, the electors are not expected to pledge themselves to a candidate and are not bound to vote for any particular candidate as a result of any popular vote. They have the power to pick anyone they admire, whether the person is an announced candidate or not, and regardless of whether he is an official designee of a party. They need not even concern themselves with whether the person will serve if elected.

Apparently it was the assumption of the authors of Article II that the states and Congress would produce several obvious presidential possibilities every four years. It was probably assumed further that there would be a "favorite son" from each of several states and that the members of the Electoral College would generally have common information about each of these favorite sons. If there were to be several such logical candidates, the Electoral College would rarely be able to produce the absolute majority required by the Constitution. That being the case, it must have been expected that, as prescribed in the Constitution, most of the final choices for president would take place in the House of Representatives, each state delegation voting as a single unit with a single vote regardless of the population of the state. Thus the November election culminating with the December meeting of the Electoral College was to be the *nominating process.*

The *electoral process* for president would then generally take place when the House of Representatives convened following the election. The authors of Article II most certainly expected a large number of candidates and an inability of the Electoral College to select a president from among them, because the original version of Section 1 provided that if no person received a majority of votes in the Electoral College, then the House would make the selection from among the top *five* on the list. This was modified by the Twelfth Amendment in 1804, which permitted the House to choose from among the top three on the list.

As soon as political parties captured the Electoral College, the situation began to change. First the electors pledged themselves to the candidate of their party. This completely destroyed the original function of the Electoral College, and it also stole away the regular opportunity of the House of Representatives to elect the president. Within a few years, the political parties developed their own method of selecting nominees for the presidency; they invented the convention system during the 1830s, and it operates in much the same way at present. In effect, the parties split the electoral atom in an entirely new way. The *nominating process* became an entirely new process completely independent of Congress, completely independent of the Electoral College, and in fact independent of the November presidential election. The *electoral process* was also freed from the Electoral College and from Congress. On the other hand, the parties did not nationalize the process but left it where it had been put by the constitutional provision that electoral votes would be allocated to each state. The parties dominated, and continue to dominate, the nominating process and the electoral process, but on a state-by-state basis—we have fifty electorates for president rather than a single national electorate.

In consequence, the selection process for president is vast and extremely complex. It has made the presidency an intrinsic part of the practice as well as the theory of representative government in the United States.

Is the Presidential Nominating Process a Good Method for Selecting Presidents?

The nominating process can be considered an arduous test we interpose between candidates and the nominations of the two major parties. The test may turn out to be so severe and so biased that it produces the wrong person with the wrong commitments at the wrong time. It may also turn out that no alternative would improve upon the result. The candidate who wishes to pass this initial test must piece together innumerable parties and factions of parties from several of the states in order to form a coalition of delegates to the party's nominating convention who will stick together at least long enough to provide the candidate with a majority of the delegate vote. For most of the last 140 years, serious contenders for the presidency have had to go through this kind of test. The details have changed, but the essentials have remained. The coalition a candidate builds for the nomination is so important that, if elected president, the victor's administration will be stable or unstable, effective or ineffective, popular or narrow, urban or rural, southern or northern largely on the basis of the composition of this coalition.

Successful coalitions tend to last longer than four years. A sitting president who wishes to be reelected can usually keep the original coalition together, so that in almost all instances renomination for a second term by the party's convention is assured. Vice-presidents who succeed to the presidency and who later run for a bona fide term of office usually face no contest because they inherit part of the original coalition and have opportunities as president to piece together additional parts of their own. Vice-presidents who do not move up to the presidency through death or resignation have a tougher time getting a presidential nomination for themselves. This was true of Nixon in 1960 and 1968, as well as Humphrey in 1968. However, generally their task is made easier by the inheritance of some of the previous coalition that had made them vice-president.

Even a successful presidential nominee who loses the general election can usually hold a coalition together long enough to have a renomination and a second chance, as did Thomas Dewey in 1948, Adlai Stevenson in 1956, and Richard Nixon in 1968. A few figures will suggest the difficulty of holding a coalition together when a candidate loses an election but remains the "titular leader" of his party for four years. In 1948, Thomas Dewey received only 39.7 percent of the delegate votes on the first ballot. In 1956, Adlai Stevenson received 66 percent of the first ballot votes, but there was great uncertainty prior to convention time. In contrast, Richard Nixon was nominated virtually by acclamation in 1968.

Because coalitions tend to endure in this fashion, there have been contested nominations—so-called open conventions, where the outcome is seriously in doubt at least up to the first day of the convention—only once every twelve to sixteen years in each party. Between 1900 and 1972, there were thirty-eight conventions held by Democrats and Republicans. In only ten of these was the outcome in doubt as late as the first ballot. The most recent open convention for the Democrats was in 1972; the most recent Republican one was in 1964. The 1968 Democratic and Republican conventions were both quite dramatic, but despite the demonstrations in downtown Chicago and rioting and tanks in Miami, these conventions were nevertheless typical of all of the other twenty-eight instances where the winning coalition was already formed and the outcome of the convention was already known before convention time.

These twenty-eight closed conventions were not useless to the parties. The rituals of popular participation prior to and during these conventions probably made a small contribution to the reinforcement of democratic values. More to the point, each convention was worth millions of dollars in free publicity. Uncontested conventions are staged almost entirely for popular coverage, especially in the age of television; the main events occur during summer evenings, and they usually get good TV ratings in competition with mid-season baseball, summer variety shows, and old westerns. This aspect of all conventions is an essential part of the electoral campaign itself.

The occasional open conventions are, however, the essential conventions. Considerable detail is necessary to appreciate how and why they work; yet each open convention is set apart from the

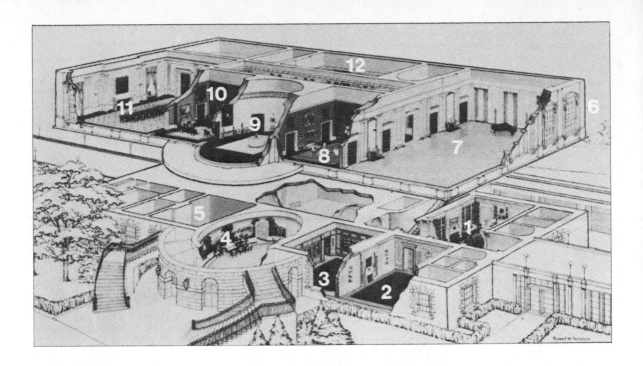

The Interior of the White House: 1) The Library; 2) The Vermeil Room; 3) The China Room; 4) The Diplomatic Reception Room; 5) The Map Room; 6) The State Floor; 7) The East Room; 8) The Green Room; 9) The Blue Room; 10) The Red Room; 11) The State Dining Room; 12) Lobby and Cross Hall (not visible on plan).

others by many years, and the parties have their open conventions at different times. Consequently, no single case study will suffice. It is necessary to present a slightly distorted abstraction of a typical case. When a party's presidential nomination is going to be contested, some candidates begin to scramble for delegates very early. George Romney began his 1968 campaign with great fanfare in 1966, following a stunning reelection as governor of Michigan. George McGovern made a rare official announcement for the Democratic nomination a year before the 1972 convention. John Kennedy started his 1960 campaign in 1956 after a bitter failure to get the vice-presidential nomination; he became increasingly explicit after the 1958 liberal landslide in Congress.

Regardless of the starting point, the test is about the same. Each candidate must line up support among state party leaders and important campaign contributors. (Campaigning for the nomination is going to be made particularly difficult by the new campaign finance laws, which set severe limits on individual contributions; but where there is a will there is likely also to be a way.) Organizing to get the nomination requires a large and personal political organization. This is necessary to gain and to keep delegate support from various parts of the country. Unless a few gains in delegates and financial support are made early in the election, the candidacy is likely to fizzle embarrassingly early. Party support is absolutely necessary in those states where delegates are not chosen by primaries; party and financial support are both important in states where important primary elections are held to select delegates.

The National Committee of each party determines the actual number of delegates to attend the convention as well as the formulas for allocating these votes among the states. The basic allocation is usually an amount roughly twice the size of the congressional delegation in each state. To that minimum is added a bonus number of delegates based upon the amount of support the state gave the party's presidential candidate in the previous election. Thanks especially to this bonus system, the size of the national conventions has grown out of all proportion to the size of the state congressional delegations.

The number of delegates and alternates has grown also because designation or appointment as a delegate or alternate is an inexpensive but rather effective form of patronage, at a time when job patronage in the home districts is getting thinner and thinner. In 1972, the Democratic National Committee provided for 3,015 votes. The official vote at the Republican National Convention tends to run about half that amount. But the actual number of persons in official attendance at a convention is a great deal larger than either because states are allowed to split their votes into a larger number of delegates, with each delegate allowed a fraction of a vote. This fractionalizing of the vote increases the patronage available to party leaders, but it also complicates the plight of the major candidates for the nomination, who thus have an extraordinarily large number of human beings to keep track of.

Of tremendous importance to each candidate is the right of each state to determine the method of selection of those delegates apportioned to it. The traditional method has been simple appointment by the party leadership or by the official state executive committee of the party. Thus earlier state delegations were usually comprised of the members of Congress, certain distinguished party donors, a few major state and local officials, and a few solid citizens. Perhaps half were allocated in singles or pairs to each of the congressional districts for appointment by the local party leaders or, eventually, election in a June primary preceding the summer convention.

In more recent years, traditions have changed to provide increasingly for selection of delegates at district levels by various forms of a primary election. One of the oldest of these is called a "preferential primary," because the delegates are elected but do not have to make pledges that bind them to go to the convention and vote specifically for the presidential candidate preferred by the voters on a separate part of the ballot. Delegates may even join with their colleagues and go to the convention to support a candidate at odds with the preference indicated at the time of the primary, or they may go without a public commitment in order to deal with each candidate for best advantage.

These older methods of selecting delegates—by party appointment, by party designation to be ratified by a state convention, or by nonbinding preferential primaries—had a highly stabilizing effect on the national conventions. Most of the delegates chosen in these various ways tended to repeat as delegates in convention after convention. There has always been something of a sour reaction to this kind of old-guard domination of convention spots, and it eventually produced a newer method of selection that is being adopted in an increasing number of states. This, of course, is the binding primary system, in which delegates pledge themselves to a certain candidate and, if elected by party members in the state primary, are bound to vote for their chosen presidential candidate until the candidate releases them from that obligation.[25]

Many experts now feel that the binding primary has spread to such an extent that it has revolutionized nominating politics, literally putting an end to the convention system. If we define an open convention as one in which no candidate receives a majority on the first ballot, then there has been no truly open convention for either party since 1952. Only by defining the open convention as a convention in which the outcome is in doubt up to the first day can we pick up any nomination contests at all. Nevertheless, the national conventions are far from finished for several reasons:

1. A substantial proportion of delegates are still chosen by older methods and are able to deal with each candidate according to age-old party methods. As recently as 1972, George McGovern received four hundred of his national convention votes from states where delegates were not chosen by binding primaries.

2. Even though at least three-fifths of all the states now choose their delegates in primaries, state provisions do vary as to the degree to which the delegates are obliged to hold their pledge. Many delegations are released from their pledge as soon as the convention goes beyond the first ballot. Such a contingency has not occurred since 1952, and there is a tendency to overlook it.

3. The probability of going beyond the first ballot is greater than any time since 1952 because of the new rules in the Democratic Party providing for *proportional* allocation of delegates in states where delegate selection is made by primary election. This means that a candidate who receives 20 percent of the vote in a state

---

[25]Compare with Paul T. David et al., *Presidential Nominating Politics,* 5 vols. (Baltimore: Johns Hopkins Press, 1954). Each of the more recent conventions has been given lively, and usually insightful, coverage by Theodore H. White in his series *The Making of the President* (New York: Atheneum, various dates), with the date of each presidential year added as part of the title to each book. A worthwhile attempt to synthesize these patterns will be found in the text by Nelson Polsby and Aaron Wildavsky, *Presidential Elections,* 3rd ed. (New York: Scribner, 1971).

Table 11.2   National Conventions—A Typical Schedule

Convention Schedule	Commentary
Preconvention 1. Months prior: Negotiation with potential convention cities, which bid up to $1 million for the convention. 2. A week or more prior: Hearings by Platform Committee, which continue through first day or two of convention. 3. Sunday evening prior: Informal first gatherings, polls.	With the convention schedule the delegates give themselves four days—Sunday afternoon through Thursday night—to get themselves a candidate, platform, running mate, and officers and rules for the next four years.
First day, Monday 1. Seating of delegates; hearings by Credentials Committee; challenges heard (decisions can be appealed to convention floor Tuesday). 2. Platform Committee continues hearings. 3. Much milling about; squabbles over seating in galleries; demonstrations. 4. Late afternoon or evening, convention officially called to order; temporary chairman gives keynote address; permanent officers elected. (Chairman is usually Speaker or Minority Leader of House of Representatives.)	Routine is most likely to be broken by credentials fights. These, or sometimes a dispute over rules or platform, can become the first test of candidate strength—often the equivalent of a first ballot.
Second day, Tuesday 1. Final reports of committees. 2. Appeals; minority reports; roll calls on disputed decisions. 3. Acceptance. 4. Memorials, movies, and other filler, if time.	Several opportunities may occur on Monday and Tuesday to let a dispute become an equivalent to a first-ballot test of strength. See text for examples (especially Taft in 1952 and the 1968 Humphrey test on the "peace plank" in the platform). In recent years top polling agencies have run delegate surveys daily. But these merely add uncertainty to claims being made by candidates or spokesmen. Early ballots on disputed planks or delegations are much more meaningful tests of candidate strength.
Third day, Wednesday 1. Nominations; roll call by states, alphabetically; nominating speech and several brief seconding speeches for each candidate; demonstrations allowed, but increasingly severely restricted. 2. Only serious candidates nominated, if at all possible; nominations closed and roll call by states for actual voting begins. 3. Second ballot, and third or more, if no candidate gets majority of all votes.	Some "favorite sons" are actually nominated. Most of them, however, withdraw in favor of one of the serious candidates at a strategic moment before balloting. The chairman of each delegation reports the vote for the entire state, unless a delegate demands polling of his or her delegation. This polling can be needed; it can also be a delaying tactic while a deal is being cooked up elsewhere.
Fourth day, Thursday 1. Roll call of states for vice-presidential nominations. 2. Roll call by states for balloting. 3. Second, or more, ballots, if no majority on first. 4. Brief appearances and acceptance speeches by presidential and vice-presidential candidates—in prime TV time if possible. 5. Adjournment *sine die;* exhaustion.	Even in open conventions, someone has usually reached a majority before the roll call reaches Wyoming. In anticipation, delegation chairmen begin to clamor for recognition to switch to the victor—and the "bandwagon" begins to roll. But even though the result is usually known before the balloting ends, it has been difficult to get a nomination during prime time (1968—Nixon at 1:50 a.m., Humphrey at 12:02 a.m.; 1972—McGovern after 3:00 a.m.).
Fifth day, Friday 1. Conventions once went into Friday night; Thursday night now seems to be the cutting point.	Except in the case of the Democrats in 1956, the choice of a running mate is left to the presidential nominee, who picks a ticket balancer. Additional vice-presidential nominations usually serve to honor some party stalwarts.

Democratic primary receives 20 percent of the delegates. Hitherto, most states with primaries provided that the candidate with the plurality of the votes would receive all of the delegates.

4. The new rules on campaign financing will actually increase the probability that no single candidate will emerge as the overwhelming choice on the first ballot. Unless the Supreme Court invalidates the new campaign finance rules—and suits are in the courts at the time of this writing—candidates are limited to a $10 million expenditure for primaries, and individuals are allowed to donate no more than $1,000 to any candidate. Wealthy donors will be severely limited, and front-running candidates will no longer be in such a dominating position.

5. Disputes over proper procedure, voter discrimination, and so on, continue to produce contested delegations. These contests are brought to the convention and have to be settled by a Credentials Committee. George McGovern gained a large number of delegates in 1972 by winning several credentials disputes.[26]

Since the possibility of contested conventions remains despite the spread of binding primaries, candidates are forced by their uncertainties to pursue, as always, a "second choice strategy." Just in case no candidate takes an unbeatable lead prior to the convention, and just in case support for the leading candidate crumbles at the last minute, each candidate must try to become the most widely acceptable second choice. The second choice strategy is purely a numbers game: "I'll support you on the second round if it turns out I have no chance of getting the nomination, but I expect you to support me as soon as you determine you have no chance."

Here is how the incorruptible Senator Robert Taft assessed his own situation after his failure to gain the Republican nomination in 1952:

> It was probably a mistake to take a vote [on the rules changes early in the convention] because it showed that the combined forces against us controlled the convention. . . . If a deadlock had been created after the first ballot, I would have been glad to reconsider the whole situation and would have been glad to withdraw in favor of some other candidate holding my general views, if it had been clear that I could not be nominated and *that he would have been stronger on the second ballot than I*.[27] (Italics added.)

---

[26]McGovern had gained considerable control of the machinery of the Democratic Convention during the course of his service as co-chairman of the Democratic Commission on Party Structure and Delegate Selection following the 1968 elections. Their report led to several important reforms in the Democratic Party, especially regarding proper representation of women, ethnic groups, and various minority groups. It was through manipulation of these rules that McGovern won several important delegation disputes, including displacement of the entire delegation of the "Daley machine" from Chicago. See *Mandate for Reform: A Report of the Commission on Party Structure and Delegate Selection to the Democratic National Committee* (Washington, D.C.: Democratic National Committee, 1970).

[27]This postmortem by Taft was published fully in the *New York Times*, November 25, 1959.

Taft had suffered an old-age fate. Many of his delegates treated the vote on the rules and two important votes on the seating of contested delegations as equivalent to a first-ballot test. Once Taft lost one or more votes, many of his delegates considered their pledges were no longer binding, and they jumped on General Eisenhower's bandwagon, fearing in their uncertainty that further delays would leave them out of the victorious presidential coalition.[28]

One of the most notorious incidences of the second choice strategy was reported in detail by Harry Daugherty in his account of his plans to secure the nomination of the obscure Ohio senator, Warren Harding, in 1920:

> I'll tell you, in confidence, what's in my mind. All I'm doing is getting in touch with the leaders and delegates who are for Wood and Lowden [the two strongest Republican candidates prior to the convention of 1920], being friendly with them. . . . When both realize they can't win, when they're tired and hot and sweaty and discouraged, both the armies will remember me and this little headquarters. They'll be like soldiers after a battle, who recall a shady spring along a country road.[29]

One further example will indicate that the second choice strategy has been employed by some of our most scrupulous politicians:

> Honorable Samuel Galloway   Chicago, March 24, 1860
> My dear Sir: I am here attending a trial in court. Before leaving home I received your kind letter of the 15th. Of course I am gratified to know I have friends in Ohio who are disposed to give me the highest evidence of their friendship and confidence. . . . My name is new in the field; and I suppose I am not the *first* choice of a very great many. Our policy, then, is to give no offense to others—leaving them in a mood to come to us, if they shall be compelled to give up their first love. This, too, is dealing justly with all, and leaving us in a mood to support heartily whoever shall be nominated. . . . Whatever you may do for me, consistently with these suggestions, will be appreciated, and gratefully remembered. Please write me again.
>
>   Yours very truly, A. Lincoln

Burns reports that Lincoln's men were still at it when the convention opened. They not only packed the galleries at the Chicago convention hall but went to great lengths to keep the second choices active. Seward polled 37 percent of the votes on the first ballot, for a commanding lead. Lincoln was nominated on the fourth ballot.[30]

---

[28]In 1932, it was said that Franklin Roosevelt carried around a little list entitled FRBC—"For Roosevelt before Chicago"—which established priorities for access to the president. In 1960, there were some FKBW buttons circulating around Los Angeles, and they were being worn primarily by delegates who had apparently supported Kennedy "before Wisconsin" and were hoping to establish the narrowest possible definition of the inner circle of the winning coalition.
[29]As told to Mark Sullivan, *Our Times: The Twenties*, vol. 6 (New York: Scribner, 1935), p. 35.
[30]James MacGregor Burns, "The Case for the Smoke-filled Room," *New York Times Magazine*, June 15, 1952, p. 9.

A few additional details about George McGovern's suprise victory in 1972 for the Democratic nomination will provide some sense of the remaining potential of the convention system. As reported earlier, McGovern had been able to add to his delegate strength by manipulation of the rules governing the seating of delegations not chosen in primaries. The new rules had also worked to McGovern's advantage inasmuch as 80 percent of the delegates finally seated were attending a convention for the first time. Usually fewer than 60 percent are attending for the first time. Of all the delegates, 27 percent were under thirty years of age, 38 percent were women (compared to 13 percent in 1968), and 15 percent were black (compared to 5 percent in 1968). Even with McGovern it took more than a few primary victories to make his nomination. Moreover, if McGovern had lost two or three important primaries, he would very probably have dropped from contention. Thus, his victory was a combination of genuine popular support, coupled with mastery of the party machinery and ability and willingness to manipulate convention rules to influence credentials and seating. As one perennial observer described the 1972 situation, "The new politics is the old politics but better."[31]

Certainly we can continue to treat national conventions as an essential element of presidential politics for at least a while longer. The national convention works as a unifying and focusing process in American national politics, especially if delegates actually form winning coalitions rather than come to a city in order to cast a pledged vote for the winner. Delegates who are elected in primaries are not so purely representative of their districts that their mere support of the candidate stamps them as representatives of a candidate popularly supported within their districts. Participation in primaries is notoriously skimpy, and candidates for delegate and alternate posts are unrepresentative inasmuch as they are better off, more politically ambitious, and usually tied to a narrower range of interests than their district at large. Primaries are not alone the ideal nominating process. A significant advance over the convention system has not yet been discovered.

Consequences for the System

Given the historic position of the presidential nominating process and the probability of its survival, at least in the immediate future, it would seem worthwhile to attempt to identify and to evaluate its place in the overall scheme of government. One apparently sys-

[31]Richard M. Scammon, as quoted in an article by Tom Littlewood in the *Chicago Sun Times*, July 9, 1972, section 2, p. 1. Good reviews of recent conventions and recent issues will be found in Joyce Gelb and Marian Lief Palley, *Tradition and Change in American Party Politics* (New York: Crowell, 1975), chapter 11.

tematic result of the nominating process is that it reinforces an already strong tendency in the party politics of the United States to choose *candidates who are inoffensive.* Someone once observed that it was a case of "the bland leading the bland." The president must of course be a great public figure, but such public stature is usually drawn from the office rather than brought by the person to the office.

Once in a great while a man with already great stature will be selected as the nominee of the party. But this ordinarily happens after some crisis, when normal party procedures are loose and unpredictable. Franklin Roosevelt may be such an example, although it is difficult to separate the pre-presidential Roosevelt from the presidential Roosevelt. Either way, he emerged at a particularly critical time in the history of the country and of his party. Eisenhower is another example; he also followed a great crisis—World War II. Some feel that John Kennedy was an example as well, although those close to him were less impressed with his charisma and far more impressed with his cool and calculating style of politics.

In any event, most other candidates are the personification of second choice strategy even if that was not their route to nomination or election. The middling personality is sought or encouraged because of the tremendous need in the party to unite, at least until the election is over. A good nominee is one who tries to avoid polarization, and failing that, has the skill to bridge it or to minimize it. We have already observed, in chapter 8, that most of the important political divisions occur inside each party during the nominating process rather than between the two parties during the election campaign.

Nowhere can this be better seen than in the national nominating process. For example, there was far greater difference between Goldwater and Rockefeller for the Republican nomination in 1964 than there was between Goldwater and Johnson in the November election of that year. There was also a greater difference between Hubert Humphrey and Eugene McCarthy in 1968 than between Humphrey and Nixon in the ensuing election. In every Democratic National Convention between 1948 and 1964 there was a profound liberal-conservative split on matters of race. There has been an abiding split between eastern and western Republicans for an equal number of years. The bland and inoffensive nominee serves a definite purpose if he or she can unify the party despite these abiding internal splits.

Some observers expected that television would all by itself revolutionize the presidential selection process, rendering the nominating convention a meeting place "to ratify the nomination for President the national favorite already determined by the agencies

. . . of mass democracy."[32] Yet, nearly two decades of mass saturation by television seem not to have changed the fact that a carload of presidential aspirants hardly produces a pound of charisma. Television has probably done more to kill off candidates than to produce them, and all the television support in the world cannot make a presidential candidate out of someone who lacks delegate support. John Lindsay, former mayor of New York, was a very good example of this in 1972.

Suppression of issues   Another cost to the system inherent in the convention method of nomination is that the price of unity involves the suppression of some of the most important issues of the day. Consistently over the past century, the nominating process for president has converted a large number of basic *social* issues into *political* "nonissues."[33] Between 1830 and 1860, for example, it would have been impossible to know from national campaigns that slavery and abolition were tearing the country apart. On the very eve of the Civil War in 1860, the Democratic Party was neither for nor against slavery; it simply took the position that slavery was an issue for each state to decide.

In the decades following the Civil War, no national campaign ever seriously raised the question of monopolies and their effect on the economy. This issue did not become explicit until 1896; but by that time the United States Congress had already committed the government on principle to fight monopolies, and the issue between the two parties was not the principle at all but rather the degree of government antitrust action. Even in the depths of the Depression in 1932 the Democratic Party was still preaching balanced budgets. By 1936 the Democrats had become more open in their differences with the Republicans, but by that time it was a matter of defending the governmental record rather than establishing the issues.

One exceptional case in recent years might be 1964, when the Republican Party under Barry Goldwater took the unusual step of attempting to distinguish itself clearly from the other party. But on the important issue of that day, foreign policy, the Democrats moved their position so close to Goldwater's that his effort did not succeed. A year later, after President Johnson had escalated the war in Vietnam, conservative columnist William Buckley could write in disgust that he had voted for Goldwater because of the Republican commitment to military defense in Southeast Asia, and that is

---

[32]William G. Carleton, "The Revolution in the Presidential Nominating Convention," *Political Science Quarterly*, June 1957, p. 224.

[33]For an effort to deal with this notion, see Peter Bachrach and Morton Baratz, "Decisions and Non-Decisions: An Analytic Framework," *American Political Science Review*, September 1968, p. 632.

exactly what he had gotten—even though Johnson was president.

Some people would cite 1948 as an exceptional case also, because the Democrats adopted a moderate civil rights platform even though it meant the secession of the southern states to form a third party. However, by 1952 the Democratic Party majority sought to soft-pedal the civil rights issue to bring the southerners back into the party, so that civil rights returned to the status of a nonissue. Congress eventually became more liberal in its willingness to deal with civil rights; but as for the parties, they moved toward this issue together like two barnacles clutching each other.

George McGovern in 1972 might be cited as an exception, too; and it is true that his wing of the Democratic Party had taken very distinguishable positions during preliminary campaigns. However, as the convention approached McGovern began to hedge, and by the time he was the nominee for president, the party had dropped most of its clearest domestic policy stands. Meanwhile, President Nixon had become such a peace candidate that the differences between the two parties on foreign policy were also erased.

Choosing outsiders One final consequence of the convention nominating process provides the link between presidential politics and presidential governing. This is the tendency of the nominating process to produce *outsiders.* It should be immediately granted that any person seriously considered for a presidential nomination must already be part of some American ruling class, no matter how that class may be defined. However, the president, who is selected through the nominating system, and most of the top people that individual will bring into the government are *outsiders to the administrative process of the national government.*

In the parliamentary systems of Western Europe, it would be almost inconceivable that a prime minister would have had no national government experience prior to taking the highest executive office. It would be equally difficult to imagine that a large number of top cabinet ministers, if any at all, would be appointed without having had long administrative experience. But in the twentieth century United States, only Presidents Taft, Hoover, and Franklin Roosevelt had had extensive federal government experience prior to their presidential nomination. Taft had served as solicitor general, governor of the Philippines, and secretary of war; Hoover had been a successful secretary of commerce for eight years immediately prior to his nomination; and Roosevelt had served a while as assistant secretary of the navy.

Many presidential nominees had been governors, or generals, or successful in business prior to their nomination, but those kinds of experience made them no less outsiders to the national bureaucracies. The typical experience was that of Truman, Johnson, and Nixon, who first held low administrative offices, then moved rather quickly into national legislative positions, and then by quirk of good fortune found themselves in a position close enough to make a claim on the presidential nomination. In the next chapter, which deals with the problems inherent in the office of chief executive, we will begin to see how important this particular pattern of electing outsiders is.

These various aspects of the presidential nominating process have been discussed in order to show the profound significance of that process in American politics. The requirements of nomination have made the presidency far different from what it otherwise might have been. Since it is the only system we have had, it is difficult to know precisely how different we would have been without it. However, a more thorough investigation of the problems of government and public policy, which will occupy the last part of this volume, will almost certainly intensify an appreciation of the importance of the broad and complex nominating process within our scheme of government. But first we must look more closely at the presidential election process and its importance to the system.

THE PRESIDENTIAL ELECTION: CONVERTING SOURCES INTO RESOURCES

The Conduct of the National Election Campaign

The two national parties seem to collapse after the conventions, despite the momentum and the publicity. Usually there is a three- to six-week moratorium on politics until Labor Day, the traditional beginning of the national campaigns every four years. But this lull is an all too brief period when several very essential political activities are taking place. First, it is a time when a campaign schedule is compiled. Presidential and vice-presidential candidates will travel more than a hundred thousand miles in the two months between Labor Day and election day. The campaign schedule is not merely a way of instructing their "advance men" and saving mileage. It is all part of a delicate balance of regional visitations that are guided by the jealousies of local leaders and by the opinion polls that suggest opportunities to make advances with voters. Thus, the schedule is intimately connected with the second objective of the campaign, which is to reorganize the victorious nominating coalition into a campaign organization.

A third objective of this early planning is the consolidation of the separate treasuries from different parts of the country and from the other candidates for the nomination. One of the most valuable properties of any political organization is its mailing list of contributors. Members of the coalition may indeed be more willing to deliver up preconvention surpluses than mailing lists. The surpluses are the golden egg, but the lists are the goose. The new campaign finance regulations are almost certain to enhance the value of these contributor lists; the quantity of *contributors* must be stressed now that the quantity of the *contribution* is limited.

Many campaigns fail or succeed during this early period. It is at this time that the nominee begins to reveal organizational skills and confirm or deny the assumptions made by all of the latecomers to the coalition, who picked the candidate as their best second choice. It was certainly during this period that the McGovern campaign fell apart in 1972. Having to face the immediate crisis of Thomas Eagleton's physical and mental fitness for the vice-presidential nomination certainly deprived McGovern of precious time to organize and plan. But his inconsistencies and confusions dealing with the decision to replace Eagleton destroyed a great deal of his credibility with party leaders and party contributors.

Actual campaign strategy is heavily influenced by the fact that the general election must be translated into electoral votes. Since 100 percent of a state's electoral vote is delivered to the candidate who gets a mere plurality of the popular votes in that state, presidential candidates must concentrate their energies in those states and regions where they are likely to win large enough blocs of the popular vote to gain the entire electoral vote. This means heavy reliance on the local party structure.

One of the reasons Richard Nixon almost won the presidency in 1960, despite the fact that it was a "Democratic year," was that, according to Gallup Poll figures, he was supported by 84 percent of all the Republican county chairmen. In contrast, only 29 percent of the Democratic county chairmen supported John Kennedy. This may also be one reason Hubert Humphrey did so much better in 1968 than did George McGovern in 1972; 70 percent of the Democratic chairmen had favored Humphrey's candidacy, while only 8 percent of the Democratic county chairmen predicted McGovern's victory.[34]

Campaign strategy is also heavily influenced by the brute need for exposure. It is not easy to make millions of people familiar with any product. A presidential candidate may not be like soap or toothpaste, but there are only two months in which to make the person's personality available and attractive. Exposure is particularly important to the Republican candidate, because there are so many more enrolled Democrats than Republicans. Millions of these habitual Democratic voters have to be encouraged to split their tickets in favor of the Republican presidential candidate. This is

---

[34]Figures for all but McGovern are reported in Frank J. Sorauf, *Party Politics in America*, 2d ed. (Boston: Little, Brown, 1973), p. 299. The McGovern figures are reported in a personal communication from Sorauf. While the form has changed from "favoring" the candidate to predicting the outcome, the latter is probably an even better indicator of the level of esteem (or lack of it) for the candidate.

The presidency and its
public: From the
Lincoln-Douglas debates
to the Kennedy-Nixon
debates, 1860 to 1960. Has
there been any progress?

*Instrumentation
of Control:
The Presidency*

why the Republican budget for advertising and television is so much larger than the Democratic budget.[35]

Perhaps this is also why President Nixon chose to run his campaign through the Committee for the Re-Election of the President (CREP) instead of the Republican Party. His chances of electing a Republican majority in the House or Senate were extremely slight, and he may have feared that a closer association with other Republican candidates would deprive him of the large personal mandate he sought in the 1972 election. Democrats can afford to be more partisan, because enrolled Democrats outnumber enrolled Republicans nearly two to one. Harry Truman ran a very successful campaign on this basis in 1948, but Barry Goldwater's attempt to follow Truman's partisan strategy as a Republican in 1964 was a fiasco. It seems quite clear that the successful Eisenhower strategy of 1952 was a distinctly personal and nonpartisan approach.[36]

Totally aside from whether to use the party or to organize a separate and personal type of campaign is the question of *what* type of appeal to make. Each campaign is of course a mixture of appeals, combining some stylistic and emotional factors with large doses of attacks on the other party. When candidates claim to be taking a stand "on the issues," they are usually doing nothing more than attacking the failures of the other party; this is particularly true of the candidate whose party has not been in office during the previous four or eight years. Occasionally there is truly a substantive appeal on the issues.[37] However, it is rare for a presidential campaign to be run strictly on substantive appeals. Usually the campaign is run at two levels. At the national level, where there is a heavy reliance on TV and the other media of mass communications, the appeals run heavily toward style and general propaganda. Substantive appeals are made at the second level, the regional and local campaign appearances. One of the most successful substantive appeals of this sort was the 1968 "southern strategy" of the Republicans, which probably made the difference between victory and defeat for Richard Nixon.[38]

---

[35]A very important case study of the role of advertising in the presidential campaign is that of Joe McGinnis, *The Selling of the President* (New York: Simon & Schuster, Pocket Books, 1969).

[36]See Donald E. Stokes, "Some Dynamic Elements of Contests for the Presidency," *American Political Science Review*, March 1966, p. 23; also Angus Campbell et al., *The American Voter* (New York: Wiley, 1960), section 2.

[37]For a historical review of these substantive appeals, see Benjamin Ginsberg, "Critical Elections and American Public Policy" (Ph.D. diss., University of Chicago, 1971); see also Julius Turner, "Responsible Parties: A Dissent from the Floor," *American Political Science Review*, March 1953, p. 143.

[38]Although the developer of the southern strategy for Nixon was probably John Mitchell, the chief theorist was a staff member, Kevin Phillips, who later published it all in a popular book, *The Emerging Republican Majority* (New Rochelle, N.Y.: Arlington House, 1969). The southern strategy mainly involved a shift of emphasis, beginning with the nomination of a southerner for vice-president and including the saturation of the South and the Wallace areas of the North with white, conservative appeals.

Actually, most of the southern votes in 1968 went to George Wallace, but this created a "negative landslide" against the Democrats, depriving them of just enough popular votes to keep them away from their normal control of the electoral votes in the southern states. Only on rare occasions, usually following some kind of catastrophe, do important substantive appeals move from the regional to the national level. When they do, they usually produce negative landslides, on a national level, where the incumbent president is thrown out of office but the opposing party does not necessarily gain proportionately.[39]

It should be clear that candidates for the presidency do not have a large range of choices in the way they will conduct their campaigns and in the terms they choose to appeal to a national electorate of over 70 million voters. One additional tactic not yet identified but widely employed is that of engaging in dishonest and illegal strategies—activities which became known in 1973 as "dirty tricks." All candidates engage in dirty tricks to some extent; it is difficult to draw the line between a clean and a dirty use of the strategies already identified. For example, a candidate can take a regional approach to substantive appeals but in so doing may decide to appeal to the very worst instincts of race hatred and class warfare, rather than to the real and relatively harmless regional differences among voters. Candidates can make appeals on the basis of style and personality that are clean and honest, even if emotional, or they can engage in smear tactics, seeking to blacken the name and reputation of the other candidates.

Beyond these activities, there are some clearly unethical and illegal strategies, such as stuffing ballot boxes, bribing voters, or destroying the physical or financial resources of the other party. Americans received a complete education in the possibilities of dirty tricks in the aftermath of the 1972 campaign. However, the Watergate incident brought out some of the limits on the use of dirty tricks. First of all, illegal tactics can be found out and punished, as many were after 1973. But there is a more effective limitation. Each candidate operates with the full realization that the adversaries can engage in the same dirty tactics. There is generally a tacit agreement between competitors for the same office not to go too far with dishonesty or illegality, because in the end all of the candidates might lose.

When used on a limited basis, dirty tricks are usually not exposed by the victims because of their awareness that they or some of their people have engaged in some of the same dirty tricks. For example,

---

[39]Walter Dean Burnham identified the negative landslide in a brilliant analysis of the 1968 election, "Election 1968—The Abortive Landslide," *TransAction,* December 1968, p. 21. Burnham showed that there was an unprecedented defection of Democratic voters between 1964 and 1968 (a loss of 18.2 percent) but no equivalent increase in Republican support during the same period (a gain of only 4.9 percent).

Perils of the presidency:
Assassinations—
successful and
unsuccessful. *Opposite
page, clockwise from top
left:* Lincoln, Garfield,
Wallace, McKinley. *This
page:* Robert Kennedy
and John F. Kennedy.

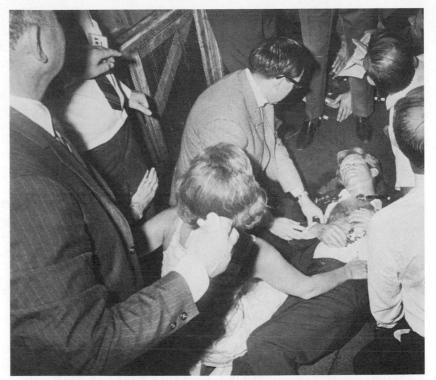

rumors flew about in 1960 that the Illinois and Texas electors had been virtually stolen for the Democrats, thus assuring the election to John Kennedy. The Nixon people claimed that Nixon refused to pursue a vote recount because he did not want to achieve the presidency through a constitutional crisis. However, beyond these noble sentiments was also the distinct awareness that a recount in those two states could easily produce recounts and perhaps evidence of Republican ballot tampering in other states.

In 1972 the Nixon people apparently broke the tacit agreement, and once all the barriers were down, the Democrats in Congress no longer felt the usual restraints about using their special congressional privileges to embarrass the other party. This was not the first time one party could have exposed the wrongdoing of the other party. This was simply the first time in our modern history that the victimized party felt it had gained the right to retaliate to the fullest.

What the Election Does Not Mean

Does victory, even a decisive victory, convert electoral sources into presidential resources? There is only one certainty about the election—that the winner is allowed by all others to take office and to use all of the formal powers vested in that office. In nearly two hundred years, and through thirty-six presidents and forty-seven presidential elections, no one has ever seriously questioned the right of the winning candidate (or his vice-presidential successor, in case of death or resignation) to occupy the office and to use all of the powers available to it. Consent was not even seriously questioned when President Hayes took office, despite the fact that his election over Samuel Tilden in 1876 was very hotly disputed and in the long run very questionable.[40]

This absolutely extraordinary stability and legitimacy of the electoral process has undoubtedly been strengthened by the fact that the outcome of the Electoral College vote has always been distorted in favor of the candidate who gained a plurality of the popular vote. For example, Kennedy beat Nixon in 1960 by less than a 1 percent margin of popular votes but received over 56 percent of the Electoral College vote. Nixon beat Humphrey by a good deal less than 50 percent of the total popular vote, thanks to a three-way split involving George Wallace; but Nixon, too, in 1968 received over 56 percent of the Electoral College vote. In each instance, the winner was given a "clear majority to govern," even though the popular vote majority was very thin or nonexistent.

This means that the election makes all presidents about equal at the beginning of their tenure in office, since the powers of the office

[40]For details see C. Vann Woodward, *Reunion and Reaction* (Boston: Little, Brown, 1951).

are available to anyone who occupies it. However, small differences in how presidents marshal their resources are thought to make great differences in presidential effectiveness. The scientist wishing to make effective use of solar energy, which is vast but diffuse, must convert that energy into a more concentrated and focused form to run machines and create light and heat. So it is with the president, who must somehow concentrate the vast but diffuse energies of popular election and bring them to focus on the "Washington community."

The Washington community includes members of Congress, the top military and civilian officialdom, the top corporate and group leaders or their representatives, the state governors and a few state and local political leaders with good access to Washington, important foreign officialdom, and the top Washington correspondents of major newspapers, television, radio, and news services. These people are the president's main constituency, and the president must serve them well or impress them vigorously; must be credible to them; must hold their respect for selfish purposes. As Neustadt put it so well over a decade ago: "The men who share in governing do what they think they must. A president's effect on them is heightened or diminished by their thoughts about his probable reaction to their doing. They base their expectations on what they can see of him. And they are watching all the time."[41]

It is best to approach the meaning of the election and the influence of presidential resources on the Washington community by considering first the meanings elections do not have. First, we can safely say that the policies espoused by a successful candidate during the campaign are not necessarily confirmed by the election victory and will not necessarily become the candidate's program once that person has taken office. As often as not, a president will seek to act in a manner totally contradictory to intentions explicit or implicit in the campaign, in order to expand popular support beyond the electoral support. President Nixon took some of the boldest steps in international affairs in our history during his first term—a move toward the left, in fact, which he himself had helped prevent Democrats from making all during the 1950s. Hardly any of his regular Republican supporters would ever have imagined he would make this move toward détente with Russia and recognition of Red China.

A second negative point—one which could have been anticipated from earlier chapters without ever examining presidential nominations and campaigns—is that the actual pattern of voting outcomes

---

[41]Neustadt, *Presidential Power*, p. 59. For a fascinating account of the original Washington community, see James S. Young, *The Washington Community: 1800–1828* (New York: Columbia University Press, 1966). For the 1970s, see Nelson Polsby, "Can a President Govern Effectively Who Systematically Alienates Himself from the Rest of Official Washington?" *Washington Post,* June 3, 1973.

Instrumentation of Control: The Presidency

rarely produces any meaning that more than a few people can agree upon. Voters in a particular income bracket almost never vote overwhelmingly in favor of a single candidate. It is not even possible to find meaning in the patterns of voting among the various regions of the country, now that the South is no longer a solid bloc. This is surely what V. O. Key meant when he observed that "the vocabulary of the voice of the people consists mainly of the words 'yes' and 'no'; and at times one cannot be certain which word is being uttered."[42]

National elections do have meaning, but almost always the meaning cannot be understood except in the long run. This is the third negative point. The meaning of a presidential election usually cannot be known in time to have any bearing upon what a president does or upon how the Washington community will want to treat him. Political scientists are good at classifying elections, especially presidential elections. Take, for example, a widely used set of categories developed by the University of Michigan Survey Research Center: (1) maintaining elections, (2) deviating elections, (3) reinstating elections, and (4) realigning or "critical" elections.[43] For certain analytic purposes these are worthwhile categories, but few if any elections can be placed in one of the four categories and have their meanings interpreted without benefit of at least two succeeding elections. With the aid of hindsight we can see that 1896 and 1932 were realigning or critical elections, in that whole segments of the electorate uniformly shifted their allegiance from one party to the other and maintained that new allegiance for several elections thereafter.

Such critical realignments have an almost definitive impact on succeeding decades of politics.[44] Yet neither President McKinley nor President Franklin Roosevelt could have assumed that the electorate had shifted more or less permanently in their direction. Many observers at the time thought that the decisive victory of President Eisenhower in 1952 was going to be another moment of critical realignment; instead it turned out to be a deviating election in which Democrats split in favor of Eisenhower but remained Democrats for all other purposes. Another critical realignment has been expected since 1964, but each succeeding presidential election has upset or altered these expectations.

This confusion of possible meanings deprives a president of a considerable amount of the potential value of the popular base. Nothing is likely to be more sobering to a president than his

---

[42]V. O. Key, *Politics, Parties, and Pressure Groups,* 5th ed. (New York: Crowell, 1964), p. 544 and note 28.

[43]Angus Campbell et al., *Elections and the Political Order* (New York: Wiley, 1966), chapters 2 and 3.

[44]Walter Dean Burnham, *Critical Elections and the Mainsprings of American Politics* (New York: Norton, 1970).

recollection of the fact that many presidents had their greatest political problems after a decisive reinstating election. Roosevelt after 1936, Eisenhower after 1956, Johnson after 1964, and even more so Nixon after 1972—all are examples of presidents returned to office by reinstating elections that were at best a mere approval of past action but no guarantee of smooth and cooperative politics to come. It is necessary to look beyond any and all electoral outcomes to understand how and under what conditions a president's popular base can become a true resource for his power to govern.

Sources into Resources: The Long, Arduous Conversion

The election gives the president nothing but the privilege of occupying the office. A popular base is a source of leadership, but the president personally must convert or translate that popular base into a resource for leadership. There are very limited methods available to any president to bring about this conversion, and few presidents have ever succeeded to their own satisfaction.

Uses and limitations of appointive power   Most often the first resort of presidents is judicious use of cabinet and other high-level appointments. In each instance the president hopes to borrow the political following of each appointee. President Nixon's first cabinet—the top twelve department heads—is an instructive example. It was composed of three governors, one lieutenant governor, one leading Republican congressman, one southern Republican Party leader, two prominent New York corporate lawyers, and two prominent members of the Chicago financial community.

Two appointments were enigmas. One was a college professor appointed secretary of agriculture; he was soon replaced by a man with a much more impressive following among agriculture groups. The other was also a professor, appointed secretary of labor. He, too, was without a personal political following; but his appointment was considered at least inoffensive to labor organizations and therefore a potential route by which Nixon could extend his popular base.[45] The president also has available a number of additional appointments to high office which can be utilized for purposes of focusing public support. The business community carefully watches appointments to the regulatory commissions, and it is probably rare for such appointments to be lacking in some kind of important political sponsorship.

Unfortunately, the use of the appointment power to marshal and focus the broad popular forces of the presidency has its limitations. First of all, those who have political support sufficient to be

[45]For further analysis of cabinets and their uses, see Richard Fenno, *The President's Cabinet* (Cambridge, Mass.: Harvard University Press, 1959).

President Nixon's chief of
staff, General Alexander
Haig: Power of the
Pentagon or power over
the Pentagon?

attractive to the president also have their own goals in life. There is
every reason to expect that they will continue to pursue their own
goals even while in the cabinet, and once in a while these goals are
likely to be in opposition to those of the president. Almost never will
the goals of a cabinet member and the president be identical. To say
the least, all top political appointees are special pleaders. It is
difficult to know when they are operating on their own behalf and
when they are disinterestedly working for the president.

A second limitation on the use of the appointive power by the
president is that the political following a cabinet member brings is
not necessarily translatable into effective control over the department the appointee is supposed to administer. For example, Robert
Finch had been a very popular lieutenant governor in California,
with a real political following and a brilliant future in politics. He
was also known to be an intimate of President Nixon. Nevertheless,

he was apparently a dismal failure as Nixon's first secretary of health, education and welfare.

Finally, the appointive power is a limited device because these very cabinet members have power primarily in terms of their ability to speak for the president and to use on his behalf the formal powers of the presidency. Thus, regardless of how much the president might be able to borrow from their political support, their ability to serve him effectively is still heavily dependent upon his independent credibility in Washington. Long after the president has shot his bolt with the appointment of his top political personnel, he must go on cultivating his credibility, never being sure whether his top officials are adding to it or detracting from it. Chief executives often come to feel that their top officials are also their "natural enemies." This is undoubtedly part of the motivation for the expansion of the White House staff over the past two decades (see chapter 12).

One of the most instructive cases of the complex relationship between the president and his cabinet is the contrast between President Nixon's first cabinet and the cabinet he organized immediately following his reelection in January 1973. Those persons with the most impressive personal constituencies from 1969 had almost completely disappeared. The governors and lieutenant governors were gone; the men with independent followings in the financial community were gone; even the congressmen and the southern Republican leaders were gone. They were replaced by what are generally called "political eunuchs." As the prominent columnists Evans and Novak put it in their review of the new cabinet, "First, the Cabinet member must fit the political grand design for a new Republican majority; second, he cannot be a genuine personage, possibly unwilling to subordinate himself to White House aides."[46]

Nixon's overwhelming reelection victory had apparently encouraged him to believe that he did not any longer need to borrow on the political followings of others and could instead concentrate on direct control of the departments and agencies by appointing persons who might know something about the departments in question but who would be personally loyal to him and personally dependent on his own popular support. Although this direction was not celebrated in Washington, it was a perfectly reasonable step for the president to have taken. The Watergate crisis and Nixon's resignation prevent us from knowing whether it was rational in the long run. But it does help show how ambivalent presidents are toward their top political appointees.

Since the appointive power is but a limited device for maintaining credibility, the president must search elsewhere for additional

[46]From a two-part review of Nixon's second cabinet in the *Washington Post,* December 9 and 21, 1972.

devices. "Keeping the initiative" is a central article of faith among presidents since John Kennedy. Presentation of the budget and the president's program have already been shown to be major aspects of this. The president also attempts to keep the initiative by regularly presenting specific legislative proposals to Congress, and by selecting from among these proposals a few to take to the population at large. Although risky, the president can also employ the technique of taking direct action. This is precisely what Kennedy tried to do in his public effort to roll back increases in the price of steel. He confronted the steel executives directly with all kinds of threatening sounds, and his attorney general (Robert Kennedy) was responsible for dispatching FBI agents to the home of one of the most important steel executives in the middle of the night in order to impress upon him the seriousness of the action. President Nixon was a great believer in gaining the top hand over history by seeking crises *or* capitalizing on them. The dramatic move on China is sufficient illustration.

Manipulating the media The president also attempts to cultivate and maintain popular support by using the news media in a variety of ways. The press conference has become the main mechanism for this, and presidents have believed in it most of the time since the end of World War II. The last three presidents have carried the press conference to a magnificently high art by appearing live and unprompted before the press corps and national television cameras. These appearances cultivate a president's popular base and at the same time keep the initiative in his hands, because the press conference helps him dominate the front page of all the newspapers and the opening minutes of virtually all network news broadcasts.[47]

News activity does not cease between press conferences but only changes form. News activity in the White House is especially vigorous while Congress is in session. Press releases emanate from the White House press secretary's office at an average of two or more per day. There has been much self-congratulation in the newspaper industry for the rise of investigative reporting during the Vietnam War and the Watergate affair. This would suggest that newspaper reporters are relying increasingly upon independent sources rather than the White House for news about presidential actions.

However, investigative reporting occupies the time of very few reporters, and these are usually young and quite ambitious people who have not yet been admitted to full membership in the Washington community. Most of the other Washington correspondents

---

[47]For various aspects of press conferences and the news, consult E. E. Cornwell, *Presidential Leadership of Public Opinion* (Bloomington: Indiana University Press, 1965), especially chapter 8.

whose assignment or "beat" is the White House or related departments usually sit around the press offices waiting for the press releases and converting them, often without much editing, into their news stories of the day. Occasionally an important reporter is granted an inside interview.

Nevertheless, "news analysis" is heavily influenced by the daily briefings that the press secretary provides the White House reporters. In this manner, the president can not only dominate the news but also to a large extent control the interpretation that will reach the newspapers.[48] Important as this opportunity is, it, too, is limited. Using the news channel as a device to maintain influence is possible only as long as the president retains credibility. When general credibility begins to decline, the same reporters who were using the press releases uncritically suddenly become distrustful, and the president's direct conduit to the public begins to be choked off.

These methods of summoning and maintaining popular support as a base of presidential power must be understood in the context of presidential action. That is to say, the president does not passively or casually utilize a press conference or a special address to Congress or a speech on prime time television. He is making use of these devices in support of one or more specific presidential actions, and at bottom it is the action that will ultimately count. Probably nothing is as generally impressive to the public and to the Washington community as a presidential action that has been demonstrably drawn from mass public interest.

Patterns of public approval—and disapproval   Public reaction to presidential action is, as should be expected, very complex. However, certain patterns seem to persist over long periods regardless of the personality of the president. Figure 11.1 is a profile of presidential popularity between 1946 and 1973, covering most of the history of the presidency since the advent of modern polling. The figure is based upon responses to a question asked consistently throughout the entire period: "Do you approve or disapprove of the way the president is handling his job?" The question is useful because it does not seek attitudes on particular presidential actions but is deliberately phrased to evoke a general, emotional feeling from the respondent. Its special beauty is that it has been asked in the same manner to about the same size random sample more than once every month for over a quarter of a century. And it can be used to gauge public reaction to presidential action without taking the responses as any kind of referendum.

---

[48]A very good assessment of the role of the press secretary and of the daily White House briefings will be found in an article by Dennis Farney, "Is Daily White House Briefing News or Just a Waste?" *Wall Street Journal*, June 13, 1975. His answer: "At times, it's hard to tell."

The most striking part of the overall pattern is that each president seems to have begun with a fairly strong base of popular support following each national election. Generally the support he received immediately after his electoral victory was in excess of the popular vote he received in the November election. It is said that the ancient Chinese believed that each emperor began his reign with a fund of support from the gods which he either squandered or spent wisely through the course of his reign. The reign came to an end when the emperor had spent all of his providential favors. If that were true of the ancient Chinese emperors, they seem to have been reincarnated in the presidency, for nothing could come closer to a statistical rendering of that belief than the profile in Figure 11.1. Note how the figure spurts upward following each presidential election, indeed beyond 65 percent approval for almost every president. Note how spectacularly popular support jumped up even for Harry Truman after his election in 1948 despite the low level of public regard for him during most of the months prior to that time.[49]

It is this fund of postelection support that a president must try to cashier into governing power; it is very much a part of what has been called the "honeymoon period." However, note the snags and disappointments that follow. It is risky to personalize on statistics, but it does not seem too far afield to observe that by all appearances presidents do seem to *use up* their popular resources as they try to *use* them. Only President Eisenhower seems to have managed to avoid this tendency. He had his ups and downs with the public—experiencing one of the severest declines in public support during the fifteen or so months following his spectacular reelection in 1956. However, during the last two years of his administration, public support was maintained and even increased slightly.

There is no definitive answer to the exception of Eisenhower's last two years, although two hypotheses are fairly strongly confirmed through the available data. One of these is that President Eisenhower was probably less active or assertive during that period than the typical post–World War II president has been. This meant that he did not use up as many of his public resources. The second hypothesis is that there were more than the usual number of international events and crises during that period; the data in Table 11.3 demonstrate that the public tends consistently to support presidents during such periods.

It is when we begin to look at specific issues that we see real meaning back of the gross profile in Figure 11.1. Table 11.3 is a presentation of a few before and after events, giving the state of public opinion according to the polls just prior to and immediately

---

[49]Since Figure 11.1 is based on quarterly averages of responses, it occasionally suppresses an unusually high or low monthly report. Thus, Truman's quarterly figure is a bit lower than some of the specific monthly reports included in the average.

Figure 11.1
A profile of presidential
popularity: Nationwide
responses to the question:
Do you approve of the
way the president is
handling his job?*

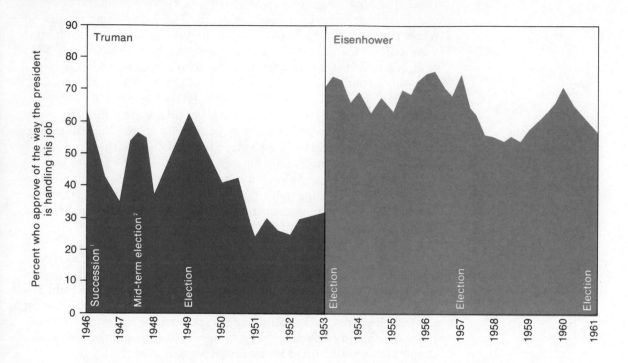

after given presidential actions. Each item in Table 11.3 involves some kind of action or event unambiguously associated with a president and his administration. Each poll was carefully chosen to be as closely associated as possible to the time of the action. Since no other events of equal importance occurred during the period in question—and care was taken to avoid such situations—it was at least possible to imagine that part, if not all, of the difference of public rating could be attributed to the event. No single instance confirms any hypothesis. However, the consistency of the pattern across all of these events cannot be taken lightly.[50]

Table 11.3 strongly confirms the proposition that the public tends to downgrade the president in response to domestic actions. There is

[50]The data and some of these passages are taken from Theodore Lowi, *The Politics of Disorder* (New York: Basic Books, 1971), chapter 4, pp. 93–95, and Tables 4–1 and 4–2.

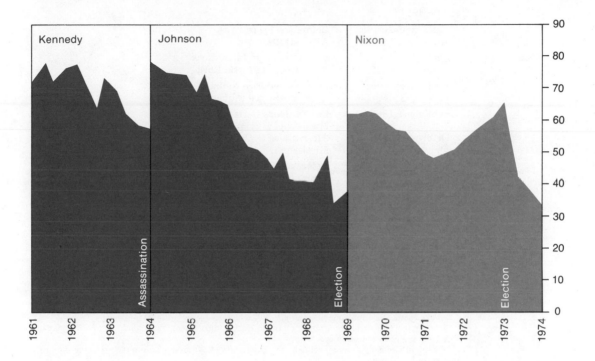

Data from American Institute of Public Opinion (Gallup Poll) through regular press releases and through courtesy of Roper Opinion Research Center, Williamstown, Mass.

*In a few instances the regular poll did not include the question on approval of the president. In those cases the point is passed over on the figure but the space is maintained.
[1] The high of 1946 was already down from 87 to 82 percent immediately following Truman's succession in 1945.
[2] Bounded up briefly despite Democrats' loss of Congress to the Republicans.

only one exception to this pattern of downward movement, and it is the public reaction to President Truman's seizure of the steel mills in 1952. However, this is the one item on that table where there was a competing event of equal importance—President Truman's announcement that he was going to retire rather than run for reelection. This could easily account for the slight upward movement in response to a domestic event. (It should also be noted that the steel seizure came very close to an "international event." See Table 11.4 for that pattern.)

Granted, the consistent downward drop for all other issues in this table is not dramatic; granted also, other events were taking place at the same time. Nevertheless, this table in conjunction with Figure 11.1 tends to substantiate the idea that presidents use up their popular support. The more analytical reader may now be wondering what these figures would look like if regions of the

Instrumentation of Control: The Presidency

441

Table 11.3

The President in the Eyes of the Public—Domestic Events

Date	Nature of Presidential Action at Issue	Percent of Sample Group Who Approved of Presidential Actions
May 1947	Before veto of Taft-Hartley bill	57
July 1947	After veto	54
Late January 1952	Before steel seizure	25
April 1952	After steel seizure	28[1]
July 1957	Before troops to Little Rock[2]	63
Late October 1957	After troops to Little Rock	57
Early April 1962	Before steel price rollback	77
May 1962	After steel price rollback	73
September 1962	Before troops to Oxford, Mississippi[3]	67
October 1962	After troops to Oxford, Mississippi	61
Late May 1963	Before civil rights message	65
Late June 1963	After civil rights message	61
July 1965	Before Medicare passage	69
August 1965	After Medicare passage	65
June 1967	After Glassboro, before troops to Detroit[4]	52
August 1967	After troops to Detroit	39

Data from American Institute of Public Opinion (Gallup Poll) through regular press releases and through courtesy of Roper Opinion Research Center, Williamstown, Mass. Reprinted from Theodore Lowi, *Politics of Disorder* (New York: Basic Books, 1971), p. 94.
[1]This survey was taken shortly after President Truman announced his retirement, and this could explain the slight increase in approval, which had gone up to 32 percent by June.
[2]During the fight over integration of Little Rock's high school, President Eisenhower sent in federal troops to maintain order.
[3]President Kennedy ordered troops to the University of Mississippi campus during the integration conflict there.
[4]President Johnson met in Glassboro, New Jersey, with Aleksei Kosygin, Soviet head of government, to discuss the Vietnam War and other issues. On July 27–28, the Detroit riots led to President Johnson's decision to send in federal paratroopers.

country were taken into account. The suspicion that reactions vary regionally is well-founded. But the reader should also be reminded that almost every domestic action a president takes will be subject to some kind of critical reaction in one or more sections of the country. This only helps explain why there is a net downward tendency in public reaction to presidential domestic actions.

Table 11.4 is concerned with public reactions to international actions or events in the international realm associated with the president. Here the tendency in public reactions is upward rather than downward. Moreover, this upward tendency is not at all affected by the character of the international action. The U-2 incident in 1960 under Eisenhower and the Bay of Pigs incident in 1961 under Kennedy were both defined in the public realm as national embarrassments. In the first instance, President Eisen-

Table 11.4   **The President in the Eyes of the Public—International Events**

Date	Nature of Presidential Action at Issue	Percent of Sample Group Who Approved of Presidential Actions
June 1950	Before Korean War outbreak	37
July 1950	After U.S. entry	46
August 1956	Before Israeli, British, French attack on Suez	67
December 1956	After U.S. opposition to the attack	75
July 1958	Before Lebanon	52
August 1958	After U.S. marine landing	58
May 1960	Before U-2 incident	62
June 1960	After U-2 debacle; collapse of summit conference	68
March 1961	Before Bay of Pigs	73
April 1961	After Bay of Pigs	83
October 1962	Eve of Cuban missile crisis	61
December 1962	After missile crisis	74
October 1966	Before tour of Pacific	44
November 1966	After tour of Pacific	48
Early June 1967	Before Glassboro conference	44
Late June 1967	After Glassboro conference	52
October 1969	Before announcement of Nixon Vietnam withdrawal plan	53
November 1969	After announcement	68

Data from American Institute of Public Opinion (Gallup Poll) through regular press releases and through courtesy of Roper Opinion Research Center, Williamstown, Mass. Reprinted from Theodore Lowi, *The End of Liberalism* (New York: Norton, 1969).

hower was caught in an outright lie concerning our use of high atmosphere airplanes to conduct surveillance operations over the territory of the Soviet Union. Yet his popular rating went up. The Bay of Pigs disaster was almost certainly a more severe embarrassment to the United States, because this time the violation of the territorial rights of a foreign nation was with ground troops rather than overflights. Yet, President Kennedy's popular support rating jumped up to the highest level of support in the entire history of polling.[51]

These figures suggest that there are two systems of public opinion regarding the presidency in the United States. One system is nationalistic. It is based on consensus; it is mobilizable, and it tends to be militaristic. It has often been properly characterized by the phrase, "Politics stops at the water's edge." The second system is

Instrumentation of Control: The Presidency

[51]The figure of 83 percent in Table 11.4 does not show up in Figure 11.1 for 1961 because of the use of quarterly averages in Figure 11.1.

domestic in orientation. It is not consensual; it is self-interested; it is segmented by class differences, regional differences, narrow economic differences, and ethnic differences. And it is definitely not a priori favorable to presidential actions.[52] These two systems of public opinion provide a very dynamic and problematic public opinion context for the president. Perhaps the best advice one could give new presidents is to hit quick and hold. Most presidents seem to try to avail themselves of their early popular support, but few seem to appreciate that this early support is most of what they are going to get. For the rest of their four-year term, as well as most of the second term, public opinion must be carefully courted on the basis of specific issues.

One method of building public opinion support at a given time is to create some kind of international incident. As indicated in Table 11.4, general public opinion is usually mobilized to a president's benefit in such cases. But alas for the president who turns on an incident which he cannot so easily turn off. If the international involvement lasts for a while, the president may be worse off than before. This was certainly true during the months after our intervention in Korea and during the months following the escalation of the war in Vietnam.

Individual polls cannot capture this sort of thing, but Figure 11.1 and related studies strongly suggest that the longer the duration of the international commitment, the stronger the probability that public approval will turn downward.[53] The president can also build public backing by launching domestic campaigns for specific causes, such as President Nixon's campaign for revenue sharing or President Johnson's campaign for civil rights legislation. But no president can do this every day for each and every issue on which he needs public support for victory. His opportunities are limited not only by the amount of attention available among citizens but by the fact that each action, especially in the domestic field, is likely to end up making the next campaign more difficult. This is simply another way of saying that active presidents use up their public support as they use it.

Presidential Resources and Presidential Power: An Assessment

Studies of the success of various presidents in getting their legislative initiatives through Congress indicate that presidential popu-

---

[52]For further discussion of these two systems of opinion, see Lowi, *The Politics of Disorder,* chapter 4.

[53]See, for example, Milton Rosenberg, Sidney Verba, and Phillip Converse, *Viet Nam and the Silent Majority* (New York: Harper & Row, 1970.) See also Kenneth Waltz, *Foreign Policy and Democratic Politics* (Boston: Little, Brown, 1967), especially his discussion of "electoral punishment."

larity does not necessarily guarantee four years of presidential leadership. For example, during the eight years of President Eisenhower's tenure, his success in getting his legislative proposals through Congress dropped from .650 to .350. President Kennedy's batting average dropped from .500 to slightly below .300. At the time of his assassination, there was a great deal of talk about the New Frontier "bogging down." Following the assassination, President Johnson began with a batting average of .600 and went up the following year to .700—the best postelection honeymoon period since the famous "100 days" of 1933. However, by early 1968 his legislative success average had dropped toward .500, although there was a slight surge during 1968 following his announcement that he was not going to be a candidate for reelection. Thus, if the first piece of advice to the president was to hit first and hold, the succeeding items of advice would be to specialize and to foray into the domestic arena only rarely—and only when there is already a good chance of winning—because domestic politics is divisive for the broader public, and the Washington community is impressed only with victory.

Yet no president is likely to heed this advice. It may be the case that the personalities of those who seek the presidency do not allow them to take on the role of restraint combined with occasionally decisive action. But it is even more probable that the Washington community will not allow the president to heed this advice. The development of presidential government has meant that each president is expected to take the initiative, and most members of the Washington community seem to need a presidency that is genuinely active every day of the year.

> Everybody now expects the man inside the White House to do something about everything. . . . But such acceptance does not signify that all the rest of government is at his feet. It merely signifies that other men have found it practically impossible to do *their* jobs without assurance of initiatives from him. Service for themselves, not power for the President, has brought them to accept his leadership in form. They find his actions useful in their business.[54] (Italics in original.)

No matter how great the president's effort to respond, all of these demands for initiative eventually chip away at his own base of power. As Neustadt puts it, support of the Washington community only guarantees that the president will be their clerk; it does not guarantee that he will be their leader. His leadership has to come from other sources.

Obviously it is extremely difficult to rely completely on any single resource or combination of resources to sustain presidential leader-

---

[54]Neustadt, *Presidential Power,* p. 6. Neustadt may not necessarily agree with the analysis here, but his statement best portrays the contemporary situation.

The occasional triumph of
being president: Signing a
bill into law.

ship. In the final analysis, the question of presidential power comes down to two basic conditions. The first is the *pattern* of electoral outcome for each president. The second is the constitutional and legal position of each president within his administration.

The electoral pattern and presidential power Where the Washington community is concerned, the acid test of presidential power is expressed in the following question: Can I buck the president and get away with it? This position of strength depends very heavily on the pattern of his electoral victory. By that we do not mean mere election, nor do we mean decisive election or reelection. There is a specific *pattern* of electoral victory which enables the president to translate popular support into leadership, and there are other patterns of electoral victory, no matter how decisive, which do not permit such translation.

Let us look first at a situation where the pattern of electoral outcome did *not* add to presidential power, despite the fact that the electoral victory itself was a decisive one—the overwhelming Nixon victory of 1972. Even without Watergate it would have been extremely difficult for President Nixon to translate his decisive victory into an enhanced power position in Washington, because he won very little besides his own reelection. For example, of all 435 seats to be filled in Congress, only 13, or about 3 percent, changed hands as a result of victories and defeats in the November election. Eight of those defeated were Democrats, but only four of them could be considered "liberal Democrats" by any stretch of the imagination. (A typical, though rough, measure of "liberal and conservative" positions is the so-called ADA score. This is a percentage based upon the proportion of times each member of the House or Senate voted for the fifteen or twenty issues chosen each year by the liberally-inclined Americans for Democratic Action. Thus, in this particular case, four of the Democrats had ADA scores of above 70 percent, while three of the defeated Democrats actually had ADA scores of below 12 percent. The average ADA score for northern Democrats, who were most likely to oppose Nixon's legislative proposals, ran well over 75 percent.) The five other defeated congressmen were strongly conservative Nixon Republicans—with an average ADA score of 27.5 percent. Three of these defeated Republicans were men of considerable influence, as measured by the fact that they had accumulated seven, nine, and fifteen terms in the House at the time of their defeat. In the Senate, only twenty-five incumbents were running for reelection, and of the five who were defeated, four were actually Republicans.

Many changes did take place during 1972, but none are attributable to Richard Nixon or his election. For example, fifty-seven members of Congress vacated office for reasons other than election defeat, as indicated:

Officially defeated for renomination 12
Vacancy in office due to voluntary retirement. 28
Vacancies due to death 2
Vacancies due to decision to run for higher office 13

Of the twelve defeated for renomination, ten were Democrats whose replacements therefore owed their victories to internal party issues far removed from the candidacy or wishes of President Nixon. Among those who voluntarily retired from office, seventeen were Republican congressmen. But since they were conservatives, having together compiled an average ADA score of 11 percent, their retirement was definitely a step backward for President Nixon. The remaining members of Congress were less susceptible to presidential influence in 1973 than they had been before 1972, despite the president's decisive reelection victory. This is because they either held safe seats, were Democrats, or were weaker (not as supportive) Republicans than those who had departed.[55]

---

[55]Another case where a decisive victory did not translate itself into presidential power is that of President Roosevelt after 1936. The election victory was of historic proportion; Roosevelt received well over 90 percent of the electoral vote and had unprecedented majorities of Democrats in the House and Senate. Yet, 1937 was filled with serious legislative defections and embarrassments for him. This is not a paradox, nor is it attributable to the mistakes he was to make later. These mistakes were in fact a response to the trouble he inherited by the 1936 election. What had happened was that the pattern of outcomes had actually gone against him but was masked by the size of the overall victory. For example, in fifteen of the forty-eight states (nearly one-third of all the states) Roosevelt experienced an actual drop in electoral support between 1932 and 1936. This drop was only slight in most instances; yet a very significant proportion of the anti-Roosevelt

The aftermath of 1964 is an example of the translation of an election into presidential power. Lyndon Johnson's victory was comparable to those of 1936 and 1972. But there was something more to the Johnson victory. In the first place, all of the liberals elected to the Senate in 1958 (known as the "Class of 1958") were reelected in 1964, despite the fact that many of them were considered marginal, or poor risks for reelection. The situation in the House was even more positive for Johnson. First, Republicans lost forty members in the election alone, comprising nearly one-quarter of their entire party in the House. Of this group, only four had ADA scores of over 25 percent in the previous Congress, and of the thirty-six remaining, twenty-three had compiled ADA scores in the zero to 5 percent range—a record of great envy among conservatives. The other thirteen had ADA scores of under 25 percent. Thus, this group of defeated members accounted for a very high proportion of all the members of Congress most likely to oppose President Johnson and his program. It also accounted for 244 years of seniority, which represented a tremendous amount of lost committee power.[56]

Better yet for President Johnson, seven of these Republicans had been serving on the Appropriations Committee; in fact, two of them were the first and second ranking members of the minority side of that committee and had ADA scores of zero. Defeated Republicans also included the first and second ranking members of the Committee on Government Operations, which investigates the executive branch; the most influential Republican member of the Rules Committee; and the second and fourth ranking Republican members of the all-important Ways and Means Committee, along with two more of the ten Republican members of that committee.

Thus Lyndon Johnson's pattern of victory provided him with a much higher degree of power in the presidency than did Roosevelt's or Nixon's, as indicated by the unprecedented success of Johnson's legislative requests in Congress (70 percent success—the only time in modern history). It was not until much later that members of the Washington community began to turn against the White House. Johnson's decline can truly be dated after the 1966 election, even though it was not certain for nearly two more years that he was a "lame duck."

The pattern of victory also helps explain why President Kennedy's program bogged down so quickly after his honeymoon period.

Democratic voting pattern in Congress in 1936 is attributable to congressmen from those fifteen States. In nine of the states the congressional defection was significant; and in three of them the defection was so significant that President Roosevelt sought to purge certain members of those state congressional delegations at reelection time in 1938. For a brief account of Roosevelt's vain effort to influence the defeat of certain recalcitrant Democrats, see William Riker, *Democracy in the United States* (New York: Macmillan, 1953), pp. 285–293.

[56]The figure of 244 years of seniority is derived by counting the years of service above the first term served by all the defeated incumbents.

Very few members of his party owed their election to Kennedy. In fact, most of the gains by the northern liberals were made in 1958; the 1960 election served primarily to reaffirm that victory. Very few seats changed hands at all in 1960, and few members of either House or Senate would have had any feeling of strong obligation to the president.

Heeding the constitutional forms   During the past twenty years political scientists and journalists have tended to stress such informal factors as leadership and will, popularity and charisma, and other "interpersonal" factors to explain political power—especially presidential power. However, the data covered so far in this chapter suggest that the informal sources of presidential power explain only marginal differences among presidents. The margins can of course be significant, as between President Roosevelt and President Hoover or between the beginning and the end of many of our presidents' terms of office. However, the real engine of the presidency is its formal construction and the formal authorizations handed over to it by Congress, through statutes and treaties, or by the courts. The construction of the engine is more important than minor differences in the quality of the fuel. The Constitution and the laws grant the president powers, limit the powers of others, and deliberately make almost every other member of the government dependent upon the moves and initiatives of the president. Presidential power is intentional. The growth of the formal *office* of president and the expansion of the informal *power* of the president are connected and related. It is the office that is powerful; it bestows the power upon the occupant, whose election and whose efforts may make slight differences in its effectiveness.

One of the most remarkable confirmations of the assertion that the formal definition of the presidency explains the power of the president can be found in the accomplishments of presidents during times when their popular support was at all-time low levels. The case of President Nixon is particularly telling in this respect. Although he could claim the support of less than 35 percent of the population and was ultimately forced to resign, he was making important decisions until the very end of his occupancy of the office. This must certainly prove that any occupant can utilize the powers of the office to the fullest until removed from that office, either by impeachment, resignation, death, or the end of the term.

Given the near equality of power among presidents, is it possible to judge and to rank them? " 'Ranking the Presidents' has always been a Favorite Indoor Sport of history-minded Americans."[57] Now that all presidents take initiatives and exert the full powers of the

[57]Clinton Rossiter, *The American Presidency,* rev. ed. (New York: Harcourt, Brace & World, Harvest Book, 1960), p. 137.

office, it is becoming an increasingly difficult game to play. If we define greatness as accomplishment, and if accomplishment requires the achievement of specifically defined goals, all presidents are closer to equal than anyone would like to admit. Perhaps we need another basis for judgment; maybe we should judge the greatness of presidents in terms of their character and of their conduct in office. We might consider, for example, the extent to which they attempt not only to take the people into account but also to raise the people's level of aspiration and ability to judge presidents. We might also consider judging presidents according to their effort to control and increase the accountability of the three million members of the executive branch.

The growth of presidential power can be considered modest in comparison to the growth of administrative organization and power in the executive branch. If the president fails to act or take the initiative in a matter concerning the economy, he may nevertheless be saved by the natural workings of the economy, just as he may be doomed (though blameless) by some natural and uncontrollable failing in the economy. However, when the president fails to exert or to accomplish effective control over administrators, the hell he pays may be our own.

The national administration of government is an institution in its own right. It is capable of expanding presidential power to an extent beyond imagination; it is also capable of nullifying the best and most vigorous efforts to govern. Everyone clamors to control it, and nearly everyone is frustrated. The president has the predominant right and obligation to deal with administrators. But Congress also has rights, as most assuredly do the courts. Every citizen has some rights in this regard, as does the press. But since the ultimate responsibility for administration in government lies with the president, the problems of administration will be analyzed best from the perspective of the presidency. In chapter 12 we will begin this enterprise—not with the assumption that the president controls administration but only with the assumption that he is always trying to cope with it.

Every modern system of conquest assumes that it has the unique capacity to create and to control the administrative apparatus necessary to ensure that conquest will be consistent with the ultimate goals of the system. No system has as yet fulfilled its assumptions. Up to this point in our history, the United States is no exception.

Chapter 12 The Chief Executive, the Executive Branch, and the Management of Conquest

The president is directed by the Constitution and supposed by the public to be chief executive. Yet, the chief executive in the American system is a product of representative government, and the executive branch is a product of bureaucratization. The two belong to the same governmental galaxy, but to tie them together as one political process would suppress the special political features of the executive branch. In our system of government there are tensions inherent in the relationship between the chief executive and the executive branch.

We begin once again with a dilemma. It is the same dilemma—incomplete conquest—in a new, complex, and more threatening form. The possibility of maintaining conquest over a large industrial nation without having an elaborate administrative apparatus is as remote as flying by

The Chief Executive, the Executive Branch, and the Management of Conquest

451

flapping one's arms. We cannot live without administration, yet we do not live very well with it. Ambivalence toward the bureaucratization of government is a great American culture trait.

Modern conquest cannot be understood without a thorough appreciation of the character of the problem at hand. Federal civil service employees alone now number nearly 3 million—almost one out of every thirty employed persons in the United States—and almost 98 percent of these people work in the executive branch. (According to 1972 statistics, about 1.6 percent of all federal employees worked for the legislative branch, and .4 percent worked for the judicial branch.) In order to assure their accountability in the expenditure of over one-third of a *trillion* dollars and their application of hundreds of thousands of coercive legal provisions, our Constitution and laws provide for lines of authority running hierarchically through the departments and agencies, culminating in a chief executive. Though at the apex of the hierarchy, the presidency has not been overwhelmingly successful in directing the bureaucratic organizations of the executive branch; here again conquest is incomplete.

Describing and evaluating the executive branch is probably the largest single undertaking of this volume. A brief overview of the discussion to follow may be of some assistance to the reader. First, we will need to define the "bureaucratic phenomenon," identifying the basic principles of organization in an administrative process. Next it will be necessary to see how and to what extent this phenomenon manifests itself in American government. Selected cases of the following types of agencies will be presented: (1) the "clientele" departments, directed by law to foster and promote a particular sector of the economy; (2) the new "service" departments, also directed to foster a clientele—but a clientele defined as a social class, usually dependent and unorganized; (3) the traditional control or "police power" agencies; (4) the survival agencies, such as the State and Defense Departments; and (5) the independent agencies.

After these detailed descriptions, we should be able to evaluate the problem of bureaucratic responsibility to the political levels of government, and the ways in which representative government manages to cope with bureaucracy—if, indeed, it ever does. The evaluation here will be made largely from the presidential perspective. Yet, no matter how it is attacked, every generation has to face this problem, and rarely does one generation leave a permanent legacy upon which the next can build.

THE BUREAUCRATIC PHENOMENON[1]

Bureaucracy is a pejorative word in the United States—a perfectly good concept corrupted by our ambivalence toward any kind of

---

[1]The title of this section is drawn from an important sociological work on the subject by Michel Crozier, *The Bureaucratic Phenomenon* (Chicago: University of Chicago Press, 1964).

Table 12.1	Characteristics of Bureaucratic Organizations (Public or Private)
	Principles of Bureaucratic Organization 1. Division of labor 2. Allocation of functions 3. Allocation of responsibility 4. Supervision along hierarchical lines 5. Full-time, salaried work 6. Career identification

government that is not loosely drawn, electoral, pluralistic. The negative connotations of the concept are not unwarranted, but the phenomenon itself is very real, enormously important, and deserving of careful and objective treatment.

Bureaucracy is nothing more nor less than a form of organization, a way to organize people and machinery together in order to accomplish a task. It is probably the most efficient means known to humans for coordinating people and machinery. Bureaucracy and administration are frequently used synonymously and interchangeably. In many contexts, this will suffice; however, it is probably preferable to treat administration as a more general term, referring to the overall process by which collective goals are pursued. Bureaucracy can then be reserved for a slightly more restricted class of phenomena, the actual agencies and principles employed in the administrative process. This distinction will be observed here.

The bureaucratic form of organization is so complex that it must be defined by listing and discussing its several basic characteristics, as in Table 12.1.

1. The division of labor is of course one of the fundamental principles of rationality in all areas of society, not only within bureaucracy. Most works of social science treat it as fundamental.[2] Division of labor enables each worker to develop a routine and a skill, which almost inevitably increases the productivity of work.

2. Allocation of functions comes immediately thereafter, because division of labor is of little value unless each worker is assigned one of the divided tasks, sticks to that task, and is assured that the other tasks are being performed by other members of the group. But note how complex this type of social organization already appears to be. No one produces a whole product; each person is dependent upon many others for the materials and services necessary to do just one small part of the overall job.

3. Allocation of responsibility must take place at this point, despite the additional complexity, because the allocation of func-

[2]For example, probably the first work in modern economics, Adam Smith's *The Wealth of Nations* (published, coincidentally, in 1776), opened not with Smith's famous disquisition about the free market and market competition, but actually with an inquiry into the division of labor.

tions must be made as dependable as possible. Each task becomes defined as a personal responsibility. The task cannot be abandoned or substituted by another task except by plan or by specific permission. Even a high-ranking account executive in an advertising agency cannot choose one morning to become an illustrator or an accountant. The assigned functions, defined as responsibilities or the rational requirements of the bureaucratic organization, would be violated by such an action.

4. Supervision is required because the bureaucracy cannot take for granted that responsibilities will be fulfilled. Most organizations usually set aside a number of jobs whose assigned responsibilities are in fact the maintenance of the organization rather than the contribution to its final product. This is probably the main reason most organizations become not only hierarchical but also pyramidal in form. Largely because of the limits of communication, no supervisor or foreman can be expected to watch over all subordinates. The "lower line administrator" may supervise the work of several dozen people. These administrators are supervised by a division head, and a very few division heads are then supervised by still fewer middle- and upper-level administrators. Those at the very top of the organization almost never concern themselves with the lowest levels of operations; they limit their concern to the broad goals of the organization and the problem of breaking these goals down into the more specialized tasks, functions, and responsibilities.

Two very important and popularly understood principles are involved here. One of these is the "span of control," a principle which holds that each supervisor should be responsible for only a limited number of subordinates; at the middle levels the upper limit may be eight or ten subordinates. The other principle is the "chain of command," which holds that communications going up and down the organization should move from level to level in an orderly fashion; no subordinate should skip his or her own supervisor in reporting a complaint or a suggestion, and no upper-level manager should communicate with employees at the lowest ranks without going through the intermediate supervisors. All of this means that each bureaucratic organization is closely bound together by rules, and most of these rules are concerned with the ways each level of organization relates to all the other levels.

5. Since most readers have been brought up in a culture where work means full-time salaried employment, it may sound trivial at first to stress this as a fundamental character of bureaucratic organization. However, in an organization of the sort described by the first four characteristics, it would be almost impossible to operate successfully unless the upper-level administrators were able to purchase the right to all of the labor output of each employee. This is the only way that assignments of function can be

allocated dependably. Moreover, this is the only way those at the top can maintain the right to *reorganize* work and functions in order to improve productivity or to iron out organizational snags. When an individual takes a job, that person agrees to abide by the terms of the organization in return for payment.

6. Following closely upon the above is the concept of the organization as a way of life, or a career. This is encouraged partly to improve the morale of individual workers by supplementing their pride in their own individual work with pride in the organization itself. But it is also encouraged in order to stabilize the organization. It reduces personnel turnover while increasing the willingness of each worker to submit to supervision. In chapter 3 we already have had occasion to see how pension plans and seniority methods are forms of conquest. Workers are encouraged to invest time and money in their organization, for then they will be far less casual about leaving.

Not all actual organizations or institutions possess all six of these attributes to the fullest extent. They can be bureaucratic to varying *degrees;* and they can be bureaucratized in different ways, depending on which of the six characteristics are significantly involved. Congress, for example, has become bureaucratized to the extent that it has taken on a good deal of specialization of labor, hierarchy, and careerism. The United States Marine Corps is obviously a great deal more bureaucratized than Congress; but the Marine Corps is also a different *type* of bureaucracy inasmuch as it requires more supervisory control over each member than does the United States Congress or, for another example, the Civil Rights Division of the Department of Justice.[3]

Table 12.2 identifies certain subjective attitudes people develop toward various objective aspects of bureaucracies. Our feelings about bureaucracies are almost never neutral; yet Table 12.2 should remind us that back of what we often view as the negative features of bureaucracy are usually sustained efforts to make organizations more rational and more efficient. No bureaucracy invents red tape merely in order to render the life of its clientele more miserable; a well-run bureaucracy is constantly organizing and reorganizing itself to eliminate inefficiency. It would be extremely difficult to find a bureaucracy in which the top administrators were not constantly trying to minimize the problems listed in the right-hand column of the table.

Nonetheless these problems become intensified in *government* bureaucracies, especially in countries which aspire to representative government. Government based on the theory of representation

[3]For further work on the phenomenon of bureaucracy, consult Max Weber, *Economy and Society,* ed. Guenther Roth and Claus Wittich and trans. Ephraim Fischoff et al. (New York: Bedminster Press, 1968), especially p. 956. A useful selection of readings will be found in Robert Merton et al., eds., *Reader in Bureaucracy,* 2d ed. (New York: Free Press, 1965).

Table 12.2 **The American Ambivalence toward Bureaucracy: Some Qualities of Bureaucracies as Seen from Two Perspectives**

Objective	Subjective
When bureaucracies affect others they are:	When bureaucracies affect me they are:
1. Strict about precedent	1. Riddled with red tape
2. Strict about rules	2. Inhumane
3. Impartial	3. Impersonal
4. Consistent, against privilege	4. Unresponsive
5. Responsive to popular control from the top	5. Undemocratic at the bottom
6. Efficient—they do a job regardless of individuals	6. Inefficient—they waste time

is expected to be efficient *and* personal, impartial *and* humane, bound by precedent *but also* quick to distinguish exceptions, committed to a task *but also* quick to respond to political decisions to change the task.

Government bureaucracies in the United States are almost inherently contradictory for at least two reasons. First, there is a constant tension between elected officials and career administrators. Elected officials are usually amateurs who only rarely have any real expertise in the areas of bureaucracy with which they become concerned. The demands made by the elected politician are almost always inconsistent in some way or another with the mission of the government agency. Some demands are inconsistent because the politician lacks the knowledge and vocabulary of the agency. Others are inconsistent because the politician is requesting individual privileges while the agency is trying to deal in general principles or trying to apply general precedents to specific cases. Political demands are inconsistent even when the politician is attempting to deal with a whole class of cases rather than with individual privileges, because any general demand made upon an agency, whether to change its policy or to coordinate itself with the work of other agencies, amounts to a distortion of the mission as it is defined by that agency.

Second, the demands made by elected officials, taken collectively, are usually inconsistent. The president and a department head rarely see things in absolutely the same way. Both will differ from the administrators subordinate to them. And all will shift their demands according to the pressures of politics within society that come to bear upon them. Politics is an effort to grapple with the nonrational, and bureaucracy is an effort to render some portion of the world as rational as possible and to insulate that portion from all of the nonrational forces around it.[4]

The mission of an agency cannot be achieved in the most professional and most efficient way if its administrators do not have the freedom and expertise to make the best use of their organization. They cannot take lightly the inconsistent and, to them, irrational demands constantly being made by the political sphere. Their reaction is a direct expression of the inherent tension of which we speak. *The more dedicated the members of an administrative agency, the stronger is the urge to independence in that agency.* The administrative agencies are problem enough for society when they are corrupt or inefficient. But they can be an even greater problem, although of a different sort, when they are sincere, honest, skillful, and efficient.

At its best, a well bureaucratized government agency will resist, and will feel an obligation to resist, the political executive. All government bureaucracies must serve two masters: their mission, as professionally defined, and the authority over them, as politically defined. The outcome is not predictable. A few specific cases of administrative agencies in the federal government will help show how these various tendencies manifest themselves, how bureaucrats make their choices, and how the bureaucracy fits into the larger scheme of government.

THE BUREAUCRACY IN AMERICAN GOVERNMENT

Figure 12.1 is a reasonable picture of almost any major department in the federal government. At the top is the secretary, the under secretary, and, in the case of agriculture, the three administrators whose functions cut across the entire department—the general counsel, the inspector general, and the assistant secretary for administration (who handles budget and personnel management). There are five other assistant secretaries of equal status. The organization chart suggests they are inferior, but that is a distortion dictated by the problem of getting all the boxes on a single chart. A more careful look will show that the solid lines moving down from the secretary—the "lines of authority"—are equivalent for all of these offices. The only difference between the first and second tier is that the five assistant secretaries on the second tier are more

---

[4]A profound and poignant treatment of this pattern will be found in Karl Mannheim, *Ideology and Utopia,* trans. Louis Wirth and Edward Shils (New York: Harcourt, Brace; Harvest, n.d.; first published in English in 1936), chapter 3. For example, "Two main sources of irrationalism in the social structure [uncontrolled competition and domination by force] constitute the realm of social life . . . where politics becomes necessary. . . . The chief characteristic of modern culture is the tendency to include as much as possible in the realm of the rational and to bring it under administrative control" (pp. 114 and 116).

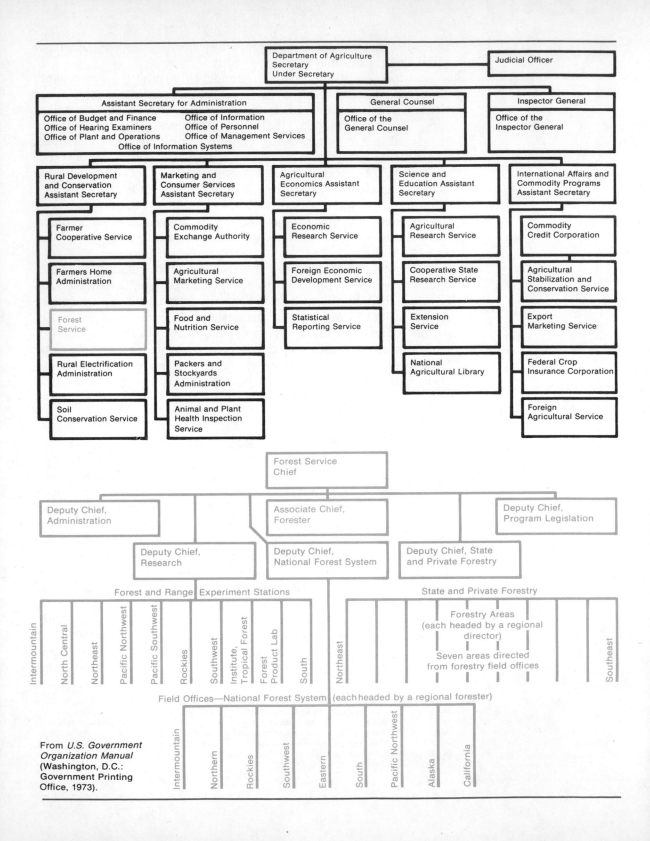

Department of Agriculture
Secretary
Under Secretary

Judicial Officer

Assistant Secretary for Administration
Office of Budget and Finance
Office of Hearing Examiners
Office of Plant and Operations
Office of Information Systems
Office of Information
Office of Personnel
Office of Management Services

General Counsel
Office of the
General Counsel

Inspector General
Office of the
Inspector General

Rural Development and Conservation Assistant Secretary
- Farmer Cooperative Service
- Farmers Home Administration
- Forest Service
- Rural Electrification Administration
- Soil Conservation Service

Marketing and Consumer Services Assistant Secretary
- Commodity Exchange Authority
- Agricultural Marketing Service
- Food and Nutrition Service
- Packers and Stockyards Administration
- Animal and Plant Health Inspection Service

Agricultural Economics Assistant Secretary
- Economic Research Service
- Foreign Economic Development Service
- Statistical Reporting Service

Science and Education Assistant Secretary
- Agricultural Research Service
- Cooperative State Research Service
- Extension Service
- National Agricultural Library

International Affairs and Commodity Programs Assistant Secretary
- Commodity Credit Corporation
- Agricultural Stabilization and Conservation Service
- Export Marketing Service
- Federal Crop Insurance Corporation
- Foreign Agricultural Service

Forest Service Chief

Deputy Chief, Administration

Associate Chief, Forester

Deputy Chief, Program Legislation

Deputy Chief, Research

Deputy Chief, National Forest System

Deputy Chief, State and Private Forestry

Forest and Range Experiment Stations
- Intermountain
- North Central
- Northeast
- Pacific Northwest
- Pacific Southwest
- Rockies
- Southwest
- Institute, Tropical Forest
- Forest Product Lab
- South
- Northeast

State and Private Forestry
Forestry Areas (each headed by a regional director)
Seven areas directed from forestry field offices
- Southeast

Field Offices—National Forest System (each headed by a regional forester)
- Intermountain
- Northern
- Rockies
- Southwest
- Eastern
- South
- Pacific Northwest
- Alaska
- California

From *U.S. Government Organization Manual* (Washington, D.C.: Government Printing Office, 1973).

Figure 12.1
An administrative agency
(Department of
Agriculture) in the
executive branch, and
one of its bureaus (Forest
Service).

specialized in their functions. Each has responsibility for a group of functions, a program area, rather than general management responsibilities.

The second tier actually begins just below the group of five assistant secretaries; it is the bureau level, the *highest operative level* in this and other departments. In the standard public administration literature these are generally referred to as *line agencies,* while the other boxes above or on the side are referred to as *staff* and *auxiliary agencies.* Another very useful term is *overhead agency,* a staff agency which generally has actual power to control and regulate the behavior of other agencies. For example, budgeting and personnel are overhead functions, usually housed in separate units within the department. Line agencies must clear their budgeting and personnel actions with these overhead units, and often this is a source of considerable friction within the department.[5]

Originally a military distinction, the distinction between line and staff (or overhead) is equally useful in ordinary domestic bureaucracies. Line agencies are actually out in the field dealing with the real world of citizens and the environment. The people being dealt with by line agencies in the military services are called the enemy; the people being dealt with by civilian agencies are called *clientele.* Staff and auxiliary units (overhead units) are distinguished by the fact that they deal almost exclusively with other government agencies rather than with nongovernmental clientele. Usually the clientele of a line agency is defined by its own name, as, for example, the Packers and Stockyards Administration. In contrast, the Office of Inspector General is an overhead unit responsible for seeing that expenditures in the department are made properly.

The second tier, the top operative level, is referred to as the bureau level, despite the fact that many bureau-level agencies avoid the actual name *bureau* in their official designation. Since the word has negative connotations, most program administrators prefer such designations as *office, service, division, agency, administration,* or *commission.* Names of this sort are all part of agency strategy to maintain a good image with the public and maximum independence from the higher authorities. In the field of public administration, there is a tendency to use the term *administrative agencies,* or simply *agencies,* as the general category. This practice will be followed here. The term *bureau* will generally be employed to designate the most important unit within a large agency, especially a department, despite the preference among more recent agencies for the other names.

In the Department of Agriculture, the Forest Service is probably

[5]For more on these very important bureaucratic facts, see Herbert Simon et al., *Public Administration* (New York: Knopf, 1950).

the most instructive single case.[6] By law, it has jurisdiction over 24 percent of all the federally owned land. As of 1972, the U.S. government owned and administered about 765 million acres of land in the continental United States, Hawaii, and Alaska. This constituted about one-third of the gross land mass of the United States (2.3 billion acres). The Bureau of Land Management in the Department of the Interior has responsibility for about 60 percent of the federally owned land, but more than half of this is in Alaska. The law of 1905 creating the agency transferred most forest preserves to its jurisdiction. In 1907, the special forest preserves under its control came to be known as national forests. The Forest Service does not exist merely to protect forests, however. It is also responsible for regulating recreational uses of the forests and commercial uses of the timber and grass lands. (The latter responsibilities often subject this bureau to various kinds of political pressure.)

As is true of most line agencies, the Forest Service employs only a small percentage of its personnel at headquarters in Washington; most of these headquarters personnel carry out overhead functions. Naturally, the main focus of activity in the Forest Service is upon the national forest system (at the bottom of the organization chart). The national system is broken up into regions, each headed by a regional forester. These regions are in turn broken down into ranger districts, varying in size from 50,000 to 500,000 acres.

Each ranger district is headed by a forest ranger, upon whom centers the basic mission of the Forest Service. The typical forest ranger is a man over the age of thirty-five, who has at least a B.S. and usually an M.S. degree in forestry and a great deal of experience with fire control, erosion control, and many other aspects of land management. Contrary to the popular image, the forest ranger is basically a manager of lands.

New personnel are recruited almost exclusively at the bottom from the major schools of forestry in the United States. Some may leave eventually to take more remunerative positions with private corporations, but anyone who has ambitions of reaching the top of the Forest Service must plan to begin a career at the bottom. There are few instances of forestry experts entering laterally into the middle or upper levels of the Forest Service after rising through occupations outside it. The Forest Service literally mirrors the nature of bureaucracy. It controls its personnel by limiting entry to

[6]As with almost all agencies, a good description will be found in the *United States Government Organization Manual,* issued annually by the Government Printing Office in Washington, D.C. However, another good reason to have picked the Forest Service as our case here is that a superb political study has been written about it providing a variety of significant data on the ranger as well as the Forest Service. See Herbert Kaufman, *The Forest Ranger* (Baltimore: Johns Hopkins Press, 1960).

the bottom level and providing for a lifetime career, step by step, through the institution toward the top. It determines the skills and qualifications requisite for appointment within the agency. The Forest Service has been more successful than most federal agencies in getting and keeping top personnel because it has a narrow and dependable source of new people in the forestry schools. And it has been able to get another step ahead of most bureaus in the United States by being able to outfit its personnel in uniforms. A uniform is a very effective way of creating boundaries around organizations, enhancing identification and morale.

"Bureaucratic power," as manifested in the organization of the Forest Service, seems less a matter of size and complexity and more a matter of professional integrity. Each bureau has its special task to perform, and each tends to develop standards and qualifications for personnel who can fulfill this task. An agency like the Forest Service becomes a way of life for those pursuing a career within it. In fact, many experts refer to this pattern as a career system, both in a sociological sense and in the jargon of the civil service personnel administration. It is no wonder that a bureaucracy comes to resent political intrusion; and given the high professional qualifications of so many of the personnel, it is no wonder that the press tends to take the side of the bureau whenever a politician tries to "coordinate" one bureau with another.

At least three other agencies in the Department of Agriculture could have been used as good case studies in bureaucratic organization and the bureaucratic power of professional integrity—the Extension Service, the Soil Conservation Service, and the Agricultural Stabilization and Conservation Service. These are only four of the twenty-two separate bureaus in the Department of Agriculture, but they account for as much as 70 percent of the department's line activities. Each of these agencies has its favorite schools of agriculture from which to draw its personnel, each has its own career system, and each has developed close relationships with organized interest groups whose members are particularly concerned with their programs.

This factor of organized clientele support is not part of the actual definition of bureaucracy, but in real political life it is so close to universal that it deserves to be considered a part of the definition of American bureaucracy. For example, the Extension Service draws its personnel and much of its support from the agriculture schools of the major land-grant colleges and universities. These schools are organized in an Association of State Universities and Land-Grant Colleges, whose lobbying has in recent years been done by a distinguished political scientist. Another supporting pressure group for the Extension Service is the famous American Farm Bureau Federation. We have already discussed (in chapter 6) the triangular trading patterns which tend to establish themselves between a bureau, an important interest group, and a congressional committee or subcommittee.[7]

The Clientele Departments

The Department of Agriculture is an example of a clientele agency. So are the Departments of Interior, Labor, and Commerce. Although all administrative agencies have clientele, certain agencies are singled out as clientele agencies because they are by law directed to foster and promote the interests of their clientele. Some clientele agencies (such as the bureaus within the Department of Agriculture that have already been described) have personnel in the field working directly with their clientele to help them use their resources better, to gain more resources, and to learn new skills. The Extension Service, with its numerous local extension agents who consult on farming and home economics, is one excellent example.

Other clientele agencies do not perform services in the usual sense of the word; they can best be called agencies for "functional representation." This means simply that they try to operate as that place in Washington where major trade associations or other clientele organizations can meet, exchange information, and pass along through the agency to the higher administrators and to Congress the prevailing needs of their sector of the economy. These agencies become the special pleaders for their clientele. The best examples of this kind of clientele agency are found in the Department of Commerce, where there has been, at least since the 1920s, a very self-conscious and explicit effort to operate as a channel of representation.[8]

Not all of the operating bureaus within these departments are clientele agencies. The Agricultural Stabilization and Conservation Service is a regulatory agency, not a promotional or clientele agency. This is also true of the Agricultural Marketing Service, which is responsible for grading and standardizing agricultural commodities in order to protect the consumer of those commodities. However, as of 1973, most of the twenty-two bureaus in the Agriculture Department exist mainly to carry out its original statutory mission—to "acquire and diffuse useful information on agricultural subjects in the most general and comprehensive sense."[9]

---

[7]In addition to chapter 6, see Charles Hardin, *The Politics of Agriculture* (Glencoe, Ill.: Free Press, 1952), and Grant McConnell, *The Decline of Agrarian Democracy* (Berkeley: University of California Press, 1953).

[8]For the development of the practice and theory of functional representation in the Department of Commerce, consult Peri Arnold, "Herbert Hoover and the Continuity of American Public Policy," *Public Policy*, Autumn 1972, p. 525.

[9]This is the Department of Agriculture's own statement, printed in the *U.S. Government Organization Manual*, 1972/73 edition, p. 93. The distinction between promotional and regulatory activities has been discussed in chapter 5 and is pursued still further in chapter 15.

The Departments of Commerce and Labor were founded as a single department in 1903 "to foster, promote, and develop the foreign and domestic commerce, the mining, the manufacturing, the shipping and fishing industries, and the transportation facilities of the United States."[10] They remained together in an uneasy marriage until 1913, but the separation did not change the fact that the mission of both departments is to promote a particular clientele. Here again, a number of the bureaus in these two departments serve as channels of functional representation. But virtually all of

[10]From the original legislation, quoted in Theodore Lowi, *The End of Liberalism* (New York: Norton, 1969), p. 116, where a longer assessment of clientele and functional representation will be found.

them are self-consciously geared toward service of some sort to their sector of the economy, usually the most organized elements of each sector.

Famous examples of promotional service bureaus in the Department of Commerce are the Bureau of Standards and the Patent Office. An example of a bureau of functional representation in the Commerce Department is the Bureau of Domestic Commerce. The most important service bureau in the Labor Department is the Bureau of Labor Statistics, source of so much of the data for the cost of living index. The only exceptional bureaus in the Labor Department are the Employment Standards Administration and the Occupational Safety and Health Administration, which are responsible for the programs of regulation of minimum wages, hours of work, public contract compliance, and general working conditions of businesses in interstate commerce. All the others are clientele bureaus.

Our Department of Interior has almost no identity except as a clientele agency. Its bureaus have responsibilities primarily in states west of the Mississippi—such as reclamation of arid lands and management of public lands in the West. The only exceptions are the Bureau of Mines, the National Parks Service, and the Bureau of Indian Affairs; but since most regulation of mines is done by state agencies, the latter two are probably the only really important bureaus in the Department of Interior.[11]

Because these departments and most of their bureaus are clientele agencies, there are considerable variations in their style of operations and the backgrounds of their personnel. But such differences are superficial compared to their common features of stability and independence, which are largely due to the separateness and integrity of their own organizations as career systems. There is a strong emphasis on control of personnel recruitment, one aspect of which is the requirement of advanced professional training. Though perhaps a paradox, these agencies oriented toward serving clientele require Ph.D.'s and other advanced degrees to a greater degree than any of the other types of agencies.[12] This stress on professional and other advanced degrees is attributable in large part to a sincere desire for professionalizing all the middle- and upper-level jobs in the agencies. This pattern is attributable as well to the urge in each of these agencies to control their own recruitment and their own sources of personnel supply. The more professionalized the appoint-

---

[11]The Bureau of Mines could take on greater importance if Congress adopts new regulatory programs controlling strip mining and other ecologically relevant aspects of the coal industry. However, if Congress sticks to form, the Bureau of Mines will continue to be less important than equivalent state agencies.

[12]Data of this sort are part of a wealth of information on the bureaucrats to be found in Judith Ann Hartmann, "Bureaucracy, Democracy, and the Government Worker" (Ph.D. diss., University of Chicago, 1973).

ments, the more easily demands by clientele or higher political authorities for a role in the personnel selection or promotion can be resisted.

This leads to still another and even more important common element among the clientele agencies. To state the matter baldly, the clientele agencies tend to be the most highly resistant to change among all the agencies. They bitterly resist efforts to change their routines, and they also tend to resist efforts to expand their powers and their jurisdictions. Popular lore would have it that bureaucracies are power hungry, but the experience of the past thirty or forty years reveals the opposite.

For example, during this period there has been vast expansion of federal regulatory power in the field of commerce; yet, none of it ended up as new bureaus or new authority in the Department of Commerce. The Interstate Commerce Commission predates the founding of the department, but the Federal Trade Commission was created at about the same time (1914) and remains completely independent of the Commerce Department. And when the U.S. government turned the railroads back to private ownership after World War I, all federal plans to create and promote a system of integrated railway traffic were turned over to agencies outside the Department of Commerce, mostly to the Interstate Commerce Commission (ICC). Control of civil aeronautics was established outside the Department of Commerce, as was the regulation of traded securities, credit, banking and currency, and the development and control of natural resources, including atomic energy. Similarly, all labor regulation in the United States (except the aforementioned) is outside the Department of Labor, as are almost all social security programs dealing with employment, unemployment, retirement, and compensation. Even the employment discrimination provisions of the civil rights acts are housed in agencies outside the Labor Department.

This peculiar phenomenon is attributable partly to the fact that new groups were reluctant to entrust their new programs to existing bureaus for fear of not enjoying complete access. But of equal, if not greater, importance is the fact that few bureaus have ever sought to add power or jurisdiction. Resistance to change, especially to added power, is not necessarily a bad thing. We are reminded of this every time a bureaucrat resists a dictator. But in a more loosely jointed society without problems of dictatorship, this kind of resistance can present three types of problems.

1. When a president or a legislature, rather than a dictator, says, "Do this, do that," something is supposed to happen. Basic to the theory of the "neutral" civil servant in the United States is the obligation of individual bureaucrats or their bureaus to respond to direction from the political authorities.

2. Resistance to new jurisdictions has produced a strong tendency in the United States toward duplication and waste, despite the bureaucrat's natural hatred of these things. Yet, adding a new agency is sometimes the only way a chief executive can get a new program going, even when a minor expansion of an existing bureau might theoretically work just as well. Many historians have observed that President Franklin Roosevelt liked to set up new bureaus that were slightly in conflict with other bureaus as a way of guaranteeing that their conflicts would generate information upwards toward the chief executive. Some political scientists have praised this pattern as a principle of administration worthy of emulation. However, despite the virtues of such interagency disputation, the lingering suspicion remains that in many of these instances President Roosevelt was merely making a virtue of necessity. It was *politically* more efficient to start a new agency, even though bureaucratically it was in the long run more efficient to expand an existing one.

3. Finally, since so much of the actual growth of the federal government in the past forty years has occurred *outside* the major departments and bureaus, many new programs are not directly within the jurisdiction of the cabinet and are far less likely to be coordinated from the top. As a result of this type of growth, the federal government lacks a lot of desired capacity to plan and coordinate its functions, particularly the new activities which are most in need of supervision from above. One could go further and say that the existence of the various clientele agencies has in fact militated against the proper location and coordination of new functions. Thus the clientele agencies actually interfere with the needs of modern administration. This is particularly unfortunate in that very few citizens would be seriously inconvenienced if all of the clientele agencies suddenly ceased to exist.[13]

The Service and Welfare Departments

Not all of the functions established outside the clientele departments remain independent of departments. Some which do will be dealt with at the end of this part of the chapter. But most agencies established outside existing departments are eventually organized as bureaus within departments other than the clientele departments; usually the solution has been to assemble a variety of independent agencies and to make them bureaus in a new department.

---

[13]The following are two excellent case studies of how, and perhaps why, clientele agencies resist new powers and functions, even when these are mandated by the president: William Greider, "Indian Runaround — How the Bureaucracy Vetoes a Nixon Vow on Schools," *Washington Post,* November 7, 1971; and the classic book-length case by Arthur Maass, *Muddy Waters: The Army Engineers and the Nation's Rivers* (Cambridge, Mass.: Harvard University Press, 1951).

The three most recently created cabinet departments—Health, Education and Welfare (1953), Housing and Urban Development (1965), and Transportation (1966)—arose out of a strongly felt need to bring various bureaus together in a more meaningful parent agency. Every time a new department is created, there tends to be a lot of self-congratulation derived from the feeling that government has finally begun to behave rationally by grouping together functions that belong together.[14] Indeed it is true that a departmental framework provides more opportunities for coordination. However, these new departments of the federal government apparently have not solved many of the problems of coordination among the bureaus and programs within their jurisdiction.

The Department of Health, Education and Welfare (HEW) is the largest of the three new departments and is also the most outstanding case study in the problems of coordinating line agencies. Most of the agencies combined in that department had existed for many years prior to its creation; most of them had enjoyed autonomy and bureaucratic integrity for a long time. For example, the Public Health Service (PHS), a clientele agency, has existed in one form or another almost since the founding of the republic. It has a very high proportion of personnel with M.D.'s and other advanced degrees, and it has been particularly stable and autonomous over the years. To the career bureaucrats in the PHS, elected officials and political appointees are birds of passage. As far as the doctors and researchers in the National Institutes of Health (the largest division within the PHS) and in the National Institute of Mental Health (yet another division in the PHS) are concerned, the higher political authorities exist to serve, not to coordinate or to control. The PHS produced the research into the question of whether smoking was hazardous to health. But as soon as their findings became the basis for mild regulatory legislation passed by Congress, the PHS quickly and successfully refused to accept responsibility for its implementation.

The Office of Education, created in 1867, has enjoyed long and supportive relationships with all of the State Boards and Superintendents of Education. It existed for most of its history as an almost unnoticed lobbying instrument used by state educational administrators. When the time came in the 1960s to add civil rights regulation to the mission of the Office of Education, it went into a period of confusion. Eventually, the responsibility for applying the education provisions of the civil rights acts went to other divisions of HEW and to the Justice Department.

The Social Security Administration (SSA), established by law in

[14]See the series of Reports of the Commission on Organization of the Executive Branch of the Government—the "Hoover Commission" (Washington, D.C.: Government Printing Office, 1953–1955).

FDR constantly wanted to increase the jurisdiction of the SEC to give it additional things to do. I fought those proposals at every step, knowing that we already were doing all we possibly could do well. That is one quarrel I had with FDR. Another was his desire to consolidate bureaus and agencies. For example, Roosevelt was always urging me to take on more duties, more responsibilities, to enlarge the SEC.

I told FDR, "Give me twice the amount of responsibility, and someone else will have to do the thinking. I won't be able to know all the facts or make good decisions. That's what's wrong with what you're doing elsewhere in the government."

William O. Douglas, *Go East, Young Man* (Random House, 1974)

1935, was almost a department in and of itself until it was brought into the Department of Health, Education and Welfare in 1953. It is probably the least prestigious of the agencies within HEW; most of its personnel have at best a B.A. degree; a much smaller proportion of them make the SSA a career; and the clientele of the agency is composed largely of dependent persons. Nevertheless, it is not much easier to coordinate or to control from the cabinet or chief executive level, because so many of its functions are purely routine administration. The categories of public assistance are set fairly clearly in the law. Another important bureau within HEW is the Food and Drug Administration, which had been playing a major role in regulating certain kinds of commerce for four decades prior to the establishment of HEW.

Most of the bureaus in the smaller Department of Housing and Urban Development (HUD) also predate the department itself and continue to be only loosely coordinated with each other. HUD's political life is shaped to a large extent by the fact that there is no clearly defined category of professional training to deal with the problems of housing or urban development. Thus HUD has fewer personnel resources. The planning profession is slowly gaining some status in the United States, but there are few professional planners in HUD agencies. For example, the community development agencies—Community Planning and Management Administration and Community Development Administration—are responsible mainly for *encouraging* planning in local agencies rather than *doing* any actual planning. Despite the hopes of many of the designers of these agencies in the 1960s, they are little more than conduits for the interest of big city mayors and their spokesmen in city planning agencies or congressional delegations.

Other agencies in HUD deal with financing construction of

housing and other urban buildings—programs under the jurisdiction of the assistant secretary for housing production and mortgage credit (who is also the federal housing commissioner) and the Federal Insurance Administration. But these bureaus are less responsive to the chief executive than they are to the savings and loan industry and to the very large and important interest group, the National Association of Home Builders. Access by new urban interests, particularly black leaders, has been better at the top level of the department than in the bureaus themselves. This was particularly true during the 1960s when the Secretary of HUD was black—the first black member of the cabinet.[15]

Coordination of related activities was even more prominently the motivation back of the movement for the Department of Transportation (DOT). This department was established in 1966 to bring together under a single authority the old and respected Coast Guard, the Federal Aviation Administration (FAA), the Federal Highway Administration (formerly the Bureau of Public Roads), the Federal Railroad Administration, and the St. Lawrence Seaway Development Corporation. Only the Urban Mass Transportation Administration and the National Highway Traffic Safety Administration were newly created and could have been said to depend upon support and coordination from the secretary of the department.

The other agencies were old and already had their independent sources of support. The Coast Guard is not only old but is a true career system like the Forest Service. Two of the agencies—the FAA and the Railroad Administration—are guaranteed most of their independence by law. The seaway agency is a public corporation with stronger obligations to bond holders than to the government. And the Highway Administration maintains the independence it enjoyed during the long period when it was the Bureau of Public Roads within the Commerce Department. For example, in 1967 the president authorized the budget director to release $1.1 billion in highway construction funds. This was passed along to the Bureau of Public Roads without any reference whatsoever to the secretary of commerce. A new secretary of a new department is likely to have even less control over such an agency. When the Bureau of Public Roads became the Federal Highway Administration in the Department of Transportation, this had virtually no effect on its independent status, its structure, or its relationships to state highway departments.

These three departments (HUD, HEW, and DOT) were set up to deal with the "problem of urban America" to which the Kennedy, Johnson, and Nixon administrations were so strongly committed. The War on Poverty was designed to do the same thing, however. In

[15]Harold L. Wolman and Norman C. Thomas, "Black Interests, Black Groups, and Black Influence in the Federal Policy Process," *Journal of Politics*, November 1970, p. 875.

fact, this was probably the most important goal of the War on Poverty. Little additional money was made available for welfare and social services or urban construction at that time. The War on Poverty, especially its Community Action Program, was expected to pull together relevant federal activities at the local level precisely because there was insufficient coordination of these same activities at the national level. In effect, the Community Action Program encouraged cities to disregard the top and try to pull together the programs at the bottom.[16]

The War on Poverty has been abandoned; it was already in a state of rigor mortis before the Nixon administration doctors declared it legally dead. Administrative coordination of urban programs, such as it is, rests with the three new departments and the White House. All we can say is that the individual services provided by the bureaus within these departments continue, but there is no sign that any department secretary or White House authority has been able to get the bureaus to work together in any kind of a common urban program.

The Agencies of Control, Traditionally Defined

During the past half century, when the federal government did most of its expanding, the stress has been so heavily upon the services and grants that the realities of government are often overshadowed and sometimes forgotten altogether. The reality of government is control, and when we speak of services we are really speaking of the use of a special kind of incentive for the purpose of control. People can be controlled with rewards as well as punishments, carrots as well as sticks.[17] However, although many people fail to perceive the controls behind services, few people miss the controls when they are explicit. And although there are variations among countries in the provision of services, there is far less variation on the more explicit, traditionally defined controls. These can be grouped into two categories: (1) control of the sources of government revenue, and (2) control of certain misbehaviors deemed an especial threat to public order. Most of the first of these types of controls will be found in the Department of the Treasury. As for the second, we have already seen that many of the most important controls have been relegated to the states in the United States. Those that have been "nationalized" are housed largely in

---

[16]For further data and an analysis of the War on Poverty, see Lowi, *The End of Liberalism,* p. 233.

[17]Conservatives are much quicker to perceive the controls behind the government services. But there are at least two works by authors from the ideological left which stress this: Lowi, *The End of Liberalism,* especially chapter 8; and Frances Piven and Richard Cloward, *Regulating the Poor* (New York: Random House, 1971). More will be said on these issues in chapter 15.

the Department of Justice. (A third department where important bureaus of domestic control are located, the Department of Defense, will be dealt with in the next section.)

Department of the Treasury The Department of the Treasury was created by one of the first actions of Congress. And probably its oldest function, now housed in the Bureau of Customs, is the collection of revenues on imports through agents at every seaport and at many airports and other terminals. (It is worthy of note that the units in these old departments are much more likely to use *Bureau* in their title.) The Bureau of Customs also engages in regulatory activities against smuggling and cooperates with other agencies on control of communicable diseases, drug traffic, and military contraband. Although a variety of related excise taxes are collected by the Bureau of Alcohol, Tobacco and Firearms on the commodities specified, this bureau also has the responsibility of regulating their consumption and use. In fact, many would say that this latter responsibility, not the tax collection function, is the real mission of the agency.

The Internal Revenue Service (IRS) is also a bureau of the Department of the Treasury. In its case, control is incidental to collection because of the enormously high proportion of total federal revenues accounted for by the income tax. But no adult reader needs to be reminded that tax and control are very closely associated even when the tax is more important than the controls. Nothing has gone further than the income tax toward converting the American citizen into a subject. The IRS is one of the largest bureaus in the federal government, with thousands of professional and clerical personnel spread throughout the various revenue districts in the country. It is also a rather loosely organized agency. Only a small proportion of the professional employees spend a lifetime career in the IRS; many of them remain only long enough to learn the taxation system and then move on to highly paid jobs in private corporations and accounting firms. It would also seem apparent from revelations following the Watergate scandal that the IRS is somewhat more responsive to central control than most of the other bureaus described so far. At least it has responded to presidential requests to audit the income tax returns of politically sensitive persons.

The IRS also has a special relationship with Congress. In addition to the Ways and Means Committee in the House and the Finance Committee in the Senate, there is a Joint Committee on Internal Revenue Taxation with a highly competent staff. This Joint Committee has no legislative authority, but the senior members of the two regular committees serve on the Joint Committee, and they and their top staff people, who generally are career and highly committed personnel, maintain a close working relationship with the IRS.[18] Finally, there is the Secret Service, a small and highly centralized professional agency. Organized largely to protect the United States currency and bonds from counterfeiting, it also has the responsibility for protecting the most important members of the United States government.

Department of Justice   Basically, the Department of Justice appears to have three rather modest powers. First, the attorney general and the deputy attorney general have authority over the United States marshals. (Wildly misrepresented by movies depicting the American West, the federal marshal is an officer of the federal district court who is responsible for carrying out court orders.) The second power available to the department is its traditional jurisdiction over all of the legal work of the United States government—that is, all of the cases to which that government is a party. (One other power, already identified, is derived from the commander-in-chief—the power to recommend the calling of federal troops to enforce court orders or to maintain vital government functions—see chapter 11.)

The main structure of the Department of Justice is influenced by its responsibility for the legal work of the government. For example, the Tax Division handles litigation arising out of actions taken by the IRS and other tax agencies. The Civil Division deals with all litigation concerning claims against the United States and also the occasional admiralty cases arising under the Constitution. The Antitrust Division is responsible for a variety of corporate laws as well as the enforcement of orders emanating from many of the independent regulatory commissions. The Civil Rights Division and the Internal Security Division take their names from the legislation for which they are responsible. The largest and most important of the divisions is the Criminal Division, which has responsibility for enforcing all of the federal criminal laws except those specifically assigned to the other divisions. The Criminal Division also supervises and directs most of the work done by the United States Attorneys, one of whom is assigned to each United States judicial district.

Over the years, the Justice Department has also added several line agencies whose responsibilities go beyond the handling of the government case load. The most important of these is the Federal Bureau of Investigation (FBI), established in 1908 and expanded to its present importance and size during the 1920s and 1930s under J. Edgar Hoover. Americans often need reminding that the FBI is

---

[18]For a review of this process, see John Manley, "Congressional Staff and Public Policy-Making: The Joint Committee on Internal Revenue Taxation," *Journal of Politics* 30 (1968), 1046.

nothing more than one of the fifteen bureaus or divisions in the department and that officially it has no higher status than any of the others. But no one needs to be told that its status really is higher than all of the others. It is the largest bureau as well; over 40 percent of the Department of Justice appropriations are for the FBI. And all of the other bureaus and divisions of the department depend in one way or another upon information provided by the FBI.[19]

Authority over these important bureaus and divisions passes from the attorney general through the deputy attorney general and the equally important solicitor general. The deputy is responsible for the political and management aspects of the department. The solicitor general is the chief of all the case activity and, consequently, is the most important officer in the federal judicial system (see chapter 13).

In line with presidential wishes, these three judicial officers make some of the most important decisions in the United States government. They decide whether to be strong or weak on antitrust, consistent or sporadic on syndicated crime, severe or permissive on internal security, tax evasion, and corporate fraud. They, particularly the solicitor general, decide which cases, among all the thousands of possible cases on appeal, to bring before the higher courts. This kind of discretion involves a tremendous amount of power, since the divisions are highly responsive to coordination from the center. Discretion of this sort makes these three officials extremely susceptible to bribery offers, since decisions *not* to prosecute are confidential and do not require reporting. Occasionally a decision not to prosecute or not to appeal leaks out to the public, and the reaction can be extremely negative.

Leaving aside the suspicions of corruption in cases of this sort, such cases serve to remind the observer that the bureaus and divisions in the Justice Department are a good deal more responsive to central direction than we found to be true of bureaus in the clientele or service departments. Even the FBI, with its famous professionalism and independence, has been regularly responsive to demands and appeals from higher authorities, especially the president. For example, in 1939 President Roosevelt put the FBI in charge of "espionage, counter-espionage, subversive activities and violations of the neutrality laws."[20] This eventually became a major activity of the FBI. In the early 1960s, the FBI at first resisted efforts by the attorney general to involve it in the fight against

---

[19]According to Victor Navasky, there at least twenty-seven federal agencies that conduct domestic intelligence, and none of these are under any obligation to cooperate with the FBI—the IRS, the Secret Service, the Post Office, and the AEC, for example. Consult Navasky's important study, *Kennedy Justice* (New York: Atheneum, 1971); references to information-gathering agencies will be found on p. 45.

[20]Navasky, *Kennedy Justice*, p. 36. Books critical of this particular function of the FBI include *Kennedy Justice, and* Fred J. Cook, *The FBI Nobody Knows* (New York: Macmillan, 1964).

WANTED

JOHN HERBERT DILLINGER

On June 23, 1934, HOMER S. CUMMINGS, Attorney General of the United States, under the authority vested in him by an Act of Congress approved June 6, 1934, offered a reward of

$10,000.00

for the capture of John Herbert Dillinger or a reward of

$5,000.00

for information leading to the arrest of John Herbert Dillinger.

DESCRIPTION

Age, 32 years; Height, 5 feet 7-1/8 inches; Weight, 153 pounds; Build, medium; Hair, medium chestnut; Eyes, grey; Complexion, medium; Occupation, machinist; Marks and scars, 1/2 inch scar back left hand, scar middle upper lip, brown mole between eyebrows.

All claims to any of the aforesaid rewards and all questions and disputes that may arise as among claimants to the foregoing rewards shall be passed upon by the Attorney General and his decisions shall be final and conclusive. The right is reserved to divide and allocate portions of any of said rewards as between several claimants. No part of the aforesaid rewards shall be paid to any official or employee of the Department of Justice.

If you are in possession of any information concerning the whereabouts of John Herbert Dillinger, communicate immediately by telephone or telegraph collect to the nearest office of the Division of Investigation, United States Department of Justice, the local addresses of which are set forth on the reverse side of this notice.

JOHN EDGAR HOOVER, DIRECTOR,
DIVISION OF INVESTIGATION,
UNITED STATES DEPARTMENT OF JUSTICE,
WASHINGTON, D. C.

June 25, 1934

Two views of the FBI. *Left:* J. Edgar Hoover orders nationwide search for most wanted criminal. *Right:* Hoover, chief bureaucrat.

organized crime; but eventually Hoover did respond. The FBI was equally reluctant to become involved in enforcement of the civil rights laws, but here, too, it eventually cooperated.[21]

Differences between the two major agencies of control   The two departments which house so many of the agencies of traditional control and regulation—Justice and Treasury—are far from identical to each other in their organizational characteristics or their relationships to the chief executive. The various bureaus and agencies in the Treasury Department tend to be a good deal more independent than those in the Justice Department. Direct presi-

[21]For coverage of these cases, see Navasky, *Kennedy Justice*. During 1963 the number of FBI agents in Mississippi increased from 3 to 153 (p. 8); and by the time Robert Kennedy had left the attorney general's office in 1964, Hoover had not only ceased calling the Mafia "baloney," but had in fact begun to cooperate in the fight to destroy it (chapter 2).

dential intervention in the Internal Revenue Service is exceptional, politically suspect, and can be illegal; in contrast, political intervention among agencies of the Justice Department is regular. The difference between these departments extends even to the top.

Traditionally, secretaries of the treasury have been rather independent figures, persons of independent followings who were brought into the cabinet to lend the president a certain type of support or access the president did not already have. Secretary Schultz under Richard Nixon was an exceptional case. Nixon's two other secretaries of the treasury, John Connally and David Kennedy, were men of independent stature; Douglas Dillon under John Kennedy was definitely his own man; he was a high-ranking Republican in a Democratic administration. Secretary Humphrey under Eisenhower was considered even more of an independent figure.

In contrast, most attorneys general have been personally or politically close to the president. Because of Watergate, President Nixon lost control of that office; but for most of his first term his alter ego, John Mitchell, was his attorney general. Almost all of Mitchell's predecessors resemble him in this respect. Ramsey Clark and Nicholas Katzenbach under Lyndon Johnson were "Kennedy men," but they were intensely political people tied to the president. Robert Kennedy was the classic instance of an attorney general close to the president. Herbert Brownell, who served during most of the eight years of the Eisenhower administration, was one of Eisenhower's original supporters. Three of the four men who served as attorney general under President Truman were definitely Truman men, and the fourth, Biddle, was almost certainly let go because he was not.

This is not the place to try to explain why these two departments are different. One productive line of exploration lies in the fact that in the Justice Department control is the primary mission, while in the Treasury Department control is generally incidental to the raising of revenue or the manipulation of credit. (See chapter 15 for a discussion of some of these differences of function.) Whatever the reason for them, the differences are illustrative of the variety of bureaucratic experience in the national government. In turn, this indicates that control by the president and politically responsible institutions is far from complete. Whether we should celebrate or lament that incompleteness is a question of personal ideology. As one high-ranking bureaucrat put the issue of bureaucratic responsibility and reorganization two decades ago, "Where you stand depends on where you sit."[22]

[22]Harold Seidman, "The Politics of Government Organization," in *Bureaucratic Power in National Politics,* ed. Francis Rourke (Boston: Little, Brown, 1972), p. 299.

The Survival Agencies: State and Defense

Since the threat to survival is usually perceived as originating from abroad, nothing should be more unified and consistent than those agencies whose mission is survival and its maintenance. Thus, it is curious how far-flung, uncoordinated, and independent our two survival departments and their agencies are. (Only the organizational problems of the survival agencies as bureaucracies are reviewed here. The substantive aspects will be discussed in chapter 14.)

The State Department The Department of State is of course the official center of all foreign affairs policies, operations, intelligence gathering, and so on. It has been in continuous operation from 1789 and ranks first in official protocol and status among all departments. The secretary of state is first in line of succession among all cabinet members to the presidency, following only the vice-president, the Speaker of the House, and the president pro tempore of the Senate. The secretary of state is also the keeper of the official seal and the commission of appointment of the president. (Some may recall that in the case of *Marbury* v. *Madison,* Madison was being sued because as secretary of state he held Marbury's commission of appointment as an inferior judge.)

Although diplomacy is probably thought of as the primary task of the department, diplomatic missions are the responsibility of only one of its sixteen bureau-level units. The other fifteen are classified into three types: functional (five units), area (seven units), and domestic (three units). The five functional units are Economic Affairs, International Scientific and Technological Affairs, Intelligence and Research, Political–Military Affairs, and Consular Affairs. The area bureaus, which many have considered the most important bureaus in the department, are concerned with geographic subdivisions of the world. There is one for each of the major world areas, plus one for international organizations. Area bureaus obviously cut across functional bureaus, trying to pull together all economic, political, scientific, social, and cultural features of the particular countries or areas in question. The three so-called domestic bureaus are concerned largely with domestic politics—including the important unit for congressional relations, headed by an assistant secretary.[23]

---

[23]Among the many very good studies of the State Department and the administration of foreign affairs, the following should be considered of particular utility: John E. Harr, *The Professional Diplomat* (Princeton: Princeton University Press, 1969); David H. Davis, *How the Bureaucracy Makes Foreign Policy* (Lexington, Mass.: D. C. Heath, 1972); William I. Bacchus, *Foreign Policy and the Bureaucratic Process* (Princeton: Princeton University Press, 1974); I. M. Destler, *Presidents, Bureaucrats and Foreign Policy* (Princeton: Princeton University Press, 1972). See also Andrew M. Scott, "Environmental Change and Organizational Adaptation," in *Bureaucratic Power in National Politics,* p. 214. My reliance on these sources is greater than indicated by the following citations.

There are two outstanding problems which prevent the State Department from developing the tight and responsive organizational structure it might like to have. The first of these is internal. The elite of the State Department have traditionally been the Foreign Service officers (FSO's). They are recruited at a young age by very rigorous standards, are assigned for a number of years to various consular and other duties in different parts of the world to gain experience, and then move slowly through the ranks until they gain high positions in the State Department and other foreign agencies throughout the government.[24]

However, the Foreign Service officer represents only one of two separately identifiable career systems within the State Department, and these have never been integrated sufficiently to provide the department with an effective ministry of foreign affairs, as in European countries. Although the Foreign Service officers are the elite, there is a large corps of domestic personnel in the State Department, and expert observers consistently report jealously and distrust between the two systems. To exacerbate the matter, the Foreign Service officers represent only 15 percent of the total employees of the department but hold most of the powerful bureaucratic posts. In addition, a substantial number (ranging from 150 to 300 FSO's) are working on detached assignment with agencies outside the State Department, such as the Arms Control and Disarmament Agency, the United States Information Agency, the Department of Defense, the White House, the National Aeronautics and Space Administration, and the Department of Commerce.[25] Consequently, there is high morale among the elite officers, but they make up too small a proportion of the total personnel and are placed in too few of the middle- and lower-level positions to constitute a unifying and integrating force in the department.

Organization and management of foreign affairs is complicated further by the second problem—the existence of many agencies of foreign affairs outside the State Department and beyond its control.[26] Table 12.3 is an illustration of this phenomenon. A good deal less than 20 percent of all the United States government employees working abroad are directly under the authority of the State Department. Another 12 percent are State Department people whose responsibilities are to some other agency. In addition, there is a still larger number of employees who are in no way under the authority of the Department of State but rather are responsible to

---

[24]For more details, consult Harr, *The Professional Diplomat*, p. 140; see also Scott, "Environmental Change and Organizational Adaptation," p. 215; and Scott, "The Department of State: Formal Organization and Informal Culture," *International Studies Quarterly*, March 1969, pp. 1–18.

[25]Harr, *The Professional Diplomat*, p. 161.

[26]For an analysis of this particular problem of coordination, consult Keith C. Clark and Lawrence Legere, *The President and the Management of National Security* (New York: Praeger, 1969); see also Lowi, *The End of Liberalism*, chapter 6.

	Table 12.3	Who's Minding Our Store Overseas?

Agency or Function	Percentage of All Employees Working Abroad
State Department—diplomacy	16.6
State Department employees—attached to other agencies	12.4
Department of Defense—attachés and intelligence	28.7
Agency for International Development (AID)	21.3
United States Information Agency (USIA)	5.6
Others (such as the Treasury, Agriculture, Commerce, and Labor Departments)	15.4
Total known	100.0
Central Intelligence Agency (CIA) and National Security Agency (NSA)	?

Data from I. M. Destler, *Presidents, Bureaucrats and Foreign Policy* (Princeton: Princeton University Press, 1972), pp. 10–11; see also John E. Harr, *The Professional Diplomat* (Princeton: Princeton University Press, 1969), p. 161.

the Department of Defense. This includes a large number of Defense Department personnel who are actually attached to diplomatic missions and are expected to cooperate with the ambassadors in those missions although they may be beholden to the Pentagon.

The same can be said of many employees of other agencies listed in Table 12.3. This kind of situation is especially problematic when one or more of the agencies is in disagreement with the State Department policy toward the country where the personnel are located. All of the agencies identified in Table 12.3 look to Washington for their leadership and their protection. And this protection is not merely a matter of friendly relations with Congress. The independence of agencies from control by the State Department is in most instances *written into the law.*

Still other agencies without installations abroad can have a similar effect on foreign policy without being beholden to the State Department. One important example is the Atomic Energy Commission (reorganized during 1974–1975 into the Energy Research and Development Administration). For another example, during the first fifteen years of its operation, foreign economic aid (under a succession of agencies beginning with the Economic Recovery Administration) was administered independently of the Department of State. The law provided that the personnel at all levels in the State Department and the Economic Recovery Administration were to keep each other "fully and currently informed. . . . If differences of view are not adjusted by consultation, the matter shall be referred to the President for final decision."[27] And even as

The Chief Executive, the Executive Branch, and the Management of Conquest

[27]Economic Cooperation Act, Section 105 (b).

President Kennedy was reducing the foreign aid agency to a unit of the State Department, he was setting up the Peace Corps as a separate operation *outside* State Department control.

Mention should also be made of the Central Intelligence Agency (CIA) and the National Security Agency (NSA), which of course also operate independently of the State Department, although figures on their personnel and the scale of their activities abroad cannot be gathered. In 1968, at the height of America's most intense involvement in cold war activities, Stuart Alsop, generally considered a "hawk" in foreign affairs, reported that the "intelligence community" was spending $3 billion a year and employing about 160,000 people. According to Alsop, more than half of that money was spent domestically by the NSA on code breaking and other such projects, with the rest going to far-flung foreign activity.[28] Accounts coming out of 1975 investigations suggest that the intelligence community now costs over $6 billion and employs around 200,000 people in ten regular agencies, of which the NSA continues to be the largest and most secretive. The Defense Intelligence Agency, formed in 1961 by Robert McNamara, has about 5,000 employees and a budget of around $100 million.[29]

As with domestic departments, these independent agencies were probably most often created in order to get a specific job done by flanking existing bureaucracies. Understanding the pressing obligations of the president may lead to some sympathy for specific instances of this strategy. However, in the long run a succession of presidents who have employed this type of strategy and the resultant proliferation of independent agencies have probably contributed to much of our frustration in the conduct of foreign affairs. Such proliferation has led to a tremendous expansion in direct diplomacy carried out by the White House or by the secretary of state. (Kissinger-type diplomacy did not begin with Kissinger. It probably started with John Foster Dulles at the very beginning of the cold war.) Direct, personal diplomacy may be brilliant and sometimes effective, but it also creates problems of trust in other nations. Their question must always be whether the agreements arrived at with the president or the secretary of state can be sustained. Sustaining agreements requires the full and enthusiastic support of administrators, and anyone who knows the United States know that this is not ever guaranteed.[30]

The Department of Defense The Department of Defense was created by legislation in 1947 and 1949. It was an effort to "unify" the three major military services, which hitherto had been housed

---

[28]Quoted in Destler, *Presidents, Bureaucrats and Foreign Policy*, p. 11.

[29]Nicholas Horrock, "The CIA Has Neighbors in the 'Intelligence Community,'" *New York Times,* June 29, 1975

[30]For an excellent statement of concern about this particular problem, see Anthony Lake and Leslie Gelb, "Don't Forget the State Department," *New York Times,* November 16, 1972.

in separate cabinet-level departments. The War Department had the responsibility for the army and a fledgling air force; the Navy Department was responsible for the naval forces and the marine corps. It is common knowledge that real unification did not occur; but actually this unification of the armed forces has been no more of an illusion than that attempted in some civilian departments already discussed (for example, the Department of Health, Education and Welfare). Some secretaries of defense, such as James Forrestal, George Marshall, and Robert McNamara, managed this enormous department with particular effectiveness. The problems of unification and responsibility to the top are not unique to this department. They are comparable to any of the "civilian" departments.[31]

As with the civilian agencies, the military services are bureaucratically organized. The military personnel are trained in special skills and infused as much as possible with intense loyalties to their separate and respective bureaus. And, as with the domestic departments, the behaviors the outsider may see as separateness and organizational jealousy are from within seen as issues of professional integrity. The bureaus in each unit of the Department of Defense are of two sorts, very much parallel to the bureaus in the State Department. One set are the line agencies—the various military commands organized along geographic lines, with army divisions and navy fleets in various parts of the United States and the world. Others are functional in character, cutting across the divisions and fleets. For example, each of the present military services has its logistics, intelligence, personnel, research and development (R & D), communication, quartermaster, and engineering bureaus, among others. At the risk of hurting the feelings of many, one could say that the marine corps is simply one bureau within the larger Naval Service.

At the top of the chain of command in each of the military services is a chief of staff (called chief of naval operations in the navy). As the organizational chart in Figure 12.2 suggests, these are the real bureau chiefs of each of the military services. Above them on the organization chart are the civilian secretaries of the army, navy, and air force; but the Unification Act which created the Defense Department essentially destroyed the status and power of these civilian secretaries. The law itself provides that "the chain of command . . . extends from the president to the secretary of defense through the joint chiefs of staff, to the commanders of the unified and specified command."[32]

---

[31]For a positive view of the Department of Defense, consult C. W. Borklund, *Men of the Pentagon* (New York: Praeger, 1966). For a somewhat more skeptical examination, see Adam Yarmolinsky, *The Military Establishment* (New York: Harper & Row, 1971); and Jack Raymond, *Power at the Pentagon* (New York: Harper & Row, 1964).

[32]*Government Organization Manual* (Washington, D.C.: Government Printing Office, 1972/73), p. 151.

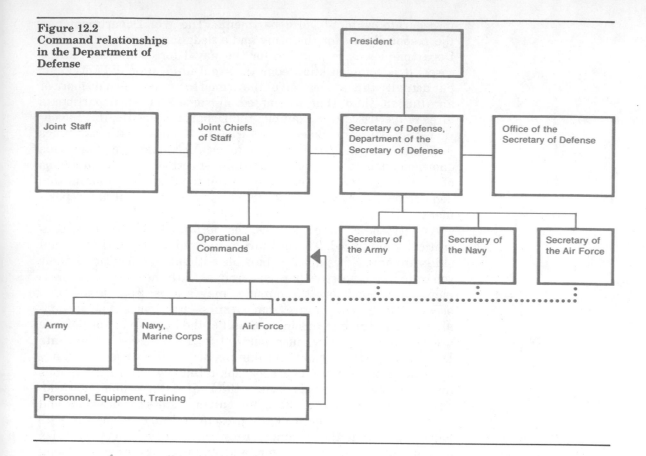

**Figure 12.2
Command relationships
in the Department of
Defense**

President

Joint Staff

Joint Chiefs
of Staff

Secretary of Defense,
Department of the
Secretary of Defense

Office of the
Secretary of Defense

Operational
Commands

Secretary of
the Army

Secretary of
the Navy

Secretary of
the Air Force

Army

Navy,
Marine Corps

Air Force

Personnel, Equipment, Training

The Joint Chiefs of Staff (JCOS) is a kind of cabinet of the "bureau chiefs," including the commandant of the marine corps. The JCOS is actually composed of four full members and one limited member. The chairman is a former chief of staff, usually of such age and seniority that he retires entirely from the service once his tenure as chairman is over. One other member of the JCOS is from the same military service as the chairman, and he is in turn joined by the chiefs of the other two services. The marine corps commandant is the fifth and limited member, who attends all the meetings but becomes the equal of the other members only when matters concerning the marine corps are up for discussion.[33]

Although the civilian secretaries of the various armed forces and their assistant secretaries have been left out in the cold, they continue to have at least one very important job to do. They are responsible for staff and auxiliary aspects of military operation,

[33]See Yarmolinsky, *The Military Establishment,* especially chapter 2.

especially the supply of personnel and the procurement of equipment. As one military reporter put it, a secretary of the navy can be responsible for developing a missile-launching submarine costing $1.3 billion but has little or no say on whether the submarine is needed or how it should be used.[34]

The one recent president with real military experience, President Eisenhower, tried earnestly to restore the position of the civilian secretaries within the operational chain of command. But after several years of effort and experimentation, he came to the conclusion that this system was "cumbersome and unreliable in time of peace and not usable in time of war."[35] In 1958, new legislation recognized this state of affairs and officially put the civilian secretaries outside the chain of military command. The civilian secretaries continue to rate a nineteen-gun salute, a personal airplane, a limousine, and most of the other status symbols. But the secretary of defense is the only civilian secretary with any legal power and strategic location to exercise influence over the Department of Defense.

Each of the armed forces is truly a career service. The top elite of each of the armed forces, with a few exceptions, are produced by the respective military academies. Lateral entry into a top military command has in the past century or more been rare in practice and unthinkable in theory. During the early months of World War II, many promotions were made out of the established bureaucratic and seniority ordering. Dwight Eisenhower was the most spectacular example, rising from colonel to top command over the heads of hundreds of senior personnel in the army. But his case was spectacular because this type of promotion has been so rare throughout most of our history. Other classic bureaucratic features of the armed services include the elaborate uniforms, the numerous gradations of status and reward, the tight and secret protocol and ritual, and perhaps above all the code of loyalty, mutual respect, and valor.[36]

Because of the Vietnam War, the armed services of the United States have not in recent years been held in the highest possible regard. However, we can all too easily fall into error by attributing those sorry adventures to military organization or military mentality. Military organization in the United States has recorded some absolutely remarkable successes during the past half century, and this must be thrown into a balanced assessment of this aspect of our government. During the decade following 1940, our armed forces

---

[34]John W. Finney, *New York Times*, July 27, 1973. See also Yarmolinsky, *The Military Establishment*, p. 17.

[35]Finney, *New York Times*.

[36]Good sources on military personnel and organization include Morris Janowitz, *The Professional Soldier* (New York: Free Press, 1960); and John W. Masland and Lawrence Radway, *Soldiers and Scholars* (Princeton: Princeton University Press, 1967).

sustained a series of spectacular military defeats and the trauma of stupendous growth without breaking down and without dragging the American people into political or military crisis.

The military forces responded flexibly, perhaps even gracefully, to the addition of a tremendous number of new technologies, new responsibilities for military government and scientific development, and new responsibilities for diplomacy, in addition to the expansion of personnel. The response of the military leadership to the extraordinarily fast and wasteful demobilization after World War II was impressively restrained, as was their response to the sudden renewal of military emphasis later during the same decade. During the 1950s, there was a rush of effort to impose a variety of civilian political tasks on the military; these seem to have been accepted without actually being sought.

Moreover, American citizens took rather for granted the acceptance by the military of the concept of limited, political wars, even when it involved the firing of one of the great military figures of American history, General Douglas MacArthur. The American public's ability to take armed forces acceptance and cooperation for granted is a remarkable expression of our success in having provided the armed forces with a stable place in our scheme of government.[37] At least through 1975, one could add that the military careerists have accepted with restraint the defeat, the embarrassments, and the recriminations following upon the Vietnam War.

There continues to be a strong concern about the involvement of American military personnel in politics, but it tends to be inaccurately focused. Concern is often expressed, for example, about the fact that Americans tend to pick military heroes as their leaders following wars. Yet, it was just such a military hero who, as president, tried to mobilize American citizens against the problems of the "military-industrial complex." This was President Eisenhower, who tried in a variety of ways to reinvigorate and to maintain civilian control of the military.

Concern is often focused also upon military lobbying and the efforts of military personnel to propagandize American citizens. One analyst meticulously counted the number of speeches made by top military officers during the first eight months of the Kennedy administration (831) and compared this "torrent" to the more moderate number of speeches made by State Department officials (540).[38] He found that many of the speeches made by military people involved efforts to mobilize the American public in favor of greater

---

[37]Compare with Janowitz, *The Professional Soldier;* also Samuel P. Huntington, *The Soldier and the State* (Cambridge, Mass.: Harvard University Press, 1957); C. Wright Mills, *The Power Elite* (New York: Oxford University Press, 1959); and David Halberstam, *The Best and the Brightest* (New York: Random House, 1972).

[38]Raymond, *Power at the Pentagon,* pp. 176–177.

Principles of
organization: The chain of
command is a military
concept.

military preparedness or against soft positions taken toward the Soviet Union. Yet, the overwhelming number of examples cited are cases of intense bureaucratic politics, in which one unit of the military is fighting another. The speeches, even those including anti-Soviet propaganda, were all part of a fight to increase the overall military budget or the share of revenue going to a particular military service.

Most of these cases suggest that the best way to understand the military in American politics is within the framework of bureaucracy. Thus the everyday political efforts of American military personnel would seem largely defensive, oriented toward maintaining the status quo of their bureaucratic organizational units. Military lobbying in Congress is most often aimed at defense of the size or integrity of an individual military unit. When self-aggrandizing propaganda is employed, it is usually with the purpose of defending the integrity of a particular military organization against encroachment by civilian politicians or the other military organizations.

Even our involvement in the most umpopular and costly war in American history was more a product of military-minded civilians than of a military-dominated government, although as the war progressed, professional military people were indeed brought closer and closer into the top decision-making channels. This certainly is a type of basic political threat; however, if one can judge from the Pentagon papers, the top military people were more often than not concerned with the effect of the war on their own organizational structure.

The army of 1965 was still organized for conventional wars and atomic wars; there was little concept of counterinsurgency and almost no organizational capacity to engage in unconventional guerrilla warfare. As a result, the military reaction to the political decision in Vietnam was to try to escalate the war up to a point where conventional warfare might give us the advantage. But this reaction was far more a politics of bureaucratic motivation and inertia than of military aggrandizement.[39]

Thus our concern about the political importance of the military in our democracy should be with the problem of bureaucracy and bureaucratic responsibility we have been facing all along. In the case of the military the problem is more pressing because military personnel have guns and bombs as well as money and specialization. But the problem is otherwise the same—a large establishment working relatively independently on the basis of its own logic to preserve itself above and before all other considerations.

There is a second, and in the long run more important, concern, although we have never actually had to face it in the United States. At some point, the military may become involved in politics by actually displacing civilian political processes and procedures with outright military rule. This is the ultimate reason we should look askance at large military establishments, even when we have a long tradition of military restraint and no precedent of any military effort to stage a coup d'etat. A military coup d'etat is not inconceivable in the United States.

It is true that recent examples of armed forces involvement in domestic affairs are actually indicative of continued military subordination to civilian wishes. For example, the army was following the orders of the Johnson administration when it put as many as 100,000 civilians under surveillance during the height of political opposition to the Vietnam War. The armed forces have never hesitated when the president has called them up to occupy disorder-

---

[39]For a brilliant analysis of Vietnam along these lines, see Josiah Bunting, "The Conscience of a Soldier," *Worldview*, December 1973, p. 6. As Bunting puts the case, the best of our military brains told us not to become involved at all, but once we did get involved, "we endorsed the ancient shibboleth, dear to generations of soldiers, that 'more means better'" (p. 9). At another point Bunting observes that "the military professional in American society is, *au fond,* a bureaucrat, usually an ambitious bureaucrat. His weakness and the weakness of the military bureaucracy have been underscored and magnified by the present war" (p. 10). See also Roger Hilsman, *To Move a Nation* (New York: Doubleday, 1967), especially part 9; and Theodore Draper, *Abuse of Power* (New York: Viking Press, 1967).

ly sections of our cities. However, what would the military authorities do if a Marxist government of the Allende type came to power as a result of a legitimate election, as in Chile? What would the military authorities do if such a government ordered them to occupy the factories and the corporate boardrooms to carry out nationalization plans rather than to occupy campuses or ghettos? What would the national guard do if the state of Ohio changed its landlord–tenant laws to favor tenants and the governor then ordered the militia forcibly to end a landlord lockout rather than use the same militia to put down a riot on the Kent State campus?

These hypothetical cases suggest that the military has played a subordinate role in American politics largely because American politics has traditionally and consistently been a very stable politics of the center toward the right of the spectrum. There has been no call for great military involvement. There has been no moment when the military had to confront the possibility that capitalism was threatened or the industrial structure was being changed. Indeed, it may well be that the military *allows* politics to take place, but only so long as it takes place within an established framework. If politics should extend outside that framework, the probability of more fundamental military involvement would be much greater.

This type of military involvement could happen in the United States not only because military leaders are on the average more conservative than most other political activists. It could happen also because the military establishment consists of several gigantic bureaucracies, each with an organizational position to protect. When we put political conservatism and organizational conservatism together, we have ample potential, at the extreme, for greater military involvement in politics than we have yet seen.[40]

The Independent Agencies

The independent agencies come last in this presentation not because they are least in importance; indeed, many exercise far more influence over the national economy or society than some of the departments. They simply represent the most extreme point in the continuum of problems facing presidents as they try to control the bureaucracies. These agencies are called independent because they have been given statutory independence from the executive branch. It is difficult to generalize about them; the four classifications in Table 12.4 provide only a rough sketch. More than a dozen hard-to-classify agencies were not included, and the distinctions between

[40]For data on political opinions and activities of military officers in the United States, consult Janowitz, *The Professional Soldier.*

Table 12.4	The Independent Agencies—A Selection and Classification

Independent Regulatory Commissions

Civil Aeronautics Board (CAB)
Environmental Protection Agency (EPA)
Federal Communications Commission
  (FCC)
Federal Power Commission (FPC)
Federal Trade Commission (FTC)
Interstate Commerce Commission (ICC)
National Labor Relations Board (NLRB)
Securities Exchange Commission (SEC)
Maritime Commission

Independent Clientele Agencies

Indian Claims Commission
Delaware River Basin Commission
National Science Foundation (NSF)
Veterans Administration (VA)
Mediation and Conciliation Service
Appalachian Regional Commission

Independent Enterprises and Public Corporations

Federal Reserve Bank
U.S. Postal Service
Home Loan Bank Board
National Aeronautic and Space
  Administration (NASA)
Overseas Private Investment Corporation
Farm Credit Administration
Panama Canal Company
Tennessee Valley Authority (TVA)
Atomic Energy Commission (AEC)*
Railroad Retirement Board

Independent Overhead Agencies

General Services Administration
  (GSA)
Civil Service Commission
Administrative Conference of the
  United States
General Accounting Office (GAO)

*The AEC was replaced by the Energy Research and Development Administration in early 1975.

categories are not logically hard and fast. Nevertheless, the classification is adequate for our purposes here. One thing can be said about them all: they are not intended to be directly responsive to presidential direction. Each operates under a broad delegation of power from Congress to administer a given area of the economy or to make decisions that regulate the behavior of participants in a given area of the economy. There will be occasion in chapter 14 to inquire more deeply into the substantive policies of the most important of these agencies. The concern here is to deal with the organizational and bureaucratic phenomena.

Independent regulatory commissions The most widely known and most controversial type of independent agency is the independent regulatory commission. Each agency of this sort has been given a broad delegation of power over a sector of the economy or a type of commercial activity, and each is expected to make its own rules and to settle disputes among parties within its jurisdiction. The making of rules by regulatory commissions is sometimes called administrative legislation, euphemistically termed "quasi-legislation," since in theory the formulation of legislation by agencies other than Congress violates the separation of powers. Similarly, when these commissions settle disputes among parties within their jurisdiction, this adjudication is called "quasi-judicial action."

Since each of these independent regulatory agencies was set up precisely to perform some regular control activity without regard to the particular wishes of the White House or of Congress, they have been viewed with a certain amount of alarm, even by persons who support the practice. The independent agencies, it has been argued, are so large in number and so powerful in resources and authority that they constitute a "Headless Fourth Branch" of government.[41] Since very few experts have been willing to insist upon more presidential supervision or stricter guidelines by Congress, the tendency has been to let these commissions go their way and to try to limit them by insisting that they provide all parties with varieties of procedural safeguards.[42]

The independent regulatory commissions appear to be organizationally a great deal more loosely structured than the bureaus organized within the regular departments. In the first place, most of these agencies are a good deal smaller. In the second place, many of them are given more leeway by law to recruit personnel outside the civil service merit system. But most importantly, they seem to be less rigidly structured because their independence has allowed them to relate more closely to their environment. These agencies were set up in response to a specific clamor for a new program or function and, once in existence, became highly responsive to the particular segment of the society they were set up to deal with. There has tended to be a great deal of osmosis between the agencies and the businesses they are supposed to be regulating. Especially during the first decade of its life, the regulatory agency tends to draw its top staff from the very industries over which its regulatory authority is to be exercised—or from related law firms. Both friends and enemies of regulatory commissions have noted this interpenetration.[43] There may be some advantages in this kind of exchange of personnel; there is, however, the ever present question of who is regulating whom.

[41]Final report of the President's Committee on Administrative Management (Washington, D.C.: Government Printing Office, 1937).

[42]See, for example, Kenneth C. Davis, *Discretionary Justice* (Baton Rouge: University of Louisiana Press, 1969). For a view favoring closer congressional control through more limited delegations of power, consult Lowi, *The End of Liberalism,* and Sotirios A. Barber, *The Constitution and the Delegation of Congressional Power* (Chicago: University of Chicago Press, 1975).

[43]For the general pattern, see Marver Bernstein, *Regulating Business by Independent Commission* (Princeton: Princeton University Press, 1955). For more specific studies, consult Gabriel Kolko, *Railroads and Regulation* (New York: Free Press, 1963); and Alan Stone, "The Politics of Trade Regulation" (Ph.D. diss., University of Chicago, 1972). Kolko and Stone analyze the pattern of regulatory commissions, paying particular attention to the Federal Trade Commission. For the case of the National Labor Relations Board (NLRB), see Francis Rourke, "Variations in Agency Power," in *Bureaucratic Power in National Politics.*

Independent enterprises and public corporations Up to a certain point, the second and third categories of independent agencies in Table 12.4 are indistinguishable. In both cases an agency is set up to produce goods or services allegedly not economically feasible for private enterprise or too important to be left to the whims of individual initiative. The major distinction between the two seems to be that the independent enterprises and public corporations category is comprised of agencies that collect part or all of their own revenues. They are either allowed to make a profit on their goods or services, which they can use to defray expenses and pay salaries, or they may be able to sell bonds to raise the capital funds necessary for their operations. Perhaps the only exception is NASA, which has no taxing authority, no product or service to sell as a source of income, and no authority to sell bonds for purposes of capital accumulation. All the other enterprises are true enterprises, even though they do not necessarily turn enough income each year to operate without federal subsidy.

Independent clientele agencies The independent clientele agencies, the third category on Table 12.4, are organized to produce goods or services without regard to demand, like the clientele departments discussed previously. No doubt these agencies would eventually wither away if there were no demand, but the outputs of the agencies are not expected to vary in any specific way in response to demands.

Few of these agencies become tightly organized career services comparable to the Forest Service or the main branches of the military. However, many of them do become highly professional in their personnel and highly routine in their activities. For example, the Tennessee Valley Authority (TVA) is one of the most professionalized agencies in the United States government, coming closer to a real career service than many of the bureaus inside regular cabinet departments. NASA is not only highly professionalized but also quite independent of the defense industry. It is one of the largest purchasers of goods and services in America, and one could say that the defense industry depends more upon NASA than NASA upon it. Even the Postal Service is more independent of its clientele than many regulatory agencies, if only because the special preference given to military veterans seeking employment in post offices has caused this agency to be dominated by veterans rather than by the primary users, such as big merchandising companies and the magazine and newspaper publishers.

Some of the independent enterprises are independent of their clientele or users because of the special obligations they develop to their sources of finance. This is particularly true of those independent enterprises called public corporations, because their primary obligation is to their bond holders rather than to their users *or* to the parent government.[44]

Independent overhead agencies   Once these agencies have been created, how shall they be supervised? Who shall guard these guardians? Part of the answer lies with the agencies listed in the fourth and final category of Table 12.4. Here we have independent overhead agencies to deal with independent line agencies. For example, the General Accounting Office is responsible for auditing all of the expenditures of administrative agencies, including the independent agencies. Its top officials, the comptroller general and the deputy comptroller general, are appointed by the president for terms of fifteen years, not removable except for special cause following a formal impeachment process. The Civil Service Commission is the agency of general responsibility for recruitment, placement, and promotion of persons with the skills required for most of the jobs in the federal service. Its authority over the independent agencies is somewhat weaker than that over the regular departmental agencies, but it is still extensive. The General Services Administration has general authority over all purchases made in all agencies, from pencils to automobiles; and it usually manages most of the buildings and real estate of the federal government as well, except as otherwise provided. The Administrative Conference has no formal power over any administrative agencies, but it has the potential for great influence through its powers to investigate legal procedures. Its full-time staff is composed of high-ranking officials drawn from various federal agencies, as well as law professors and other experts of high standing in private life.

All of these independent overhead agencies are capable of exercising great influence over the other independent agencies as well as the departments. However, the limitations should be obvious. First, these agencies have no authority over the substantive policies being pursued by the other agencies. Basically, the independent overhead agencies are responsible for maintaining "clean government," but they have no right to consider the desirability of any program or agency action. The second great limitation is that these agencies are also independent of central political responsibility. As such, they can be just as subversive of presidential programs or congressional intent as any other bureaucracy.

For example, one observer noted that once the "merit system" (under the Civil Service Commission) was extended to include virtually all but the very top government personnel, the top

[44]Some of the agonizing problems of public authorities are dealt with dramatically in Robert Caro, *The Power Broker* (New York: Knopf, 1974).

leadership of the major line agencies, who are supposed to direct policy for the president, began "to pray for deliverance from their guardians. They do not deny that it would be impossible to conduct effective administrative operations if their staffs were inexpert. . . . But they add that good administration is difficult also if personnel management is taken partly out of their hands."[45]

It is thus clear that the independent overhead agencies do not solve the problem that central political authorities have to face; that is, these agencies may help by improving the quality of service, but they cannot determine policy for themselves or for the higher authorities. As James Q. Wilson put the point in an eloquent essay, "Coping with the bureaucracy problem is inseparable from re-thinking the objectives of the programs in question."[46] When governments face new problems of conquest, it is overwhelmingly rational to organize a bureaucracy around those problems, to routinize the bureaucracy, to arrange for its administration by specialists, and to gain continuity by promoting careerism and professional dedication among those specialists. But it is in this way that each bureaucracy becomes singularly incapable of considering all the consequences of its own actions or of taking into account the related actions of other agencies. The real "bureaucracy problem" is this: Can we design agencies to solve the various problems of conquest in one period of time without mortgaging our future permanently to those particular solutions? Is a government that is capable of responding appropriately to one round of problems incapable by that very fact of responding to the next?

Our initial observation should now be taking on stronger and stronger elements of somber truth. The most formidable barrier to responsible central political control of bureaucracy is not size or complexity but *integrity*—the integrity of the separate bureaus, the integrity of professional specialties, and the integrity of careers that begin with advanced training and end in a lifetime of dedication to a particular problem of conquest. Is it possible to balance this kind of integrity against the demands of representative government?

BUREAUCRACY AND THE FIFTY-YEAR STRUGGLE FOR RESPONSIBLE CONTROL

The centers of political responsibility in our government are not entirely bereft of power over the bureaucracy. But the power is limited or specialized, or both. From the perspective of the presiden-

---

[45]Herbert Kaufman, "The Growth of the Federal Personnel System," in *Bureaucratic Power in National Politics*, p. 269.
[46]James Q. Wilson, "The Bureaucracy Problem," in *The Politics of the Federal Bureaucracy*, ed. Alan A. Altshuler (New York: Dodd, Mead, 1968), p. 31.

cy, the problem begins with the tendency of the nomination and election process to produce outsiders (see chapter 11).

During the last fifty years of American government, no president has taken office with any significant experience in national administration. This pattern of administrative inexperience extends beyond the president to most of his top political appointments. For example, the first Nixon cabinet was long on political experience, but the experience of its members with the federal bureaucracies prior to their elevation to the cabinet was almost nonexistent. The same could be said for President Kennedy's cabinet, with the exception of Secretary of State Dean Rusk, who had accumulated five years of experience in the State Department between 1946 and 1951. President Johnson's cabinet was exceptional only inasmuch as Johnson tried to retain as much continuity as possible with the Kennedy administration immediately following the assassination.

Such are the dictates of presidential politics that when it comes to the appointment of the top officialdom, ability to run a department or bureau seems to be the last qualification considered. Secretaries of defense have tended to come out of big industry and may have knowledge of it. Secretaries of state have usually come from the top East Coast law firms and may be familiar with the ruling classes of other powerful nations. Secretaries of labor usually bring some expertise in labor-management relations. Secretaries of interior tend to be known and respected among Western interests, especially the users of natural resources. However, extremely few of them know their agencies or are known well by the top career personnel in their agencies.

It has been suggested that staffing the top presidential offices "resembles a continuous performance of the Battle of Bull Run with new actors for each show and a minimal build-up of knowledge from the experience."[47] Interviews with top White House aides of Kennedy, Johnson, and Nixon all tend to confirm the observation that the so-called talent hunts were haphazard and filled with mistakes. The fact is, in the presidency there is *great power to commit but very little power to guide.* Most of the expansion of the executive branch has taken place during the past fifty years. At every step along the way this has been accompanied by efforts to accumulate the formal powers and the staff to enhance the presidential capacity to guide as well as to commit.

Before 1920, each president made some effort to provide himself with a staff of trusted advisers who could help him keep track of what was going on in the agencies. This inner circle has always generated a certain amount of mystery as well as fear. Sometimes it

---

[47]This quotation by Norton Long, and other observations on staffing, will be found in Thomas E. Cronin, "Presidents as Chief Executives," in *The Presidency Reappraised,* ed. Rexford Tugwell and Thomas Cronin (New York: Praeger, 1974), chapter 14.

In the beginning was the
"kitchen cabinet":
Andrew Jackson's White
House staff as depicted
by a period cartoonist.

has been called the "kitchen cabinet," at other times the "tennis cabinet" or the "inner cabinet." During the 1930s, the presidential staff grew to such size and status that it was referred as the "brain trust." But since the 1930s this type of arrangement has been considered inadequate. The skills of the staff tend to be the same as those of the president; they tend to reproduce his ignorance. Perhaps this is why recent presidents have had such poor luck in the search for administrative talent.

In their effort to cope with the bureaucracies, most presidents resort to three types of strategies, the first of which is selective attention. That is to say, they concentrate upon a few agencies crucial to the most pressing problems and let the rest fend for themselves. Sometimes the president's attention is a matter of free choice. But most often this choice is imposed by events over which presidents have little control. President Nixon would probably have chosen to concentrate on foreign affairs, but events pulled him in that direction in any case—as they did President Johnson, despite his preference for domestic issues. President Kennedy had to work with agencies that could deal with civil rights because of the impressive march on Washington in 1963. The inflationary tendencies of the years 1970 and 1971 forced President Nixon to deal with agencies that could cope with wage and price controls despite his inclination to leave this administrative area alone.

As a second strategy presidents tend to go to Congress for new legislation directing an existing agency to do something—even directing the agency to coordinate its activities with all other agencies related to it. President Johnson clearly attempted this with his War on Poverty program. Presidents Johnson and Nixon engaged in this sort of strategy in their efforts to expand the Environmental Protection Agency to coordinate all other agencies as well as to deal with the environment at large. However, even though this may in the long run be the best way of directing agencies, such laws are not self-executing, and their passage does not guarantee the president any kind of an enforcement procedure. New legislation of this sort begins to look more like a new commitment rather than an increased capacity to guide.

Still a third strategy of coping with the bureaucracies is to disregard existing bureaucracies altogether and to create a new agency which is much more likely to be responsive to presidential leadership. For the president who creates the agency, this is probably a solution. But for succeeding presidents such an established agency and its loyalties to the previous president may make the agency all the less responsive to later presidential leadership and guidance. President Franklin Roosevelt was the most frequent user of this flanking technique; but it was also President Roosevelt who once threw up his hands in despair, comparing efforts to control the bureaucracy to the futile activity of punching a large featherbed.

The futility of these strategies goes far toward explaining the continuous fifty-year effort to build overhead functions around the president. Table 12.5, which itemizes periods and aspects of government expansion, is a chronicle of good intentions. It begins with the Budgeting and Accounting Act of 1921, which was a very substantial response to the expansion of government under the administration of Woodrow Wilson. From that point onward, every period of government expansion has been accompanied and succeeded by expansion of overhead controls in and around the White House. The diligence of these efforts is underscored by the fact that responses to governmental expansion have been neither partisan nor antagonistic among presidents. For example, although Republicans enacted the Budgeting and Accounting Act in response to a Democratic administration, the Democrats accepted budgeting and pursued the theory and practice of budgeting far beyond anything the Republicans had originally had in mind. Beginning in the late 1930s, the Democrats brought the Budget Bureau into the Executive Office of the President and expanded its powers until it became the central overhead control in the national government. (Note in Table 12.5 the several instances under Roosevelt and Truman where budgetary functions were expanded.)

The 1940s and 1950s were years of expansion in our government's foreign and military agencies, as well as in domestic agencies; and the expansion in all of these areas seems to have been accompanied by innovations in presidential overhead capacity. The Joint Chiefs

Table 12.5 Toward an Executive Establishment

Period of Government Expansion	Responses of the Presidency to Expansion
Wilson—World War I, 1914–1918: Budget up from average $800 million to over $18 billion in 1919 and $6.5 billion in 1920.	Budgeting and Accounting Act, 1921: (1) Bureau of the Budget in executive branch and (2) General Accounting Office as agent of Congress.
Roosevelt—New Deal period, 1933–1936: Growth, plus great addition of new agencies, the "alphabetocracy."	Executive Office of President, 1939; Budget Bureau from Treasury; new Office of Legislative Clearance; reorganization of powers, 1939.
Roosevelt—World War II, 1940–1944: Mobilization and maintenance.	Council of Economic Advisors, 1946; Secretary of Defense, 1947; National Security Council, 1947; Joint Chiefs of Staff, 1947.
Truman—Postwar, Korean period, 1947–1951: Contraction, followed by growth.	*Truman:* Spread of legislative clearance and emergence of "president's program," 1948+; Office of Secretary of Defense, 1949; Emergence of White House Staff, 1950+.
	Eisenhower: Formalizing of White House Staff; institutionalizing of "president's program"; enhancement of the National Security Council; Schedule C; departmentalization*; Hoover Commission.
Kennedy—1961–1962: Aggressive effort to work out a comprehensive program.	Status of White House personnel increased; functions of White House Staff begin to parallel those of departments; task forces of outside people; use of Cabinet intimates instead of National Security Council; Planning–Programming–Budgeting System (PPBS) applied to Defense Department.
Johnson—1964–1966: Guns *and* butter.	Expansion of White House—more counterparts to departments; PPBS applied to domestic agencies; War on Poverty (1964–1965); departmentalization (HUD and the Department of Transportation), 1964–1966; presidential commissions; Office of Management and Budget; ultimate formalization of White House Staff.
Nixon—1969–1972: Increased mandated costs of social security and defense; expansion of diplomacy; price controls	Super-departmentalization; fusion of White House with super-department heads; downgrading of cabinet, 1972–1973.

*Created new Department of Health, Education and Welfare as part of the effort to coordinate and control social agencies.

of Staff was almost certainly an institution created in the midst of preoccupations about central overhead control of military planning. This wartime innovation was followed in 1947 by the National Security Council (NSC), a kind of specialized super-cabinet made up of the president, the vice-president, the secretary of state, the secretary of defense, and any other participant invited by the president. The NSC also appoints a senior staff, which in recent years has been headed by the assistant to the president for national security affairs—an office held by such political luminaries as Henry Kissinger and McGeorge Bundy. Table 12.5 shows a parallel growth in the domestic side of presidential overhead, beginning after World War II with the establishment of the Council of Economic Advisors.

Each president, whether strong or weak, has had his own style of overhead control. No president has seen fit to abandon the efforts and innovations of his predecessors, but each has added something of his own. For example, President Eisenhower had intended to depart from the Truman practice of using the Budget Bureau to develop a "president's program," so he took the enlarged Truman White House staff and organized it along military lines as a much more formal and hierarchical method of receiving and processing information on the activities of the bureaucracies. Within two years, however, Eisenhower not only had accepted the work of the Bureau of the Budget but also found himself making regular use, as Truman had, of the National Security Council.[48]

President Kennedy, following eight years of Republican rule, accepted the Eisenhower military staff approach almost completely but deemphasized the National Security Council in favor of individual consultation with cabinet members in the foreign affairs and defense areas. His most important cabinet member, Robert McNamara, developed a very high-powered systematic budgeting approach (the Planning–Programming–Budgeting System—PPBS) to administrative control that had proved successful in parts of the Defense Department.

When President Johnson took over the White House, he not only left the Kennedy staff intact but specialized it still further. He fully accepted the McNamara budgeting idea and tried conscientiously to apply it to all domestic agencies. He also followed an Eisenhower approach by trying to control certain independent agencies through departmentalization calling for the creation of two new departments, Housing and Urban Development and Transportation. In addition, Johnson made more use than ever of presidential commissions composed of distinguished outsiders, whose recommendations might lead to programmatic approaches that would tie various agencies and departments together in a common mission. His most dramatic effort to cope with administrative coordination and control was the War on Poverty, which was above all an effort to create a capacity in and near the White House to coordinate social service agencies.

President Nixon, during his first four years in office, seems to have brought to a culminating point several tendencies that had been present since the 1950s. He, too, enlarged the White House staff greatly, and he took the departmentalization approach still further in his efforts to combine all or parts of existing departments into a smaller number of super-departments. Congress turned down his legislative request for this formal reorganization, but he managed to achieve some of the same results by informally deem-

[48]For a comparative look at the practices of Roosevelt, Eisenhower, and Kennedy, see Richard Neustadt, "Approaches to Staffing the Presidency," *American Political Science Review,* December 1963, pp. 855–863.

phasizing certain departments (Interior, Labor, Commerce, and Transportation) and elevating the status and influence of others (especially Treasury, HEW, Agriculture, and HUD).[49] At the same time, Nixon was still promoting the Bureau of the Budget; he gave it additional powers and a new name, the Office of Management and Budget (OMB).

Presidential Efforts toward Continuity

Budgeting Reviewing presidential efforts over the past fifty years to develop effective overhead controls, two patterns emerge fairly clearly—continuity and futility. Each deserves some discussion. The longest continuous line of development in overhead control is of course budgeting. Since the introduction of the "executive budget" in 1921, the budgeting function has gone up in status and outward in its domain of influence until it has become an essential tool of the president. Its prestige and influence are respected by bureaucrats and members of Congress alike. A budget has never been anything more than a detailed statement of who is going to get how much money to buy what kinds of goods and services. However, once it was discovered in the 1930s that a budget is a way of translating important policy decisions into routine administrative action, it was not long before the budget became the single most important overhead weapon of the president. Some policy makers see it as a way of gaining efficiency and restraint, while others see it as an opportunity to gain program effectiveness; but all sides agree overwhelmingly on its importance in controlling the everyday activities of the line agencies.

The story of budgeting is far from over, but it does have a recent chapter: the Planning–Programming–Budgeting System. PPBS took the notion that budgetary items should be categorized within larger objectives, rather than merely detailed in a budget for each agency, and went as far with it as the computer would allow. PPBS requires all departments and agencies to define their major objectives or programs and then systematically to identify two or more alternative ways by which these programs can be attained. The program alternatives, defined in terms of budgetary implications, are accumulated for the higher authorities. With these alternatives in hand, so goes the theory, the higher authorities can make more rational decisions which can also be implemented more effectively back through the lower administrators.

However, PPBS has proven itself effective mainly in those agencies where objectives can be clearly translated into monetary

---

[49]Although this would seem a natural culmination of earlier developments, it was not greeted with universal praise. Even some of the more conservative members of the press criticized it. See, for example, Rowland Evans and Robert Novak, "Behind Purge, a Super-Cabinet Emerges," *Washington Post*, December 21, 1972.

quantities. This is why it has been working well enough in the Department of Defense, where so many objectives can be translated into amounts of goods, personnel, and services. But where the objectives are unclear, especially where Congress or the president hopes that an agency will be able to work out the objectives on its own, PPBS is simply not relevant. Another limitation is political. PPBS is rarely opposed as a system of budgeting within a specific agency, since it may offer ways of increasing rationality and efficiency. But it is quite another matter when it is used as a method of overhead control, especially when the higher authorities employ it in attempts to force agencies to cooperate with each other. PPBS may offer some hope for future presidents, but it is not likely to be the panacea it has been held to be by some of its proponents.[50]

Preparation of the president's program A second dimension of continuity during the past fifty years of struggle for a "presidential establishment" is an offshoot of budgeting which has gained its own

---

[50]As one of the most careful students of PPBS put it, "We are now at the dawn of a new era in budgeting; high noon is still a long way off." Allen Schick, "The Road to PPB: The Stages of Budget Reform," in *Politics, Programs, and Budget,* ed. James W. Davis (Englewood Cliffs, N. J.: Prentice-Hall, 1969), p. 227. Also in the Davis volume, see Aaron Wildavsky, "The Political Economy of Efficiency," pp. 230–252. Wildavsky is even more skeptical of the benefits and the prospects of PPBS. His article also adds an assessment of some related planning techniques, such as cost-benefit analysis and systems analysis, or operations research.

separate identity—the preparation of the president's program. This process is largely an outgrowth of the success of the Office of Legislative Reference in the Bureau of the Budget (OMB since 1970), which was charged with the simple but fundamental responsibility of receiving all agency requests for new legislation. The responsibility of the Office of Legislative Reference was called legislative clearance, which amounted to review of each request for legislation by an executive branch agency in order to determine whether it was in accord with the wishes of the president. Hundreds of actual drafts of legislation are cleared by this process every year.

Legislative clearance was used by Franklin Roosevelt as a negative device, mainly to keep check on such requests to avoid the embarrassment of later having to oppose or veto enactments that actually came out of his administration. As recently as 1946, there was still an "absence of cohesion in the legislative program of the chief executive—absence, in fact, of a program clearly designated as such."[51] By 1954 the preparation of the president's program had become "customary" and "institutionalized."[52] We have already seen how it has become a key to legislative action. It is also an essential feature of presidential efforts to cope with the bureaucracies.

Although there is no denying the importance of the president's program, it is a weapon better suited for commitment than for detailed guidance. Since it is based upon a well-established and systematic legislative clearance procedure, it offers the president an excellent chance for comprehensive review of the bureaucracies. However, it is only good at catching initiatives that agencies propose to take. It does not give the president an analysis of what the agencies are doing or an investigatory tool for discovering things agencies might like to keep hidden. Its inadequacies in this regard must be one of the reasons that presidents continue to add more agencies and more staff for central control of administration, despite heavy reliance on the legislative clearance procedure.

Development of counterpart units A third dimension of continuity does not have as extensive a history, but it has grown in significance in recent years and could eventually overshadow the other two. This is the development of *counterpart units* in the White House and in the Executive Office of the president. Counterpart

---

[51]Quoted in Richard E. Neustadt, "Presidency and Legislation: Planning the President's Program," in *The Presidency,* ed. Aaron Wildavsky (Boston: Little, Brown, 1969), p. 559. This article and a companion in the same volume, also by Neustadt, "Presidency and Legislation: The Growth of Central Clearance," p. 601, are essential to any treatment of the development of the overhead functions of the president, including this one.

[52]Neustadt, "Presidency and Legislation: Planning the President's Program," p. 559.

units are either separate offices or individual advisers whose jurisdiction for overhead or advisory tasks corresponds to one or more line agencies in the executive branch. For example, at the beginning of the Nixon administration there was already a "special adviser" or "special assistant" in the White House for each of the following areas: international security affairs, military affairs, the draft, social security, poverty, narcotics, labor, and science and technology. There was one special assistant with general domestic responsibilities, and over all these advisers was the chief of staff (H. R. Haldeman).

This was altogether consistent with steps already taken by Presidents Eisenhower, Kennedy, and Johnson. During the 1960s no year passed without considerable growth and specialization of the central offices of the White House and the Executive Office of the president. And although these two units—the White House and the Executive Office—are legally separate and are housed in separate buildings, the specialization of the presidential staff has led to an increasing amount of interchange between the two. Before the disruptions of the Watergate crisis, the president's White House staff had 510 authorized positions, with 606 people actually employed. At the same time the Executive Office of the president employed around 5,000. (This figure is reported in round numbers because there was a disagreement between adviser John Ehrlichman and the Civil Service Commission on the actual numbers. The commission claimed that there were over 5,200 while Ehrlichman claimed that there were more like 3,600 or 3,700.[53])

Figure 12.3 provides an overview of presidential staff and organization toward the end of the Nixon administration—mid-1973, before the onset of the confusion and uncertainties attributable to the Watergate affair. Note first how centralized presidential staff had become. Virtually all communications passed through the White House chief of staff. The extent of this centralization was not fully appreciated until the public testimony of various witnesses before the Ervin Committee.

But the most outstanding feature of these counterpart units illustrated in Figure 12.3 is the extraordinary number of high-level offices—special assistants and special consultants on full-time assignments for a special area. Twelve of these functionaries had jurisdictions described by their titles—for example, the special assistant for military affairs and the special assistant for national security affairs. But it would be a mistake to overlook the twenty-one other deputy special assistants whose assignments also tended to be in rather specialized and stable areas of administration. For example, presidential counselor Donald Rumsfeld was responsible

[53]*Congressional Quarterly Weekly Report,* January 20, 1973, p. 12.

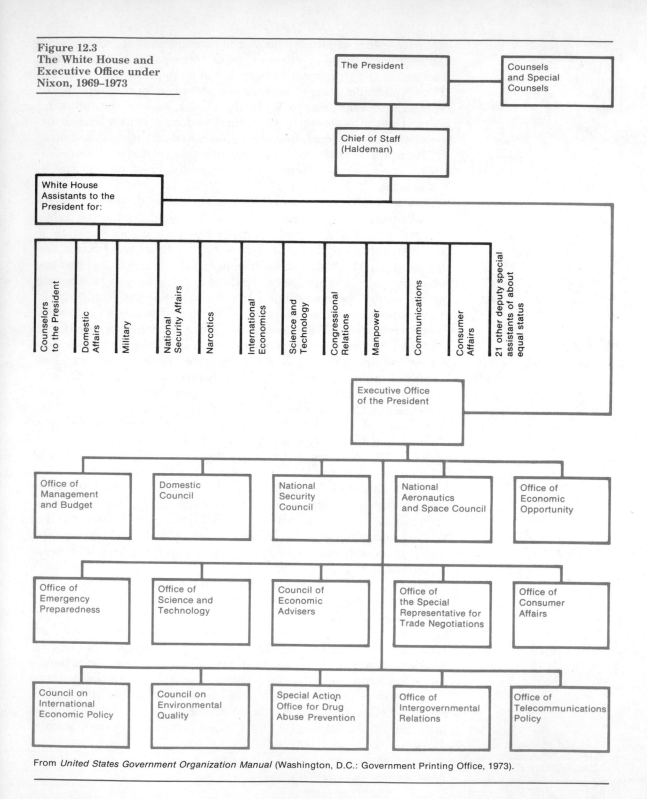

**Figure 12.3
The White House and
Executive Office under
Nixon, 1969–1973**

The President

Counsels and Special Counsels

Chief of Staff (Haldeman)

White House Assistants to the President for:

Counselors to the President

Domestic Affairs

Military

National Security Affairs

Narcotics

International Economics

Science and Technology

Congressional Relations

Manpower

Communications

Consumer Affairs

21 other deputy special assistants of about equal status

Executive Office of the President

Office of Management and Budget

Domestic Council

National Security Council

National Aeronautics and Space Council

Office of Economic Opportunity

Office of Emergency Preparedness

Office of Science and Technology

Council of Economic Advisers

Office of the Special Representative for Trade Negotiations

Office of Consumer Affairs

Council on International Economic Policy

Council on Environmental Quality

Special Action Office for Drug Abuse Prevention

Office of Intergovernmental Relations

Office of Telecommunications Policy

From *United States Government Organization Manual* (Washington, D.C.: Government Printing Office, 1973).

for watching over the whole area of wage and price control, including the Cost of Living Council and relevant departments and agencies.

The placement of the Executive Office of the president in Figure 12.3 should not be taken to mean that it is collectively less influential than the White House staff. True, the Executive Office is a sort of "outer circle"; but its influence is very substantial, although different from that of the White House staff. The difference may in part be represented by the fact that the Executive Office is housed in the Executive Office Building, which is next door to the White House but outside the White House compound. This large Victorian building once housed the entire State Department, and it is still referred to as Old State.

The Executive Office has come a long way since 1939, when it was basically little more than the Bureau of the Budget. Its greatest growth took place during the 1960s, but its greatest period of formalization and specialization was during the first four years of the Nixon administration. The most important units, already iden-tified, are the OMB, the Council of Economic Advisors, and, until the end of the Nixon administration, the Office of Economic Opportunity (an evolved form of Johnson's War on Poverty). Each of these three, and each of the other units identified in Figure 12.3, is a small bureaucracy organized for the purpose of controlling other bureaucracies—the line agencies. Each unit is strictly an overhead agency, the result of the efforts of one president or another to cope with the line agencies; and all of these units are coming closer and closer to having jurisdictions parallel to those of one or more important line agencies or programs.

Two units not on the official chart of the Executive Office belong in this discussion. These are the CIA and the FBI. The CIA was organized to report foreign intelligence to the National Security Council and through that to the president. This is one thing it does, but the CIA is also an overhead agency to the extent that the president is able to use it to make confidential checks on activities of sensitive personnel in all other agencies, particularly agencies with international responsibilities. Although the practice is definitely illegal, the CIA has on occasion been used also to put domestic government personnel and private citizens under surveillance. Despite the public investigations of 1975, no one knows exactly what the president's secret budget is for this kind of surveillance; but it is definitely an overhead activity.

This is also true of the FBI, whose agencies are more frequently, and more legally, assigned the task of investigating government personnel. The FBI is responsible for building the dossiers for top-secret clearance, without which no civil servant can participate in highly responsible policy-making activities. Yet, despite its impressiveness, this kind of power does not guarantee that an

The Chief Executive, the Executive Branch, and the Management of Conquest

503

employee or an agency will be more responsive to presidential guidance. Its possibilities as an axe in the corner have not, however, gone unnoticed by presidents who may resort to the data, hearsay, and unevaluated information in a bureaucrat's dossier as a form of blackmail.[54] Examples of FBI and CIA misuse by the president are contained in the presidential transcripts of the Watergate tapes as well. For example, one excerpt from a conversation between President Nixon and John Dean:

President Nixon: We have not used the Bureau [FBI] and we have not used the Justice Department but things are going to change now. . . .
John Dean: What an exciting prospect.
President Nixon: Thanks. It has to be done.[55]

Plans proposed by President Nixon immediately following his reelection in 1972 recognized the supremacy of the White House staff and the attempted final downgrading of the cabinet (see Figure 12.4). In these plans the chief of staff and the assistant for domestic affairs were retained. Four cabinet officers were then designated to serve jointly as secretaries and presidential assistants. The secretary of the treasury would serve also as presidential assistant for economics; the secretary of health, education and welfare would serve jointly as presidential assistant for human resources and presidential assistant for community development; and the secretary of agriculture would serve as presidential assistant for natural resources. They were to be given jurisdiction over the departments in which they served as secretaries and all other domestic departments and agencies with related areas of concern. The other departments—Interior, Labor, Commerce, and Transportation— were to become inferior departments reporting only indirectly to the president. The four super-cabinet secretaries would also serve as a high-powered Domestic Council. Many of the previous members of the White House staff were to remain in the White House, while many others were to be reassigned to sensitive positions in the departments, maintaining their loyalties to the White House.[56]

President Nixon was attempting as best he knew to fuse all overhead activities in the White House with those in the cabinet. The departure from traditional overhead was that the fusion was to

---

[54]See, for example, Navasky, *Kennedy Justice,* p. 372; also the testimony of various members of the "plumbers group" before the Ervin Committee concerning the burglary of the office of Daniel Ellsberg's psychiatrist.

[55]From *The President's Transcripts* (New York: Dell–Washington Post, 1974), p. 38.

[56]Good surveys of these developments just before they were choked off by the Watergate revelations will be found in columns by Evans and Novak, "Behind the Purge, a Supercabinet Emerges"; and "Cabinet: Faceless, Symbolically Political," *Washington Post,* December 9, 1972. See also John Herbers, "Watergate's Impact on Agencies," *New York Times,* July 9, 1973.

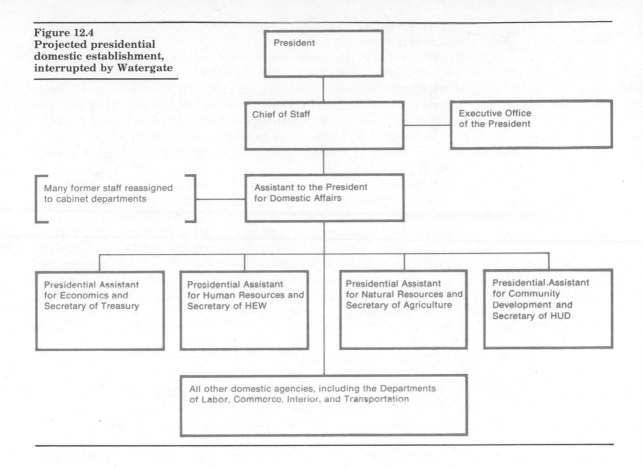

Figure 12.4
Projected presidential
domestic establishment,
interrupted by Watergate

President

Chief of Staff

Executive Office
of the President

Many former staff reassigned
to cabinet departments

Assistant to the President
for Domestic Affairs

Presidential Assistant
for Economics and
Secretary of Treasury

Presidential Assistant
for Human Resources and
Secretary of HEW

Presidential Assistant
for Natural Resources and
Secretary of Agriculture

Presidential Assistant
for Community
Development and
Secretary of HUD

All other domestic agencies, including the Departments
of Labor, Commerce, Interior, and Transportation

take place *directly in the White House* rather than at cabinet or subcabinet levels or in the Executive Office. This would have given him a slightly better chance of having advisers loyal to him. A second advantage to the president would have been that these holders of the top command posts would be far less responsible to Congress. This would be true by dint of their greater loyalty to the president, but also legally true to the extent that personal advisers in the White House would have been able to make more effective claims of executive privilege when testifying before congressional committees.

Many reporters spoke in grave terms about the disadvantages of these plans. The gravest charge of all was that combining cabinet secretary and White House adviser would close off from the president all the news he might not want to hear, or all the news his advisers suspect he might not want to hear. Combining line and overhead functions in the White House increased the risk of isolation by reducing the number of people and the number of types of people reporting to the president.[57]

But actually these reactions seem rather farfetched, probably based more on suspicions of President Nixon's paranoia than on a dispassionate assessment of his proposals. If a president personally does not want to hear bad news, almost any institutional arrangement of the White House will accommodate him. On the other hand, a president who truly wants to keep in touch with reality can get some inkling of world activity by clicking on the television and by issuing invitations to critics.

Since Nixon's plan for the fusion of super-cabinet positions and White House overhead did not go into full effect after the Watergate crisis, it is not possible to evaluate the arrangement as another round in presidential efforts to cope with the bureaucracies. Yet the Nixon effort was very consistent with many of the developments and contributions of his predecessors, and Nixon's successors are very likely to toy around with the same ideas even if they eventually choose some other means by which to bring the bureaucracies under presidential control.

BUREAUCRACY AND THE PRESIDENCY

Where does all this lead the presidency? We have the fossil remains of thousands of encounters between the president and the bureaucracy, the president and the public, the president and the outside world, the president and the corporate elite. Following the science of archaeology, we may be able to construct a meaningful picture of this gigantic institution.

First, we can be fairly confident that the bones we labeled chief of state are substantial; when brought into our archaeological construct they will work well enough as legs to prop up the beast. We can be almost equally sure that the osseous remains we sometimes call chief legislator are also substantial and will fit in place to give the beast some degree of form. The neck and jaw bones called chief diplomat give the animal additional shape, and we can be reassured by the teeth of commander-in-chief. Unfortunately this leaves us without backbone—all we have is a rubbery spinal cord, the chief executive. The weakness of the spine leaves us with an archaeological find that may stand up well enough to put on view at the Smithsonian for our bicentennial celebration but may not stand up to actual stress. This fossil creature—the presidency—shows evi-

---

[57]One eloquent statement concerning the general risks of isolation in the presidency is that of George Reedy, *The Twilight of the Presidency* (New York: World Publishing, 1970). An important article stressing the insidious effect of Nixon's new White House organization is that of David Broder, "Nixon's Guardians," *Washington Post,* January 1974 (reprinted in the *International Herald Tribune,* January 11, 1974).

dence of all kinds of surgical effort to strengthen its backbone with bits of baling wire and string, but few fragments have been turned up on digs to indicate that it ever had the real strength of spine that a large beast would need.

Indeed, nothing we have found so far will detract from the original proposition that the president has power to commit but not to guide. The president can get us into a war and sometimes get us out of one, can manipulate countries so well that many potential wars have been rendered unnecessary, can manipulate us to mount every sort of success in getting the desired domestic policies. This is perhaps why we all look to the president so optimistically to put us and the world to rights. But this optimism is to a large extent unfounded. In its relationship to the bureaucracy the presidency provides us with a system that is at best well run but not very well governed.

This is the essence of the bureaucracy problem anywhere in the world. Successful conquest requires commitment, and commitment through a government program involves a commitment to a bureaucracy to administer it. This provides dependability and efficiency, but it also involves an obligation to do the same thing the same way for a long time. The advantages and the disadvantages of that are self-evident. Bureaucracy is one of the great secrets of success in all of the "developed countries" of the world. It underlies governments in capitalist nations and the productivity of capitalism, but it is also at the foundation of socialist nations, for planning in the public sector requires solutions to the same problems of overhead and overhead control of line agencies that we have been dealing with here. No matter what the system of government, bureaucracy makes modern conquest possible and in turn sets severe limits on the freedom of each generation to choose its own form of conquest.

The enormous stature and energy of a single chief executive, coupled with the constitutional authority of the office of president, ought to be adequate to control bureaucracy. The trouble is that the president, like a modern prime minister or military dictator, is confronted by an almost equal formal authority held by the bureaucracy. The formal position of the bureaucracy is not explicitly granted by the Constitution, but it does have a statutory, judicial, professional, cultural, and historical basis. There will never be sufficient presidential power to cope with these large institutions, because there can never be a sufficient amount of formal authority plus informal power in the presidency to overbalance the position of the bureaucracies.

This is something our theory of government has not yet begun to grapple with, and it must. There may be some profit in returning to the older effort to separate the presidency into its component aspects—as in Table 12.1. This kind of separation has been criticized by sophisticates of the recent past, because they see the president as one person with many sources of power. But the truth may indeed lie the other way around. There is not one presidency but rather a president for each of the formal missions built by the Constitution into the executive branch. The president, by virtue of formal authority and the particular utility of certain resources, may be strong with respect to certain purposes and permanently inadequate with respect to others. It may simply be that the president cannot cashier these resources into power as chief executive, even though the same resources might pay off very well in terms of effectiveness as chief legislator or chief diplomat. Each of the many forms of the presidency may possess a different amount of informal power. The whole thrust of modern social science is to perceive individuals and institutions as highly differentiated. Why in that context do we continue to insist that the presidency is an undifferentiated unity?

The solution to the problem of presidential power is not going to be more presidential power. This may simply equip a president for the wrong battle. Yet, due to their insistence on the informal unity of the presidency, members of Congress and many learned observers continue to believe that more "delegation of power" from Congress to the president will eventually make the president powerful enough to cope with the bureaucracies and, through them, with society at large. What is actually delegated from Congress to the president, however, is not power, but responsibility—for which there may never be sufficient power. Such delegation of responsibility to the president only assures the decline of that office into disgrace as it fails to fulfill even a small part of what is expected of it.

There may be no available solution to the problem of presidential power. Some small progress may be made toward a solution, however, through a more thorough appreciation of the bureaucracy problem. Progress of this sort would have to start with recognition of the possibility that no single occupant of a single office can cope with the problems of modern conquest. This would lead to some substantial reforms in the American approach to conquest, after which the presidency would amost certainly never be the same. But why should it be? Is it a perfect institution?

Chapter 13 The National Judiciary and the "Administration of Justice"

Scarcely any question arises in the United States that is not resolved, sooner or later, into a judicial question.
Alexis de Tocqueville, 1831

The prophecies of what the courts will do in fact, and nothing more pretentious, are what I mean by the law.
Associate Justice Oliver Wendell Holmes, 1897

I am older and slower and less acute and more confused. However, as long as things continue as they are, and I am able to answer in my place, I must stay on the court in order to prevent the Bolsheviki from getting control.
Chief Justice William Howard Taft, 1929

THE JUDICIARY AS AN ADMINISTRATIVE AGENCY

Each and every year more than 10 million cases are tried in American courts. The overwhelming majority of these cases arise under state laws, local ordinances, and state common law. The United States federal district courts handled 145,000 cases in 1972; and although this is up from 92,000 cases in 1962, it still constitutes only 1.5 percent of the judicial action in the United States. The federal courts of appeals hear only about 4,200 of these cases. The United States Supreme Court reviews about 4,500 cases, of which only around 250 get full-dress review before the Nine Men. This is quite a pyramid.

Most of the 10 million cases come up under the heading of *private law*—cases which arise out of disputes between citizens who resort to the courts in preference to fights, feuds, or force of arms. Marriage, divorce, and human rights cases (for

The National Judiciary and the "Administration of Justice"

Table 13.1   **Types of Laws and Cases**

Type of Law	Definition	Form of Case
1. Private law	Disputes between private citizens, taken to court, arising out of property rights, civil damages, etc.	*Smith* v. *Jones.*
2. Civil law	Disputes between private citizens or between government and citizen where no crime is alleged. Two types: (1) contracts—disputes arising out of voluntary actions, and (2) torts—obligations imposed by virtue of living in civil society (for example, negligence and slander).	*Smith* v. *Jones,* or *U.S.* v. *Jones,* or *N.Y.* v. *Jones.*
3. Criminal law	Cases arising under actions that allegedly violate laws protecting public order (government is always the plaintiff).	*U.S.* v. *Jones,* or *New York* v. *Jones (Jones* v. *New York),* or *Jones* v. *U.S.* if Jones lost and is appealing to a higher court.
4. Public law	All cases where the powers of government or rights and obligations of citizens are involved (government is always the defendant). Two types: (1) constitutional law—issues of procedural rights, powers of government, etc., and (2) administrative law—disputes arising out of the actions, jurisdictions, or procedures of specific administrative agencies. Any and all private civil or criminal cases can become public law. The bigger and less technical issues are considered constitutional law.	*U.S.* v. *Jones* or *In re Jones* (or *Smith* v. *Jones,* if a license or statute is the cause of action).

example, libel and slander suits) are all aspects of private law adjudication.

Table 13.1 identifies the form of such cases, and places private law in the context of the other categories of cases. These categories are not mutually exclusive, but they will in any event help clarify some of the vocabulary in the judiciary field. *Civil law* is almost synonymous with *private law,* and is often confused with it. However, civil law is a larger category, which includes both private law and actions by government where the issues do not involve criminal penalties. The opposite of civil *or* private law is *criminal law,* in which some public agency is always the plaintiff. Any of these cases can become *public law,* including disputes between purely private parties, if either side of the case argues that a license is unfair, or a law is inequitable, or an agency has acted unfairly or violated a procedure.

One additional distinction does not show up in the table—the distinction between law and equity. Equity proceedings arose out of the feeling that the law can sometimes be too rigid and that the remedy available through the precedents of earlier laws and cases would not be appropriate for a given case. They began as an appeal to the ruling monarch but ultimately became simply a separate feature of the judiciary. For example, whereas at law the payment of monetary damages is most often sufficient to redress a grievance, in some cases the courts deem this insufficient, demanding not only redress but that defendants actually change their conduct in order to prevent recurrence in the future. Out of this notion of equitable relief, of prevention of future damage rather than redress for past damage, grew the modern administrative process.[1]

As mentioned earlier, of the 10 million cases handled each year, only about 145,000 are dealt with by the trial courts of the national judiciary. These are the United States district courts, of which there are ninety in the fifty states, the District of Columbia, and the Commonwealth of Puerto Rico. These federal trial courts, or courts of original jurisdiction, handle cases that are indistinguishable from the cases in the state court systems. Thus, from the standpoint of ordinary disputes and crimes, the national judiciary is unimportant. Were it not for the District of Columbia and other federal territories not belonging to or existing within various states, and were it not for a few other issues where no state possesses jurisdiction, the "trial court level" of the national judiciary could disappear with no untoward effect.

The Appellate Courts

What makes the national judiciary indispensable is the 10 percent of all cases handled by the lower courts that are later accepted for appeal by the federal courts of appeals and the Supreme Court.[2] For these appeals above the district courts, the country is divided into eleven judicial circuits, and in each circuit there is a United States

---

[1]For a discussion of equity and how it becomes a problem for courts in their effort to avoid "political questions," consult Philippa Strum, *The Supreme Court and "Political Questions": A Study in Judicial Evasion* (University, Ala.: University of Alabama Press, 1974), especially chapter 1.

[2]Lawyers for clients in trial cases would be considered professionally negligent if they did not write eloquent briefs to appellate courts seeking to show errors in the record or oversights in important constitutional issues. Briefs are simply the written statements by the lawyers presenting the facts of their cases and the arguments in their favor. Many courts do not require written briefs, but the federal system is quite formal, with the Supreme Court being particularly stodgy on the matter. All petitions and briefs must be printed according to very careful specifications, except for paupers, who are released from these requirements.

court of appeals. Each of the states is assigned to one of these circuits; there is also a circuit—one of the most important—for the District of Columbia; and all of the territories are assigned to a circuit according to their proximity to the continental United States. These appellate courts were created by an act of Congress in 1891 to relieve the Supreme Court of the responsibility of having to consider all cases appealed above the district courts.

Thus, the courts of appeals have exclusively appellate jurisdiction, which means that they restrict their own review to the facts as presented in the lower courts. New evidence may not be presented before an appellate court, including the Supreme Court. These appellate courts are expected to review issues of law and the Constitution; the facts in the lower court record are not at issue. The courts of appeals are not limited to reviews of cases arising from a district court. Certain regulatory agencies (especially the Securities and Exchange Commission, the National Labor Relations Board, the Federal Trade Commission, and the Interstate Commerce Commission) have the legal right to appeal their own cases directly to the court of appeals without first going to the district court at all. In this sense, each regulatory agency enjoys the status of a district court, and as with district courts, the record of facts compiled in the original proceeding is taken as the exclusive factual record for review by the appellate court.

Except for those cases selected for review by the Supreme Court, the decisions made by the courts of appeals are final and are subject to no further action, unless the appellate court itself chooses to reconsider. Consequently, certain safeguards are built into the appellate system; the most important one is the provision of more than one judge for each case. Each court of appeals has from three to fifteen permanent judgeships, depending on the work load of that circuit. In all, there are ninety-seven appellate judgeships, plus the services of all retired appellate judges, who can be called upon to take cases at the behest of the chief justice of the United States. Normally, each case before a court of appeals is heard by three judges, but in some instances several judges sit together *en banc.*

Another safeguard is provided by the assignment of one justice of the Supreme Court as the circuit justice for each of the eleven circuits. Before the creation of the appeals courts in 1891, this was an important and burdensome assignment for the justices of the Supreme Court.[3] Congress has built still another safeguard into the appellate system by providing that whenever a case before a district

[3]Riding circuit was not only onerous but could be dangerous. In the late 1880s, Justice Field, an associate justice of the Supreme Court, was riding circuit in California when his life was threatened by a Mr. Terry, a dissident former California chief justice. A U.S. marshal was assigned as Justice Field's bodyguard, and in the line of duty, Marshal Neagle shot and killed Mr. Terry. This reached the Supreme Court in the important case of *In re Neagle,* 135 U.S. 1 (1890).

court appears to present a constitutional issue, the single judge and jury are to be replaced by a three-judge court, with a circuit court judge presiding.

The Supreme Court

The Supreme Court is without question the "supreme court" of the American judicial system. It is the Supreme Court of the United States and not just of the federal judiciary. Article III of the Constitution vests "the judicial power of the United States" in the Supreme Court, and virtually all official documents make reference to the Supreme Court of the United States and to the chief justice of the United States. This court is supreme in fact as well as form by virtue of its powers to review any and all cases from any and all courts in the land, whenever there is reason to believe that a substantial issue of public law is involved. The famous power of judicial review over acts of Congress is actually nothing more than the power of the Supreme Court to review decisions of lower courts in which one or more provisions of a statute are at issue.

In fact, it is generally agreed that the most important aspect of judicial review is the power of the Supreme Court to review the decisions of state courts in order to determine whether these decisions and the state laws they are applying are consistent with the U.S. Constitution. Congress could in fact be its own arbiter of constitutionality, and generally the Supreme Court tries its best to defer to congressional judgment on these matters. One of the cardinal rules of the Supreme Court is to avoid questions of constitutionality of congressional statutes as far as possible.

In contrast, judicial review of state action is normal, and probably indispensable to the integration of the Union. The power to review state decisions is neither granted by the Constitution nor inherent in the coexistence of two judicial systems in one country. However, the logic of the supremacy clause of Article VI is very strong (see chapter 4). Moreover, Congress conferred power on the Supreme Court in its first judiciary act (1789) to reverse state constitutions and laws whenever they are clearly in conflict with the U.S. Constitution, its laws, or its treaties.[4] This literally gives the Supreme Court effective jurisdiction over all of the 10 million cases handled by American courts each year. Little wonder at the widespread use of the term *administration of justice,* which serves to emphasize the vastness of the job the appellate judiciary has to do.

As the department head in this organization, the Supreme Court performs mainly overhead functions. The Constitution does give the

[4]Review power was affirmed in *Martin* v. *Hunter's Lessee,* 1 Wheaton 304 (1816). For a good review of all aspects of judicial review, see Alexander Bickel, *The Least Dangerous Branch* (Indianapolis: Bobbs-Merrill, 1962), especially chapter 1.

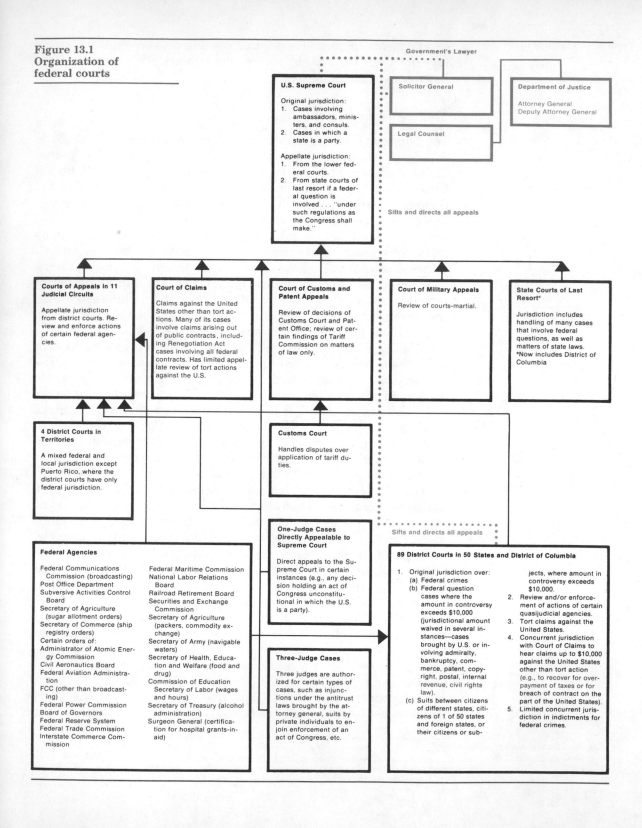

Figure 13.1
Organization of federal courts

Government's Lawyer

U.S. Supreme Court

Original jurisdiction:
1. Cases involving ambassadors, ministers, and consuls.
2. Cases in which a state is a party.

Appellate jurisdiction:
1. From the lower federal courts.
2. From state courts of last resort if a federal question is involved . . . "under such regulations as the Congress shall make."

Solicitor General

Legal Counsel

Department of Justice

Attorney General
Deputy Attorney General

Sifts and directs all appeals

Courts of Appeals in 11 Judicial Circuits

Appellate jurisdiction from district courts. Review and enforce actions of certain federal agencies.

Court of Claims

Claims against the United States other than tort actions. Many of its cases involve claims arising out of public contracts, including Renegotiation Act cases involving all federal contracts. Has limited appellate review of tort actions against the U.S.

Court of Customs and Patent Appeals

Review of decisions of Customs Court and Patent Office; review of certain findings of Tariff Commission on matters of law only.

Court of Military Appeals

Review of courts-martial.

State Courts of Last Resort*

Jurisdiction includes handling of many cases that involve federal questions, as well as matters of state laws.
*Now includes District of Columbia

4 District Courts in Territories

A mixed federal and local jurisdiction except Puerto Rico, where the district courts have only federal jurisdiction.

Customs Court

Handles disputes over application of tariff duties.

One-Judge Cases Directly Appealable to Supreme Court

Direct appeals to the Supreme Court in certain instances (e.g., any decision holding an act of Congress unconstitutional in which the U.S. is a party).

Sifts and directs all appeals

Federal Agencies

Federal Communications Commission (broadcasting)
Post Office Department
Subversive Activities Control Board
Secretary of Agriculture (sugar allotment orders)
Secretary of Commerce (ship registry orders)
Certain orders of:
Administrator of Atomic Energy Commission
Civil Aeronautics Board
Federal Aviation Administration
FCC (other than broadcasting)
Federal Power Commission
Board of Governors
Federal Reserve System
Federal Trade Commission
Interstate Commerce Commission

Federal Maritime Commission
National Labor Relations Board
Railroad Retirement Board
Securities and Exchange Commission
Secretary of Agriculture (packers, commodity exchange)
Secretary of Army (navigable waters)
Secretary of Health, Education and Welfare (food and drug)
Commission of Education
Secretary of Labor (wages and hours)
Secretary of Treasury (alcohol administration)
Surgeon General (certification for hospital grants-in-aid)

Three-Judge Cases

Three judges are authorized for certain types of cases, such as injunctions under the antitrust laws brought by the attorney general, suits by private individuals to enjoin enforcement of an act of Congress, etc.

89 District Courts in 50 States and District of Columbia

1. Original jurisdiction over:
   (a) Federal crimes
   (b) Federal question cases where the amount in controversy exceeds $10,000 (jurisdictional amount waived in several instances—cases brought by U.S. or involving admiralty, bankruptcy, commerce, patent, copyright, postal, internal revenue, civil rights law).
   (c) Suits between citizens of different states, citizens of 1 of 50 states and foreign states, or their citizens or subjects, where amount in controversy exceeds $10,000.
2. Review and/or enforcement of actions of certain quasijudicial agencies.
3. Tort claims against the United States.
4. Concurrent jurisdiction with Court of Claims to hear claims up to $10,000 against the United States other than tort action (e.g., to recover for overpayment of taxes or for breach of contract on the part of the United States).
5. Limited concurrent jurisdiction in indictments for federal crimes.

Supreme Court original jurisdiction (line functions) over a few types of cases, but these are minor in comparison to its appellate jurisdiction.[5] Since the Court and Congress have given concurrent original jurisdiction in most of these cases to the federal district courts, only a few cases arise where the Supreme Court hears all the facts like an ordinary trial court. The problem for the Supreme Court is about the same as the problem for the head of any big organization: how to keep as much as possible of the flow of decisions at the lower, working level. To do this, the Court must keep tight control over the number of cases that are allowed to be brought before it for review. Although litigants have the right to appeal their decisions, the Court habitually dismisses over 60 percent of all writs of appeal presented by their lawyers. A case may be brought up on appeal with a writ of *certiorari,* which is granted whenever at least four of the nine justices agree to issue it.

Decisions handed down in lower courts can reach the Supreme Court for review in one of three ways. The first is the *writ of appeal,* usually called simply appeal, which expresses the right of every party to a case. Virtually all of these are turned down. While the court is not required to give its reasons for refusal, it usually says the rejection is "for want of a substantial federal question." The second procedure is *certification,* where the judges of a court of appeals certify that a case involves an important federal question. This is rarely resorted to. The third is the *writ of certiorari.* Until 1925 the Court was flooded by all sorts of writs; in that year Congress passed laws granting the power to issue *writs of certiorari* by which the Court could decide for itself the cases which should be reviewed.[6]

Another means by which the Supreme Court tries to keep the main actions at the lower levels is the issuance of leading opinions. We call these the "rule of the case," or judicial law, and they do add up to law inasmuch as lawyers advise their clients that an action contrary to such a ruling would be futile. But the direct effect of leading opinions is upon the *actions of judges in the lower courts.* Administratively speaking, the higher courts have to be careful about their decisions, because a vague decision could inundate them

---

[5]The Court's original jurisdiction includes cases between the U.S. and one of the fifty states, cases between two or more states, cases involving foreign ambassadors or other ministers, and cases brought by one state against citizens of another state or against a foreign country. The most important ones are disputes between states over land, water, or old debts. Between 1789 and 1961, the Supreme Court rendered decisions in only 123 cases under the original jurisdiction clause of the Constitution, according to Henry J. Abraham, *The Judicial Process* (New York: Oxford University Press, 1962), p. 157.

[6]See Abraham, *The Judicial Process,* chapter 5, for a good analysis of all these types of review. The Court's Rule 19 gives some of the circumstances justifying the grant of *certiorari.* All of the circumstances have to do with possible inconsistencies of rulings among lower courts. For a discussion of these instances and other aspects of review, see Herman Pritchett, *The American Constitution* (New York: McGraw-Hill, 1959), p. 107.

later when lawyers or judges discover that courts in one district or circuit are making decisions inconsistent with the decisions on the same subject in other districts or circuits. For example, a vague ruling such as "all deliberate speed" in the school segregation cases inundated the courts eventually because in the lower courts school boards and lawyers were getting poor guidance from the earlier decisions. Thus, there is a *direct administrative reason* for higher court rulings.

Administration is stressed as the form of the judicial process because it conveys best the reality of the judiciary as an institution of government. In their own distinctive and peculiar way the courts govern, even though they have no closer relation to the law than Congress or, for that matter, the executive branch. There is a special relationship between courts and law, but it is not a simple fact that can be asserted. It must be identified as part of the complex pattern of governing. We think of courts and law as synonymous because of the high legitimacy of our courts and because of the monopoly of access to the courts held by lawyers. But to identify courts and law as one and the same is a misrepresentation. The courts govern, and it is their role as an institution of government which will concern us here. This is not a lawyer's or judge's analysis. The courts must be placed in the scheme of government.

ADMINISTRATION OF JUSTICE: JUDGES IN SEARCH OF A PURPOSE

The purpose of the judiciary is judging, not lawmaking. One of the cardinal principles of operation is that the jurisdiction of the federal courts, under the Constitution, extends only to cases or controversies. The federal judiciary has consistently refused to give advisory opinions as to the constitutionality of laws or actions, even when these are requested by high-ranking officials. Such features as law, politics, administration, or justice are secondary. They qualify the *type* of judging that may go on, but they are not part of the definition of the purpose of the judiciary. The verb *to judge* is defined in the *Oxford English Dictionary* as synonymous with "to try" or "to pronounce sentence upon a person in court"; "to sit in judgment upon"; "to condemn"; "to decide" or "to form an opinion about."[7] In the act of judging, disputes are settled.

Of course, it takes a great deal of history, culture, and education before members of a society will submit their disputes to a judge, and the judiciary is filled with formality, ritual, and procedure—so

[7]*Compact Edition of the Oxford English Dictionary* (New York: Oxford University Press, 1971).

much so that a specialist in judicial routines is indispensable for dealing with the judiciary. But these aspects of the judiciary should not mask its purpose. Judges make choices. They may or may not listen carefully to evidence. They may or may not give full respect to both sides of the dispute. They may be strict or lenient about procedures. But they make choices about who gets the money, or who is liable, or whether a law was violated.

Juries and Adversary Proceedings

The two aspects of our judicial system which most consistently interfere with an understanding of the basic purpose of the judiciary are juries and adversary proceedings. These two factors are often mistaken for the judicial purpose itself when in fact they are merely qualifiers of it. In trial courts—courts of original jurisdiction—judges usually have juries to help them make their choices. The jury helps weigh the evidence and decide on the basis of the facts who gets the money or who is liable. But the jury is part of judging; it is not the judicial process itself. The jury is in fact under the judge's thumb; the judge defines what the facts are, what facts are admissible, what facts are relevant, and whether facts about previous cases are relevant. Granted, where juries are involved, the jury, not the judge, makes the final choice. But that only reinforces the definition of the purpose of a judiciary, which is to judge—to settle disputes between parties with an immediate stake in the dispute.

Jury verdicts are almost never directly overturned,[8] but it is not at all rare for an appeals court to reverse a trial court decision where an error of procedure was made—even when the appeals court might actually be in sympathy with the decision itself. Indeed, since cases are often reversed on appeal because some procedural requirement was not observed, lawyers can easily conclude that precedents and procedures—the ritual, that is—are what courts exist to produce. The formalized argumentation of the adversary process is a good example of these procedural rituals of the judiciary.

The basic assumption underlying the entire American judiciary is that the best way to provide judges and juries with the materials necessary to make a wise choice is to allow each side in a dispute to present only those arguments most favorable to it. In the words of the old adage: "When two men argue, as unfairly as possible, on opposite sides, it is certain that no important considerations will

---

[8]One exception to this general rule is the negligence field. Juries often get carried away and hand down extremely generous verdicts in favor of persons suing large corporations for damages. See *New York, New Haven, and Hartford* v. *Hennagan*, 364 U.S. 441 (1960).

altogether escape notice." It would be impossible ever to prove that the adversary process produces the truth. A good argument could in fact be made that judges might provide themselves with a better basis for a decision by dispensing with the lawyers, investigating the situation for themselves, and interrogating the witnesses for themselves. Everyone is aware that there are enormous differences of talent among lawyers. Why assume that an adversary process will produce the truth if one side of the case is so much better represented than the other?

This very preoccupation was the basis for one of the most important constitutional cases in the past two decades, *Gideon* v. *Wainwright,* 372 U.S. 335 (1963). In that case the Supreme Court reversed Gideon's conviction, holding that henceforth all defendants in criminal cases have a right to legal counsel. Immediately following that case, Congress responded with the Criminal Justice Act of 1964, to provide more adequate representation of defendants in all cases. By 1966, the legislatures and courts of twenty-three states had taken action to improve upon the requirements of the *Gideon* case. All of this suggests a preoccupation with the inadequacies of adversary proceedings in practice.[9]

Actually, the adversary process constitutes very strong evidence in favor of the definition of the judicial purpose as judging. For, although the adversary process provides no guarantee that trials will produce truth, it possesses three other virtues that enormously facilitate judging. The first of these virtues is the *presumption of innocence* in criminal cases. We universally give lip service to the idea that the accused is innocent until proven guilty. But without the adversary process, this presumption would hardly ever be more than lip service. Second, the adversary process helps preserve the *equality of contending parties* in criminal and civil cases, even when one of the parties is the state. This is accomplished by providing a means by which the defendant can face the accusers, can cross-examine them, and can present contrary evidence. There are many flaws in the theory and practice of equality of the parties, but the routines of adversary proceedings do in fact help keep the judge in the middle.

The third virtue of the adversary process is that it helps maintain the judicial principle of *passivity*—enabling courts to wait for real cases to be brought by contending parties. Time after time this will be encountered as a key to the secret of the political power of the judiciary, especially an appointed federal appellate judiciary in a society committed to democratic forms of governing.

---

[9]For more on this case and those issues, see Anthony Lewis, *Gideon's Trumpet* (New York: Random House, 1964). See also Henry Abraham, *Freedom and the Court* (New York: Oxford University Press, 1972), especially pp. 65–66.

Do the Appellate Courts Make Law?

The appellate courts may not take initiatives and may also refuse to accept cases on appeal from lower courts. However, when an appellate court does accept a case on review and is dealing only with a single case, *it is immediately and unavoidably involved in reaffirming or rejecting all previous relevant rules or making new rules affecting all future cases of the same sort.* This is most of what there is to the appellate courts and their relationship to law and to great power. Some important examples may help pave the way toward an understanding of this phenomenon in its fullest sense.

First, return to *Gideon* v. *Wainwright* and the decision of the Supreme Court to order a new trial on the grounds that Gideon had been deprived of legal counsel. In effect, the Court was saying to all trial judges, all prosecutors, all defendants, and all defense attorneys that henceforth they would be wasting their time if they tried to cut corners in trials concerning indigent defendants. Ponder for a moment the question of whether or to what degree this holding was a law, as that term would be used to describe a decision by a legislature.

Meanwhile, take the recent history of the Supreme Court on capital punishment. Caryl Chessman was put to death in a California electric chair in 1960, eleven years after receiving the death penalty for the crimes of kidnapping and attempted rape. At least twenty-eight appeals to the federal courts and sixteen petitions for review to the Supreme Court culminated in the Court's final decision to dismiss the case and to reaffirm the state court decision by declining to interfere.[10] In deciding to let stand the California decision, the Supreme Court upheld the Chessman conviction and the death sentence. But in the process, it also upheld all other state laws and decisions applying to the death penalty. In allowing the California decision to stand, the Supreme Court had ruled that capital punishment is not an unconstitutional deprivation of the Eighth Amendment safeguard against "cruel and unusual punishment." This holding had the same *effect* as a state legislature refusing to rescind its own capital punishment statute or passing a new one.

But was the Court's decision *law* in the same sense as the legislature's decision? Twelve years after the Chessman ruling the Supreme Court reversed itself, holding that capital punishment—as applied in theUnited States at that time—was indeed a violation of the Eighth Amendment.[11] To many observers, and certainly to the occupants of Death Row in the prisons of the United States, this

[10]*Chessman* v. *Teets,* 362 U.S. 966 (1960).
[11]*Furman* v. *Georgia,* 408 U.S. 238 (1972).

> The judiciary, from the nature of its functions, will always be the least dangerous to the political rights of the Constitution, because it will be least in a capacity to annoy or injure them.
> Hamilton, *Federalist* 78

> It is emphatically the province and duty of the judicial department to say what the law is. . . . If two laws conflict with each other, the courts must decide on the operation of each. . . . This is the essence of judicial duty.
> Chief Justice John Marshall, *Marbury* v. *Madison,* 1803

> A justitiable controversy is . . . distinguished from a difference of a hypothetical or abstract character. . . . The controversy must be definite and concrete, touching the legal relations of parties having adverse legal interests . . . admitting of specific relief through decree of conclusive character.
> Chief Justice Charles Evans Hughes, *Aetna Life* v. *Haworth,* 1937

> *Stare decisis* is usually the wise policy, because in most matters it is more important that the applicable rule of law be settled than that it be settled right. . . . But in cases involving the Federal Constitution . . . this Court has often overruled its earlier decisions. The Court bows to the lessons of experience and the force of better reasoning, recognizing that the process of trial and error, so fruitful in the physical sciences, is appropriate also in the judicial function.
> Justice Louis Brandeis, *Burnet* v. *Coronado Oil and Gas,* 1932

> I do not think the United States would come to an end if we lost our power to declare an act of Congress void. I do think the union would be imperilled if we could not make that declaration as to the laws of the several states. . . .
> Justice Oliver Wendell Holmes, *Law and the Court,* 1913

decision had the same effect as simultaneous decisions in all of the state legislatures to soften or eliminate their laws on capital crime. But again, is the Supreme Court decision in this case the same kind of law as the decisions in the state legislatures, even though the effect on citizens and condemned prisoners may be the same? Since the court did not hold that capital punishment is absolutely a violation of the Eighth Amendment but rather that the inconsistencies of laws and their applications were a violation, this gave rise to a whole series of legislative revisions leading toward capital punishment statutes that would be constitutional. Consequently, we may still see some executions before the Court decides to invalidate all capital punishment.

How can we settle the question which these two cases pose? The higher court accomplishes two things when it hands down the decision on cases it brings up for review. First, of course, it decides who wins—the person who won in the lower court or the person who lost in the lower court. Second, the appellate court expresses its decision in such a manner that it provides some kind of guidance to the lower courts for the handling of future cases and controversies in the same area. Sometimes the appeals court, even the Supreme Court, is silent or vague on such guidance—or rulings. But, as often as possible, the appellate courts try to give their reasons and their rulings in such a manner that the "administration of justice" can take place most of the time among the lower judicial units. When the court is not satisfactorily clear on its rulings, there is a considerable amount of guessing and speculation on the part of all officers of the court (prosecutors, defense counsels, and judges), in hopes of anticipating what the appellate courts will do the next time the same problem arises. Since vagueness produces more cases, appellate courts cannot avoid clearly defined rulings without producing chaos at the lower levels.

These rulings are watched by counsel more carefully even than the Washington community watches the actions of the president or lobbyists watch the movements of Congress. These rulings are laws. But *they are laws governing only the behavior of the judiciary.* They are constituent laws inasmuch as they affect citizens only indirectly, by providing a structure within which governmental activity takes place. If they influence citizen conduct, that is only because legal counsel is, in the words of Justice Holmes, making "prophecies of what the courts will do in fact."[12] Another case may help clarify the distinction.

One of the most widespread and insidious forms of racial discrimination in the United States was the practice of including racially restrictive clauses in contracts to sell private housing. A clause of this nature is a restrictive covenant, a contract whereby the purchasers must agree that if they later decide to sell the house, they will not sell it to anyone but a Caucasian. When a test case finally reached the Supreme Court, the Court ruled unanimously that individual citizens have a right to include racially restrictive clauses in their private contracts, and that a racially restrictive covenant on a house purchase is a private contract. However, the Court argued that such contracts may not be enforced in the courts, because such enforcement would constitute state action in violation of the Fourteenth Amendment provision that no state shall "deny to any person within its jurisdiction the equal protection of the law" (*Shelley* v. *Kraemer,* 331 U.S. 1 [1948]).[13]

This is a pure case of judicial lawmaking, in the spirit of judicial action extending in an unbroken line back to *Marbury* v. *Madison.* In that case, Chief Justice John Marshall invalidated an important

[12]Oliver Wendell Holmes, Jr., "The Path of the Law," *Harvard Law Review* 10 (1897), 457.
[13]See also Clement E. Vose, *Caucasians Only: The Supreme Court, the NAACP, and the Restrictive Covenant Cases* (Berkeley: University of California Press, 1969).

piece of congressional legislation (and at the same time first established the power of judicial review over congressional legislation) on the grounds that the Court was *unable to enforce the legislation.* Marshall did not argue about the right of Congress to make laws or to make laws that might be in conflict with each other. As the Court was later to do in *Shelley* v. *Kraemer,* he dealt only with what the Court *would and could do in future court cases.* This is what Holmes meant in his definition of the law as "prophecies of what the court will do in fact"[14]; and this is undoubtedly what Charles Evans Hughes meant when he said, before his appointment to the Supreme Court, that "the Constitution is what the judges say it is."[15] This widely misunderstood remark takes on special meaning in the present context, because the judges are saying what the Constitution is in order to guide other judges and related officers of the court.

We may be warranted in calling this law, because as citizens we will ultimately be affected by what courts decide. We win or lose money, we go to jail or go free on the basis of what judges decide; but we must nevertheless be able to appreciate the differences in the way judges govern from the way other institutions govern. Their reasoning processes, their manner of expression, their criteria of action, their reason and purpose for making law are all very different from other types of governing processes. At the local trial court level, it is more difficult to make this distinction, because courts of original jurisdiction apply laws directly to citizens and are in effect closer to part of the legislative process because they are implementing legislative or administrative rulings. Most agencies in fact have to get a court order to apply their rulings to recalcitrant citizens. But at the appellate level, we can truly say that courts are only legislating for one another.[16]

This is the essential difference between the national appellate judiciary in the United States and all of the lower courts (and, to a large extent, most of the higher courts) in the world. Its purpose is expressed in its form. The form is a higher court decision on a real case or controversy, ending in a set of instructions about what lower courts ought to do in this and future cases. The purpose of such an appellate system is primarily *to open and close access to the courts.* This is what is meant by the passivity of our courts. It is the limitation and the source of power in our court system. No law or tradition requires that disputing parties make all their settlements judicially. No court can go out and take cases, and no court has the

---

[14]Holmes, "The Path of the Law."

[15]Speech at Elmira, New York, May 3, 1907.

[16]For a longer treatment of some of these distinctions, see Phillip B. Kurland, *Politics, the Constitution and the Warren Court* (Chicago: University of Chicago Press, 1970), chapter 5. For Kurland's observation that the common law courts are "where the analogy to legislation is closer and easier," see p. 175.

power to see that its determinations are followed to the letter by the disputing parties or others. Courts only have the power to say what is fruitful and what is futile to pursue through the judicial process.

An important illustration of this passivity is judicial power over civil liberties and police behavior. A police commissioner of New York City in the 1930s once swore that "there's a lot of law at the end of a night stick."[17] What he really meant was that there is a lot of *force* at the end of a night stick. The law is behind the night stick and in front of it. Nothing the courts say can directly prevent policemen from bashing heads or forcing confessions; in fact, courts have no power to eliminate abuses of power and authority in any of the branches of government. All they have power to do is to make it easier or more difficult for the recipient of the mistreatment to gain redress. That in turn may affect the policeman, but not necessarily. Court decisions either raise or lower the probability of redress.

Today's Court decisions affect future citizens and policemen primarily by giving citizens a cause of action, or by taking away a cause. When the Court said that it was unable to cooperate with the Florida courts in keeping Gideon in jail without a retrial, it was not able to free Gideon without the goodwill and cooperation of the Florida authorities. Nevertheless, it probably did lead to his freedom, and at the same time it gave all future Gideons a cause of action against all local police officials. The initiatives would then be taken by lawyers (including jailhouse lawyers), who could read the Gideon case and see that it was no longer futile to bring actions against the police and the courts for retrials with legal counsel.[18]

Another case in point is the so-called law of capitalism. Insofar as capitalism was fashioned or facilitated by courts, this was done largely by decisions that (1) limited the power of state governments over contracts and (2) gave the business world access through the courts to the police and the army for assistance in enforcing contracts.[19] As far as the federal appellate judiciary is concerned, capitalism is composed primarily of messages to judges and lawyers about the conditions of access to the court and, through that, the conditions of legal use of violence against trespassers, defrauders, contract breakers, or strikers. It is necessary to note only one particular example to see the importance of this—the willingness of lower courts to issue injunctions and of appellate courts to uphold these injunctions against efforts by workers in the nineteenth century to organize for purposes of striking, raising wages, and

---

[17]Lewis J. Valentine, *Police Night Stick* (New York: Dial Press, 1947).

[18]For excellent reviews of court cases that have influenced the power of local police, see Kurland, *Politics, the Constitution and the Warren Court,* especially chapters 3 and 4; see also Abraham, *Freedom and the Court,* especially chapter 5.

[19]The superiority of law, especially the law of property, as a form of conquest has been discussed in chapter 2. For good coverage of judicial involvement, see Arthur S. Miller, *The Supreme Court and American Capitalism* (New York: Free Press, 1968).

changing working conditions. If the efforts continued despite the injunction, the employees were held to be in contempt of court, which is a crime punishable without trial and jury. This gave the employer legal justification for mayhem and murder, either through his own private police or through the official police of state and local governments.

Once the laws were changed by courts and legislatures so that injunctions against labor organizations were no longer issued, employers lost this route to the judiciary; this did not necessarily end the use of private police and employer-supported violence. Once the legal justification was withdrawn, however, the advantage of access to the court was almost reversed; and that very probably did lead eventually to the reduction of employer violence against employees.

Many other areas of law have been constructed in about the same way, by judicial messages to other judges. These may or may not be codified eventually into legislative enactments. Take for another example the area of liability for injuries sustained by employees. This potent source of disputes in an industrial society was stabilized by court decisions to such an extent that it has become virtually useless for employers to go to court to fight injury cases. It has become "the law" that employers are liable for all such injuries, without regard to questions of negligence. But "the law" is basically a series of messages to lawyers that it would be useless for them to advise their employer clients to go to court.

One final area of importance is the court's relation to Congress. In the *Schechter* case in the late 1930s, the Supreme Court declared an important piece of legislation unconstitutional on the grounds that Congress had delegated too much of its legislative power to administrators and to private associations. This meant that businesses with reason to doubt the authority of an administrative agency could hope to win in suits against the agency on the grounds that the agency authority from Congress was too broad.[20]

But as the years went by, the Court chose not to be guided by its ruling in the *Schechter* case and consistently refused to review cases brought by parties arguing that some vague piece of legislation failed to pass the constitutional standard established by the Court in that case. Even though the Court has never reversed its *Schechter* ruling, its disregard of that ruling in the past forty years has communicated the message to lawyers that it would be useless to try to follow that rule. At present, if Congress bases its authority on the power to regulate commerce, it is almost certain that the Court will accept the legislation as valid; and this means that corporate lawyers would be wasting their time if they brought suits question-

[20]*Schechter Poultry Company* v. *United States*, 295 U.S. 495 (1935).

ing the constitutionality of the authority of an administrative agency to regulate commerce. Thus, here is an instance where the Court has "made law" by its refusal to take action, without ever making a new ruling.[21]

By now it should be possible to see form and purpose in the appellate judiciary—and how the two relate to each other. The *form* (case and controversy) shapes and is shaped by the *purpose* (judging); the *result* in government is what we call law, but law of a very special sort (access to the courts). We now need to speculate on the place of this kind of form and purpose in the general scheme of

The National Judiciary and the "Administration of Justice"

[21]The Court does continue to exercise judicial review of congressional enactments in such areas as congressional investigation and the First Amendment. See *United States* v. *Rumely,* 345 U.S. 41 (1953). A good review of the present situation will be found in Bickel, *The Least Dangerous Branch,* p. 156. An appeal for restoration of the *Schechter* rule will be found in Theodore Lowi, *The End of Liberalism* (New York: Norton, 1969), chapter 10.

government. Sociologically, we refer to this as the *function* of the institution—our judgment or hypothesis as to the long-run influence of the institution within the larger system.

Many have said that the place or function of the judiciary in the larger scheme of government is the "provision of legitimacy" for public action. That is, when a court backs an action as legal it is certainly putting the stamp of legitimacy on the action and on all of its consequences. Nothing could be closer to an explicit example of "putting the stamp of legitimacy" on an action than a Supreme Court decision declaring a law constitutional or a police action legal.

However, it would be too easy to stop with that characterization when in fact it begs a very important question. One analyst of the judiciary has argued that there must already be a tremendous fund of governmental legitimacy from which the judiciary itself must draw, and that the "legitimating function" is sufficient neither to explain the existence of judicial review nor to justify its existence.[22] Moreover, another student of the judicial process adds that (1) the other government institutions very rarely need an extensive and explicit stamp of approval, and (2) the Court reverses itself or disregards its own past decisions frequently enough to make it impossible for other institutions to depend upon that legitimacy.[23]

The point is that the judiciary does not legitimize conquest the way a priesthood anoints a new heir to the throne, or the way an electorate gives its consent to a democratic elite. The legitimacy given to government by the judiciary is the result of a history of hundreds, perhaps thousands, of individual decisions that cumulate toward legitimacy in the larger sense. The court legitimizes conquest in a very special sense, *by distributing and redistributing access to the Court.* We cannot repeat too often that courts participate in government according to the form of their action, and the effect of their action is to open and close access, making certain causes of action easier or more difficult to pursue and thus changing the long-range advantages and disadvantages various interests have. Small cases make big rulings, and big rulings may have the effect of law as well as legitimacy.

It may now be more meaningful to look once again at the principle of passivity and to appreciate how it can produce an institution in which small cases make big laws. The same principle that keeps the courts out of many social issues requires that the courts *accept all real cases;* it also requires appellate courts to deal with all cases where a rule of law or constitutionality is questioned. As long as there are lawyers to bring future litigation, a decision by a higher

---

[22]Bickel, *The Least Dangerous Branch,* p. 29.

[23]Kurland, *Politics, the Constitution and the Warren Court,* p. 36. Kurland and Bickel take issue with a thesis about the function of legitimation proposed by Charles L. Black, *The People and the Court* (New York: Macmillan, 1960).

court to deal with an appeal by refusing to take it can be as significant a "rule of law" as taking the appeal and handing down an opinion. For example, if the Supreme Court had continued to avoid taking a school segregation case in the 1950s, this would have amounted to a reaffirmation of existing laws in the southern states. Eventually the Supreme Court had to take a case if it wanted to convey some other impression.

The inevitable next question is whether this form of judicial process works to the benefit of certain interests over others. Is there any indication that the judicial process is more conservative than the legislative or administrative processes, as has often been charged? Tocqueville observed in 1831, "If I were asked where I placed the American aristocracy, I should reply without hesitation . . . that it occupies the judicial bench and the bar." But is that true today? Or if true, are the "aristocratic" officers of the court able to give consistent benefit to members of their own class? This takes us beyond the realm of form and function into the realm of evaluation. Rather than go directly into a treatment of this issue, we will first observe closely the appellate judiciary in action.

BLIND JUSTICES: SEE HOW THEY RUN

On May 25, 1965, Dr. Jeremiah Stamler, a major scientist in world heart research, was named winner of the Albert Lasker Award for his coauthorship of a series of articles on the prevention of heart attacks. Immediately following the presentation of this award by the vice-president of the United States, Stamler rushed from New York back to his home in Chicago, where he had been subpoenaed to appear before the House Committee on Un-American Activities (HUAC) as a witness in an investigation of alleged resurgence of Communist activities in Chicago. Yolanda Hall, a research colleague of Stamler, was also ordered to appear.

Stamler objected to the whole process, as well as to HUAC, but he also did not want to appear as a witness and to cite the Fifth Amendment as his basis for noncooperation.[24] Over the years, the use of the Fifth Amendment had become increasingly dangerous because its interpretation, thanks largely to HUAC and to Senator Joseph McCarthy, had made it tantamount to the admission of guilt in the eyes of the public. Stamler faced this situation in 1965 and responded to it as no citizen ever had. He decided to take the

---

[24]The Fifth Amendment is actually a safeguard extended to a person accused of a crime, who shall not "be compelled . . . to be a witness against himself." However, over the years the courts have extended the privilege to include witnesses before congressional committees, who are allowed to invoke it if their fear is that answering the question might "furnish a link in the chain of evidence needed to prosecute." Out of this came the peculiar plea, "I refuse to answer on the grounds that it might tend to incriminate me." *Blau* v. *U.S.*, 340 U.S. 59 (1950).

initiative. Instead of answering the subpoena and refusing to cooperate, he decided to follow the advice of a former classmate—a lawyer of some prominence in civil liberties litigation—to bring a civil suit in the federal district court to enjoin the Chicago hearing on the grounds that the committee's enabling act was an unconstitutional invasion of the First Amendment as well as an overly vague delegation of power to a committee.

Stamler's civil suit The suit brought by Stamler was aimed at reversing the usual relationship between committee and witness by making the *committee* rather than the witness the defendant. Thus, although the adversary process does guarantee equality between parties, even the most professional lawyers would agree that in a criminal case, especially one involving political beliefs, all the social opprobrium is visited upon the defendant. With his injunction, Stamler and his prestigious attorney, Albert E. Jenner, hoped to avoid this.[25]

This unusual suit was not welcomed in the Court. Federal District Judge Julius Hoffman immediately dismissed the suit as "premature." He ruled that despite the past conduct of HUAC, there was no reason to assume that the committee would abuse its witnesses; and there would be ample protection later on if the committee did run true to form. Although the decision was immediately appealed to the U.S. Court of Appeals of Chicago's Seventh Circuit, it still meant that the HUAC hearing could proceed. Stamler therefore had no choice but to appear before the committee in response to his subpoena.

Fearing that cooperation with the committee would render the civil action moot (hypothetical, no longer a case or controversy), the Stamler lawyers advised him to refuse to testify. Stamler did not testify, and the committee initiated action to have him and Hall cited for contempt of Congress—a criminal charge requiring passage of a resolution by the entire House of Representatives.

Stamler's "second" civil suit After these hearings, Stamler resumed his civil suit with a second "updating" suit, describing in detail what had actually taken place at the hearings (including an episode during which Stamler's lawyers were physically mistreated). An attempt was made to demonstrate that Judge Hoffman's original assumption of proper conduct on the part of the committee had been unfounded. Nevertheless, Judge Hoffman summarily

---

[25]A review of abusive committee techniques was put together by the Stamler lawyers as part of their brief to the Supreme Court in 1968. Parts of this have been edited and reprinted as "HISC Investigates: The Strategy of Exposure, With and Without a Legislative Purpose," in *Legislative Politics U.S.A.*, ed. Theodore Lowi and Randall Ripley (Boston: Little, Brown, 1973), p. 352. HISC (House Committee on Internal Security) was the name HUAC adopted after 1970.

dismissed the second suit, this time claiming that it was too late, since the hearings it challenged had already occurred.

The court of appeals reversed the decision to dismiss the civil suit, arguing that Judge Hoffman had been in error because he had overlooked substantial constitutional questions. The fact that constitutional issues were involved meant that a trial with a three-judge court was necessary. A request by the government—that is, the U.S. Attorney—to reconsider this ruling was turned down by the court of appeals.

This was a very important victory for Stamler, but one that did not come until autumn 1967, one year and five months after the original suit had been instituted. The wait of nearly a year and a half had been costly to Stamler, for, despite the existence of the civil suit, and despite the fact that the issues in the civil suit were the same as those to be covered in any criminal action, HUAC vigorously pressed the Eighty-ninth Congress to pass their request for a citation of criminal contempt. Scarcely three weeks before the court of appeals decision reversing the Hoffman ruling, the House of Representatives voted the contempt citation against Stamler and Hall. Opposition to HUAC on the floor of the House was unprecedentedly large, considering that most members of the House usually did not oppose HUAC for fear their vote would be construed as unpatriotic. Nevertheless, the contempt citations were passed, and the basis for a criminal suit against Stamler and Hall was established.

Judicial delays The government was now able to move vigorously on two fronts. First, it had been restored to the status of plaintiff, or prosecution, rather than defendant. On the second front, it produced a variety of strategies to gain dismissal or delay in the civil suit in order to keep the initiative with the criminal case. Consideration by the three-judge district court carried the civil case well into its second year. While the government was trying by every conceivable means to get another dismissal of the civil suit, the Stamler lawyers were trying every possible argument to get the court to bring the civil case finally to trial. Every postponement added cost and continued jeopardy to Stamler and Hall personally.[26]

At one point as the case plodded into its third year, it seemed that the government strategy of delay might be foiled and the civil trial

---

[26]Once Stamler was put under indictment following the congressional citation for contempt, Mayor Daley's administration placed him on "inactive status" as Heart Disease Control Officer for the Chicago Board of Health. Stamler was allowed to continue his work for the board, but his salary was put in escrow for an indefinite time. During that period, Stamler was able to draw a partial salary from research grants from foundations and other government agencies, including the National Institutes of Health. This testifies to one of the great advantages of the loose federal structure; Stamler was being prosecuted—some say hounded—by some government agencies while being supported by others.

might finally get under way, because the three-judge district court indicated it was going to deny the government's second motion to dismiss the case. However, just as steps were being taken to go to trial, the three-judge court, in a surprise move, chose to dismiss the civil suit on the grounds that the committee members were immune from civil suit under the protection from arrest granted all members of Congress while doing congressional business (Article I, Section 6, of the Constitution). This unprecedented ruling, already seven months coming, required still further delays, expense, and jeopardy. It was immediately appealed to the Supreme Court, and another six months were to pass before there was a response.

The Supreme Court's response was a victory, but a very narrow one, for the Stamler cause. Its decision kept the civil suit alive, but the grounds were so narrow and technical that it left the central issues unsettled. The Court's ruling was that an appeal of the dismissal by a three-judge court should be taken to the court of appeals, not directly to the Supreme Court. Back it went, with the same arguments, the same issues, the same briefs, the same personnel.

The civil suit is sustained   On August 5, 1969—four and one-third years after the subpoena to appear before HUAC, one and one-fourth years after the three-judge court decision, and nearly six months after the Supreme Court decision—the court of appeals finally made a clear determination on all of the preliminaries that had been delaying the civil trial for so long. The dismissal decision of the lower court was reversed, and the trial was ordered to begin, finally, on its merits.

The court of appeals, however, did not rule on whether Article I, Section 6, actually protects members of Congress from such suits. Instead, it held that the suit could be sustained (that relief was available) against the U.S. attorney general and his staff in Chicago. The revived case was consequently retitled *Stamler* v. *Mitchell* (Attorney General John Mitchell). The appeals court also ordered the government to defer prosecution of the criminal case pending efforts to find a remedy through the civil action. For the first time it was officially recognized that the issues of the two cases were identical and that the civil suit should be the dominant route.

The government immediately appealed the decision to the Supreme Court, because the court of appeals ruling, though narrow, would be extremely significant if allowed to stand. If Stamler had "standing to sue"—that is, if the questions raised constituted a real "case or controversy"—this meant that all citizens could, in a civil action, raise questions about the legality or constitutionality of a congressional committee without having to wait until after their refusal to cooperate had put them in jeopardy of criminal action.

But the implications of the holding went even beyond that. The relief which the court was allowing Stamler to seek through an injunction against the attorney general might one day come to apply to *all* government agencies, not simply congressional committees. The mind boggles at the idea of a citizen's right to enjoin any public agency, stopping it from its tasks until the agency can show that its authorization is constitutional and that its actions against a citizen are legal. If these points could survive the court of appeals decision, a tremendous amount of law would result from one minor case before one circuit court.

In June of 1970—another ten months after the court of appeals victory for Stamler—the Supreme Court in its second review handed down a decision *per curiam*. This is a decision, without a written opinion, that refuses to review the decision written by a lower court. It amounts to a reaffirmation of the lower court's opinion. A *per curiam* affirmation is not as strong and does not have as high a status as a Supreme Court opinion that explicitly accepts the doctrines established by the court of appeals. But the *per curiam* decision did let stand the appeals court ruling that the suit against the U.S. attorney general was valid as "good law" in the Seventh Circuit. This was likely to be influential throughout the eleven circuits until a leading opinion to the contrary was handed down.

More delays   It seemed at last after five years that the Supreme Court decision was sufficient to get the trial of HUAC on substantive issues under way. But several delaying moves were still available to the government. HUAC had already tried in 1969 to render the civil case moot by getting new legislation through Congress changing its name to House Committee on Internal Security (HISC) and its charter to add a few safeguards for witnesses. This was accompanied by a notable change in the treatment of witnesses in public hearings and might well have impressed the courts enough to hold that the changes mooted the civil suit.

Following the 1970 Supreme Court decision, the committee then moved to deny the request of the Stamler attorneys to inspect its clipping file. It also refused to produce the unedited versions of old HUAC hearings, although this record constitutes the only more or less official source of data on whether, or to what extent, the committee had departed from proper rules of procedure. To avoid the possible confrontation of a court order to produce these materials, HISC secured from the House of Representatives a resolution *ordering the committee not to comply* with any order to render up the material. This meant that the courts would have to face Congress itself rather than a mere committee in signing such an order; and that simply was not likely to happen.

It also meant that the brief for the plaintiff would be much more difficult and expensive to put together. The Stamler brief thus had to include equivalent materials gathered from public sources, data gathered from depositions (written testimony) of former witnesses and public opinion experts, and other data concerned with the treatment of former witnesses before the committee. The purpose was to add social science data to logic and precedent in order to establish the unconstitutionality of the committee on the grounds that investigations into political beliefs not only caused irreparable injury to individual witnesses but also had a "chilling effect" on the community at large and its willingness to tolerate political dissent.[27]

A case of Catch-22   The government's best tactic came last. On the very eve of the trial in January 1972, the committee, through the United States Attorney, presented the Stamler attorneys with a series of demands for data in pretrial discovery proceedings. Their demands included questions on political beliefs and associations. In

---

[27]The Stamler attorneys were trying to draw on the earlier Supreme Court ruling against a State of Louisiana prosecution, *Dombrowski* v. *Pfister*, 380 U.S. 479 (1965). A brief with arguments drawing on empirical data is called a Brandeis brief, following precedents set by Louis Brandeis while he was still a private practitioner before being appointed to the Supreme Court. The effort is to try to convince a court with arguments based upon the study of the social impact of cases rather than from legal precedent alone.

effect, the committee was saying that in order to prepare their defense for the trial, they needed answers to the very questions that had given rise to the original suit.

By answering these questions, the defendants would have yielded on the principles most fundamental to the case. Yet refusal would mean at least dismissal, once again, of the civil suit and the probable resumption of the criminal case. As the Stamler lawyers put it in their final report to the Stamler Legal Aid Fund officers, "In order to maintain their civil suit challenging the government's right to answer the questions, our clients must first answer them!"[28]

In one of his last decisions before retiring from the bench in 1972, Judge Hoffman accepted the pretrial discovery demands of the committee. Judge Hoffman's successor, Richard McLaren, also affirmed the validity of the pretrial discovery procedure, but he may have done so to pressure the parties into a settlement. He met with the attorneys of both sides to urge settlement. At first the committee was most adamant in its refusal to drop criminal charges, and the Stamler attorneys were equally adamant against yielding to the pretrial discovery questions. Finally, with the aid of the Department of Justice, the U.S. Attorney managed to get the committee to drop its criminal charges in return for an agreement by the Stamler attorneys not to appeal another dismissal of the civil suit. The criminal case was before another district court in Chicago, presided over by Judge Abraham Lincoln Marovitz. Judge Marovitz's official concurrence was needed, and it was not until he accepted the government's request for a dismissal of the criminal charges that the case was officially ended, on December 21, 1973.

Some victories Jenner advised his clients to accept the arrangement, arguing that a significant victory had already been achieved and must be weighed against additional years of litigation—a good part of which would be on technical rather than substantive issues—with no guarantee of a greater victory in the Supreme Court. The clients ultimately accepted that advice. When the agreement was announced in December of 1973, the case ended—after eight and a half years without ever having gone to trial.

Even though the plaintiffs had been deprived of ultimate victory, they could rightly claim numerous lesser victories:

1. Stamler and Hall were freed of the burdensome criminal charges and financial drain.

2. Their position had been more than vindicated in the eyes of the community. Three of the four Chicago daily newspapers had issued strong editorials of approval, and generally the outcome was interpreted as a victory over HUAC-HISC.

[28]Letter of Albert Jenner and Thomas Sullivan to Dr. Robert Wissler, treasurer, and Theodore Lowi, secretary, Legal Aid Fund, January 10, 1974.

3. HUAC-HISC had been held virtually at bay during those eight years. It had tried for a new image by changing its name and rules and its treatment of witnesses at hearings.

4. Within a year of the termination of this case the House voted to terminate the committee altogether.[29]

5. Finally, the 1969 court of appeals decision still stands. It reaffirms the right of citizens to examine the legal and constitutional basis of all congressional committees, making this right more practical by providing remedies through civil action. It provided a foundation for applying the same rights, with the same civil process, to all government agencies and officials.

THE JUDICIAL POWER: ON BOTH SIDES OF CONQUEST

The appellate judiciary can neither escape the making of law nor evade the responsibility for being an arbiter in the process of conquest. The judicial power in the federal scheme is enormous, all the more so because it is not sought but sought after. Every case that involves government, government authority, or claims to remedy for private rights—every case of *public law,* that is—involves the national appellate judiciary in an act of judicial review.

Little is served anybody but legal scholars by long inquiries into whether the founders intended to provide the appellate judiciary with this power. We are closer to the truth if we aver that judicial review in our appellate system *cannot be avoided.* True, the courts avoid review of the constitutionality of many acts of Congress. But the effect of judicial review on law and government emanates from every appellate action. Never did the old oath, "Damned if they do and damned if they don't," apply any more literally and instructively than to the appellate courts in the American system of government.

For the appellate judiciary, law is the impression given by a decision. The impression can be implied by placing one decision in line with or apart from previous decisions, strengthening or weakening *stare decisis.* Or the impression of the law can be carefully articulated, as in a leading opinion, where the appeals court tries to formulate rules and reasoning to settle future cases. But either way, the appellate judiciary gives an impression when it hands down a

---

[29]By 1966, the status of HUAC-HISC had begun to decline. More House members began to vote against the annual appropriation for the committee. Another measure of the declining status of the committee was the appointment of a liberal firebrand, the Jesuit Father Robert Drinan, as a member of the committee. Drinan was one of the early and outspoken sponsors of the Stamler Legal Aid Fund. In 1973, a Select Committee on Committees in the House recommended abolition of HISC and the relinquishment of its few, if any, legislative functions to the Judiciary Committee.

case. This is simply another way of saying that the appellate judiciary is making law.

Stamler v. *Mitchell* offers a good prismatic view of the situation. In the very first instance, Judge Hoffman was presented with a case full of public law issues and basically had only two alternatives. Instead of dismissing the case, he could have taken the opposite extreme, accepting the complaint and ordering a civil trial to begin. But either way, the case could, and probably would, have been appealed. If Stamler had lost, it certainly would have been appealed. If Stamler had won, the government most certainly would have tried to appeal because of the serious constitutional issues involved. Either way, the appellate court had no choice but to review the case eventually. Then, in its disposition of the case, it had only three alternatives. It could have affirmed the dismissal, it could have reversed it and ordered Judge Hoffman to begin the civil trial at once, or it could have taken the middle course of avoiding the issue on technical grounds. The third alternative is the one it chose, by ordering the three-judge panel to convene. The same set of alternatives would have faced the Supreme Court at any point.

There are several interesting features to this situation.

1. When litigants have standing to sue in the courts, it is extremely difficult, if not impossible, to avoid indefinitely some kind of judicial response, even if it is not a satisfactory response.

2. The response always has legal implications; that is, the response always makes law. The higher up the appeal, the more law is made. The appellate courts have the power to confine or broaden the law that is implicit in any case. A written opinion is often an attempt to *limit* the law implied in a decision. It depends upon the kind of impression the case will make. Thus, the courts may define and guide the direction of the law they make, but they cannot quite avoid making it.

3. The impact of judge-made law is heavily in favor of the status quo. Note that two of the three options available to the appellate courts favor the status quo. One is an explicit embrace of the status quo by a decision that reaffirms the existing legal and power patterns. The second is the avoidance of public law issues by some technical consideration, remanding the case to the lower levels for further argument and another decision; but this is itself a form of reaffirming existing practices and leaving power relationships about where they were before the complaint was made.

When one adds the tremendous cost of litigation to the fact that two of three options favor the status quo, one is faced with the realization that the courts are, in composition, an upper bourgeois institution and, in tendency, basically conservative. Yet that does not square entirely with our knowledge that the judiciary has been the source or cause of many of the most dramatic changes in American life during the past fifty years. It is very probable that no changes in race relations would have occurred had not the 1954 Supreme Court rendered a decision redefining the rights of blacks in relation to state governments. The treatment of criminals and those accused of crimes was changed dramatically by one case in 1963[30] and two cases on the same day in 1966.[31]

Of the numerous other examples, one of the most significant is the revolution in representation unleashed with *Baker* v. *Carr* in 1962, when the Supreme Court held that it could no longer avoid reviewing complaints about the malapportionment of state legislatures.[32] Following that case, the Court went on to force an almost complete revamping of all of the state, county, and local legislatures in the country on the basis of the rule of "one man–one vote."[33]

Indeed, there are many experts who criticize the Court for being too willing to introduce radical change, and not all of these critics are on the far right of the political spectrum. Some may even agree with the general direction of the changes but are troubled by the willingness of the Court to enter into such cases prematurely.[34] However, from the perspective of members of the Supreme Court, who often may very well agree with this kind of criticism, the situation is probably one of choosing between the lesser of two evils. The Court must take the cases as they come and then weigh the risks of opening new options against the risks of approving things as they are.

Thus, calling the judiciary conservative will establish little and misrepresent much. It is indeed conservative with regard to the procedures that make the institution what it is. But the actual impact of the judiciary on society depends most upon how it is used by the forces around it. Among all the possible influences on the behavior of the judiciary and on its ultimate impact on society, three stand out above all the rest and will be dealt with to the exclusion of the others. The first is the Nine Men on the Supreme Court, the attitudes they bring with them, and the influences they have upon each other. The second is the Justice Department, especially the solicitor general, who regulates the flow of cases involving public law issues. The third is the actual pattern of cases.

IMPACT OF THE JUDICIARY: WHAT MAKES IT RUN

The study of judicial decisions has a very long history. Lawyers have been studying judges for as long as there have been judges.

---

[30]*Gideon* v. *Wainwright.*
[31]*Miranda* v. *Arizona,* 384 U.S. 436; and *Escobedo* v. *Illinois,* 384 U.S. 436 (1966).
[32]*Baker* v. *Carr,* 396 U.S. 186 (1962).
[33]One of the best efforts to identify the role of the courts in bringing about change in the United States is Clement E. Vose, *Constitutional Change* (Lexington, Mass.: Lexington Books, 1972).
[34]This is often the gist of Kurland's analysis in *Politics, the Constitution and the Warren Court,* especially chapters 3–5.

The so-called "professionalization of the law" is very much a matter of the study of what makes judges run. Professionalization implies the training of lawyers in the handling of complex procedures at law. It implies lawyers with experience in judging judges—when to move, how to move, what motions will be effective. And most important, the law is professionalized to the extent that the lawyer is relied upon almost completely as a judge of precedent—of how judges have behaved in the past and how they are likely to move next time.

Political scientists have also studied judicial decisions. One entire subdiscipline, constitutional law, had, until recent years, concerned itself almost exclusively with what judges decide. The concerns of political scientists have been different from those of lawyers, inasmuch as lawyers have been interested in winning cases and academicians have been interested in patterns of decision for their own sake. But until recently the *focus* was the same. During the past two decades the academic student of judicial decisions has tended to change focus slightly but significantly. The switch has been from the study of judicial decisions to the study of judicial behavior—that is, the political behavior of judges. Cases are handled statistically in terms of the voting behavior of judges. Academicians now question how judges relate to each other, whether they form voting blocs, whether their votes tend to be consistent with earlier decisions, how they vote a second time on a similar issue, and what seems to influence their vote.[35]

Unfortunately, the study of judicial behavior, no matter how well it explains the behavior of judges, will not explain the decisions made by their Court. The behavior of individual justices is only one of three main influences on the Court. Because they may be the most fascinating of the influences, the Nine Men will be treated first. (The Nine Men, or Nine Old Men, is an old, popular reference to the justices.) But are the justices the most important influence on their own Court?

The Nine Men: Influential or Influenced?

If any judges have a personal influence over the judiciary, and, through it, over the American system of government, it would be the justices of the Supreme Court. The Supreme Court is the final arbiter in many of society's most fundamental disputes. Congress and the state legislatures do have the power to reverse Court

---

[35]Perhaps the largest and most substantial contribution toward the systematic study of judicial behavior in political science has been that of Glendon A. Schubert. See, for example, his book, *The Judicial Mind: Attitudes and Ideologies of Supreme Court Justices, 1946–1963* (Evanston, Ill.: Northwestern University Press, 1965).

decisions by remedial legislation.[36] Generally, however, despite the grumbling that follows any major Court decision, it has been extremely difficult for state legislators or members of Congress to summon up the majorities necessary to react directly against the Court. With these few exceptions, the Court is final. As the eloquent Justice Robert Jackson once put it, "The Court is not final because it is infallible; the Court is infallible because it is final."

Most presidents have appreciated the importance of the Supreme Court but have overly relied on the influence they could gain over the Court by appointment of justices. This kind of influence is often not attained, since the newly appointed justices must ultimately adjust their positions to the other members of the Court. President Nixon had the best opportunity since President Roosevelt to make a sufficient number of appointments to the Supreme Court to have an effect on its decisions. Indeed, many of the decisions made by the Nixon Court did run according to his hopes. Under Chief Justice Burger the Court has been more favorable than the Warren Court toward the powers of police and prosecuting attorneys over accused persons, the power and flexibility in making of arrests, and those matters that come under the category of "search and seizure."

The Court behaved to President Nixon's liking in the area of obscenity and morals legislation as well. But weighing heavily against these pleasures for Nixon was the pain of such Burger Court decisions as those against capital punishment, and, perhaps of more lasting importance, those which struck down existing state laws making abortion a crime. Of course the ultimate blow of the Nixon Court to President Nixon was their 1974 ruling that the president's executive privilege did not extend to the famous White House tapes. It was this decision that led to Nixon's resignation.

Nixon's dogged consistency in appointing so-called conservatives to the bench produced a situation not experienced in the judiciary since the 1930s. His appointments polarized the Court. When Nixon left office he left the Court with one voting bloc composed of the four men he had appointed: Chief Justice Burger and Associate Justices Blackmun, Powell, and Rehnquist. The opposite voting bloc was composed of the four remaining members of the Warren Court: Justice Douglas, the oldest (appointed by Roosevelt); Justices Brennan and Stewart (appointed by Eisenhower); and Justice Marshall, the only black ever to serve on the Court (appointed by Johnson). In the middle was a "swing man," Justice White (appointed by Kenne-

---

[36]For one instance, see Frank J. Sorauf, "*Zorach* v. *Clauson:* The Impact of a Supreme Court Decision," *American Political Science Review,* September 1959, pp. 777–791, on the reaction of the states to Court decisions on "released time" for religious instruction in the public schools. See also Kurland, *Politics, the Constitution and the Warren Court,* pp. xx and 80. An area to watch closely in the future for legislative revision of Supreme Court decisions is capital punishment. Some of the best reports on congressional reactions to court decisions will be found in Walter Murphy, *Congress and the Court* (Chicago: University of Chicago Press, 1962).

Table 13.2	Percentages of Federal Judicial Appointments Adhering to the Same Political Party as the President, 1888–1973

President	Party	Percentage
Cleveland	Democrat	97.3
B. Harrison	Republican	87.9
McKinley	Republican	95.7
T. Roosevelt	Republican	95.8
Taft	Republican	82.2
Wilson	Democrat	98.6
Harding	Republican	97.7
Coolidge	Republican	94.1
Hoover	Republican	85.7
F. D. Roosevelt	Democrat	96.4
Truman	Democrat	90.1
Eisenhower	Republican	94.1
Kennedy	Democrat	90.9
L. B. Johnson	Democrat	93.2
Nixon	Republican	93.7

From Henry J. Abraham, *Justices and Presidents* (New York: Oxford University Press, 1974), p. 60.

In the American judicial system, are federal judgeships partisan offices?

dy). This organized split turned out to possess as many potentialities for perplexing decisions as did many earlier Courts.[37]

Polarized voting The Supreme Court's polarized voting structure is problematical for at least two reasons. First, it tends to produce a large number of five-four decisions, which have severely limited credibility. Earlier Courts produced five-four decisions as well, but under the Burger Court they are likely to be more troublesome because of the unusual consistency of voting within the two factions on the bench. There is a great likelihood for public officials and private attorneys to look at each disadvantageous decision and console themselves with, "While there's death, there's hope."

The second reason that this polarized voting structure causes problems brings our analysis closer to the reality of Supreme Court decision making and to an understanding of the enormous limitations on each individual justice's influence upon the Court. The five-four decision hands over too much power to the man in the middle. The man in the middle is likely to be an indecisive person,

[37]For example, the Court under Chief Justice Earl Warren, 1953–1969, presented just such a picture of nine individuals applying the Constitution, each in his own way. Despite the dominance of the so-called liberal position, Justice Douglas wrote thirty-three dissenting opinions in the 1952–1953 term alone; he wrote eleven in the 1958–1959 term. During the same term, the more conservative Justices Frankfurter and Harlan wrote thirteen and nine, respectively. In that term, seventy-two dissenting opinions were filed by all the justices in the cases on which written opinions were handed down. The ultimate example in this period, although it occurred before Warren had become chief justice, was probably the steel seizure case (*Youngstown Sheet and Tube Co.* v. *Sawyer*, 343 U.S. 306 [1952]), where seven separate opinions were filed.

The National Judiciary and the "Administration of Justice"

Native Born (there have been but six exceptions, the last, Austrian-born Felix Frankfurter); **White** (the first nonwhite, Thurgood Marshall, was appointed in 1967); **Male** (there have been no women to date); **Generally Protestant** (six Roman Catholic and five Jewish Justices); **Fifty to Fifty-five** years of age at the time of appointment; **Anglo-Saxon Ethnic Stock** (all except six); **Upper-Middle to High Social Status; Reared in an Urban Environment; Member of a Civic Minded, Politically Active, Economically Comfortable Family; B.A. and LL.B. Degrees** (usually from prestigious institutions); **Service in Public Office.**   Abraham, *Justices and Presidents* (1974)

characterized by vagueness of position or style. For example, the "swing man" in the 1930s, when the Court was last split between stable voting blocs, was Justice Owen Roberts, who was widely considered one of the weakest judges ever to serve the Supreme Court.

The "swing man" in the 1970s has most often been Justice Byron White. During his first decade on the Court (1962–1972), his role in decisions was usually marked simply by "joined by White." Near his tenth anniversary, one of his former law clerks published a popular article on White, in which the most positive thing he could say was, "The sense of propriety that made him a patient junior Justice may be encouraging more active intra-court leadership, now that he has served ten years and is on the middle of the seniority ladder."[38]

But whether the Court is in an era of judicial free-for-all or of organized polarization, the perplexities of judicial determination are always great. A good Supreme Court decision is one that is clear and meaningful to all those who need to understand it, one that at the same time enjoys a clear enough majority of the Court so that it is not likely to be overturned in the foreseeable future. A review of the problems of producing such a decision will explain to a great extent why presidents are frustrated, why the Court often tries to avoid taking controversial cases, and why statistics on judicial backgrounds and judicial behavior do not predict very much about judicial decisions.

Opinion writing   Each Friday during the term of the Court, the Justices sit in conference to discuss the cases they heard in oral argument the first four days of that week.[39] The Chief Justice presides and is first to present his views of each case. He is followed in order of seniority by each of the eight associate justices, and at

---

[38]Lance Liebman, "Swing Man on the Supreme Court," *New York Times Magazine,* October 8, 1972, p. 94.

[39]This is true except for alternate Mondays of each month, which are called Opinion Days, when several hours are devoted to the announcement of decisions and the formal reading of opinions.

the end of discussion a tentative vote is taken. On the vote, the seniority ordering is reversed; tradition has it that this method avoids bringing undue pressure or influence upon the youngest justices.

Following this tentative vote on a case, the chief justice must assign the writing of the opinion to himself or to one of his associates. This can be the most sensitive point in the process, and it is also the point where the chief justice is likely to have his greatest influence. For a unanimous Court and for many of the most important cases, the chief justice assigns himself as the author of the opinion. If he is in the majority on a split decision, he is still free to assign himself, or anyone in the majority. When he is in the minority, the job of assigning the opinion goes to the senior associate justice in the majority. Those in the minority may get together and agree on one of their company to write a dissenting opinion; but when there are dissents and concurring opinions, every justice may write an opinion.[40]

Assignments of opinion writing rest upon a number of important considerations.[41] On a rare occasion, the chief justice may select one of his associates on the basis of a specialty that the particular justice is known to have. Or he may take into account some early experience with writing a related opinion. But almost certainly he has to take into account the public image presented by the author of an opinion. For example, he may select the most liberal member of the majority to write a conservative opinion and the most conservative member of a majority to write an opinion that is likely to be on the liberal side.

One of the most dramatic instances of such a consideration occurred when Chief Justice Stone chose Justice Frankfurter to write the opinion in the "white primary" case. The chief justice believed that such a sensitive case, involving the rejection of the southern practice of prohibiting black participation in political primaries, required the most brilliant and scholarly jurist on the Court. However, the day after the assignment, Justice Jackson wrote a letter to Chief Justice Stone urging a change of assignment, arguing that Justice Frankfurter, a foreign-born Jew from New England, would not win the South with his opinion, regardless of its brilliance. Chief Justice Stone accepted Justice Jackson's advice and substituted Justice Stanley Reed, an American-born Protestant from Kentucky and a southern Democrat in good standing. Few

---

[40]For a good discussion of dissenting opinions, their sources, and the Court's attitude toward them, see David Danelski, "Conflict and Its Resolution in the Supreme Court," in *The American Political System,* ed. Bernard Brown and John Wahlke (Homewood, Ill.: Dorsey Press, 1971), p. 242.

[41]Since it is rare for justices to reveal their private deliberations, we tend to know about these patterns by analysis of those who have written the opinions rather than from direct testimony from the justices.

southerners were going to like the Court's decision, but it was a pill more likely to be swallowed if coated with the words of Justice Reed.[42]

The question of which justice is most likely to write an opinion that the largest number of justices can go along with is the most important consideration in the assignment of a case for an opinion. There is always the possibility that an opinion may be written that will bring over to the majority side some of the members who had cast their tentative votes the other way.[43] An unusually revealing story with respect to this possibility is told by Justice Brandeis. He was about ready to write a dissent on an opinion being drafted by Justice McReynolds when it was decided "the corrections weren't adequate, and finally the Chief took over the opinion and put out what is now the Court's opinion and I *suppressed my dissent,* because, after all, . . . the worst things were removed by the Chief."[44] (Italics added.)

Thus the actual drafting of these opinions requires not only good reasoning but the formulation of arguments aimed at keeping and expanding the support of the justices. A draft is usually printed and circulated so that the author of the majority opinion can learn what the dissenters are planning to say and try to take it into account in his opinion. Very often, therefore, the dissent has an extraordinary influence on the majority opinion, goading the majority to take up aspects of law that it would not otherwise take up. The author of the majority opinion is to be considered particularly successful if he finds a way to bring one or more of the dissenters over to a concurrence, or at least to a position of "concur, dissenting in part," which is still a vote in favor of the majority position.

Sometimes the effort to bring one of the dissenters over to the majority involves a significant change in the majority opinion's reasoning. For instance, Chief Justice Stone brought Justice Byrnes from dissent to majority support in an important case arising out of the depression, when the Okies were being stopped by state laws from migrating into California. The Court had already voted eight to one in conference to reverse the California laws, but the chief justice made the vote unanimous by agreeing with Byrnes to switch the *grounds* of the decision from the privileges and immunities clause to the interstate commerce clause.[45]

It should now be clear why we do not know very much if we know

---

[42]Reported in Abraham, *The Judicial Process,* pp. 186–187.

[43]A good selection of examples drawn from personal memoirs and letters will be found in Abraham, *The Judicial Process,* p. 186. See also David Danelski, "The Influence of the Chief Justice in the Decisional Process," in *Courts, Judges, and Politics,* ed. Walter Murphy and C. H. Pritchett (New York: Random House, 1961).

[44]Reported in Abraham, *The Judicial Process,* pp. 192–193.

[45]Ibid., p. 191. The case was *Edwards* v. *California,* 314 U.S. 160 (1941). Four of the justices in this case wrote a concurring opinion indicating a preference for the privileges and immunities clause, but the decision itself was unanimous.

only *how* the justices voted. To produce a majority decision is difficult enough. But *to write the reasons,* knowing these are to become law, is infinitely more difficult. Often it is impossible to anticipate the character of the ruling even when the decision itself might be predictable. We can easily know, for example, that on certain kinds of civil liberties, race relations, and free speech cases, Justices Brennan, Marshall, and Douglas (until his recent retirement) vote on the liberal side. But the opinion any one of them may write for the majority on such a case will depend upon the views of the two or three other justices who will ultimately make up the majority.

Justice Warren worked for two years on an opinion in order to get a unanimous decision in the segregation cases of 1954 and 1955. We may never know exactly what he started with and how he had to revise his reasoning, but we do know that it was a very complex matter. In getting his unanimous vote, he may have enhanced the legitimacy or authority of the decision; but he also reduced its clarity and effectiveness. The famous decree that integration was to be accomplished with "all deliberate speed" gave the liberals of the country a sense of real progress, but it also functioned as a message to knowledgeable southerners that the courts were not going to require immediate and drastic change. The decision committed the federal courts to looking at the degrees of progress in desegregation rather than to a definitive case-by-case approach to the presence of segregation. The latter approach would have been far easier to implement at the district court level.[46]

Because there is no need to please a majority, dissenting opinions can be more eloquent and less guarded than majority opinions. Some of the greatest writing in the history of the Court will be found in dissents; and some of the most famous justices, such as Holmes and Brandeis, were notable dissenters. The dissent plays a very special role in the work and the impact of the Court. It can have an impact far beyond the justices because it amounts to an appeal to lawyers all over the country to keep bringing cases in this area. That is to say, an effective dissent influences the flow of cases through the courts as well as the arguments that counsel may use in later cases. Perhaps most importantly, the dissent underlines and emphasizes the fact that the Court speaks with a single opinion— the opinion of the majority. The American Supreme Court is a policy-making body, a body made up of men who actually vote, men who might one day vote the other way on the same cases.

Throughout all of the considerations back of the deliberations and

[46]For a related argument, see Kurland *Politics, the Constitution and the Warren Court,* chapter 5. In a rare television interview years later, Justice Black conceded that the "all deliberate speed" decree had probably been a mistake. Reference to this concession by Justice Black is also made in James MacGregor Burns, *Uncommon Sense* (New York: Harper & Row, 1972), pp. 166–167.

decisions of the Supreme Court, it would seem inevitable that the Court is unable to view each case merely "on its merits." Each case brought to the Court for review must, to repeat, be a real case or controversy. Yet it is inevitable that the specific decision the Court will make on the case is incidental to the reasons for reviewing the case and for handing down the opinion. In a rare moment of confession, one chief justice observed, "To remain effective, the Supreme Court must continue to decide only those cases which present questions whose resolution will have an immediate importance far beyond the particular facts and parties involved."[47]

Limits on individual justices   All these patterns of case selection, voting, and opinion writing tend to emphasize the severe limits on each of the individual members of the Supreme Court. Even if each individual justice remained true to the ideologies and policy positions because of which he was appointed, these might have little bearing on decisions, even in the cases where he is on the majority side. He may not get to write the opinion, and his vote is thus amalgamated with all of the others. Or, if he does get to write the opinion, he may be forced to contort his reasoning to such an extent that his original position is vitiated.

Even in combination with a voting bloc, the influence of individu-

[47]Chief Justice Fred Vinson, 1944, quoted in Abraham, *The Judicial Process,* p. 163.

al justices is limited, though palpable. There is no question that the four Nixon appointees to the Court have contributed to some important legal changes, even some reversals of recent Court positions. During the 1972–1973 terms, these four justices voted together 70 percent of the time; during the 1973–1974 terms, they voted together 75 percent of the time. However, these percentages are based on all of the cases considered, including a large number of unimportant cases, some important cases that reaffirmed rather than reversed previous Court positions, and many important cases where the four voted together but in the minority. This has happened frequently enough for Justice Rehnquist to develop quite a reputation as a dissenter.

Bloc voting provides a limited form of influence also because it can have a counterproductive effect on other justices, whose support may be necessary for a majority. In one case during the 1974 term, the Court reversed an earlier four-three decision by a five-four decision, with the Nixon appointees constituting four of the five members of the new majority. In his dissent to this decision, Justice Potter Stewart, who frequently votes with the Nixon bloc, expressed grave concern as to its significance: "The only perceivable change that has occurred since [the earlier ruling] is in the make-up of this Court. . . . A basic change in the law upon a ground no firmer than a change in our membership invites the popular misconception that this institution is little different from the two political branches of the Government."[48]

Ironically, the only sure way a justice can exercise a direct and clear influence beyond casting his vote is to prevent unanimity on a ruling. Justice Learned Hand said, "Disunity cancels the impact of monolithic solidarity on which the authority of a bench of judges so largely depends. People become aware that the answer to the controversy is uncertain, even to those best qualified, and they feel free, unless especially docile, to ignore it."[49]

Every justice occasionally exercises his right to dissent, precisely because he understands its importance. In 1928 Chief Justice Charles Evans Hughes commented, "A dissent in a court of last resort is an appeal to the brooding spirit of the law, to the intelligence of a future day, when a later decision may possibly correct the error into which that dissenting judge believes the court to have been betrayed."[50] Yet, in the end the direct influence that each of the nine men on the supreme judicial body of the country has is certainly not nearly as great as might be expected. Their

[48]Quoted in Warren Weaver, "Mr. Justice Rehnquist, Dissenting," *New York Times Magazine,* October 13, 1974, p. 94.

[49]Learned Hand, *The Bill of Rights* (Cambridge, Mass.: Harvard University Press, 1958), p. 72.

[50]Quoted in Abraham, *The Judicial Process,* p. 182.

influence is not negligible, but it is so severely limited that we must look for other forces that help shape the national judiciary and its impact.[51]

Controlling the Flow of Cases (Justice According to Justice)

Individual Supreme Court justices have a certain amount of influence on the judiciary by virtue of their participation in choosing cases for review by the Supreme Court. As already suggested, one of the reasons the Court uses the *writ of certiorari* rather than other methods of selecting cases is that it thereby retains some initiative in the choice of cases. There is little question that the Court grants and denies *certiorari* with the nature and function of each case clearly in mind.[52] However, since it takes four justices to grant *certiorari,* it should be added that the only occasion when a single justice can direct the Court is in the exercise of his right to grant a stay of execution or a writ of habeas corpus.

Far greater influence over the flow of cases toward the Supreme Court is in the Justice Department, in the hands of the solicitor general.[53] The solicitor general is third in line of status in the Justice Department, but he is the top government lawyer in almost all cases before the appellate courts where the government is a party. Although other hands can turn the faucet on and off, his is overwhelmingly the strongest hand, and there is no review of his actions by any higher authority in the executive branch. Over 50 percent of the Supreme Court's total work load is comprised of cases under the direct charge of the solicitor general. He and his staff supervise all government briefs filed in the Court regarding appeals, opposition to *certiorari,* and substantive agruments on cases coming up before the Court.

The influence of the solicitor general begins very early in the history of each and every case that may eventually come before the Supreme Court. In *all* cases where the U.S. government or one of its agencies is the losing party in a lower court, the solicitor general is the final authority on whether there will be an appeal. The Supreme Court justices rely on him explicitly to "screen out undeserving litigation and furnish them with an agenda to government cases that deserve serious consideration."[54] Agency heads may lobby the

---

[51]Compare with Abraham, *The Judicial Process,* pp. 181–185.

[52]For additional reports on the consciousness of the judges in picking cases, see Lewis, *Gideon's Trumpet;* and Daniel Berman, *It Is So Ordered* (New York: Norton, 1966).

[53]For his place in the organizational scheme of the Justice Department, see chapter 12. The following discussion relies heavily on a superb treatment of the solicitor general in Robert Scigliano, *The Supreme Court and the Presidency* (New York: Free Press, 1971), chapter 6. More detail will be found in William E. Brigman, "The Role of the Office of the Solicitor General of the United States in the Judicial Process" (Ph.D. diss., University of North Carolina, 1966).

[54]Scigliano, *The Supreme Court and the Presidency,* p. 162.

Virtually a lifetime
appointment: Justice
Douglas served on
the Court from 1939
to 1975.

Virtually a lifetime
appointment: Justice
Douglas served on
the Court from 1939
to 1975.

president and otherwise try to circumvent the solicitor general; and some of the independent agencies have a statutory right to make direct appeals without clearing them with the solicitor general. However, such strategies and appeals are almost inevitably doomed to *per curiam* rejection by the Court if the solicitor general refuses to participate.

The solicitor general can enter a case even when the United States government is not a direct litigant by writing an *amicus curiae* ("friend of the court") brief. Frequently the Supreme Court invites him to submit such a brief. And he has the power to invite others to enter a case as *amici curiae,* as well as to take the initiative himself to join a case in that role. Many important groups seek to submit *amicus curiae* briefs, but it is the solicitor general who gives or withholds consent. The Supreme Court can invite such briefs, but in practice the controlling influence is the solicitor general.

Of all the various statistics on the work of the solicitor general, the following seem to be the most indicative of the amount and nature of his influence. In a study of ten Supreme Court terms through June 1968, the Court accepted 72 percent of the appeals made through the solicitor general by the government while accepting only 9 percent of the appeals made by the adversaries of the government. Moreover, many of the successful adversaries were helped in their appeals by the solicitor general. In one term, for example, one-third of the successful *certiorari* writs granted to adversaries of the government were made with the support of the solicitor general's office. In some ways it is more impressive that when the solicitor general enters a case as *amicus curiae* rather than as the appellant, the courts grant *certiorari* over 80 percent of the time—as compared to 70 percent when the government is its own petitioner and a mere 7 percent in petitions for writs of *certiorari* where the government was neither a direct party nor an *amicus curiae.*[55]

In addition to substantial control over the flow of cases, the solicitor general is in a position to shape the terms of discourse used in argument before the Court. The Court tends to give special attention to the way the solicitor general characterizes the issues. Although the justices pride themselves on their ability to develop effective arguments and opinions, they tend nevertheless to rely heavily on the "government" for the development of the relevant arguments. The solicitor general is the most frequent face before the Court and, theoretically at least, the most disinterested. He is known to reject more requests for appeals than he accepts, and his

[55]Ibid., pp. 174–176.

credibility is not hurt when several times each year he comes to the Court in order to withdraw a case with the admission that the government has made an error.

Of course, the solicitor general's sway over the flow of cases should not be allowed to overshadow entirely the influence of the Department of Justice in which he serves. As indicated in chapter 12, the solicitor general is counsel for the major divisions in the department—including Antitrust, Tax, Civil Rights, and Criminal. Their activities generate a great part of the agenda with which he must deal. This is particularly true of the Criminal Division, whose cases come before the solicitor general on appeal every day; these are generated by initiatives taken and mistakes made by the United States Attorneys and the district judges before whom they practice. (The Stamler case demonstrates how many opportunities there are for mistakes and some of the reasons why the U.S. Attorneys or the citizen appellants might want to appeal cases.)

Another important influence on the flow of cases through the appellate judiciary is the FBI, one of the other bureaus of the Department of Justice. Its work provides data for numerous government cases against businesses, individual citizens, and state and local government officials. Its data are the most vital source of material for cases in the national security field, as well as in the field of organized crime. The FBI also has the important function of linking the Justice Department very closely to cases being brought by state and local police and other government officials. The FBI has a long history of cooperation with state and local police forces, and this is one of the most important reasons why the solicitor general often finds himself joining a state case as *amicus curiae*.

This has its good side, in that the FBI is probably better at getting relevant data on accused persons and may be more solicitous of proper procedure than many local police authorities. But its bad side is that the FBI's cooperation with state and local government officials means that it is not necessarily a disinterested participant when private citizens bring suits against one of these state or local governments charging that their civil rights have been denied. During the turbulent 1960s, the FBI was constantly being asked to investigate allegations made by black residents against local police and other state and local authorities. Surely, there must be more than a nagging doubt about the ability of the FBI to investigate the very persons with whom they have been cordially cooperating over the years.

Although our main concern here is to locate the FBI and the other bureaus of the Justice Department in the appellate judicial process, it should be noted that the relationship between the FBI and local authorities is indeed an area in need of some drastic reform. Whenever any governmental office is accused of depriving a citizen of civil rights, civil liberties, or due process of law in general, a special procedure seems to be called for; this merits some serious attention.[56]

The Third Influence: The Case Pattern

The case pattern has been back of all of the other influences. Cases are the environment—the reason for being—of the judiciary. The *pattern* of cases that are brought through the appellate judiciary is treated as an independent influence because it is something that cannot be entirely controlled by the solicitor general, the justices, or anyone else. Although the solicitor general can shape the flow of cases, he cannot suppress permanently a particular current of significant litigation as long as litigants continue to try to bring it before the appellate court. He has the power to choose which of several cases raising the same basic issue to favor on appeal, but he does not have the choice to suppress a line of litigation altogether. Moreover, despite the great influence of the solicitor general and the various divisions in the Department of Justice in generating cases and in controlling the process of appeal, it is nevertheless true that a significant number of important cases reach the Supreme Court totally without their intervention.

The Supreme Court picks up some of these cases independently through the issuance of writs of *certiorari,* and a few additional cases come up through the other routes of appeal identified earlier.[57] Many of the important segregation cases reach the Supreme Court through appeals other than *certiorari.* Recently some substantial independent challenges have been made against state education laws and local zoning codes. In any of these instances, the solicitor general may join afterwards in support of the case; but he neither creates the case nor plays any significant part in getting it to the Supreme Court.

New problems in the society create disputes. Some of these are settled privately; others are settled by legislation; and still others are settled by legal action that never comes before a court or, if adjudicated, is never appealed. Yet, few lawyers feel they have served their clients properly if they have failed to appeal a case when, in their opinion, an issue of law or constitutionality is involved. The appellate courts must wait for cases to come to them,

---

[56]Victor Navasky, *Kennedy Justice* (New York: Atheneum, 1971), chapters 3–5. For more on the organizational problems of the Justice Department, see Theodore Lowi, "An Irresistible General, an Immovable Justice," *Washington Monthly,* February 1972, pp. 57–62.

[57]Nearly 10 percent of all of the cases reviewed by the Supreme Court come up under these other forms of appeal. Cases are almost certain to gain Supreme Court review if a federal law or treaty has been brought into question by a lower court decision, if a federal appellate court strikes down a state law as being contrary to federal law or the Constitution, or in certain instances where statutes provide an avenue of appeal. See Abraham, *The Judicial Process,* p. 160.

but there are thousands of lawyers who consider it their job to give the appellate courts something worth waiting for. A problem in society, such as race relations or labor-management relations, is very likely to produce a flow of litigation that will bring into question existing laws and interpretations of the Constitution that were developed out of an earlier period. The Court will eventually take one or more of these cases for review and action, because continued refusal to do so will amount to a rule of law just as much as if the courts handed down a written opinion. It is in this sense that the "pattern of cases" influences the behavior and shape of the appellate judiciary.

THE ADMINISTRATION OF JUSTICE AND THE JUSTICE OF ADMINISTRATION

Many would maintain, for good reason, that among the various influences, the solicitor general's remains the most important, because the Supreme Court has relied upon him to "speak for the government" virtually since the creation of that office in 1870. Another reason for his importance is that he knows the Court and is most often able to keep his positions in harmony with it.

Numerous studies of judicial behavior report findings along these lines. For example, during the years of the liberal Warren Court, the solicitor general was four to five times more successful when he assumed the liberal position than when he assumed the conservative position; and he took the liberal position far more frequently during that period.[58] In the 1920s and 1930s, a more conservative solicitor general had a higher batting average before a more conservative Supreme Court. However, from the perspective of the larger governmental scheme, this classification is beside the point.[59] There is a continuity that deserves neither *liberal* nor *conservative* labels and that links the historical periods and the courts and solicitor generals; it is the continuity of a *pro-government disposition.*

When the solicitor general—that is, the government—is defending the authority of one of the independent regulatory commissions, for example, he is generally defending also its jurisdiction and its freedom to act according to its professional judgment with regard to the conduct of a business or individual within its jurisdiction. The

---

[58]A whole variety of related studies can be found in a single volume edited by Glendon Schubert, *Judicial Decision-Making* (New York: Free Press, 1963).

[59]As the various students of judicial behavior make clear, their distinction between the two positions is drawn from the popular distinctions, wherein the liberal position is one that favors the little people, small business versus big business, poor versus rich, free speech and equality, etc. The conservative position is usually defined as the opposite of these. More of this will be discussed in chapter 15.

defense of the Federal Trade Commission, for example, is something that the solicitor general often takes on, and when he does so he is likely to win his case in the federal appellate courts.[60]

Or, when the solicitor general takes a case initiated by the Criminal Division of the Justice Department and goes through the appeals process to the Supreme Court, he is very probably defending the actions of the U.S. Attorneys against the objections of some private defendant. The private defendant could be someone in business, or a kidnapper, or a congressional committee witness being prosecuted for contempt. In any event, the job of the solicitor general is generally one of defending the government.

What we are talking about here, then, is conquest. The entire Justice Department, of which the solicitor general is a servant, is set up to defend the social order, that is, to maintain conquest. It would be impossible to imagine a stable society that does not have one or more institutions which specialize in defending the social order. And it would be extremely difficult to imagine a Department of Justice that would not be one of those institutionalized defenses. Granted, the cards could be stacked against the citizens more than they are; after all, the solicitor general does occasionally join cases against the government on the side of civil liberties and political freedom. But these cases are indeed rare. The overwhelming number of cases where the Justice Department is said to be taking a "liberal" position are cases where the government is actually defending the power or authority of one of the administrative agencies of government against the businessman who would like to see a limit put upon that power.

In the United States, recourse against complete conquest lies heavily upon the appellate judiciary. The Justice Department *and* the solicitor general will always be more on the side of conquest than will the Supreme Court. This should be easy to understand. *In every case that involves a serious question of public law, the government is inevitably the defendant.* This is merely an extension of the very definition of public law. Public law is formulated through the art and science of asking questions about governmental control—that is, about the balance between conquest and incomplete conquest. In these issues, the Justice Department is the paid and institutionalized partisan of the government. The appellate judiciary has the role of an arbiter, even though it is part of the government, because of the very fact that it deals in real cases and controversies.

As a partisan of the government, the Justice Department tends to handle cases of public law with two basic strategies. The first is to

[60]Compare with Alan Stone, "The Politics of Trade Regulation" (Ph.D. diss., University of Chicago, 1972).

"John Marshall has made his decision, now let him enforce it." *President Andrew Jackson, 1832.* "Failure to act [to enforce the judicial order integrating Little Rock High School] would be tantamount to acquiescence in anarchy and the dissolution of the Union." *President Dwight D. Eisenhower, 1957.*

avoid and to suppress cases insofar as possible, precisely because the government is a defendant. The second strategy follows if the first one fails. When the department cannot avoid or suppress an important case of public law, its only other choice is to pursue it as vigorously as possible toward a conclusion that leaves the government intact.[61] This is the obligation and the mission of the Department of Justice and its top legal office, the office of the solicitor general. Every case of public law, if not fought vigorously and with care, could easily end up depriving the government of some vital power to control the population. This is not a mission to be taken lightly, unless we take conquest lightly. It is a mission to be respected, and feared.

Fortunately, the batting average of the solicitor general must always fall below 1.000 because the Supreme Court is not the Department of Justice and is not in complete harmony with its mission. The Court's historic task has been to balance the overwhelming need of conquest against the strongly felt ideal of protecting those individuals who do not wish to be conquered. When dissenting individuals become too numerous or too intense for the tastes of the Court at a given time, it is likely to render decisions which strike the balance in favor of conquest.

For example, when the Court speaks of "clear and present danger" in a free speech case, it is preparing to say that the

The National Judiciary and the "Administration of Justice"

---

[61]There are ample instances in the Stamler case, for example.

individual or individuals in question are interfering with maintenance of conquest. But, while it does give the government the benefit of the doubt, the Court is at least free to consider nongovernment as well; and the litigation of the last two decades on free speech and criminal procedure suggests that the Court is able to exercise its power to restrain conquest by the government.

This is precisely the point at which differences between the judiciary and the executive branch can be perceived. The equivalence of the two institutions has been stressed strongly enough in this chapter, and there are others who may stress the equivalence even more strongly.[62] But the equivalence should not be allowed to overshadow the fundamental differences between the two forms of administration.

1. The courts are passive, while the administrative agencies in the executive branch can take the initiative. In this respect, administrative agencies are vastly superior. The ability to take initiatives and to prevent problems, rather than to wait for them to develop, is one of the primary advantages back of the historic expansion of administrative agencies over courts.

2. The members of the judiciary are amateurs and nontechnicians except with respect to legal procedure, whereas each administrative agency is run by those persons who have expert knowledge in the aspect of society over which the agency has jurisdiction. (These first two differences help explain the rather dramatic displacement of the courts by administrative processes during the past century.[63] The following distinctions between the two branches help explain the persistence of judicial power despite its clear inferiority to administrative agencies.)

3. The formal, constitutional status of the appellate judiciary is so much higher than that of administrative agencies that the legal effect of its decisions is far more important and far longer-lasting than that of the decisions of administrative agencies.

4. The appellate judiciary receives disputes on appeal that administrative agencies are unable to settle. This makes the national appellate judiciary the *overhead agency* above all other overhead agencies.

5. The appellate courts are formally constituted with the power to make rulings that affect the power of government itself, including the power of specific administrative agencies. Each administrative agency has great power over its own jurisdiction, and through that

---

[62]See, for example, Martin Shapiro, *Law and Politics in the Supreme Court* (New York: Free Press, 1964).

[63]There are many works which recognize and celebrate the fact that these advantages of administrative power have led to a displacement of the judiciary by administrative agencies. One of the most learned and eloquent is that of James M. Landis, *The Administrative Process* (New Haven: Yale University Press, 1938).

power it participates very effectively in conquest. But the agencies do not have power to alter the boundaries of their jurisdiction. In fact, the most severe limitation we put upon administrative power is the requirement that each administrative unit stay as carefully as possible within its jurisdiction.[64] The appellate courts have power over such questions.

6. Another distinction in favor of judicial power is the ability of the appellate judiciary to deal with small and unorganized minorities. This had once been argued as a virtue of administrative agencies, but in practice this has turned out less and less to be the case. Experience in the United States leads to the inevitable conclusion that administrative agencies deal primarily with sectors, that is, the organized economic elements in the society. Administrative agencies have been created largely as a response to organized demands, and the expertise of each administrative agency tends to be defined in terms of an organized sector of the economy. At bottom, *administrative law* usually means *sector law.* For example, as far as the real working classes are concerned, the National Labor Relations Board (NLRB) hardly exists. The *labor law* developed by the NLRB should more accurately be called *union law* or *management law;* it is distinctly not labor*er* law. For better or worse, the law of labor*ers* will be found in the common law systems of state judiciaries and in a few principles of public law in the rulings within the appellate system. It will not be found in the national administrative agencies.[65]

Because of our ability to apply with equal meaning such terms as *administration* and *lawmaking* to both the executive branch and the judiciary, the tendency has been to assess the two institutions as equivalent when placed within the larger framework of the governmental system. That is to say, in the eyes of sophisticated analysts, the functions of these agencies appear to be the same. Both, according to this view, are conservative, inasmuch as they are dedicated to preserving the social order. Both are formal, costly, and forbidding to the lower classes. Both tend to be hostile to social change, consenting to it only when all other avenues are closed; and both exist to control on the one hand and to provide legitimacy for control on the other hand.

The differences, however, are as significant as the similarities. In the first place, the politics within the judiciary is a good deal more competitive than in the administrative process. Granted, adminis-

[64]For a good treatment of some of the limitations on administrative power that derive from this problem of limited jurisdiction, see Victor A. Thompson, *Modern Organization* (New York: Knopf, 1969). See also Karl Mannheim, *Freedom, Power and Democratic Planning* (New York: Oxford University Press, 1950).

[65]A comprehensive treatment of the organized basis of regulatory agencies and their constituencies will be found in Marver Bernstein, *Regulating Business by Independent Commission* (Princeton: Princeton University Press, 1955).

trative agencies employ adversary proceedings and attempt to maintain open and public processes, just as courts do. Nevertheless, the judiciary is a more competitive institution, because it is open to a far wider range of interests than those to which the individual administrative agencies are open. The very specialization of each agency reduces its own access to those citizens who have a very special and sustaining interest in the jurisdiction of that agency.

Since the judiciary has no specialized subject matter limitations, it exists in a "competitive market." In contrast, the administrative agency seems to function within an "oligopolistic" market. The two are so small in number that they are capable of communicating their needs to each other and, through mutual accommodation, avoiding the destructive aspects of competition, including costly litigation.

The job of legal counsel in a judicial proceeding involving an issue of public law is to keep the case in court. The job of legal counsel representing corporations before administrative agencies is to keep the case out of court. The judicial system differs from the administrative process in that it produces more legal principles. Every case kept out of court by an accommodation, in which an administrative agency may serve as umpire, is a case in which the government successfully avoided becoming a defendant over an issue of how much power the government possesses or what rights citizens have.

Ultimately this means two things about the appellate judiciary process in the United States. First, the judicial system is far more capable than the administrative process of making a radical departure from existing governmental practices or powers. Its bias, like that of the administrative process, is in favor of not making such radical departures; but it has the capacity to do so, and the *pattern of cases* occasionally forces the courts into radical departures. Knowledge of this potential encourages many persons of radical persuasion to seek political action through public law litigation.

Second, the judicial process is an important source of criteria for judging the conduct of government, including the administrative agencies. The appellate judiciary, especially the Supreme Court, is a primary, perhaps the primary, *source of political theory in the United States.* The rulings and opinions of leading decisions of the Court constitute our most important source of standards about what is good and what is bad for the public, what is good or bad government, and what are the acceptable conditions of conquest.

Obituaries for the American judiciary would be, therefore, a bit premature. Judiciaries not only have a place in modern government but are important precisely because of the emergence of modern administration. The judiciary facilitates our acceptance of power and often serves as a handmaiden to administrative needs. But at the same time that it helps to maintain conquest in these ways, it, more than any other institution, maintains our sense of what is *il*legitimate. If police forces, armies, and other governmental agencies do not choose to be guided by the judicial stamp of illegitimacy and illegality, that is not the fault of the courts. The courts are a continual reminder of how far our society falls below its own level of aspiration for a well-ordered, yet incomplete, conquest.

Part Five
Policy

Policy is conquest updated. Foreign policy is a precondition of domestic policy, since its purpose is to keep our sovereignty credible in the eyes of all of the nations. The primary purpose of domestic policy is to maintain order by controlling behavior or producing new behavior. Each domestic policy is implemented by one or more techniques of control. But how can general social benefit be derived from controls? Who wants controls? Is government nothing more than the tool of those who have power and access in government? Can a recognition of the realities of control produce better policies even for the powerless?

Chapter 14   Maintaining the Right to Conquer: The Foreign Policies of One Sovereignty in a Predatory World of Sovereignties

CONQUEST, SOVEREIGNTY, AND THE PURPOSE OF A FOREIGN POLICY

It is fit and proper to turn abruptly from the judiciary to foreign policy. A judiciary is an expression of domestic order, while foreign policy arises out of international chaos. The two extremes define each other. When individuals live near one another and have a dispute, they can take their dispute to court. But that presupposes conquest and the establishment of sovereignty and stable government. When there is no sovereignty, relationships become chaotic, tending toward violence. Chaos at the level of the individual is called alienation, the absence of familiarity—or anomie, the absence of identity. Chaos at the level of the community within a nation is usually called anarchy, the absence of government. Chaos at the level of nations is often euphemistically called international relations.

Maintaining the Right to Conquer: The Foreign Policies of One Sovereignty in a Predatory World of Sovereignties

International relations refers to the phenomenon of relations among nation-*states,* not among nations. A nation-state is a nation after it has conquered itself, has established its sovereignty among other sovereignties, and has a government able to deal with other governments. The formation of a nation-state is one way of avoiding occupation and conquest by outsiders, and the relationships among nation-states are the single most important source of influence on the world level of violence—now and throughout history.

Sovereignty means recognition by all other nation-states (and other peoples, however they may be organized) that the government of a particular country is indeed the government of that country in the fullest sense. (It is for this reason that from the moment of the Declaration of Independence until after the War of 1812, establishing sovereignty was of the greatest importance to the United States.) Sovereignty is a relationship between and among existing governments which changes in response to a variety of factors. That relationship is precisely what defines foreign policy and its purpose. Foreign policy is comprised of all actions by the ruling classes of a nation-state to maintain in the world at large an acceptance of or respect for the conquest they claim to have achieved or inherited. Even one "foreign" government which fails to be convinced of a nation's sovereignty can take action that could influence that nation's government without its consent. Susceptibility to actions of other governments is the opposite of sovereignty.

No state is *completely* sovereign. For example, the United States suddenly became a good deal less sovereign after 1973, when the oil producing states organized their cartel—the Organization of Petroleum Exporting Countries (OPEC)—to control oil production and prices. When a country is regularly susceptible to the influence of another country, we tend to call the weaker country the satellite of the stronger, as is the case of Eastern European countries and the Soviet Union and many Latin American countries *vis-à-vis* the United States.

Governments of many countries seem satisfied with something less than complete sovereignty. For many years the government of South Vietnam operated almost as a fifty-first state of the United States; this was virtually a condition of their survival. The governments of Hungary and Czechoslovakia seem, at least since 1956 and 1968 respectively, to exist stably enough without full sovereignty. In contrast, the governments of Rumania, Yugoslavia, Cuba, and India have sipped enough from the cup of traditional Western ideas about sovereignty to be eager to have more and more of their own.

Countries often reach a crisis point in their own domestic politics, when they have to decide whether to demand more sovereignty or to settle for less. In recent years this has been frequently true of the Caribbean republics and commonwealths, including Puerto Rico. Those people within a smaller country who oppose more sovereignty

are not necessarily against independence as such; they are likely to be concerned over whether there are sufficient resources in their country to provide them with real sovereignty after they have achieved more independence.

Sovereignty is not altogether a matter of choice. As long as there are a few strong countries and a large number of weak countries, the amount of sovereignty enjoyed by any one of the weaker countries depends to a great extent upon the foreign policies of the stronger countries. That is to say, the sovereignty of most weaker countries is guaranteed by the stronger countries as long as the stronger countries define such guarantees as within their national interests. This has been explicitly true of the historically neutral countries, such as Switzerland, in whose sovereignty virtually every other country seems to be interested, in order to have at least one spot on earth where diplomacy can always take place.

Other countries, such as Sweden, Finland, the middle-European states, and most of the states of the so-called Third World, could never sustain their claim to sovereignty without a constant guarantee by stronger countries. But even for the weaker countries, the problem of foreign policy is retaining credibility as a nation-state so that guarantees of some sovereignty remain within the national interest of one or more stronger nation-states.

Consequently, nation-states tend to look fearfully and antagonistically upon each other. Although some nation-states may be defensive in their foreign policies, while others are aggressive, the

Maintaining the Right to Conquer: The Foreign Policies of One Sovereignty in a Predatory World of Sovereignties

563

general tendency on the part of responsible policy makers is to assume their sovereignty will be encroached upon. Sovereignty, almost by definition, has a predatory spirit: Prey upon your neighbors, or be prepared to be preyed upon. The purpose of foreign policy may be maintenance of sovereignty; but, to judge from the results, foreign policy is almost always predatory.

THE FOREIGN POLICY OF ONE "PREDATORY DEMOCRACY"[1]

Nation-states whose internal politics may be democratic do not necessarily bring anything new or better to international relations. Alexis de Tocqueville early identified the problems of foreign policy which would face new democratic nations:

> Foreign policies demand scarcely any of those qualities which are peculiar to a democracy; they require, on the contrary, the perfect use of almost all those in which it is deficient. . . . A democracy can only with great difficulty regulate the details of an important undertaking, persevere in a fixed design, and work out its execution in spite of serious obstacles. It cannot combine its measures with secrecy or await their consequences with patience.[2]

In this context, it was providential that the first hundred or more years of the development of our republic took place during a period of relative international stability in Europe. One historian referred to that century as the "hundred years' peace."[3] Because of the "balance of power" foreign policies of the European countries, especially Great Britain, the United States managed to pursue and complete the conquest of the American continent almost completely free of foreign interference.

Without the balance of power system in Europe, American policies in the nineteenth century might well have invited foreign intervention. Seizure of land on this continent involved violence against the Indians and regularly affected the interests of one or another European power. Moreover, although American foreign affairs in the nineteenth century were primarily commercial, the policies were aggressive and often exploitative. The two basic and persistent aspects of American foreign policy during that period were the tariff and the Monroe Doctrine.

Our tariff was extremely high and manipulative, serving a dual

---

[1]The term *predatory democracy* is taken from Barrington Moore, Jr., *Reflections on the Causes of Human Misery* (London: Penguin Press, 1972), chapters 5–6.

[2]Alexis de Tocqueville, *Democracy in America,* vol. 1, trans. Phillips Bradley (New York: Knopf, Vintage Books, 1945), p. 243.

[3]This terminology and an excellent analysis of the period will be found in Karl Polanyi, *The Great Transformation* (Boston: Beacon Press, 1957), p. 5.

purpose: (1) to raise revenue, and (2) to protect American industries from foreign competition. This was, to say the least, aggressive.[4] The Monroe Doctrine of American responsibility for shielding the entire Western Hemisphere from "foreign intervention" was not only an aggressive stance but would have been worth little more than the paper it was constantly reprinted on without the jealousies of the European powers toward one another—particularly without the vigilance of Great Britain. (In this manner even our expansionist adventures were protected by Great Britain.[5])

At least one very important institutional development is attributable to the freedom from big power intervention during the early stages of our history—the intermingling of domestic and foreign policy. In most countries, foreign and domestic policies are made in two rather separate and distinct institutions. This has been true in practice and is generally supported in theory.[6] Sometimes the separation has been extreme, as in the case of the autocratic Bismarck, who, when questioned on his foreign policy in the German legislature, exploded in great shock and frustration with the observation that it was difficult enough to conduct foreign policy without "three hundred asses" trying to tell him what to do.[7]

Even where domestic influences have been allowed full play in foreign policy decisions, the two have been institutionally separate, as in the case of the British system. (Many students of international relations have attributed the decline of balance of power politics to the rise of nationalism and the requirement that rulers conduct all of their policies in terms of broad popular support.[8])

After 1918 we attained world power status, and we took our place in world leadership as an imperial power after 1945. We would never again be completely dependent on other national powers. However, we would continue to mix domestic and foreign policy processes, and we would continue to try as much as possible to treat the rest of the world as a receptacle for our internal problems, as we had done with our tariff policies in the nineteenth century. There is absolutely no consensus among expert observers on the description, let alone the evaluation, of United States foreign policy since our emergence after 1945 as a world power. However, it is clear that any well-balanced analysis of our foreign policy must treat at least three dimensions of the problem:

---

[4]Frank W. Taussig, *The Tariff History of the United States* (New York: Capricorn Books, 1964).

[5]Dexter Perkins, *A History of the Monroe Doctrine* (Boston: Little, Brown, 1963); and Samuel F. Bemis, *The Latin American Policy of the United States* (New York: Harcourt, Brace, 1943).

[6]Compare with William Wallace, *Foreign Policy and the Political Process* (London: Macmillan, 1971), pp. 7–10.

[7]Quoted in Kenneth Waltz, *Foreign Policy and Democratic Politics* (Boston: Little, Brown, 1967), p. 9.

[8]Compare with George Quester, *The Continuing Problem of International Politics* (Hinsdale, Ill.: Dryden Press, 1974), p. 157; also Waltz, *Foreign Policy and Democratic Politics,* p. 3 and the many footnote citations.

Maintaining the Right to Conquer: The Foreign Policies of One Sovereignty in a Predatory World of Sovereignties

Some of the Architects of Anti-Communist Policy in America

The original strategic concept:
"From Stettin in the Baltic to Trieste in the Adriatic, an iron curtain has descended across the continent. Behind that line lie all the capitals of the ancient state of central and eastern Europe. . . . all these famous cities and the populations around them lie in the Soviet sphere and . . . far from the Russian frontiers and throughout the world, Communist fifth columns are established and work in complete unity and absolute obedience to the directions they receive from the Communist center. . . . I do not believe that Soviet Russia desires war. What they desire is the fruits of war and the indefinite expansion of their power and doctrines. . . . For that reason the old doctrine of a balance of power is unsound. . . . "
Winston Churchill's Iron Curtain Speech, 1946

Containment of international Communism:
"It would be an exaggeration to say that American behavior unassisted and alone could exercise a power of life and death over the Communist movement and bring about the early fall of Soviet power in Russia. But the United States has it in its power to increase enormously the strains under which Soviet policy must operate. . . . Soviet pressure against the free institutions of the Western world is something that can be contained by the adroit and vigilant application of counter-force at a series of constantly shifting geographical and political points, corresponding to the shifts and maneuvers of Soviet policy. . . . "
George F. Kennan, *The Sources of Soviet Conduct,* 1947

Containment of domestic Communism:
"We of the F.B.I. need your help now even more than during the war years if the battle for a safe and secure America is to be won. . . . During the past five years, American Communists have made their deepest inroads upon our national life. In our vaunted tolerance for all peoples the Communists have found our "Achilles heel! . . . "
J. Edgar Hoover, *Loyal Americans Must Stand Up and Be Counted,* 1946

Judicial approval of the conspiracy theory of Communism:
"It is argued that if Congress may constitutionally enact legislation requiring the Communist Party to register . . . , Congress may impose similar requirements upon any group. . . . Nothing we decide here remotely carries such an implication. The Subversive Activities Control Act applies only to *foreign-dominated* organizations, . . . controlled by a *particular* country, the leader of a movement which, Congress has found, is 'in its origins, its development, and its present practice, . . . a world-wide revolutionary movement whose purpose it is . . . to establish a Communist totalitarian dictatorship in the countries throughout the world through the medium of a world-wide Communist organization.'"
Supreme Court in *Communist Party* v. *Subversive Activities Control Board,* 1961

1. Values. What goals are being sought? What counts as success? What *are* national interests?

2. Roles. What roles do we attempt to play in world politics consistent with our values and rationally designed to fulfill those values?

3. Instruments. What institutions, administrative arrangements, statutes, and programs have we established in order to enable the government to choose among values and roles and to pursue them on a sustained basis?

These three dimensions are not entirely independent of one another. For example, the employment of certain instruments will usually be some indication of the kind of role the country is trying to play; or the role being played often indicates far better than the rhetoric of the president or secretary of state the actual values being pursued at a particular time through foreign policy. Thus, it is best to consider the three dimensions as three different ways of looking at the same phenomenon—the exercise of sovereignty for the purpose of making sovereignty secure.

On the basis of these three dimensions we will be able to evaluate the influence of the United States as a world leader. Toward the end of the chapter we will look once again at the general purpose of foreign policy in any nation-state as compared to the purpose or purposes of American foreign policy during the past three decades. We will want to judge whether American foreign policy has made any difference, whether the difference has been for better or worse, and whether it could have been better. Can a nation-state, which is inherently predatory in its international relations, have foreign policies that can be judged as good or bad? Should the foreign policies of representative democracies come under more severe judgment than the foreign policies of other nations? Can any improvements be made in the conduct or impact of our foreign policy without endangering the very sovereignty that foreign policy seeks to uphold?

Values in United States Foreign Policy: The Anti-Communist Impulse[9]

Emerging out of World War II, leaders in the United States discovered that they and most of the public had made a fundamental about-face in values and attitudes. Our unilateral approach to international economics was over. Our ability to depend upon the foreign policies of other nations had ended. Our role in World War II had made the other great powers dependent upon us and upon the

---

[9]The title of this section is drawn from Michael Parenti's book, *The Anti-Communist Impulse* (New York: Random House, 1970).

foreign policies we might pursue. Even the unexcelled traditionalist (often called isolationist) Senator Robert Taft was heard observing after World War II that there was no such person as an isolationist left in the United States. There was clear memory of our contribution to the failure of the League of Nations, and there was a strong sense that our aloofness had contributed to the suffering of people subjected to German and Japanese occupation. The countries of traditional world leadership had been left flattened by the war. Many had been our allies in arms; more importantly, all of them would be our customers in peace, but only if their economies could be rebuilt.

The change in values took two steps. The first step was a commitment to the defense of democracy everywhere and the pursuit of peace through the United Nations. This was a substantial commitment but did not last very long. Well before the end of the first three postwar years, the basic value position of the leaders and active followers in the United States had become anti-Communism rather than pro-democracy.[10] That is, anti-Communism became our foreign policy—the single most important criterion guiding virtually all strategic and tactical decisions made in the White House, the State Department, and the Department of Defense. Four factors promoted the change in emphasis from pro-democracy to anti-Communism.

1. The switch is attributable in part to the real world situation immediately after the war. Soviet troops were still stationed throughout eastern Europe, and when there was no longer a common enemy, the older distrust and antagonism between the United States and the Soviet Union reemerged. The Soviet Union was probably no more at fault for this renewal of antagonisms than the United States; in fact, many American specialists believe the United States was considerably more to blame.

2. Democracy was either too hard to define cross-culturally, or, if defined according to American ideals, would in fact have yielded too few countries to qualify for our defense. Apparently, anti-Communism was a global notion that could enable us to conduct day-to-day foreign affairs without having to make fine discriminations and judgments in the flow of information received every day in dispatches from the field to the State Department and the White House. Subtle distinctions in political forms would have required more information and more patience to see how changes in regimes were developing and how new political movements were organizing.

For an example of how far away we had moved by the mid-1960s from pro-democracy toward anti-Communism as our automatic criterion, note the following admission by the former assistant

[10]Compare with Parenti, *The Anti-Communist Impulse.*

secretary of state for inter-American affairs:

> A majority of the Guatemalan people voted in free elections for Arbenz, a candidate for President. Later the Guatemalan people discovered that Arbenz was a Marxist-Leninist. Colonel Castillo led a successful revolt and was widely acclaimed by his people. . . . Had we been unconditionally committed to the support of all constitutional governments under all circumstances, we would have been obliged to do everything within our power to bring about the overthrow of Castillo and to restore a Marxist-Leninist power against the will of the Guatemalan people.[11]

3. Anti-Communism seems to have better suited our needs for maintaining *internal* conquest at a time when we were new and uncertain in our peacetime relations with the rest of the world. The single, simple notion of anti-Communism persisted, even in the face of the breakup of the single world Communist front, because policy makers could use anti-Communism at home as a weapon against political dissent just as they could use it abroad as a gauge for our policies. McCarthyism, as it was called, was a transition in a long effort to control domestic dissent and to mobilize domestic consent by tying it to international threats.[12] In order to be sure that there was sufficient public support for a massive commitment to Europe and in order to prepare the way for the building of our military and the rearming of our former adversary, West Germany, it was going to be necessary to sell as strongly as possible the danger of Soviet power and intentions.

4. Finally, anti-Communism was attractive as doctrine because it could be more easily translated into military terms. Political notions are inherently ambiguous. Ambiguity is the stock in trade of diplomats. As military factors entered more and more into our foreign policy thinking, our criteria required something more martial than a pro-democracy attitude.

Anti-Communism was the value fundamental to the general theory of *containment.* Generally speaking, the theory of containment involved recognition of existing lines of influence dividing the "Communist world" from the rest and then the vigorous resistance of any expansion of Communist influence. Basic to the popular version of containment were the terms *cold war* and *iron curtain,* the former denoting the constant need for mobilization in the absence of a shooting war and the latter the existence of territories into which we could not pierce but around which we should

---

[11]Quoted in Theodore Draper, "The Dominican Crisis," *Commentary,* December 1965, p. 35.

[12]Compare with Earl Latham, *The Communist Controversy in Washington* (Cambridge, Mass.: Harvard University Press, 1966); see also Hans Morgenthau, *Politics in the Twentieth Century* (Chicago: University of Chicago Press, 1962), especially chapter 7. A useful collection of documents is Barton Bernstein and Allen Matuso, eds., *The Truman Administration* (New York: Harper & Row, 1966).

maintain constant surveillance. Technically, the situation characterized by these two terms can be called *bipolarity*.[13]

There was, of course, always some basis to our fears of Soviet and Chinese expansionism. However, American leaders often forgot that expansion has been a constant in international relations. In acting as though Soviet and Chinese efforts to increase their own security was something new and particularly aimed at the United States, American policy makers developed the reductio ad absurdum of their own theory by operating as though all domestic civil wars and guerrilla actions in the world were interrelated, cumulative, and part of a carefully planned conspiracy against the United States.

These values and practices were first developed by Democrats under President Truman, but they were expanded with nonpartisan zeal under President Eisenhower, mainly through his secretary of state, John Foster Dulles. They were extended and articulated with uncommon eloquence by President Kennedy and his associates and continued to be utilized to guide our foreign policy choices until the end of the Vietnam War. They remain strong today, even though there are signs that reevaluations of American national interests have been taking place.

Did all of our foreign policy leaders from Truman through Nixon come to be victimized by our own cold war propaganda? Or were these rhetorical flourishes a mask for a more sophisticated analysis underneath? Although anti-Communism and its related operational criteria were probably espoused sincerely by almost all American governmental leaders, it is also true that Democrats had been so stung by McCarthy-Nixon charges of being Communist collaborators that they were especially fearful of taking a position of flexibility toward radical and guerrilla activities in various countries living under dictatorships.

But for all our country's leaders, foreign policy responsibilities were easier to bear, and judgments about the foreign situation easier to make, if they could operate on the assumption that every disturbance of the status quo was engineered by a Communist conspiracy and would ultimately benefit Communist national and international interests. This is, however, only one observer's hypothesis. A sound analysis requires a closer look at the actual roles played by the United States during the years since World War II.[14]

---

[13]One of the best treatments of these various concepts, including an analysis of the most important cases in which we sought to deter what we thought were violations of our containment policy, is that of Alexander George and Richard Smoke, *Deterrence in American Foreign Policy* (New York: Columbia University Press, 1974).

[14]Well-balanced treatments of the cold war as a theory and the sincerity with which it was applied will be found in Paul Y. Hammond, *The Cold War Years: American Foreign Policy since 1945* (New York: Harcourt, Brace, & World, 1969); Walter LaFeber, *America, Russia, and the Cold War* (New York: Wiley, 1967); and George and Smoke, *Deterrence in American Foreign Policy*.

Senator McGovern and
Premier Castro: In the
American system senators
can carry on their own
diplomatic missions.

Roles: The Behavioral Components of World Leadership

A role is a character or part one assumes or is assigned. The concept
has been taken over from the theater by sociologists and indicates
behavior that is highly predictable. Once a role is established,
assumed, or assigned, it becomes something that others learn to
expect. Individuals play many different roles in different situations.
Some roles are chosen deliberately and self-consciously; some are
pressed upon the individual by other individuals or by circumstances. The same is true of groups and nation-states. Balance of power
was not only an observable pattern of international relations during
the seventeenth, eighteenth, and nineteenth centuries. It can also
be seen as a role that leaders of many nation-states expected each
other to play.

The role may have been assumed voluntarily by some members of
the international system; it may have been imposed upon other
nation-states against their will. Either way, there are at least two
great advantages to role-playing behavior. One of these is that it
makes the task of decision or choice much easier in the face of
incomplete information and great uncertainty. In complex international situations, when the full story cannot be known, a few
indications can trigger off a whole series of decisions that are
inherent in a particular role. The second advantage is that the
assumption of a role reduces the difficulty of ascertaining who are
friends and who are adversaries. This is very important in international relations, where a miscue, to draw from the words of theater
and billiards, can be a matter of life and death. The disadvantage, of

*Maintaining the Right to
Conquer: The Foreign
Policies of One Sovereignty
in a Predatory World of
Sovereignties*

571

course, is that the wrong role played at the wrong time in the wrong situation can produce a whole series of irrational or inappropriate behaviors. Some examples of this will be found in the ensuing analysis.

The more powerful the nation, the more capable it will probably be of choosing its own role. The opportunities of the United States for choice were greatly enhanced by the devastated condition of almost all of the other major nation-states following World War II. On the other hand, there are probably a limited number of roles available for any nation-state, regardless of its power. Since these roles are to a great extent defined by history, we shall let history define the major roles for our analysis here.

Four roles drawn from history are identified in Table 14.1, with a brief phrase that seems best to capture the orientation of each role. This is not an exhaustive categorization; other observers might be able to identify several additional roles. However, most would agree that these four are distinct and have been important in the recent history of the United States. This is sufficient for the purposes of the analysis in this chapter.[15]

During the nineteenth century and much of the twentieth, before the United States had any regular role at all in foreign affiars, the country's self-image came closest to being Napoleonic. Only in Napoleon's own France was the sentiment any stronger that the system of government was the best. The sentiment in America that no people could consider themselves truly free until they had adopted some variant of the American system was nurtured in our own independence movement, and it was reinforced by our own particular brand of domestic imperialism in the conquest of the western regions of the continent.

It was considered, for example, our "manifest destiny" to take Texas and California from Mexico. However, our very sporadic and occasional intrusions into international relations were heavily influenced by the Napoleonic spirit. For example, President Woodrow Wilson explained our involvement in World War I on the basis of the fact that "the world must be made safe for democracy."[16]

It was, therefore, quite in character for the United States to adopt the Napoleonic role after World War II, when we finally decided to become a regular member of the international diplomatic communi-

---

[15]It should be emphasized also that these roles and the international systems of which they were a part were a phenomenon largely of the Western world until some point during the latter part of the nineteenth century. In our day, however, it seems fairly clear that the non-Western countries are mostly organized along nation-state lines, have come to share the Western definition of national sovereignty, and would now tend to behave within the classification scheme of Table 14.1. This is a major example of the influence of the West on the world—an influence expressed concretely in such organizations as the United Nations, which encounter great difficulty when dealing with problems except at the level of the nation-state. This has virtually forced tribal and national leaders to take on Western definitions of their territory.

[16]Address to Congress, for a declaration of war, April 2, 1917.

Table 14.1	**The Four Primary Roles of Nation-States in the Conduct of Their Foreign Policy**	
	Role	**Orientation**
	Balance of power	Political opportunism
	Holy Alliance	Antirevolutionary intervention
	Napoleonic	Ideology-based imperialism
	Capitalistic	Economic expansionism

ty. Our concepts of participation and human rights implanted in the charter of the United Nations were indicative of the kind of role we chose to play. The Marshall Plan was to a large extent Napoleonic. Despite the undoubted mixture of economic motivations in the Marshall Plan, the idea of rebuilding Europe was nevertheless a feverishly pro-democracy commitment. Since the State Department had traditionally served commercial interests in our foreign policy, the Marshall Plan was placed outside the State Department; it was given its own international envoys and its right to make "foreign policy" independent of the State Department (see also chapter 12). Even our dogged opposition to Communist parties in the Western European countries arose as much out of our commitment to remaking those countries along the lines of American party politics as out of fear that the parties would stage Communist revolutions.

Another interesting example of our Napoleonic role was our policy toward Spain. Spain never did fully cooperate with Hitler; in fact, Spain's World War II record under Franco was a good deal less disreputable than that of Vichy France under Pétain. Nevertheless, since postwar France was a democracy more to our liking than postwar Spain, the United States singled out Spain for tremendous pressure, making it quite clear we would continue our pressure until the Spanish government made measurable improvements in the political rights of its citizens. One indication of our shift away from the Napoleonic role was the development of close military ties with Spain after 1950.[17]

The zeal to impose our way of life on the people of other countries continues to be strong. But as a dominant role, the Napoleonic gave over to the Holy Alliance role. A Napoleonic role is an interventionist role motivated largely by antagonism to dictatorship; in contrast, a Holy Alliance role is deeply antagonistic to disorder. This role has put the United States on the side of dictatorships as often as democracies, perhaps more often. A well entrenched dictator is more

Maintaining the Right to Conquer: The Foreign Policies of One Sovereignty in a Predatory World of Sovereignties

[17]Several important case studies of American foreign policy which chart our shift away from the Napoleonic role will be found in Harold Stein, ed., *American Civil-Military Decisions: A Book of Case Studies* (University, Ala.: University of Alabama Press, 1963).

often than not a force for stability. Thus, even though these roles are both interventionist, they are as far apart as two roles could possibly be—as far apart as Napoleon was from Metternich.

Even the form of intervention is different. The Napoleonic role is likely to be played upon the sentiments of large masses of people, exhorting them to resist their own rulers as well as love the enemy of their rulers, the United States. In contrast, the intervention of the Holy Alliance role is much more likely to be secretive, involving quiet but forceful threats by a diplomat, a CIA involvement with the local military, or a trade arrangement or import quota that may shore up the economic elites.

The so-called policy of containment was the main expression of the American Holy Alliance role. Because the theory of containment sounded so realistic and could apparently account for so much of Soviet conduct, the Holy Alliance role became the strongest and most frequently adopted role throughout the second term of Truman and the succeeding terms of Eisenhower, Kennedy, and Johnson.[18] Containment theory and the Holy Alliance role made the United States a status quo power throughout the more than two decades following World War II. Anti-Communism was the main pretext, and there is probably little question that our interventions were most frequently against socialist movements. But any disorder qualified for American concern, and within the Holy Alliance point of view it was almost coincidental that the largest number of organized disorders were socialist in leadership. To be against international disorder meant being prepared to oppose any and all sources of disorder.[19]

Investigations by the Rockefeller Commission and by Senator Church's committee in 1975 revealed that the CIA accepted the possibility of disorder when their interventions were against what they defined as a Communist-dominated ruling group. However, although anti-Communism was the dominant value, the criterion of success was the preservation of the status quo. As with Yugoslavia in the late 1940s, we have often been very quick to make our peace even with socialist governments if they are a proven force in favor of the status quo.

The most concrete manifestation of the Holy Alliance role is to be found in the military pacts and mutual security alliances that were

---

[18]George Kennan, the originator of the theory of containment and one of the major architects of its employment by American policy makers, was a widely respected intellectual and a high-ranking State Department diplomat in the 1940s. Given his sensitive position, he published his original ideas under the pseudonym Mr. X, in "The Sources of Soviet Conduct," *Foreign Affairs* 25 (1947), 556. In an elaboration of his theory, two critics of American foreign policy have argued that containment policies should really be called "containment of socialism" policies: Paul Baran and Paul Sweezy, *Monopoly Capital* (New York: Monthly Review Press, 1968); useful excerpts have been reprinted in Michael Parenti, ed., *Trends and Tragedies in American Foreign Policy* (Boston: Little, Brown, 1971), p. 105.

[19]For a good review of American interventions, both covert and overt, see Thomas Ross and David Wise, *The Invisible Government* (New York: Random House, 1964).

begun with NATO and extended year after year throughout the 1950s. These alliances, to be discussed below as instruments of foreign policy, were all cumulative along the lines of containment or anti-Communism, and they were established with the expectation that they would be maintained over a very long period of time. Reinforcing this worldwide Holy Alliance role, the American defense posture was tied in with the definition of the world as bipolar, with freedom at one pole and slavery at the other, and with the mind-boggling notion of "the delicate balance of terror."

This definition of world relationships in military terms by some of the most scientific and clear-headed analysts in the American foreign policy establishment is not an entirely false one.[20] After all, the primary adversary of the United States was for most of these years the Soviet Union, and the Soviet Union felt and expressed a mutual antagonism and a commensurate definition of the world. One could say that the United States forced a Holy Alliance role on the Soviet Union, or that the Soviet Union forced the role on us, or that the two countries imposed the role on each other. Whatever the case, a Holy Alliance role seems to underlie the great varieties of treaties and strategic arrangements we developed during most of the years of our international involvement since 1945 and the formation of NATO.

Some of our mutual security alliances are undoubtedly formed with mutual enthusiasm; but in many instances membership is a result of military and economic pressure from the United States. A very concrete example of our approach is the integration of Western Europe. A balance of power approach might well have called for a Europe of several independent powers; a Holy Alliance approach called for a unified Europe operating under permanent treaty arrangements with the United States, regardless of the differing national interests among the European powers.

We have apparently felt even stronger pressure to pull weaker countries on the periphery of the iron curtain into protective alliances because of our belief that Communism is a world conspiracy. An assessment of this pattern appears at the conclusion of a massive study of American efforts to "deter" the Russians and Chinese:

The different parts of the international system were seen as tightly "coupled," so that perturbation in one locale, it was feared, could cause

_____

[20] A good compilation of readings on American strategic thinking is that edited by Henry Kissinger while still a Harvard professor, *Problems of National Strategy* (New York: Praeger, 1965). See also Albert Wohlstetter, "The Delicate Balance of Terror," *Foreign Affairs* 37 (1958). For a massive review of the military and theoretical considerations back of containment, consult George and Smoke, *Deterrence in American Foreign Policy*. For an assessment of the most important of American "think tanks" and its close relationship to the air force and other strategic agencies, see B. L. R. Smith, *The RAND Corporation* (Cambridge, Mass.: Harvard University Press, 1966).

strong repercussions in other areas that might throw the rest of the international system (like a row of dominoes) into greater disequilibrium. . . . The parallel belief that a setback to "international communism" in one area would increase the likelihood of setbacks in other areas tended to increase the value assigned by American policy-makers to maintain noncommunist regimes in all peripheral areas. The conception of the American interest in preserving the "freedom" of weaker countries was thus inflated by the Cold War significance imputed to them. . . . This view of the international system, besides encouraging a proliferation of American commitments, tended (1) to increase the perceived importance of protecting countries in peripheral areas; (2) to homogenize rather than differentiating the commitments made to various countries, and (3) to encourage a belief in the "interdependence of commitments" i.e., the belief that failure of the United States to honor any one commitment effectively would weaken the credibility of all other American commitments and, hence "invite" further challenges.[21]

A number of developments during the late 1960s tended to weaken our Holy Alliance role. The failure to define and deal adequately with the civil war in Vietnam may have been the most important of developments that eventually led to a reevaluation of our postures. But there were other factors too: our acceptance of the split between China and Russia as a new aspect of world affairs; the increased independence of Europe; the emergence of the Third World as an important idea, even if not yet any kind of organized relationship; and the new-found ability of the Arab countries to operate occasionally as an economic, if not a political, unit.

For all these and perhaps other reasons, theorists of international relations, inside and outside the government, have most surely begun to revise their theoretical outlook. Multipolarity is replacing bipolarity as a description of world relationships.[22] The world had probably been becoming multipolar for a long while, but this reality had been masked and suppressed by the energy and resources the United States had been putting back of its theory of bipolarity and the alliances made on the basis of that theory. It took our own recognition of the world's multipolar potentialities to help make multipolarity a reality.

Probably the most important step toward recognition of multipolarity and the actualization of a new role was the reversal of the position of the United States toward mainland China. This was dramatized particularly by the fact that the reversal, after over twenty years of opposition, was accomplished by Richard Nixon, one

---

[21]George and Smoke, *Deterrence in American Foreign Policy,* pp. 552–553. See also Max Singer and Aaron Wildavsky, "A Third World Averaging Strategy," in *U.S. Foreign Policy: Perspectives and Proposals for the 1970's,* ed. Paul Seabury and Aaron Wildavsky (New York: McGraw-Hill, 1969).

[22]See, for example, Richard Rosecrance, "Bi-Polarity, Multi-Polarity and the Future," *Journal of Conflict Resolution,* September 1966.

of the very leaders of the 1950s responsible for the original position
of aggressive opposition to mainland China. In his successive roles
as congressman, senator, and vice-president, Nixon was one of
several leaders who defined all positions other than total hostility to
Communist China as prima facie evidence of treason. The official
change in U.S. attitude toward China during his presidency meant
that the United States was finally ready to recognize that the
so-called Communist world is not monolithic. And this recognition
ultimately involved the breakup of the theory of bipolarity, of the
interconnection of all world disorders, and ultimately of total
reliance on the Holy Alliance role.

The United States now fully recognizes at least five and perhaps
six major national units or alliances that are capable of playing
significant and independent roles in world politics: the United
States, the Soviet Union, the Western European Alliance, China,
and Japan. (The Arab states could constitute a sixth unit, unless
American policies manage to prevent the Arab countries from
developing an effective political alliance.) We have come to understand that small shifts in Soviet-Chinese relationships can have a
great effect on our interests, despite the fact that China is not at the
moment a credible nuclear power. We have discovered that small
shifts among members of the NATO powers can also affect us, as in
the case of the decision by several of these countries to reject our
support of Israel in 1973 in the Middle East.

Recognition of the multipolarity of the world is not likely to
suppress the Holy Alliance attitude completely. Our distrust of

*Maintaining the Right to
Conquer: The Foreign
Policies of One Sovereignty
in a Predatory World of
Sovereignties*

countries with Marxist domestic goals continues to be too strong to allow our leaders to play a completely opportunistic role as called for by the balance of power and the capitalistic models identified in Table 14.1. The existence of nuclear weapons and the ability to deliver them by MIRV missiles from land and submarine bases renders impossible a balance of power relationship between the United States and the Soviet Union. However, the stalemate between the two countries in terms of their capacity for mutual destruction has opened up all sorts of possibilities for variation in the relationships among all of the other countries and between the United States and those other countries. The same is true of the Soviet Union and its relationship to countries other than the United States and China.

What seems to be happening is that the United States now has begun to adopt *all four* of the roles and play them in a specialized but sustained manner in different parts of the world. In all matters pertaining to and affecting the Soviet Union, Holy Alliance role playing is still very much a reality. Our commitment to NATO, even when it is not necessarily within our economic interests, remains steadfast. The particular stridency of the Defense Department and its secretary, James Schlesinger, following the collapse of the South Vietnamese government in early 1975 also testifies to the seriousness with which we continue to take our various military alliances (worked out during the Holy Alliance period) that surround the Soviet Union.

All during 1974 and 1975 Schlesinger stressed the ability and the willingness of the United States to use its nuclear force to support its alliances against the Soviet Union. For example, in testimony to Congress, made public on May 29, 1975, Schlesinger said that to avoid defeat in Europe by a conventional attack from Russia or its allies in the Warsaw Pact (the Russian counterpart of NATO), the United States could authorize the use of its 7,000 battlefield "tactical" nuclear warheads on a *first strike* basis.[23] The notion of our using nuclear weapons first under any circumstances was something we had insisted for nearly two decades we would not do. This statement and others of its kind provided a new way of underlining the seriousness of our pact commitments at the very time when we were engaging in other kinds of international roles, which might seem to deemphasize those commitments.

Nevertheless, Schlesinger's stridency serves here mainly to emphasize the new willingness of the United States to recognize that there are regions of the world and problems in the world that are not directly related to the Soviet Union, and that for relations with these a different kind of role must be assumed. For example, our

[23]*New York Times,* May 30, 1975, pp. 1 and 7.

role in the Middle East has not been one of the Holy Alliance type. Not only were we unable to stop the Yom Kippur War, there is no evidence that we sought to. Moreover, we then intervened to help end the war on a stalemate and took a position which seemed to the Israelis to favor Arab interests. The full measure of our balance of power role in the Middle East can be taken by recognition of the fact that we were, and remained through 1975 a least, the only important friend of the Israelis and at the same time conducted ourselves so evenhandedly (or opportunistically) that the Egyptians restored full diplomatic relations with us after a gap of seven years following the 1967 war in the Middle East.

The frequent shifting of relationships between Syria and Jordan, Egypt and Syria, and Libya and the several other Arab nations is probably in large part attributable to differences of national interest sewn into the histories of these countries. But the role of the United States in recent years has certainly contributed to that instability to such an extent that—although war could still break out between Isreal and one or more Arab countries—there is not at the moment a sense that war in the Middle East could ignite World War III between the U.S. and the Soviet Union.

The situation was so flexible and confused, in the sense of balance of power, during 1974 and 1975 that there was considerable talk of a settlement being imposed upon Israel and the Arab countries by the United States and the Soviet Union together. Yasar Arafat, leader of the militant Palestine Liberation Organization (PLO), became the officially recognized spokesman for Palestinians in November 1974, and six months later he was back fighting violently not only against the Israelis but also against the Lebanese. This kind of changeability was typical of relations among the European countries in the nineteenth century.

Meanwhile, although economic considerations color many of our actions throughout the world, there are certain regions where the United States has played and continues to play a capitalist expansionism role. This is probably most true in Latin America, despite the frequency with which we justify our interventions there as part of our struggle against Communism. Many of our actions in Latin America have to be understood in the context of the enormity of American investments and profits in that area. Table 14.2 gives a general indication of American economic relationships on the eve of the American adoption of the Alliance for Progress early in the Kennedy administration.

Without any question, the figures show that the greatest efficiency in the employment of capital has been in the Latin American region of the world, where we have asserted our strongest right to intervene and where we have most frequently taken strong and direct interventionist measures. By the same token, however, many of our actions in other parts of the world would be totally

Table 14.2 U.S. Investments and Profits around the World

	Percentage Distribution of:	
	Assets	Profits
United States and Canada	67	34
Latin America	20	39
Eastern hemisphere	13	27
Total	100	100

From Paul A. Baran and Paul M. Sweezy, *Monopoly Capital: An Essay on the American Economic and Social Order* (New York: Monthly Review Press, 1968), p. 194.

inexplicable in terms of arguments based upon economic interests and economic expansionism. The expenditure of over $30 billion per year for the several years of the Vietnam War cannot possibly be explained in terms of capitalistic interests in Vietnam or in Southeast Asia. Moreover, it does not take a very close look at the structure of American industry to understand that only one segment, albeit a large segment, of the entire capitalist class gains directly from defense contracts and loses directly from withdrawals or defeats in far-flung areas of the world.[24]

Any overview of American foreign policy within the context of the system of government in the United States should render quite acceptable the proposition that the U.S. cannot play only one role in international affairs. One role may dominate at a particular point in time; one role may dominate in one region of the world. But there are too many conflicting interests within the United States (and too many channels by which these conflicting interests can express themselves) for there to be a complete severance of foreign from domestic policy and a consistent role in foreign affairs regardless of international challenges and contingencies. This is very probably why so much of our foreign policy has been conducted with extreme secrecy during the past decade. Every time it is revealed that our government subsidized some corporations in order to encourage a foreign operation, or that we cooperated in an effort to undermine a regime, there is an indignant reaction.

Perhaps the world would be safer if we were able to separate foreign from domestic politics and were consequently able to adopt one role from among the four and play it consistently. Our behavior would then be predictable, allowing other countries to plan their

---

[24]Compare with Stanley Leiberson, "An Empirical Study of Military-Industrial Linkages," *American Journal of Sociology*, January 1971, p. 571. For a well-balanced assessment of arguments about the degree of involvement of capitalist interests in American foreign policy, see Moore, *Reflections on the Causes of Human Misery*, p. 119.

own foreign policies in a manner which would reduce violent conflict. At the present time, it is extremely difficult to know just what kind of world events will bring about what kind of a sustained role on the part of the United States as it begins it third century as a republic. Meanwhile, movement back and forth among the four major roles may already be an advancement over the rigid anti-Communism of the period of nearly thirty years which we may someday identify as a distinctive postwar era.

Of one thing we can be sure: the United States was never isolationist. The choice in foreign affairs roles in modern times has not been and never will be between isolationism and internationalism. The choice is and always has been one of *what kind* of involvement, and *how much.* The era called isolationist was really a period during which the United States was acting out a special form of capitalistic expansionism. The yearning for isolationism among many different elements of American society following our vain adventure in Vietnam bears no relation to any present or future realities. Isolationism would mean no involvement beyond our own borders except where an absolutely vital interest is involved.

But where would the line be drawn? Would it be drawn with Korea and Thailand? Would it include or exclude the Middle East? Would it exclude or include our present military alliances? Would those who argue that the line should be drawn around the continental United States (so as to exclude sending armed forces to defend property and contracts held by American citizens abroad) also draw the line tightly enough to prohibit American intervention in cases of genocide? What about extradition? Do we want to forego the prospect of retrieving an embezzler who escapes to a foreign land in order to evade criminal prosecution in the United States? Do we bring to an end all of our efforts to gain information about the intentions of other nation-states, as the left might want? Or do we redouble our efforts to keep our own intentions secret, as the right might want?

Instruments of Foreign Policy: Manipulating Other Sovereignties

An instrument is a tool with which or through which something is accomplished. It is a neutral apparatus that can serve any hand. Each instrument, of course, has its inherent limitations. Indeed a machine gun is a poor instrument of defense against an attack by a swarm of bees. There are many major instruments of foreign policy—things with which or through which one country tries to manipulate other countries. These instruments are often called foreign policy, but in fact they are instruments or capabilities with which many roles may be played and many goals may be sought.

No attempt has been made here to provide an exhaustive study of all possible instruments. The basic concepts and information in our discussion should help the reader develop a personal capacity to identify instruments and to analyze them. The instruments to be covered are the United Nations, foreign aid, collective security, the military establishment, and propaganda.

The United Nations For a while after World War II the United Nations was probably the key instrument of U.S. foreign policy. Through support of the United Nations we expected to be able to play something of a balance of power role, influencing other countries without actually intervening in their affairs, and perhaps keeping a shaky peace without too much military preparedness or involvement. The United Nations was to be a sort of permanent alliance of all states hostile to fascist aggressiveness in foreign policy.

American use of the U.N. as its own instrument probably reached its height during the Korean War, when the United States was able to use its own troops in Korea under the umbrella of the official U.N. "peace-keeping force." Within three years after the termination of the Korean War, the United States lost control of the admission of new members to the U.N.; the Third World decolonization led to the expansion of the official U.N. membership from around 60 nation-states to 130. These developments made it inevitable that the United States would lose its sway within the U.N. and rely on it less and less as an instrument for the pursuit of American foreign policy goals.

Nevertheless, the U.N. does continue to function as an effective force in some sensitive areas, as its role in the Congo and the Middle East during the 1960s testifies. Thus, although the lion's share of the U.N. annual budget is provided by the United States, it would be difficult to deny that the United States has received more value than many other countries from the U.N. (Article 19 of the United Nations charter obliges all member countries to pay their proper share of U.N. expenses, including peace-keeping activities.)

A large number of people in the United States have always questioned the value of the United Nations, and that number has probably grown. However, the U.N. was never expected to be the only instrument of American foreign policy, and very soon after World War II several other important instruments were added. By our own actions we made certain that the U.N. charter provided for recognition of other instruments, as well as for activities independent of the U.N.

Most particularly, the charter anticipates the development of collective security—alliances among several states (multilateral alliances) providing for their mutual defense. Almost as soon as the United Nations was accepted by the American people as a reasonable type of peacetime involvement for this country, campaigns were undertaken by the government to establish popular acceptance of two additional instruments—foreign aid and collective military security—which would lead to far greater U.S. entanglement in the affairs of foreign countries than anything for which our traditions and experiences had prepared us.

Foreign aid and other economic instruments If the United States was ever going to be a major power in international relations, it was inevitable that its vast economic power would have to come into play. Economic instruments take two forms—economic aid in the form of grants and loans and the creation and maintenance of an institution to replace the gold standard as the means by which countries can get proper currencies (especially dollars) for engaging in international trade.

Plans for the involvement of our economic resources got under way almost as early as plans for joining the United Nations, and by 1947 a public commitment had been made. It had begun with an international crisis brought on by the sudden British decision that they would no longer be able to maintain their commitments to Greece and Turkey to support the existing regimes against guerrilla forces. Within three weeks of the British announcement, President Truman had recommended a $400 million military aid program for the two countries, and by mid-May of 1947 Congress had passed a bill to that effect. All along, however, President Truman had placed this action within the larger context of a world commitment to help rebuild and defend countries whose leadership wished to develop democratic systems (at first) and ward off Communism (eventually).[25]

Use of foreign aid as an instrument has varied according to which of the four roles has been dominant. Foreign aid was overwhelmingly compatible with the Napoleonic and capitalistic roles of the U.S. during the early years after World War II. The European Recovery Plan (Marshall Plan) was very well designed for assisting the rebuilding of the great industrial, capitalistic democracies of Western Europe, making them showplaces of democracy, bulwarks against Communism, and dependable customers for U.S. exports.

Table 14.3, however, suggests that this was never more than part of the story. As the Napoleonic and capitalistic roles were utilizing assistance programs to rebuild Western Europe, other agencies were employing other foreign aid appropriations for military purposes. The column showing total grants and loans under foreign assistance programs is an almost precise record of expenditures under the popularly understood foreign aid program. This program

Maintaining the Right to Conquer: The Foreign Policies of One Sovereignty in a Predatory World of Sovereignties

[25]A detailed account of the developments of the Truman Doctrine and the Marshall Plan will be found in Joseph M. Jones, *The Fifteen Weeks* (New York: Viking, 1955). A different kind of an assessment will be found in Gabriel Kolko, *The Politics of War* (New York: Random House, 1968).

Table 14.3   U.S. Foreign Economic Assistance, 1946–1973

Year	Total Grants and Loans under Foreign Assistance Programs	Total Grants and Loans, All Foreign Programs	Percentage of Foreign Programs for Military Assistance
1946–1948	—	14,536	3.30
1949–1952	14,505	22,190	12.79
1953	1,958	6,885	62.00
1954	2,228	5,831	58.51
1955	1,821	5,195	48.29
1956	1,506	5,598	53.21
1957	1,627	5,421	39.36
1958	1,620	5,313	45.24
1959	1,916	5,567	38.80
1960	1,866	5,123	36.01
1961	2,012	5,642	25.98
1962	2,508	6,376	23.94
1963	2,297	6,738	27.91
1964	2,136	6,134	24.82
1965	2,026	6,140	21.38
1966	2,677	7,074	32.37
1967	2,419	6,883	42.72
1968	2,176	6,920	40.70
1969	1,690	6,772	47.96
1970	1,877	6,647	44.69
1971	1,861	7,705	55.32
1972	2,072	8,538	53.84
1973	2,001	8,363	50.75

Data from U.S. Agency for International Development, *U.S. Overseas Loans, Grants, and Assistance* (Washington, D.C.: Government Printing Office, 1963 and 1973), and U.S. Office of Business Economics, *Foreign Grants and Credits by the U.S.* (Washington, D.C.: Government Printing Office, 1963 and 1973).

was administered by a succession of agencies beginning with the Marshall Plan and continuing under the Mutual Security Act and the Agency for International Development.

The agencies were independent of the State and Defense Departments and to a large extent were able to pursue their own foreign policy (see Chapter 11). Some of the expenditures listed under the column of total grants and loans for all foreign programs also served the same purposes, such as food for peace programs and programs of technological assistance. But note in the column showing the percentages of expenditures for military assistance what a high proportion of all economic assistance was being used for this purpose. The amounts varied from year to year, dropping to something of a low during the early 1960s. In the past decade the proportion of foreign assistance going to military programs has passed the 50 percent mark and promises to remain there.

We can never know whether American economic and military assistance actually kept the Russians and Chinese from taking over countries anywhere in the world. It is impossible to know how hard the Russians and Chinese tried to subvert African, Latin American, or Southeast Asian countries. It is also impossible to relive the period without American foreign aid in order to determine what would have happened. However, it is undeniable that foreign aid constituted a significant proportion of the gross national product (GNP) of several countries in the Third World. While this money seldom filtered down to the masses of the people, there was certainly an ample amount to help stabilize and maintain the existing ruling classes. During the 1960s, foreign aid to India amounted to nearly 2 percent of the Indian GNP. During the same period, nearly 3 percent of the Pakistani GNP was attributable to American foreign aid. The proportion of GNP provided by American economic assistance in the somewhat smaller countries of Korea and Vietnam amounted to more than 10 percent.[26]

American policy makers have good reason to believe that foreign aid rates high as a counterrevolutionary instrument. And it also seems to be adaptable to the different roles we may play at a particular time or in a particular region of the world. Just as it was compatible with the Napoleonic and capitalistic roles in Western Europe, so it seems to serve other roles elsewhere. Combined economic and military aid in the Middle East has probably been significant in keeping Arab states from becoming too dependent upon the Soviet Union and at the same time may have helped keep them from uniting into one common front against Israel.

Our military assistance may have aided them in waging war, but our economic and political activities have kept them from waging it too efficiently as a unified multinational force. For another example, a generous combination of economic and military aid for more than twenty years kept Spain strong, yet independent of NATO and Europe and dependable as an alternative base for U.S. strategic naval and air operations. This paid off handsomely in military dividends during the Yom Kippur War of 1973, when the NATO countries decided to refuse Americans access to their bases to send emergency military aid to Israel.

Since the major preoccupation of the United States in Latin America has been economic stability, it is highly probable that our foreign aid would have been used there in an entirely capitalistic role, except for the presence of Fidel Castro. Castro has been the pretext used to justify our Holy Alliance activities in Latin Ameri-

[26]A related treatment, with additional figures, will be found in Waltz, *Foreign Policy and Democratic Politics,* p. 182.

ca. Take, for example, the Alliance for Progress, President Kennedy's effort to revive our "good neighbor policy" through economic assistance. As one observer noted, "The first years of the Alliance saw a notable shift toward the right in Latin American politics."[27]

Brazil may be the most instructive case in Latin America. In 1961, the United States used its economic and political power to oppose the new Brazilian President Goulart as an apparently left-leaning politician. After Brazilians began to find his position acceptable, the U.S. government extended over $400 million in financial aid to Brazil. But when the policies of the Goulart regime began to appear to be too interventionist and inflationary for private investment, Washington proceeded to cut the aid as a means of pressuring the regime. In 1964, Goulart was replaced by a right-wing military regime. Ten years later Brizil was being governed by the very same regime.[28] This does not mean that American economic aid directly caused the military take-over of Brazil. After all, there were many military take-overs and interventions in Latin America during the early 1960s—in Guatemala, the Dominican Republic, Honduras, Peru, Ecuador, and Argentina. But it would be difficult to deny that American foreign aid, motivated so heavily by anti-Communism and anti-Castroism, was a reinforcing influence in Brazil and elsewhere.

Foreign aid, once the darling of the liberal internationalists, began to decline in popular esteem during the 1960s, until it came to be appreciated for what it really was—one of several instruments of foreign policy. And as such an instrument, it shows no signs of disappearing. Loans and grants to a great many nations continue to be administered by the State Department, the agencies of the Commerce Department, the Defense Department, and so on. Each of these departments and agencies sometimes seems to be conducting its own independent foreign policy. But the overall impact of our various influences on Latin America has tended to be strongly in favor of American corporate interests.

Economic assistance must also be considered a significant element in world monetary relationships. The United States and its capitalist elites are not alone in their concern for world commerce. Stable and dependable currencies and terms of exchange are the absolute prerequisite of international trade, and international trade is not a vital interest limited to capitalists. No country is self-sufficient, and therefore no country can get along without some fairly honest arrangements for trade.

For nearly twenty years after World War II, an overwhelming international problem was the dollar gap, an insufficient supply of

[27]Hammond, *The Cold War Years*, p. 193. See pp. 174–195 for a good general assessment of foreign aid and other types of politics in the underdeveloped world.

[28]Ibid., pp. 192–193.

dollars around the world to fulfill the demand for international exchange. Most of the major countries had come out of World War II seriously in debt to the United States, and yet they had a tremendous need for additional dollars to buy necessary capital and consumer goods. American foreign aid was an essential element, therefore, in the reconstruction of international trade as well as the domestic economies of the various industrial countries.

Of perhaps greater importance was the founding of the International Monetary Fund (IMF), which enables all countries to establish comparable values for their currencies in order to engage in the transfer of money for goods or investments. Up until the early 1930s, the gold standard enabled countries to exchange currencies for goods, functioning as an automatic determiner of the comparable value of currencies. That worked well enough as long as most countries were willing to take measures to reduce comsumption inside their own economies during any period when they suffered an unfavorable balance of trade. Once increasing numbers of governments committed themselves to internal economic growth, they were no longer willing to make the sacrifices necessary to live by the gold standard.[29] Another medium of exchange was necessary, and this was contrived in establishment of the IMF.

The International Monetary Fund works on the basis of an actual fund composed of gold and the currencies of member countries. The fund, which exceeded $10 billion in the early 1970s, was made available for lending to member countries to help them overcome temporary trade deficits without unduly contracting their imports of goods. The IMF system worked well enough as long as there was such a demand for dollars that the dollar could operate as an alternative to the old gold standard. Countries could even commit themselves to long-range economic growth, as long as the United States continued to support their deficits by foreign economic aid and through the IMF. The combination of IMF and U.S. foreign aid in effect constituted the international monetary system.

During the decade following 1965, however, when the dollar gap became a dollar glut, the international monetary system began to face a crisis. This was due largely to the American expenditure of $30 billion per year on the Vietnam War, our maintenance of American troops in Europe under NATO obligations, our continued foreign economic and military assistance, and our almost unquenchable thirst for oil and a variety of foreign goods. After

Maintaining the Right to Conquer: The Foreign Policies of One Sovereignty in a Predatory World of Sovereignties

[29]Under the gold standard, each government established by law the value of its currency in terms of a fixed quantity of gold—so many grains of gold per unit, such as 23.22 grains of gold per dollar and 113 grains of gold for the British pound sterling. These values were maintained by the willingness of each government to buy and sell unlimited amounts of gold at the established price. Under these circumstances, if there was a continual flow of gold from a country, due to its buying more goods abroad than it sold, then the only way it could live by the gold standard was to contract its domestic economy, throw people out of jobs, and reduce its consumption.

several years in which the United States had a large unfavorable balance of trade, there were billions of dollars in world trade that could not be converted into gold or into other currencies at existing prices. Countries holding a surplus of dollars had to accumulate them in their national banks or risk breaking up the monetary system within the IMF.

The break came in the early 1970s when the European banks and private speculators finally broke the fixed price of gold, and it more than tripled in price. The United States finally recognized the breakup of the postwar monetary system by actually devaluing the dollar in 1971. Since the United States was the primary designer of IMF, and since our contribution had been roughly one-thrid of the total, a change in the official value of the dollar, especially coupled with a dramatic increase in the price of gold, produced changes throughout the world. All of this had been unthinkable before 1971; and even now a new international monetary system has not yet been stabilized. In the meantime, countries are improvising through the IMF, thanks largely to the invention of Special Drawing Rights (SDRs). SDRs are actually international currency set up by vote of the IMF members to be made available to countries with heavy trade deficits. Since these SDRs function just like gold, they are usually called "paper gold."

Continued heavy U.S. trade deficits and an alarming flow of gold from the United States to European and Japanese markets probably contributed seriously to the inflation and recession of 1974 and 1975. Nevertheless, despite our heavy trade deficits, and despite the fact that we are the heaviest user of SDRs, our foreign aid programs have continued unabated. Foreign economic and military assistance continues because it never was merely a monetary instrument, despite its value in that regard. Economic and military assistance has been and continues to be an important instrument of foreign policy in virtually any such role the United States may choose to play.[30]

Collective security   Coming slightly later in the postwar apparatus, collective security eventually surpassed all of the other instruments of foreign policy in the extent of our reliance upon it, and it remained probably the primary instrument for nearly a decade. Whether we were ever really more secure by virtue of our collective security arrangements is something that can never be known. Nevertheless, these collective defense treaties were almost universally respected in the United States and remain important even in their declining years.

[30]For a thorough, critical review of the United States in the world of international money and trade, consult Raymond Aron, *The Imperial Republic: The United States and the World 1945–1973*, trans. Frank Jellinek (Englewood Cliffs, N.J.: Prentice-Hall, 1974), part 2.

Our first collective security arrangement was the Rio Treaty, signed in September of 1947. It provided for the Organization of American States (OAS), established in 1948. It also provided that an armed attack against any one of the members "shall be considered as an attack against all of the American states," against which each member was strongly bound to assist all of the others. This arrangement became typical of the later treaties, as Table 14.4 shows. The North Atlantic Treaty (NATO is the North Atlantic Treaty Organization) was next, with quite similar terms, in April of 1949. The ANZUS Treaty of September 1951, between Australia, New Zealand, and the U.S., committed the United States to the defense of one corner of the Pacific. Three years later, the Southeast Asia Treaty (SEATO is the abbreviation for the treaty organization) committed the United States to mutual defense of a still larger corner of Asia, along with countries in that area or countries that had overwhelmingly strong interests in the area.

Table 14.5 is a list of bilateral treaties between the United States and one other country. These were formed directly and self-consciously as a supplement to collective security treaties (multilateral treaties). They were made mostly during the same decade, a period characterized by some experts as one of "pactomania."[31] For various political and strategic reasons these arrangements for bilateral treaties included countries that were not fated to become members of multilateral United States treaties.

Each of these treaties helped fill out a portion of the perimeter around the Soviet Union and China, giving physical expression to the theory of containment. If the Central Treaty Organization (CENTO), of which the United States is a strong supporter but not a signatory power, is included, the line of containment established by these treaties extends from Europe through the Middle East, around the underbelly of Asia from Pakistan to Thailand, and upwards through the Philippines, Japan, and Korea.[32]

Having accepted the presence of an "iron curtain" around the Soviet sphere of influence, the United States proceeded to materialize that curtain by encompassing it with a chain. This tended to confirm the Soviet view, first enunciated by Stalin, that the country was being encircled by the capitalists. Our alliance pattern, coupled with their point of view and their eventual alliance pattern against ours (the Warsaw Pact), led to a situation during the 1950s and 1960s when the two major powers were almost literally encircling one another.

[31]Hammond, *The Cold War Years*, p. 67.

[32]CENTO was promoted by the United States, but objections from certain nonsignatory Middle Eastern countries, most particularly Egypt, convinced the U.S. that it was better not to be a member. However, our support was known to everyone, and we depended on the joint membership of Pakistan in SEATO and CENTO to link CENTO to all of the other multilateral and bilateral alliances that made up what we thought was our strong chain of containment.

Table 14.4

Treaty	Date Signed	Treaty Terms	Members	
Rio Treaty[1]	September 2, 1947	An armed attack against any American State "shall be considered as an attack against all the American States," and each one "undertakes to assist in meeting the attack."	Argentina Bolivia Brazil Chile Colombia Costa Rica Cuba[2] Dominican Republic Ecuador El Salvador	Guatemala Haiti Honduras Mexico Nicaragua Panama Paraguay Peru United States Uruguay Venezuela

North Atlantic Treaty[3]	April 4, 1949	"The parties agree that an armed attack against one or more of them in Europe or North America shall be considered an attack against them all"; and each party "will assist the . . . attacked by taking forthwith, individually and in concert with the other parties, such action as it deems necessary including the use of armed force."	Belgium
			Canada
			Denmark
			Federal
			  Republic
			  of Germany[4]
			France[5]
			Great
			  Britain
				Greece[6]
				Iceland
				Luxembourg
				Netherlands
				Norway
				Portugal
				Turkey[6]
				United States

ANZUS Treaty[7]	September 1, 1951	Each party recognizes that "an armed attack in the Pacific Area on any of the parties would be dangerous to its own peace and safety," and each party agrees that it will act "to meet the common danger in accordance with its own constitutional processes."	Australia New Zealand United States	
Southeast Asia Treaty[8]	September 8, 1954	Each party "recognizes that aggression by means of armed attack in the treaty area against any of the parties . . . would endanger its own peace and safety," and each will "in that event act to meet the common danger in accordance with its own constitutional processes."	Australia France Great Britain New Zealand Pakistan Philippines Thailand United States	

From Paul Y. Hammond, *The Cold War Years: American Foreign Policy since 1945* (New York: Harcourt, Brace, & World, 1969), p. 256.
[1]The Organization of American States, called for by the Rio Treaty, was established in April 1948.
[2]Suspended from the OAS in 1962.
[3]The North Atlantic Treaty Organization (NATO) was established in September 1950.
[4]Joined in 1954.
[5]Withdrew forces by 1967 but remains a NATO member.
[6]Joined in 1951.
[7]This abbreviation is made up of the first letters of the names of the member nations.
[8]The Southeast Asia Treaty Organization (SEATO) was established in September 1954.

Since in all mutual defense arrangements credibility is the key, the United States sought credibility by mutual promises to consider an attack on one country tantamount to an attack on the United States as well as on all other member countries. Credibility is strongest in treaties where the contingent action is automatic, as is

Table 14.5 — Collective Security—Bilateral Treaties between the U.S. and Individual Nations

Treaty	Date Signed	Treaty Terms	Members
Philippine Treaty	August 30, 1951	Each party recognizes that an "armed attack in the Pacific Area on either of the parties would be dangerous to its own peace and safety," and each party agrees that it will act "to meet the common dangers in accordance with its constitutional processes."	Philippines United States
Republic of Korea Treaty	October 1, 1953	Each party recognizes that "an armed attack in the Pacific Area on either of the parties . . . would be dangerous to its own peace and safety," and each party agrees to "act to meet the common danger in accordance with its constitutional processes."	Republic of Korea United States
Republic of China Treaty	December 2, 1954	Each party recognizes that "an armed attack in the West Pacific Area directed against the territories of either of the parties would be dangerous to its own peace and safety" and that each would "act to meet the common danger in accordance with its constitutional processes. (The territory of the Republic of China is defined as "Taiwan and the Pescadores.")	Republic of China United States
Japanese Treaty*	January 19, 1960	Each party recognizes that "an armed attack against either party in the territories under the administration of Japan would be dangerous to its own peace and safety," and each party would "act to meet the common danger in accordance with its own constitutional provisions and processes."	Japan United States

From Paul Y. Hammond, *The Cold War Years: American Foreign Policy since 1945* (New York: Harcourt, Brace, & World, 1969), p. 256.
*Replaced the bilateral security treaty of 1951.

almost the case with NATO. Credibility probably shades off as the treaty arrangement provides a member country with the opportunity to exercise discretion over its decision to respond to an attack—for example, "in accordance with its constitutional processes," as in the case of the ANZUS Treaty. Yet regardless of the wording of a treaty, there will always be a credibility problem.

Long-term treaties, such as those included in Tables 14.4 and 14.5, do provide the United States with a certain advantage inasmuch as they may tend to improve relations among member countries. This in turn may contribute to the credibility of the mutual defense treaty. Relationships may be further improved to the extent that each treaty provides for a treaty organization,

Maintaining the Right to Conquer: The Foreign Policies of One Sovereignty in a Predatory World of Sovereignties

sometimes called an infrastructure, of military and civilian bureaucracies. NATO is so far advanced along this line that military troops of the different countries are stationed on the soil of some of the member countries. War games are engaged in, and all kinds of information may be exchanged in a way that improves the military technology of each country and reduces uncertainty about its international motivations.

Although all of this helps, the credibility of our mutual defense linkages seems always to have fallen short of what our policy makers would consider satisfactory. One inherent shortcoming of mutual defense alliances is the ambiguity of the threat against which the member nations have united. What kind of aggression is sufficient to activate the treaty? Is the discovery of subversion sufficient aggression? Is outright sabotage, such as an Arab terrorist attack on a passenger plane owned by one of the member nations, a sufficient aggression? Is the occupation of a nonmember neighbor state, such as the Soviet occupation of Czechoslovakia in 1968, a sufficient aggression against NATO? Or does the treaty require a direct and unambiguous armed attack upon one of the member countries?

In the past, when we have considered aggressive actions sufficient to activate a treaty, we have tended to spend a great deal of time and money convincing member nations that the aggression was sufficient. For example, we paid a very handsome price (some would call it a ransom) to Korea, Australia, and the Philippines to induce them to define the Vietnam conflict as an aggression sufficient to activate mutual defense treaties. This suggests still another reason why our defense alliances have fallen short of satisfactory credibility. Our alliances tend to be one-sided, something the United States seems to want more than the member nations. Indeed, we are a producer rather than a consumer of security.[33] We have occasionally tried to deny this, but the lurking suspicion is that, although we would automatically act if France were attacked by the Soviet Union or a Warsaw Pact nation, France would be very slow to join us if we reported an attack on Alaska or Puerto Rico.[34]

This is not to say that the alliance system has been useless. Each

---

[33]Quester, *The Continuing Problem of International Politics*, p. 229.

[34]In the summer of 1975, Turkey was threatening to shut American bases unless Congress removed its ban on arms shipments imposed after Turkey's invasion of Cyprus, and West Germany was complaining about having to help finance American troops stationed in their country as part of the NATO alliance. Secretary of State Kissinger lectured the allies of the United States about the fact that they were not "doing us a favor by remaining in alliance with us. . . . No ally can pressure us by threat of termination; we will not accept that its security is more important to us than itself." *(New York Times, June 29, 1975, sec. 4, p. 2).* However, this need to remind our allies of their own interests is an indication of the different intensities the members feel toward the commitments they have made to the alliances. There may be even greater credibility problems in the future. On September 24, 1975, the foreign ministers of SEATO voted to phase out the organization "in view of the changing circumstances" in the region—meaning the end of the war in Indochina (*New York Times*, September 25, 1975, p. 22).

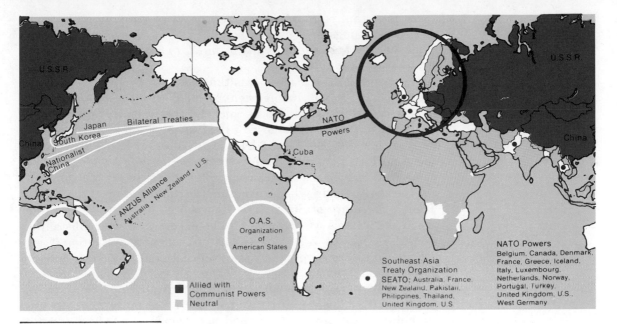

Allied with Communist Powers
Neutral

NATO Powers
Belgium, Canada, Denmark, France, Greece, Iceland, Italy, Luxembourg, Netherlands, Norway, Portugal, Turkey, United Kingdom, U.S., West Germany

Southeast Asia Treaty Organization SEATO: Australia, France, New Zealand, Pakistan, Philippines, Thailand, United Kingdom, U.S.

O.A.S. Organization of American States

ANZUS Alliance Australia · New Zealand · U.S.

Bilateral Treaties

NATO Powers

Japan
South Korea
China
Nationalist China
Cuba
U.S.S.R.
China

**Figure 14.1
The world of U.S. collective security in the 1970s**

alliance has had some credibility; each has been something more than a useless instrument of United States foreign policy. Even the weaker alliances have provided an umbrella of justification for direct United States intervention; that is to say, if the alliance had not existed, certain instances of U.S. intervention would have been much more difficult to justify. The alliance system may also have helped detain the proliferation of nuclear capacity. Without these alliances, Japan and Germany would almost certainly have sought to develop their strategic nuclear weapons capacity. This would have put pressure on other countries, such as the Soviet Union and China, to devote greater amounts of their resources and technology to nuclear weaponry.

There is still the lurking question as to whether the advantages have been worth the price.[35] Most member nations would probably not have developed nuclear capacity anyway; and even if the alliances help delay nuclear development in some of the stronger countries, delay and prevention are two very different things. Arguments can be made either way, but the fact remains that the alliance system has never been considered adequate even by the

Maintaining the Right to Conquer: The Foreign Policies of One Sovereignty in a Predatory World of Sovereignties

[35]For a good discussion of our alliance system and the need to reassess most alliances, see Paul Warnke, "Should We Reassess Old Alliances?" *Center Magazine,* November/December 1973.

most important policy makers. The answer of the United States to the shortcomings of alliances has been *to build a capacity in the United States to act unilaterally by military means inside or outside an alliance umbrella.*

The original hope of 1947 was that our world influence could be exercised by economic involvement alone. That was a vain hope, and it was probably recognized as such by many policy leaders who voiced it; indeed, they followed the Marshall Plan almost immediately with a plan for mutual defense alliances. This, too, was sold to the American public as though treaty obligations would be sufficient unto themselves to make our influence for peace felt throughout the world. During the hearings on the confirmation of the NATO Treaty, Secretary of State Dean Acheson assured the Senate that the United States was not going to be expected to send substantial numbers of troops to Europe as part of the treaty obligation.[36]

Secretary Acheson probably knew at that point that he was lying to the Senate; but his assurances were accepted by many who had yearned for world involvement without expanding our military presence. That was in 1949, and by 1951 Secretary Acheson was explaining that, although we had not been "expected to" commit troops (as he had assured the Senate in 1949), this did not mean we had not "intended to" send them. His testimony was accompanied by a brief statement that the president, as commander-in-chief, needed no congressional authority for committing the troops.[37]

Eventually the Senate came to realize that *entanglement in world affairs necessitates military preparedness.* The more powerful the nation, the greater the proportion of its gross national product that must go to peacetime military expenditure. As with the rich and their bodyguards, if the country can afford an army, it will probably need one. And the army that it will need will almost always be slightly more expensive than the army it can afford. In sum, collective security will not hold much promise as a meaningful instrument of foreign policy unless it is associated with a large military establishment.

The military establishment as an instrument of foreign policy
The professional military man has traditionally chafed at the idea that he is an instrument of politics. In the United States, "keeping the military out of politics" meant not only self-restraint on the part of the military in domestic politics but also equal self-restraint by civilian politicians dabbling in military affairs. American involve-

---

[36]U.S., Congress, Senate, Committee on Foreign Relations, *Assignment of Ground Forces of the United States to Duty in the European Area: Hearings on S. Con. Res. 8,* 82nd Cong., 1st sess., 1951, p. 111.
[37]Ibid.

The military basis of
foreign policy: Appeals
for manpower, 1860 and
1917.

MEN WANTED FOR CAVALRY.

The undersigned having been appointed to raise a Company of Cavalry for the war, calls upon the young men to come forward and volunteer for that purpose.

$100 BOUNTY

will be paid to each man as soon as mustered into service; plenty to eat and good clothes will be furnished by the Government.
Men who come and bring their horses will be paid **24** dollars per month. Those who have good shot guns can get a good price for them.
JOHN A. WREN.
Volunteers will for the present address me at Greensboro, N. C.

I WANT YOU FOR U.S. ARMY
NEAREST RECRUITING STATION

ment in world affairs drastically altered that balance; just as it was inevitable that world affairs would come to mean military commitment, so military commitment would eventually play a major role in determining the political point of view. Over the years, the military professionals have tended to adjust themselves to this kind of relationship.[38]

We have already gone about half the distance toward understanding the military establishment as an instrument of foreign policy by simply studying its size, structure, and outlook (see chapter 12). But that is only the static aspect, the Maginot Line of the military in modern international affairs. The military must have a dynamic aspect if it is to remain credible as an instrument of foreign policy relevant to the problems at hand. For our purposes of analysis, we shall call this dynamic element research and development.

Research and development (R and D), rather than the emotionally charged term *the arms race,* provides just the proper connotation, because the effort to maintain a credible military force is very largely a technological effort. Between the 1860s and the 1940s, military capacity was measured largely in terms of the relative size of each national armed force, coupled with the ability of each general staff to mobilize the total population quickly enough to meet

*Maintaining the Right to
Conquer: The Foreign
Policies of One Sovereignty
in a Predatory World of
Sovereignties*

[38]See footnote citations on civil-military relations in chapter 12. Perhaps the best starting point for an inquiry into the adjustment of military professionals to the political point of view is Morris Janowitz, *The Professional Soldier* (Glencoe, Ill.: Free Press, 1960). For an effective fictionalized account of the realization that limited wars are fought for political, not military, goals, see S. L. A. Marshall, *Pork Chop Hill* (New York: Morrow, 1956).

any hot war. This was the age of democratic armies and mass ground warfare.[39]

Technology was, of course, always important, even in the era of mass, democratic armies. For example, the invention of the stirrup, making possible the use of cavalry, was of immense importance in the development of Chinese history.[40] Technological superiority may have often made the difference in the outcome of wars before World War II. However, it was probably not until World War II and afterward that technology became the key feature in the dynamics of maintaining military credibility as a political instrument. The most important factors back of the switch to contemporary stress on technology were most likely the emergence of nuclear weaponry, missile delivery technology, and the computer. In terms of strategic planning and budgetary decisions, the technological tail began to wag the military dog.

The history of defense expenditures (Table 14.6) is accurate in showing a steady growth, except for a brief period just prior to Vietnam. It is not altogether accurate in absolute amounts, however. In the first place, totals depend on how one accounts for defense-related appropriations in other departments. More important, for the most recent years the table does not account well for supplemental appropriations voted by Congress months after a budget was adopted. For instance, the actual expenditures for 1974 were at least $2 billion over the estimates without even counting carefully the defense-related expenditures by all civilian departments. Even the revised *estimates* for 1975 raised the figure to $90 billion, and that does not allow for the inevitable supplemental actions Congress will have to take in the spring of 1976, when defense officials return, hat in hand, with stories about inflation, new Russian discoveries, and "cost overrides" on a new craft or weapon. All things considered, the total defense budget will surpass $100 billion during or not long after 1976.

Up to a point it is also accurate to show, as does Table 14.6, that defense expenditure has declined slightly as a proportion of the gross national product. But that is also misleading to the extent that it suggests some kind of defense deemphasis. Military production has probably gone up steadily as a proportion of all domestic production. Moreover, we should note the enormous significance of defense contracts to the twenty largest industrial companies in the United States (see Table 14.6).

---

[39]On the importance of manpower to the war policies of the nineteenth century democracies, see Elliot J. Feldman, "An Illusion of Power" (Ph.D. diss., Massachusetts Institute of Technology, 1972).

[40]H. G. Creel, "The Role of the Horse in Chinese History," *American Historical Review* 70 (1965), 647–672. For an argument that the chariot was not as important a piece of military technology as modern mythology would have it, see Creel, *The Origins of Statecraft in China*, vol. 1 (Chicago: University of Chicago Press, 1970), chapter 10.

Table 14.6			Defense Expenditures, 1960–1975

Year	Defense Budget (in Billions)	Defense as Percent of GNP
1960	$44.9	8.9
1961	$47.8	9.2
1962	$51.6	9.2
1963	$50.8	8.6
1964	$50.0	7.9
1965	$50.1	7.3
1966	$60.7	8.1
1967	$72.4	9.1
1968	$78.0	9.0
1969	$78.8	8.5
1970	$75.1	7.8
1971	$71.4	6.8
1972	$78.3	7.1
1973	$76.1	6.2
1974	$80.0 (est.)	
1975	$85.8 (est.)	

Data from *Economic Report of the President* (Washington, D.C.: Government Printing Office, annual); *Associated Press Almanac* (New York: Almanac Publishing, 1973), p. 620. Figures include the Defense Department, military assistance, atomic energy, and defense-related activities of civilian agencies.

Military production has also been given a post-Vietnam boost by a dramatic increase in military sales to the Middle Eastern countries. The great upsurge began in 1973, at the time of the formation of OPEC, the oil cartel, with an Iranian contract to buy $2 billion of U.S. weapons, planes, and helicopters. This was termed the largest single arms deal ever negotiated by the Pentagon, but it was followed by many other deals from 1973 to 1975. These sales are significant in the economic sense that they shore up our defense industry and they help our balance of trade. But the sales are also significant in that they use the military as an instrument of foreign policy. In brief, "the more advanced and expensive the weapons traded, the more dependent the buyer becomes [on the U.S.]."[41]

Table 14.7 is also indicative of the scale of the research and development aspect of military expenditures. Most of these expenditures involved contracts to produce a particular piece of hardware for one of the military services. But an indeterminate portion of the expenditure on each of these contracts went toward the actual

Maintaining the Right to Conquer: The Foreign Policies of One Sovereignty in a Predatory World of Sovereignties

[41]Michael J. Klare, "The Political Economy of Arms Sales," *TransAction*, September/October 1974.

Table 14.7 — The Value of U.S. Defense Contracts—The Top Twenty Companies, 1963–1971

Company	Total 1963–1971
Lockheed Aircraft	$15,302,000,000
General Dynamics	12,321,000,000
General Electric	10,365,000,000
McDonnell Douglas	10,324,000,000
United Aircraft	7,948,000,000
Boeing	7,752,000,000
American Telephone and Telegraph	6,696,000,000
North American Rockwell	6,564,000,000
Grumman	4,755,000,000
Ling-Temco-Vaught	4,440,000,000
General Motors	4,030,000,000
Sperry-Rand	3,721,000,000
Raytheon	3,444,000,000
Hughes	3,373,000,000
Martin-Marietta	3,282,000,000
AVCO	3,219,000,000
Westinghouse	3,158,000,000
Ford (Philco)	2,396,000,000
Textron	2,850,000,000
General Tire	2,623,000,000

research and development of the hardware. These companies were awarded contracts very largely in terms of their ability and reputation for inventing new hardware according to the abstractly defined needs of one of the services. Some of this activity may be in the explicit R and D budget, but it is extremely difficult in every instance to determine just where the development ends and the manufacturing and delivery begins.

Why so much pressure to grow and to innovate in the military field? Why is there a technological imperative, or an arms race? Former Secretary of Defense Robert McNamara probably answered for every high-ranking American foreign policy and defense official of the past generation when he proposed that "the cornerstone of our strategic policy continues to be to deter deliberate nuclear attack upon the United States or its allies . . . by *assured-destruction capability.*"[42] (Italics in the original.)

But where is the point of assurance when each of the two major

---

[42]From the memoirs of Robert McNamara, *The Essence of Security: Reflections in Office* (New York: Harper & Row, 1968), p. 52.

powers possesses ten to twenty times overkill capacity? Overkill is calculated by taking the number of megatons of nuclear destructive capacity in the arsenal of a country, calculating the amount of that megatonnage that would probably be left after an enemy attacked and tried to knock it out (this is called second strike capacity), and then dividing that remaining megatonnage by the number of inhabitants in the enemy country. Even after allowing for a certain proportion of misfired missiles, and for the successful defense by the other side against some of the oncoming missiles, the remaining second strike capacity must be capable of eradicating the other country. Our second strike capacity is capable of eradicating the Soviet Union or any other countries several times over. This is overkill.[43] But somehow an overkill factor of ten, or twenty, is not enough. The most probable position is that nothing is enough.

Why is nothing enough? One plausible answer is that there is a kind of ratchet effect to technological commitment. The argument would be that although it takes only a small sum to get a piece of technological research or testing under way, it becomes very difficult to let go of it once the development begins to show promise. At some point along the line there may be a decision, either by the scientists or by the politicians, that any price may be worth the payoff. The ratchet effect of upward flexibility and downward inflexibility in budget decisions is produced by the fear that cutting a promising project is a tremendous political liability. Research on a project such as the nuclear submarine of the Trident class mushroomed from a few million dollars to $13 billion. It would be virtually impossible to do a thorough cost accounting on the research aspects of the multiple warhead missiles (MIRV).

But that kind of explanation is woefully incomplete. After all, the Skybolt program was terminated after a significant investment. The project to develop the Supersonic Transport (SST) was also scratched. The decision to stop a research project is not all that much more difficult than any other decision on strategic issues. There has to be some additional dynamic force behind the ratchet effect that impels us to generate more and more money for present and future military items.

It seems to me that the explanation has to be found in the problem of maintaining *credibility* in a situation where the nuclear balance between the United States and the Soviet Union is extremely close and the probability of actually using any of the weapons is extremely low. If it is assumed that all nations are predators, then nuclear parity between the United States and the Soviet Union also opens up opportunities for each to pursue its lesser goals while stopping

Maintaining the Right to Conquer: The Foreign Policies of One Sovereignty in a Predatory World of Sovereignties

[43]A very accessible treatment of these calculations will be found in Adam Yarmolinsky, *The Military Establishment* (New York: Harper & Row, 1971), p. 101.

each other short of ultimate aggression. In this context, credibility means everything.

But why assume that all nations are predators? Here again is Robert McNamara's response:

> In 1961 when I became Secretary of Defense, the Soviet Union had a very small operational arsenal of intercontinental missiles. However, it did possess the technological and industrial capacity to enlarge that arsenal very substantially over the succeeding several years. We had no evidence that the Soviets did plan, in fact, fully to use that capability. But . . . a strategic planner must be conservative in his calculations; that is, *he must prepare for the worst plausible case and not be content to hope and prepare merely for the most probable.*[44] (Italics added.)

In this passage, McNamara was probably speaking once again for virtually every Republican and Democratic foreign policy maker of the 1950s and 1960s.

By the time he wrote the following observation, in 1970, he was expressing some misgivings. The above passage continues as follows:

> Thus, in the course of hedging against what was then only a theoretically possible Soviet build-up, we took decisions which have resulted in our current superiority in numbers of warheads and deliverable megatons. But the blunt fact remains that if we had had more accurate information about planned Soviet strategic forces, we simply would not have needed to build as large a nuclear arsenal as we have today.[45]

Many policy makers may have the same misgivings after they are out of office; but during their incumbency they seem impelled to make their decisions on the assumption of the worst case. Theoreticians in the field of international relations compare this arms race mentality, or its source, to the "prisoner's dilemma." In this situation, two vagrants are arrested by an unscrupulous sheriff on false burglary charges. The two are held in separate prison cells, and the sheriff attempts to extract confessions from each. Here are the alternatives he lays out for each prisoner:

1. If you confess your part in the burglary and that of the other prisoner, and if he does not confess meanwhile, he will get ten years and you will go free.

2. If you plead innocence but the other prisoner says you did it, you will get ten years and he will go free.

3. If both of you confess, each will get a slightly lighter sentence of six years.

---

[44]McNamara, *The Essence of Security*, pp. 57–58.
[45]Ibid, p. 58.

4. If both of you insist upon your innocence, you will get very light sentences of one year.

Since the prisoners are not allowed to communicate with each other, each must make his decision on the basis of his assumption about what the other prisoner will do. According to most students of the "prisoner's dilemma," each prisoner turns out to be better off confessing, no matter what the other prisoner does, and despite the fact that an absolutely honest approach to their real innocence would have gotten both of them off with a one-year sentence.[46]

Robert McNamara's confession reveals quite clearly that American policy makers tend to operate on the basis of the "prisoner's dilemma," despite the fact that nation-state prisoners on this earth have a good deal more information about each other than the prisoners in the story. But since there is always uncertainty, we have traditionally led ourselves to assume the worst—that any country with the capability also has the willingness. No longer can we merely say, "If we can afford an army, we must have one"; in the past generation we have gone even further to say, "If *they* have something, *we* must have it too." One of America's wisest political figures, Adlai Stevenson, when a candidate for president in 1956, asserted that "the answer lies in Moscow." Lesser minds in foreign affairs seem to espouse this view, and as long as our answer lies in Moscow, and Moscow's answer lies in Washington, we have the basis for an endlessly accelerating whirligig of credibility rites.

The United States and the Soviet Union are constantly trying to ease the pressure on military growth and development. Both countries seem seriously committed to the development of a Strategic Arms Limitation Treaty (SALT). However, even as this progresses, the credibility problem continues to make the nuclear calculus extremely sensitive—to words as well as to actual developments.

One of the most recent case studies in this sensitivity and instability of nuclear parity is the announcement by Secretary of Defense James Schlesinger in February of 1974 that the United States was considering a change in "targeting doctrine" for nuclear missiles. Technically called a "counterforce strategy," it involves changing the aim of some American missiles away from cities and other "soft targets" toward the actual land-based launching pads or silos which house the Soviet missiles. The change appears attractive because it implies a shift away from the terrifying business of threatening millions of people in a single city with a single bomb.

But the attractiveness is only superficial. In the first place, our ability to destroy Soviet launching sites would seriously reduce the

[46]See Quester, *The Continuing Problem of International Politics*, pp. 3–6. For games and strategies generally, see T. C. Schelling, *The Strategy of Conflict* (New York: Oxford University Press, 1960).

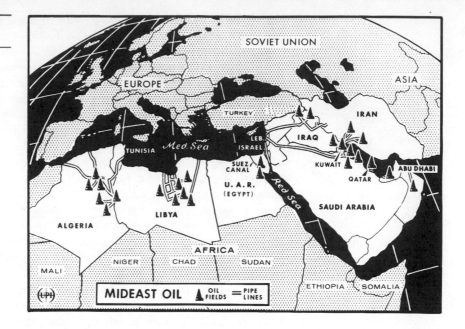

MIDEAST OIL ▲ OIL FIELDS = PIPE LINES

credibility of *their* nuclear capacity. Even though a first strike by the United States against Soviet land-based sites could never disarm the Soviet Union as long as it had submarine bases, the Soviet Union would not be able to tolerate vulnerable land-based sites. Thus, a decision by the United States, even as only proposed by Secretary Schlesinger, could set off a tremendous Soviet drive to develop a defense against our potential counterforce.

In the second place, if we developed this new capability to aim our nuclear force toward the bombs rather than toward the people, we would then have the capability of engaging in limited nuclear war by using nuclear weapons in a "surgical" or "precision" attack. This would increase the likelihood of limited nuclear war and directly reduce the security of the Soviet Union.

Assuming a Soviet reaction to any such move on our part, this would mean that our credibility might go up a bit in the short run but that our security would go down. Since the United States probably already has the technical capacity to aim its missiles toward the silos and away from the cities, it would take a very small initial investment to gain counterforce capacity. But this in turn would lead the Russians to greater efforts in military research and development and to greater intransigence in the SALT talks. All of this suggests how easy it is to affect world psychology.[47]

---

[47] A very good analysis of this case was reported in John C. Baker and Robert P. Berman, "Counter-Force Strategy and U.S. Defense," *International Herald Tribune*, February 26, 1974. My analysis follows theirs.

As of 1975, there are no signs that this upwardly spiraling tendency is weakening. One full decade before 1984, a year made significant by George Orwell's novel, we already hear Orwellianisms such as "billions for defense but not enough for security" and "arms spending lags while soaring."[48]

People of good will continue their efforts to make marginal improvements in international relations, leading toward a breaking of the upward spiral in arms development. A switch from the Holy Alliance orientation toward a balance of power role could improve the international environment by giving major powers more room for maneuver. Relaxation of relationships between the United States and China could go far to improve diplomacy and to deemphasize the great need for maintaining military credibility. Even such little improvements as the Hot Line between the White House and the Kremlin may have helped a bit, inasmuch as the prisoner nations are able to impart to each other a bit more information about their dilemmas. Perhaps it might help further if some of the families of the elites in the United States and the Soviet Union made exchange visits for months at a time to live as hostages in the major cities or near the major missile silos.

But all efforts are probably doomed to marginality. It is difficult to imagine a time in the near future when military preparedness and innovation will disappear as a key instrument of foreign policy. Even as collective security alliance systems weaken, as surely they must, the military instrument remains strong. Even as balance of power politics expands, as it probably will, the military instrument will remain vital, if only as a continuing means of stalemating the two major powers in order to allow for balance of power politics. And the problems for American democracy will continue accordingly.

For a while after the Vietnam War, the rejection of the military draft in favor of a professional army was seen as some kind of an answer. But alas, the switch to a professional army was more expensive. (In 1973, manpower counted for 56 percent of the Defense Budget, as against 43 percent in 1964.) More to the point, professionalization of the armed forces could prove to be a greater danger than military conscription of civilians. If the military ever becomes fully professionalized, we may face the problem of how to civilianize it or otherwise keep it from becoming a separate social class or hierarchy in our society.

There is at least one other sign that we have institutionalized ourselves for at least another generation of commitment to military

---

Maintaining the Right to Conquer: The Foreign Policies of One Sovereignty in a Predatory World of Sovereignties

[48]The first of these quotes is the title of an article by former Secretary of Defense Clark Clifford after his 1969 retirement from office and his almost complete disenchantment with America's involvement in the Vietnam War (*New York Times,* July 2, 1972, sec. 4, p. 9). The second comes from a title of a syndicated article by journalists Rowland Evans and Robert Novak, *International Herald Tribune,* January 7, 1974.

credibility; science itself has become an instrument of foreign policy. Probably since Sputnik in 1957, manpower discussions have been more likely to be about the number of scientists and engineers than about the number of soldiers. The number of scientists and engineers in our country has actually become a matter of public policy.

For example, in its February 11, 1974, cover story on Secretary of Defense Schlesinger, *Time* reported rather gravely on the "research gap." According to *Time*'s sources, the Soviet Union will "pull ahead, both in terms of strategic and conventional forces," unless we loosen the purse strings on research. One measure of the research gap used in this article was apparently the difference in manpower. For example, according to *Time,* in 1960 the Soviet Union had 225,000 research scientists and engineers, and the U.S. had 400,000. As of 1974, the Soviet Union reportedly had 625,000 and the U.S. 550,000. No reference was made in the article to the extraordinarily large number of unemployed or underemployed research scientists and engineers in the United States. What is relevant to *Time,* and probably to most policy makers, is the existence of science manpower as a "resource"—and the maintenance and expansion of this resource as a producer of military innovations and a symbol of American power.

It would seem that when a country engages in world politics on a large scale, it has to make a number of adjustments in its domestic institutions. These adjustments are not altogether consistent with American tradition or its self-image of democracy—precisely because they are consistent with conquest. Maintenance of sovereignty in the eyes of other nation-states requires regular proof of ability to defend that sovereignty. This in turn requires regular reinforcement of internal conquest in order to be able to operate with maximum flexibility in the outside world.

There seems to be no escape, especially for a major power. Sovereignty *will* be defended, and that may involve going to the defense of the sovereignties of other weaker powers. It is highly probable under the circumstances that every available technology will be considered for its ability to improve the defense of sovereignty. Perhaps the only check against this primordial urge to defend sovereignty is awareness that there are better and worse ways of adjusting domestic institutions to it. But that leaves open one of the most profound questions—whether mass democracies are capable of mature and deliberate calculation.

Propaganda as an instrument of foreign policy Nation-states have given propaganda a bad name. As with bureaucracy, propaganda has an objective definition, referring to a body of doctrine or ideas that someone *propagates* in order to convince others of the virtue of that position. (Since the seventeenth century the Roman

Table 14.8

U.S. Government Propaganda Agencies—A Selection

United States Information Agency (USIA)
    Voice of America
    Publication programs
    Movie service
    Liaison with State and other departments

State Department
    Cultural exchange program
    Information and political officers in each mission

Central Intelligence Agency (CIA)

White House
    Director of communications
    Office of telecommunications
    Press secretary

Department of Defense
    Assistant secretary for international security affairs
    Military missions and attachés at embassies

Agency for International Development (AID)

Departments of Treasury, Agriculture, Labor, Commerce, Armed Services
    Each has at least one bureau of information and other agencies to present
    American point of view to international gatherings

Catholic church has had its College of Propaganda, whose purpose it is to oversee foreign missions in regard to their propagation of Christian doctrine.) Once propaganda becomes part of a struggle for power, there is an overwhelming tendency to abuse it by making false claims, using false logic, or making false statements about alternative ideas. No country has a clean record in this respect, but the record of the U.S. seems particularly poor when compared to our *own* commitment to truth and our *own* denunciation of closed societies.

The importance of propaganda to United States foreign policy can be appreciated quite concretely by pondering the number of agencies whose mission is the propagation of the American faith. Table 14.8 is a list of only the important agencies. It is not intended to be exhaustive but rather to give a general impression of the significance of the propaganda instrument.

Probably only one agency on the list is dedicated entirely to propaganda. This is the United States Information Agency (USIA). It attaches one or more skilled persons to the major embassies throughout the world and also has missions of its own in many of the major cities. For example, one of the more active USIA installations is in Bologna, Italy, which happens also to be a city run by the Italian Communist Party. The best known activity of the USIA is the Voice of America, and one of its virtues is that it runs a very large number of interesting and useful programs that are only loosely tied to an official message. It is reassuring to find occasional-

Maintaining the Right to Conquer: The Foreign Policies of One Sovereignty in a Predatory World of Sovereignties

ly an agency which considers that the best propaganda may be conveyed by a good example.

The State Department is itself an agent of propaganda, although the precise importance of this activity is hard to measure. Its various embassies and consulates facilitate the work of the USIA and other propaganda activities, including those of the military attachés. But its own information and political officers are as skilled as the USIA officers at public relations.

The Central Intelligence Agency (CIA) has as its primary mission the collection and evaluation of information produced in other countries. However, the CIA's function in the dissemination of American propaganda is probably very considerable. We get some sense of its importance when "the cover is blown" on a CIA agent or activity. For example, the first major CIA embarrassment was not Watergate but the discovery during the mid-1960s that it was subsidizing several respectable American organizations, such as the National Students Association. This organization had been subsidized for many years by the CIA in order to carry out a program of attendance at international student meetings, supposedly to provide a response to Communist propaganda. At the same time the public learned that certain commercial and university publishers were receiving subsidies to encourage the publication of books that the CIA decided would be effective when distributed abroad through USIA libraries.

It goes almost without saying that the White House and the Department of Defense engage in all sorts of propaganda activities. Every statement made by the president is carefully designed for symbolic value, especially with regard to its international impact. President Kennedy was probably most self-conscious of the international value of what presidents say. President Nixon, being aware of the value of this activity and perhaps aware of his own shortcomings as a media figure, equipped the White House with an unusual capacity for planning and administering information for propaganda value. He not only had a press secretary and an assistant press secretary but also a director of communications, an office held by a man known to be skillful at communications planning.

The Department of Defense is one of several departments with responsibility for international propaganda activities of some sort. The Department of Labor has been particularly active in international affairs, and the Department of Agriculture has considerable propaganda value through its promulgation of new techniques in agriculture and new agricultural products. Our agents abroad are constantly conveying the message that American technological superiority is a result of our democratic and capitalistic system.

None of these activities should be considered insidious in themselves. But two problems arise which have given all propaganda activity a bad name. The first of these is the very simple and straightforward problem of lying. How often do we misrepresent our case and our cause abroad? How often do we suppress unhappy information about ourselves in order to make our image look rosier abroad? Any misrepresentation is too much. It has probably contributed to the general state of distrust in the world. More importantly, it tends to give other countries, especially the elites of other countries, the wrong information about our own intentions or about the seriousness of threats against the security of other countries.

A tragic example of our use of propaganda occurred in 1956, when Hungarian revolutionaries were encouraged by Voice of America propaganda to think that the United States would come to their aid in their attempt to overthrow the Stalinist regime. When their revolution did begin and we did nothing, the reaction against the United States was probably very bitter. It is difficult to judge the reactions of other countries to our propaganda, but the thought of its impact should, as in the Hungarian sitution, leave us uneasy. To what extent did American propaganda exacerbate the hatreds of non-Communist parties in Indonesia, hatreds which led to political assassinations on a massive scale in the 1960s? How often has anti-Soviet, anti-Chinese, and anti-Castro propaganda from the United States provided military groups with the justification for staging a coup d'etat in Latin America?

The second problem of propaganda is even more serious. This is the tendency of American officials to turn their foreign policy propaganda upon their own citizens. Whether or not American leaders are sincere in their beliefs, they often use their propaganda on American citizens in hopes of maintaining public support for current administration policies or for some particular international adventure. Sometimes this propaganda effort takes the form of suppressing information at home that is openly known outside of the United States.

Note the revelations from the Pentagon Papers. The war leaders in Washington had maintained to the bitter end that (1) the various guerrillas in South Vietnam (known as the Viet Cong) were puppets of the North Vietnamese and (2) Americans were bombing *only* those areas in North Vietnam that were related to the war effort. Most scholarship on Vietnam concludes that at least some of the indigenous opposition to the Thieu regime was bona fide and distinctly not an instrument of North Vietnam; and the Pentagon Papers revealed that B-52's were bombing all sorts of nonbelligerent sites in Vietnam as well as areas of Cambodia. Everyone seemed to know these things but the American people.

This tendency, which exists in peacetime as well as during war, has produced a two-part approach to domestic propaganda: (1) overselling the nature of the threat posed to the United States by some other country or some action that country proposes to take, and (2) overselling the value of the remedy available to solve the

Maintaining the Right to Conquer: The Foreign Policies of One Sovereignty in a Predatory World of Sovereignties

Public opinion and
foreign policy: Dissent
and support.

problem or to meet the threat.[49] One of the most effective jobs in overselling the threat was the argument, affirmed regularly, that every domestic disorder in any part of the world is tied to an international Communist conspiracy against the United States. This was related in turn to the overselling of the remedy, in effect, "If we beat them here, we have them beat all over the world."[50]

Thanks to the Pentagon Papers, the press, and the congressional hearings during the years 1971 to 1975, we know a lot more about American propagandizing than we ever did before. Whether such revelations and embarrassments will restrain future American leaders and agencies is another question, because the pressure on them to gain and maintain popular support will continue to be strong. Eventually, perhaps, the American people and their leaders will become more mature in their involvement in foreign affairs. As suggested before, one of the disadvantages of having been protected by the European countries during the nineteenth century was that American leaders were deprived of real experience in international affairs. When we emerged as the imperial power after World War II, we were simply green to the ways of diplomacy.

There are signs that the United States may be coming of age. The change of our official position toward mainland China is one indication of this. The slow but almost certain change in our position toward Cuba is another. These moves are still accompanied by occasional rattlings of the sabre, as, for example, the very intense American reaction toward the *Mayaguez* seizure by Cambodia. Nonetheless, there seems to be some development in the United States toward greater self-restraint, greater respect for the sovereignty of other nations, and greater tolerance for the ambiguities and disorders that are inevitably produced by a world of predatory sovereignties.

WAR, DIPLOMACY, AND THE PURPOSE OF FOREIGN POLICY

Many Americans consider diplomacy another instrument of foreign policy. But this point of view is simply one more expression of American immaturity in the conduct of international relations. Diplomacy is the fine hand of the state, employing all the instruments identified above, plus any others available. Foreign policy properly conducted should subordinate everything else to diplomacy, the purpose of which is to pursue national goals in a manner that makes as many gains as possible for one's own country without

[49]These patterns and other examples of them are discussed at length in Theodore Lowi, *The End of Liberalism* (New York: Norton, 1969), chapter 6.

[50]Ibid., pp. 174–181, where other examples of oversell are provided.

making these gains unacceptable to other countries. Clarity of goals
and ambiguity of results are the key to diplomacy. Since unambiguous defeat is unacceptable to other countries, unambiguous victory
is not an acceptable result of diplomacy.

The recent history of American diplomacy is part of an arduous
coming of age. Our history began with a tiny diplomatic corps made
up of intelligent dilettantes. As recently as the 1920s George
Kennan could still refer to the State Department as "a quaint old
place, with its law-office atmosphere."[51] Practically until World War
II, diplomacy was used as an instrument of domestic public opinion,
or as an instrument of corporations. Since World War II diplomacy
has become more professionalized and frequently is able to subordinate all interests and instruments to diplomatic methods and
purposes. However, as we shall see, diplomacy is still much too often
used as an instrument of the military, rather than vice versa. And

---

[51]George Kennan, *American Diplomacy, 1900–1945* (Chicago: University of Chicago Press,
1951), pp. 91–92. This work is a good starting point for the study of the history of diplomacy.
Kennan's original "Mr. X" article, "The Sources of Soviet Conduct," is reprinted in this volume,
p. 107. For a good brief treatment of the history of ambassadors and diplomacy, see Carl
Friedrich, *Constitutional Government and Democracy* (Boston: Ginn, 1950), pp. 78–84.

when that is not the case, there is a tendency to shunt diplomacy aside altogether.

As Kennan put it: "I see the most serious fault of our past policy formulation to lie in something that I might call the legalistic-moralistic approach to international problems. This approach runs like a red skein through our foreign policy of the last fifty years."[52] As illustrated by our collective security treaties, our attempt very often has been to obviate diplomacy by making international relationships automatic, so that they are self-regulating or, if that fails, they trigger off a full-scale war.[53]

A large part of the problem of conducting foreign policy in the United States is organizational, as discussed already in chapter 12. It is difficult to conduct foreign policy through a regular and professionalized diplomacy when foreign aid is administered outside the State Department (as it was until 1962), or when atomic energy is controlled in an independent agency outside both the State *and* the Defense Departments, or when the Defense Department and several other major departments are able to conduct their own brand of international affairs.

More recent ventures suggest that this pattern of proliferating independent foreign affairs agencies has not yet come to an end. For example, the United States sought the development of satellite communications with an agency independent not only of the State Department but of the government itself. The Communications Satellite Corporation (COMSAT) is a corporate board run mainly by representatives of large corporations in the communications business and responsible to the holders of the bonds and stocks sold by COMSAT to finance its operations. The permissive, almost nonexistent, policy toward the new multinational corporations is another example. Such corporations as International Telephone and Telegraph (ITT) and other international conglomerates operate virtually as international cartels free of any government or diplomatic controls. Each, in essence, has its own foreign policy, inasmuch as it must decide whether new governments are stable and worthy of new investments, how to deal with moves to nationalize property, and other problems on an international scale.[54]

A major part of the problem in all this is the tendency to define

---

[52]Kennan, *American Diplomacy, 1900–1945*, p. 95.

[53]Ibid., p. 101.

[54]For an important analysis of multinational corporations and their influence on foreign policy and defense, see Jonathan Galloway, "The Military-Industrial Linkages of U.S.-Based Multinational Corporations," *International Studies Quarterly*, December 1972, p. 491. Galloway observes, for example, that of the top 100 Department of Defense contractors in the fiscal year 1971, 39 were multinational corporations—defined as corporations which hold 25 percent or more of manufacturing enterprises located in six or more foreign countries. The interests of these multinational corporations are distinct from most other corporations, and they have a very distinct type of influence on American interests abroad. (See especially p. 503 of Galloway's article.)

Maintaining the Right to Conquer: The Foreign Policies of One Sovereignty in a Predatory World of Sovereignties

611

international political issues in military rather than diplomatic terms. The American attitudes toward the Soviet Union and containment, the need to have military backing for "legalistic-moralistic" arrangements, and the special interest of multinational and national corporations in maintaining defense sales have all combined to help subordinate diplomatic to military considerations, although it is probably true that the diplomatic side has slowly gained in strength over the years.

One instructive example of a military approach preferred over a diplomatic approach even when there is freedom of choice is that of the Dominican Republic in 1965. In December of 1962 a well-known member of the non-Marxist left, Juan Bosch, won the presidency of the Dominican Republic in the first valid election held in that republic for forty years. Within nine months, the Bosch regime was

The beginning, middle,
and end of the
post–World War II era of
American foreign policy.
Left: Iwo Jima. *This page:*
Korea and Vietnam.

*Maintaining the Right to
Conquer: The Foreign
Policies of One Sovereignty
in a Predatory World of
Sovereignties*

613

overthrown by a military coup d'etat. However, the military regime did not enjoy the firm support of the Dominican people, and within weeks a whole series of popular uprisings broke out, involving trade unions, workers, students, and others.

Nevertheless, during that period the Johnson administration extended economic and military support, as well as diplomatic support, to the military regime, on the basis of arguments made by that regime that military control and military suppression were necessary in order to avoid a Communist takeover. Yet, the military junta eventually did install its own civilian regime, which ruled with military support until April of 1965. At that point, a group of junior officers and former members of the Bosch regime attempted to stage a countercoup in the name of a return to constitutional rule under the election of 1962. Immediately the original military group resumed control and attempted to crush the countercoup. A reported two thousand Dominicans were killed, but the rebellion was not effectively ended.

At this point the military junta sought intervention from Washington, and their request was granted. The American ambassador reported that twenty-four hundred Americans needed protection. He also reported that there was danger of a "Communist takeover," and apparently to document his point he produced a CIA-compiled list of fifty-three Dominican Communists who were part of the rebellion. He also produced reports of horror stories regarding atrocities committed by the rebels. These so-called facts were widely reported in American newspapers.

On the basis of the reports, President Johnson dispatched over 500 marines on the aircraft carrier *Boxer*, and within two weeks of the original request, 32,000 marines, a flotilla of ships, and over 250 aircraft, artillery, and mobile machine-gun units followed to join in fighting against the rebels. The American generals boasted that the revolutionaries would be taken in two hours; but after three nights and two days of bitter fighting, the marines had advanced only two blocks and had managed to kill an estimated 3,000 to 4,000 Dominicans. It was estimated that some 12,000 Dominican rebels were in the sector under attack. These figures of the total number of rebels and the total number of estimated deaths stack up peculiarly against the CIA-based ambassador's report of 53 Communists.

Following the bitter fighting, there was a stalemate during which the Americans sought to play an intermediary role between the government and the rebels. The U.S. government paid the expenses of the civil servants and the military personnel on both sides. The peace discussions were conducted by a personal envoy of the president, not the ambassador. The first mission failed to accomplish the task, and the stalemate continued. This led to a U.S. effort to create an inter-American peace force made up of contingents from all of the Americas.

Under great financial pressure, plus the skillful guidance of presidential troubleshooter Averill Harriman, an international peace force was finally put together under the umbrella of the OAS. The stalemate persisted, however, and President Johnson dispatched still another team of presidential representatives, headed this time by Special Assistant for National Security Affairs McGeorge Bundy. This mission also failed, and there were five additional peace missions during the ensuing six weeks before a new regime was finally worked out.

This is a clear case in which diplomacy was the tool of the military, rather than the other way around. The presence of fifty-three Communists seems to have brought about an instantaneous and massive military response, and the military dominance was not displaced even after the first confrontations were over. It should be added that at no time did the U.S. Embassy try to check the figures or verify the sources for the atrocities or for reports on the number of Communists involved. Thus, not only was the proportion of Communist involvement tiny in relation to the total effort; there was no certainty that even this much actually had existed. (The American ambassador eventually blamed the American press for having reported the "unverified rumors" of atrocities, but all of these false figures and the hearsay information had already had their effect.)

Until the end of his days, President Johnson considered the role of the United States in the Dominican affair a triumph.[55] Johnson failed to recognize during or after the affair that the original report of fifty-three Communists, against which we sent a division of marines, had never been verified. He also failed to recognize that his action was very probably a violation of the charter of the OAS, which provides that no member country "has the right to intervene, directly or indirectly for any reason whatever, in the internal or external affairs of any other state." And he failed to realize that the American fear of Castro had displaced diplomacy with military action in this incident.[56]

An approach to world affairs that renders diplomacy an instrument of the military is dangerously neurotic. Certainly, the massive response of a modern army and a modern flotilla to a small rebellion in a tiny country is neurotic. But perhaps neurotic countries, as well as individuals, can be given therapy. The consequences of Vietnam may be a kind of therapy for the United States. There would probably be a therapeutic influence if our policy makers recognized

---

Maintaining the Right to Conquer: The Foreign Policies of One Sovereignty in a Predatory World of Sovereignties

[55]Lyndon B. Johnson, *The Vantage Point* (New York: Holt, Rinehart and Winston, 1971), pp. 187–205.

[56]Other sources on the Dominican action are Draper, "The Dominican Crisis," pp. 33–65; James M. Burns and Jack Peltason, *Government by the People* (Englewood Cliffs, N.J.: Prentice-Hall, 1969), pp. 518–521; and James Petras, "The Dominican Republic: Revolution and Restoration," in *Trends and Tragedies in American Foreign Policy*, p. 128.

and provided safeguards against the fact that all large industrial nations are under a special kind of pressure to pursue vigorously the necessary markets and resources abroad and at the same time to sustain mass popular support at home. This requires elaborate and intricate involvement abroad, and it also requires overly simplified communication with the mass domestic public.

Mass publics probably have a universally low tolerance for the ambiguity of diplomacy, especially where a vital interest, such as oil, is involved. The more nationalistic a people, the more difficult it is for them to put any faith in diplomacy, inasmuch as diplomacy depends upon realistic definitions of the national interest and ambiguous definitions of gains and losses. In the old monarchies and autocracies, the conduct of diplomacy was not so difficult because of the separation of domestic and foreign politics and domestic and foreign instruments and institutions.

United States diplomacy was overshadowed but not completely set aside during the containment era. Table 14.9 is sufficient illustration of that fact, since treaties and executive agreements are arranged and implemented through diplomacy. It is also clear from this table that there are far more executive agreements than treaties. Some people feel this has created constitutional problems, inasmuch as the executive agreement has the same force and effect as a treaty yet does not have to be approved by a two-thirds vote of the Senate.[57] But there were always more executive agreements than treaties, because the bulk of the executive agreements are on lesser matters that carry out the commitments of earlier treaties or ordinary acts of Congress.

Executive agreements make possible such things as international postage, international copyrights, international exchange of patents and other technology, and most of the normal commercial dealings between nations. Even during the stormy years between 1950 and 1969, the United States made at least eighty executive agreements and only two treaties with the Republic of Vietnam.[58] A few of these executive agreements with Vietnam were strictly military in nature; however, the overwhelming portion had to do with the exchange of agricultural commodities, the mutual recognition of trademarks, admission of Vietnam to multilateral banking pacts, and so on. And virtually all of them were diplomatic actions directed toward implementation of some congressional intent.

The diplomacy inherent in executive agreements suggests that the importance of diplomacy at any point in time or at any place on

---

[57]*U.S.* v. *Pink,* 315 U.S. 203 (1942).

[58]These figures are qualified with "at least" because they had to be drawn from official sources and do not necessarily include secret agreements, as well as other diplomatic actions that were too trivial to be published. See also Amy M. Gilbert, *Executive Agreements and Treaties, 1946–73* (Endicott, N.Y.: Thomas-Newell, 1973).

Table 14.9   **Treaties and Executive Agreements Ratified by the United States, 1789–1969**

Year	Number of Treaties Approved	Executive Agreements Approved and Published by State Department
1789–1839	60	27
1840–1889	215	238
1890–1939	524	917
1950	12	94
1951	13	200
1952	17	359
1953	16	124
1954	13	249
1955	20	295
1956	5	247
1957	19	227
1958	3	182
1959	10	231
1960	5	264
1961	5	258
1962	7	332
1963	10	230
1964	19	221
1965	5	193
1966	14	231
1967	8	224
1968	0	200
1969	0	188
Total, 1950–1969	183	4,549

Data from Department of State, *U.S. Treaties and Other International Agreements,* 1789–1939. Materials since 1950 drawn from Series 2010 (1950) to Series 8001 (1975). See also Wallace McClure, *International Executive Agreements* (Ithaca, N.Y.: Cornell University Press, 1941). Figures here compiled by Joel Levin, in his senior paper in public affairs, University of Chicago, 1972. The first three rows are taken from McClure, and the later rows are provided by Levin.

the globe will depend on what kind of foreign policy role we are playing. It might be useful to review the relation of each of these roles to diplomacy as a way of anticipating the future of United States foreign policy.

Diplomacy is obviously strongest whenever and wherever the capitalist international role is being played most strongly. Capitalists, of course, make their own investments and conduct their own negotiations for contracts. But in the international realm, most of these arrangements depend upon conditions maintained through diplomatic channels. This dependence of international capitalism

Maintaining the Right to Conquer: The Foreign Policies of One Sovereignty in a Predatory World of Sovereignties

upon effective diplomacy has always been strong; for this reason it can justifiably be said that the State Department was once an adjunct of international commerce. On the other hand, even though many of the commercial relationships are maintained regardless of what role is being played, commercial relationships *and* diplomacy take a back seat once the foreign policy role shifts away from capitalist expansionism.

Diplomacy, then, tends to move into the back seat as soon as commercial affairs are subordinated to some larger goal, such as keeping Vietnam out of the hands of the Communists. The more pronounced the Holy Alliance role or the Napoleonic role, the smaller the place for real diplomacy—or the greater the likelihood diplomacy will be an instrument rather than a user of instruments. This is particularly clear under conditions of the Holy Alliance role, because in that situation no cost is felt to be too great to keep a status quo regime in power or to help arrange for a regime in one country that appears to be conducive to world status quo. During the past thirty years, it was generally true that our diplomats did not look as good as the young generals and the young technicians in the Defense Department and elsewhere. But these relative statuses were very largely products of the prevailing roles—Holy Alliance and Napoleonic—which tended to rely more heavily upon military and technological, rather than diplomatic, skills.

The balance of power role is also a great deal more conducive to diplomacy than the Holy Alliance or Napoleonic roles. Since there are signs, as suggested earlier, that the balance of power role seems to be spreading, this may indicate an advance of diplomacy. In the Middle East, for example, we have for some time been playing a balance of power role, maintaining our steadfast friendship with Israel but at the same time playing with Israeli interests in such a manner as to keep the Arab nations from complete unification.

As it turns out, the Middle East was also probably the only large area of substantial responsibility in the hands of the State Department, at least during the four years of President Nixon's first administration. William Rogers, Nixon's secretary of state for almost that entire period, had left virtually the rest of the world to the White House and Henry Kissinger. Kissinger did take direct responsibility for Middle East relationships eventually, but not until *after* he had become secretary of state. Since an elaborate balance of power posture even in one region of the world would require considerable diplomatic apparatus, it does not seem at all strange that this role arose out of the State Department, which is, so to speak, made to order.

Our review suggests that if balance of power and commercial roles prevail, diplomatic relationships among nations will also prevail. Perhaps this can also be turned about, suggesting that if we can somehow give diplomacy the upper hand (over military and

Maintaining the Right to Conquer: The Foreign Policies of One Sovereignty in a Predatory World of Sovereignties

619

technological personnel) it may produce for us more of the balance of power and commercial relationships that a peaceful world will require.

Looking at the past, there will probably never be widespread agreement on the nature and value of United States influence as a world power since World War II. Due to the predatory character of international relationships, assessment will always be on a balance sheet, and perhaps always with costs outweighing gains. Yet, with all the costs, there is the fact that the rate of world economic growth was probably unprecedentedly high during the period of America's greatest world influence.

Earlier in the twentieth century it is probable that no more than a fraction of a percent of the world's population lived above the level of bare subsistence. In the 1970s that figure probably has risen to 30 percent; and it continues to be governments, churches, and other groups *in the United States* who are most responsive to the needs of the other 70 percent. The dramatic reconstruction of Europe is another development directly attributable to the role of the United States; although motivated in large part by our need for markets, it did not have to be done in a way that would eventually encourage European independence of the United States.

Moreover, the United States has not always tried to dominate or domineer. The contribution of the United States to India has been consistently significant for over two decades, despite Indian tendencies toward socialism and neutrality in world affairs. The rebuilding of Germany and Japan, although motivated heavily by fear of the Soviet Union, has nevertheless been an important contribution to the emergence of a more flexible, multipolar world. These factors help counterbalance the sadder history of American involvement in Latin America, Africa, and Southeast Asia.

The record of the United States in world affairs since World War II probably compares favorably enough with the past records of other major world powers. However, when we judge our record by *our own aspirations,* it begins to look far worse. Other Holy Alliance powers in the past were undoubtedly a great deal more antidemocratic than the United States. Deliberate subversions of electoral processes or elected regimes—in Vietnam (1956), in the Dominican Republic (1965), and in Chile (1970–1973)—are so deeply contrary to American values that they must be weighted more heavily against our policies than similar actions on the part of other world powers.

The same is true of foreign assassination plots (Castro) and the killing of nonbelligerents (Vietnam, Cambodia, Laos). Support for totalitarian dictatorships is, according to American values, universally and absolutely unacceptable; yet, our recent record of support includes dictatorial regimes in Greece, South Korea, Vietnam, Taiwan, and Brazil. Outright bribery of foreign elites is surely a regular tool of all nation-states but cuts sharply across the grain of American values, whether the bribery involves Chilean legislators or oil potentates in the Middle East. All too often our foreign policy has been kept a secret only to hide our actions from our own citizens, because those actions were so deeply in violation of American values.

Perhaps American values will have to change now that we are regularly involved in world affairs. But it is more important for American elites to quit appealing to the American people as though each foreign policy action were consistent with and in pursuit of the basic ideals. Herein lies the significance of continual study and assessment of foreign policy. If the judgments resulting from such study lead Americans to a more modest evaluation of their government's virtues and thus encourage American policy makers to be more tolerant of the ambiguities inherent in the international situation, then such study has enormous value.

Improvements in our world record will ultimately require American elites to change in a whole variety of ways. But above all they must begin by being able to accept the actions of other nations as not always a conspiracy against the United States. And if American elites have now come to recognize this fact, they must communicate their understanding of it to the American people rather than filling our heads with the nonsense that our national interest requires us to tie ourselves to the regimes of any and all countries and to consider every minor disorder a matter of American responsibility.

An essential flaw in the United States approach to foreign policy has been characterized as "the illusion of American omnipotence."[59] Events in Southeast Asia have proved that the United States is not omnipotent, that there are certain kinds of indigenous social forces against which we may be totally impotent. If American policy makers can avoid being captured by the illusions of omnipotence and of a single world conspiracy against us, then there is a favorable probability that the greatest power on earth will give itself a chance to mature into the greatest force for peace on earth.

[59]Sir Dennis Brogan, "The Illusion of American Omnipotence," *Harper's*, December 1952, p. 21.

Chapter 15 Domestic Policy: Conquest Maintained

The most successful foreign policy can only establish and secure recognition from all other countries of the right to control, with a minimum of hindrance, a designated territory and population. But the right is only the beginning of the reality. The United States is an instructive case, for its recognition as a powerful sovereign state has been matched only by its inability to keep its own people in line.

Social control is the never-ending problem which governments are established to deal with—through the institutionalization of control. Even the Declaration of Independence, with all its stress on individuals and their rights to life, liberty, and the pursuit of happiness, also avows, "That to secure these rights, Governments are instituted among men." Governments may choose to do many distinctive things for individuals. The political process may impose upon the government some special obligation to bestow benefits, but neither government nor politics can choose not to control. Governments do make choices; but these choices of what types of controls, over whom, and for whose benefit only qualify controls and should not be allowed to overshadow the underlying reality.

As governments attempt to adjust themselves to old failures and new needs, they contrive new controls. These are called laws, edicts, orders, rules, and so on. In recent years the preferred terminology is *public policy.* A public policy is an expressed intention of a government or one of its agencies or agents. A policy usually implies an intention backed up by a sanction—with a reward or punishment corresponding to the adherence to the policy. The policy can be vague or clear in its intent; the sanctions can be strong or weak. But policy should be understood to include the intentions of public officers and the sanctions accompanying those intentions. Government affects society in ways not attributable to policies; unauthorized actions by police, unanticipated failures in a research and development project, and the loss of a war are examples of government impact that is not government policy. This chapter will focus itself primarily upon the intentional actions of government—the policies.

Two case studies are provided at the outset to give the reader some understanding of the phenomenon of control and its problems; following these cases will be an analysis of a variety of actual policies of the national government.

STICK AND CARROT: TWO CASES OF CONTROL

When Ali Said No

All during the years of his spectacular rise to the world heavyweight championship, Cassius Clay was also fighting a quieter and less successful battle with his draft board. In 1962, Clay had been classified I-A (no exemption). In 1964 he was classified I-Y (exemption from military service except in case of war or national emergency). However, on February 17, 1966, Clay, who by that time had become Muhammad Ali, was reclassified I-A. Personal appearances before his draft board and before the appeal board failed to achieve a reclassification as I-O (conscientious objector exemption). The case was then referred to the Department of Justice, where a hearing officer took testimony from Ali's parents and a minister representing the Nation of Islam faith, and got a report from the FBI on Ali's character. The Justice Department hearing officer recommended in favor of reclassification, but his superiors in the department wrote a letter recommending rejection of Ali's claim. Following that, Ali's lawyers added still another letter claiming

IV-D status (ministerial exemption), on the grounds that Ali had been a minister of the Nation of Islam since 1964 but had not been aware of the special exemption privileges of such a role. Counter-balancing this was the Justice Department's recommendation for denial on the grounds that, "It seems clear that the teachings of the Nation of Islam preclude fighting for the United States not because of objection to participation in war of any form but rather because of political and racial objections to the policies of the United States as interpreted by Elijah Muhammad."[1]

Almost immediately the national director of the Selective Service System ordered the local board to reopen the classification, and Ali was returned to I-A status. A transfer of induction to Houston and still another appeal in early 1967 was in vain. Houston ordered Ali to report for induction April 28, 1967. Ali reported but refused induction. He was then tried and convicted in June of 1967 by a U.S. district court, which sentenced him to a maximum penalty of five years in prison and a $10,000 fine.

Muhammad Ali had been a free man, one of the freest of human beings. He was free to choose, and he was rich enough to be able to realize most of his choices. But the day he said no, he revealed the extent to which he was involved in an elaborate and complex web of controls.

Once he was denied the special status of conscientious objector, Ali was immediately subjected to the power of the state to require the labor of all its able-bodied citizens and otherwise to deprive them of their freedom of choice. Ali's greatest problem was with the athletic (or boxing) commissions in the various states where the big professional matches are held. State legislatures have given to each such commission the power of life and death over all persons who wish to participate in boxing for money. This power exists in the form of licensing, which, it should be recalled, is a permission by authorities to do something that is otherwise illegal. Licensing is the chief instrument of control over professional boxing.

In March of 1967, Ali defended his crown. On April 28, 1967, the New York State Athletic Commission suspended Ali's license on the grounds that "your refusal to enter the Service and your conviction in violation of Federal law is regarded by this Commission to be detrimental to the interests of boxing."[2] Most states followed the lead of New York, and the various business interests began immediately to seek a new champion, for, without the licenses, Ali could not defend his championship. It did not seem to matter that the New York State decision was taken two months *before* the actual trial

---

[1]Quoted in the briefs of *Clay* v. *U.S.*, 403 U.S. 698–710 (1971).

[2]A letter from the chairman of the New York State Athletic Commission, quoted in Ernest Easton, "Muhammad Ali v. the Selective Service System and the New York State Athletic Commission: A Policy Perspective" (unpublished research paper, Cornell University, 1974). My thanks to Mr. Easton for unearthing many of the items used in this case report.

and conviction in the district court and over three years *before* the appeal to the Supreme Court was completed. Due largely to the licensing problem, Ali spent three years unable to earn an income as a boxer.

Figure 15.1 is an attempt to capture a few of the most important controls in the web around Muhammad Ali. Some of these controls are of course not governmental. Ali's church (and especially its leader, the late Elijah Muhammad) had tried always to keep close control of its members. Ali was in hot water for a period of time because of the wishes of his church that he not continue to engage in prizefighting.

Every boxer, including a champion, is under tight financial and promotional control by the professional sports industry. The world of sports journalism exercised one of the most interesting types of control in the case of Ali. Ali had never been one of their favorites because of his role as an antihero. As soon as Ali said no and followed that up at a press conference with the observation that he did not have any special grudge against the Viet Cong, it became very difficult to find a prominent sports journalist writing in Ali's defense.[3]

In contrast to the decision on Ali was the fact that in the twenty years from 1950 through 1969, the New York State Athletic Commission issued 247 boxing licenses to applicants who had prior records of conviction. The overwhelming proportion of these people had actually served time in prison. When queried about the policy in these cases, the commission lamely stated that boxing is a good form of rehabilitation.[4] The hostile public opinion almost certainly had some bearing upon the New York State Athletic Commission's decision on Ali.

Many of the important controls over Ali shown in Figure 15.1 appear to be nongovernmental. Yet appearances are misleading in some cases. In the professional sports industry, for example, private businesses, private sporting clubs, and private syndicates of investors control the access to participation. This access is virtually a monopoly, but only because of the willingness of state commissions to discourage competing sports businesses and state agencies to refuse licenses to anyone not in good standing with the private businesses or clubs. Some of the professions with higher status, such as law, medicine, and dentistry, are allowed by each state to

---

[3]For example, in a very large and expensive advertisement in *Esquire* of November 1969, over a hundred celebrities in the arts, sports, and journalism signed an appeal to allow Ali to defend his title. The only prominent sportswriter or editor on the list was Howard Cosell.

[4]See NAACP briefs in the Ali case, and Easton, "Muhammad Ali v. the Selective Service System and the New York State Athletic Commission." Given the timing, especially of the New York State licensing decision, a case could be made that Ali had been deprived of his livelihood without due process of law under the Fourteenth Amendment. For additional discussion of licensing and the control of the professions, see Corrinne Gilb, *Hidden Hierarchies* (New York: Harper & Row, 1966); and Milton Friedman, *Capitalism and Freedom* (Chicago: University of Chicago Press, 1962).

Figure 15.1
The day Ali said no. A
web of controls binds
each citizen. Controls are
usually not appreciated
until the citizen persists
in doing something
unpopular.

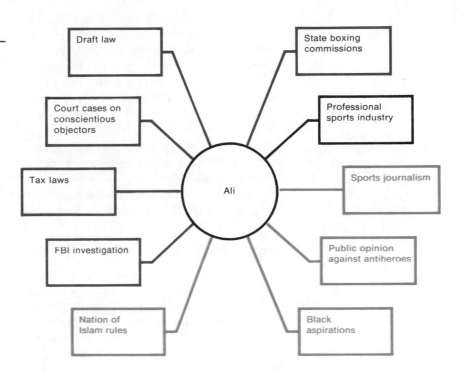

Actually three types of controls are shown here: (1) The red controls are formal government controls based on statutes or court decisions. Violation results in fines or imprisonment. (2) The black control is quasi-governmental, imposed by private corporations but recognized and supported by the government. Violation can result in loss of income. (3) The blue controls are purely private. Violation can mean ostracism or other informal means of punishment.

regulate themselves and their own members without need of a government agency composed of persons independent of the profession. But in all of these occupations and professions, the state controls through licensing and through cooperation with the major businesses or organizations in the industry.

A truly private sphere does exist, but it is not easy to identify, and most definitions of it are filled with ignorance and myth. As seen already, many areas of private endeavor are privately administered controls made possible by government sponsorship. Others are outright public controls not recognized as controls because they are perceived as beneficial. This would most probably have been Ali's

Domestic Policy: Conquest Maintained

own view of stiff gambling regulations in the boxing industry. Much of what is left of the private sphere is actually the freedom of one person made possible by control over others. This is necessarily a large part of what the words of the Declaration of Independence mean.

The private sphere has a basis in empirical realities, but its size and its limits are philosophical. However defined, the sphere of completely uncontrolled private activity is not as large as we would like to believe or as the prevailing American ideology would have us believe. Moreover, it is likely to grow smaller for at least two reasons, neither of which has anything to do with a bureaucratic lust for power. First, few people recognize private controls *as controls,* particularly private controls that are made possible by government sponsorship. Second, as we shall see in more detail throughout this chapter, *there is almost always strong popular support in favor of practically any proposal to expand government controls.* Let it not be forgotten that contemporary controls are in a long line of continuity with ancient conquest.

But What about Benefits? A Case of Saying Yes

Stress on government as control may seem at first to be an unbalanced view. Take, for instance, the *Encyclopedia of U.S. Government Benefits,* a 1,013-page guide to government benefits "for *every* American . . . from *all* walks of life." It claims, *"Right now,* there are thousands of other American Taxpayers who are missing out on valuable Government Services, *simply because they do not know about them* . . . . Start your own business. . . . Discover valuable minerals. . . . Take an extra vacation. . . . Here are all the opportunities your tax dollars have made possible."[5] (Italics in original.) It is difficult to argue against a thousand pages and five thousand different types of benefits provided by the federal government alone. Indeed, something is there for everybody, and citizens have a right to know what is coming to them. Government can be considered a bundle of benefits available to those with the wit and energy to claim them.

Appearances can be deceptive, however. Take the single case of a young woman with two small children, no husband, and no dependable source of income. Figure 15.2 is a sketch of the important benefits she can claim on the basis of a review of the *Encyclopedia of U.S. Government Benefits.* Some of the programs provide her with actual cash for living expenses. Some provide her with essential

---

[5]Roy A. Grisham and Paul D. McConaughy, eds., *Encyclopedia of U.S. Government Benefits* (Union City, N.J.: Wise, 1972; published annually since 1965). The quote is taken from the dust jacket. There is a comparable guide published by the *New York Times,* called *Federal Aid for Cities and Towns* (New York: Quadrangle Books, 1972). It contains 1,312 pages of federal government benefits that cities and towns, rather than individuals, can apply for.

Figure 15.2
The web of benefits
around one young woman
on welfare

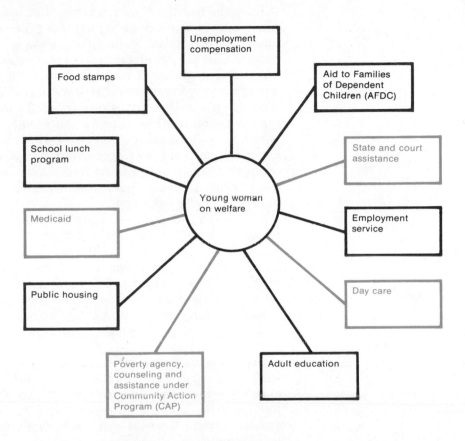

Programs in red are provided and administered by federal agencies and are available throughout the country on a more or less uniform basis. Programs in blue are state programs made possible by federal grants-in-aid. Programs in black are state programs assisted by federal money; they are highly discretionary and vary in access and amount from state to state and city to city.

services, such as medical services and babysitting. Others are directed toward getting her off the welfare roles and on a regular job. At least two of the services provide her with opportunities to improve her status and her income-earning capacity.

All of these are benefits, in the strictest sense of the word. The government cannot deny them to her if she makes her claim and proves her eligibility. Their existence cannot be denied by those who contend that the federal government does nothing for the poor.

There are probably very few poor people who would be eager to see these various benefits discontinued. Yet the issue here is not whether such benefits exist. Our concern is with the nature of those benefits. Figure 15.3 brings us a bit closer to an understanding of this.

All of the benefits shown in Figure 15.2 are indicated in red in the inner ring of the web in Figure 15.3. They are surrounded by an outer ring of activities (in blue), some governmental and some private, that are not precisely what one would call benefits but are a direct and meaningful part of the everyday environment of the young woman. For example, welfare inspection is as meaningful to her as is the welfare assistance check. To maintain her eligibility for payments, she has to prove continually that she is not living with a man—husband or otherwise—who is helping support her and her children. Some will argue that this is necessary; others will argue that because of this requirement the social security system is contributing to her permanent dependency by forcing her to live alone or to avoid marriage.

Either way, no one could claim that the welfare inspection is a benefit; nor could anyone claim that the welfare benefit can be considered independently of the welfare inspection. The welfare inspection can even determine specifically how the welfare income is spent. For example, there is a limit on liquor, cigarettes, and other consumer luxuries. The various requirements convert typically well-meaning welfare workers into a police squad concerned with vices and moralities. Similiar controls are associated with the provision of public housing.

One of the greatest controls over the single woman on welfare—as well as a very large number of persons not on welfare—is a quasi-governmental system of controls, the credit bureau. A negative report by a credit bureau is tantamount to a complete withdrawal of credit from the applicant. This kind of deprivation could not be more definitive if the credit bureau were a government agency. Moreover, credit bureaus are governmentally supported inasmuch as they are licensed by state governments and are officially recognized in litigation.

A comparable quasi-governmental system of private controls is insurance companies, especially those dealing with home insurance and automobile liability insurance. Decisions by these companies or their agents directly affect the price of fire and theft insurance; they also determine whether insurance is available at all. There are areas in every city of the United States that are "red-lined" by insurance companies—whole neighborhoods where insurance is either priced exhorbitantly high or is simply not available regardless of the condition of the specific home or car. This could not be more effective if it were a decision by a city zoning board or a state planning commission.

Figure 15.3
The web of benefits and controls for a welfare mother. Controls are never far from benefits.

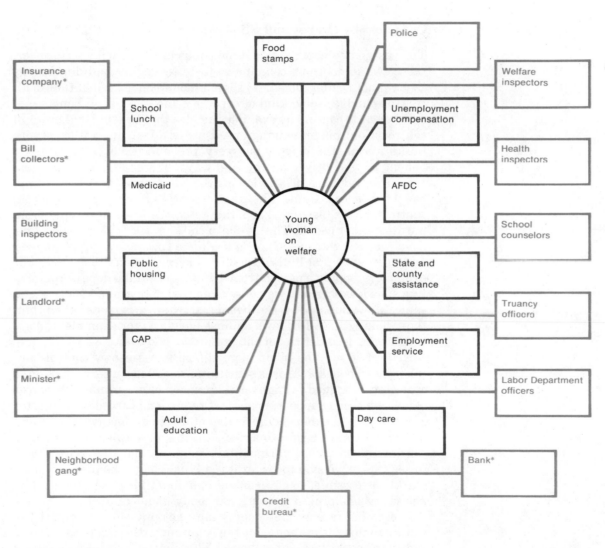

The inner circle, in red, is composed of the benefits identified in Figure 15.2. The outer circle, in blue, is composed of controls.
*Nongovernmental controls.

These decisions are even more governmentalized because certain official government programs rely upon the decisions made by insurance companies. For example, the mortgage insurance available under the Federal Home Administration (FHA) and the Veterans Administration (VA) has been very difficult to get in red-lined neighborhoods or in other neighborhoods where private insurance companies are reluctant to enter. Consequently, private insurance and governmentally-insured mortgage loans have been virtually nonexistent in the very areas where people such as the young mother in our case must live and earn their living.

Conquest by Carrot and Stick

The cases cited capture two dimensions of public policy. However, these two dimensions combine to form two additional dimensions that cannot be diagramed: (1) some kind of benefit is inherent in all controls, and (2) some kind of control is inherent in all benefits.

It is easy to capture by example the idea that benefit is inherent in control. Controls on driving speed are a direct and rather severe limitation on the driver, but very probably such controls are a benefit to that driver on the highways. Traffic accidents dropped measurably during 1974 following the adoption of the fifty-five mile per hour speed limit. The reason back of most governmental controls is the need to keep the activities of some people from harming other people. That is one of the secrets of public support for governmental controls. Once in a while a specific control is imposed on the grounds that it also benefits the very person subject to it. For example, stopping a person from drinking or taking dope or committing suicide is seen as a way of serving that person and society at the same time. But mostly the benefit accrues to persons other than those being controlled; laws against burglary, for example, control the burglar in order to benefit the property owner.

At first it may be a bit more difficult to see how controls are inherent in benefits. This is something so-called conservatives have consistently argued—that every expansion of government, however beneficent it may appear, is a direct reduction of freedom. But after a generation of expanded government, there are many liberals and leftists who have begun to agree with the conservatives. They may continue to support governmental expansion, but they have begun to see this expansion for what it really is. To put the proposition as starkly as possible, no government benefit will last very long if it is not seen as helpful in keeping somebody under control.

Those who receive the benefits may not immediately detect the controls inherent in them, but the relationship between benefit and control is never very far removed. The United States was actually late to see the political value of benefits. Most other capitalist nations recognized it as early as the fourth quarter of the nineteenth century. Bismarck expressed one aspect of the political value of benefits in a speech to the Reichstag in 1899: "I will consider it a great advantage when we have 700,000 small pensioners drawing their annuities from the state, especially if they belong to those classes who otherwise do not have much to lose by an upheaval and erroneously believe they can actually gain much by it."[6]

Back of the consensus that produced America's social security system in 1935 was a tremendous fear that the country was headed for revolution. Dissatisfaction with the depression had to be placated somehow.[7] The same kind of concern was strongly associated with the expansion of social security and social programs in the 1960s. Debate in Congress was checkered with expectations that a more generous national government would help put an end to ghetto rioting, which during the 1960s was popularly referred to as "the long hot summer."

The control aspects of welfare and other benefits go well beyond the theory that benefits to the poor will buy off violence and coopt support for the regime. There are two aspects of the welfare system as an important instrument of control, far beyond any influences it

---

[6]Quoted in Gaston Rimlinger, *Welfare, Policy and Industrialization in Europe, America and Russia* (New York: Wiley, 1971), p. 121.

[7]Theodore Lowi, *The End of Liberalism* (New York: Norton, 1969), p. 217. See also G. William Domhoff, *The Higher Circles* (New York: Random House, 1970), p. 207. For more on attitudes and motivations, see Roy Lubove, *The Struggle for Social Security* (Cambridge, Mass.: Harvard University Press, 1968); and Edwin Witte, *The Development of the Social Security Act* (Madison: University of Wisconsin Press, 1963).

may have upon the individual recipients through inspection and cooptation; and it is because of these two aspects that welfare can be so strongly supported by the capitalist system.

1. The social security system helps control extremes of the business cycle. Some economists call this *maintenance of aggregate demand.* As unemployment rises during a recession, the printing presses are activated, the unemployment checks go out, and buying power is maintained for a good while despite the downturn in employment. This provides entrepreneurs with added optimism, encouraging them to maintain production and investment despite economic contraction; if buying power is maintained and optimism is supported long enough, the recession may stop before it becomes a depression.

2. The other aspect of this broader type of control back of the welfare system is best understood as *forced savings.* The overwhelming proportion of all employees in the United States are subject to a social security tax, deducted from the paycheck. (In 1974 this was about 5.85 percent.) This tax forces employees to provide at least part of the savings necessary for their own later dependency and for the dependency of many who do not contribute. The assumption in this instance is that the average person when left to his or her own devices will not adequately provide for old age, unemployment, or disability. Some call the social security system "liberal," because they see benefits going to the deprived groups in the society. Perhaps it would be better to call it paternalistic, inasmuch as the benefits we derive from it are contingent upon a very strong compulsory element, even though it is "for our own good."

The relationship between benefits and controls becomes more intricate and more intimate the higher the income brackets and the further up the corporate world. Almost all the laws related to property and contracts passed by state legislatures are benefits to the corporate structure precisely because they are controls upon trespass, fraud, and all other crimes against ownership and commerce. If there are a few effective federal controls restricting big business, it is because a large number of smaller businesses lobbied for these controls in the expectation that legal limits upon big businesses would benefit small businesses.[8]

There are regulations on airlines, because airline companies have perceived that regular schedules and limitations on competition, although controls, are greatly beneficial to them in the long run. In agriculture there are numerous federal controls over the quality of agricultural products, not only to protect the public (for whom these

---

[8]Instances of federal controls that work as benefits will be found in Walter Adams and Horace Gray, *Monopoly in America* (New York: Macmillan, 1955); for a general treatment of the need for control in capitalism, see John R. Commons, *Legal Foundations of Capitalism* (New York: Macmillan, 1924).

may be a benefit) but also in order to prevent a large number of farmers from selling their lower quality products at a lower price and thus cutting the price of all products. It is impossible in instances of this sort to know just where the benefit ends and the control begins. But the distinction becomes less and less necessary. The inescapable significance of all these instances is control. Some controls are by stick, while others are by carrot. But control is the common element.

CONQUEST AND POLICY: TECHNIQUES OF CONTROL

Although a good beginning for an analysis, it is insufficient merely to assert that all government is control and that policy is conquest updated. While no government is free to choose not to control, every government has some freedom to choose *whom* to control, *how* to control, and *for what.* This means that there will be a range of different types of controls with different consequences. It is important to identify those differences and to understand what they mean. That is what the study of public policy ought to be about.

This chapter began with a definition of public policy as an expressed intention by a government to exert its influence over a particular person, action, or object. This statement of intention by a government usually involves three elements: (1) The subject matter—the people, behaviors, or objects whose situation the government tends to influence. (2) Implementation—designation of the person or agency to be responsible for applying the policy; in the twentieth century provision is usually made for an administrative agency. (3) Sanctions—provision of some technique of control by which to increase the probability that the expectations will be fulfilled. (Sanctions can be rewards or punishments or both.) These can ordinarily be discovered by an intelligent reading of the formal statement of public policy. In fact, if educated citizens cannot determine these elements from their own reading of a statute, there is something wrong with the statute. After all, statutes are intended for citizens; citizens must understand if they are to comply on the basis of something other than blind obedience.

Little need be said of the first two elements. Although it is frequently a matter of contention as to who actually benefits, the *subject matter* of a policy is usually quite clear. A problem exists in time and space—an economic sector needs adjustment, a class or region is at odds with the rest of the country; a new discovery about the cause or cure of a disease gives rise to new public health proposals. Members of Congress often feel Congress has made a policy statement when it has in fact only enunciated some broad sentiment: "There is too much inflation; something ought to be done about it." Or, "The air and water are polluted. Every citizen has a right to a clean environment; therefore, let there come to pass an agency that can give us clean air in five years." "Programs" like these have subject matter but lack some essentials. They are often passed by Congress; but they serve as nothing more than a measure of the extent to which power has come to be centered in the executive branch, since the missing elements in such programs must be supplied by administrators.

Nevertheless, many members of Congress, along with many political scientists and journalists, feel that nothing further is needed except an appropriation to implement the program. There is no doubt that such an appropriation is an essential aspect of implementation. However, it is a necessary but insufficient condition for a full-fledged policy. In the first place, there has to be a sufficient administrative arrangement, so that the sentiments expressed in the subject matter of the policy can be pursued on a routine and systematic basis. But more is needed than an administrative agency that can "throw money at" the problem.

Important as the first two elements of a policy are, the test of a policy is whether it embodies a sanction, and if so, what kind and how substantial a sanction. A preferred synonym for *sanctions* is *techniques of control,* a term which stresses two things about sanctions: (1) control is the common factor, and (2) there are several distinct types of sanctions available to governments.

Table 15.1 is a selection of important techniques of control available to government. The listing is not a logical categorization, nor is it intended to exhaust all the possible techniques of control. Each, however, is of fundamental importance. It would be difficult to imagine the formulation of any important public policy that did

Table 15.1 **Techniques of Public Control—A Selection of Important Weapons for Keeping Conquest Up-to-date**

Weapons	Comments
Licensing	Precondition for private endeavor. Permission by the state to do something that is otherwise illegal. Permits, franchises, licenses, incorporation, "certificates of convenience and necessity."
Subsidizing	Promotion of private activity through unconditional gifts or services.
Civil penalties	Fines, exposure.
Criminal penalties	Heavy fines and imprisonment, forced labor, removal of citizenship, expulsion from country.
Regulatory taxation	Added costs to eliminate or keep production or consumption down. Used on liquor, cigarettes, gasoline, and so on.
Contracting powers	Power to buy goods and services and set the conditions (such as no defense contract to employers who discriminate).
Other market powers	Power to buy and sell U.S. bonds and notes (open market operations) and thus affect prices. In this way, for example, TVA can compete with private power companies to keep prices down.
Expropriation	Eminent domain—the power to seize private property for a public use. Nationalization is one variant.
Macroeconomic (fiscal) techniques:	
Fiscal use of tax	Altering quantity of money or its distribution by setting and changing tax rates and deductions.
Fiscal use of budgeting powers	Deliberate budgeting surplus or deficit to affect private consumption.
Fiscal use of credit	Manipulation of interest rates and other conditions of investment to affect demand.
Fiscal use of insurance	A variant of credit power, which works through reduction of risk rather than by changing the pay-off for taking risk (interest rate).
Macrosocial and macropolitical controls	Propaganda, censorship, education for citizenship, creating a state church, martial law—the reassertion of complete conquest.

Domestic Policy: Conquest Maintained

not include a serious consideration of one or more of these techniques as the means by which the intention of the policy would be carried out. In any instance where the policy or program does not include some kind of sanction, the policy is likely to be an empty gesture, a merely symbolic response to a demand for governmental action.[9] When listed together, the techniques in Table 15.1 almost speak for themselves.

Licensing has already been discussed in this volume, and its importance as a traditional technique of control can hardly be overestimated. One type of license which has not been mentioned is the corporate charter, a grant of a privilege to the owners, who are liable for the actions or failures of the corporation only up to the amount of their stock in it.

Subsidies are at first glance the easiest of all techniques to understand. One could simply characterize them as "giveaways" to anyone who has access and political pull. Be that as it may, subsidies have also been a traditional and time-tested method of encouraging important activities that might not otherwise have taken place. A subsidy should be thought of as a positive sanction, the use of a reward rather than a punishment to influence private activity. The first planning document ever written for the federal government—Alexander Hamilton's *Report on Manufactures* (1791)—was based heavily on the assumption that industry could be encouraged primarily by federal subsidies.[10]

The next two types—civil penalties and criminal penalties—are the ones most widely understood as sanctions backing up policies. Perhaps these are also the most widely employed sanctions, although they appear somewhat less important when they are seen as part of a long list of sanctions, as in Table 15.1. For example, regulatory taxation and the contracting powers are being used with increasing frequency.

Regulatory taxation is a method of control over moral conduct as well as commercial activities. For example, heavy taxes are traditionally placed on liquors and cigarettes not only for the purpose of raising revenue but also on the theory that if the price is high enough, the consumption will be moderate. More recently this type of control has been manifested in the gasoline tax, through which the government hopes to discourage excessive use of automobiles and to gain for the United States "energy independence."

The contracting, or purchasing, power is in one respect another form of subsidy. Indeed, nothing is more valuable to an airplane manufacturer than a defense contract. But the government can also use contracts as a sanction. One of the most effective civil rights programs in the field of job discrimination is based upon the power

---

[9]Some of the best reading on techniques of control will be found in older textbooks. See, for example, Harold Koontz and Richard Gable, *Public Control of Economic Enterprise* (New York: McGraw-Hill, 1956), especially chapter 3; see also Melvin Anshen and Francis Wormuth, *Private Enterprise in Public Policy* (New York: Macmillan, 1954), especially chapters 1, 3–4, 6–10. See also Andrew Shonfield, *Modern Capitalism* (New York: Oxford University Press, 1965).

[10]This is surely one of the most interesting documents in American history and can still be read with great profit as a source of insight into government and into the American attitude toward government. An edited version of this document will be found in Theodore Lowi, ed., *Private Life and Public Order* (New York: Norton, 1968), p. 111.

of the federal government to set specific conditions in contracts and to refuse to honor old contracts or issue new ones to any company in violation of the civil rights provisions of the contract.

There are still other uses of the purchasing power of government as control over individuals or over the economy at large. Because they are so various, they are listed as "other market powers" in Table 15.1. One of the most important uses of government marketing power can be found in the everyday activity of the Federal Reserve Board, which buys and sells bonds and short-term notes in order to affect interest rates and prices. For over thirty years the federal government has also tried to support prices for certain agricultural commodities, such as cotton and corn, by buying enormous amounts of these commodities and storing them during bountiful years for use during lean years. There is more to the price support programs than buying and selling commodities, but the use of these market powers is an essential sanctioning device back of most of the federal efforts to support farm prices.

Expropriation might seem at first to be an alien and little-used technique of control in the United States. We think of it as a method used by a new military dictator in Latin America or a new socialist revolutionary government dedicated to the eradication of capitalism. Yet, expropriation in various forms is and has been a widely used technique of governmental control in the United States. While we have only rarely nationalized an industry, the way it might be done by a socialist government, similar techniques of expropriation exist whenever one of our government agencies uses its eminent domain power to take a piece of private property for a public purpose.

As discussed already in chapter 5, every time a piece of land is taken by a government agency for a highway or a site for urban renewal or atomic research projects, it should serve as a reminder that there is a fundamental public dimension to all private property. Expropriation also includes the right of the government to force individuals to work for the state. This includes conscription for the armed forces and forcing laborers on strike to return to their jobs in industries considered essential to national security.

The macroeconomic techniques of control are distinguished from all of the others by the fact that they are *indirect* sanctions. They are called macroeconomic to indicate that they are methods of control that manipulate the *environment of conduct* rather than conduct itself.

Note, for example, that a criminal penalty is an arrest, a trial, and a fine and/or imprisonment of a specific person whose behavior is allegedly in violation of some governmental policy. The purpose is not only to punish the violation but to deter the violator and all potential violators from future actions of the same sort; the sanction is placed against the individual and the conduct of each and every

The concepts *police* and *policy* have common roots. *Above:* Enforcing the law before the National Labor Relations Act—the Haymarket Riot of 1886 in Chicago. *Below:* Enforcing the law today—the Civil Disturbance Unit of the Washington, D.C., police department.

individual who is, or is likely to be, involved in certain kinds of activity. In contrast, a macroeconomic or fiscal technique influences behavior by changing the conditions within which persons operate, rather than bearing on the persons themselves. For example, a cut in the income tax is likely to increase consumption even though no individual consumer is approached by the government. A decrease in interest rates is likely to encourage more home buying simply because the value of borrowed money suddenly goes up.

The use of these fiscal techniques has been expanding in the United States since 1946, but they are not new to us. The decision in the 1790s to assume the war debts of the individual states was a fiscal decision. The founding of the Bank of the United States was also a fiscal decision. The printing of paper money in the 1860s was a fiscal decision. The decision to go off the gold standard in the 1930s was a fiscal decision. Each in its own way sought to affect the economy by changing its structure or by affecting the value of the dollar rather than by controlling the behavior of specific individuals.

Macrosocial and macropolitical controls may be the most pernicious of all sanctions. Nevertheless, techniques of this sort are utilized by all governments, including democracies. They are aimed at getting behind behavior and altering the values held by individuals or manipulating the information by which those individuals operate. Propaganda, of course, is one such sanction. Perhaps of even greater importance in this category is censorship—all efforts to remove from individuals important bases for making their choices. These controls are "macro" in the sense that they involve government in efforts to change the atmosphere rather than impose influences directly upon individuals.

PROBLEMS, POLICIES, AND TECHNIQUES OF CONTROL: SELECTED CASES OF CONTEMPORARY CONQUEST

The techniques of governmental control are neutral instruments which can be used by any regime to implement its goals. Ideologists have tried on occasion to associate a particular technique with the opposing camp, as though the technique represented the ultimate failure or discredit of that camp. Nineteenth century liberals tried to argue that the government interventionism of eighteenth century aristocratic regimes, through criminal penalties or licensing to limit or guide commerce, was responsible for the failures of the old regimes. What they did not realize was that the type of government demanded by the nineteenth century liberal required the use of similar techniques, although for different goals.

For example, free enterprise required maintenance of open markets and protection of property and contracts; yet, these could not be maintained without rather vigorous use of such techniques as currency control and property protection through provision of severe criminal penalties for trespass and breach of contract. Twentieth century liberals turned things on their head, or feet, by making government intervention into commerce a matter of liberalism, branding nineteenth century liberals "conservatives," as though their opposition to government licensing and interventionism through criminal penalties or regulatory taxation was inherently conservative.

Table 15.2 should lay all of that to rest. It is composed of a variety of public policies and private policies or practices. They are ar-

Table 15.2   Selected Public and Private Policies Arranged According to Probable Effect on Society

← Favoring Change   Against Change →

Public ("Liberal") Policies

Social security programs based on graduated income tax	Luxury taxes	Growth fiscal policies	Countercyclical fiscal policies	Social security programs based on insurance principles (as in U.S.)	Farm price support programs	High tariffs
Civil rights laws with sanctions	Real antitrust	Graduated income tax (as in U.S.)	Sales taxes	Direct regulation (FCC, ICC, CAB)	Restraint of competition (NRA, fair trade, anti-price discrimination)	Import quotas
Low tariffs	"Yardstick" regulation (TVA)	Civil rights laws without sanctions	Aids to small business	Antitrust by consent decree	Tax on colored margarine	Utilities (licensed monopolies)
			1970 wage-price controls		Revenue sharing	Very high bond reserve requirements
			Mortgage insurance			

Private ("Conservative") Policies or Practices

Competition in agriculture	Competitive business	Oligopoly with research competition	Oligopoly without competition (steel, cigarettes)	Trade associations	Monopoly
New interest groups	Competition by closely matched political parties	Corporate philanthropy	Brand names	Market controls through:	Old interest groups (NAM, AFL-CIO, TWU)
	Merit hiring and promotion		Ethnic appeals of political campaigns	Pools	
				Basing points	
				Price leadership	
				Union policies against automation	

From Theodore J. Lowi, *The End of Liberalism* (New York: Norton, 1969).

ranged according to the two major dimensions of contemporary ideological discussion in the United States. Since liberals have been thought to be persons who favor the "public sector," the liberal, public policies are placed above the line, and the policies geared to the "private sector," supposedly favored by contemporary conservatives, are below the line. All of these are then ranged from left to right according to present arguments as to the *probable effect* on society. Liberals are thought to favor policies that may bring about change and that are identified with the "left"; conservatives are thought to oppose those policies and favor policies, public or private, that would tend to maintain existing conditions or statuses and that are identified with the "right."

If there were any consistency or meaning to these two points of view, we would expect to find that the policies which have been publicly identified as "liberal" would be above the line tending toward the left of the table, while conservative policies would be below the line and distinctly toward the right of the table. What we find instead is that private and public policies are spread all across the continuum. Many public policies are extremely conservative inasmuch as they are designed to fight social change. Many private practices, if left unregulated by government, would bring about considerable social change. An example of the former would be the farm price support programs of the past generation. Artificially high supports on farm products keep a far larger number of people in farming than the market would otherwise support. By the same argument, an unregulated agricultural economy, supposedly preferred by conservatives because it would be in the private sector, would have brought about a tremendous amound of socioeconomic change in the United States.

Experts disagree on precisely where to place any public or private policy on the continuum. Some argue that a strict gold standard is not necessarily antagonistic to social change. Others argue that the American social security program has brought about a great deal of social change by forcing the young to support the old, even if it has not redistributed much income between the rich and the poor. But these kinds of arguments confirm the broader point made by Table 15.2. Although the experts disagree about the placement of any single policy, their evaluation of the ten, twenty, or thirty major policies of any regime is likely to produce a considerable spread across the continuum.[11]

As Table 15.2 suggests, and our cases of public policies tend to confirm, ideologies are not and should not be defined by one or more techniques of control. Instead they must be defined by the actual goals being sought. If liberalism is dedicated to equal opportunity,

[11]This table and a more lengthy discussion of these issues will be found in Lowi, *The End of Liberalism,* chapter 3.

then liberal regimes will be found using a variety of techniques to achieve it. No one technique is inherently capable of achieving it, nor will any one technique bring about improvements in equal opportunity *unless the user of the technique is dedicated to that improvement.* For example, while socialism is dedicated to the eradication of economic class and status differences, socialist regimes nevertheless find themselves using the same techniques of control that Table 15.1 ascribes to our government. The purpose of their use is different, and that is what defines the ideology and direction of the regime. The techniques must be appreciated for what they are.

Since there is no way to deal adequately with the hundreds of government policies of a large system like the United States, wisdom would seem to dictate the selection of a few cases for close scrutiny. In order to do this, we must first identify a few social and economic problems that any nation-state will have to cope with—or risk losing control of territory and population, thus endangering conquest. The problems we will examine have no permanent solution; each generation must contrive workable solutions for itself.

Although the same problems might best be defined in somewhat different terms in another country, they will be stated here in terms of the approaches taken in the United States: (1) public order and private property, (2) making and maintaining a market, (3) making and maintaining a capitalist economy, (4) socializing poverty and dependency, (5) inequality, and (6) human and community resources. The identification of these problems must, of course, be followed by an identification of the major public policies which American governments have produced in their efforts to solve or to avoid each of the problems. Finally, we must, where possible, assess the significance and potential consequences of these policy choices.

Public Order and Private Property

With the exception of the defense of sovereignty, no problem is more fundamental or more incessantly demanding than that of maintaining public order. Yet, paradoxical as it may seem, the federal government of the United States was nearly inactive in this area for the first century or more of its development. As already reported in chapter 5, throughout the nineteenth century the federal government paid only scant attention to the protection of individuals and their property, leaving almost all of this protection to the "police power" of the states.

The responsibility of the state governments for the fundamental decisions on public order and private property has remained a strong tradition, even though the federal government has expanded its role in this area during the past forty years. For example, although there has been a considerable increase in federal controls

Local and national
policies are often in
conflict.

NOTICE
IT IS REQUIRED BY LAW, UNDER
PENALTY OF FINE OF $5.00 TO $25.00,
THAT WHITE AND NEGRO PASSENGERS MUST
OCCUPY THE RESPECTIVE SPACE OR SEATS
INDICATED BY SIGNS IN THIS VEHICLE.
TEXAS PENAL CODE: ARTICLE 1659, SEC.4
DALLAS CITY ORDINANCE: NO. 2904

on interstate commerce and on the businesses that engage in
interstate commerce, there is still no federal property law and still
no important federal law on corporations or on capitalism. Even
though the constitutional power of the federal government to
exercise police power has been recognized since the 1930s, most
federal policies in this area have concerned themselves either with
interstate crimes (such as crossing state lines to avoid arrest, white
slavery, and gambling by use of the wire services) or a few crimes
defined as being so inherently evil that they should be made
interstate crimes (such as kidnapping, narcotics trade, counterfeiting, and political agitation).

The national government has so few policies concerning basic
public order that it has never developed a national police force. The
size and duties of the FBI, coupled with the power of the
commander-in-chief to use the army or to call out the national
guard may sound like a great deal of national police force. There are
also the various independent regulatory commissions whose staffs
are able to police many corporations. But it is a matter of great
significance that these various federal policing agencies are spread
all over the government and are not under a single authority.

Making and Maintaining a Market:
Policies toward Commerce and Industry

Maintenance of a national system of production and exchange is a
problem second only to the maintenance of basic public order. It has

always been especially demanding in the United States, where the ideal of small government is combined with the reality of a vast and rich continent. We have already seen how the movement to reject the Articles of Confederation arose out of the frustrations encountered by trade among separate and overly independent states. It was clear from the beginning that making and maintaining a viable market economy would not be left strictly to private incentives.[12] It was clear from the beginning that the federal government, though limited, would have a much stronger role in maintaining a market than in maintaining basic public order.

Nineteenth century federal policies were immensely important to the building of a national economy. Land distribution plus protection by federal troops distributed populations across a vast territory. Federal policies of specific land grants to railroad companies greatly accelerated the time when the entire continent would be tied together by trade. Protective tariffs also went a long way toward building an industrial economy. The myth of a totally free enterprise system persisted mainly because of the *form* which government intervention took. At the federal level, it consisted primarily of direct benefits, with the purpose of husbanding rather than regulating or coercing commerce. At the state level, there were many coercive interventions by government into commerce; however, these were largely restrictions on those who would trespass or otherwise interfere with private property and exchange. There were few direct regulations on the conduct of commercial activity itself.

In the twentieth century, scale and form changed. Aid to the economy through the provision of direct subsidies did continue, of course. For example, since the late 1950s, the federal government has paid for 90 percent of the construction costs of the interstate system of 42,500 miles of highway; the federal government also maintains, on a 50-50 basis with the states, 870,000 additional miles of other federal roads in the system, begun on a large scale in the 1930s. The federal government spends billions to encourage air transportation and the maintenance of a gigantic aerospace industry. However, once the national economy was fully established and thousands of firms were engaging in commerce on a national and international scale, the nature of the economic problem changed, and government policies changed accordingly. There was a shift from policies that encouraged commerce to policies that sought to govern commerce in specific respects. This is usually called regulation.

---

[12]For a look through the mythology into the reality of governmental involvement of the American private enterprise economy, consult the volumes of statutes of any state in any good law library. See also Louis Hartz, *Economic Policy and Democratic Thought: Pennsylvania, 1776–1860* (Cambridge, Mass.: Harvard University Press, 1948); and Lee Benson, *The Concept of Jacksonian Democracy* (Princeton: Princeton University Press, 1961).

The main preoccupation was that many businesses had become large enough to possess *market power*—the ability to influence the market and market prices directly rather than merely function within the general system of economic competition. This violated the classical theory of how a market system works.[13] Those who were victimized by this new economic power—the power to coerce other firms, individual entrepreneurs, and individual employees, as well as do irreparable injury to the environment—were unable to cope on an individual basis with it. Inevitably, they organized and turned to government to demand some kind of control.

The problem is that it is insufficient simply to rave against economic injustice and rant in favor of general governmental control of the economy. Unless the government chooses the right technique of control for the appropriate industry at the appropriate time, it is very likely that government intervention will be counter-productive.[14]

The first modern effort by the federal government to influence the national economy by direct regulatory policy was the Interstate Commerce Act of 1887, which was specifically designed to control a few important aspects of the transportation industry—mainly the railroad companies, whose monopolistic position, supported in the first place by federal subsidies, enabled them to exploit farmers and other small business people. The Interstate Commerce Act established our first federal independent regulatory commission, the Interstate Commerce Commission (ICC). The ICC was given power to control the rates that railroads could charge for their services and to forbid certain kinds of practices that monopolies are known to utilize, including discrimination between clients for coercive purposes, pooling and other forms of collusion in order to reduce competition or increase prices, and other practices alleged by farmers to be discriminatory against them. By establishing an independent administrative agency, the hope also was to attract personnel with enough dedication and expertise to understand the

---

[13]For a critique of the market system by economists, see Paul A. Samuelson, *Economics,* 9th ed. (New York: McGraw-Hill, 1973). For a critique from the point of view of politics, see Robert A. Dahl and Charles E. Lindblom, *Politics, Economics and Welfare* (New York: Harper & Bros., 1953); also Lowi, *The End of Liberalism,* chapters 1 and 2.

[14]Every student of government should try to gain some minimum knowledge of a few of the basic sectors of the American economy. From the standpoint of studying government, the very best starting point for such an economic education is probably Walter Adams, ed., *The Structure of American Industry,* 4th ed. (New York: Macmillan, 1971). For some engaging and sophisticated thoughts about the highlights of the modern industrial economy, see John Kenneth Galbraith, *Economics and the Public Purpose* (Boston: Houghton Mifflin, 1973). Despite his eagerness to generalize about the economy, Galbraith is quick to insist that there is no single theory or single explanation about the structure or behavior of all the different sectors of the economy:

An advanced electronic, chemical or computer firm . . . will set more store by technical innovation as a goal than a meat packer or a steel company. In other cases there will be differing emphasis on security of earnings as opposed to growth. The choice of the largest firms on these matters will differ from that of the less large. . . . The social consequences of those choices, as well as the power with which they are pursued, can . . . be considerable (pp. 108–109).

particular technologies and particular requirements of one sector of industry in order to regulate it effectively.

Three years later the ICC was followed by the more generalized Sherman Antitrust Act, which was to police the behavior of all large firms attempting to use their market power in a monopolistic manner to reduce competition or set prices without regard to competition. Because economic power was defined as contrary to the basic assumptions of a free, competitive market economy, the antitrust act was seen as a profound effort by the government to protect the economy, even though regulatory measures were involved. Businesses did not have to be absolute monopolies to come under the jurisdiction of the Sherman act.

In addition to a few monopolies, there are many oligopolies. An oligopolistic sector is one in which two or three companies dominate, even though there may be several small companies in the sector and even though the three or four largest companies do occasionally compete. The governmental problem has been how to keep these large monopolistic and oligopolistic businesses from unfair economic practices. Many have argued that bigness *as such* is a restraint of trade that ought to be outlawed. But very early in the history of the antitrust movement, stress was put upon unreasonable practices rather than size itself.

John Kenneth Galbraith was engaging in his usual hyperbole when he observed: "Were there only a handful of great corporations . . . perhaps their dissolution into smaller units and therewith the dissolution of their power might be possible. But a government cannot proclaim half of the economic system illegal."[15] However, Galbraith's observation is founded on historical fact inasmuch as the federal government has avoided head-on collisions with major industries. For example, it confronts the automobile industry with the rather tame charges of illegal franchise withdrawals, while the leading automobile producer accounts for more than 50 percent of the total market and the Big Three automobile producers account for about 90 percent of production and sales.[16]

The federal government sought to identify additional commercial practices in need of regulation by passing the Federal Trade Act, which established the Federal Trade Commission (FTC), and the Clayton Act of 1914, which was to be administered by the FTC. These were the last major efforts to deal with the behaviors of business throughout the economy. Beginning with the Federal

---

[15]Galbraith, *Economics and the Public Purpose*, p. 216. For an excellent general statement about original attitudes toward monopoly and how they have changed, see Walter Adams, "Public Policy in a Free Enterprise Economy," in *The Structure of American Industry,* chapter 13.

[16]The closest thing to modern trust-busting is the long and weary, and only partially successful, effort to force duPont to get rid of its controlling share of General Motors stock. For that story and a good treatment of the general problem of economic concentration and power in this industry, see Robert Lanzilotti, "The Automobile Industry," in *The Structure of American Industry,* chapter 8.

Reserve Act (1913) and its Federal Reserve Board and system to deal with the banking industry, Congress enacted a series of regulatory policies aimed at specific sectors of the economy. In 1920, legislation expanded federal regulatory policies directed at the railroads and truckers. Later in the 1920s, Congress made its first try at regulating a new sector, radio communication; this regulation was later expanded to cover all forms of communication.

With the advent of the Roosevelt administration in 1933, Congress began to act more vigorously and more frequently to set up policies with administrative agencies to regulate the behaviors in many sectors, including stock markets, the investment community (primarily holding companies), air transportation, commercial agriculture, the extraction and transportation of basic energy resources (primarily oil, natural gas, and coal), and the drug and cosmetic industries. Several basic sectors and the primary federal policies toward them are summarized in Table 15.3.

Although in the earlier parts of the twentieth century Congress concentrated mightily on regulating one sector of the economy at a time, it did not completely abandon the federal effort to formulate policies applicable to the economy as a whole. There was already a history of effort to defend natural resources from encroachment. Once called conservation policy, the more recent effort, called environmental policy, should not mask this earlier history. With the passage in 1938 of the so-called Robinson-Patman Act amending the original Clayton and Federal Trade Acts, Congress also revised and expanded its regulation of all commercial behavior in the field of price discrimination and mergers. Most important, with the enactment of the National Labor Relations Act (Wagner Act) of 1935, Congress attempted to change *throughout the economy* the basic relationship between employees and employers.

In order to gain a majority for passage of this act in Congress, a few sectors of the economy were exempted from coverage. But most sectors were included, and within each sector the policies protecting labor's right to organize and bargain collectively were applicable to all firms involved in interstate commerce.[17] The federal government has also seen fit to pass general regulatory policies concerned with maximum hours, minimum wages, and general working conditions of a large proportion of employees. These laws very definitely cut across the separate sectors of the economy. The era of growth in economic regulation by the federal government did not end with the New Deal. Nor did it end with Presidents Kennedy and Johnson. Many economic regulations produced during the 1960s and early

---

[17]Except in civil rights legislation, where firms employing fewer than twenty-five employees are explicitly exempted from coverage, the limitation to interstate commerce is no longer meaningful. Since even the smallest firms buy or sell at least one commodity that is shipped through interstate commerce, the federal law can reach as far as unions and the National Labor Relations Board (NLRB) would ever want.

Table 15.3 Highlights of Federal Government Policy in Selected Sectors of Commerce and Industry

Policies	Agriculture	Consumer Industries	Energy Industries	Basic Industries	Communications Industries	Transportation Industries
Subsidy	Grants to improve land productivity; education on how to do this; aids to facilitate marketing.	Traditional tariffs against foreign competition; development of new products, for the benefit of government research.	Tariffs and quotas against foreign sources; results of government research (especially atomic); access to public mineral resources; construction of dams or other direct support for generating capacity.	Stockpiling contracts; highways; benefit of government research.	Government-sponsored research; defense contracts; cash and services for satellite development.	Land and cash (for rail and shipping); mail contracts; highway building and airport construction; grants for rapid transit.
Regulatory	Control of uniform standards, measures, quality of products; support of increased prices by keeping down the amount of land under cultivation (the so-called parity program); control of soil erosion; control of timber use on public lands.	Policing price discrimination and mergers (food), and policing safety and advertising claims (drugs, cosmetics, and cigarettes).	Control of rates, assignment of amounts to extract (oil and gas), licensing to enter market (atomic energy and oil-gas transport).	Policing price discrimination and bid rigging; threats (rarely serious) against monopoly size; some policing of product safety.	Licensing to control frequencies; policing access and "equal time"; regulation of mergers and interlocking ownerships; policing of telephone rate charges and services.	Antitrust regulation; policing of rates and services; licensing entry and schedules of airlines; policing of safety.

continued on next page

Policies	Agriculture	Consumer Industries	Energy Industries	Basic Industries	Communications Industries	Transportation Industries
Fiscal	Credit extended on a below-market basis to protect farm mortgages and to encourage expanded investment in farms.	Tax deductions for a high proportion of the business expenses of research, advertising, and building.	Tax allowance for depletion of resources to encourage exploration.	Tax credits on investments and research; tax deductions on interest payments; mortgage guarantees; long-range loans and loan guarantees.	None especially for these industries; only the usual tax breaks for investment.	Taxes on gasoline to finance part of highway construction and to discourage use of automobiles; reduced excise taxes to encourage purchase of automobiles.

The *consumer industries* include over-the-counter food, drugs, cigarettes, and cosmetics. The *energy industries* include oil, gas, coal, water, and atomic energy. The *basic industries* include steel, chemicals, automobiles, housing construction, and defense. The *communications industries* include telephone, radio and television, computer transmission, and satellite communication. The *transportation industries* incluce rail, air, trucking, and water.

1970s were extensions and amendments of the policies coming out of the New Deal, but expansion in some entirely new areas has also occurred. For example, in 1970 a Democratic Congress enacted legislation establishing an entirely new basis for federal regulation of wages and prices. President Nixon opposed the enactment, promised he would not use the controls, and then proceeded within two years to employ them with great fanfare.

Although the wage and price control programs of 1972 and 1973 failed to stem the tide of inflation, the basis for additional attempts to regulate incomes and prices has been established. Wage-price control in the 1970s has been bad policy, because the laws setting it up gave entirely too much discretion to the executive branch and entirely too little guidance to the unions, managers, and proprietors affected by the regulations. But clearly this form of control is here to stay, and we should seek ways to improve it and make it more just rather than object to it unconditionally.[18]

Table 15.3 is a bird's-eye view of the actualities and potentialities of governmental control of commerce and industry. Efforts at regulation have often been so paltry or completely permissive as to constitute encouragement rather than limitation of the activities supposedly being policed. Antitrust policy is so far out of date that it is almost irrelevant to the new developments of conglomerate merger and other restraints of trade that are not, strictly speaking, monopolistic. Many regulatory policies continue to depend upon data drawn from the regulated companies themselves and are thus not capable of the independence we would expect from government agencies that are supposed to regulate and police commercial abuses.

Nevertheless, the techniques of control reviewed here are capable of a great deal more influence over the economy than most administrations or congressional majorities have sought. Failure to provide adequate regulation is much more often due to ignorance, corruption, or plain lack of will than to any inherent limitations on the powers to license, subsidize, contract, or tax that a serious government might wish to use to eradicate business fraud, price discrimination, or other restraints of trade that interfere with the workings of a dynamic industrial economy.

Making and Maintaining a Capitalist Economy

American propaganda is full of praise for American capitalism. Capitalism is juxtaposed with Soviet communism; it is associated with limited government, personal freedom, and prosperity. Indeed, there is much to praise about American capitalism, and it should be

[18]For some good suggestions, see Galbraith, *Economics and the Public Purpose,* pp. 194–197 and 313–316.

no surprise that Americans have strongly supported public policies that support capitalism. What is surprising is the myth that capitalism exists free of government, has needed no government support, and suffers to the extent that government seeks to support or to control it.

Every modern government does something to provide for a uniform national currency—including governments in capitalist countries. The special distinction of capitalist government is manifested in banks, savings institutions, stock markets, and insurance companies, where private wealth is accumulated and used as *capital*. Currency *as such* is involved in only a tiny proportion of all transactions in a developed economy; the question, then, is how provision is made for the vast majority of economic transactions.

Money policies: Federal banks, credit, and insurance   During the first century of our republic, banking was provided for and regulated by the states.[19] As the economy became more and more national and international, federal rather than state control became more appropriate and began to emerge soon after the Civil War. States continued to have the power to charter and regulate their own system of state banks, and state banks continue to outnumber banks in the national system. But they are less important in the overall financial picture.

When the federal government did enter the picture, it behaved more or less consistently with the American ideal of free enterprise by not setting up a publicly supported national bank, even though there were good models in capitalistic England and France. Instead, it sought primarily to regulate banks in order to help provide for a consistent and dependable method of making commercial transactions anywhere in the country. State banks had been notoriously inconsistent and unstable, creating their own bank notes, failing to honor checks, overextending credit. This was altogether too uneven and unstable for any national economic system, especially a capitalistic system.

Banks are a mainstay, perhaps *the* mainstay, of a capitalist economy, not only because they are a channel for money and credit, but because they create money. For example, a bank can take a new deposit of $1,000 and immediately loan a large proportion of that amount to a new customer. If the authorized proportion is 80 percent, the bank can loan $800 to the new customer. Assuming that this customer leaves his or her loan as a deposit in the bank, drawing on it only as needed, the bank can then loan up to 80

---

[19]Congress did provide for a Bank of the United States from 1791 to 1811 and for a Second Bank of the United States between 1816 and 1836. But these were of minor importance in the full history of banking and capitalism in the United States. For the early history of banking and its problems, see Bray Hammond, *Banks and Politics in America* (Princeton: Princeton University Press, 1956).

percent ($640) of that deposit. This means that in two transactions the original $1,000 deposit can grow to $2,440.

Assuming a closed banking system, where most money borrowed from any bank goes to that bank or to other banks in the form of deposits, economists estimate that each new deposit can create as much as five times its own value in new credit. This is called the *multiplier effect.* As suggested in chapter 7, the practice of *fractional reserve banking* is made possible by our knowledge of mass behavior and the very small likelihood that a large proportion of depositors will go to the bank at the same time to withdraw their money. On the rare occasions when this happens, it creates a panic, and banks may fail by the dozens simply because they never keep enough money on hand to satisfy all the demands of all depositors.

This immense capacity of banks for expansion of credit is a very productive but also a very dangerous element in the economy. An economy that can expand at the exponential rate of the multiplier effect is an economy that can also deflate at the same exponential rate if demand begins to drop, investment begins to fall, and no new deposits are generated. Thus, although the American federal government does not operate as the banker, it is very heavily involved in keeping the multiplier effect from becoming a "divisor effect."

The earliest governmental device for establishing and maintaining a stable national banking system was, as could probably be expected, chartering (licensing) on condition that the bank follow relatively conservative lending practices. Thus banks would be chartered only if they kept around 20 percent of all deposits on hand—the fractional reserve requirement. National bank chartering also included periodic bank examinations and reports, both of which were done under the supervision of the Treasury Department and the comptroller of the currency.

The national government began building some foundations for a real national banking system by establishing the Federal Reserve system in 1913. The purpose of this system was to provide a central reservoir of money that could be made available to member banks in times of serious deflation to help meet the demand for credit if there were insufficient deposits from individuals. This had a great nationalizing effect, because the Federal Reserve could facilitate the transfer of surpluses from regions with low credit demands toward regions where the demand for credit was stronger than the supply of money.

Each member bank is able to borrow money from the Federal Reserve, using as collateral the very notes on the loans already made by that bank. In this way, by allowing each member bank to pass along its loan obligations to the center and to get further currency and credit flexibility in return, the multiplier effect can work to its fullest. In order to provide some control over borrowing

The railroad was to
government in the 19th
century as the pipeline is
to government in the 20th
century.

from the fund, the Federal Reserve Board (FRB) was given legislative authority to charge interest on the money its member banks borrow. This is called the discount rate, and the power of the FRB to raise or lower the rate was expected to act as a brake or an accelerator on the availability of credit and therefore on the level of business activity in the economy.

When the FRB raises the discount rate charged to member banks, this is popularly called a hard money policy; the lowering of discount rates is supposed to lower the interest rates charged by banks to borrowers and is therefore called an easy money policy. Some would argue that this power lodged in the FRB has done more harm than good; many critics have even gone so far as to blame the 1929 stock market crash on irrational monetary policies of the FRB. Others have defended the system while conceding that it has its limitations.

For example, when the country is in a severe deflation, even the most extremely low discount rate will probably not be sufficient to encourage the investment necessary to pull the economy out. Nevertheless, by 1935 the Federal Reserve system had sufficient stature and was given additional authority to use its control over reserve requirements and discount rates as techniques of control over the economy at large—that is, as macroeconomic controls (see

Table 15.1). The FRB is independent of the president and the Treasury Department, but every president since Roosevelt has looked to the FRB to help get us out of economic trouble.

Of equal importance in maintaining a stable national banking system, the federal government established deposit insurance under the Federal Deposit Insurance Corporation of 1933. Each deposit in a nationally chartered bank is insured up to a maximum of $40,000 per individual deposit. If a bank fails and is unable to meet all its obligations, depositors do not have to fear the loss of their money. The theory is that insurance of this sort will eliminate bank panics, because no one will feel the need to run down to the bank and remove his or her deposit as soon as the economy begins to look bad.

The federal approach to banking, particularly deposit insurance, became a kind of model for a distinctly American approach to its capitalist economy. Deposit insurance is quite clearly a method of *putting a floor under risk.* It is in fact a reassurance to every individual in the market that the economy will be allowed to contract only so far; of still greater importance is the reassurance it gives investors, making possible their willingness to take greater and greater risk. This same device has been employed in a number of other areas since the 1930s, and it promises to increase in use as the years go by.

Perhaps the most important area where this method of government insurance has been used as a very effective policy is in the home construction industry. Several important federal agencies have been insuring mortgage loans for years. (For the administrative side of this, see chapter 12.) If a veteran goes to an office of the Veterans Administration (VA) and gets their approval for the purchase or building of a house, the veteran can take that approval to a private bank and get a mortgage loan on terms a good deal more favorable than the terms otherwise available in the credit market. Billions and billions of dollars in private housing investments have been influenced and facilitated by these programs of mortgage insurance. Yet, it costs the federal government a very small amount, since its main job is to put the word of the government back of each mortgage and then to pick up the losses on that small proportion of mortgages that are foreclosed.

The whole sector of the housing industry is propped up still further by government insurance on the deposits made in savings and loan associations. The Federal Savings and Loan Insurance Corporation (FSLIC) performs for the savings and loan institutions as the FDIC performs for the nationally chartered banks.

Similar public policies for insuring private investment (setting a floor under risk) can be found in the area of loans for small business disasters; economic development; business and farming investments by the VA; economic opportunity (by the Small Business Administration) for businesses, especially in the ghetto, which find conventional borrowing difficult; students attending college; certain defense contracts; many types of community facilities and community land acquisition; community health care facilities; and certain kinds of agriculture improvement (although most agriculture loans are provided directly by government).

The willingness to take risks is apparently such an important resource in the United States that the federal government considers itself obligated to protect it and to husband it by a federal system of insurance. There is no national government health insurance in the United States except for the elderly; but there is a national risk insurance. The United States may never adopt socialism in its classical form. However, it may obviate the need for socialism through the socialization of risk.

The national government has in effect socialized risk by agreeing to repay all depositors in the event of a bank failure; by agreeing to repossess homes and to indemnify investors, including banks, in cases where home buyers cannot maintain their federally insured mortgages; by agreeing to repay banks in those instances where a defense industry proves unable to honor its debts. There are many other examples of this national risk insurance, which has a dual political advantage: (1) It meets with the approval of capitalists and potential capitalists. (2) It is not costly to the federal government, for reasons already suggested. Risk insurance is not yet fully appreciated in the United States, but it could easily become the most important device for economic planning in the country.

Federal taxation and spending policies   In the United States, taxation has the reputation for being the most important technique of fiscal policy. Long ago it was discovered that every method of taxation has its own special effect on society. That is to say, all taxes discriminate; it is the essence of fiscal policy to decide what kind of discrimination to build into the tax structure.

One aspect of fiscal policy is the choice between a progressive and a regressive tax structure. The former is designed to place a much heavier tax burden on higher income brackets than lower income brackets. The rationale behind the progressive tax is that those most able to pay should pay the most on a percentage basis. This is called "ability to pay." A highly graduated income tax is an example of a progressive tax. A sales tax on food and clothing is considered a regressive tax inasmuch as a very high percentage of the income of persons in lower brackets goes to these essential expenditures. An even more regressive tax is our social security tax, since it is applied only to the first $15,300 of income. This means that people earning up to that amount pay exactly 5.85 percent of their income to social security (7.9 percent if self-employed), whereas those making twice as much income pay only half the same rate to social security. (More

Jonathan Swift observed
250 years ago that no
system of taxation can
be neutral—*Gulliver's
Travels*, 1726.

I heard a very warm Debate between two Professors, about the most commodious and effectual Ways and Means of raising Money without grieving the Subject. The First affirmed, the justest Method would be to lay a certain Tax upon Vices and Folly; and the Sum fixed upon every Man, to be rated after the fairest Manner by a Jury of his Neighbours. The second was of an Opinion directly contrary; to tax those Qualities of Body and Mind for which Men chiefly value themselves; the Rate to be more or less according to the Degrees of excelling; the Decision whereof should be left entirely to their own Breast. The highest Tax was upon Men, who are the greatest Favourites of the other Sex; and the Assessments according to the Number and Natures of the Favours they have received; for which they are allowed to be their own Vouchers. Wit, Valour, and Politeness were likewise proposed to be largely taxed, and collected in the same Manner, by every Person giving his own Word for the Quantum of what he possessed. But, as to Honour, Justice, Wisdom and Learning, they should not be taxed at all; because, they are Qualifications of so singular a Kind, that no Man will either allow them in his Neighbour, or value them in himself.

The Women were proposed to be taxed according to their Beauty and Skill in Dressing; wherein they had the same Privilege with the Men, to be determined by their own Judgment. But Constancy, Chastity, good Sense, and good Nature were not rated, because they would not bear the Charge of Collecting. . . .

on these aspects of fiscal policy will be treated under the category of inequality.[20])

There are other fiscal aspects of taxation which require a brief review. The most important of these is probably the tax structure itself and the ability of the federal government to manipulate it in order to manipulate aggregate demand. The government tries to set up the income tax structure in such a way as to maximize revenue and minimize the effect of taxation on consumption and investment. Even when the tax rates are not manipulated, they have a fairly significant countercyclical effect on the economy. Consequently, the tax structure is considered one of the important automatic stabilizers of the economy.

When the economy is on the upward side of the business cycle, the established rates of taxation draw in increasingly large amounts of revenue, and this operates as something of a check on inflationary pressures. During the downward swing of the business cycle, the same tax rates will produce proportionately lower revenues, leaving somewhat more than otherwise in the hands of the income earner. If the expenditure side of the government remains the same or increases during the downward swing, the reduced revenues plus

---

[20]A good analysis of some of these issues will be found in Louis Eisenstein, *Ideologies of Taxation* (New York: Ronald Press, 1961); see also Joseph Pechman, "The Rich, the Poor and the Taxes They Pay," *Public Interest*, Fall 1969, pp. 21–43.

the budgetary deficit will produce a slight inflationary effect that could encourage more investment.

Tax subsidies—sometimes called loopholes or deductions, depending on the vantage point of the speaker—are important in that they work an enormous incentive on economic behavior, especially on capitalistic behavior. When people are allowed to deduct the interest they pay on mortgages or other loans from their taxable income, this means that the tax structure is encouraging them to be capitalists—that is, to engage in investment. Government is essentially subsidizing the borrower; if the borrower is in a high tax bracket, say where 40 percent of income is taxable, then the government is essentially subsidizing 40 percent of any interest payments the person has to make, because that is the amount of the interest that can be deducted from taxes. Other business expenses that can be deducted from taxable income are further examples of ways in which the federal government subsidizes people who agree to behave like capitalists.[21]

People are generally against tax loopholes in principle but rarely recognize as a loophole the tax advantage that applies to them. There would be a great clamor against any effort to eliminate the right to deduct medical expenses from taxable income; and there would be an even greater clamor if Congress ever tried to put an end to tax deductions for contributions to religious and charitable institutions. Yet these are seen as loopholes to those not benefited by the deductions, because obviously not every type of person benefits equally from allowable deductions in the income tax structure. Table 15.4 suggests that the more capitalistic the behavior of an individual or corporate group, the more likely it is that advantageous deductions which apply to that individual or group can be found in the income tax code. The table seems to indicate that on the way to raising enough revenue to run the government, the United States would like to encourage as many people as possible, in all walks of life, to behave like capitalists.

If taxpayers will use some of their surplus to invest rather than to buy an extra television set, they can deduct their losses; and if they make a profit on their investment, they can pay a capital gains tax at half the rate of their personal income tax. There is even greater advantage if the investment is made from borrowed money, particularly in the purchase of real estate. In addition to the very high proportion of the interest payments which can be deducted from taxes, many other advantages in the tax structure go to home ownership. Very few go to home or apartment rental. Probably even more deductions can be claimed if one owns an apartment house and

[21]A devastating study of the character and extent of tax subsidies or loopholes is that of Phillip M. Stern, *The Rape of the Taxpayer* (New York: Random House, 1972). See also Stanley S. Surrey, *Pathways to Tax Reform* (Cambridge, Mass.: Harvard University Press, 1974).

Table 15.4	Some Tax Incentives to Behave Like a Capitalist
Invest.	Write off depreciation; pay capital gains rather than personal income tax, at half the rate.
Borrow.	Deduct interest payments.
Buy your house.	Deduct interest, fees, taxes, insurance, depreciation. If you rent, you cannot deduct any of these costs.
Expand your business.	Deduct losses; spread income peaks over bad years; plow back profits instead of paying out taxable salaries and dividends; pay capital gains tax instead of income tax.
Incorporate your business.	Corporate income taxes reach a peak at 52 percent. In contrast, personal income taxes can reach a peak at over 70 percent.

takes one of the apartments as living quarters. Incentive for expansion is added by the allowance for deduction of many losses and by the allowance for any sudden increases in profit to be dealt with on a five-year income averaging plan, which in many instances can keep a taxpayer in a lower tax bracket. Finally, there are great incentives to incorporate, so many that even individuals are incorporating themselves and small business is rejecting ancient proprietorship in favor of incorporation. There is a lower tax rate for corporate income; moreover, the owners or the officers of the corporation are able to manipulate the amount of taxes they pay by minimizing the amount paid in salaries, retaining earnings in the firm as investments, or reporting them as corporate rather than personal income. The tax structure is also supportive of the industrial capitalist economy by its enormously stable support of the middle and upper-middle income brackets. This is conservative from the standpoint of redistribution of wealth, and at the same time it is an encouragement to the investment and savings habits of the middle classes.

The stability of the tax structure is dramatically portrayed in Table 15.5. In the sixty years covered by this table, the proportion of money income going to the richest 20 percent of the country has not changed appreciably. It has dropped slightly, but it has remained over 40 percent. There has been a slight improvement in the shares going to the second highest income bracket, but the general impression is one of almost no change during the twentieth century. The lowest 20 percent—perhaps the lowest 40 percent—may have been made more comfortable by social security, a more stable income through union membership, and more government services outside the welfare system. But none of these has changed the general

Table 15.5	Has There Been Any Redistribution of Wealth in the U.S. in the Twentieth Century? Not According to Studies of Shares of "Total Money Income" Received by Five Income Brackets, 1910–1972.

Family Income Bracket	1910	1929	1934	1944	1950	1960	1969	1972
Lowest fifth	8.3	5.4	5.9	4.9	4.5	5.0	6.0	5.0
Second fifth	11.5	10.1	11.5	10.9	12.0	12.0	12.0	11.0
Third fifth	15.0	14.4	15.5	16.2	17.4	18.0	18.0	18.0
Fourth fifth	19.0	18.8	20.4	22.2	23.5	24.0	23.0	24.0
Highest fifth	46.2	51.3	49.7	45.8	42.6	42.0	41.0	43.0

Figures for the period 1910 through 1950 are provided by Allan Rosenbaum, "State Government, Political Power, and Public Policy: The Case of Illinois" (Ph.D. diss., University of Chicago, 1974), chapters 10–11; figures for 1960 through 1972 are from Edward S. Greenberg, *Serving the Few* (New York: Wiley, 1974), pp. 132–133. See also Gabriel Kolko, *Wealth and Power in America* (New York: Praeger, 1962).

distribution of wealth appreciably, and this kind of stability has to have a buoying effect on the savings and investment habits of the higher income brackets.[22]

Not all of this stability or conservatism is attributable to the federal income tax structure. In fact, it is slightly redistributive, inasmuch as the rate of taxation on very high incomes is disproportionately higher than on very low incomes. However, that redistributive effect is blunted by several features of revenue policies in the United States. The progressive rates of the internal revenue structure are weakened by all of the deductibles, which are typically more applicable in the upper income brackets than in the lower. Then, too, most taxes other than the federal income tax are quite clearly regressive. That is to say, they hit the lower brackets at a *higher rate* than the upper brackets. Among the regressive taxes (some of which were mentioned earlier) are the sales tax on necessary items, social security taxes (which are taken at a constant rate regardless of the total annual income), local gasoline and cigarette taxes, property taxes, and local school taxes.

These are the *structural* features of the federal taxing system. That is to say, these provisions are written into the law—the Internal Revenue Code—and do not change appreciably from year to year. They constitute the so-called tax structure. And their regular impact tends strongly to favor capitalist behavior, whether the taxpayer is wealthy or only of modest means. That is, the

[22]Good discussions will be found in Robert J. Lampman, *What Does It Do for the Poor? A New Test for National Policy* (Madison: University of Wisconsin, Institute for Research on Poverty, October 1973); also Edward S. Greenberg, *Serving the Few* (New York: Wiley, 1974), chapter 4.

greater benefits tend to go to those who are willing to save, to invest, to buy their home, and generally to improve themselves through increasing their wealth rather than their regular income.

There are also some *dynamic* uses of taxation, where the government—mainly the president and the secretary of the treasury—attempt to change the tax structure or some particular part of it on specific occasions to meet a problem in the economy. Sometimes these changes are temporary, and sometimes they become a regular part of the tax structure; but the changes are adopted in response to a particular challenge. These dynamic elements tend also to favor the capitalistic elements of the economy, although generally the theory is that helping the larger investor will allow others to gain as well, because the tax cut may maintain aggregate demand, or the tax increase may check inflation.

In 1961, when a new and aggressive president anticipated the continuation of a recession, his most dramatic action was to cut taxes for any business willing to make new investments. This was called the investment tax credit and was a multibillion dollar boost to capitalist enterprise, not directly a shot in the arm to the consumer. In 1971, when the prosperity of the 1960s was beginning to suffer from inflation, a Republican president chose almost the same measures. In addition to the investment tax credit, President Nixon also suspended the automobile excise tax in order to bail out one of the ailing industries by forcefully directing consumer activity into the purchase of new automobiles. Manipulation of interest rates—moving from a hard money policy to easy money and back again—is another measure frequently relied upon to affect the economy through changes in investment behavior.[23]

So far we have dealt with the taxation and credit techniques of planning for capitalism in the United States. There is a third element, the *spending* side of fiscal policy. The American public in the past forty years has come overwhelmingly to accept the fact that the federal government will engage in countercyclical spending by letting the national budget go into great deficits during downward sides of the business cycle and then by trying to reduce the deficit—though rarely producing a surplus—whenever the upward side of the business cycle is so vigorous as to produce inflation rather than prosperity. Sometimes the budget deficit is attributable to the maintenance of existing levels of spending coupled with reduction of revenues. However, there are also occasions when the deficit is produced by deliberate increases in the amount of spending.

Most presidents and their economic advisers since the mid-1940s have been followers of the great British economist John Maynard Keynes, who propounded theories of the modern capitalist economy

[23]If one can cut through the jargon, Galbraith's analysis of the recent uses of taxation can be most enlightening. See his *Economics and the Public Purpose*, p. 303.

to guide governments on how and when to intervene. Part of the enormous attractiveness of Keynes's theories is attributable to his real insights into the relationship between savings and investment and how and when to manipulate the one or the other in order to achieve a predictable result. Another part of his attractiveness is that his theories gave policy makers a strong rationale for *intervention,* particularly for larger and larger budget deficits.[24]

However, despite the faith of policy makers that governments can spend their way out of depressions and out of inflations, the expenditure side of fiscal policy has not worked well in the United States, for several reasons.

1. Although it is true that public spending can supplement private spending to produce higher aggregate demand in the economy, there is no guarantee that public spending will get money into the hands of consumers who will spend it on prosperity-producing items, such as durable goods like automobiles and washing machines.

2. It is not easy for the government to increase its expenditures quickly enough or spend the money fast enough to head off pessimistic psychology in the economy. New blueprints for public works have to be designed or old ones have to be dusted off, contracts have to be let, and people have to be hired before new public money begins to circulate. This takes time, and the opportunity to avert economic contraction may pass before such projects can be begun.

3. Probably most important in the United States, the spending side of public policy is a great deal more decentralized and fragmented than the taxing or credit sides. The so-called budget deficit may look like a single item in published documents, and the total size of that deficit may be a significant figure. But the budget deficit is the result of literally hundreds of different programs and agencies where money is being spent.

We already know from earlier treatments of bureaucracy that the president can influence only a few of these programs in time to have them meet his commitment toward the economy. But when time is short, a president's limitations are particularly severe. It would be impossible to bring to an immediate halt all the government programs that are deemed contributors to inflation, and it would be impossible to generate quite suddenly a doubling or tripling of action in agencies where the president sees a chance of improving the battle against a recession.

4. In contrast to the attempts at manipulating the economy

---

[24]John Maynard Keynes, *The General Theory of Employment Interest and Money* (New York: Harcourt, Brace, 1936). For an insight into the prominence of Keynes in the basic outlook of American economics, see Samuelson, *Economics,* 9th ed. For a fascinating account of how Keynes was brought into central economic planning in the United States through the Employment Act of 1946, see Stephen K. Bailey, *Congress Makes a Law* (New York: Columbia University Press, 1950), chapters 1–3.

through government spending, taxing, credit, and insurance are far less fragmented techniques of stimulating the economy. The president seems to have more control over the dynamic aspects of these powers, where influence has to be exerted through a limited number of Treasury officials, the Federal Reserve Board, and two congressional committees (Senate Finance and House Ways and Means). There is the usual political fragmentation in the process of making basic changes in the tax structure, but many taxing and credit actions do not require full-fledged congressional enactments. The Federal Reserve is an independent agency and can make its decisions on tight money and easy money without the clearance of any other government agency. The president, the Treasury, and the Federal Reserve Board all have some direct power to affect the amount of money in circulation, the value of bonds being exchanged, and the attractiveness of investment over saving. And, although the president has no power to raise or lower tax rates to meet economic needs, cooperation is usually available from the congressional committees on tax policy.[25]

The taxing and credit aspects of fiscal policy are also more efficacious in planning for the U.S. economy to the extent that leaders of the largest capitalist enterprises prefer tax policies to spending policies. It is quite clear that they prefer tax cuts to increased spending whenever there is perceived need to give the economy a boost. Perhaps this preference is attributable to the fact that there are fewer agencies to deal with on the tax and credit side, or perhaps it is attributable to the ability of business people to adjust more easily to changes in the tax structure than to the very diffuse results of shifts in government spending. In any case, for all these reasons and others, it is probable that the growth of economic planning in the United States will be much more on the tax, monetary, credit, and insurance side.

This seems to be consistent with the American tradition of keeping most capital in private hands. Government can become heavily involved in private economic matters yet can limit its involvement to two basic areas, one for the individual investor and the other for the business community at large. The areas are: (1) the reduction of risk, mainly through the principle of insurance; and (2) a perpetual war against the downward side of the business cycle, mainly through manipulation of the tax and the interest rates. Government spending will always be an important factor in the

---

[25]President Kennedy sought discretionary taxing power in 1962 without success; however, the political process of tax policy is decidedly centered in the executive branch and is dominated by the president. Compare with Stanley S. Surrey, "How Special Tax Provisions Get Enacted," *Public Policies and Their Politics*, ed. R. B. Ripley (New York: Norton, 1966). Surrey observes that Congress is very jealous of its power to provide the various details of the tax structure, such as equities, deductibles, and specific taxing brackets. However, as to the general principles of taxation, Surrey observes that the wishes of the president and the Treasury prevail.

economy, but its potential as an instrument of planning is blunted
by the inability of the chief executive to coordinate the activities of
all the individual agencies. Consequently, spending will remain a
pork barrel activity whose cumulative effect will never be susceptible to a coordinated or planning approach to the economy.

Socializing Poverty and Dependency

In the United States, poverty and dependency tend to be separated
into two classes, the deserving poor and the undeserving poor. We
have traditionally assumed that the undeserving poor far outnumber the deserving poor, and that if the poor would only exert
themselves they would no longer be dependent.

A very large system of voluntary, private philanthropy was built
up during the nineteenth century on the basis of these attitudes.
Churches and related religious groups, ethnic and fraternal societies, and communities and smaller neighborhoods had charities in
one organized form or another. Individual charitable contributions
by the extremely rich were common phenomena long before foundations systematized their good works. Public involvement in charity
was very slight until the end of the nineteenth century, not only
because of our preference for private enterprise but also because
there was confidence that all of the deserving poor could be taken

care of by private effort. Even as late as 1928, only 11.6 percent of all relief granted in fifteen large cities came from public funds.[26]

The traditional American theory of poverty and dependency crumbled under the stark realities of the 1929 depression. The scale of the failure of the economic system revealed some ugly facts that mythology and prosperity had kept hidden for a long time. Thousands upon thousands of workers suddenly became dependent through no fault of their own. Misfortune was suddenly shared by millions and was threatening to last beyond any period that even the most frugal wage earner could have provided for.

The Great Depression finally proved to Americans that poverty is an aspect of the economic system and is only seldom a product of individual effort or irresponsibility. Poverty, in other words, is a social class in a capitalist system, just as it is in any other system. Poverty is one of the evidences of imperfection in any economic system. Thus in 1969, when an annual income of $3,720 was the public definition of the poverty line for a nonfarm family of four, 24.3 million Americans were, by definition, poor. For the ten years prior to 1969 there had been a decline in the number of poor, as well as a decline in the proportion of the poor in the total population.[27] In 1970–1971 there appeared to be a slight increase in the number of poor Americans, but it is quite probable that the poor will continue to constitute over 10 percent of the population. The percentage figure varies, of course, depending on where the line of poverty is defined.

Once poverty was seen as a phenomenon inherent in the economic system, a more systematic approach to it by governments was probably not far away. With the new administration in 1933, the issue of poverty and dependency was high on the public agenda. There was no longer any question of whether we would socialize poverty; from that time forward it was a question of how large the poverty class was going to be and how comfortable we were going to try to make dependent persons.[28]

Figure 15.2 provides some indication of the extent to which federal, state, and local governments now provide programs for the poor and dependent. However, by far the most important programs are the two popularly known as social security and public assistance. The distinction between these two is based on the type of

---

[26]From a WPA study by Anne E. Geddes, reported in Merle Fainsod et al., *Government and the American Economy* (New York: Norton, 1959), p. 769.

[27]Using 1969 criteria, there were 39.5 million poor in 1959, comprising 22.4 percent of the population. In 1969, this proportion had dropped to 12.2 percent. These figures and others like them can be drawn from the United States Bureau of the Census, *Current Population Reports,* (Washington, D.C.: Government Printing Office, periodically). A particularly useful report by the bureau is *Twenty-four Million Americans: Poverty in the United States, 1969* (Washington, D.C.: Government Printing Office, 1970, no. 76).

[28]There is a third question: What types of persons will be allowed to enter and leave the poverty class? This will be held over to the next section, since it turns out to be a very different kind of question.

Table 15.6

Contributory ("Insurance") System

1. Old Age and Survivors, Disability and Health (OASDHI): Title II of 1935 act, plus Title XVIII (Medicare, 1965). National system financed by taxes on employer and employee, plus subsidy from general revenue.

2. Unemployment: Title III. State systems, National Trust Fund with state accounts. Financed by tax on employers of eight or more persons, 90 percent of which is credited against contributions to an approved state program (sections 903 and 902, Title IX).

Noncontributory System (Public Assistance)

1. Old Age Assistance: Title I. Grants to state for one-half of all payments up to $30 per month to individuals of 65 and over, if state program is approved by social security board.[1]

2. Aid to Families with Dependent Children (AFDC): Title IV. Grants to states for one-third of payments of up to $18 per month for first child and $12 for each additional child.[2]

3. Aid to the Blind and the Permanently and Totally Disabled: Title X, as amended. Grants to states for one-half of payments of up to $30 per month, subject to approval by social security board.

4. Maternal and Child Welfare: Title V. Nonmonetary welfare. Payments based on number of births and financial need to states providing hospital, nursing, and public health services under plans. Up to one-half the cost of services is provided by Secretary of Labor and children's bureau.

5. Vocational Rehabilitation: Title V. Extension of act of 1920. Nonmonetary welfare.

6. Public Health: Title VI. Nonmonetary welfare. Grants to states for improved services, personnel, or sanitation.

---

[1]Federal grants may be terminated if states violate federal standards, but the program works mainly through incentives. The federal government reimburses each state for a substantial proportion of state outlays for old-age assistance.
[2]Supervision and incentives are the same as for old-age assistance.

beneficiary or client. Social security is for those who *contribute* from their wages prior to receiving benefits, and public assistance is for persons who *do not contribute* or have not contributed to a trust fund but who can show some specifically defined need for welfare assistance.

Table 15.6 outlines the major categories within each of the two parts—contributory and noncontributory—of the welfare system. Both these parts define poverty and dependency as a class; and the categories of assistance tend strongly to provide for modes of dependency that are associated with capitalist modes of production or capitalist modes of organizing for work. That is to say, these categories are comprised of people who are either "not needed" in an industrial economy or who, even if able-bodied, have nothing to offer the industrial system.

Since our social security is a contributory system, it is sometimes referred to as social insurance; however, this is not an accurate

Domestic Policy: Conquest Maintained

designation. Although it is true that only those persons who contribute for a certain minimum number of months during their years of employment are eligible to receive social security benefits, their contributions are not sufficient to pay for the benefits. That is to say, the social security system is not actuarially sound, as a true insurance system would have to be. In fact, the rates of taxation for old age or for unemployment compensation were never set high enough to come anywhere near actuarial soundness. Moreover, as the number of old people in the United States increased, and as benefits increased and coverage was extended, subsidies drawn from general revenues for the Social Security Trust Fund began to expand also.

This is not necessarily a bad thing. Since the social security tax is a highly regressive tax (as earlier observed), about the only way to introduce a slight redistribution of wealth in the welfare system is to draw contributions directly from general revenues, because the general income tax is more progressive than the social security tax. Yet those who want the federal government to contribute to the redistribution of wealth should not want the welfare system to be completely self-sustaining. A completely self-sustaining welfare system would, among other things, tend to redistribute wealth from the young to the old, drawing as it does upon those who are working to pay for those who are retired or disabled. While some of this may be desirable, it is not necessarily desirable to base the entire social security system upon it.

Noncontributory welfare comprises six separate categories in Table 15.6. The most important are the first three, which provide actual cash payments. These are truly the public assistance categories, a direct outgrowth of earlier state and local welfare programs; federal programs "nationalized" state and local activities and were influenced by the fact. Federal law requires each state to have these programs, in which a predetermined proportion of the payments made is contributed by federal grants. Thus each state is free to be as generous as it wishes in establishing the schedules of payments but is bound by law not to opt against these programs.

There are both advantages and disadvantages to the American welfare system. The major advantage of the American approach is that it touches upon virtually every conceivable type of dependency relevant to an industrial capitalist economy. Each category is defined with considerable clarity, so that administrators and citizens will know who can benefit and who cannot. Moreover, this kind of categoric approach to welfare enables the government to extend the welfare system as new problems in the industrial economy are discovered. For example, permanent and total disability was added in 1951. This categoric approach may seem rigid, but there is, perhaps, compensating flexibility in certain of the noncontributory programs, especially Aid to Families with Dependent Children

(AFDC). This is the sort of thing that cannot be handled on a routine basis, since no one knows which father will desert his family or which individual will be born or rendered blind or crippled. Such haphazard occurrences are provided for in the American welfare system.

There are also some specific advantages to the contributory system of social security. Forced savings may seem a harsh technique for benefiting the individual, but the system does operate as a continual reminder that people ought to provide for themselves as much as possible. The contributory aspect also helps limit the use of the welfare system as a political football. Another advantage is that people can approach old age or unemployment with the confidence that they have a *right* to support rather than having to go to the government as a supplicant for a grant or a dole. For many individuals, workers as well as business people, this is a very strong feature of the American system.

Despite all these virtues, there are many negative aspects of American welfare.[29] The biggest disadvantage to contributory programs is that they often do not reach the most needy, who do not work long enough to make adequate contributions to retirement or to medicare or unemployment. Moreover, the contributory system at present discriminates heavily against retired persons by setting severe limits upon the amount of money that may be earned between the ages of sixty-five and seventy-two without losing welfare benefits. If, for example, a person earns more than $2,100 a year, the social security pension is reduced by one dollar for every two dollars earned. This amounts to a tax rate of 50 percent, and it does not apply to money received from dividends, interest, or other pensions. Thus it hits most heavily those who are willing to supplement their pensions with effort.

Neither of these disadvantages is of course inherent in the system. Both are, rather, the result of choices made in Congress to limit government provisions for the poor. The barrier to supplementing the social security pension with other earnings could be overcome by simple reform; and as the number of elderly increases, the likelihood of this reform grows. The fact that social security does not reach those who are permanently unable to work and to make the minimum contribution to the system is substantially overcome by the noncontributory programs. Here, too, it is a question only of how generous Congress chooses to be.

The main criticisms of the noncontributory programs have been hurled against the single largest category, AFDC, which accounts for more than half of all public assistance payments. At the

[29]These led to the War on Poverty in 1964. However, as already discussed in chapter 12, the War on Poverty did not actually involve very much new welfare but was instead an effort to coordinate, and thereby make more effective, existing programs for the poor.

Policies begin with
problems: A hunger
march in the 1930s.

beginning of the decade of the 1970s, AFDC covered 7.3 million recipients, while Old Age Assistance provided coverage for 2 million. Moreover, the latter is on a declining slope, whereas AFDC has been continually on the upswing. For example, in 1960, only 30 percent of all public assistance went to AFDC recipients, as compared to 50 percent by the end of the decade.

Critics on the left and the right of the ideological spectrum have denounced AFDC for actually contributing to dependency. Conservatives say that it encourages people to refuse low-paying jobs; that is, public assistance may be anticapitalistic to the extent that it reduces the supply of labor for low-status or exploitative wages. Critics of the left argue that AFDC encourages dependency by refusing aid to households where a breadwinner is present. This has the effect of encouraging many otherwise responsible heads of households to remain absent in order to gain or to maintain eligibility for welfare. Moreover, until 1962, AFDC payments were reduced one dollar for every one dollar earned—a 100 percent tax on outside earnings. Between 1962 and 1967 the rules were liberalized, but only up to the point where further generosity might begin to encourage others to go on assistance rather than seek work.

This points to the single problem inherent in any welfare system—ours or any conceivable alternative. If the support is too skimpy, many poor will not be able to subsist; if too generous, many able-bodied persons will prefer assistance to work. Many alternatives or reforms for the present system have been proposed, and some have been experimented with; but none seem to meet the basic problem any better. The most recent proposals have been a variant of a guaranteed annual income. They are called income maintenance plans, family assistance plans, negative income taxes, or "demogrants." Each could easily contribute a significant improvement to the present system; however, each will also contribute some problems of its own. None of the reforms has a solution to the problem of the balance between too little assistance and too much.[30]

Apparently, most people have always had to work in order to survive. Capitalism invented neither labor nor the exploitation of labor. However, capitalism has provided a few new and special problems by converting the overwhelming proportion of the population into laborers—people who must work for other people for a wage of some sort. Other economic systems have depended much more upon the land and upon communal and traditional economic relationships.[31] The capitalist system has proven immensely productive; it produces a surplus far beyond minimal social requirements. But will assignment of that surplus to the poor kill the very productivity by which the surplus was produced? Does a system based upon industry and employed labor rather than agriculture and a peasantry depend upon having a whole class of poor to give laborers the proper incentives? Should people be removed so far from their families and from the land that they have no alternatives but wage labor, welfare, or starvation? A farm family must work or starve. Why not the laborer? Or are the two situations really comparable?

These questions are not intended to discourage welfare or efforts to reform the welfare system. The main point is that people on all sides of the welfare issue need regular reminders of the place and significance of welfare in any system of government. Conservatives need reminding that capitalism must have a plan for its poor just as socialism must. Liberals need reminding that there is a limit to welfare, both as to the individual amounts that might discourage the will to work and in terms of the total amounts that are supportable in the economic system as a whole.

---

[30]See Daniel Patrick Moynihan's book-length report on the efforts to work out an acceptable family assistance plan, *The Politics of a Guaranteed Income* (New York: Random House, 1973). See also James Welsh, "Welfare Reform: Born August 8, 1969; Died October 4, 1972," *New York Times Magazine,* January 7, 1973, p. 14. One of the most poignant efforts was that of George McGovern, who proposed an extremely generous approach during the 1972 campaign, called popularly the "demogrant." This involved cash grants to individuals, on the basis of right rather than contribution. As he and his staff began to study the implications of his proposal, in terms of the number of people covered and the effect the grant would have on the working poor, they began to back away, until they ended up without a distinctive program at all. Part of this account will be found in Welsh's article.

[31]For a description of systems of economics with communal settings, see Marc Bloch, *Feudal Society,* trans. L. A. Manyon (Chicago: University of Chicago Press, 1961). For a well-balanced treatment of the change from communal to capitalistic relationships in the economy, consult Karl Polanyi, *The Great Transformation* (Boston: Beacon Press, 1957).

To engage in a proper assessment of these problems, one must set aside sentiment to ponder the intimate relationship between any economic system and the imperfections in it that produce poor and dependent persons.[32] What we do about the relationship between the economic system and the poor is a matter of political choice and will thus vary from culture to culture and perhaps generation to generation. The welfare system of the United States is quite clearly different from that of France, England, or the Scandinavian countries.[33]

However, the level of public welfare expenditure in the United States is fully comparable to that of the European so-called socialist countries, because a capitalist system must be committed to public welfare for its lowest classes just as much as a socialist system. The reasons should by now be apparent. A large dependent class is essential in an industrial society; and the government in an industrial society, regardless of its specific economic or governmental system, must contrive means to keep that class alive, and conquered. The ideal situation is to conquer the poor with comfort and satisfaction, because the alternative may be to conquer them with suppression and fear. Once again, the common denominator is conquest.[34]

Inequality: Who Shall Be Poor?

Poverty and inequality are related but quite independent problems. Granted, members of the lowest income brackets seem to have less of everything, whether the measurement is in terms of the amount and quality of possessions, the opportunities available to their children, their working conditions, their hopes of developing their physical and intellectual capacities, or their self-esteem. At one level, this unequal distribution of goods and opportunities is an objective fact which can be changed by altering the amounts of valued things that go to each class or income bracket. But inequality, especially in the context of government and public policy, must refer to something more. In these pages, inequality will be taken to refer to the *rules and practices in a society that determine who shall be poor.* (We could complicate the argument by adding to our concerns rules that determine who shall be detested, who shall be spat upon, and who shall be hidden from view. But in a society where money is valued so greatly as a symbol of worth as well as a

---

[32]Probably the best preparation for the effort to assess the relationship between an economic system and its welfare system will be found in Polanyi, *The Great Transformation.* See also Frances F. Piven and Richard A. Cloward, *Regulating the Poor* (New York: Pantheon, 1971).

[33]See Rimlinger, *Welfare, Policy and Industrialization in Europe, America and Russia;* see also Arnold Heidenheimer, "The Politics of Public Education, Health and Welfare in the U.S.A. and Western Europe," *British Journal of Political Science* 3 (1973), 315–340.

[34]A comparable point of view is expressed in Piven and Cloward, *Regulating the Poor.*

mark of wealth, "poor" is an adequate focus.) Policies concerned with inequality are policies that are concerned with making or changing the rules that determine who shall be poor.

Equality and inequality are impossible to define for all times and circumstances. In some contexts, equality refers to the right of individuals to expect and receive fair treatment under law, as is implied by due process. It is also legitimate to use the notion of equality in all matters of economic opportunity, where one may very well be content with equality of chances despite great inequality in results. But it is equally legitimate to speak of equality in the strict sense of the absence of differences in the possession of goods, status, and other things of value in the society. Any or all of these may be used as a criterion when the central concern is with the rules that determine who shall be poor.

These examples of types of inequality capture the many things that governments are attempting when they use the rhetoric of equality and inequality. Perhaps the best example is the adoption of "incomes policies" in the social democratic countries of the West. An incomes policy is designed not to equalize income or anything else but actually to hold all social classes or income groupings in the society *to their current relationships to each other,* changing these relationships only insofar as the changes are related to changes in actual productivity. With such a policy, the political battle is not over the absolute redistribution of wealth but over how to handle the marginal increases or decreases in national wealth each year. This could change in the future, but at the moment a real incomes policy is a far cry from the rhetoric of socialist and social democratic parties about achieving equality in some absolute sense.[35]

Capitalism, left to its own devices, tends to create its own particular brand of inequality in several specific ways.

1. Capitalism in an industrial society tends to produce a broad layer or class of poverty. It is made up of everyone who cannot adjust to the demands and skills of commerce, the division of labor, collective working conditions, supervision, a money economy, and the ability to follow rules made by others. The subsistence farmer, the home manufacturer, and many kinds of artisans suffer as the commercial economy takes over.[36]

2. All poverty is cruel, but the distinctive feature of capitalist poverty is that it makes no distinction—it is objective. As in war, so in a capitalist system, poverty is a random harvest. If a disproportionate number of blacks, Chicanos, and other ethnic groups are

---

[35]For an assessment and a thorough criticism of the theory and practice of "incomes policies," see Shonfield, *Modern Capitalism,* p. 217.

[36]For a multi-country look at the coming of capitalism, see Barrington Moore, *The Social Origins of Dictatorship and Democracy* (Boston: Beacon Press, 1966). Or, see *Grapes of Wrath* by John Steinbeck. If his treatment seems unfair, consult any study sponsored by the United States Senate during the 1960s on migratory labor or poverty in Appalachia, or on hunger anywhere in the United States.

Policies begin with problems: The 1963 civil rights march on Washington.

found in poverty, this is due to general social prejudice rather than to biases built into capitalist economic practices. More will be said of this below.

3. Capitalist poverty sets no limit upon how poor the poverty class can be—no limit except subsistence itself. One of the earliest and most important of the modern political economists, David Ricardo, made a permanent place for himself in the history of ideas with the formulation of his "iron law of wages."[37] Basically, Ricardo proposed that when capitalism has finally reduced every economic relationship to a matter of wages and prices, competition for the available work will reduce the price of labor to the point below which it cannot go without endangering the physical survival of the worker. Any effort to improve the income of workers can have only temporary success, because the resultant improvement will encourage population growth through more childbirth, lower death rates, and expanded immigration from subsistence farming and outmoded occupations; this growth will in turn produce a surplus of labor, which will push the wages paid labor back down to subsistence level.[38]

---

[37]Published in his *Principles of Political Economy and Taxation,* 1817.

[38]Compare with Polanyi, *The Great Transformation,* chapter 6. For some very startling and prophetic insights into the consequences of having an upper class made up of capitalists in a democratic society, see Alexis de Tocqueville, *Democracy in America,* vol. 2, trans. Phillips Bradley (New York: Random House, Vintage, 1955), chapter 22. Reprinted in Lowi, *Private Life*

Given the undoubted power of capitalist leaders in our society, there would probably never be any changes in the rules determining who shall be poor if there were a basic conflict of interest between capitalism and changes in the composition of the poverty class. But the fact is that some public policies have changed the rules. It is fair to say that public policy has had a very good record in some respects, although a poor one in others. Opposition to such changes has simply not come from capitalists as a class.

There is the usual fear of change in any bureaucracy, and large business is definitely a bureaucracy. However, most of the opposition to recruiting or promoting blacks, women, or other groups comes from co-workers in their capacity as human beings rather than as capitalists. For example, one very important study conducted several years before the passage of the federal civil rights act against job discrimination reported that the mobility of employees from humble origins is a good bit greater in large, publicly-owned corporations than in the more traditional family-owned corporations, even when the family-owned corporation is large, like Ford Motor Company.[39]

The most important change in the rules determining who shall be poor in the entire history of the United States was of course the decision to abolish slavery. This change was brought about by civil war rather than by the normal political process. Nevertheless, it is a case of an important change in the rules, effected by a series of constitutional provisions and government policies regarding the right to own other persons as property and the right to exact labor from them with no regard for their wishes.[40]

We do not have to go back that far in history, however, to find examples of basic changes in the rules governing who shall be poor. By far the most important contemporary change in these rules was the change made during the 1930s which gave wage laborers more power to influence the conditions of their work and the levels of their pay. We need not go over this well-known story, but it should be emphasized that national labor relations policies and policies concerning the conditions of work in factories and plants are excellent examples of the potential there is in the political process for influencing the economic system and, in turn, shaping social classes. Allowing workers to develop their own form of market

and Public Order, p. 13. It was Tocqueville's feeling that an upper class in a capitalist society will lack the common bonds of land and tradition that bound upper and lower classes in preindustrial societies; thus the new "aristocracy" would not be limited by anything but economic rationality, which Ricardo goes on to argue will inevitably push all workers toward subsistence.

[39]W. Lloyd Warner and James C. Abegglen, *Occupational Mobility* (Minneapolis: University of Minnesota Press, 1955), pp. 168–169.

[40]For a discussion of these issues, see Moore, *The Social Origins of Dictatorship and Democracy.* For a recent statistical picture of conditions under slavery, suggesting that freed blacks were not necessarily economically any better off during the remainder of the nineteenth century, see Robert Fogel and Stanley Engerman, *Time on the Cross* (Boston: Little, Brown, 1974).

power was the twentieth century's answer to the iron law of wages.

Yet because of the great social heterogeneity in the United States, rules applying at large to wage labor have proven to be inherently inadequate. This is because there are segments of the population which are kept from many opportunities for a reason which has nothing to do with the random harvest of capitalism. The reason is pure and simple bigotry, which is culturally rather than economically determined. It affects opportunity with organized labor as well as management. Trade unions, for example, tend to develop their own rules about who shall be poor; this is especially the case in the skilled trades, where minority groups have found it extremely difficult to get the training and the apprenticeship jobs that the unions control.

Racial bias is sometimes mistakenly attributed to capitalism because of the very large number of racial minorities imported into a country to perform the least desirable and lowest-paying tasks. But the fact may be that capitalism is simply receptive to any population willing to accept the low-paying jobs. Thus, there are blacks in America, but there are also Irish and Italians, who were attracted in large numbers by low-paying industrial jobs. Post–World War II capitalist France has imported large numbers of Portuguese as well as Algerians; Germans have imported Italians and Turks. The British used the Irish to build their capitalism. If blacks and Chicanos have been held back in the United States, the responsibility lies more with the social and cultural values than the economic structure. For whatever reasons, the composition of our poverty class is decidedly not random. Whites outnumber blacks in the poverty class, simply because whites outnumber blacks four to one in the population at large. However, in 1969, whereas 10 percent of all the whites in the population were defined as poor, over 31 percent of the nonwhites fell into that category.[41]

Given the specific problem of blacks in the United States, civil rights legislation was probably the only appropriate approach for public policy. Blacks were unlike other ethnic groups in the United States. Blacks were a caste—that is, a whole people subjected to separate systems of law and ethics. Even as the separate systems of law began to break down during and after World War II, ethical practices, habits, and traditions imbedded in the white community continued to operate as though the caste system continued.

Agitation for civil rights legislation began almost immediately

---

[41]For a statistical picture of the distribution of poverty in America, see Bureau of the Census, *Twenty-four Million Americans*. For a poignant and effective statement concerning the lack of progress during the decade 1959–1969, when the federal government was making its most concerted efforts to change the distribution of income without trying to change the rules determining who shall be poor, except in the South, see Michael Harrington, "The Other America Revisited," *Center Magazine,* January 1969, pp. 36–41. For the picture of discrimination against women at lower and higher levels of the economy, see part 4 of Jo Freeman, ed., *Women: A Feminist Perspective* (Palo Alto, Calif.: Mayfield Publishing, 1975).

after World War II, which had been a period of unprecedented opportunity and prosperity for blacks in the United States. These efforts succeeded only in splitting the Democratic Party in 1948, and no serious effort was made again until the mid-1950s. Most of the effective attempts to change the rules for blacks came first through the judicial system. Even when the liberal Democrats came to power in 1961, there was a self-conscious urge to avoid the civil rights approach in favor of a general welfare approach.

Rather than singling blacks out as a specific social unit against which the rules discriminated, the Kennedy administration sought to make the economy so prosperous that poverty would be virtually eliminated for blacks as well as whites. Kennedy did succeed in liberalizing welfare payments somewhat and quite clearly was able to stimulate the economy toward full employment and prosperity. But no amount of stimulation could change the already established relationship of the black to the white-dominated economy. In fact, efforts to improve the relative and absolute economic situation of blacks contributed to the radicalization of black politics.

President Johnson's War on Poverty sought to improve the condition of blacks by making welfare money disproportionately available to them. The main point of the War on Poverty was essentially, "Whoever organizes best in each community will get the most—and we will help you organize." Within a few years there was general consensus that this approach had failed to reach blacks in any disproportionate degree, except where the payments were a reaction to rioting in the ghetto. There seemed also to be consensus that even where blacks proved themselves to be good at organizing, they tended to alienate city hall, bringing a few wealthy leaders (derisively called the limousine liberals) to their support and consolidating the rest, especially the white professional politicians, against them.[42]

The trouble with all of the fiscal or welfare approaches is precisely that they do not seek to change the rules that determine who shall be poor. The fiscal approach can only indemnify damages; it cannot right wrongs. The only way wrongs can be righted on a systematic basis is by identifying the wrongful conduct and regulating it as other wrongful conduct is regulated. In 1964, the federal government finally turned in earnest to this route. Its steps were faltering and meek, especially considering it was by then a decade after the landmark civil rights decision of the Supreme Court in 1954; but even so these modest steps of 1964 and 1965 have had some profound effects.

The 1954 Supreme Court decision on school segregation, coupled

---

[42]Lowi, *The End of Liberalism*, chapters 7–9; also J. David Greenstone and Paul E. Peterson, *Race and Authority in Urban Politics* (New York: Russell Sage Foundation, 1973). See also William Goldsmith, "The Ghetto as a Resource for Black America," *Journal of the American Institute of Planners*, January 1974, p. 20.

with subsequent civil rights legislation, takes a very high place among the most important efforts in the United States to eradicate inequities. In 1954 the lawyers who argued the cases leading to *Brown* v. *Board of Education*—under the guidance of Thurgood Marshall, who later became our first and only black Supreme Court Justice—had to walk the long half-mile between the Supreme Court building and the railway station to find a place to eat. This was our nation's capital; yet blacks could not find a lunch counter in the business and government areas of the city. Even the illustrious National Theater closed its doors in order to avoid desegregation. Washington in 1954 was in every way a representation of the moral outlook and habits of the United States. The changes since 1954 are almost altogether due to small changes in the rules of inequality.

No matter that the changes took place mainly in response to court orders and the threat of troops. No matter that eventually the mobilization of blacks and occasional outbreaks of racial violence were required to bring about desegregation. The fact is that once the rules were changed, first by Supreme Court decisions and then by civil rights legislation dealing with public accommodations, schools, voting, and employment, places of ancient black suppression like Jackson, Mississippi, became peacefully integrated. Jackson is no model of racial justice, but it is now more integrated than most northern metropolitan areas. It was once a place where any equal association between blacks and whites was a punishable offense. The University of Alabama is another interesting representation of change in the South. In 1974, Governor George Wallace and black leader Reverend Ralph Abernathy stood on the same platform to receive honorary doctoral degrees. This was the same governor who had "stood in the school house door" little more than a decade earlier to prevent Autherine Lucy from integrating the university.[43]

Two conclusions seem to be thrust upon anyone who is cognizant of the long history of racial exploitation, fear, and hostility in the United States. The first conclusion is that there has definitely been progress in the behavior of whites toward blacks, even where local fears and bigotries remain. The second conclusion is that the progress was not natural or inevitable. It was imposed on white communities by laws, administrative regulations, and court orders dealing with specific behaviors of whites toward blacks. To emphasize the importance of even small changes in the rules governing equality, it is worth mentioning that the South has gone farther in racial changes not merely because it had farther to go but because federal court decisions and federal civil rights laws were responsive to and designed for southern practices. Federal efforts to change the

[43]For a well-balanced assessment of the situation twenty years after the Brown decision, see Robert Reinhold, "Brown Decision 20 Years Later: Gains, Setbacks," *International Herald Tribune,* May 13, 1974; Anthony Lewis, "The Brown Decision: A Time to Celebrate," *International Herald Tribune,* May 14, 1974. These articles were reprinted from the *New York Times.*

Table 15.7

Federal Civil Rights Laws, 1957–1968

Key Provisions

Act of 1957	Established the Civil Rights Commission. Elevated Civil Rights Division, headed by an assistant attorney general. Made it a federal crime to attempt to intimidate or to prevent a person from voting.
Act of 1960	Increased the sanction against obstruction of voting or obstruction of court orders enforcing the vote. Established federal power to appoint referees to register voters wherever a "pattern or practice" of discrimination was found and declared by the federal court. Declared it a crime to destroy any voting records for 22 months.
Act of 1964	*Voting:* Title I made 6th grade education (in English) a presumption of literacy.
	Public accommodations: Title II barred discrimination in any commercial lodging (more than 5 rooms) for transient guests, any service station, restaurant, theatre, or commercial conveyance. Complainant could bring suit or attorney general could take initiative if he saw a "pattern or practice" of discrimination.
	Public schools: Title IV empowered attorney general to sue for desegregation whenever he found a segregation complaint meritorious. Title VI authorized withholding of federal aid to segregated schools.
	Private employment: Title VII outlawed discrimination in a variety of employment practices on basis of race, religion, *and* sex (sex added for the first time). Provided an agency (EEOC), but required it to defer enforcement to state or local agency for 60 days following each complaint.
Act of 1965	*Voting rights only.* Empowered attorney general, with Civil Service Commission: (1) to appoint voting examiners to replace local registrars wherever he found fewer than 50 percent of the persons of voting age not voting in 1964 presidential election, and (2) to suspend all literacy tests where evidence was found that they were used as a tool of discrimination.
Act of 1968	*Open housing:* Made it a crime to refuse to sell or rent a dwelling on basis of race or religion, if a bona fide offer had been made, or to discriminate in advertising or in the terms and conditions of sale or rental. Administered by HUD, but the burden of proof is on complainant, who must seek local remedies first, where they exist.

rules of inequality were oriented toward the South almost exclusively until the late 1960s, when the courts made new formulations and Congress passed modest legislation dealing with school segregation, housing segregation, and voting in northern communities.

Table 15.7 is a sketch of existing federal legislation on civil rights. Although it is self-explanatory for the most part, a few points deserve some attention. It is clear that the only preoccupation of legislators for the first decade following the 1954 Supreme Court school segregation decision was to secure effective voting rights for blacks, especially in the South, where they had so clearly been

Domestic Policy: Conquest Maintained

discriminated against. The preoccupation was due to the blatant nature of this type of discrimination as well as to the fact that voting was the only area in which it was possible to get a majority on civil rights decisions in Congress. The need for legislation of this sort was compelling, and the prospect for enforcement was fair, considering that most of the acts of discrimination required cooperation and complicity by actual employees of state and local governments.

The second decade of civil rights legislation began with the most significant piece of civil rights action ever taken by Congress, the Civil Rights Act of 1964. This act very effectively tightened voting rights by making it enormously easier to enforce the earlier provisions. But it went even further, finally breaking through the barriers to regulation of actions outside the voting rights area by incorporating some very significant provisions covering discrimination in public accommodations, public school systems, and, at long last, in the conduct of employers advertising for applicants and filling job openings. One of the less noted but more significant aspects of that act was the inclusion of sex as an unfair basis of discrimination.[44]

Title IV of the 1964 act covering public schools went far beyond provision for suits against school systems by authorizing government agencies to withhold federal aid to any school system whose board practiced segregation. It is this provision that became the central weapon for enforcing civil rights action outside the South. School segregation in the North was not provided for by law but was a de facto result of residential segregation. This was a more subtle problem and required more positive administrative action. As it turned out, the only way to satisfy the provision that any system defined as segregated could not receive federal money was to overcome residential segregation by busing. Efforts to apply these provisions have caused tremendous "white backlash" in northern cities and suburbs, exposing at long last the reality of racial prejudice outside the South.[45]

Title VII of the 1964 act finally applied civil rights laws to the economic system by provisions against discrimination in recruitment, hiring, and promotion. It is of equal significance that the act

[44]In 1963 Congress also passed the Equal Pay Act, which eventually had as much significance for women as did Title VII of the 1964 Civil Rights Act. For coverage of all these actions, especially in relation to sex discrimination, see Jo Freeman, *The Politics of Women's Liberation* (New York: David McKay, 1975), chapter 6. A "title" is a major subsection of a statute. Some very large subsections may be called "chapters." Small subsections are usually called "sections."

[45]The Nixon administration sought to head off this kind of enforcement by legislation that would prevent the Department of Housing and Urban Development and the Department of Health, Education and Welfare from withholding funds or in any way providing for the busing of children to comply with conditions for receiving the funds. For an excellent account of civil rights enforcement outside the South, consult Gary Orfield, "The Politics of Civil Rights Enforcement," in *Politics in America,* ed. Michael P. Smith (New York: Random House, 1974), chapter 3.

This report of the
President's Committee on
Civil Rights (1947) stands
as one of the great
documents on the positive
power of the federal
government.

There is nothing in the Constitution which in so many words authorizes the national government to protect the civil rights of the American people on a comprehensive basis. . . . There are [however] several specific constitutional bases upon which a federal civil rights program can be built. Some have been recognized and approved by the courts. . . . The several specific constitutional bases for federal action in the civil rights field brought to our attention follow. . . . Power to protect the right to vote. . . . Power to protect the right to freedom from slavery and voluntary servitude. . . . Power to protect rights to fair legal process, to free speech and assembly, and to equal protection of the laws. . . . The war power. . . . Power to regulate activities which relate to interstate commerce. . . . The taxing and spending powers. . . . The postal power. . . . Power over the District of Columbia and the Territories. . . . Power derived from the Constitution as a whole to protect the rights essential to national citizens in a democratic nation. . . . Power . . . to protect civil rights which acquire a treaty status. . . . Power derived from the "republican form of government" clause in Article IV, Section 4 of the Constitution, to protect rights essential to state and local citizens in a democracy. . . .

outlawed discriminatory practices of trade unions, including discriminatory exclusion of a person from a union, attempting to cause an employer to discriminate against a worker, discriminating in any apprenticeship or training program, and discriminating against employees who have attempted to use their rights under the act. Title VII and the Equal Employment Opportunity Commission (EEOC), the administrative agency set up by it, were the program civil rights activists had sought since 1948.

The Civil Rights Act of 1965 focused once again on the problem of voting, but this time the provisions began to have the desired effect. Since 1965 there has been a tremendous increase in the number and proportion of black voters in the South and in the number of elected black legislators, mayors, congressional representatives, and other officials. Judging from the behavior of such white political leaders as Governor George Wallace, the increase in black voting has had a notably liberal effect on white politicians.

In 1968 a new civil rights act opened up an area of regulation that could become as large as, perhaps even larger than, any in the 1964 act. In making it unlawful to discriminate in the sale or rental of housing, that act touches virtually every person in the United States. Perhaps more to the point, it comes closer than any other to a direct attack on the worst racial abuses in the northern cities and suburbs. There are two very important reasons why we have heard so little of the 1968 open housing laws. The first is, of course, the profound opposition to the implementation of these laws in the white community, including most of the politicians and bureaucrats responsible for their application. A few modest efforts by Secretary of HUD Romney from 1970 to 1971 produced such a furor that he

Domestic Policy: Conquest Maintained

was led eventually to disclaim any plan for "forced integration of the suburbs."[46]

The second reason for less than vigorous pursuit of civil rights in the housing field is that the attitudes of many black leaders range from ambivalence to outright opposition. Some of the opposition stems from the new-found feeling for black nationalism and black separatism. Some of the opposition and a lot of the ambivalence comes from the urgently felt need to bring housing to the ghettos even if they remain ghettos. Many other blacks who are dedicated to the ultimate goal of desegregation are nevertheless pushing for immediate housing for people who need it.[47]

Even a great deal of progress in civil rights regulation would not necessarily gain for the present generation of blacks the share in the economy they feel rightfully belongs to them. Thus, they are prepared to demand special economic treatment even before the general rules of inequality are changed in ways that would bring a greater share more naturally to the blacks of the next generation. This is precisely why so many blacks supported President Johnson's War on Poverty despite the fact that it drew many leaders away from the fight for civil rights for the black population.

Still, there is dilemma inherent in the demand for immediate gains without changing the rules; the immediate gains could easily interfere with the attainment of the ultimate goal of changing the rules. For instance, greatly improved housing conditions in the ghetto could make the ghetto a permanent place for blacks and the suburbs a permanent haven for whites. This amounts to a governmentally supported commitment to "two nations." Since whites would remain in control of the terms of discourse and the terms of promotion in most of the businesses, this type of cultural separation would continue to work a great hardship upon blacks.

"Black capitalism" is in a sense an answer to the problem of cultural separation producing economic disadvantage, since it provides blacks, as a matter of policy, with their own "separate but equal" corporations. In reality, however, black capitalism is a hopelessly futile commitment to long-range economic improvement without changing the rules. Since blacks comprise one-fifth of the American population, the extent of black capitalism necessary to provide opportunities for a culturally separate black nation in the United States is a ridiculously visionary goal. It is much more realistic to imagine changing the racially discriminatory behavior of whites! Leaving aside the morally compelling need for civil rights and for changing of white behavior toward blacks, the single biggest long-range advantage to changing the rules of inequality is that when capitalism is required by law to take competence and

[46]Compare with Orfield, "The Politics of Civil Rights Enforcement," p. 68.
[47]Ibid., pp. 72–73.

efficiency into account, blacks with the appropriate training will indeed be able to take their appropriate share of income on an equal and dignified basis.

Human and Community Resources

Although the policy area of human and community resources may appear new to many, the federal government has been producing policies on one aspect or another of this area for a very long time. The long history of federal effort might be more quickly identified by conventional labels, such as public health and conservation. The label used here was not chosen for reasons of obscurity but because it seems best to capture the more recent types of effort.

Up until the 1960s, federal policies related to human and community resources followed a pattern quite familiar to state programs, especially in the field of public health. The earliest federal efforts were, as mentioned earlier, limited to a few domestic problems related to international trade, such as quarantine at the ports. They also included regulation of the drug traffic, although serious efforts to regulate narcotics from the public health standpoint did not really take shape until 1919, over a decade after passage of the first important domestic federal public health statute, the Food and Drug Act of 1906.[48] It was during this period, too, that Congress attempted to eliminate the use of child labor (although this was declared unconstitutional by the Supreme Court) and to initiate federal action in the field of conservation by creating large forest preserves and parks and by regulating access to them.[49]

The 1930s was another creative period in federal efforts to regulate the factors affecting human and environmental resources. Some of these efforts were amendments to earlier legislation, extending and strengthening regulatory powers. There were a few new twists, some of which anticipated the growth in federal public health and environmental policies of the 1960s and 1970s. For example, the New Deal took the notion of conservation and extended it from control of public lands to regulating public and private lands where exploitation might end in waste and irreparable injury. Conservation laws were extended to include laws limiting the way

---

[48]The Harrison Act prohibiting commercial use of drugs, especially the sale of drugs to addicts, was passed in 1919 after several successful federal efforts to control the meat-packing industry, to regulate the sale of adulterated medicines, to eliminate manufacture of white phosphorous matches, and to deal with other health hazards, including efforts to protect the quality of rivers and streams and to prevent harmful or misleading advertising of drugs, cosmetics, and other kinds of merchandise. For a useful account of the development of the federal government's position toward narcotic drugs, see David Musto, *The American Disease: Origins of Narcotic Control* (New Haven: Yale University Press, 1973).

[49]Compare with Samuel Hays, *Conservation and the Gospel of Efficiency* (Cambridge, Mass.: Harvard University Press, 1959). A good history of the politics and policies in the conservation area will be found in Grant McConnell, *Private Power and American Democracy* (New York: Knopf, 1966), chapters 2 and 7.

farmers could cultivate their lands and the way mine operators and oil drillers could tap their resources.

Other regulatory efforts, such as the regulation of the fluid milk industry, made use of established powers of conservation to justify regulation of the prices of important agricultural commodities. Federal powers over conservation thus came to justify a great variety of regulatory programs and also prepared the way for the 1960s efforts to impose very broad environmental and ecological controls. The concept of public health also began to expand into the larger realm of human resources. Serious regulation of child labor was finally adopted, as a public health measure. The Resettlement Administration in the Agriculture Department was created to help displaced farmers, and the independent Civilian Conservation Corps (CCC) was established primarily to provide work for unemployed youth. In both instances, the concept was a human resource concept, despite criticisms that such programs were communistic.

These policies anticipated an approach not fully developed until the 1960s, which recognized the environment and the human being as parts of an interdependent and all-encompassing system. This point of view acknowledges that ultimately *any* recurring phenomenon can become a menace to public health or to the environment *even though the phenomenon may be the farthest thing from an evil in itself.* This distinction between behaviors evil in themselves and behaviors evil in their consequences, made more than once before, became increasingly important in the 1960s, when the language of the ecosystem and the theories of the interdependence of all things came into popular currency.[50]

If we had ever lagged behind the democratic socialist countries in our efforts to deal with the interdependence of food supply, population, and the environment, we seem to have determined during the 1960s not to continue to do so. Books on the environment helped blast us out of our complacency. A new Democratic administration committed to discover a "new frontier" had a lot to do with this awakening. But if one single event triggered it off, it was probably Sputnik. Our national embarrassment over the spectacle of Communist Russia in space ahead of us was of cataclysmic proportion. Since our immediate concern was the technological superiority implied in Sputnik, our first response was the passage of the National Defense Education Act of 1958, which authorized expendi-

---

[50]The notion of interdependence was already in the air, but the sense of urgency about it was probably created by three enormously influential books of the 1960s: Paul Ehrlich, *The Population Bomb* (New York: Ballantine, 1968), a culmination of Ehrlich's articles, beginning with a pamphlet by the same name in 1954; Rachel Carson, *Silent Spring* (Boston: Houghton Mifflin, 1962); and Barry Commoner, *The Closing Circle* (New York: Knopf, 1971). A good bibliography of important books in the same genre will be found in *The Population Bomb*, pp. 218–220.

Is there a limit to public control?: An Amish family signs bond papers for release after being jailed for refusing to send their children to a public high school.

tures for the improvement of teaching in the sciences and mathematics, in foreign languages, and in general education at all levels, including scholarships and loans for a variety of majors in college. Soon, more than half the research conducted in colleges and universities was federally financed.[51]

The connection between national defense and human resources was neither unprecedented nor accidental. The concept expressed in the term *manpower* comes closer than almost any other to catching the rationale back of many social programs in democracies. It is not that democracies lack human sympathy. It is that human sympathy becomes a compelling force for good works when it is *reinforced* by an awareness of what it takes for the survival of the country itself.

Fears have occasionally been expressed that rulers will try to maintain conquest by keeping the people docile. For example, when the drug scare hit the United States immediately after World War I, conservatives were concerned that drugs were an effort by Communists and anarchists to take over the country. During the 1950s, the movements for fluoridation of water and vaccination against polio were opposed by many on the same grounds. They argued that the Russians used these techniques to keep their own population docile. In the 1960s, proposals for greater permissiveness in the treatment of drug abuse were opposed by many blacks, who feared drugs were being used as a device by whites to hold the black community

[51]For a concise treatment of this and other "social programs," see James E. Anderson, *Politics and the Economy* (Boston: Little, Brown, 1966), chapter 8.

down.[52] However, the truth is that the elites of most countries, democratic and otherwise, have probably preferred to maintain conquest by other means, because the health and welfare of their population is so vital for national defense. There is some solace in the idea that the most selfish calculations of elites would lead them to wish for a healthy population.

The relationship between health, human resources, and national defense became more and more prominent during the 1960s. The National Defense Education Act was expanded; eventually it was supplemented by still another important congressional enactment, the Elementary and Secondary Education Act of 1965, through which virtually every school district in the country was expected to receive federal assistance. In the spirit of the War on Poverty, the grants under this act were turned over to the states on condition that a particular effort be made to assist school districts where there were substantial numbers of children from low-income families. Programs intended to be supported from these grants included Head Start, special services to remedial and adult education, job retraining, the teaching of English to non–English-speaking children, special aids to schools attempting to integrate the races, and some experimentation with the use of school vouchers to improve the access of poor children to better schools.

Americans also discovered hunger in the 1960s and made a concerted effort to improve the nutrition of low-income families outside existing categories of welfare support. The established school lunch program was significantly expanded. The food stamp program began slowly during the 1960s, but between 1960 and 1971 the numbers of persons and families benefiting from the direct distribution of commodities actually doubled. Under the food stamp program low-income persons can take the amount of money they usually spend on food and buy government issued food stamps, which, in the food store, have far higher purchasing power. Food stamps are a special kind of currency for low-income individuals and families.

Inasmuch as these compensatory health programs in the nutrition field are administered largely by the Agriculture Department and are part of an effort to support farm prices, many may be dubious about their value. But we can say once again that the presence of a second or third motivation behind a health program does not necessarily discredit the program itself.

Federal policies in the 1960s also expanded public health in the

---

[52]For more on the drug scare, see Musto, *The American Disease.* For the politics of an entirely different kind of public health issue, see Matthew A. Crenson, *The Un-Politics of Air Pollution* (Baltimore: Johns Hopkins Press, 1971). See also Ralph Ellsworth and Sarah Harris, *The American Right Wing* (Washington, D.C.: Public Affairs Press, 1962), especially for observations on fluoridation and on the use of the Salk vaccine. See also Anderson, *Politics and the Economy.*

traditional sense. An ancient agency, the Public Health Service (PHS), was made into one of the largest activities in the welfare field. (For its place in the government, see chapter 12.) At one time nearly half the biomedical research in the country was either conducted directly by one of the units of the PHS or under contracts with universities and other laboratories heavily subsidized by the PHS. A vast program of federal assistance for the construction of hospitals and other medical facilities is another part of the program of activities conducted by the PHS or one of its agencies. When one adds to this the modest effort by the FDA to protect the public from adulterated commodities, and the immense program of free medical care to veterans under the VA, one gets the sense that public health is a large and serious industry within the federal government structure.

To aid in understanding the scale of these efforts, note that as of March 1972 there were nearly 29 million veterans, virtually all of whom were eligible for VA health and hospitalization assistance. Nearly a million veterans were receiving some kind of VA medical care annually. To this should be added around $10 billion per year for the outlays under the federal medicare program for the aging and federal support to state programs under medicaid.

Most of the policies of the 1960s identified up to this point did attempt to define specific problems in terms of a larger system. However, each relied almost exclusively upon subsidies as the primary technique of control. In this respect, most of these policies are a throwback to the nineteenth century; the effort was to avoid as much as possible making a fundamental decision about how the society ought to be but to throw enough money at it to hope that its problems would solve themselves and go away.

However, not all policies of the 1960s relied completely on subsidy approaches. The medicare and medicaid programs, for example, are associated with the social security system and rely more on a fiscal technique. Medicare is in fact an amendment to the Social Security Act and is administered like the other contributory programs identified in Table 15.7. Medicare does not actually redistribute much wealth from the rich to the poor, but it does a lot of redistributing between the young and the aged. In the same act of 1965 (Title XIX), Congress established medicaid, a program of grants to individual states contingent upon their provision of free medical services to persons already receiving public assistance—as well as to other classes of individuals the state legislature might designate. Additional federal grants were provided to the states for inpatient and outpatient hospital services, laboratory and x-ray services, and nursing home care. Only a few states have opted for a recognizable medicaid program, but the political and juridical precedents have been established, and the United States has moved a very significant step toward what has derisively been called

CITY of DE KALB, ILLINOIS
LICENSE

FOR AND IN CONSIDERATION OF THE RECEIPT OF

$..............

LICENSE IS HEREBY GRANTED TO

_____

_____

_____

PROVIDED that for any violation of the ordinance of said City this License may be declared forfeited and revoked by Mayor or Council.

Given under our hands and the Seal of the City this_____day

of_____19____   _____

MAYOR

_____

CITY CLERK

This License is not transferable by sale or assignment

socialized medicine. Other steps in this direction are almost certain to be taken during the 1970s. Much of the hospital and medical industry may remain private, but doctors, especially the payment of doctors, will increasingly come under public programs.

Regulation, in addition to subsidies, has become a more prevalent technique used by the government when confronted with problems of human resources and the environment. Not only is there increasing willingness to "regulate the poor" through restrictive provisions in public assistance programs; the federal government has also taken steps to regulate others "for their own good" with more comprehensive programs of drug control and warnings against cigarettes, as well as programs which attempt to regulate false advertising, to mention just a few.

Probably the most important recent regulatory approaches to human and community resources is in the environmental field. Since the late 1960s, the federal government has been taking meek but significant steps toward reduction of activities that pollute the air and water. Most of the tough decisions were turned over to a new agency, the Environmental Protection Agency, which has been authorized to develop rules and regulations covering water and air quality. Once this step was taken, further decisions and additional policies became more likely. Since there is a considerable amount of popular support for air and water pollution controls, there is likely to be a continual interplay during the 1970s between demands for policies that will clean the air and water and protests by industry and many unions against regulations that will add too many costs to production.[53]

Policy and Conquest

Policy innovation comes in fits and starts. The onset of a major new program proposal may be a major technological breakthrough, a disaster, a social movement, or one of these followed by the others. Very often a proposal, such as medicare and environmental regulation, develops a major following and then runs into severe reaction. When the movement for a new policy succeeds, the reaction may also take the form of a public policy seeking to limit or to reverse that success. For example, the trade unions made their big breakthrough with the Wagner Act of 1935; immediately after World War II their gains were severely limited by the Taft-Hartley Act of 1947 and again twelve years later with the Landrum-Griffin Act. The very popular poverty programs of the 1960s suffered a reaction in the 1970s with revenue sharing—which became an effort by the Nixon administration virtually to turn governing powers back to the states.

The next round in human resource policies may be national health insurance. But the pattern of thrust and reaction can already be seen. For example, Senator Edward Kennedy in 1972 and 1973 was sponsoring a bold national health care plan whereby all patients would be free to choose their own doctor and their own clinic or other facility, and to proceed very much as they do now under private medicine. In the spring of 1974, to the dismay of many of his supporters, Senator Kennedy abandoned his plan for a far less comprehensive one. The reaction, for the time being, had set in.

Where will the next major policies and programs be? Some may be in old and continually unresolved areas, such as civil rights and energy. Some may be in areas of long-settled public policies which will come unstuck—such as trade unionism, liability for accidents, and the copyright laws (thanks to such new inventions as xerography and cable television). A social movement against the income tax may turn our attentions entirely toward the redistribution of wealth. In the meantime, some currently hot issues (such as gun control, narcotics control, and automobile safety) may find themselves resolved with definitive public policies.

---

[53]Crenson, *The Un-Politics of Air Pollution.* For a very good account of the politics of air pollution and of the potential for public support, see Paul Sabatier, "Social Movements and Regulatory Agencies," *Policy Sciences,* forthcoming. See also Mark Nadel, *The Politics of Consumer Protection* (Indianapolis: Bobbs-Merrill, 1971).

But whatever happens, we can be sure of at least two things: (1) There will be nothing natural, inherent, or divine in what becomes an issue or in what becomes *of* an issue. Policy making will continue to revolve around interests, support, and calculations as to how much the public will accept. (2) As soon as enough people feel that a problem exists in the society, there will be public support for dealing with the problem governmentally.

There is likely to be popular support for governmentalizing part or all of the problem, even though there is no guarantee whatsoever that government is equipped to deal with it. Indeed, the policy-making process, like society, moves in fits and starts. But as long as something is left to conquer, it will never stand still.

Chapter 16

Prospects of Conquest:
With Liberty and
Justice for Some

The inevitable is seldom what anybody
expected.
Barrington Moore, 1973

It is impossible to look into the future of the United States
without seeing a much larger national government using
more coercive power on larger and larger numbers of people.
The national government is growing because there are no
longer any constitutional barriers against its growth. It will
continue to grow because so many individuals feel that, as a
condition of their own freedom, they need to support government control over others while trying to displace it from
themselves.

Control by the national government will increase also
because more and more individuals and corporations will
seek governmental controls upon *themselves*. Economic stability seems often to be possible only if private contracts are
enforced by government agencies rather than courts, through
such arrangements as the licensing of commercial airlines by

the Civil Aeronautics Board or the regulation of competition by the Federal Trade Commission.

Wide popular support for more government tends to produce an impression of natural harmony between government and the private sphere. Nevertheless, the notion that natural harmony prevails is a myth, and a dangerous myth at that. It encourages acceptance of unfavorable terms of conquest. Those who are willing to accept the idea of government as a friendly force are much more prone to give unconditionally their consent to be governed; they are much more willing to accept administrators who give orders without authority and who claim authority without warrant.

Most modern politicians foster the myth of natural harmony precisely because it encourages consent. When Republicans are in power, they are likely to speak of "business-government partnership and cooperation." When Democrats are in power, they tend to say the same thing with a slightly different stress. One of the favorite comments during the two Democratic administrations of the 1960s was "Anti-trust is pro-business."[1] Nevertheless, harmony is a myth, and it has enormous potency because it has some basis in fact. Many programs receive little vocal opposition, especially where the actual burden or cost of the program is unclear. Nevertheless, some segment of society is always bearing the brunt of the controls or paying the main share of the costs. At the very least, claims to harmony and partnership between government and private individuals should always be suspect.

Suspicion about the myth of harmony is not merely the mark of conservatism, or of laissez-faire orthodoxy, or of a defense of entrenched interests. In fact, entrenched interests usually have the most to gain from the myth of harmony. Skepticism about harmony is derived from a definition of government as conquest; if government by definition means control—conquest updated—then also by definition government will always involve the reduction of somebody's freedom. This does not mean that government expansion is never supportable. It simply means that the expansion has to be justified.

Skepticism gives rise to a belief in the natural *dis*harmony of relationships between government and the individual. This too is a myth, but it has the advantage of encouraging vigilance. Skepticism about harmony is more likely to force a proper accounting of the costs along with the gains of control. Although resistant to the expansion of government, skepticism is at the same time a safeguard against disappointment. In the long run, legitimacy is very sensitive to a false picture of government and to falsely high

[1]For example, Robert F. Kennedy, *The Pursuit of Justice*, ed. Theodore Lowi (New York: Harper & Row, 1964); Hobart Rowen, *The Free Enterprisers* (New York: Putnam, 1964); and Jim Heath, *JFK and the Business Community* (Chicago: University of Chicago Press, 1969).

expectations of government. Abraham Lincoln must have had something like this in mind when he observed:

> You can fool some of the people all of the time;
> You can fool all of the people some of the time;
> But you cannot fool all of the people all of the time.

To this we should add:

> You can control all of the people some of the time;
> You can control some of the people all of the time;
> But you cannot control all of the people all of the time.

REACTIONS TO BEING CONQUERED: THE MEANINGS OF POLITICAL VIOLENCE

What, then, of the rest of the people the rest of the time? How do people react when the terms of conquest seem permanently antagonistic to them? Most of us are so well conquered that we obey nevertheless, hoping perhaps that someday the balance of advantages will shift favorably. But no matter how successfully we are socialized to obey, obedience cannot always be a comfortable or a permanent condition. Dissidence is a fact of life, and although most dissident minorities obey most of the time, their dissidence is a factor of fundamental importance to the state.

All countries are organized to deal with dissidence. For example, Great Britain's newspapers are controlled far more strictly than newspapers in the United States.[2] French television and news reporters are accustomed to "news management." Most European countries require all adults to carry a government identity card, which helps the large national police forces keep track of political dissidents.

Indignation over revelations of FBI surveillance and illegal domestic spying activities by the CIA and the army, expressed by so many millions of Americans during the 1970s, is a very healthy reaction. But it also reveals massive ignorance of the fact that our own government does have regular policies to control dissidence despite the absolute prohibition against such policies in the First Amendment. In fact, the Supreme Court doctrine of "clear and present danger" was developed as an escape hatch from that absolute prohibition, giving the courts a means of allowing government agencies to censor and restrain dissidents whenever their

---

[2]For an excellent review of British practices and problems, see Anthony Lewis, "Edited by Lawyers," *New York Times,* July 31, 1975. As Lewis puts it, "American editors and publishers are rightly sensitive to anything that looks like an infringement of their freedom. But before their next speech about the First Amendment, some of them would do well to visit Britain. . . . Editing a newspaper in this country is a bit like walking through a minefield."

words or actions, in the opinion of an official, tend to disrupt public life.[3]

Politics in the Extreme:
Three Models of Reaction to Conquest

Leaving aside muttering in the marketplace and ordinary crimes against persons and property, dissidence can be appreciated as a reaction against being conquered—a reaction against the state, its authority, its symbols, its apparatus. But dissidence is not a single phenomenon; there are several forms of it. Three distinct models of extreme reaction require special attention. The first is extreme but nonviolent—the *withdrawal model.* The other two are both extreme and violent, because they involve deliberate disobedience. One is the *revolution model;* the other is the *rebellion model.*

The withdrawal model Withdrawal has not been strong in the American tradition of political extremism. A few thousand have decided to return to their homelands after immigrating to the United States. A few hundred citizens may trickle away each year to new countries or new frontiers beyond the authority of the United States. A few thousand American youths of draft age chose to emigrate each year rather than be part of the Vietnam War during the 1960s. Other persons withdraw into themselves by forming communes, by taking refuge in drugs, or by embracing some separate ethnic or religious community. Still others withdraw by rejecting active participation in politics. Since participation is a technique of conquest—a technique much needed by politicians who believe in consent—withdrawing participation on an organized scale can have a profound effect, because it amounts to withdrawal of support for the regime. This form of withdrawal could increase in significance if Americans ever discover that participation is a favor citizens do for politicians.

All of these various styles of withdrawal can obviously have a deep effect on political authority. Yet, government agencies can do very little about withdrawal, either to reduce it or to control its political effects. Withdrawal into oneself or into separate ethnic or religious communities cannot be punished as long as those who withdraw do not violate a law along the way, giving the authorities pretext. Emigration to another country can be controlled by the state, but this is very risky. If would-be emigrants are prevented from leaving the country, their dissatisfactions could curdle into more active and antisocial forms. If they are allowed to leave, their leaving can be a terrible reflection upon established authority.

---

[3]Consult chapters 4 and 5 for discussions of the First Amendment. See also Henry Abraham, *Freedom and the Court,* 2d ed. (New York: Oxford University Press, 1972), pp. 190–205.

American leaders have been very outspoken in the international sphere about the rights of citizens of other countries to immigrate to the United States. During the 1970s Congress publicly pressured the Soviet Union to change its policy against emigration of Soviet Jews. However, those same American authorities look very differently upon American emigration. The actual number of persons who emigrated from the United States during the Vietnam War has very probably been suppressed. Of perhaps greater significance is the fact that the *Statistical Abstract of the United States,* an official government document, publishes ample statistics on immigration into the United States but none whatsoever on outward migration or repatriation.

The revolution model Revolution is the most particular, the most fundamental, the most radical of extreme reactions against conquest. Far from withdrawal, revolution involves disobedience. It is an organized effort to change *by force* the regime, the rules by which the regime operates, and the social class and social values that prevail in the regime. Organized radical activity should be called revolutionary only if the clear intent and theory of the group is revolutionary. To paraphrase Lenin, there is no revolutionary party without a revolutionary theory.

Because some of the important revolutionary parties in Europe have been relatively quiet and obedient in recent years, some observers have been led to speculate upon the "twilight of revolution." For example, the French and Italian Communist parties, largest in the West, have for many years been cooperating with the more conventional political parties. The French Communist Party even went so far as to oppose the revolutionary agitation of 1968, and both the French and the Italian parties have been trying to reassure their countries that they are ready to participate as a conventional party in a conventional democratic government.

But it is equally possible that their cooperativeness is a matter of self-conscious strategy. The revolutionary model usually calls for patience, warning against "adventurism." Sometimes it is better to wait for things to get worse before seizing the initiative. The point here is that the extremist following the revolutionary model is loyal to a system that does not yet exist.[4]

When revolution is defined fairly strictly as a deliberate effort to change the entire course of history in a country,[5] or "an insurrection, an act of violence by which one class overthrows another,"[6] or

---

[4]For a worthwhile statement on these phenomena, see Octavio Paz, "Twilight of Revolution?" *Dissent,* Winter 1974, pp. 56–62.

[5]Hannah Arendt, *On Revolution* (New York: Viking Press, 1963), p. 21. This definition and several others are identified and compared in an excellent study: David V. J. Bell, *Resistance and Revolution* (Boston: Houghton Mifflin, 1973), pp. 7–13.

[6]Mao Tse-tung, *Quotations from Chairman Mao* (Peking: Foreign Language Press, 1967), p. 7. Quoted in Bell, *Resistance and Revolution,* p. 8.

an "internal war . . . designed to overthrow the regime or dissolve the state . . . by extensive violence,"[7] the observer is immediately struck by the notable lack of such experience in the history of the United States. This absence of revolutionary tradition has been explained largely on the basis of the assumption that, for the most part, America was born "free and equal" and did not have to tear down an old feudal society to achieve that status.[8] I am aware of no better general explanation for why the revolutionary tradition was not brought over from Europe to the United States.[9]

However, two features of the American experience have to be added to this thesis. First, totally aside from the absence of a feudal tradition, the United States was extremely slow to develop a large central government. In European terms, we had a "weak state." Second, although it is true that we have had little *revolutionary* experience, it is distinctly not true that we have lived all those generations in conditions of social peace and political consensus. There is much violence in the history of the United States, and it cannot be explained away as exceptional. While it is not revolutionary violence, it is still violence; and we need another name for it: *rebellion.*

The rebellion model Rebellion, like revolution, is an extreme reaction to authority. Rebellion also involves disobedience, and it is a violent political activity. But rebellion is not revolution. Rather than using violence to displace one regime with another and one dominant class and dominant set of rules with another, rebellion seeks to use violence and disobedience to *change the behavior of the existing regime.* If a rebellious group or movement has a theory at all, that theory will be aimed at bringing behavior into closer proximity with existing rules rather than changing those rules entirely; it will be oriented toward joining the ruling class rather than displacing it.

Civil disobedience is the classic example of rebellious action. It virtually defines itself as deliberate violation of law in order to shock authorities into appreciating the anomaly or the injustice of the law. The purpose of the action is not to avoid application of the law but to make a political cause out of the law. Sometimes the appeal is in terms of an abstract moral principle, such as the attack on British property called the Boston Tea Party, which was based upon the standard of "no taxation without representation." At other times civil disobedience is based on the claim that a local or state

[7]Ted R. Gurr, *Why Men Rebel* (Princeton: Princeton University Press, 1970), p. 11, assessed in Bell, *Resistance and Revolution,* p. 9.

[8]See especially Louis Hartz, *The Liberal Tradition in America* (New York: Harcourt, Brace, 1955), chapter 1.

[9]For the best brief review, see Charles Tilly, "Collective Violence in European Perspective," in *The History of Violence in America,* ed. Hugh Davis Graham and Ted Robert Gurr (New York: Bantam Books, 1969), chapter 1, p. 41.

law is in violation of the Constitution or in conflict with other state or federal laws. This would have been true of much of the civil disobedience of blacks in the South during the 1950s and 1960s.

Some people disobey for personal gain—for example, by not paying their taxes for fun and profit. This is not a political act. Nonpayment of taxes becomes a political act—an act of rebellion—when its aim is to protest the tax burden, to object to a war in which the taxes are being used, or to fight against expansion of public education. The whole purpose of civil disobedience as an act of rebellion is spoiled unless the disobedience is public and carried out in a way calculated for maximum effect. If the act is not public, not organized, and not eventually punished, it is unlikely to draw the attention of the public or bring the appropriate response from the authorities. America's most famous proponent of civil disobedience, Henry David Thoreau, engaged in acts of civil disobedience as well as writing about them. However, his acts gained far less attention than his writings, because he tried to have a political effect as one peaceful malcontent.

Rebellion is at its very basis organized political violence. Either the rebellious group will use violence in its disobedient action against the state, or the government will use violence to suppress and punish the disobedience. The more political the explicit motivation of the rebellion, the more likely the government will use violence against it. In fact, governments have a way of converting a haphazard riot into a movement of political significance by treating it as though it were a politically significant action. For example, the race riots of 1917, 1919, and 1943 all seem to have begun as direct and nonpolitical confrontations of white and black *individuals* in some public place, such as a bathing area. In many instances the authorities did not even try to intervene until blacks organized themselves to retaliate against whites.[10]

Not all rebellious acts warrant being called civil disobedience. In the 1960s when blacks burned homes and businesses in their own neighborhoods in the urban ghettos, they were clearly engaging in rebellious acts, but their aims were a good deal more vague and general than is implied by civil disobedience. In these instances, "the rebellion becomes a community event; for once, the ghetto is united, and people feel they're acting together in a way they rarely can. . . . As in all rebellions throughout history, eventually agitators and professional revolutionaries come into the picture, but only after the ordinary and usually law-abiding ghetto residents have begun the rebellion."[11]

---

[10]For a comparison of earlier race riots to the ghetto protests and rebellions of the 1960s, see Robert M. Fogelson, "Violence as Protest," in *Proceedings of the Academy of Political Science* 29, no. 1 (1968), 25–41.

[11]Herbert Gans, "The Ghetto Rebellions and Urban Class Conflict," in *Proceedings of the Academy of Political Science* 29, no. 1 (1968), 43–44.

Revolutions and rebellions are both imbued with hope and optimism. Each operates under the banner of some utopian goal. But there the similarity ends. Revolution holds no hope for the existing political order; it is optimistic only in its belief that the organized actions of the revolutionary movement can eliminate injustice and create new institutions within a short (revolutionary) span of time. Revolutionaries may look for the worst only because the worst provides the opportunity to strike out for the best. Revolutionaries have a tremendous tolerance for contemporary injustices and inconveniences, because these are a sign for opportunities to come. In contrast, rebellion accepts the existing political order. Its optimism is its belief that rulers are redeemable and institutions are reformable. The violence committed by or in the name of a rebellion is virtually a result of the belief that the existing system can be everything it claims to be.

Extreme Reactions to Conquest, in the American Tradition

The student revolts of the 1960s in France and the United States provide a good case study of the difference between the tradition of revolution and the tradition of rebellion. In France, the explicit purpose of the student movements was to bring down the Fifth Republic in the name of one fundamental critique or another. Their strategies included nightly demonstrations in the important public places, provocation (barricades) to test the police and to encourage the police to make mistakes, exhortation of unions to join them in strikes, and many disobedient actions aimed at disrupting life in Paris (and eventually in other cities) to such an extent that it would be impossible for the regime to conduct public business. President de Gaulle ultimately did fall, and the regime came closer to falling than anyone let on at the time. Even though the protests may have been on new issues, the strategy of disruption aimed at overthrow was very much a part of the French tradition.

Although there has been only one major revolution in France, there have been many lesser revolutions and organized revolutionary efforts. It is no coincidence that the label for lesser revolutions, coup d'etat, is a French term. Since the Revolution of 1789, French regimes have had an average life of only twelve years. In 1968, the Fifth Republic was in its tenth year. It did not fall, but French political activists in the 1960s must have been aware of the pattern and of the tradition.[12] Although there are also many examples of rebellion in the history of France, the revolutionary model is clearly

[12]Compare with Stanley Hoffmann, "Protest in Modern France," in *The Revolution in World Politics,* ed. Morton Kaplan (New York: Wiley, 1962), p. 72.

available and is obviously thought to be a rational, if extreme, reaction against political authority.[13]

American student movements of the 1960s were in many ways more dramatic than the French. Public manifestations were frequent, and acts of disobedience involved far more injury and death in the United States than in France. But the great distinction between the French and American movements of the 1960s was not in the greater number of injuries and deaths in the United States but in the fact that American students were by and large not committed to revolutionary theory—in fact, most were virtually unaware of revolutionary ideas.

The most self-consciously committed part of the student movement of the 1960s, the Students for a Democratic Society (SDS), had many leaders whose ideas were intensely revolutionary, but these ideas did not become a central part of the SDS strategy until rather late in the history of the organization. During most of the 1960s, its members followed an almost pure strategy of rebellion, attempting to use campus obstruction to activate the larger society toward changes in foreign policy, military involvement, the draft, and race and labor relations.[14]

At no point did the student actions seek to overturn the national government or to rewrite the rules for selecting elites. Most student actions were aimed at specific and programmatic goals and took place far from Washington. At the most general level, students were seeking to redeem the American system, to take actions, however shocking, that might bring American leaders to policies more in keeping with an ideal standard. Here again, we find that the student demands virtually defined the nature of rebellion—to redeem the system, not to bring it down. Only a few at the fringe spoke of and organized for revolution in the classical sense.

H. Rap Brown, an early leader of the Student Nonviolent Coordinating Committee (SNCC, pronounced "snick"), made the widely quoted observation that "violence is as American as cherry pie." Brown's observation is more than confirmed by the history of labor in the United States, which has been "the bloodiest and most violent . . . of any industrial nation in the world."[15] Major instances of organized political violence in our country have been catalogued and studied by historians and sociologists. These will be reviewed here, in the context of two major hypotheses: (1) Some of the most important changes in American history were brought about by

---

[13]The best brief review of this history will be found in Tilly, "Collective Violence in European Perspective."

[14]See, for example, Irwin Unger, *The Movement—A History of the American New Left, 1959–1972* (New York: Dodd, Mead, 1974), especially pp. 101–116.

[15]Philip Taft and Philip Ross, "American Labor Violence: Its Causes, Character, and Outcome," in *The History of Violence in America*, p. 281. See also Richard Rubenstein, *Rebels in Eden* (Boston: Little, Brown, 1970), p. 81.

violent political action, not by normal or consensus politics; and (2) radicalism and political violence in the United States belong to the *tradition of rebellion.*

The American Revolution   Our own so-called revolution was itself a rebellion and was so understood by the British and the American loyalists. Acts of rebellion preceding the Declaration of Independence were aimed largely at pushing Parliament toward important reforms in the British system and its relation to its colonies. And although the war itself resulted in a new and independent nation, the American leaders moved rather steadfastly toward the reconstitution of the United States on the British model. The patriots were not concerned with the British system, except to adopt parts of it for their own. This is the basis of Edmund Burke's famous distinction between the American and the French Revolution, leading him to support the former and bitterly oppose the latter.[16]

Agrarian rebellion   Farmer rebellions also preceded independence but did not disappear afterwards. Many were given names, such as the Whiskey Rebellion in Pennsylvania. Although no single farmer rebellion rates as a historic moment, this series of early rebellions probably created the conditions or experiences for far more important nonviolent farmer movements after the Civil War. Farmers could be radicalized, and were. The pitchfork was one of the great symbols of agrarian radicalism; it beautifully combined the ideas of sword *and* ploughshare. But in most of the cases of farmer action—violent and nonviolent—the primary goals were redemption and reform, not revolution. Although some of the Populists in the nineteenth century dreamed of fending off or transforming the capitalist system, most of the actual farmer movements made demands for basic reforms of the system in order to make it work better for agriculture.[17]

Southern white rebellion   For the South, the Civil War, ending in military occupation, was in many respects a repeat of the Revolutionary War. The South conducted the Civil War against actions and tendencies of the national government that were thought to be intolerable. The northern states treated secession, quite properly, as rebellion. President Lincoln tried desperately to treat the situation as a state of "insurrection" by trying to frame

---

[16]Edmund Burke, *Reflections on the Revolution in France* (London, 1790).
[17]See, for example, M. R. Benedict, *Farm Policies of the United States, 1790–1950* (New York: Twentieth Century Fund, 1953); and Grant McConnell, *The Decline of Agrarian Democracy* (Berkeley: University of California Press, 1953), especially his treatment of the rise and decline of the most radicalized segment of agriculture in the late nineteenth century, the People's Party.

concessions that would prevent the South from going to war or would end the war quickly and maintain the Union. For example, in Lincoln's second State of the Union Address, in January of 1864, he proposed a scheme of "compensated emancipation," by which the national government would indemnify each slave owner in a manner very much comparable to acquisition through eminent domain.

In its turn, the South would have been satisfied either with drastic changes in national policies or with secession to form a new entity. There were no plans to win the war in order to remake the entire United States. Victory for the South would have meant the establishment of a separate nation-state, leaving the United States as a smaller, nonslave nation-state with the system of government it already had. Defeat did not turn southern whites away from rebellion and from the causes of the original rebellion. For example, the Ku Klux Klan, founded immediately after the surrender, was a significant type of rebellion, aimed at reversing, if not terminating, Reconstruction policies and the military government. The Klan's violent actions were part of a larger effort of guerrilla action aimed at reform, not at any goals comparable to the guerrilla actions of the Viet Cong during the 1960s.

The labor movement In the context of twentieth century trade unions in the U.S., the notions of either rebellion *or* revolution seem terribly remote. However, given the laws and attitudes of American leaders and governments in the nineteenth century, most efforts to improve the condition of labor involved disobedience. The main question was, of course, what kind of disobedience. The revolutionary model was tried briefly as a means of violently changing the policies of state governments and the actions of state and local police. However, nonrevolutionary political action became dominant long before the situation had developed into nonviolent, ordinary politics.[18] Even after the Soviet Revolution there is no indication that revolutionaries made much headway inside American labor.

The only element of political violence left in the labor movement is the strike, and it provides us with telling evidence of the importance of the rebellion model. In Europe, the strike is frequently used as a broad political weapon, a class-conscious act by workers against the state. In the United States, the strike is a specialized weapon of momentary obstruction aimed at altering management behavior at the bargaining table. The strike in the United States assumes the persistence of the existing power structure. Even when

[18]J. David Greenstone, *Labor in American Politics* (New York: Knopf, 1969).

it has been used as a political weapon in the United States, the purpose has been to extract specific concessions from the government. These actions have included laws providing for shorter hours, better conditions, the right to organize, and expansion of welfare legislation. The strike, or threat of it, has almost always followed a rebellion model in the United States.[19]

Urban protest Violence in American cities seems to have followed the rebellion model for at least the past century. Many white urban riots and gang wars were violent actions by a nativist or older ethnic group to oppose the advance of some newer ethnic group, without public intervention at all—a form of "private self-government" or direct-action politics, as described in chapter 3.[20] Other radical urban actions were aimed at getting the local police and other government officials to intervene more forcefully against encroachment by new immigrants.[21]

Violent action by blacks in the cities has also followed the rebellion model. Many of the most spontaneous uprisings have developed into collective protests, despite the spontaneity of their origins. Protests which started as a reaction to an arrest of a single individual may have grown into widespread attacks against white landlords and merchants and eventually have been drawn up by a few articulate leaders into a protest against the injustices throughout the system. "Hence," observes Fogelson, "the riots were meant to alert America, not to overturn it. . . . For the great majority of Negroes, the American dream, tarnished though it has been for centuries, is still the ultimate aspiration."[22] Another expert observer of civil strife notes that:

> With few exceptions, the demands or apparent objectives of participants in civil strife in the United States have been limited ones. Civil-rights demonstrators have asked for integration and remedial governmental action on Negro problems; they have not agitated for class or racial warfare. Peace marchers vehemently oppose American foreign policy and some of the men who conduct it; none of them have attempted to overthrow the political system. Black militants talk of revolutionary warfare; such sentiments are rarely voiced by those who participate in ghetto riots. By the testimony of most of their words and actions, they have been retaliating against the accumulated burden of specific grievances. . . . The United States has experienced chronic conspiratorial violence in the past decade, but it has been almost entirely defensive.[23]

---

[19]Compare with Daniel Bell, *The End of Ideology* (New York: Free Press, 1960), pp. 212–215.
[20]See also Fogelson, "Violence as Protest," especially pp. 28–31.
[21]For example, see Rubenstein, *Rebels in Eden,* p. 31.
[22]Fogelson, "Violence as Protest," p. 35.
[23]Ted Robert Gurr, "A Comparative Study of Civil Strife," in *The History of Violence in America,* chapter 17, p. 587.

CONQUEST AND PUBLIC MORALITY:
THE OBLIGATION TO JUSTIFY

The rebellion model is so much a part of our experience that some of our wisest observers have taken it as the definition of the entire phenomenon of political radicalism. For example, in one of the best available treatments, political violence is defined as acts of disruption whose purpose is to "modify the behavior of others in a bargaining situation."[24] While this is the essence of the rebellion model, there is at least one other type of political violence—the revolutionary model, which is oriented toward replacement of the bargainers as well as the bargaining table.

A model operates as a guide. When people are radicalized by their exasperation with the regime, they tend to imitate the past. There is a form to extreme action just as there is a form to conventional action. Rebellion tends to take place some distance from the political center, out where the specific grievances and the specific symbols exist.[25] The demands of the rebellious leaders tend to be demands that can be met, in whole or in part, by the authorities. In fact, one of the great self-designated American radicals, Saul Alinsky, laid down as one of the cardinal rules of radical action that the behaviors ought to be extreme but the demands ought to be concrete and achievable.[26]

The rebellion model guides rulers as well as dissidents. Since extreme action violates the law, or threatens to violate the law, state intervention is usually unavoidable. But extreme action must be perceived and defined by the authorities: How dangerous are the dissidents? How much force is needed, and when and where? Acts that are defined as rebellions will almost certainly be treated in the United States less violently than acts defined as revolutionary. Unquestionably, rebellion does threaten public authority; and the police feel themselves implicated even when their own position is not directly attacked—all the more so because they tend to be drawn from the same social classes as the rebels.[27]

However, when a revolutionary group turns to violent action, the heat of official reaction is disproportionately greater. For example, the Black Panthers, who were never more than a few dozen members, became the object of nationwide surveillance and suppression, not merely because they had threatened to use weaponry,

---

[24]H. L. Nieburg, *Political Violence* (New York: St. Martin's Press, 1969), p. 13.

[25]Compare with Allan Silver, "Official Interpretations of Racial Riots," *Proceedings of the Academy of Political Science* 29, no. 1 (1968), 146.

[26]Saul Alinsky, *Reveille for Radicals* (Chicago: University of Chicago Press, 1946). See also Charles F. Levine, "The Political and Organizational Theory of Saul Alinsky" (Ph.D. diss., Stanford University, 1976).

[27]Gans, "The Ghetto Rebellions and Urban Class Conflict," pp. 42–51.

but because the Panthers had developed an eclectic but nevertheless explicit revolutionary theory to accompany their local actions. The elimination of the Panthers was carried out by a carefully planned and heavily armed police detachment led by the state's attorney in Chicago. Yet, "withall in the perspective of American history, the Panthers were less violent than white minorities had been as they fought their way up the social and economic scale."[28]

Even when quiescent and conventional, a group with a revolutionary theory in the United States is badly off, subject to infiltration, surveillance, discrimination. Let it just hint at intellectual espousal of direct action, and the official reaction is disproportionately swift and severe. The revolutionary model is apparently so unusual in the American tradition that revolutionaries are treated almost by definition as foreigners.

Actually, since there are inevitably going to be occasional outbreaks of political violence in any country, an elite should count itself fortunate if its dissidents tend naturally to pattern their behavior on the rebellion model. The demands of a rebellious movement can almost always be met. Although it is the inevitable urge of the officials to suppress, they usually end up making substantial concessions; and in the process of doing so, they tend to coopt the movement—satisfying many of the members even if not entirely placating all of the rebellious leaders. Either way, in the wake of rebellion, the regime tends to be reinforced.

Our tradition of rebellion seems also to have saved us from radical action of one segment of our elite against another. It is unimaginable that the stakes of a dispute between two segments of the American corporate elite were never high enough to warrant an attempted coup d'etat. Yet, there is no record of so much as a plan of this sort. Why, for example, did Richard Nixon not attempt to suspend the Constitution in 1974 as Indira Gandhi did in India in 1975? The record shows that President Nixon never hesitated violating the law to suppress the opposition and to concentrate power in his own hands. Yet, when it became certain he was doomed to go down in disgrace, he yielded rather than try to overturn the legal situation or suspend constitutional procedures.

Nixon's chief of staff was a high-ranking and highly respected military officer, who went on to become the commanding officer of NATO. Nixon's own standing with the military and with the "civilian hawks" was very high. He was respected by most conservatives, revered by many. It is useless to suggest that we are such a diverse nation and so love our Constitution that the president would never have succeeded. Perhaps that is true, but why did he not try? By July 1974, he had so little to lose by attempting to remain in power through extraconstitutional means.

[28]Alexander Kendrick, *The Wound Within* (Boston: Little, Brown, 1974), p. 263.

Perhaps the answer is that such a course of action would probably never have occurred to President Nixon. Or if it had occurred to him, *he would not have known how to behave.* Revolution, even a small palace revolution, is so far outside American experience that there is no scenario for it. Who should be called in first? What kinds of deals ought to be made? What are the contingencies?

In a very important sense, rebellion has become part of the institutionalized politics of the United States. Most of the time the political process works through elections, bargaining, secret deals, legislative action, and consensus. Competition is between two unprogrammatic parties on the same side of property, industry, employment, and poverty. Change usually takes place at the margins of the existing system, and when there is violence, they are simply extended until the rebellion is placated or palliated.

However, traditions can change. If our tradition of violence is explained by the absence of an old aristocracy and the weakness of the state, what will happen to that tradition if one of those conditions changes? There is no old aristocracy to reemerge, but the state can be "Europeanized" and become a strong center of national life. How far can the state go in responding to the demands for more conquest without becoming the kind of force and symbol that confirms the revolutionary critique and converts rebellious leaders into revolutionaries? The very optimism of American leaders toward the capacity of the national government has brought the country some distance already along this route.

Note, for example, how far we have come toward the nationalization of response to local disorders. During the nineteenth century there were of course occasions when the president called out the militia to deal with a local rebellion. President Washington sent 12,950 troops drawn from four states to meet the Whiskey Rebellion.[29] However, these instances were few and far between until the 1960s, especially the late 1960s. In the twenty years between September 1945 and August 1965, federal intervention by the use of the national guard and other military troops became a regular occurrence. Eighty-three call-ups involving 44,927 troops have been identified during that period of time. Then, in the three and one-half years between August 1965 and December 31, 1968, there were 179 call-ups involving 184,133 federal troops.[30]

One response to these statistics might be that the years of the late 1960s were unusual because of the culmination of war opposition and of civil rights militancy. Nevertheless, the significant feature during that time is the regularity of federal response to local disorder. The national government seems to have become a regular party to each and every rebellion anywhere in the country. Local

[29]Adam Yarmolinsky, *The Military Establishment* (New York: Harper & Row, 1971), p. 154.
[30]Ibid., pp. 162–163.

disorder has been nationalized. The national government has not only used federal troops on a regular basis, it has also gotten into the business of regular surveillance and infiltration of local organizations. Revelations during the Watergate investigations showed not only that the CIA and the FBI were engaged in local surveillance during the Nixon administration but that these activities, including civilian surveillance by the army, had been going on at least since 1965.[31]

It is too early to assess precisely the extent to which the nationalization of response to local disorder indicates a basic change in our system. However, it is not too soon to view this development with alarm. When the state makes itself a party to all disputes, it must prepare itself for the consequences. There are great advantages to a national approach, as, for example, in the matter of civil rights. But as the national government moves out of its nineteenth century conception of weak-centered federalism, it must enrich its appreciation of control and must concern itself increasingly with the requisites of justifying control at every turn. And now that our modernized and sophisticated citizenry no longer responds to appeals to obedience based upon God or nature, community, or tradition, a stronger central government must search for ever stronger justification for its control.

One of the great tragedies is that human beings must be conquered and governed at all. But if this to be our lot, let us resolve to be conquered only by a good argument and to be governed only by ample justification. The requirement of justification is the only dependable defense the powerless have against the powerful.

Equally tragic is the requirement that rulers must rule. But if they must, let us teach them to justify their actions. The obligation to justify can only make them better rulers. Nothing will make them good rulers, since rulers must coerce, and coercion can never be absolutely good. Rulers deal in necessity, and the best they can do with necessity is to justify it within the forms of governing provided for them long before they ever took power.

If the American system has any claim to greatness, do not look for it in the goodness of its rulers but rather in its forms and how proportionately these forms deal with everlasting contradictions between control and freedom, control and representation, control and justification—between conquest and incomplete conquest.

Few governments in all history have coped any better with the contradictions inherent in incomplete conquest. Through two centuries we have persisted as a system of government while perhaps making some modest strides toward the advancement of individual

---

[31]Ibid., p. 374; Christopher H. Pyle, "CONUS Intelligence: The Army Watches Civilian Politics," in *Blowing the Whistle,* ed. Charles Peters and Taylor Branch (New York: Praeger, 1972), pp. 44–76; and Victor Navasky, *Kennedy Justice* (New York: Atheneum, 1971).

dignity. Yet, persistence proves nothing, except that human beings will strive for progress despite inhuman odds, despite the certainty that for the everlasting problems of government there are no lasting solutions.

> Do I contradict myself?
> Very well then I contradict myself;
> (I am large, I contain multitudes.)
> Walt Whitman, 1855

> It is my fate. . . . to swing constantly from optimism to pessimism and back, but so is it the fate of anyone who writes or speaks of anything in America—the most contradictory, the most depressing, the most stirring, of any land in the world today.
> Sinclair Lewis, 1930

The Articles of
Confederation

Agreed to by Congress November 15, 1777; ratified and in force March 1, 1781

To ALL TO WHOM these Presents shall come, we the undersigned Delegates of the States affixed to our Names send greeting. Whereas the Delegates of the United States of America in Congress assembled did on the fifteenth day of November in the Year of our Lord One Thousand Seven Hundred and Seventy seven, and in the Second Year of the Independence of America agree to certain articles of Confederation and perpetual Union between the States of Newhampshire, Massachusetts-bay, Rhodeisland and Providence Plantations, Connecticut, New York, New Jersey, Pennsylvania, Delaware, Maryland, Virginia, North-Carolina, South-Carolina and Georgia in the Words following, viz. "Articles of Confederation and perpetual Union between the states of Newhampshire, Massachusetts-bay, Rhodeisland and Providence Plantations, Connecticut, New-York, New-Jersey, Pennsylvania, Delaware, Maryland, Virginia, North-Carolina, South-Carolina and Georgia.

Art. I. The Stile of this confederacy shall be "The United States of America."

Art. II. Each state retains its sovereignty, freedom and independence, and every Power, Jurisdiction and right, which is not by this confederation expressly delegated to the United States, in Congress assembled.

Art. III. The said states hereby severally enter into a firm league of friendship with each other, for their common defence, the security of their Liberties, and their mutual and general welfare, binding themselves to assist each other, against all force offered to, or attacks made upon them, or any of them, on account of religion, sovereignty, trade, or any other pretence whatever.

Art. IV. The better to secure and perpetuate mutual friendship and intercourse among the people of the different states in this union, the free inhabitants of each of these states, paupers, vagabonds and fugitives from Justice excepted, shall be entitled to all privileges and immunities of free citizens in the several states; and the people of each state shall have free ingress and regress to and from any other state, and shall enjoy therein all the privileges of trade and commerce, subject to the same duties, impositions and restrictions as the inhabitants thereof respectively, provided that such restriction shall not extend so far as to prevent the removal of property imported into any state, to any other state of which the Owner is an inhabitant; provided also that no imposition, duties or restriction shall be laid by any state, on the property of the united states, or either of them.

If any Person guilty of, or charged with treason, felony, or other high misdemeanor in any state, shall flee from Justice, and be found in any of the united states, he shall upon demand of the Governor or executive power, of the state from which he fled, be delivered up and removed to the state having jurisdiction of his offence.

Full faith and credit shall be given in each of these states to the records, acts and judicial proceedings of the courts and magistrates of every other state.

Art. V. For the more convenient management of the general interests of the united states, delegates shall be annually appointed in such manner as the legislature of each state shall direct, to meet in Congress on the first Monday in November, in every year, with a power reserved to each state, to recal its delegates, or any of them, at any time within the year, and to send others in their stead, for the remainder of the Year.

No state shall be represented in Congress by less than two, nor by more than seven Members; and no person shall be capable of being a delegate for more than three years in any term of six years; nor shall any person, being a delegate, be capable of holding any office under the united states, for which he, or another for his benefit receives any salary, fees or emolument of any kind.

Each state shall maintain its own delegates in a meeting of the states, and while they act as members of the committee of the states.

In determining questions in the united states, in Congress assembled, each state shall have one vote.

Freedom of speech and debate in Congress shall not be impeached or questioned in any Court, or place out of Congress, and the members of congress shall be protected in their persons from arrests and imprisonments, during the time of their going to and from, and attendance on congress, except for treason, felony, or breach of the peace.

Art. VI. No state without the Consent of the united states in congress assembled, shall send any embassy to, or receive any embassy from, or enter into any conference, agreement, or alliance or treaty with any King, prince or state; nor shall any person holding any office of profit or trust under the united states, or any of them, accept of any present, emolument, office or title of any kind whatever from any king, prince or foreign state; nor shall the united states in congress assembled, or any of them, grant any title of nobility.

No two or more states shall enter into any treaty, confederation or alliance whatever between them, without the consent of the united states in congress assembled, specifying accurately the purposes for which the same is to be entered into, and how long it shall continue.

No state shall lay any imposts or duties, which may interfere with any stipulations in treaties, entered into by the united states in congress assembled, with any king, prince or state, in pursuance of any treaties already proposed by congress, to the courts of France and Spain.

No vessels of war shall be kept up in time of peace by any state, except such number only, as shall be deemed necessary by the united states in congress assembled, for the defence of such state, or its trade; nor shall any body of forces be kept up by any state, in time of peace, except such number only, as in the judgment of the united states, in congress assembled, shall be deemed requisite to garrison the forts necessary for the defence of such state; but every state shall always keep up a well regulated and disciplined militia, sufficiently armed and accoutred, and shall provide and constantly have ready for use, in public stores, a due number of field pieces and tents, and a proper quantity of arms, ammunition and camp equipage.

No state shall engage in any war without the consent of the united states in congress assembled, unless such state be actually invaded by enemies, or shall have received certain advice of a resolution being formed by some nation of Indians to invade such state, and the danger is so imminent as not to admit of a delay, till the united states in congress assembled can be consulted: nor shall any state grant commissions to any ships or vessels of war, nor letters of marque or reprisal, except it be after a declaration of war by the united states in congress assembled, and then only against the kingdom or state and the subjects thereof, against which war has been so declared, and under such regulations as shall be established by the united states in congress assembled, unless such state be infested by pirates, in which case vessels of war may be fitted out for that occasion, and kept so long as the danger shall continue, or until the united states in congress assembled shall determine otherwise.

Art. VII. When land-forces are raised by any state for the common defence, all officers of or under the rank of colonel, shall be appointed by the legislature of each state respectively by whom such forces shall be raised, or in such manner as such state shall direct, and all vacancies shall be filled up by the state which first made the appointment.

Art. VIII. All charges of war, and all other expences that shall be incurred for the common defence or general welfare, and allowed by the united states in congress assembled, shall be defrayed out of a common treasury, which shall be supplied by the several states, in proportion to the value of all land within each state, granted to or surveyed for any Person, as such land and the buildings and improvements thereon shall be estimated according to such mode as the united states in congress assembled, shall from time to time direct and appoint. The taxes for paying that proportion shall be laid and levied by the authority and direction of the legislatures of the several states within the time agreed upon by the united states in congress assembled.

Art. IX. The united states in congress assembled, shall have the sole and exclusive right and power of determining on peace and war, except in the cases mentioned in the sixth article—of sending and receiving ambassadors—entering into treaties and alliances, provided that no treaty of commerce shall be made whereby the legislative power of the respective states shall be restrained from imposing such imposts and duties on foreigners, as their own people are subjected to, or from prohibiting the exportation or importation of any species of goods or commodities whatsoever—of establishing rules for deciding in all cases, what captures on land or water shall be legal, and in what manner prizes taken by land or naval forces in the service of the united states shall be divided or appropriated.—of granting letters of marque and reprisal in times of peace—appointing courts for the trial of piracies and felonies committed on the high seas and establishing courts for receiving and determining finally appeals in all cases of captures, provided that no member of congress shall be appointed a judge of any of the said courts.

The united states in congress assembled shall also be the last resort on appeal in all disputes and differences now subsisting or that hereafter may arise between two or more states concerning boundary, jurisdiction or any other cause whatever; which authority shall always be exercised in the manner following. Whenever the legislative or executive authority or lawful agent of any state in controversy with another shall present a petition to congress. stating the matter in question and praying for a hearing, notice thereof shall be given by order of congress to the legislative or executive authority of the other state in controversy, and a day assigned for the appearance of the parties by their lawful agents, who shall then be directed to appoint by joint consent, commissioners or judges to constitute a court for hearing and determining the matter in question: but if they cannot agree, congress shall name three persons out of each of the united states, and from the list of such persons each party shall alternately strike out one, the petitioners beginning, until the number shall be reduced to thirteen; and from that number not less than seven, nor more than nine names as congress shall direct, shall in the presence of congress be drawn out by lot, and the persons whose names shall be so drawn or any five of them, shall be commissioners or judges, to hear and finally determine the controversy, so always as a major part of the judges who shall hear the cause shall agree in the determination: and if either party shall neglect to attend at the day appointed, without shewing reasons, which congress shall judge sufficient, or being present shall refuse to strike, the congress shall proceed to nominate three persons out of each state, and the secretary of congress shall strike in behalf of such party absent or refusing; and the judgment and sentence of the court to be appointed, in the manner before prescribed, shall be final and conclusive; and if any of the parties shall refuse to submit to the authority of such court, or to appear to defend their claim or cause, the court shall nevertheless proceed to pronounce sentence, or judgment, which shall in like manner be final and decisive, the judgment or sentence and other proceedings being in either case transmitted to congress, and lodged among the acts of congress for the security of the parties concerned: provided that every commissioner, before he sits in judgment, shall take an oath to be administered by one of the judges of the supreme or superior court of the state, where the cause shall be tried, "well and truly to hear and determine the matter in question, according to the best of his judgment, without favour, affection or hope of reward:" provided also that no state shall be deprived of territory for the benefit of the united states.

All controversies concerning the private right of soil claimed under different grants of two or more states, whose jurisdictions as they may respect such lands, and the states which passed such grants are adjusted, the said grants or either of them being at the same time claimed to have originated antecedent to such settlement of jurisdiction, shall on the petition of either party to the congress of the united states, be finally determined as near as may be in the same manner as is before prescribed for deciding disputes respecting territorial jurisdiction between different states.

The united states in congress assembled shall also have the sole and exclusive right and power of regulating the alloy and value of coin struck by their own authority, or by that of the respective states—fixing the standard of weights and measures throughout the united states.—regulating the trade and managing all affairs with the Indians, not members of any of the states, provided that the legislative right of any state within its own limits be not infringed or violated—establishing and regulating post-offices from one state to another, throughout all the united states, and exacting such postage on the papers passing thro' the same as may be requisite to defray the expences of the said office—appointing all officers of the land forces, in the service of the united states, excepting regimental officers.—appointing all the officers of the naval forces, and commissioning all officers whatever in the service of the united states—making rules for the government and regulation of the said land and naval forces, and directing their operations.

The united states in congress assembled shall have authority to appoint a committee, to sit in the recess of congress, to be denominated "A Committee of the States," and to consist of one delegate from each state; and to appoint such other committees and civil officers as may be necessary for managing the general affairs of the united states under their direction—to appoint one of their number to preside, provided that no person be allowed to serve in the office of president more than one year in any term of three years; to ascertain the necessary sums of Money to be raised for the service of the united states, and to appropriate and apply the same for defraying the public expences—to borrow money, or emit bills on the credit of the united states, transmitting every half year to the respective states an account of the sums of money so borrowed or emitted,—to build and equip a navy—to agree upon the number of land forces, and to make requisitions from each state for its quota, in proportion to the number of white inhabitants in such state; which requisition shall be binding, and thereupon the legislature of each state shall appoint the regimental officers, raise the men and cloath, arm and equip them in a soldier like manner, at the expence of the united states, and the officers and men so cloathed, armed and equipped shall march to the place appointed, and within the time agreed on by the united states in congress assembled: But if the united states in congress assembled shall, on consideration of circumstances judge proper that any state should not raise men, or should raise a smaller number than its quota, and that any other state should raise a greater number of men than the quota thereof, such extra number shall be raised, officered, cloathed, armed and equipped in the same manner as the quota of such state, unless the legislature of such state shall judge that such extra number cannot be safely spared out of the same, in which case they shall raise officer, cloath, arm and equip as many of such extra number as they judge can be safely spared. And the officers and men so cloathed, armed and equipped, shall march to the place appointed, and within the time agreed on by the united states in congress assembled.

The united states in congress assembled shall never engage in a war, nor grant letters of marque and reprisal in time of peace, nor enter into any treaties or alliances, nor coin money, nor regulate the value thereof, nor ascertain the sums and expences necessary for the defence and welfare of the united states, or any of them, nor emit bills, nor borrow money on the credit of the united states, nor appropriate money, nor agree upon the number of vessels of war, to be built or purchased, or the number of land or sea forces to be raised, nor appoint a commander in chief of the army or navy, unless nine states assent to the same: nor shall a question on any other point, except for adjourning from day to day be determined, unless by the votes of a majority of the united states in congress assembled.

The congress of the united states shall have power to adjourn to any time within the year, and to any place within the united states, so that no period of adjournment be for a longer duration than the space of six Months, and shall publish the Journal of their proceedings monthly, except such parts thereof relating to treaties, alliances or military operations as in their judgment require secrecy; and the yeas and nays of the delegates of each state on any question shall be entered on the Journal, when it is desired by any delegate; and the delegates of a state, or any of them, at his or their request shall be furnished with a transcript of the said Journal, except such parts as are above excepted, to lay before the legislatures of the several states.

Art. X. The committee of the states, or any nine of them, shall be authorised to execute, in the recess of congress, such of the powers of congress as the united states in congress assembled, by the consent of nine states, shall from time to time think expedient to vest them with; provided that no power be delegated to the said committee, for the exercise of which, by the articles of confederation, the voice of nine states in the congress of the united states assembled is requisite.

Art. XI. Canada acceding to this confederation, and joining in the measures of the united states, shall be admitted into, and entitled to all the advantages of this union: but no other colony shall be admitted into the same, unless such admission be agreed to by nine states.

Art. XII. All bills of credit emitted, monies borrowed and debts contracted by, or under the authority of congress, before the assembling of the united states, in pursuance of the present confederation, shall be deemed and considered as a charge against the united states, for payment and satisfaction whereof the said united states, and the public faith are hereby solemnly pledged.

Art. XIII. Every state shall abide by the determinations of the united states in congress assembled, on all questions which by this confederation are submitted to them. And the Articles of this confederation shall be inviolably observed by every state, and the union shall be perpetual; nor shall any alteration at any time hereafter be made in any of them; unless such alteration be agreed to in a congress of the united states, and be afterwards confirmed by the legislatures of every state.

AND WHEREAS it hath pleased the Great Governor of the World to incline the hearts of the legislatures we respectively represent in congress, to approve of, and to authorize us to ratify the said articles of confederation and perpetual union. KNOW YE that we the under-signed delegates, by virtue of the power and authority to us given for that purpose, do by these presents, in the name and in behalf of our respective constituents, fully and entirely ratify and confirm each and every of the said articles of confederation and perpetual union, and all and singular the matters and things therein contained: And we do further solemnly plight and engage the faith of our respective constituents, that they shall abide by the determinations of the united states in congress assembled, on all questions, which by the said confederation are submitted to them. And that the articles thereof shall be inviolably observed by the states we respectively represent, and that the union shall be perpetual. In Witness whereof we have hereunto set our hands in Congress. Done at Philadelphia in the state of Pennsylvania the ninth Day of July in the Year of our Lord one Thousand seven Hundred and Seventy-eight, and in the third year of the independence of America.

The Constitution of the United States of America

Annotated with references to the *Federalist Papers*

[PREAMBLE]

84 (Hamilton)

We the People of the United States, in Order to form a more perfect Union, establish Justice, insure domestic Tranquility, provide for the common defence, promote the general Welfare, and secure the Blessings of Liberty to ourselves and our Posterity, do ordain and establish this Constitution for the United States of America.

ARTICLE I

Section 1

[LEGISLATIVE POWERS]

45 (Madison)

All legislative Powers herein granted shall be vested in a Congress of the United States, which shall consist of a Senate and House of Representatives.

Section 2

[HOUSE OF REPRESENTATIVES, HOW CONSTITUTED, POWER OF IMPEACHMENT]

39 (Madison)
45 (Madison)
52–53, 57 (Madison)

The House of Representatives shall be composed of Members chosen every second Year by the People of the several States, and the Electors in each State shall have the Qualifications requisite for Electors of the most numerous Branch of the State Legislature.

52 (Madison), 60 (Hamilton)	No Person shall be a Representative who shall not have attained to the Age of twenty-five Years, and been seven Years a Citizen of the United States, and who shall not, when elected, be an inhabitant of that State in which he shall be chosen.
54 (Madison)	Representatives and *direct Taxes*[1] shall be apportioned among the several States which may be included within this Union, according to their respective Numbers, *which shall be determined by adding to the whole Number of free Persons, including those bound to Service for a Term of Years,* and excluding Indians not taxed, *three*
54 (Madison)	*fifths of all other Persons.*[2] The actual Enumeration shall be made within three Years
58 (Madison)	after the first Meeting of the Congress of the United States, and within every subsequent Term of ten Years, in such Manner as they shall by Law direct. The Number of Representatives shall not exceed one for every thirty Thousand, but each
55–56 (Madison)	State shall have at Least one Representative; *and until such enumeration shall be made, the State of New Hampshire shall be entitled to chuse three, Massachusetts eight, Rhode-Island and Providence Plantations one, Connecticut five, New-York six, New Jersey four, Pennsylvania eight, Delaware one, Maryland six. Virginia ten, North Carolina five, South Carolina five, and Georgia three.*[3]
	When vacancies happen in the Representation from any State, the Executive Authority thereof shall issue Writs of Election to fill such Vacancies.
79 (Hamilton)	The House of Representatives shall chuse their Speaker and other Officers; and shall have the sole Power of Impeachment.

Section 3
[THE SENATE, HOW CONSTITUTED, IMPEACHMENT TRIALS]

39, 45 (Madison), 60 (Hamilton), 62–63 (Madison)	The Senate of the United States shall be composed of two Senators from each State, *chosen by the Legislature thereof,*[4] for six Years; and each Senator shall have one Vote.
59 (Hamilton)	Immediately after they shall be assembled in Consequence of the first Election, they shall be divided as equally as may be into three Classes. The Seats of the Senators of the first Class shall be vacated at the Expiration of the second Year, of the second Class at the Expiration of the fourth Year, and of the third Class at the Expiration of the sixth Year, so that one third may be chosen every second Year: *and*
68 (Hamilton)	*if vacancies happen by Resignation, or otherwise, during the Recess of the Legislature of any State, the Executive thereof may make temporary Appointments until the next Meeting of the Legislature, which shall then fill such Vacancies.*[5]
62 (Madison), 64 (Jay)	No person shall be a Senator who shall not have attained to the Age of thirty Years, and been nine Years a Citizen of the United States, and who shall not, when elected, be an Inhabitant of that State for which he shall be chosen.
	The Vice President of the United States shall be President of the Senate, but shall have no Vote, unless they be equally divided.
	The Senate shall chuse their other Officers, and also a President pro tempore, in the Absence of the Vice President, or when he shall exercise the Office of President of the United States.
39 (Madison), 65–67, 79 (Hamilton) 65 (Hamilton)	The Senate shall have the sole Power to try all Impeachments. When sitting for that Purpose, they shall be on Oath or Affirmation. When the President of the United States is tried, the Chief Justice shall preside: And no Person shall be convicted without the Concurrence of two thirds of the Members present.
84 (Hamilton)	Judgment in Cases of Impeachment shall not extend further than to removal from Office, and disqualification to hold and enjoy any Office of honor, Trust or Profit under the United States: but the Party convicted shall nevertheless be liable and subject to Indictment, Trial, Judgment and Punishment, according to Law.

Section 4
[ELECTION OF SENATORS AND REPRESENTATIVES]

59–61 (Hamilton)	The Times, Places and Manner of holding Elections for Senators and Representatives, shall be prescribed in each State by the Legislature thereof; but the Congress

---

[1]Modified by Sixteenth Amendment.
[2]Modified by Fourteenth Amendment.
[3]Temporary provision.
[4]Modified by Seventeenth Amendment.
[5]Ibid.

may at any time by Law make or alter such Regulations, except as to the Places of chusing Senators.

The Congress shall assemble at least once in every Year, and such Meeting shall be on the first Monday in December, unless they shall by Law appoint a different Day.[6]

Section 5

[QUORUM, JOURNALS, MEETINGS, ADJOURNMENTS]

Each House shall be the Judge of the Elections, Returns and Qualifications of its own Members, and a Majority of each shall constitute a Quorum to do Business; but a smaller Number may adjourn from day to day, and may be authorized to compel the Attendance of absent Members, in such Manner, and under the Penalties as each House may provide.

Each House may determine the Rules of its Proceedings, punish its Members for disorderly Behavior, and, with the Concurrence of two thirds, expel a Member.

Each House shall keep a Journal of its Proceedings, and from time to time publish the same, excepting such Parts as may in their Judgment require Secrecy; and the Yeas and Nays of the Members of either House on any question shall, at the Desire of one fifth of the present, be entered on the Journal.

Neither House, during the Session of Congress, shall, without the Consent of the other, adjourn for more than three days, nor to any other Place than that in which the two Houses shall be sitting.

Section 6

[COMPENSATION, PRIVILEGES, DISABILITIES]

The Senators and Representatives shall receive a Compensation for their Services, to be ascertained by Law, and paid out of the Treasury of the United States. They shall in all Cases, except Treason, Felony and Breach of the Peace, be privileged from Arrest during their Attendance at the Session of their respective Houses, and in going to and returning from the same; and for any Speech or Debate in either House, they shall not be questioned in any other Place.

55 (Madison), 76 (Hamilton)

No Senator or Representative shall, during the time for which he was elected, be appointed to any civil Office under the authority of the United States, which shall have been created, or the Emoluments whereof shall have been encreased during such time; and no Person holding any Office under the United States, shall be a Member of either House during his Continuance in Office.

Section 7

[PROCEDURE IN PASSING BILLS AND RESOLUTIONS]

66 (Hamilton)

All Bills for raising Revenue shall originate in the House of Representatives; but the Senate may propose or concur with Amendments as on other Bills.

69, 73 (Hamilton)

Every Bill which shall have passed the House of Representatives and the Senate, shall, before it become a Law, be presented to the President of the United States; if he approve he shall sign it, but if not he shall return it, with his Objections to that House in which it shall have originated, who shall enter the Objections at large on their Journal, and proceed to reconsider it. If after such Reconsideration two thirds of that House shall agree to pass the Bill, it shall be sent, together with the Objections, to the other House, by which it shall likewise be reconsidered, and if approved by two thirds of that House, it shall become a Law. But in all such Cases the Votes of both Houses shall be determined by Yeas and Nays, and the Names of the Persons voting for and against the Bill shall be entered on the Journal of each House respectively. If any Bill shall not be returned by the President within ten Days (Sundays excepted) after it shall have been presented to him, the Same shall be a Law, in like Manner as if he had signed it, unless the Congress by their Adjournment prevent its Return, in which Case it shall not be a Law.

69, 73 (Hamilton)

Every Order, Resolution, or Vote to which the Concurrence of the Senate and House of Representatives may be necessary (except on a question of Adjournment) shall be presented to the President of the United States; and before the Same shall

---

[6]Modified by Twentieth Amendment.

take Effect, shall be approved by him, or being disapproved by him, shall be repassed by two thirds of the Senate and House of Representatives, according to the Rules and Limitations prescribed in the Case of a Bill.

Section 8
[POWERS OF CONGRESS]

The Congress shall have Power

30–36 (Hamilton),
41 (Madison)
56 (Madison)

To lay and collect Taxes, Duties, Imposts and Excises, to pay the Debts and provide for the common Defence and general Welfare of the United States; but all Duties, Imposts and excises shall be uniform throughout the United States;

To borrow Money on the Credit of the United States;

42, 45, 56 (Madison)

To regulate Commerce with foreign Nations, and among the several States, and with the Indian Tribes;

32 (Hamilton), 42 (Madison)
42 (Madison)
42 (Madison)

To establish an uniform Rule of Naturalization, and uniform Laws on the subject of Bankruptcies throughout the United States;

To coin Money, regulate the Value thereof, and of foreign Coin, and fix the Standard of Weights and Measures;

42 (Madison)

To provide for the Punishment of counterfeiting the Securities and current Coin of the United States;

42 (Madison)
43 (Madison)

To establish Post Offices and post Roads;

To promote the Progress of Science and useful Arts, by securing for limited Times to Authors and Inventors the exclusive Right to their respective Writings and Discoveries;

81 (Hamilton)
42 (Madison)

To constitute Tribunals inferior to the supreme Court;

To define and Punish Piracies and Felonies committed on the high Seas, and Offences against the Law of Nations;

41 (Madison)

To declare War, grant Letters of Marque and Reprisal, and make Rules concerning Captures on Land and Water;

23, 24, 26 (Hamilton),
41 (Madison)
41 (Madison)

To raise and support Armies, but no Appropriation of Money to that Use shall be for a longer Term than two Years;

To provide and maintain a Navy;

To make Rules for the Government and Regulation of the land and naval forces;

29 (Hamilton)

To provide for calling for the Militia to execute the Laws of the Union, suppress Insurrections and repel Invasions;

29 (Hamilton), 56 (Madison)

To provide for organizing, arming, and disciplining, the Militia, and for governing such Part of them as may be employed in the Service of the United States, reserving to the States respectively, the Appointment of the Officers, and the Authority of training the Militia according to the discipline prescribed by Congress;

32 (Hamilton), 43 (Madison)

To exercise exclusive Legislation in all Cases whatsoever, over such District (not exceeding ten Miles square) as may, by Cession of particular States, and the Acceptance of Congress, become the Seat of the Government of the United States, and to exercise like Authority over all Places purchased by the Consent of the Legislature of the State in which the Same shall be, for the Erection of Forts, Magazines, Arsenals, dock-Yards, and other needful Buildings;—And

43 (Madison)

29, 33 (Hamilton)
44 (Madison)

To make all Laws which shall be necessary and proper for carrying into Execution the foregoing Powers, and all other Powers vested by this Constitution in the Government of the United States, or in any Department or Officer thereof.

Section 9
[SOME RESTRICTIONS ON FEDERAL POWER]

42 (Madison)

The Migration or Importation of such Persons as any of the States now existing shall think proper to admit, shall not be prohibited by the Congress prior to the Year one thousand eight hundred and eight, but a Tax or Duty may be imposed on such Importation, not exceeding ten dollars for each Person.[7]

83, 84 (Hamilton)

The privilege of the Writ of Habeas Corpus shall not be suspended, unless when in Cases of Rebellion or Invasion the public Safety may require it.

84 (Hamilton)

No Bill of Attainder or ex post facto Law shall be passed.

[7]Temporary provision.

No Capitation, or other direct, Tax shall be laid, unless in Proportion to the Census or Enumeration herein before directed to be taken.[8]

No Tax or Duty shall be laid on Articles exported from any State.

32 (Hamilton)

No Preference shall be given by any Regulation of Commerce or Revenue to the Ports of one State over those of another; nor shall vessels bound to, or from, one State, be obliged to enter, clear, or pay Duties in another.

No Money shall be drawn from the Treasury, but in Consequence of Appropriations made by Law; and a regular Statement and Account of the Receipts and Expenditures of all public Money shall be published from time to time.

39 (Madison), 84 (Hamilton)

No Title of Nobility shall be granted by the United States: And no Person holding any Office of Profit or Trust under them, shall, without the Consent of the Congress, accept of any present, Emolument, Office, or Title, of any kind whatever, from any King, Prince, or foreign State.

Section 10
[RESTRICTIONS UPON POWERS OF STATES]

33 (Hamilton), 44 (Madison)

No State shall enter into any Treaty, Alliance, or Confederation; grant Letters of Marque and Reprisal; coin Money; emit Bills of Credit; make any Thing but gold and silver Coin a Tender in Payment of Debts; pass any Bill of Attainder, ex post facto Law, or Law impairing the Obligation of Contracts, or grant any Title of Nobility.

32 (Hamilton), 44 (Madison)

No State shall, without the Consent of the Congress, lay any Imposts or Duties on Imports or Exports, except what may be absolutely necessary for executing its inspection Laws: and the net Produce of all Duties and Imposts, laid by any State on Imports or Exports, shall be for the Use of the Treasury of the United States; and all such Laws shall be subject to the Revision and Control of the Congress.

No State shall, without the Consent of Congress, lay any Duty of Tonnage, keep Troops, or Ships of War in time of Peace, enter into any Agreement or Compact with another State, or with a foreign Power, or engage in War, unless actually invaded, or in such imminent Danger as will not admit of Delay.

ARTICLE II

Section 1
[EXECUTIVE POWER, ELECTION, QUALIFICATIONS OF THE PRESIDENT]

39 (Madison),
70, 71, 84 (Hamilton)
69, 71 (Hamilton)
39, 45 (Madison),
68, 77 (Hamilton)

The executive Power shall be vested in a President of the United States of America. *He shall hold his Office during the Term of four years and, together with the Vice President, chosen for the same Term, be elected, as follows:*[9]

Each State shall appoint, in such Manner as the Legislature thereof may direct, a Number of Electors, equal to the whole Number of Senators and Representatives to which the State may be entitled in the Congress: but no Senator or Representative, or Person holding an Office of Trust or Profit under the United States, shall be appointed an Elector.

The electors shall meet in their respective States, and vote by ballot for two Persons, of whom one at least shall not be an Inhabitant of the same State with themselves. And they shall make a List of all the Persons voted for, and of the Number of Votes for each; which List they shall sign and certify, and transmit sealed to the Seat of the Government of the United States, directed to the President of the Senate. The President of the Senate shall, in the Presence of the Senate and House of Representatives, open

66 (Hamilton)

all the Certificates, and the Votes shall then be counted. The Person having the greatest Number of Votes shall be the President, if such Number be a Majority of the whole Number of Electors appointed; and if there be more than one who have such Majority and have an equal Number of Votes, then the House of Representatives shall immediately chuse by Ballot one of them for President; and if no person have a Majority, then from the five highest on the List the said House shall in like Manner chuse the President. But in chusing the President, the Votes shall be taken by States, the Representation from each State having one Vote; A quorum for this Purpose shall

[8]Modified by Sixteenth Amendment.
[9]Number of terms limited to two by Twenty-second Amendment.

719

consist of a Member or Members from two-thirds of the States, and a Majority of all the States shall be necessary to a Choice. In every Case, after the Choice of the President, the person having the greatest Number of Votes of the Electors shall be the Vice President. But if there should remain two or more who have equal vote, the Senate shall chuse from them by Ballot the Vice President.[10]

The Congress may determine the Time of chusing the Electors, and the Day on which they shall give their Votes; which Day shall be the same throughout the United States.

No Person except a natural born Citizen, or a Citizen of the United States, at the time of the Adoption of this Constitution, shall be eligible to the Office of President; neither shall any Person be eligible to that Office who shall not have attained to the Age of thirty-five Years, and been fourteen Years a Resident within the United States.

In Case of the Removal of the President from Office, or his Death, Resignation, or Inability to discharge the Powers and Duties of the said Office, the same shall devolve on the Vice President, and the Congress may by Law provide for the Case of Removal, Death, Resignation, or Inability, both of the President and Vice President, declaring what Officer shall then act as President, and such Officer shall act accordingly, until the Disability be removed, or a President shall be elected.

The President shall, at stated Times, receive for his Services, a Compensation, which shall neither be encreased nor diminished during the Period for which he shall have been elected, and he shall not receive within that Period any other Emolument from the United States, or any of them.

Before he enter on the Execution of his Office, he shall take the following Oath or Affirmation:—"I do solemnly swear (or affirm) that I will faithfully execute the Office of President of the United States, and will to the best of my Ability, preserve, protect and defend the Constitution of the United States."

Section 2
[POWERS OF THE PRESIDENT]

The President shall be Commander in Chief of the Army and Navy of the United States, and of the Militia of the several States, when called into the actual Service of the United States; he may require the Opinion, in writing, of the principal Officer in each of the executive Departments, upon any Subject relating to the Duties of their respective Offices, and he shall have Power to grant Reprieves and Pardons for Offences against the United States, except in Cases of Impeachment.

He shall have Power, by and with the Advice and Consent of the Senate, to make Treaties, provided two thirds of the Senators present concur; and he shall nominate, and by and with the Advice and Consent of the Senate, shall appoint Ambassadors, other public Ministers and Consuls, Judges of the Supreme Court, and all other Officers of the United States, whose Appointments are not herein otherwise provided for, and which shall be established by Law: but the Congress may by Law vest the Appointment of such inferior Officers, as they think proper, in the President alone, in the Courts of Law, or in the Heads of Departments.

The President shall have Power to fill up all Vacancies that may happen during the Recess of the Senate, by granting Commissions which shall expire at the End of their next Session.

Section 3
[POWERS AND DUTIES OF THE PRESIDENT]

He shall from time to time give to the Congress Information of the State of the Union, and recommend to their Consideration such Measures as he shall judge necessary and expedient; he may, on extraordinary Occasions, convene both Houses, or either of them, and in Case of Disagreement between them, with Respect to the Time of Adjournment, he may adjourn them to such Time as he shall think proper; he shall receive Ambassadors and other public Ministers; he shall take Care that the Laws be faithfully executed, and shall Commission all the Officers of the United States.

---

[10]Modified by Twelfth and Twentieth Amendments.

64 (Jay)

73, 79 (Hamilton)

69, 74 (Hamilton)

74 (Hamilton)

69 (Hamilton)
74 (Hamilton)
42 (Madison), 64 (Jay),
66 (Hamilton)
42 (Madison),
66, 69, 76, 77 (Hamilton)

67, 76 (Hamilton)

77 (Hamilton)
69, 77 (Hamilton)
77 (Hamilton)
69, 77 (Hamilton)
42 (Madison),
69, 77 (Hamilton)
78 (Hamilton)

Section 4

[IMPEACHMENT]

39 (Madison), 69 (Hamilton)

The President, Vice President and all civil Officers of the United States shall be removed from Office on Impeachment for, and Conviction of, Treason, Bribery, or other high Crimes and Misdemeanors.

ARTICLE III

Section 1

[JUDICIAL POWER, TENURE OF OFFICE]

81, 82 (Hamilton)
65 (Hamilton)

78, 79 (Hamilton)

The judicial Power of the United States, shall be vested in one supreme Court, and in such inferior Courts as the Congress may from time to time ordain and establish. The Judges, both of the supreme and inferior Courts, shall hold their Offices during good Behavior, and shall, at stated Times, receive for their Services, a Compensation, which shall not be diminished during their Continuance in Office.

Section 2

[JURISDICTION]

80 (Hamilton)

The judicial Power shall extend to all Cases, in Law and Equity, arising under this Constitution, the Laws of the United States, and Treaties made, or which shall be made, under their Authority;—to all Cases affecting Ambassadors, other public Ministers and Consuls;—to all Cases of admiralty and maritime Jurisdiction;—to Controversies to which the United States shall be a party;—to Controversies between two or more States;—*between a State and Citizens of another State;*—between Citizens of different States,—between Citizens of the same State claiming Lands under Grants of different States, *and between a State,* or the Citizens thereof, *and foreign States, Citizens or Subjects.*[11]

81 (Hamilton)

In all Cases affecting Ambassadors, other public Ministers and Consuls, and those in which a State shall be Party, the supreme Court shall have original Jurisdiction. In all the other Cases before mentioned, the supreme Court shall have appellate Jurisdiction, both as to Law and Fact, with such Exceptions, and under such Regulations as Congress shall make.

83, 84 (Hamilton)

The Trial of all Crimes, except in Cases of Impeachment, shall be by Jury; and such Trial shall be held in the State where the said Crimes shall have been committed; but when not committed within any State, the Trial shall be at such Place or Places as the Congress may by Law have directed.

Section 3

[TREASON, PROOF AND PUNISHMENT]

43 (Madison), 84 (Hamilton)

Treason against the United States, shall consist only in levying War against them, or in adhering to their Enemies, giving them Aid and Comfort. No Person shall be convicted of Treason unless on the Testimony of two Witnesses to the same overt Act, or on Confession in open Court.

43 (Madison), 84 (Hamilton)

The Congress shall have Power to declare the Punishment of Treason, but no Attainder of Treason shall work Corruption of Blood, or Forfeiture except during the Life of the Person attained.

ARTICLE IV

Section 1

[FAITH AND CREDIT AMONG STATES]

42 (Madison)

Full Faith and Credit shall be given in each State to the public Acts, Records, and judicial Proceedings of every other State. And the Congress may by general Laws prescribe the Manner in which such Acts, Records and Proceedings shall be proved, and the Effect thereof.

---

[11]Modified by Eleventh Amendment.

Section 2

[PRIVILEGES AND IMMUNITIES, FUGITIVES]

80 (Hamilton)

The Citizens of each State shall be entitled to all Privileges and Immunities of Citizens in the several States.

A person charged in any State with Treason, Felony or other Crime, who shall flee from Justice, and be found in another State, shall on Demand of the executive Authority of the State from which he fled, be delivered up to be removed to the State having Jurisdiction of the Crime.

No person held to Service or Labour in one State, under the Laws thereof, escaping into another, shall, in Consequence of any Law or Regulation therein, be discharged from such Service or Labour, but shall be delivered up on Claim of the Party to whom such Service or Labour may be due.[12]

Section 3

[ADMISSION OF NEW STATES]

43 (Madison)

New States may be admitted by the Congress into this Union; but no new State shall be formed or erected within the Jurisdiction of any other State; nor any State be formed by the Junction of two or more States, or Parts of States, without the Consent of the Legislatures of the States concerned as well as of the Congress.

43 (Madison)

The Congress shall have Power to dispose of and make all needful Rules and Regulations respecting the Territory or other Property belonging to the United States; and nothing in this Constitution shall be so construed as to Prejudice any Claims of the United States, or of any particular State.

Section 4

[GUARANTEE OF REPUBLICAN GOVERNMENT]

39, 43 (Madison)

The United States shall guarantee to every State in this Union a Republican Form of Government, and shall protect each of them against Invasion; and on Application of the Legislature, or of the Executive (when the Legislature cannot be convened) against domestic Violence.

ARTICLE V

[AMENDMENT OF THE CONSTITUTION]

39, 43 (Madison)
85 (Hamilton)

The Congress, whenever two thirds of both Houses shall deem it necessary, shall propose Amendments to this Constitution, or, on the Application of the Legislatures of two thirds of the several States, shall call a Convention for proposing Amendments, which, in either Case, shall be valid to all Intents and Purposes, as Part of this Constitution, when ratified by the Legislatures of three fourths of the several States, or by Conventions in three fourths thereof, as the one or the other Mode of Ratification may be proposed by the Congress; *Provided that no Amendment which may be made prior to the Year One thousand eight hundred and eight shall in any Manner affect the first and fourth Clauses in the Ninth Section of the first Article;*[13] and that no State, without its Consent, shall be deprived of its equal Suffrage in the Senate.

43 (Madison)

ARTICLE VI

[DEBTS, SUPREMACY, OATH]

43 (Madison)

All Debts contracted and Engagements entered into, before the Adoption of this Constitution, shall be as valid against the United States under this Constitution, as under the Confederation.

27, 33 (Hamilton),
39, 44 (Madison)

This Constitution, and the Laws of the United States which shall be made in Pursuance thereof; and all Treaties made, or which shall be made, under the Authority of the United States, shall be the supreme Law of the Land; and the Judges

---

[12]Repealed by the Thirteenth Amendment.
[13]Temporary provision.

27 (Hamilton), 44 (Madison)

in every State shall be bound thereby, any Thing in the Constitution or Laws of any State to the Contrary notwithstanding.

The Senators and Representatives before mentioned, and the Members of the several State Legislatures, and all executive and judicial Officers, both of the United States and of the several States, shall be bound by Oath or Affirmation, to support this Constitution; but no religious Test shall be required as a Qualification to any Office or public Trust under the United States.

ARTICLE VII

39, 40, 43 (Madison)

[RATIFICATION AND ESTABLISHMENT]

The Ratification of the Conventions of nine States, shall be sufficient for the Establishment of this Constitution between the States so ratifying the Same.[14]

Done in Convention by the Unanimous Consent of the States present the Seventeenth Day of September in the Year of our Lord one thousand seven hundred and Eighty seven and of the Independence of the United States of America the Twelfth. *In Witness* whereof We have hereunto subscribed our Names,

G:⁰ WASHINGTON—
Presidt, and Deputy
from Virginia

New Hampshire	JOHN LANGDON
	NICHOLAS GILMAN
Massachusets	NATHANIEL GORHAM
	RUFUS KING
Connecticut	WM SAML JOHNSON
	ROGER SHERMAN
New York	ALEXANDER HAMILTON
New Jersey	WIL: LIVINGSTON
	DAVID BREARLEY
	WM PATERSON
	JONA: DAYTON
Pennsylvania	B FRANKLIN
	THOMAS MIFFLIN
	ROBT MORRIS
	GEO. CLYMER
	THOS. FITZSIMONS
	JARED INGERSOLL
	JAMES WILSON
	GOUV MORRIS
Delaware	GEO READ
	GUNNING BEDFOR JUN
	JOHN DICKINSON
	RICHARD BASSETT
	JACO: BROOM
Maryland	JAMES McHENRY
	DAN OF ST THOS. JENIFER
	DANL CARROLL

[14]The Constitution was submitted on September 17, 1787, by the Constitutional Convention, was ratified by the conventions of several states at various dates up to May 29, 1790, and became effective on March 4, 1789.

Virginia	JOHN BLAIR— JAMES MADISON JR.
North Carolina	WM BLOUNT RICHD DOBBS SPAIGHT HU WILLIAMSON
South Carolina	J. RUTLEDGE CHARLES COTESWORTH PINCKNEY CHARLES PINCKNEY PIERCE BUTLER
Georgia	WILLIAM FEW ABR BALDWIN

Amendments to the Constitution

Proposed by Congress and Ratified by the Legislatures of the Several States, Pursuant to Article V of the Original Constitution.

Amendments I–X, known as the Bill of Rights, were proposed by Congress on September 25, 1789, and ratified on December 15, 1791. Federalist Papers *comments, mainly in opposition to a Bill of Rights, can be found in #84 (Hamilton).*

AMENDMENT I

[FREEDOM OF RELIGION, OF SPEECH, AND OF THE PRESS]

Congress shall make no law respecting an establishment of religion, or prohibiting the free exercise thereof; or abridging the freedom of speech, or of the press; or the right of the people peaceably to assemble, and to petition the Government for a redress of grievances.

AMENDMENT II

[RIGHT TO KEEP AND BEAR ARMS]

A well regulated Militia, being necessary to the security of a free State, the right of the people to keep and bear Arms, shall not be infringed.

AMENDMENT III

[QUARTERING OF SOLDIERS]

No Soldier shall, in time of peace be quartered in any house, without the consent of the Owner, nor in time of war, but in a manner to be prescribed by law.

AMENDMENT IV

[SECURITY FROM UNWARRANTABLE SEARCH AND SEIZURE]

The right of the people to be secure in their persons, houses, papers, and effects, against unreasonable searches and seizures, shall not be violated, and no Warrants shall issue, but upon probable cause, supported by Oath or affirmation, and particularly describing the place to be searched, and the persons or things to be seized.

AMENDMENT V

[RIGHTS OF ACCUSED PERSONS IN CRIMINAL PROCEEDINGS]

No person shall be held to answer for a capital, or otherwise infamous crime, unless on a presentment or indictment of a Grand Jury, except in cases arising in the land or naval forces, or in the Militia, when in actual service in time of War or in public danger; nor shall any person be subject for the same offence to be twice put in jeopardy of life or limb; nor shall be compelled in any Criminal Case to be a witness against himself, nor be deprived of life, liberty, or property, without due process of law; nor shall private property be taken for public use, without just compensation.

AMENDMENT VI

[RIGHT TO SPEEDY TRIAL, WITNESSES, ETC.]

In all criminal prosecutions, the accused shall enjoy the right to a speedy and public trial, by an impartial jury of the State and district wherein the crime shall have been committed, which district shall have been previously ascertained by law, and to be informed of the nature and cause of the accusation; to be confronted with the witnesses against him; to have compulsory process for obtaining Witnesses in his favor, and to have the Assistance of Counsel for his defence.

AMENDMENT VII

[TRIAL BY JURY IN CIVIL CASES]

In suits at common law, where the value in controversy shall exceed twenty dollars, the right of trial by jury shall be preserved, and no fact tried by a jury shall be otherwise re-examined in any Court of the United States, than according to the rules of the common law.

AMENDMENT VIII

[BAILS, FINES, PUNISHMENTS]

Excessive bail shall not be required, nor excessive fines imposed, nor cruel and unusual punishments inflicted.

AMENDMENT IX

[RESERVATION OF RIGHTS OF PEOPLE]

The enumeration in the Constitution, of certain rights, shall not be construed to deny or disparage others retained by the people.

AMENDMENT X

[POWERS RESERVED TO STATES OR PEOPLE]

The powers not delegated to the United States by the Constitution, nor prohibited by it to the States, are reserved to the States respectively, or to the people.

AMENDMENT XI

[*Proposed by Congress on March 4, 1794; declared ratified on January 8, 1798.* RESTRICTION OF JUDICIAL POWER]

The Judicial power of the United States shall not be construed to extend to any suit in law or equity, commenced or prosecuted against one of the United States by Citizens of another State, or by Citizens or Subjects of any Foreign State.

AMENDMENT XII

[Proposed by Congress on December 9, 1803; declared ratified on September 25, 1804. ELECTION OF PRESIDENT AND VICE-PRESIDENT]

The Electors shall meet in their respective states, and vote by ballot for President and Vice-President, one of whom, at least, shall not be an inhabitant of the same state with themselves; they shall name in their ballots the person voted for as President, and in distinct ballots the person voted for as Vice-President, and they shall make distinct lists of all persons voted for as President, and of all persons voted for as Vice-President, and of the number of votes for each, which lists they shall sign and certify, and transmit sealed to the seat of the government of the United States, directed to the President of the Senate;—The President of the Senate shall, in presence of the Senate and House of Representatives, open all the certificates and the votes shall then be counted;—The person having the greatest number of votes for President, shall be the President, if such number be a majority of the whole number of Electors appointed; and if no person have such majority, then from the persons having the highest numbers not exceeding three on the list of those voted for as President, the House of Representatives shall choose immediately, by ballot, the President. But in choosing the President, the votes shall be taken by states, the representation from each state having one vote; a quorum for this purpose shall consist of a member or members from two-thirds of the states, and a majority of all states shall be necessary to a choice. And if the House of Representatives shall not choose a President whenever the right of choice shall devolve upon them, before the fourth day of March next following, then the Vice-President, shall act as President, as in the case of the death or other constitutional disability of the President. The person having the greatest number of votes as Vice-President, shall be the Vice-President, if such a number be a majority of the whole number of Electors appointed, and if no person have a majority, then from the two highest numbers on the list, the Senate shall choose the Vice-President; a quorum for the purpose shall consist of two-thirds of the whole number of Senators, and a majority of the whole number shall be necessary to a choice. But no person constitutionally ineligible to the office of President shall be eligible to that of Vice-President of the United States.

AMENDMENT XIII

[Proposed by Congress on January 31, 1865; declared ratified on December 18, 1865.]

Section 1

[ABOLITION OF SLAVERY]

Neither slavery nor involuntary servitude, except as a punishment for crime whereof the party shall have been duly convicted, shall exist within the United States, or any place subject to their jurisdiction.

Section 2

[POWER TO ENFORCE THIS ARTICLE]

Congress shall have power to enforce this article by appropriate legislation.

AMENDMENT XIV

[Proposed by Congress on June 13, 1866; declared ratified on July 28, 1868.]

Section 1

[CITIZENSHIP RIGHTS NOT TO BE ABRIDGED BY STATES]

All persons born or naturalized in the United States, and subject to the jurisdiction thereof, are citizens of the United States and of the State wherein they reside. No State shall make or enforce any law which shall abridge the privileges or immunities of citizens of the United States; nor shall any State deprive any person of life, liberty, or property, without due process of law; nor deny to any person within its jurisdiction the equal protection of the laws.

Section 2
[APPORTIONMENT OF REPRESENTATIVES IN CONGRESS]

Representatives shall be apportioned among the several States according to their respective numbers, counting the whole number of persons in each State, excluding Indians not taxed. But when the right to vote at any election for the choice of electors for President and Vice-President of the United States, Representatives in Congress, the Executive and Judicial officers of a State, or the members of the Legislature thereof, is denied to any of the male inhabitants of such State, being twenty-one years of age, and citizens of the United States, or in any way abridged, except for participation in rebellion, or other crime, the basis of representation therein shall be reduced in the proportion which the number of such male citizens shall bear to the whole number of male citizens twenty-one years of age in such State.

Section 3
[PERSONS DISQUALIFIED FROM HOLDING OFFICE]

No person shall be a Senator or Representative in Congress, or elector of President and Vice-President, or hold any office, civil or military, under the United States, or under any State, who, having previously taken an oath, as a member of Congress, or as an officer of the United States, or as a member of any State legislature, or as an executive or judicial officer of any State, to support the Constitution of the United States, shall have engaged in insurrection or rebellion against the same, or given aid or comfort to the enemies thereof. But Congress may by a vote of two-thirds of each House, remove such disability.

Section 4
[WHAT PUBLIC DEBTS ARE VALID]

The validity of the public debt of the United States, authorized by law, including debts incurred for payment of pensions and bounties for services in suppressing insurrection or rebellion, shall not be questioned. But neither the United States nor any State shall assume or pay any debt or obligation incurred in aid of insurrection or rebellion against the United States, or any claim for the loss of emancipation of any slave; but all such debts, obligations and claims shall be held illegal and void.

Section 5
[POWER TO ENFORCE THIS ARTICLE]

The Congress shall have power to enforce, by appropriate legislation, the provisions of this article.

AMENDMENT XV

[*Proposed by Congress on February 26, 1869; declared ratified on March 30, 1870.*]

Section 1
[NEGRO SUFFRAGE]

The right of citizens of the United States to vote shall not be denied or abridged by the United States or by any State on account of race, color, or previous condition of servitude.

Section 2
[POWER TO ENFORCE THIS ARTICLE]

The Congress shall have power to enforce this article by appropriate legislation.

AMENDMENT XVI

[*Proposed by Congress on July 12, 1909; declared ratified on February 25, 1913.*]
AUTHORIZING INCOME TAXES]

The Congress shall have power to lay and collect taxes on incomes, from whatever source derived, without apportionment among the several States, and without regard to any census or enumeration.

AMENDMENT XVII

[Proposed by Congress on May 13, 1912; declared ratified on May 31, 1913. POPULAR ELECTION OF SENATORS]

The Senate of the United States shall be composed of two Senators from each State, elected by the people thereof, for six years; and each Senator shall have one vote. The electors in each State shall have the qualifications requisite for electors of the most numerous branch of the State Legislature.

When vacancies happen in the representation of any State in the Senate, the executive authority of such State shall issue writs of election to fill such vacancies: Provided, That the Legislature of any State may empower the executive thereof to make temporary appointment until the people fill the vacancies by election as the Legislature may direct.

This amendment shall not be so construed as to affect the election or term of any Senator chosen before it becomes valid as part of the Constitution.

AMENDMENT XVIII

[Proposed by Congress December 18, 1917; declared ratified on January 29, 1919.]

Section 1
[NATIONAL LIQUOR PROHIBITION]

After one year from the ratification of this article the manufacture, sale, or transportation of intoxicating liquors within, the importation thereof into, or the exportation thereof from the United States and all territory subject to the jurisdiction thereof for beverage purposes is hereby prohibited.

Section 2
[POWER TO ENFORCE THIS ARTICLE]

The Congress and the several states shall have concurrent power to enforce this article by appropriate legislation.

Section 3
[RATIFICATION WITHIN SEVEN YEARS]

This article shall be inoperative unless it shall have been ratified as an amendment to the Constitution by the legislatures of the several states, as provided in the Constitution, within seven years from the date of the submission hereof to the states by the Congress.[15]

AMENDMENT XIX

[Proposed by Congress on June 4, 1919; declared ratified on August 26, 1920. WOMAN SUFFRAGE]

The right of the citizens of the United States to vote shall not be denied or abridged by the United States or by any state on account of sex.

Congress shall have power, by appropriate legislation, to enforce the provision of this article.

AMENDMENT XX

[Proposed by Congress on March 2, 1932; declared ratified on February 6, 1933.]

Section 1
[TERMS OF OFFICE]

The terms of the President and Vice-President shall end at noon on the 20th day of January, and the terms of the Senators and Representatives at noon on the 3rd day of January, of the years in which such terms would have ended if this article had not been ratified; and the terms of their successors shall then begin.

Section 2
[TIME OF CONVENING CONGRESS]

The Congress shall assemble at least once in every year, and such meeting shall begin at noon on the 3rd day of January, unless they shall by law appoint a different day.

---

[15]Repealed by the Twenty-first Amendment.

Section 3
[DEATH OF PRESIDENT-ELECT]

If, at the time fixed for the beginning of the term of the President, the President elect shall have died, the Vice-President elect shall become President. If a President shall not have been chosen before the time fixed for the beginning of his term, or if the President elect shall have failed to qualify, then the Vice-President elect shall act as President until a President shall have qualified; and the Congress may by law provide for the case wherein neither a President elect nor a Vice-President elect shall have qualified, declaring who shall then act as President, or the manner in which one who is to act shall be selected, and such person shall act accordingly until a President or Vice-President shall have qualified.

Section 4
[ELECTION OF THE PRESIDENT]

The Congress may by law provide for the case of the death of any of the persons from whom the House of Representatives may choose a President whenever the right of choice shall have devolved upon them, and for the case of the death of any of the persons from whom the Senate may choose a Vice-President whenever the right of choice shall have devolved upon them.

Section 5

Sections 1 and 2 shall take effect on the 15th day of October following ratification of this article.

Section 6

This article shall be inoperative unless it shall have been ratified as an amendment to the Constitution by the legislatures of three-fourths of the several States within seven years from the date of its submission.

AMENDMENT XXI

[*Proposed by Congress on February 20, 1933; declared ratified on December 5, 1933.*]

Section 1
[NATIONAL LIQUOR PROHIBITION REPEALED]

The eighteenth article of amendment to the Constitution of the United States is hereby repealed.

Section 2
[TRANSPORTATION OF LIQUOR INTO "DRY" STATES]

The transportation or importation into any State, Territory, or Possession of the United States for delivery or use therein of intoxicating liquors, in violation of the laws thereof, is hereby prohibited.

Section 3

This article shall be inoperative unless it shall have been ratified as an amendment to the Constitution by conventions in the several States, as provided in the Constitution, within seven years from the date of the submission hereof to the States by the Congress.

AMENDMENT XXII

[*Proposed by Congress on March 21, 1947; declared ratified on February 26, 1951.*]

Section 1
[TENURE OF PRESIDENT LIMITED]

No person shall be elected to the office of President more than twice, and no person who has held the office of President, or acted as President, for more than two years of a term to which some other person was elected President shall be elected to the Office of the President more than once. But this Article shall not apply to any person holding the office of President when this Article was proposed by the Congress, and shall not prevent any person who may be holding the office of President, or acting as President, during the term within which this Article becomes operative from holding the office of President or acting as President during the remainder of such term.

Section 2

This Article shall be inoperative unless it shall have been ratified as an amendment to the Constitution by the legislatures of three-fourths of the several states within seven years from the date of its submission to the States by the Congress.

AMENDMENT XXIII

[Proposed by Congress on June 21, 1960; declared ratified on March 29, 1961.]

Section 1

[ELECTORAL COLLEGE VOTES FOR THE DISTRICT OF COLUMBIA]

The District constituting the seat of Government of the United States shall appoint in such manner as the Congress may direct:

A number of electors of President and Vice President equal to the whole number of Senators and Representatives in Congress to which the District would be entitled if it were a State, but in no event more than the least populous State; they shall be in addition to those appointed by the States, but they shall be considered, for the purposes of the election of President and Vice President, to be electors appointed by a State; and they shall meet in the District and perform such duties as provided by the twelfth article of amendment.

Section 2

The Congress shall have power to enforce this article by appropriate legislation.

AMENDMENT XXIV

[Proposed by Congress on August 27, 1963; declared ratified on January 23, 1964.]

Section 1

[ANTI-POLL TAX]

The right of citizens of the United States to vote in any primary or other election for President or Vice President, for electors for President or Vice President, or for Senator or Representative of Congress, shall not be denied or abridged by the United States or any State by reasons of failure to pay any poll tax or other tax.

Section 2

The Congress shall have power to enforce this article by appropriate legislation.

AMENDMENT XXV

[Proposed by Congress on July 7, 1965; declared ratified on February 10, 1967.]

Section 1

[VICE PRESIDENT TO BECOME PRESIDENT]

In case of the removal of the President from office or his death or resignation, the Vice President shall become President.

Section 2

[CHOICE OF A NEW VICE PRESIDENT]

Whenever there is a vacancy in the office of the Vice President, the President shall nominate a Vice President who shall take the office upon confirmation by a majority vote of both houses of Congress.

Section 3
[PRESIDENT MAY DECLARE OWN DISABILITY]

Whenever the President transmits to the President pro tempore of the Senate and the Speaker of the House of Representatives his written declaration that he is unable to discharge the powers and duties of his office, and until he transmits to them a written declaration to the contrary, such powers and duties shall be discharged by the Vice President as Acting President.

Section 4
[ALTERNATIVE PROCEDURES TO DECLARE AND TO END PRESIDENTIAL DISABILITY]

Whenever the Vice President and a majority of either the principal officers of the executive departments, or of such other body as Congress may by law provide, transmit to the President pro tempore of the Senate and the Speaker of the House of Representatives their written declaration that the President is unable to discharge the powers and duties of his office, the Vice President shall immediately assume the powers and duties of the office as Acting President.

Thereafter, when the President transmits to the President pro tempore of the Senate and the Speaker of the House of Representatives his written declaration that no inability exists, he shall resume the powers and duties of his office unless the Vice President and a majority of either the principal officer of the executive department, or of such other body as Congress may by law provide, transmit within four days to the President pro tempore of the Senate and the Speaker of the House of Representatives their written declaration that the President is unable to discharge the powers and duties of his office. Thereupon Congress shall decide the issue, assembling within 48 hours for that purpose if not in session. If the Congress, within 21 days after receipt of the latter written declaration, or, if Congress is not in session, within 21 days after Congress is required to assemble, determines by two-thirds vote of both houses that the President is unable to discharge the powers and duties of his office, the Vice President shall continue to discharge the same as Acting President; otherwise, the President shall resume the powers and duties of his office.

AMENDMENT XXVI

[Proposed by Congress on March 23, 1971; declared ratified on June 30, 1971.]

Section 1
[EIGHTEEN-YEAR-OLD VOTE]

The right of citizens of the United States who are eighteen years of age or older to vote shall not be denied or abridged by the United States or by any State on account of age.

Section 2

The Congress shall have power to enforce this article by appropriate legislation.

AMENDMENT XXVII [PROPOSED]

[Proposed by Congress on March 22, 1972; ratification incomplete as of publication.]

Section 1
[EQUAL RIGHTS FOR WOMEN]

Equality of rights under the law shall not be denied or abridged by the United States or by any State on account of sex.

Section 2

The Congress shall have the power to enforce, by appropriate legislation, the provisions of this article.

Section 3

This amendment shall take effect two years after the date of ratification.

Acknowledgments

Chapter 2

Print, p. 21, from New York Public Library. Photo, p. 24, courtesy of Bettmann Archive. Prints, p. 25, clockwise, from top left: Treaty with Massasoit from Henry G. Watson and J. Harris Patton. *History of the United States of America from the Discovery to the Present Time.* New York: Thomas Kelly, 1879. Courtesy of New York Public Library. Sale poster from New York Public Library. Magna Carta courtesy of Bettmann Archive. Cortez and Montezuma courtesy of Bettmann Archive. Print, p. 28, courtesy of Bettmann Archive. Poster, p. 32, from New York Public Library. Poster, p. 36, courtesy of Time-Life Picture Agency. Ben Schneider–The State Historical Society of Colorado. Poster, p. 38, from New York Public Library. Poster, p. 40, from New York Public Library.

Chapter 3

Table 3.2, p. 46, data copyright Hammond Almanac, Incorporated. Table 3.3, p. 47, reprinted by permission of NEA. Photos, p. 49. Top, courtesy of UPI; middle, courtesy of Bettmann Archive; bottom, courtesy of Bettmann Archive. Photo, p. 56, courtesy of UPI. Photo, p. 59, courtesy of UPI. Photo, p. 61, by Robert A. Isaacs. Print, p. 64, courtesy of Bettmann Archive. Photos, p. 66. Top, courtesy of UPI; bottom, courtesy of Bettmann Archive. Photo, p. 70, courtesy of Time-Life Picture Agency, by Ralph Morse. Photo, p. 74, courtesy of UPI.

Chapter 4

Figure 4.1, p. 83, after George E. Frakes and W. Royce Adams. *From Columbus to Aquarius.* Hinsdale, Ill.: Dryden Press, in press. Reprinted by permission. Print, p. 88, courtesy of Bettmann Archive. Figure 4.2, p. 89, after George E. Frakes and W. Royce Adams. *From Columbus to Aquarius.* Hinsdale, Ill.: Dryden Press, in press. Reprinted by permission. Print, p. 94, courtesy of Bettmann Archive. Print, p. 99, courtesy of Bettmann Archive. Cartoon, p. 101, courtesy of Bettmann Archive. Photo, p. 103, courtesy of UPI. Print, p. 106, courtesy of the New-York Historical Society.

Chapter 5

Photos and clipping, p. 120, from *Chicago Tribune,* July 24, 1975. Reprinted courtesy of the Chicago Tribune. Photo, p. 123, courtesy of Time-Life Picture Agency, by Hansel Mieth. Print, p. 127, from John Dawson Gilmary. *Child's History of the United States.* New York: McMenamy, 1872. Courtesy of New York Public Library. Photo, p. 133, courtesy of Bettmann Archive. Clipping, p. 136, from *Chicago Tribune,* August 6, 1975. Reprinted courtesy of the Chicago Tribune. Clipping, p. 137, from *Chicago Tribune,* August 10, 1975. Reprinted courtesy of the Chicago Tribune. Photo, p. 148, courtesy of UPI. Photos, p. 149, courtesy of UPI. Poster, p. 155, from New York Public Library.

Chapter 6

Photo, p. 169, courtesy of UPI. Document, p. 171, courtesy of Bettmann Archive. Photos, p. 173, courtesy of Bettmann Archive. Photo, p. 177, courtesy of Wide World Photos. Photos, p. 179, courtesy of UPI. Box, p. 185, courtesy of the Chesapeake and Potomac Telephone Company of Washington. Photo, p. 187, courtesy of UPI. Advertisement, p. 190, courtesy of General Electric. Cartoon, p. 192, courtesy of Bettmann Archive.

Chapter 7

Cartoon, p. 211, reprinted by permission of Jules Feiffer. Box, p. 217, from Victor Marchetti and John D. Marks. *The CIA and the Cult of Intelligence.* New York: Alfred A. Knopf, 1974. Photo, p. 224, courtesy of UPI. Photo, p. 226, courtesy of UPI. Questionnaires, pp. 228–229, courtesy of National Opinion Research Center. Photo, p. 239, courtesy of Wide World Photos. Cartoon, p. 248, courtesy of Bettmann Archive. Photo, p. 252, courtesy of UPI. Photo, p. 255, courtesy of UPI.

Chapter 8

Box, p. 264, from E. E. Schattschneider. *Party Government.* Dryden Press, 1942. Reprinted by permission of Holt, Rinehart and Winston. Print, p. 266, courtesy of Bettmann Archive. Photo, p. 266, courtesy of UPI. Photos, p. 274, courtesy of UPI. Photos, p. 276, courtesy of UPI. Photo, p. 287, courtesy of UPI. Photo, p. 297, courtesy of UPI.

Chapter 9

Prints, p. 308, courtesy of Bettmann Archive. Photo, p. 317, courtesy of UPI. Photo, p. 319, courtesy of UPI. Print, p. 326, courtesy of Bettmann Archive. Print, p. 328, courtesy of Bettmann Archive. Photo, p. 330, courtesy of UPI.

Chapter 10

Print, p. 337, courtesy of Bettmann Archive. Photo, p. 349, courtesy of UPI. Photo, p. 356, courtesy of UPI. Photo, p. 358, courtesy of UPI. Photo, p. 361, courtesy of Wide World Photos. Photo, p. 368, courtesy of UPI. Box, p. 372, excerpts from "The Car Is All Right, But Your Crabgrass Is Illegally Parked," by Flora Johnson and Ron Berler. *Chicago Magazine,* August 1975. Copyright 1975 by Chicago Magazine. Reprinted by permission. Photo, p. 378, courtesy of UPI. Photos, p. 386, courtesy of UPI.

Chapter 11

Photo, p. 393, courtesy of UPI. Photo, p. 397, courtesy of UPI. Photo, p. 403, courtesy of UPI. Photo, p. 405, courtesy of UPI. Drawing, p. 411, courtesy of Tim Hall, House of Representatives. Photos, p. 420. Top two, courtesy of Wide World Photos; bottom two, courtesy of UPI. Photos, p. 421, courtesy of UPI. Print, p. 425, courtesy of Bettmann Archive. Photo, p. 425, courtesy of UPI. Poster, p. 428, from New York Public Library. Prints, p. 428, courtesy of Bettmann Archive. Photo, p. 428, courtesy of UPI. Photos, p. 429, courtesy of UPI. Photo, p. 434, courtesy of UPI. Photos, p. 437, courtesy of UPI. Table 11.3, p. 442, from Table 4-2, "The President's Relation to His Public—Domestic Events," from *The Politics of Disorder*, by Theodore J. Lowi, © 1971 by Basic Book, Inc., Publishers, New York. Table 11.4, p. 443, reprinted from *The End of Liberalism* by Theodore J. Lowi. Copyright © 1969 by W. W. Norton & Company Inc. With permission of the publisher. Photo, p. 446, courtesy of UPI.

Chapter 12

Photo, p. 463, courtesy of UPI. Poster, p. 474, from New York Public Library. Photo, p. 475, courtesy of UPI. Table 12.3, p. 479, reprinted by permission of Princeton University Press. Photo, p. 485, courtesy of Bettmann Archive. Print, p. 494, courtesy of Bettmann Archive. Photo, p. 499, courtesy of UPI.

Chapter 13

Figure 13.1, p. 514, reprinted with permission from *American Government 73/74.* Copyright © 1973 by The Dushkin Publishing Group, Inc., Guilford, Connecticut. Photo, p. 525, courtesy of UPI. Photo, p. 531, courtesy of UPI. Box, p. 540, from Henry J. Abraham. *Justices and Presidents.* New York: Oxford University Press, 1974. Photo, p. 544, courtesy of UPI. Photos, p. 547, courtesy of UPI. Photo, p. 553, courtesy of UPI.

Chapter 14

Cartoon, p. 563, courtesy of Bettmann Archive. Photo, p. 571, courtesy of UPI. Photo, p. 577, courtesy of UPI. Table 14.2 p. 580, Copyright © 1966 by Paul M. Sweezy. Reprinted by permission of Monthly Review Press. Tables 14.4 and 14.5, pp. 590, 591, from *The Cold War Years: American Foreign Policy since 1945* by Paul Y. Hammond. Copyright © 1969 by Harcourt Brace Jovanovich, Inc., rearranged and printed with their permission. Figure 14.1, p. 593, from Oscar

Acknowledgments

735

Handlin. *America: A History*. New York: Holt, Rinehart and Winston, 1968. Reprinted by permission. Posters, p. 595. Left, from New York Public Library; right, by James Montgomery Flagg. Table 14.6, p. 597, data copyright Hammond Almanac, Incorporated. Map, p. 602, courtesy of UPI. Photos, p. 608, courtesy of UPI. Photo, p. 610, courtesy of Time-Life Picture Agency, by Alfred Eisenstaedt. Photo, p. 612, courtesy of UPI. Photos, p. 613, courtesy of UPI. Photos, p. 618, courtesy of UPI. Print, p. 618, courtesy of Bettmann Archive.

Chapter 15

Box, p. 633, excerpts from *New York Times,* June 5, 1972. © 1972 by The New York Times Company. Reprinted by permission. Photo, p. 635, courtesy of UPI. Print, p. 640, from New York Public Library. Photo, p. 640, courtesy of UPI. Photo, p. 645, courtesy of UPI. Photos, p. 655, courtesy of UPI. Photo, p. 665, courtesy of Bettmann Archive. Photo, p. 670, courtesy of Bettmann Archive. Photo, p. 674, courtesy of UPI. Photo, p. 685, courtesy of UPI. License, p. 688, courtesy of City of DeKalb.

Glossary

absolutism A system of government in which the sovereign has unlimited powers; despotism.

administrative law The branch of law pertaining to administrative agencies.

amicus curiae "Friend of the court"; individuals or groups who are not parties to a lawsuit but who seek to assist the court in reaching a decision by presenting additional briefs.

appropriation The process by which Congress approves in statutes (bills) actual amounts each unit or agency of government can spend.

authorization The process by which Congress enacts or rejects proposed statutes (bills) embodying the positive laws of government.

auxiliary agency A bureau or other unit of administration whose primary purpose is to service other agencies; housekeeping agency.

balance of power A system of political alignments by which stability can be achieved.

bandwagon effect A situtation wherein reports of voter or delegate opinion can influence the actual outcome of an election or a nominating convention.

bellwether districts Towns or districts that are microcosms of the whole population or that have been found to be good predictors of electoral outcomes.

bicameralism Having a legislative assembly composed of chambers or houses; opposite of unicameralism.

bilateral treaty Treaty between two nations; contrast with multilateral treaty.

bill of attainder A legislative act which inflicts guilt and punishment without a judicial hearing or trial, it is proscribed by Article I, Section 10, of the Constitution.

bill of information Official opinion of a government prosecutor or district attorney that there is sufficient evidence of a crime to bring a case to trial; in some places the equivalent of an indictment by a grand jury.

Bill of Rights The first ten Amendments to the U.S. Constitution, ratified in 1791, they ensure certain rights and liberties to the people.

binding primary Primary election (usually a presidential election) in which delegates pledge themselves to a certain candidate and are bound to vote for that person until released from the obligation.

bipartisanship Close cooperation between two parties; usually an effort by the two major parties in Congress to cooperate with the president in making foreign policy.

Brandeis brief A brief presented to an appellate court, containing substantial nonlegal information, usually about the impact of a law or a court decision on the society.

Calendar Wednesday A procedure in the House whereby a committee chairman can bypass the Rules Committee and bring proposed legislation directly to the floor for consideration.

capitalism The economic system in which most of the means of production and distribution are privately owned and operated for profit.

categoric aid Grants by Congress to states and localities, with the condition that expenditures be limited to a problem or group specified in the law.

caucus A normally closed meeting of a political or legislative group to select candidates, plan strategy, or make decisions regarding legislative matters.

certificate of convenience and necessity Permission granted by a regulatory agency to an individual or group to conduct a particular type of business; license.

charisma A special gift of attraction held by an individual; an attribute of leadership based on the qualities of a particular person.

chauvinism Unreasoning enthusiasm for the glory of one's own country.

citizenship The duties, rights, and privileges of being a citizen of a political unit.

civil law A system of jurisprudence, including private law and governmental actions, to settle disputes that do not involve criminal penalties.

clientele agencies Departments or bureaus of government whose mission is to promote, serve, or represent a particular interest.

closed primary A primary election in which voters can participate in the nomination of candidates, but only of the party in which they are enrolled for a period of time prior to primary day.

closed rule Provision by the House Rules Committee limiting or prohibiting the introduction of amendments during debate.

cloture rule Rule allowing a majority in a legislative body to set a time limit on debate over a given bill.

coattail effect Result of voters casting their ballot for one candidate and "automatically" voting for the remainder of the party's ticket.

commerce power Right of Congress to regulate trade among the states and with foreign countries.

common law Law common to the realm in Anglo-Saxon history; unwritten law based on custom, usage, and the decisions of law courts.

concurrent power Authority possessed by both state and national governments, such as the power to levy taxes.

confederation League of independent states.

congressional veto Legislative veto; a statutory arrangement under which Congress delegates power to an agency but requires the agency to submit its plans to Congress or to one of its committees for approval.

conquest Bringing a territory and its population under control.

constituency The district comprising the area from which an official is elected.

constitutionalism An approach to legitimacy in which the rulers give up a certain amount of power in return for their right to utilize the remaining powers.

control agencies Agencies which have the power to intervene in the private sphere to regulate the conduct of individuals, groups, or corporations.

cooptation Strategy of bringing an individual into a group by joint action of the members of that group, usually in order to reduce or eliminate the individual's opposition.

correlational analysis Analysis of two or more items that involve a mutual relationship; effort to determine the degree of relative correspondence between two sets of data.

coup d'etat Sudden, forcible overthrow of a government.

criminal law The branch of law that deals with disputes or actions involving criminal penalties (as opposed to civil law), it regulates the conduct of individuals, defines crimes, and provides punishment for criminal acts.

democratic centralism In Communist Party doctrine, members can dispute with one another and the leadership until a decision is made, after which militant adherence to the decision is obligatory.

discharge petition Procedure of the House whereby an absolute majority of the members can force a bill out of committee when the committee itself has refused to report it out for consideration.

doctrine of expressed power The national government can exercise only those powers explicitly granted to it by the Constitution; all other powers are to be retained by the states or the people.

double jeopardy Trial more than once for the same crime. The Constitution guarantees that no one shall be subjected to double jeopardy.

due process The right of every citizen against arbitrary action by national or state governments.

elastic clause See *necessary and proper clause.*

Electoral College The presidential electors from each state who meet in their respective state capitals after the popular election to cast ballots for president and vice-president.

electorate All of the eligible voters in a legally designated area.

elite Those people at the top who exercise a major influence on decision making.

eminent domain The right of government to take private property for public use, with reasonable compensation awarded for the property.

equity Law providing a remedy to a dispute where common law does not apply.

exclusive power Power belonging exclusively to and exercised only by the national or state government.

executive agreement Agreement with a foreign power that has the force and effect of a treaty but that does not require approval by the Senate.

executive privilege The claim that confidential communications between a president and close advisers should not be revealed without the consent of the president.

ex post facto law "After the fact" law; law that is retroactive and that has an adverse effect on someone accused of a crime. Under Article I, Sections 9 and 10, of the Constitution, neither the state nor the national government can enact such laws; this provision does not apply, however, to civil laws.

expropriation Confiscation of property with or without compensation.

faction Group of people with common interests, usually in opposition to the aims or principles of a larger group or the public.

federalism System of government in which power is divided by a constitution between a central government and regional governments.

franchise The right to vote; see also *suffrage.*

full faith and credit clause Article IV, Section 1, of the Constitution provides that each state must accord the same respect to the laws and judicial decisions of other states that it accords to its own.

gerrymandering Apportionment of votes in districts in such a way as to give unfair advantage to one political party.

government Institutionalization of conquest; exercise of authority over an organization, group, state, and so on.

habeas corpus A court order demanding that the individual in custody be brought into court and shown the cause for detention. Habeas corpus is guaranteed by the Constitution and can be suspended only in cases of rebellion or invasion.

home rule Power delegated by the state to a local unit of government to manage its own affairs.

ideology The combined doctrines, assertions, and intentions of a social or political group that justify its behavior.

illusion of central tendency The assumption that opinions are "normally distributed"—that responses to opinion questions are heavily distributed toward the center, as in a bell-shaped curve.

illusion of saliency The assumption that something is important to the public when actually it is not.

independent agencies Agencies set up by Congress to be independent of direct presidential authority. Congress usually accomplishes this by providing the head or heads of the agency with a set term of office rather than allowing their removal at the pleasure of the president.

indirect election Provision for election of an official where the voters first select the delegates or "electors," who are in turn charged with making the final choice. The presidential election is an indirect election.

indoctrination The act of teaching or being taught a doctrine, belief, or principle.

jingoism Extreme or militant devotion to one's country.

Johnson rule Senate rule, adopted while Lyndon Johnson was majority leader, providing that no senator could receive an assignment to a second major committee until all senators had received consideration for a major committee assignment.

judicial review Power of the courts to declare actions of the legislative and executive branches invalid or unconstitutional. The Supreme Court asserted this power in *Marbury* v. *Madison.*

laissez-faire An economic theory first advanced by Adam Smith, it calls for a "hands off" policy by government toward the economy, in an effort to leave business enterprises free to act in their own self-interest.

latent functions Regular but unintended consequences of an activity or an institution.

legislative intent The supposed real meaning of a statute as it can be interpreted from the legislative history of the bill.

legitimacy Widespread agreement that government is founded upon certain values that are fundamental to the history and philosophy of the nation.

license The sovereign's grant of a privilege to do something that is otherwise illegal.

line agency Department, bureau, or other unit of administration whose primary mission requires it to deal directly with the public; contrast with auxiliary or overhead agency.

lobbying Strategy by which organized interests seek to influence the passage of legislation by exerting direct pressure on members of the legislature.

logrolling A legislative practice wherein reciprocal agreements are made between legislators, usually in voting for or against a bill. In contrast to bargaining, parties to logrolling have nothing in common but their desire to exchange support.

majority rule Rule by vote of more than half of those voting.

manifest functions Regular and intended consequences of an activity or an institution; same as *purposes* and opposite of *latent functions.*

Marxism The system of thought developed by Karl Marx, it is predicated upon a history of class struggle between those who control production and distribution (the owners) and the workers, culminating in the overthrow of the owners, the redistribution of wealth and power, and the "withering away of the state."

multilateral treaty A treaty among more than two nations.

multiple-member constituency Electorate which selects all candidates at large from the whole district; each voter is given the number of votes equivalent to the number of seats to be filled.

multiple-member district See *multiple-member constituency.*

nationalism The widely held belief that the people who occupy the same territory have something in common, that the nation is a single community.

national supremacy A principle, rooted in Article VI of the Constitution, which asserts that national law is superior to all other law.

nation-state A nation that has conquered itself; a people with some common cultural experience (nation) who also share a common political authority (state), recognized by other sovereignties (nation-states).

necessary and proper clause Article I, Section 8, of the Constitution, it enumerates the powers of Congress and provides Congress with the authority to make all laws "necessary and proper" to carry them out; also referred to as the "elastic" clause.

open primary A primary election in which the voter can wait until the day of the primary to choose which party to enroll in to select candidates for the general election; see *closed primary.*

overhead agency A department, bureau, or other unit of adminstration whose primary mission is to regulate the activities of other agencies; it generally has no direct authority over the public. Contrast with line or auxiliary agency.

patriotism Love of one's country; loyalty to one's country.

patronage The resources of higher officials, usually the opportunities to make partisan appointments to offices and to confer grants, licences, or special favors to supporters.

per curiam Decision by an appellate court, without a written opinion, that refuses to review the decision of a lower court; amounts to a reaffirmation of the lower court's opinion.

petition Right granted by the First Amendment to citizens to inform representatives of their opinions and to make pleas before government agencies.

pluralist democracy System of democracy in which political elites actively compete for leadership, voters choose from among these elites, and new elites can emerge in quest of leadership.

plurality rule Victory to the individual who gets the most votes in an election, not necessarily a majority of votes cast.

police power Power reserved to the state to regulate the health, safety, and morals of its citizens.

political socialization Induction of individuals into the political culture; learning how to accept authority; learning what is legitimate and what is not.

polity A society with an organized government; the "political system."

poll tax A state-imposed tax upon the voters as a prerequisite to registration, it was rendered unconstitutional in national elections by the Twenty-fourth Amendment and in state elections by the Supreme Court in 1966.

populism A late 1870s political and social movement of western and southern farmers that protested eastern business interests.

pork barrel legislation Appropriations made by legislative bodies for local projects which are often not needed but which are created so that local representatives can carry their home district in the next election.

positive law Law made in and by legislatures self-consciously to fit an occasion; contrast with divine law, natural law, judge-made law.

preferential primary Primary election in which the elected delegates to a convention are instructed, but not bound, to vote specifically for the presidential candidate preferred by the voters on a separate part of the ballot.

private bill A proposal in Congress to provide a specific person with some kind of relief, such as a special exemption from immigration quotas.

private law A system of jurisprudence designed to settle disputes between citizens who prefer the courts to the use of personal force.

privileges and immunities clause Article IV of the Constitution, it provides that the citizens of any one state are guaranteed the "privileges and immunities" of every other state, as though they were citizens of that state.

procedural due process The Supreme Court's efforts to forbid any procedure that shocks the conscience or that makes impossible a fair judicial system. See *due process.*

promotional agency See *clientele agency.*

proportional representation A system which allows each political party representation in proportion to its percentage of the vote.

public corporation An agency set up by a government but permitted to finance its own operations by charging for its services or by selling bonds.

public law Cases in private law, civil law, or criminal law in which one party to the dispute argues that a license is unfair, a law is inequitable or unconstitutional, or an agency has acted unfairly, violated a procedure, or gone beyond its jurisdiction.

quorum The minimum number of members of a deliberative body who must be present in order to conduct business.

random sample polling Polls in which respondents are chosen mathematically, at random, with every effort made to avoid bias in the construction of the sample.

reapportionment The redrawing of election districts and the redistribution of legislative representatives due to shifts in population.

regulatory agencies Departments, bureaus, or independent agencies whose primary mission is to eliminate or restrict certain behaviors defined as being evil in themselves or evil in their consequences.

revenue acts Acts of Congress providing the means of raising the revenues needed by the government. The Constitution requires that all such bills originate in the House.

revenue districts For purposes of collecting federal income taxes, the country is divided into a number of regions and districts; each has a field office of the Internal Revenue Service.

revenue sharing One unit of government yields a portion of its tax income to another unit of government, according to an established formula.

revolution A complete or drastic change of government and the rules by which government is conducted.

roll call vote Each legislator's yes or no vote is recorded as the clerk calls the names of the members alphabetically.

select committee A legislative committee established for a limited period of time and for a special purpose; not a standing committee.

selective polling A sample drawn deliberately to reconstruct meaningful distributions of an entire constituency; not a random sample.

seniority Priority or status ranking given to an individual on the basis of length of service in an organization.

separation of powers The principle that power must be distributed among three branches of government—the executive, the legislative, and the judicial—if tyranny is to be avoided.

service agencies Departments or other bureaus whose primary mission is to promote the interests of dependent persons or to deal with their problems.

single-member constituency An electorate which is allowed to elect only one representative from each district; the normal method of representation in the United States.

single-member district See *single-member constituency.*

sovereignty Supreme and independent political authority.

standing committee A regular legislative committee which considers legislation within its designated subject area; the basic unit of deliberation in the House and Senate.

stare decisis Literally "let the decision stand." A previous decision by a court applies as a precedent in similar cases until that decision is overruled.

state A community that claims the monopoly of legitimate use of physical force within a given territory; the ultimate political authority.

statute A law enacted by a state legislature or by Congress.

substantive due process A judicial doctrine used by the appellate courts, primarily before 1937, to strike down economic legislation the courts felt was arbitrary or unreasonable.

supremacy clause Article VI of the Constitution, which states that laws passed by the national government and all treaties are the supreme laws of the land and superior to all laws adopted by any state or any subdivision.

suffrage The right to vote; see also *franchise.*

survival agencies An informal designation for the departments and other agencies whose primary missions are diplomacy, war, or defense of sovereignty.

teller vote A legislative vote wherein votes are counted as members march by a teller (counter); the record of individual votes is not kept.

ticket balancing Strategy of party leaders to nominate candidates from each of the major ethnic, racial, and religious affiliations.

ticket splitting The practice of voting for candidates of different parties on the same ballot.

totalitarianism A system in which the government or state is completely controlled by one party or group and in which attempts are made to eliminate all competing loyalties.

treaty A formal agreement between sovereign nations to create or restrict rights and responsibilities. In the U.S. all treaties must be approved by a two-thirds vote in the Senate.

tyranny Oppressive and unjust government which employs cruel and unjust use of power and authority.

vested interests Fixed or established interests; interests not varying with changing conditions; privileges respected or accepted by others.

whip system Primarily a communications network in each house of Congress, whips take polls of the membership in order to learn their intentions on specific legislative issues and to assist the majority and minority leaders in various tasks.

writ of *certiorari* A decision concurred in by at least four of the nine Supreme Court justices to review a decision of a lower court; from the Latin "to make more certain."

Index

Nadel, Mark, 178n, 689n
Nader, Ralph, 178, 178n, 179
Nader's Raiders, 178
Nagel, Stuart, 249n
Napoleonic international role, 572–574; and diplomacy, 619
Narbutovich, Vikenty, 305
Nation, Carrie, 148
National Academy of Sciences, 199
National Aeronautics and Space Administration, 478, 490
National Association for the Advancement of Colored People (NAACP), 176, 203, 207
National Association of Counties, 373
National Association of County Agricultural Agents, 185
National Association of Electric Companies, 202
National Association of Home Builders (NAHB), 182–183, 469
National Association of Land Grant Colleges and Universities, 197
National Association of Manufacturers, 167, 202
National Association of Real Estate Boards, 202
National Association of Soil Conservation Districts, 185, 197
National Coal Association, 202
National Cooperative Milk Producers, 185
National Cotton Council, 197
National Defense Education Act of 1958, 684–685, 686
National Farmers' Union, 169
National Governor's Conference, 373
National guard, increasing use of, 705
National Guard Association, 199
National Highway Traffic Safety Administration, 469
National Institute of Health, 467
National Institute of Mental Health, 467
Nationalism, 55–58, 84
Nationalization: of crime, 142–143; of rights, 143–150
National Labor Relations Act (Wagner Act) 649
National Labor Relations Board (NLRB), 555
National Labor Relations Board v. Jones and Laughlin Steel Corporation, 131–132
National Labor Union, 170
National Legislative Conference, 373
National Opinion Research Center, 230
National Organization for Women (NOW), 178
National Parks Service, 464
National Security Agency (NSA), 480

National Security Council (NSC), 496, 497
National Society of State Legislators, 373
National Students Association, 606
National supremacy, 100–105
see also Supremacy clause.
Nation of Islam, 176
Nation-state, 5–7, 562
Navasky, Victor, 187n, 473, 475n, 504n 550n
Navy Department, 199, 481
Navy League, 199
Necessary and proper clause, 104, 108
negative knowledge, 242
negative landslide, 427
Neustadt, Richard E., 105, 225n, 369n, 387n, 393n, 403n, 431, 431n, 445, 445n, 497n, 500n
New Deal, and conservation, 683–684
New England Company, 28
New England Confederacy, 31–32
New Jersey Plan, 97
New math, 68
New Mexico, capital punishment laws in, 139
New science, 68
New York:
capital punishment laws in, 139; gerrymandering in, 248–249; party organization in, 266–267; ticket balancing in, as cooptation, 76
New York, New Haven, and Hartford v. Hannagan, 517n
New York State Athletic Commission, 625, 626
New York Times, and Pentagon Papers, 125
New York Times Company v. United States, 125
Nieburg, H. L., 703n
Ninety-second Congress (1971–1972), conservative vs. liberal voting in, 311
Nixon, Richard M., 124, 201, 277, 280, 282, 370, 371, 376, 379, 385, 391, 395, 395n, 401, 422, 426n, 494; and bombing in Cambodia, 395; cabinets of 433–435, 504–506; campaign strategy of, 426; and China, 576–577; county chairman support for, 424; and control of administrative agencies, 497–498; election pattern of, 446–447; and executive privilege, 406; and Gulf of Tonkin Resolution, 398; and impoundment of funds, 404–405; influence of Supreme Court, 538, 545; issue orientation of supporters in 1972, 243, (fig.) 244; and mail strike of 1970, 404;